THE
LUFTWAFFE
OVER GERMANY

THE LUFTWAFFE OVER GERMANY

Defense of the Reich

Donald Caldwell and Richard Muller

GREENHILL BOOKS, LONDON
MBI PUBLISHING, ST PAUL

Greenhill Books

The Luftwaffe over Germany
Defense of the Reich

This edition published in 2007 by Greenhill Books/Lionel Leventhal Ltd,
Park House, 1 Russell Gardens, London NW11 9NN
and
MBI Publishing Co. Galtier Plaza, Suite 200, 380 Jackson Street,
St Paul, MN 55101-3885, USA

British Library Cataloguing-in Publication Data

Caldwell, Donald L.
The Luftwaffe over Germany : defence of the Reich
1. Germany. Luftwaffe – History – World War, 1939–1945
2. World War, 1939–1945 – Aerial operations, German
I. Title II. Muller, Richard, 1961–
940.5'44943

ISBN: 978-1-85367-712-0

Library of Congress Cataloging-in Publication Data available

For more information on our books, please visit www.greenhillbooks.com, email
sales@greenhillbooks.com, or telephone us within the UK on 020 8458 6314. You can
also write to us at the above London address.

The figures and map in this book were created by Les Butler.

Printed and bound in China through Printworks Int. Ltd.

CONTENTS

ACKNOWLEDGEMENTS

The history of the Luftwaffe, although a subject of great inherent interest, has posed an almost insurmountable challenge to serious historians owing to a grievous lack of primary documentation. Some was lost as a result of bomber raids on Luftwaffe headquarters in Berlin. Most of the records of the combat units were destroyed deliberately, burned by order of the High Command just before the surrender. It has been estimated that 95 percent of the records were lost. Many valuable documents have since turned up: in the personal effects of pilots who refused to turn over their logbooks to be burned, in the files of various Allied agencies, and even "found" in the German archives themselves. But the data needed for this book, especially the details of combat operations, had to be pulled together and reconciled from hundreds of sources, many of them private archives maintained by the small band of Luftwaffe historians and enthusiasts. A computer with a good database program is the *sine qua non* for this type of research (thanks, Appleworks®!).

Pride of place in any list of individuals to whom we owe our gratitude must go to the Luftwaffe veterans, whose numbers are unfortunately but inevitably growing fewer by the year. Those who provided material for this volume during our ten years of independent data-gathering and, after joining forces, ten years of writing were: Willi Andiel, Hans Berger, Karl Boehm-Tettelbach, Hans-Ekkehard Bob, Walter Bohatsch, Oskar Bösch, Hans Bott, Hermann Buchner, Eberhard Burath, Josef Bürschgens, J. E. Clade, Martin Drewes, Georg-Peter Eder, Günther Ehrlich, Fritz Engau, Wolf Falck, Richard Franz, Adolf Galland, Georg Genth, Heinz Gomann, Alfred Grislawski, Klaus Hahn, Alois Höhn, Hans-Joachim Jabs, Robert Jung, Jörg Kiefner, Otto Kleinert, Gerhard Kroll, Heinz-Günter Kuring, Erwin Leykauf, Fritz Marktscheffel, Wilhelm Mittag, Werner Molge, Theo Nau, Johannes Naumann, Karl-Heinz Ossenkop, Dietrich Peltz, Horst Petzschler, Douglas Pitcairn, Günther Rall, Willi Reschke, Arno Rose, Wolfgang Schenck, Ernst Scheufele, Dieter Schmidt-Barbo, Gerhard Schöpfel, Ernst Schröder, Erich Schwarz, Günther Sinnecker, Georg Spies, Peter Spoden, Otto Stammberger, Heinrich Staniwoga, Karl-Heinz von den Steinen, Fritz Ungar, Willi Unger, Hans Weik, Berthold Wendler, Gerd Wiegand, Günther Wolf, Helmut Zittier, and Paul Zorner.

The families of deceased veterans Otto Behrens, Gerhard Herzog, and Heinz Rose also provided photographs and information.

Our thanks go to the following American and Canadian airmen for their cooperation: William Binnebose, Kenneth Blyth, Ed Burford, Harry Coleman, Arthur Fiedler, Robert Goebel, Al LaChasse, Steve Pisanos, Robert Seelos, and Hubert Zemke.

The fraternity of airwar historians and enthusiasts helped us with generous gifts of time, information, leads, photographs, documents, and/or photographic assistance. We wish to acknowledge: Arno Abendroth, Bernd Barbas, Nick Beale, John Beaman, Paul Berg, Dénes Bernád, Christer Bergström, Tami Davis Biddle, Steve Blake, Winfried Bock, Manfred Boehme, Andreas Brekken, David Brown, Eric Brown, Edwina Campbell, Carl Charles, Steve Coates, James Corum, Jerry Crandall, A. J. Cranston, Jim Crow, Curt Deatrick, Arie De Jong, Ivo De Jong, Wim de Meester, Russ Fahey, Bob Fletcher, Stephen Fochuk, John Foreman, Jim Forsyth, Robert Forsyth, Norman Franks, Garry Fry, R. B. Gill, Steve Gotts, Richard Goyat, Timothy Gravelle, John Gray, Lewis Griffith, Russell Guest, Ian Hawkins, Bill Hess, Larry Hickey, Michael Holm, Kevin Holzimmer, Budd Jones, Peter Kassak, Jim Kitchens, Werner Kock, Malcolm Laing, Gerd Lanio, Jean-Yves Lorant, John Manrho, Lex McAulay, Ian McLachlan, Michael Meyer, Robert

Michulec, Kenneth Minor, Kees Mol, Eric Mombeek, George Morrison, Williamson Murray, Wesley Newton, Frank Olynyk, Neil Page, Robert Peczkowski, Doug Peifer, Gordon Permann, Jim Perry, Toni Petito, Peter Petrick, Dick Powers, Alfred Price, Jochen Prien, Lorenz Rasse, Jean-Louis Roba, Barry Rosch, Brown Ryle, Chris Shores, Barry Smith, Evelyn Smith, Sam Sox, Klaes Sundin, Günter Sundermann, Lothair Vanoverbeke, John Vasco, Luc Vervoort, Dave Wadman, Edward Westermann, and Tony Wood. We apologize to anyone whose name has been inadvertently omitted from this list.

The Bundesarchiv-Bildarchiv (Koblenz) and ww2images.com have granted permission to reprint photographs from their collections. We also greatly appreciate the following publishers and authors for kindly granting permission to reproduce quoted passages from published works: W. W. Norton for Bert Stiles, *Serenade to the Big Bird*; the British National Archives (Public Record Office) for Air Ministry, *The Rise and Fall of the German Air Force* and Denis Richards, *Royal Air Force 1939–1945*; Ian Allan Publishing for Armand van Ishoven, *Messerschmitt Bf 109 at War*; and author Eric Mombeek for *Defending the Reich: The History of Jagdgeschwader 1 "Oesau."*

We wish to acknowledge the help given us by the professional staffs of the British Public Record Office, the Bundesarchiv-Militärarchiv (Freiburg), the Lake Jackson Public Library, the Auburn University Library, the Military Archives Division of the U.S. National Archives, the Air University Library, the Air Command and Staff College, the School of Advanced Air and Space Studies, and the United States Air Force Historical Research Agency.

A special thanks is owed to Les Butler for the maps and figures.

Last but by no means least, our thanks go to our wives for their patience and support.

Any book of this size and scope will contain errors of both omission and commission. We welcome correspondence with anyone who has information to share pertaining to this fascinating period in aviation history. We wish to state further that all quotations in the book that were originally written or spoken in the German language were translated into English by one of us, with the exception of those identified as wartime or postwar Allied official translations. The responsibility for any consequent errors in fact or tone is our own.

PREFACE

From September 4, 1939, through the end of the war in Europe in May 1945, the Luftwaffe's day-fighter force struggled to defend German airspace against enemy attack, first by the Royal Air Force's Bomber Command, and later by the four-engine bomber fleets of the United States Army Air Forces (USAAF). The battle to defend the homeland was not one the Germans planned to fight, yet by 1944 it had evolved into a titanic campaign involving thousands of aircraft, Flak guns, sophisticated radar and fighter-control equipment, and highly trained personnel. In the process, the German day-fighter arm was shattered, leaving the combat fronts stripped of air cover. By any measure, the aerial defenders of the Reich—the *Reichsluftverteidigung* (RLV)—were part of one of the most important campaigns of the entire Second World War.

Many excellent books have examined aspects of this six-year battle. There are first-rate histories of the Luftwaffe as a whole, detailing its overall strategy, methods of employment, and ultimate inability to wage a protracted war of attrition. Over the past several decades, historians have produced some outstanding studies of individual air battles. There are also minutely detailed unit histories of some of the most important units of the RLV, offering a microcosmic yet invaluable view of the campaign. Technical studies of the principal—and even the more obscure—Luftwaffe aircraft abound, and many display thorough research and a high degree of technical accuracy. Several prominent commanders and aviators have left their memoirs—although far too few did so. There are also outstanding comprehensive histories of the Flak arm and the German night-fighter force. Yet the day-fighter effort has not received similar treatment. This is understandable, since it would be a daunting task, covering as it does not only the activities of dozens of flying units in action against hundreds of major Allied raids, but also touching upon Luftwaffe doctrine and strategy, command and control principles, organization, technological development, and the German war economy.

Ten years ago, in recognition of the scope of the task, we decided to combine our expertise and research interests to produce a new account that we believe to be the most complete available in a single volume. The book you are holding traces the theoretical underpinnings of Luftwaffe fighter defense concepts, and shows how these played out during six long years of combat. It offers a concise examination of the major phases of the defensive campaign, and provides new and meticulously researched accounts of the major air actions. Themes such as pilot training, technological evolution, tactical innovation, and command and control development run throughout the narrative. Especially noteworthy are dozens of firsthand accounts by the surviving pilots and commanders themselves—many provided to historians for the first time. From the corridors of power at the Luftwaffe high command, to the division operations rooms, to the cockpits of the fighters bearing the distinctive colored fuselage bands of the RLV, this account examines for the first time the entire conduct of the German day-fighter effort against the Allied bombers. We believe it is a unique contribution to the history of Word War II in the air.

Donald Caldwell, Lake Jackson, Texas
Richard Muller, Montgomery, Alabama

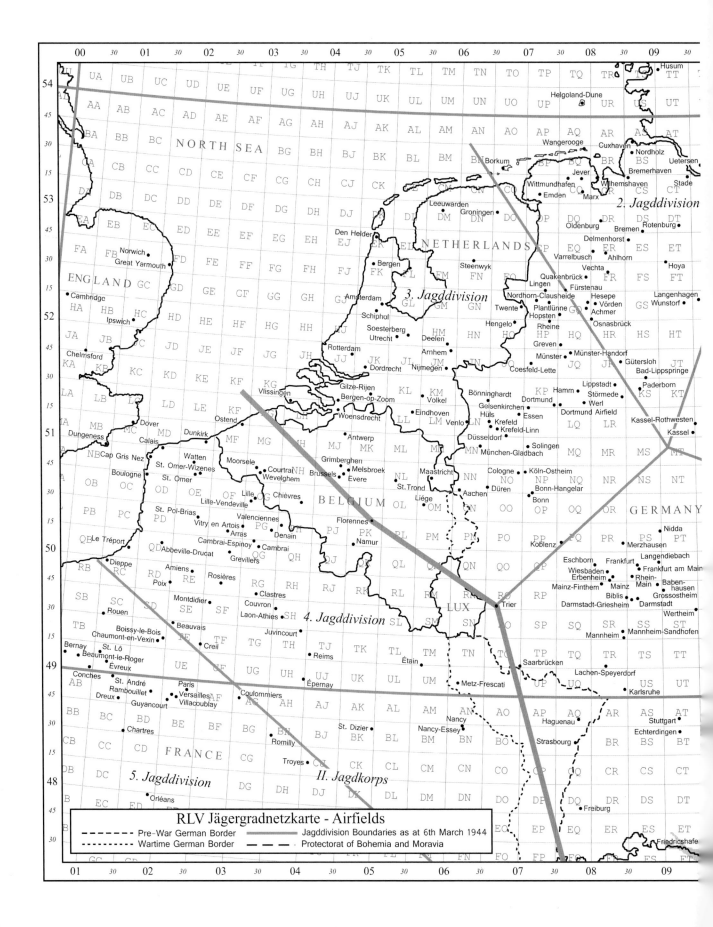

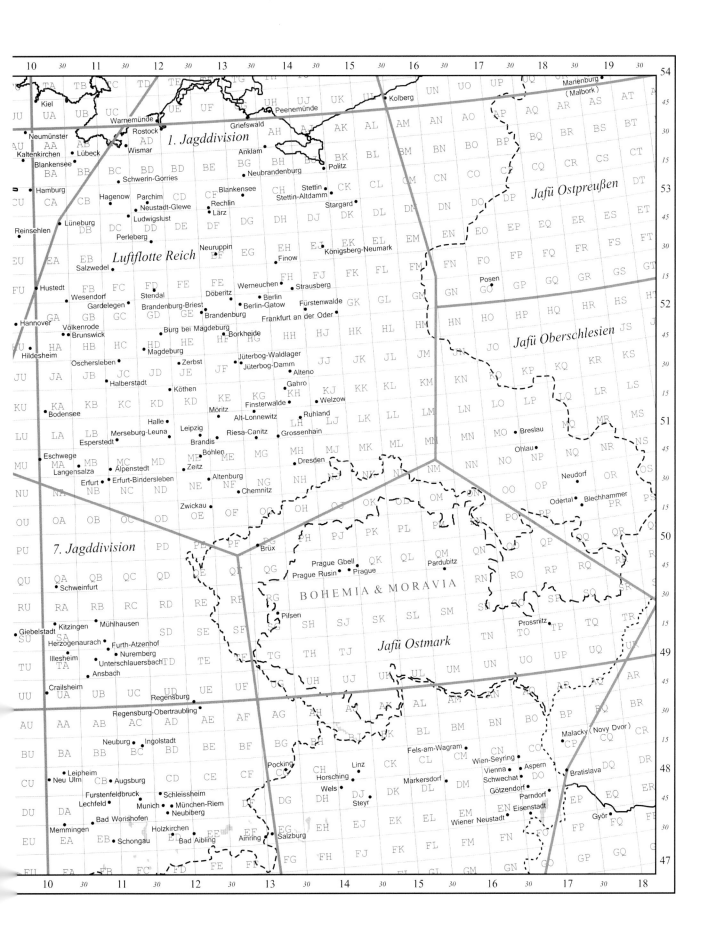

CHAPTER 1

GERMAN AIR DEFENSE:
EARLY HISTORY AND THEORY 1914–1939

In early 1944 the air defense of Germany (*Reichsluftverteidigung*, *RLV*) was the responsibility of Luftflotte Reich, an organization containing more than 1,300 day and night fighters and thousands of heavy Flak (anti-aircraft) guns backed up by a sophisticated early warning and command and control system. Little of this structure, and few of these components, existed four years previously. The rapid growth and great strength of Luftflotte Reich certainly owed much to wartime improvisation and the deteriorating military situation, yet many of its organizational elements, operational concepts and command arrangements could trace their origins back to the dawn of German aviation, and particularly to the fertile period of aerial rearmament and doctrinal formulation in the 1930s.

Beginnings: The First World War, 1914–1918

The First World War was the crucible of military aviation, and the story of German day-fighter defense begins there as well. The great powers began the conflict with small air arms, which by 1916 had evolved into formidable military organizations, laying claim to large shares of their defense budgets and industrial capacity. The bulk of this effort went into aviation supporting the titanic battle of attrition on the Western Front, and innovative commanders honed operational capabilities such as observation, artillery spotting, close air support and interdiction to a fine edge. The increase in performance and effectiveness of the fighter aircraft of Germany and the western powers was particularly dramatic, although, again, most of these fighters were committed to the battle for air superiority over the front lines. The stalemate also ushered in the age of "total war" with the development of strategic bombardment—aerial attacks aimed not at the fighting forces of the enemy, but at the industries, transportation networks, and population sustaining

the war effort. Early in the war, these raids took the form of isolated attacks by small groups of aircraft against targets such as blast furnaces, which were easily spotted at night. German raids by Zeppelin dirigibles and heavy bombers against London and other urban targets in Great Britain spurred not only the creation of the Royal Air Force (RAF) on April 1, 1918, but also the growth of Britain's air defenses and calls for

Organized glider flying was a prime outlet for aviation-minded German youth between the wars. This is Gerhard Herzog in a Grunau Baby, *c.* 1933–4. Herzog later served in the Condor Legion in Spain and became the first war casualty of JG 26, going into captivity on May 11, 1940. (*Herzog*)

A pair of He 51 fighters of the *Reklamestaffel* (advertising squadron) *Mitteldeutschland* from Döberitz, displaying civilian markings; the Luftwaffe had not yet come into being. (*Galland*)

reprisals. The Independent Force, commanded by Sir Hugh Trenchard, carried out a sustained air campaign against German industrial and transportation targets for the last five months of the war.

The increasing strength of Allied bombing compelled the Germans to think more seriously about homeland air defense. Early raids into German territory led to the creation of five air-defense districts in 1915. The *Flugmeldedienst* (Aircraft Reporting Service) had been created the previous year, and was eventually linked to searchlight and Flak units by telephone. At the onset of the war, the German military believed that anti-aircraft artillery would bear the largest share of the burden of defending the airspace over the homeland. By 1915, aircraft had

begun to play a role as well: "The fighter units stationed at the front aided the air defense of the homeland indirectly by battling the bombers" as they crossed the lines. But daylight fighter defense of Germany really began in the fall of 1915, when a fighter pilot training school assumed the task of defending the huge and vulnerable Zeppelin sheds in northern Germany against British air attacks.[1]

On December 8, 1916, the *Luftstreitkräfte* (Air Service) leadership created the position of "Commander of Home Defense," directly subordinate to the *Kogenluft* (the commanding general of the Air Service), charged with overseeing "all arrangements and measures which are necessary for the defense of the homeland against air attacks."[2] These changes in organization were accompanied by improvements in tactics, and cooperation between the Flak and fighters steadily improved. By the end of the war, home-defense forces disposed of 896 heavy Flak guns, 454 searchlights, 204 anti-aircraft machine guns, and nine fighter squadrons.[3] German air defense, following this "combined-arms" philosophy, gave a good account of itself, by day and by night. Some of the raids of the RAF's Independent Force in the summer of 1918 sustained appalling losses. For example, a mission against railroad installations at Saarbrücken on July 31, 1918, cost No. 99 Squadron seven out of 12 de Havilland DH 9s committed; all fell to the guns of German fighters.[4] In a 1920 official volume commemorating the achievements of the various German air units, Major Hugo Grimme recounted the following tale of combat, this time against French raiders:

The "Weimar Air Force," photographed at Breslau on October 28, 1934. The nearest airplane is a Klemm 25; the second is a Heinkel 72 Kadett. (*Herzog*)

General Walther Wever, the first Chief of Staff of the new Luftwaffe. Wever cast the German air arm in an offensive mold while recognizing that defense of German airspace required attention. Milch regarded him as the only Chief of Staff of any service who approached von Moltke the Elder, the father of the German General Staff, in ability. (*USAFHRA*)

Already, before morning dawned, several fighting squadrons were ready to take off—indeed, every minute was precious—and precisely at 3:15 a.m., a report came via the Aircraft Reporting Service regarding a "squadron approaching Stuttgart." It must not reach its target. Thanks to the excellent work of the Air Reporting Service, two fighting squadrons had time to cut between Stuttgart and the French squadrons so as to climb above the latter, and—guided by direction shots fired by the Flak—ruthlessly dove to the attack. A true air battle resulted; soon the enemy fled after three aircraft were shot down in flames. The French lost four more during the pursuit, and eventually escaped with two only, thanks to the appearance of cloud cover.

Nowhere else in the air service must the various branches work as closely together as the units involved in homeland air defense. Airmen, Flak, airships, searchlights, machine guns, air reporting and meteorological services, all worked together in harmonious and successful cooperation . . . Germany's Air Service protected Germany's homeland.[5]

Indeed, the Germans by their own count sustained no fewer than 1,200 air raids on the Western Front during the war, with 650 (mostly daylight) raids taking place in 1918. Actual damage to German war potential was negligible, even though the air-defense forces had not been able to prevent the attackers from reaching their targets. General Herhudt von Rohden, the chief of the Luftwaffe General Staff's historical division, was therefore more measured in his assessment. He noted, "Towards the end of the war in 1918 one could neither speak of aerial warfare, nor of

A He 51B-1 of the 4. Staffel of JG 132 (later 4./JG 2 *Richthofen*) at Jüterbog-Damm, *c.* 1936–7. The colorful markings are typical of the world's fighter forces in the interwar period. The identification color of this unit was red, in honor of the Red Baron. (*Herzog*)

an organized air defense as we conceive it today."[6] Yet most of the elements that made up the powerful air defenses of the Third Reich in 1943–5 were in evidence. These included: an early-warning system, regional defense commands, dedicated interceptor units, and ever-changing tactics to maximize the effectiveness of both Flak and fighters. Future generations of German airmen would have good reason to revisit these lessons from the first air war. It is important to note, however, that the central command that controlled these defenses in 1916–18 was not re-established until 1944, more than four years after the onset of the Second World War.

The Weimar Years

After the abdication and flight of the Kaiser at the end of the war, Germany established a federal democracy with a weak central government, the Weimar Republic. The Versailles Treaty permitted Germany a modest defensive force, the 100,000-man *Reichswehr*, but no combat aviation units or aircraft. Under the guiding hand of General Hans von Seeckt, the "genius with the monocle," a small number of aviation officers were allowed to join the Reichswehr; for several years they were necessarily limited to staff duties. Along with their ground force comrades, they embarked on a rigorous analysis of the late conflict. These officers studied the major air power problems of the 1914–18 war, including tactical aviation, the struggle for air superiority, strategic bombardment, and air defense. The analysis took place in a spirit of critical self-examination, and concluded that the Luftstreitkräfte had been oriented too much toward

A close-up view of a 2./JG 131 Ar 68F-1 at Jesau. (*Herzog*)

Ar 68F-1s of 2./JG 131 (later 2./JG 1) at Jesau, c. 1937–8. The Geschwader is denoted by the trim color, black; the bands of its II. Staffel are white. (*Herzog*)

defense. The technique of creating a *Luftsperre* (aerial barrier) of defensive fighter patrols, as employed during the Battle of Verdun in 1916, came in for particular criticism; it had wasted scarce resources and had failed to stop the French from seizing control of the skies over the battlefield. The preferred German tactic of waiting for French and (especially) British aircraft to cross the lines before engaging them had indeed inflicted heavy losses on the Allies, but it had also forfeited the initiative. A future German air arm would not make this error. While defense of key cities and installations could not be ignored, the primary task of both single- and two-seat fighters was to ensure the freedom of action of friendly air power while denying the same to the enemy.[7] The analysts also pointed out the huge quantity of manpower and material—including pursuit squadrons desperately needed at the front— that the British used to defend against a handful of German Zeppelin and Gotha raids.

The fruits of the postwar analysis project found expression in the 1926 manual *Richtlinien für die Führung des operativen Luftkrieges* ("Guidelines for the Conduct of Operational Air Warfare"). This remarkable document spelled out the many ways in which a modern air arm might operate in a future war. It was the first clear articulation of the German idea of "operational air warfare." According to this concept, the Luftwaffe was to contribute to the overall war effort in a variety of ways: by aggressively gaining and maintaining air superiority, assisting the surface forces through interdiction and direct support, and through attacks on key "centers of gravity" and the enemy's "sources of power."

The manual had much to say about air defense, but a good part of the discussion highlighted the futility of relying on a defensive posture in modern air warfare. It asserted:

> A delaying battle in the air or a pure defense denies the essential character of the air force ... Aircraft cannot be used like machine-gun nests on the ground, to fire at the enemy flanks. The sky contains no strong or weak points such as exist in ground warfare ... The breadth of the sky and its three-dimensional character make defense impossible.[8]

It further noted, "Air tactics do not recognize the term 'defense,'" and decried "the wasteful and pointless use of personnel and material" in employing large numbers of aircraft in defensive barriers. In a statement foreshadowing British Prime Minister Stanley Baldwin's observation that "the bomber will always get through," the authors of the 1926 manual warned, "Soldiers and civilians must know that the overflight of their own territory cannot be hindered, and that they need to take necessary measures for defense and cover."[9]

What is striking about the 1926 regulation is its similarity to the thinking of the other major air-power thinkers of the interwar period. Hugh Trenchard spoke of "attack as the best defense," while Giulio Douhet regarded air defense as futile and auxiliary aviation as "worthless, superfluous, harmful."[10] Douhet unequivocally stated:

> Viewed in its true light, aerial warfare admits of no defense, only offense. *We must therefore resign ourselves to the offensives the enemy inflicts upon us, while striving to put all our resources to work to inflict even heavier ones upon him.* That is the basic principle which must govern the development of aerial warfare.[11]

In his classic 1925 polemic *Winged Defense*, General

The He 51B of Hptm. Oskar Dinort, the first Kommandeur of I./JG 234 (later I./JG 26 *Schlageter*) on the firing stand at Köln-Ostheim in early 1937. The fighter's cowling is orange, the unit's ID color. The figure on the left is the Gruppe's chief armorer. (*Meyer*)

William "Billy" Mitchell argued:

> It was proved in the European war that the only effective defense against aerial attack is to whip the enemy's air forces in air battles. In other words, seizing the initiative, forcing the enemy to the defensive in his own territory, attacking his most important ground positions, menacing his airplanes on the ground, in the hangars, on the airdromes and in the factories so he will be forced to take the air and defend them. To sit down on one's own territory and wait for the other fellow to come, is to be whipped before an operation is even commenced.[12]

Yet German air power thinkers were keenly aware that their nation was vulnerable to attack from the air. A prisoner of central European geography, the Reich found itself potentially outflanked by hostile bomber fleets based in France, Poland, Great Britain, or the U.S.S.R.[13] The Reichswehr planners could therefore not neglect the need for air defense and pursuit aviation to the same extent as, for example, airmen in the United States or Great Britain. Attack may have been the best defense, but the manual did lay out methods for building a home air-defense system that might "hinder, or at least greatly limit, the effects of air bombardment" against certain key objectives. This organization, a "single, unified organization for home air defense" was to be led by a Commander of Home Air Defense as existed during the Great War. Its missions were:

1. Observation of the air space (Air Reporting Service)
2. Engaging enemy aircraft in close proximity to their targets (Air Defense)
3. Warnings for businesses and the populace (Alert Service)
4. Protection from enemy aerial observation (Camouflage Service)

Its final paragraph, however, returned to the overall Douhetian thrust of the document: "The best defense against attack is to create the strongest possible air force, which can destroy the enemy attack forces at their bases and carry out thorough retaliation."[14] It is important to remember that the 1926 regulation was in many ways a theoretical document to be used as a basis for future planning; Germany possessed no air force. Yet even in contingency planning, the use of fighter aircraft for home defense was downplayed. The June 30, 1927, war mobilization plan of the *Reichs-*

He 51Bs of 2./JG 234 (later 2./JG 26) on field maneuvers in July 1937. During peacetime such maneuvers were always highlights of the year for unit personnel. (*Meyer*)

wehrministerium (Defense Ministry) called for the creation of a home-defense headquarters incorporating the aircraft warning service and the Flak, but noted that any available fighter squadrons were not to be employed in home defense but instead placed at the disposal of the front-line combat commanders.[15]

The World War I lessons were analyzed and digested. A comprehensive air warfare doctrine was on the shelf, patiently awaiting the day Germany rearmed in the air. In a future war the Luftwaffe would operate offensively, warding off strikes against the homeland by launching powerful air attacks of its own. The Flak forces, searchlights, and Air Reporting Service would guard against enemy air attack. The architecture for creating a modern air-defense system, incorporating early warning, anti-aircraft guns, fighters, command and control, and civilian air raid protection began to emerge.

Air Defense under the National Socialists

The Nazi accession to power on January 30, 1933, galvanized the growth of German air power. Within two years the hitherto camouflaged air arm would be ready to be unveiled. The aircraft industry was expanding, and the theoretical treatises of the Reichswehr era were being refined into practical operational doctrines. Yet, in the first months after Adolf Hitler's rise to power, Germany was still virtually disarmed. An October 25, 1933, directive from the Defense Ministry somewhat fatalistically noted: "Without regard for the prospects of military success, the Reich government is determined to offer local armed resistance to any hostile action." The Luftwaffe was responsible for "defense in the air over

Berlin and the industrial region of central Germany, with main emphasis on Berlin."[16] The Luftwaffe forces available to implement this modest goal were themselves limited to:

1. One fighter group, equipped with Arado 65 aircraft, still in the process of activation at Döberitz;
2. One fighter training school at Schleissheim, where it would have been possible to activate one to two improvised tactical squadrons, using the Ar 64 and Ar 65 aircraft available for training purposes. The instructor crews were from the Reichswehr and from the German Commercial Aviation School, and had received fighter pilot training at Lipetsk (Russia) and in Italy;
3. A serviceable aircraft reporting system;
4. The authority to order passive air-raid-protection measures.

Indeed, German air planners recognized that 1933–4 would be a dangerous time for the new regime. Accordingly, one air theorist, Dr. Robert Knauss, proposed the creation of a "Risk Luftwaffe," a powerful force of bombers quickly assembled to act as a deterrent while more broadly based rearmament was in progress.[17] The territory of the Reich itself was to be protected by "powerful anti-aircraft units, so that fighter production could be restricted in favor of

bomber production."[18] Knauss's scheme proved beyond the capability of the German aircraft industry at the time, yet it fitted in well with the new service's offensive direction.

The Luftwaffe throughout its short existence was an amalgam of the professional German General Staff ethos and a strong dose of National Socialism. In questions of offensive versus defensive orientation, these two traditions reinforced each other. The professional officer corps believed that the experience and lessons of the 1914–18 war suggested that the Luftwaffe should carry the fight to the enemy, even if the unfavorable military balance called for a temporary tactical defense. In this they echoed earlier German military thinkers such as Scharnhorst, Clausewitz and von Moltke.[19] At the same time, the ambitious goals set forth in Hitler's foreign policy agenda demanded that the Luftwaffe build up its offensive forces in the shortest practicable time. Hitler's program of open rearmament, vastly increased defense budgets, and his promise to wipe away the shame of the Versailles years found many ready adherents among the officer corps, among them General Walther Wever,[20] the first Chief of the Luftwaffe General Staff.

The new Luftwaffe was established on March 1, 1935. It benefited from the political patronage of Hermann Göring,[21] its Commander-in-Chief, and held a privileged place in the new Germany. Göring in

A single He 51B of 2./JG 234 (later 2./JG 26), photographed in July 1937. (*Meyer*)

Ar 68s of II./JG 234 (later II./JG 26) during an inspection at Düsseldorf in 1937. The closest aircraft appears to lack individual or unit markings. It is either new, or a harbinger of toned-down camouflage. (*Spies*)

fact commanded all aspects of German aviation, civilian and military, from his *Reichsluftfahrtministerium* (RLM—German Air Ministry). Field Marshal Werner von Blomberg, the War Minister, enthusiastically transferred first-class Army and Navy officers to the new air service with the comment that the Nazi air arm must become "an elite corps with a tempestuous spirit of attack."[22] Wever's selection as General Staff chief was one obvious manifestation of von Blomberg's largesse; Blomberg told Göring that the Army was giving up its very best prospect (and most likely a future Chief of the Army General Staff).[23] While Hitler and Reich Air Minister Hermann Göring charted the Luftwaffe's political direction, and former Lufthansa chief Erhard Milch[24] saw to its technical and industrial foundation, it was able professionals such as Wever and his staff officers who would shape the actual fighting capability of the new service.

Most of these officers professed awareness of Germany's vulnerability to air attack. They noted that the Reich's geopolitical position, population density, concentration of vital industries linked to available raw materials by a well-developed transportation network, and complicated electrical supply grid, made it susceptible to air attack from many quarters. Yet, in Wever's view, "It [was] not possible to create an unlimited number of areas adequately defended against air attack and at the same time build up a strong air force."[25] Another officer maintained that attaining total air superiority, either over the battlefield or the homeland, was a "fantasy."[26] Accordingly, he believed that only a small percentage of Luftwaffe fighter strength should be allocated for home air defense.

Wever and his collaborators ensured, therefore, that the Luftwaffe would continue to exhibit a strong and almost single-minded offensive orientation. The German concept of "operational air warfare," greatly developed from its 1926 roots, called for the Luftwaffe to achieve a strategic decision in conjunction with the other two services, especially the Army. Its first task at the onset of any major war was the gaining of air superiority. The whole of the Luftwaffe was to participate in this effort, through bombing raids on airfields and aircraft factories as well as air-to-air combat.[27]

All of this found cogent expression in a most significant doctrine manual—*Luftwaffendienstvorschrift 16: Luftkriegführung* ("Luftwaffe Manual 16: Conduct of Aerial Warfare"—hereafter L.Dv. 16).[28] Drafted by a team of officers in 1935, and slightly revised in 1940, it remained in force throughout the Second World War. The manual maintained:

> One's own armed forces and one's own country are constantly threatened by the enemy air force. This danger cannot be opposed merely by defensive measures in one's own territory. The danger of air attack against one's land requires that the air force carry out offensive action against the enemy's air force in his own territory.[29]

Adolf Galland,[30] in a postwar statement, sharply criticized this prevailing attitude when he stated: "I still remember a period when the talk was all of strategic bombers and one referred with something of pitying condescension to 'home-defense fighters.'"[31] Many Luftwaffe generals interrogated after the war agreed with Galland's assessment; Milch and General Josef "Beppo" Schmid,[32] among others, criticized the unwavering fixation on the offensive and the corresponding lack of home-defense capability.

It is only fair to record another participant's view. In 1943 one member of the *Jagdwaffe* (Fighter Arm) concluded that the USAAF, in carrying the fight into the Reich territory, was correctly applying German prewar doctrine. He ruefully noted:

> Now they're showing us how we ought to have fought the battles over Britain . . . I've just been reading a manual, usually the last sort of thing I do. L.Dv. 16 is the one, and it describes exactly how to set about it. Written by General Wever himself . . .[33]

Members of the Luftwaffe General Staff's historical analysis division agreed; in 1944 they concluded, "The enemy has learned from our conduct of the air war, and the pupil has become the master!"[34] In any case, the Luftwaffe would ultimately prove incapable of either securing victory through offensive means or of providing an adequate aerial defense.

Armed with this knowledge of how the air war of 1939–45 actually turned out, the 1935 air war regulation makes for fascinating reading. While the section entitled "The Defense" was clearly subordinate to the sections dealing with operational employment of offensive combat power, the 1935 regulation proved remarkably

A mixed lineup photographed during 1937 field maneuvers. I./JG 234 Bf 109Bs are in the foreground, with II./JG 234 Ar 68s in the rear. (Meyer)

prescient in addressing the general form—and indeed some of the specific details—of the Luftwaffe's daylight battle against the USAAF in 1942–5. It made a case for unity of command: a senior air commander provided overall guidance for the employment, command relationships, and coordination of defense forces—Flak and fighters—as well as the aircraft reporting and air-raid-warning services and civil defense.[35] The manual recommended the creation of operations centers, equipped with "a complete and effective communications net, linking the air reporting system to subordinate units."[36] The commander, in cooperation with neighboring air-defense districts, was "to build a picture of the situation, as well as possible enemy courses of action. By taking timely and appropriate actions and by making effective use of time and space, he can minimize the effect of enemy attacks."[37]

Wever's manual envisioned a forward defense, with the defending fighters stationed as close to the front line as practicable. His instructions emphasized timely location of the enemy formation "so that the enemy is identified before reaching the air-defense area and is brought to battle before, during and after his attack."[38] Although effective air defense required a measure of centralized control, success rested on the initiative and judgment of the flying unit commanders:

> Success depends on minutes; giving orders via the defense commander costs time. The commander of fighters, therefore, has independent authority concerning the moment of takeoff, for deploying his forces, and for leading battle operations.[39]

The manual further recognized that the First World War concept of combined operations between Flak and day fighters was valid. It proposed a rather rigid delineation between Flak and fighter defense zones as a means of maximizing the effectiveness of each weapon, while at the same time implying that the fighters were the junior partner in the arrangement:

> Cooperation between fighter and Flak forces requires the most thorough liaison. Simultaneous attack by anti-aircraft weapons and fighters against the same enemy formation will normally not be carried out owing to the danger to our own fighters.
>
> Fighters should engage the enemy before he enters the anti-aircraft zone; an attack at the right moment can disperse the bombing formation and create favorable conditions for anti-aircraft defense. When

Maneuvers in the field in early 1938. 4./JG 234 (foreground) now has Bf 109Bs; the Ar 68s of the rest of II./JG 234 are in the rear. (*Meyer*)

the enemy reaches the anti-aircraft zone, the commander of the fighter unit must decide whether to disengage and allow the anti-aircraft to take over the defense, or to continue to press the attack. Taking into account the possibility of loss from our own fire, he may decide to allow some fighters to hunt the enemy freely into the target area.[40]

Although one might fault L.Dv. 16's overly optimistic view of offensive air operations, the manual certainly shared this trait with the air theories of the other emerging air powers. Indeed, in at least addressing some of the problems inherent in modern air defense, it was certainly more realistic than most. Command arrangements, cooperation with Flak, the importance of communications, the need for tactical and operational flexibility and mobility, and even tactical details such as the likelihood of encountering enemy escort fighters covering the bombers' withdrawal—all were clearly delineated in the 1935 Luftwaffe manual.

The Practice

L.Dv. 16 spelled out the big questions about the employment of air power, while leaving a myriad of operational details unaddressed. Luftwaffe General Staff officers and operational commanders attempted to devise workable tactics, command arrangements,

and operational procedures. Oberst Paul Deichmann, a General Staff officer who was one of the key contributors to L.Dv. 16, argued that successful defense of key industrial areas in Germany would require effective and flexible coordination between Flak and fighters.[41] Foreshadowing a debate that would rage throughout the Second World War, Deichmann insisted that: "The concentration of offensive and defensive power in one hand is the strength of our air defense."[42] He clearly meant that an aviator, instead of a Flak commander, should have overall control of air-defense forces, in keeping with the prevailing idea that even "defensive" problems had "offensive" solutions.

After the war Deichmann elaborated further on the principles of day-fighter defense:

In 1936 the doctrines for the fighter forces were compiled by the Operations Division of the Luftwaffe General Staff. According to these doctrines, fighter units in adequate numbers were to be stationed in Germany in times of peace in such a manner that a fighter defense line would be established extending along the entire length of the frontiers, backed by further fighter units stationed in a checkerboard pattern throughout Germany, with proper regard for areas of main effort in air defense, so that any enemy air force penetrating into Germany in a surprise attack would encounter fighter defenses everywhere and would come under constantly repeated attacks . . .

A source of concern in planning this system was caused by the small striking range of the existing fighters . . . [43]

Other staff officers and commanders focused more on the operational details of handling fighter forces in combat. A presentation entitled "Technology, Organization and Operations of the Fighter Forces" was delivered by Major Johann Raithel of the Fighter and Dive-Bomber Inspectorate on October 22, 1936.[44] The opening portion of the lecture was vintage L.Dv. 16. Since Germany was unusually vulnerable to enemy air attack, the first task was to gain air superiority in order to fend off this threat. He argued that the best way to achieve this was to apply all air power in a concentrated fashion against the enemy air force, in the air and on the ground, thereby requiring an independent air force command. After this obligatory preamble, he turned to his main subject: how the fighters might engage and destroy enemy bomber and reconnaissance aircraft in order to protect the homeland.[45]

Raithel was aware that there was insufficient fighter strength to treat all of Germany as a "single large air-defense region," so it was necessary to identify specific objects to be protected.[46] These objects were to be protected by a series of defensive zones—a refinement of Deichmann's checkerboard concept and L.Dv. 16's air-defense zone. These consisted of the *Flakzone*, in the immediate vicinity of the target and within the effective range of the anti-aircraft artillery protecting it. Next was an inner *Schutz-Zone* (protection zone), in good weather conditions usually a 30–40 kilometer (18–25 mile) radius around the target, which represented the last opportunity for fighters to engage the incoming enemy bombers. Operations in the Schutz-Zone required a great degree of coordination between Flak and fighters. Next was the *Einsatz-Zone* (zone of operations), within which most of the air combat between enemy bombers and German fighters would take place. The dimensions of this zone depended upon both the speed of the enemy bomber formation and the response time and speed of the German interceptors. Raithel calculated that the Einsatz-Zone for a Heinkel (He) 51, a standard German fighter, was 80 km (50 miles) wide; for a Messerschmitt Bayerische Flugzeugwerke 109 (abbreviated as Bf 109; at the time still under development), he envisioned it would extend to 100 km (62 miles). Obviously, it was desirable to engage the enemy aircraft as early as possible.

In order to ensure success, Raithel stressed the importance of the aircraft reporting network for informing both fighter and Flak defenses of the

II./JG 234 at Düsseldorf in 1938; the Gruppe is now fully equipped with Bf 109s. (*Meyer*)

altitude, bearing and strength of enemy formations. The system had evolved in complexity and efficiency since its First World War origins, but the basic requirements were unchanged (and indeed would endure well into the radar era). A May 12, 1937, directive laid out those requirements concisely:

1. Surveillance of hostile air activities to provide the data necessary for constructing an estimate of the air situation;
2. Speedy reporting of hostile aircraft sighted to ensure timely counter-action by the defending forces, in particular to give fighter forces time enough to reach operating altitude before the arrival of the enemy;
3. The timely reporting of approaching hostile aircraft to the air raid warning service . . . to make possible the implementation of preplanned air-raid-precaution measures before the actual air attack can commence . . .[47]

The Aircraft Reporting Service consisted of a number of aircraft reporting centers that collected reports from individual air observation posts spaced some 9–11 km (6–7 miles) apart. "Through their air observers they provide continuous lines of air observation, which criss-cross the entire territory of Germany. The parallel lines are spaced approximately 80–100 km [50–60 miles] apart, with smaller spacing near the frontiers." Control of the Air Reporting Service rested with the Luftgaukommandos in the interior of Germany; in the zone of operations it was run by the Luftwaffe general (*Koluft*) assigned to Army headquarters.[48] When early-warning radar became available, it was integrated into this system, primarily to economize on observers.

Most interestingly, Raithel also proposed the use of German long-range-reconnaissance and bomber aircraft to reconnoiter enemy bases, detecting take-offs of enemy bombers and reporting these to fighter units based close to the front. He also proposed using these reconnaissance planes to "inconspicuously accompany" the incoming enemy formations, constantly reporting on their course, speed and altitude. This must be one of the earliest references to the concept of *Fühlungshalter* (contact keeper) aircraft that would play such an important role shadowing USAAF Fortress and Liberator formations during the great air battles over Germany in 1943–4.[49]

Air tactics to engage the enemy formations were

Erwin Leykauf (*left*), his mechanic, and their Ar 68 before a mission to Czechoslovakia in 1938. This fighter of ZG 176 (later ZG 26 *Horst Wessel*) bears hastily applied "Munich" camouflage. (*Leykauf*)

also being developed and refined. In 1936, German fighter *Staffeln* (squadrons) still employed the *Kette* (three-aircraft element) as the basic flying formation; the famed *Schwarm* or "finger-four," developed in Spain, lay in the future. German air tacticians viewed the problem of interception as a fairly straightforward task of acting quickly upon receipt of information from the Air Reporting Service, scrambling the fighters, and bringing them into contact with the enemy in Staffel strength or greater. Ideally, the fighters would find themselves in a favorable firing position, above and behind the bombers.

To accomplish this task, the Luftwaffe's fighter units relied on a well-established German command principle—that of *Auftragstaktik* (mission-oriented tactics). The concept is most associated with German

Army doctrine and regulations, but it was well established in the Luftwaffe as well. According to one student of the German Army:

> The success of *Auftragstaktik* rested on subordinate commanders understanding the intent of their commander and acting to achieve his goal even if their actions violated other guidance or orders they had received. According to this concept, which was deeply ingrained in the German officer corps and essentially acted as a philosophy of command, a commander could act according to the circumstances of the moment and perhaps ignore a directive or a control measure such as a boundary if his actions contributed to the accomplishment of the unit's mission. Though an officer did this at his own risk, the results could be astounding, for the concept of *Auftragstaktik* permitted, if not encouraged, an officer to use his initiative to solve a tactical problem.[50]

A German fighter commander described its application in air defense:

> The larger and more composite the assigned air-defense forces are, and the wider the areas to which they are committed, the more it will become necessary to direct their operations through mission assignment rather than through direct orders. The significance of the mission assignment or directive [*Auftrag*] is that it states the purpose to be achieved in an action *but leaves it to the unit commander assigned the mission to decide on the timing, nature and scope of the action to be taken.*[51]

Hptm. Walter Grabmann, Kommandeur of I./JG 234 (later I./JG 26), in his Bf 109B at Köln-Ostheim in 1938. These fighters were painted in menacing dark green camouflage at the Messerschmitt factory. (*Boehm-Tettelbach*)

The many successes of German fighter units in the Second World War, therefore, stemmed in part from the same tradition that produced General Heinz Guderian's decisive victory at the Meuse in May 1940.

All of the emerging air powers attempted to learn lessons from observing the limited wars that took place during the 1930s. For the Luftwaffe, the most significant of these was its own participation in the Spanish Civil War, 1936–9. The story of the Condor Legion and its impact on future Luftwaffe operations, particularly air-to-air combat tactics, is well known. Yet the lessons learned in Spain for homeland air defense were at best ambiguous. Some commanders believed that the Spanish intervention "had a decisive influence on the shaping of air-defense principles."[52] They noted that the conflict highlighted the vulnerability of unescorted bombers in daylight (which spurred the development of the Messerschmitt Bf 110 long-range fighter). The fact that the standard Luftwaffe fighters, the He 51 and Ar 68, were inferior to the latest Soviet and Western designs helped advance the Luftwaffe's modernization program. Other observers maintained that the war in Spain offered few lessons for a future air war between the great powers. They argued that strategic targets were too few, and the size of the forces committed too small, to enable the Luftwaffe leadership to draw meaningful conclusions for the aerial defense of Germany.[53]

The Technology

"With no other weapon is the interaction of tactics and technology so great as in the air force."[54] Wever's observation at the opening of the Luftwaffe's Air War Academy in November 1935 certainly applied to the development of air-defense weaponry and techniques. Throughout the 1930s, the limitations of German aircraft and communications technology shaped tactics and command relationships, while desired improvements in procedures in turn accelerated the development of improved hardware. Fighter design, weaponry, communications equipment, and detection apparatus all made dramatic advances in an effort to close the gap between theory and practice.

The first generation of Luftwaffe aircraft was of mixed quality, and German planners and airmen were keenly aware of their shortcomings. The 15 years lost during the Versailles era retarded German engine and aircraft development, and much work needed to be done in all aircraft categories.[55] The Ar 64, generally acknowledged as the new Luftwaffe's first fighter aircraft, appeared in 1930. This was a conventional biplane with undistinguished performance, but it did serve as a test-bed for the much improved Ar 65, the first Luftwaffe fighter aircraft to enter series production.[56] Its limited endurance (1 hour 15 minutes) and speed (240 km/h—150 mph) greatly circumscribed its usefulness in air-defense operations. The Ar 65 and the He 51 equipped the first (still camouflaged) fighter squadrons in 1934; the first Luftwaffe fighter wing, JG 132 (later JG 2 *Richthofen*), began life as a *Reklamestaffel* (a military unit masquerading as a commercial advertising squadron).[57] The He 51 was one of the most aesthetically appealing aircraft in the Luftwaffe's inventory, but by 1936 its shortcomings as an air-defense machine were becoming evident. A biplane with a top speed of approximately 280 km/h (175 mph) at 4,000 meters (13,000 ft.), it had weak armament (two MG 17 7.9-mm machine guns), limited ceiling, and (most problematical for air defense) limited range.[58] It also acquired a reputation among Luftwaffe pilots as difficult to handle.[59]

A third aircraft carried the fighter force through its formative years: the Ar 68, the Luftwaffe's last biplane fighter. It was considered a slight improvement over the Heinkel design, but exhibited the same overall weaknesses in armament and range. These early aircraft did serve one very important purpose: they helped prime the minuscule German aircraft industry for mass production, and they gave the embryonic German fighter squadrons valuable practical experience and tactical development.[60]

Perhaps less dramatic than aircraft performance figures, but equally important in terms of contemplating controlled interception of enemy air raids, was the state of German radio development in the mid-1930s. The radio equipment in use in the He 51 and Ar 68 (the FuG VI and FuG VIa sets) had an air-to-ground range of only 80 km (50 miles). Newer radio equipment (the FuG VII) was in the development and testing stages and promised better performance.

Given the limited performance of aircraft and their radios, it is not surprising that German air-defense concepts and tactics in the 1930s tended to emphasize point-defense of a few selected objectives, rather than a centrally controlled air defense capable of massing interceptors from some distance against incoming bomber formations. General Walther Grabmann, a Luftwaffe air defense commander and author of a postwar study for the USAAF[61] laid out the problem in stark terms:

A fighter plane which, after the time required for take-off, climbing, combat action, and landing had been deducted, had a maximum striking range of only 145 km [90 miles] could only be considered a weapon for local air defense . . . for this reason there was no possibility to concentrate fighter units during an action to form a point of main defensive effort at any point farther than 145 km from their bases.[62]

The promise of a new fighter design in 1936 seemed to open up new possibilities for effective air defense. The Messerschmitt Bf 109, known as the Me 109 to most Allied and German airmen, was one of the great planes of World War II. It represented Germany's leap to parity in international airplane design, a move away from biplanes and toward all-metal cantilever monoplanes with more powerful armament, retractable landing gear, and improved speed and rate of climb. It was a contemporary of the British Supermarine Spitfire and Hawker Hurricane and the French Morane M.S. 406 and Dewoitine D. 520. It was also a response to a specific German requirement for a second-generation "light" fighter.

In 1937, the RLM issued guidelines for fighter development along two parallel tracks—"light" and "heavy" fighters. A German instructional manual noted:

According to their missions, the fighter forces are organized in heavy and light fighter units.

The light fighter units stationed within or close to the zones of operations attack hostile bomber formations before they cross the front lines or after, and interfere with the operations of hostile reconnaissance aircraft and hostile fighter units over the zones of operations of the Army and over coastal defense areas . . .

Light fighter units committed in locally restricted air-defense missions in close cooperation with the anti-aircraft artillery will prevent attacks by hostile units against the installations they are assigned to protect . . .

Generally speaking, heavy fighter units will have the following missions:

1. Pursuit of hostile units engaged in attack operations over friendly and enemy territory;

2. Protection of friendly bomber formations over their target areas;

3. Attack against hostile defenses.[63]

In addition to its defensive tasks, the light fighter was to provide escort for friendly reconnaissance aircraft and bombers over the battlefield, conduct offensive fighter sweeps, and attack ground targets with gunfire and light bombs. The Bf 109, employed as an interceptor and air superiority fighter, would carry out these roles with great success during the opening years of the war. With steadily improved engine power, armament, altitude performance and range, the 109 would remain the backbone of the German air-defense forces until 1945.

As the Luftwaffe fighter force evolved, German airmen recognized a need for a "heavy fighter," not unlike the two-seat "infantry aircraft" or "escort aircraft" that equipped the *Schlachtstaffeln* (ground-attack squadrons) and *Schutzstaffeln* (protection squadrons) of the First World War.[64] As early as 1936, officers in the fighter inspectorate were taking note of foreign development of twin-engine heavy fighters (notably in the French Armée de l'Air) for operations in homeland air defense as "destroyer aircraft"— *Zerstörer* in German. Early proposals called for heavy armament (including a 3.7-cm shell-firing cannon and 1.5-cm and light machine guns).[65] Experience in the Spanish Civil War also suggested the need for a heavy fighter for use as a bomber escort. From an air-defense perspective, the chief advantage of the heavy fighter was its increased range. This extended operational reach would free the Luftwaffe fighter forces from a reliance on point defense and allow the building of a true "defensive point of main effort." Another 1937 study, this one by Josef Schmid, at that time a major on the General Staff, specifically mentioned the requirement "to attack even the heaviest type of bomber aircraft, to pursue enemy formations returning from an attack far into enemy territory in order to prevent their return to their bases and destroy them."[66] Specifications resulting from

Communications troops of 4./JG 234 take a break while on maneuvers at Jever in 1938. *(Sundermann)*

these deliberations eventually resulted in the Messerschmitt Bf 110, although production delays held up its appearance in quantity until 1939.

Radar, although it was to play a dramatic role in the day and night defense of Germany later in the war, had little place in the Luftwaffe's prewar calculations. In fact, the Freya radar, the most important German early-warning radar up to the middle of World War II, was a naval development. Luftwaffe interest in the new device, which quickly demonstrated its utility in tests and maneuvers, was lukewarm. An early radar pioneer recounted a conversation with Ernst Udet, the chief of the Luftwaffe's Technical Office, who reportedly told him, "If you introduce that thing you'll take all the fun out of flying!" Historian Alan Beyerchen concluded:

> One can extract from this episode not only the distress of a vanishing breed of World War I pilots, but a sense of the pervasiveness of inter-service rivalry and the visceral preference for the offensive spirit over technical advances in the defense of the Third Reich.[67]

It was not until October 1938 that Luftwaffe General Wolfgang Martini began experimenting with borrowed naval Freya sets. Martini, in his capacity as chief of the Luftwaffe signals branch, subsequently began to acquire Freyas for the Luftwaffe. Yet the peacetime Luftwaffe failed to create any kind of an integrated air-defense system using radar to full advantage. It would be years before it occurred to the Luftwaffe leadership that this was a serious omission— another hidden cost of the "dogma of the offensive."

Devising a Command Structure

Without a workable command arrangement through which to implement the newly developed operational concepts, aerial defense of the Reich territory would be stillborn. Luftwaffe command organization underwent considerable revision during the late 1930s as thinking and technology improved, and as German rearmament gathered momentum.[68] In 1936, Germany was divided into seven *Luftkreis-kommandos* (Air Regional Commands) overseeing all Luftwaffe activity within a particular geographic region. Within each *Luftkreis*, the senior commander of the Flak forces in that region was designated the commander of a *Luftgau* (Air District Command). On October 12, 1937, the Luftgau boundaries were altered to conform to the Army's corps command areas in Germany; to the end of the war Luftgaukommandos were identified by Roman numerals following the Army practice for designating corps.

A further reshuffle on February 4, 1938, abolished the Luftkreiskommandos, replacing them with three *Luftwaffengruppenkommandos* (Air Force Group Commands) and two separate air commands for East Prussia and naval aviation. These new commands were the precursors of the *Luftflotte* (Air Fleet) commands with which the Luftwaffe entered war in 1939, and now contained the Luftgaukommandos. The command relationships were as follows:

Luftwaffe Air Defense Organization, February 1938 [69]

Luftwaffengruppe 1 (East)	*Berlin*	*Kesselring*
Luftgaukommando III	Berlin	
Luftgaukommando IV	Dresden	
Luftgaukommando VIII	Breslau	
Luftwaffengruppe 2 (West)	*Brunswick*	*Felmy*
Luftgaukommando VI	Münster	
Luftgaukommando X	Hamburg	
Luftgaukommando XI	Hannover	
Luftwaffengruppe 3 (South)	*Munich*	*Sperrle*
Luftgaukommando VII	Munich	
Luftgaukommando XII	Wiesbaden	
Luftgaukommando XIII	Nuremberg	
Luftwaffenkommando Ostpreußen	*Königsberg*	*Keller*
Luftgaukommando I	Königsberg	
Luftwaffenkommando See	*Kiel*	*Zander*

Each Luftgaukommando controlled the administrative, ground organization, and supply functions within the district, and was also responsible for the Air Reporting Service and for "coordinating the actions of

A clean lineup of Bf 109Bs of I./JG 21 (later III./JG 54) at Gutenfeld, East Prussia, c. 1938. (*Spies*)

fighter and Flak forces in air defense."[70] This provided for the aforementioned "checkerboard" defense of the Reich territory, but it soon became apparent that Berlin, Leipzig, Hamburg and Düsseldorf merited their own dedicated air-defense forces. Accordingly, in recognition of the need to protect these especially vital political and industrial centers, special *Luftverteidigungskommandos* (Air Defense Commands) were added. Fighter aviation proponents took a dim view of these, as they reduced the flexibility of the participating fighter units.

On February 3, 1939, another major step toward a true wartime organization took place as the three Luftwaffengruppen were redesignated as Luftflotten, each with a number of assigned flying units grouped into *Fliegerkorps*. When hostilities commenced, these operational headquarters and their assigned flying units would deploy forward. The Luftgau commands still retained control over fighter units assigned to home defense. The rub was that these same fighter units were also needed at the front, and Luftwaffe doctrine and force structure dictated that the front took priority. Hence, the Luftgaukommandos later assumed the character of anti-aircraft commands, and were usually led by a Flak general.

One exception to the decentralized approach to air defense was the creation of an air-defense zone to protect the Ruhr industrial region.[71] In June 1938 the German high command extended the *Westwall* frontier fortifications into the third dimension with the construction of the *Luftverteidigungszone West* (Western Air Defense Zone). Although the defensive zone was backed up by some four to five Gruppen of Bf 109 fighters, the German command placed primary reliance on light and heavy anti-aircraft guns, sound detectors and searchlights in what was billed as a "gapless barrier." The entire project cost the staggering sum of 400 million Reichsmarks.[72] Significantly, the commander of Luftverteidigungs-zone West was to report directly to Göring. This was not primarily an attempt to achieve unity of command in air defense. More prosaically, the Luftver-teidigungszone West command was created to minimize friction between Luftflotten 2 and 3, whose command areas each encompassed parts of the *Westwall*. In any case, the German conquests of spring 1940 would shortly render the zone irrelevant, and it was never fully established. *Westwall* air defense was taken over by *Höherer Kommandeur der Festungs-Flakartillerie III*, which contained no flying units.

On the Eve of War

As relations with Poland soured in the summer of 1939 and war began to appear inevitable, the Luftwaffe scrambled to fill its existing tables of organization with units, equipment and personnel. The basic combat and administrative unit was the *Gruppe* (light fighters were in *Jagdgruppen*; heavy fighters, *Zerstörergruppen*). The Gruppe was equivalent in function to the USAAF group or the RAF wing, and for fighters had a fixed structure comprising a *Stabsschwarm* (staff flight) of four aircraft, and three 12-plane *Staffeln*. The latter were thus equivalent to small American or British squadrons. The Luftwaffe organization contained a larger unit, the *Geschwader*, which was the largest mobile, homogeneous flying unit. Although similar to a USAAF wing or an RAF group, it was unlike them in having a permanent structure, typically for fighters a Stabsschwarm and three Gruppen, totaling 124 aircraft. The commanding officers of Staffel, Gruppe, and Geschwader were known respectively as the *Staffelkapitän*, *Kommandeur* and *Kommodore*, whatever the actual rank they held. There were many holes in the organization in 1939; some Geschwader did not have three Gruppen, and some Gruppen were "orphans," without a parent Geschwader. It took a year to tidy things up.

Luftwaffe unit designations were a model of consistency. Gruppen and Staffeln were numbered according to their home Geschwader. Gruppen had Roman numbers; Staffeln, Arabic, in a single sequence within the Geschwader. Accordingly, the First Gruppe of Jagdgeschwader 1 (I./JG 1) contained the 1st, 2nd, and 3rd Staffeln, designated 1./JG 1, 2./JG 1, 3./JG 1. II./JG 1 had the 4., 5., and 6. Staffeln; III./JG 1 had the 7., 8., and 9. The establishment strength of a Jagdgeschwader doubled over the course of the war, but the basic component numbering system never changed.

During the 1930s, two underlying assumptions had guided the development of the German homeland air-defense system. First, there was a general belief that an offensively oriented Luftwaffe could strike hard and quickly and neutralize a hostile air force before it could do grievous damage to German cities. Second, it was hoped that the German fighter force at the front could fend off incoming air raids, and that the Flak and remaining fighter forces in the interior would deal with any bombers getting through. The Luftwaffe's five-fold expansion in front-line strength ordered after the Munich Agreement in the fall of 1938 was nowhere near complete, but new aircraft were flowing into the squadrons and providing real teeth to the Luftwaffe's striking power. In the last summer of peace, the expanding Luftwaffe fighter force was formally assigned the duty of protecting specific geographic regions within Germany. "Besides Berlin, with its importance as an industrial center and

By mid-1939 most Jagdgruppen had been equipped with the Bf 109E-1, the model in which they would go to war. This is the airplane of Major Gotthardt Handrick, the I./JG 26 Kommandeur. It has the Geschwader emblem, his personal top hat emblem, Gruppenkommandeur chevrons, and the temporary white bands around the fuselage and tail tip that it bore during the summer 1939 maneuvers. (*Roba*)

as the center of government and Munich as the main center of the National Socialist Party, the fighter arm was intended to protect all important industrial regions."[73] Many of the soon-to-be-famous wartime Jagdgeschwader were part of this air-defense scheme.

These units were to be buttressed by a number of twin-engine fighter units that were just forming in the summer of 1939. Most would eventually be equipped with the Bf 110, but at the time a good number of the Zerstörergruppen flew obsolescent Bf 109B, C and D models while awaiting their complement of Bf 110s. The continued expansion of the fighter arm was to provide an additional 13 Jagdgruppen and six Zerstörergruppen by November 1, 1939. When one considers the minimal state of German home defenses in early 1943, these deployments look impressive, until one realizes that, with the onset of war, nearly every one of these units left its peacetime base to take its place in the front line. The demand on the heavy fighter units was especially great. Conceived as they were as offensive fighters, the Bf 110s (apart from a brief moment of glory in defending the north German naval bases in late 1939) did not reappear in a daylight air-defense role until the second half of 1943. Those homeland defense forces remaining were to be directed through the Luftgaukommandos, whose final prewar arrangement reflected the addition of Luftflotte 4, created in part out of the Austrian Air Force after the *Anschluss* (union) of March 1938 and commanded by an Austrian, General Alexander Löhr.

The German homeland air-defense system in 1939 was not created out of nothing. The First World War had laid the foundations, and the basic concept of an aircraft warning system, interceptors,

and Flak defense was well established. Yet the amount of progress made between 1933, when a single Gruppe of obsolete short-range aircraft defended the Reich capital, to 1939, when many Gruppen of state-of-the-art single- and twin-engine fighters were deployed across Germany, is nevertheless remarkable. This progress was achieved against formidable opposition from within the Luftwaffe, the Armed Forces High Command, and the government. Without a doubt, offensive concepts of air power employment predominated in Germany, no less than in Britain and the United States. Bomber production outstripped fighter manufacture by approximately 3:1 during most of this period, and bomber and Stuka (dive-bomber) units siphoned off many of the best pilots in the training establishments. Historian Horst Boog recently offered a harsh verdict on the prewar defensive preparations:

> The significance of a centrally led defense of air-space by fighters was to be grasped only in the later stages of the war . . . "Air defense" was seen as a "local matter" as regards "both active and passive defense" . . . The fighters were there only "as an extension of the AA guns," as Adolf Galland, the long-serving *General der Jagdflieger* (General of the Fighter Arm), expressed it after the war.[74]

There were certainly theorists and commanders in the 1930s who attempted to think beyond this localized view of air defense, yet lack of resources, technological limitations, and the ever-present "dogma of the offensive" hindered their efforts.

Fighter Protection Zones, June 1, 1939

Unit	Strength	Base	Objective Protected
I./JG 1	1 Gruppe	Jesau	Königsberg/E. Prussia
JG 2	1 Gr + 1 Staffel	Döberitz	Berlin
I./JG 2	1 Gruppe	Garz	Stettin/Greifswald
JG 3	1 Gruppe	Zerbst	Halle-Leipzig
JG 26	2 Gruppen	Cologne/Düsseldorf	Rhineland/Ruhr
I./JG 51	1 Gruppe	Bad Aibling	Rosenheim/Munich
I./JG 52	1 Gruppe	Böblingen	Stuttgart
JG 53	2 Gruppen	Wiesbaden/Mannheim	Frankfurt/Mannheim
I./JG 76	1 Gruppe	Vienna/Aspern	Vienna/Wiener Neustadt
I./JG 77	1 Gruppe	Pilsen	Bohemia/Moravia
1./JGr 186	1 Staffel	Kiel	Kiel

On September 1, 1939, Germany and its Luftwaffe went to war. The bulk of the nearly 1,200 single- and twin-engine fighters in the Reich territory were committed to the campaign in Poland. But within days of the war's outbreak, enemy bombers would seek to hit targets in Germany. Thus began a struggle between Allied bombers and German defenders that would last for nearly six years—the longest and costliest air campaign of the Second World War.

Luftwaffe Air Defense Organization, September 1, 1939[75]

Luftflotte 1	*Berlin*	*Kesselring*
Luftgaukommando I	Königsberg	
Luftgaukommando III	Berlin	
Luftverteidigungskommando	Berlin	
Luftgaukommando IV	Dresden	
Luftverteidigungskommando	Leipzig	
Luftflotte 2	*Brunswick*	*Felmy*
Luftgaukommando VI	Münster	
Luftverteidigungskommando	Düsseldorf	
Luftgaukommando XI	Hannover	
Luftverteidigungskommando	Hamburg	
Luftflotte 3	*Munich*	*Sperrle*
Luftgaukommando VII	Munich	
Luftgaukommando XII	Wiesbaden	
Höherer Kommandeur der Festungs-Flakartillerie III	Wiesbaden	
Luftgaukommando XIII	Nuremberg	
Luftflotte 4	*Vienna*	*Löhr*
Luftgaukommando VIII	Breslau	
Luftgaukommando XVII	Vienna	

The 6. Staffel of JG 26, photographed during the last prewar maneuvers, August 10, 1939. The tail assembly and wing tips of "yellow 12" in the foreground carry temporary white paint. (*Dölling via Rasse*)

CHAPTER 2

REPELLING RAF BOMBER COMMAND'S DAYLIGHT ASSAULT 1939–1941

Opening Rounds over the North Sea

The longest defensive air campaign of the Second World War began on the afternoon of September 4, 1939, with German forces slashing across the Polish plains and only one day after Britain and France declared war on Nazi Germany. On that day, 15 RAF Bristol Blenheim light bombers of Nos. 107, 110 and 139 Squadrons and 14 Vickers Wellington medium bombers from Nos. 9 and 149 Squadrons took off from their bases and gamely set out to attack the warships of the German fleet. A daring low-level Blenheim reconnaissance mission earlier in the day had identified several capital ships lying at Wilhelmshaven, the Schillig Roads, and Brunsbüttel.

Through a combination of bad weather and faulty navigation, only ten Blenheims and eight Wellingtons actually located their targets. The Blenheims pressed home their attack on the pocket battleship *Admiral Scheer* in the Schillig Roads. They attacked at an altitude of only 150 meters (500 ft.), and the alerted German Flak defenses took a terrible toll—five Blenheims, including four of the five from No. 107 Squadron, failed to return. The *Scheer* was struck by several bombs, all of which failed to explode. One of the crashing Blenheims slightly damaged the light cruiser *Emden*.

The Wellington force arrived over Brunsbüttel in the late afternoon. The battlecruisers *Scharnhorst* and *Gneisenau*, then the largest warships in the German Navy, lay below them. Again, poor visibility and intense anti-aircraft fire made the Wellington crews' job difficult. In addition, Messerschmitt Bf 109E-1 interceptors of II./JG 77, commanded by Oberstleutnant (Obstlt.) Carl Schumacher, rose to the attack from Nordholz airfield. Although the precise sequence of events has never been resolved, two Wellingtons of No. 9 Squadron did not return from

the mission. Bf 109 pilots Feldwebel (Fw.) Alfred Held and Fw. Hans Troitsch both claimed victories.

Held gave the following account to a war correspondent shortly after the event:

> We were alerted around six in the afternoon. In the shortest time possible we were off towards the enemy. Now at last things were getting started! Our formation

The leaders who took the Luftwaffe to war: Reichsmarschall Hermann Göring, the Commander-in-Chief, and Genobst. Hans Jeschonnek, his Chief of Staff. (*Cranston*)

A Rotte of 4./JG 26 Messerschmitts patrols the western German border in late 1939. This was the principal task of the Jagdwaffe (fighter force) after the conclusion of the Polish campaign. (*Meyer*)

soon reached Wilhelmshaven, but nothing was to be seen over the harbor. So we turned away towards the Jade Bight, where we could hear AA guns booming even above the noise of our engines. But while we were turning away I spotted three unidentified aircraft with AA shells exploding among and behind them. We raced towards them, gratefully noticing that the AA guns were holding their fire. But the enemy aircraft had disappeared. They had been engaged by the AA guns of a German warship that we were then flying over and when I glanced down I could see two English aircraft lying in the water—twin-engined bombers, one of them still burning. So the first Tommies had met their fate.

But while we were circling above this memorable spot I suddenly observed, very far away, another twin-engined aircraft which I recognized as English. Our formation curved towards it. The Leutnant leading our formation positioned himself above the Tommy in order to attack, but unfortunately he was still too far away to shoot at him with any chance of success; I was much nearer to the Englishman and did not hesitate to engage him.

With my Staffel comrades still relatively far behind me, I already had the Englishman in my sights. Calmly and confidently I fired the first bullets into his aircraft, feeling as hardened to combat as if I had already shot down a dozen Englishmen. However, the bomber's

rear gunner wasn't going to allow me to be complacent. As I streaked in he fired one burst after another at me. Despite fiercely concentrating all my senses on the job, I managed to make out every single detail of the Wellington bomber, even its various crew members. Whether that rear gunner was a good shot and had hit me I could not see for the moment. So, unperturbed, every time I had a free field of fire I shot at the enemy aircraft. Was I a better shot than the Englishman? Time and again we rushed past each other, machine guns hammering away and engines howling like maddened beasts, and thus twisting about we strayed far out over the Jade Bight.

As if the Englishman sensed the death-blow coming he dove his bomber to get more speed and escape from my fire. Lower and lower I forced the Tommy, but still he defended himself desperately. Then—I could hardly believe my eyes—a long flame shot from the left side of the bomber. Was this the finale? Already the aircraft seemed to be out of control and wallowing about. A last burst from my guns—and that was enough. The aircraft dropped its nose and fell. I throttled back and circled to follow the Englishman's descent, but already there was just a burning pile in the water, and that lasted only a few seconds. Then the waves closed the grave and foaming wavetops glided over it as before.[1]

Held's kill was hailed in the press as the first *Abschuss* (shootdown) of an RAF aircraft. However, some participants, including Schumacher, the II./JG 77 Gruppenkommandeur, believed that Troitsch actually scored first. Troitsch gave the following account to the German press:

We were flying above the German Bight off the Elbe estuary. I noticed the Englishmen far below us, very low over the water. As my comrades had apparently not yet spotted the enemy formation, I told them. I was flying at the front of our formation so I was the first to fire. When we got nearer I recognised the Englishmen as Wellington bombers, twin-engined aircraft with a rear gunner at the end of their fuselages.

Two of the aircraft immediately turned towards the low-hanging clouds and disappeared. The third one was right in front of my guns and I closed to 100 meters [110 yards] to be sure of hitting him. At 50 meters the Englishman's left wing broke off and a flame shot from the fuselage. Shortly before the Englishman had returned my fire, though without hitting my machine, I found out later. By the time the bomber was engulfed in flames I was only 20 meters behind him. The burning tail fell off and streaked past, just above my machine, so that I had to dive to avoid being swallowed by the flames. I dove away to the right and followed the bomber, which dropped from some 400 meters into the water, where it quickly disappeared, leaving just an oil slick.[2]

Troitsch also reported engaging another bomber, but lost it in cloud after making several attacks and exchanging fire with its gunners.

Even if one assumes that these accounts were perhaps embellished for the benefit of the Nazi propaganda machine, they bear out certain time-honored tenets of German air-defense procedures dating back to the First World War. The aircraft warning service seemed to function smoothly, as reports from naval Freya radar stations reached the fighters in time to ensure an interception.[3] Flak and fighter forces had worked together to frustrate an enemy attack; Held spoke of finding the enemy by spotting the Flak bursts. Yet this first success—and others to follow in the next three months—would also breed overconfidence.

In the short term, the conclusions RAF Bomber Command drew from this first action were less accurate than those of the Luftwaffe. The danger from Flak was clear enough, as the loss of five Blenheims

During the winter of 1939–40, all Bf 109s were repainted. Their dark green camouflage hid them well against the ground, but was felt to be too "defensive"; the new pale gray fuselage sides would better disguise them while waging "offensive" war at high altitude. Before the beginning of the Western Campaign on May 10, 1940, during which most of the Jagdwaffe left the Reich, daily life in most units was monotonous. Here the 6./JG 26 line chief enforces discipline among his ground crews. (*Petrick*)

Obstlt. Carl Schumacher, the first Kommodore of the first RLV unit, JG 1. The Bf 109E-3 behind him has the standard Kommodore markings of "< – + –". The photo was taken at Jever on December 19, 1939, the day after the famous Battle of Heligoland Bight. At this time JG 1 comprised only a headquarters staff and flight, with a number of independent Gruppen coming under its command for operations. (*Bundesarchiv 321-855-33*)

demonstrated. Yet the reports from the returning Wellington crews tended to downplay the effectiveness of the German fighters. RAF aircrew reported that even modest evasive action—"the slightest skid"—was enough to spoil the aim of the Luftwaffe interceptors.[4] Evidently, no returning witness had observed the Wellingtons fall to the 109s, so the British assumed that anti-aircraft fire was responsible for all of the losses that day. Future raids would therefore be flown at a much greater altitude in order to avoid this menace. Not for the first time, nor for the last, were operational results assessed incorrectly.

The RAF bombers (and the German fighters that opposed them) were over the north German coast that day as the culmination of years of prewar predictions and planning. Sir Hugh Trenchard had conceived the RAF as a force capable of carrying the war to the enemy in a sustained strategic air offensive. Yet political realities, interservice rivalries, and a severely constrained defense budget ensured that the Bomber Command of 1939 was impressive in numbers, but very limited in actual capability. As a result, Trenchard's successors commanded a force that lacked target-finding and navigational aids, adequate defensive armament, and even bombs of effective design and large enough size. Lack of real combat experience—or even realistic exercises—during the

1930s left its leadership with little grasp of the real problems that would arise in prosecuting such a novel form of warfare.[5] Simply put, the outbreak of war in 1939 found RAF Bomber Command unprepared for the complex challenges that would face it.

These shortcomings extended to the types of twin-engine aircraft in service with Bomber Command squadrons in 1939. All were of conventional design. The Bristol Blenheim had excellent performance for its day, but was only a light bomber. Two medium bombers—the Handley-Page Hampden and the Armstrong Whitworth Whitley—were obsolescent. One Whitley pilot noted that it was "not the sort of vehicle in which one should go to pursue the King's enemies."[6]

The best of the first-generation RAF wartime bombers was undoubtedly the Vickers Wellington, designed by the brilliant inventor Barnes Wallis. The

A Kette of II./JG 77 Bf 109Es, photographed on a broad, desolate north German landing ground, probably Jever, on December 19, 1939, one day after taking part in the Battle of Heligoland Bight under the command of JG 1. (*Bundesarchiv 321-855-5*)

Wellington had a large bomb load and impressive range for the day (4,100 km/2,550 miles) but cruised at only 266 km/h (165 mph) and in its early marks was defended by only three .303-inch machine guns. It did boast power-operated turrets, and its geodesic construction gave it enormous structural strength.[7] But all in all, British capabilities in the fall of 1939 were quite modest.

During his long tenure as Chief of the Air Staff, Trenchard spoke grandly of heavy attacks upon "vital centers" bringing about the swift collapse of an adversary.[8] Yet he had always been somewhat vague about the precise nature of these "vital centers," and as war loomed, the Air Staff set about drawing up a series of specific plans that attempted to take into account the available target intelligence, the limitations of the British bomber force, and other operational factors. These were the so-called Western Air (WA) Plans.[9] WA 1 called for a comprehensive attack on the Luftwaffe, both its front-line strength and its industrial underpinnings; WA 4 targeted the German transportation system (railroads, canals, roads), and the ambitious WA 5 focused on German war production writ large, including the Ruhr factories and the oil industry. Sir Edgar Ludlow-Hewitt, Commander-in-Chief Bomber Command in

September 1939, believed that even these plans exceeded his command's operational abilities. Political and international legal restrictions also combined to limit the opening phases of the RAF's offensive to a more restricted character. The Air Minister had even stated publicly that the Ruhr industries were off limits to bombing because they were "private property." Bomber Command would only strike targets of an undoubtedly military nature. Therefore, when Britain declared war on September 3, 1939, RAF Bomber Command put in motion WA 7b, an attack against the German fleet at Wilhelmshaven.[10] Thus, the "strategic air offensive against Germany," as it later became officially known, began as it did on September 4. In retrospect, one must agree with the assessment of the official RAF historian:

The overoptimistic view of what might be achieved; the care taken to avoid harming the German civil population; the large proportion of aircraft failing to locate the objective; the ineffective bombs and inconsiderable results; the expectation that crews would be skilful enough to find and bomb in atrocious weather a precise and hotly defended target on the other side of the North Sea; and the unflinching courage with which the attacks were pressed home—all these were typical, not merely of September 1939, but of many months to come.[11]

The events of September 4 were analyzed; the campaign against the Kriegsmarine continued. RAF planners noted that the time delay between the receipt of a reconnaissance report and the mounting of an attack reduced the chances for success. Thus was born the concept of the "reconnaissance in force." The bomber formation itself would conduct the reconnaissance and strike appropriate targets as they presented themselves.[12] This policy proved disastrous on September 29. Eleven Hampdens in two formations were sent to seek out and attack German warships. One flight, consisting of five Hampdens of No. 144 Squadron, was wiped out by a "hornet's nest" of German fighters.[13] Such a disaster does not seem to have shaken the RAF's confidence in the viability of the self-defending bomber formation. The armed reconnaissance sweeps continued through October and November.

This was, of course, the curious pause in the war known as the *Sitzkrieg* or "Phony War." Yet the war at sea was continuing apace, and pressure began to mount on RAF Bomber Command to step up the attacks on the German fleet. Therefore, on December 3, 1939, 24 Wellingtons launched a major attack on Heligoland. Taking off from Marham and Mildenhall airfields, the bombers, flying in eight vics of three, climbed to 10,000 feet (3,000 meters) for the run-up to the target. Again, the Wellingtons encountered fierce anti-aircraft fire, which damaged two bombers, but all maintained formation and pressed the attack. Results of the bombing were inconclusive, but the anemic Luftwaffe fighter response reinforced the belief that well-disciplined bomber formations could survive in daylight. The Bf 109s and 110s failed to close the range, and the Wellington gunners reported that the enemy pilots seemed to treat the rear turret with great respect.[14] No bombers were lost to any cause, and their gunners claimed one Bf 109, which was flown by Oberleutnant (Oblt.) Günther Specht of

A 4./JG 77 Bf 109E, photographed on December 19, 1939, the day after the Staffel took part in the Battle of Heligoland Bight. The Staffel emblem, a skeleton riding on a scythe, is visible beneath the cockpit on the original print. (*Bundesarchiv 321-855-32*)

I./ZG 26. Specht lost an eye but was rescued after ditching in the sea.[15]

On December 14, another armed reconnaissance took place, this time over the Schillig Roads. Twelve Wellingtons of No. 99 Squadron took off at 1145. Atrocious weather forced the formation down first to 180 meters (600 ft.), then 60 m. (200 ft.). The Wellingtons were victims of cruel fate; the semi-armor piercing bombs they carried required an altitude of at least 610 meters (2,000 ft.) to be effective. The cloud base was at 240 meters (800 ft.) and standing orders prohibited the crews from attacking in such poor visibility for fear that civilians might be killed or their property damaged.[16] Nevertheless, the British bombers remained in the area for 30 minutes, plenty of time for the Bf 109s of 5./JG 77 and the Bf 110s of 2./ZG 76 to intercept.[17] British observers noted not only greater determination on the part of the German fighter pilots, but also commented that cooperation between fighters and Flak was "excellent . . . the latter ceasing fire each time the fighters came in."[18] Five bombers were lost; one crashed in England. In stark

Obstlt. Carl Schumacher (*left*) and Oblt. Gert Müller-Trimbusch, Kommodore and Adjutant of JG 1 (Jagdgeschwader *Schumacher*) at Jever, *c.* 1939–40. (*Behrens*)

terms, half of the British bomber formation had been destroyed. The Wellingtons' gunners downed a Bf 109 of 4./JG 77, killing the pilot. Five other 109s were slightly damaged by .303-inch machine-gun fire.

The British post-battle analysis sought to put the best possible face on the debacle. Air Commodore Norman H. Bottomley of the Air Staff made the following astonishing assessment:

> It is by no means certain that enemy fighters did in fact succeed in shooting down any of the Wellingtons. Considering that enemy aircraft made most determined and continuous attacks for 26 minutes on the formation, the failure of the enemy must be ascribed to good formation flying. The maintenance of tight, unshaken formations in the face of the most powerful enemy action is the test of bomber force fighting efficiency and morale. In our Service it is the equivalent of the old "Thin Red Line" or the "Shoulder to Shoulder" of Cromwell's Ironsides.[19]

Other RAF officers closer to the debacle were less sanguine; the group commander compared the operation to the Charge of the Light Brigade. Nevertheless, RAF Bomber Command would persist, setting the stage for one of the most important air battles of the Second World War.

December 18, 1939—The Battle of Heligoland Bight

The first "named" air battle of the war involved tiny forces by the standards of 1943–4. Just over 100 aircraft from RAF Bomber Command and the Luftwaffe's fighter defenses took off, and not all of those were engaged. Although a small-scale battle, its impact was profound. It helped transform RAF Bomber Command into a night-bombing force, and thereby lulled the Luftwaffe command into neglecting its day-fighter defenses for two critical years. British and German official historians refer to this battle in almost identical terms: it was "among the most important actions of the entire war."[20]

The Luftwaffe's organization for air defense went through a number of changes during the first months of the war. The command organization for the defense of the north German ports posed special challenges. Normally, the defense of an important target in Germany would come under the appropriate Luftverteidigungskommando. In this case, protecting the German fleet would be the responsibility of Luft-verteidigungskommando Hamburg.[21] Two factors—one geographic, one personality-dependent—rendered this impractical. The short-range fighter units were based on the coastline, while the Luftwaffe Flak units of the Hamburg air-defense command were located well inland protecting other vital targets, since the Navy's anti-aircraft units would defend the coast. The fighters and the Luftwaffe Flak were located too far apart for effective coordination.[22] On the human level, relations between Göring and the Commander-in-Chief of the German Navy, Grand Admiral Erich Raeder, had never been particularly warm.[23] A situation in which Navy

Oblt. Otto Behrens, *Technischer Offizier* **(technical officer) of JG 1 at Jever from February 1940–May 1941. Behrens left to become Kommandeur of ErprKdo 26, charged with debugging the Fw 190 and introducing it to service in II./JG 26. After a brief tour as Kapitän of 6./JG 26, Behrens spent the rest of the war in critical technical positions. He was killed in Argentina in 1952 while testing a new Kurt Tank jet fighter.** (*Behrens*)

Flak, Luftwaffe fighters, and warning and signals units drawn from both services would have to work together was fraught with potential friction.

The solution was twofold. The fighter units defending the North Sea coastline were subordinated directly to Luftgaukommando XI in Hannover. These fighter forces would function as an autonomous fighter command, in effect, a prototype *Jagdflieger-führer*, or regional fighter command.[24] This command was entrusted to the former commander of II./JG 77, Obstlt. Carl Schumacher. Schumacher was a former Navy man who had fought at the Battle of Jutland as an officer cadet.[25] With his nautical background and easygoing personality, he seemed a good choice to smooth Luftwaffe–Kriegsmarine relations. His task was to wring the necessary cooperation out of the various Luftwaffe and Navy Flak, aircraft reporting (radar and observer posts), and fighter units. The arrangement still lacked unity of command, as he and the Navy Flak commander were peers.

His new command was designated Stab/Jagd-geschwader 1, sometimes referred to as JG Nord or JG Schumacher. In addition to short-range Bf 109D and E interceptors, Schumacher's units also boasted a number of Bf 110 long-range fighters. Because of the Phony War and the lack of significant British or French air activity on the western front, these powerful aircraft, always in demand by the "offensive" air fleets, were available for the defense mission. JG Nord and its naval counterparts in mid-December therefore stood ready to meet the next RAF incursion. Stab/JG 1 had the following units at its disposal on December 17, 1939,[26] with approximately 80–100 operational fighters:

Unit	Type	Base	Commander
II./JG 77	Bf 109E	Jever	v. Bülow
II./TrGr 186 [27]	Bf 109E	Nordholz	Seeliger
JGr 101	Bf 109D/E	Neumünster	Reichardt
10.(Nacht)/JG 26	Bf 109D	Jever	Steinhoff
I./ZG 76	Bf 110C	Jever	Reinecke
I./ZG 26 (1 Staffel)	Bf 110C	Jever	—

On the morning of December 18, 24 Wellingtons of Nos. 9, 37, and 149 Squadrons assembled over King's Lynn.[28] Two bombers aborted early, one due to engine trouble, the other simply following the lame duck back to base; 22 continued, and the day turned beautifully clear as the formation approached the target area—"fighter weather." The bombers flew a course taking them well north of the Frisian Islands to avoid the Flak, then made a sharp dog-leg south.[29] Wing Commander Richard Kellett, commanding the formation, had orders to attack from a minimum altitude of 3,000 meters (10,000 ft.). As the official historians noted, "The belief that previous disasters were due to the lethal effect of the Flak at low level was written into the operational orders."[30]

The course the formation flew might have protected them from the Flak, but it gave the aircraft reporting system an extended opportunity to alert the fighter defenses. In late 1939 the German fleet was protected by several Freya early warning radar installations, both naval (on Heligoland, or Helgoland in the German spelling) and Luftwaffe (on Wangerooge).[31] The fragmented command structure wasted valuable time. Major Harry von Bülow-Bothkamp, the Kommandeur of II./JG 77, recalled:

On December 18, 1939, when radar control called us up, no one could believe it. Many enemy aircraft were en route for our sector—it must have been some kind of interference. However, a few minutes later, a naval "Freya" radar gave us identical information, which was confirmed by eye-witness sightings. This time, there was no doubt. The alarm was raised . . .[32]

As a result of these miscues within the German command, the bombers almost made landfall without encountering any German fighters. The first contact did not take place until nearly an hour after the Luftwaffe Freya had first picked up the formation. Heavy Flak fire—from Bremerhaven, Wilhelmshaven,

and ships in the Schillig Roads—caused the formation to open up slightly as it searched for targets. Ultimately, the Welllingtons dropped no bombs; Wing Commander Kellett had orders not to attack warships in close proximity to land. The bomber formation split into two flights as it began the homeward leg, a northern flight and a southern flight, flying a parallel course approximately 19.3 km (12 miles) apart. Just as the formation separated, at approximately 1430 Central European Time, the German fighter assault began.

Oblt. Johannes Steinhoff's 10.(Nacht)/JG 26, accompanied by a Rotte from 6./JG 77, was the first to hit the northern group after the Flak barrage ceased. The 109s claimed seven Wellingtons, including two by Steinhoff himself. At 1440, a patrolling Rotte of Bf 110s from 2./ZG 26 led by Hauptmann (Hptm.) Wolfgang Falck claimed four Wellingtons in short order. Falck himself, hit in the starboard engine, was forced to make an emergency landing on Wangerooge. At the same time, a Rotte from 3./JGr 101 claimed two more Wellingtons. The formation was set upon by more patrolling 110s from 2./ZG 76, which claimed five more of the British bombers. One of the 110's gunners recalled his excitement at spotting the Wellingtons, with their "distinctive shark-like tail assembly."[33] By 1505, the engagement involving the northern formation was over as the remaining bombers passed out of range.

The netting-draped Bf 109E-3 "yellow 1" of 3./JG 1 Staffelkapitän Oblt. Paul Stolte at De Kooi in the spring of 1941. Many of this unit's aircraft still have the light fuselage camouflage of early 1940. Those units of the Jagdwaffe taking part in the Battle of Britain the previous summer had found it necessary to darken the sides of their fuselages to minimize sun reflections at altitude. (Hess)

As Steinhoff's men engaged the northern formation, the JG 1 Kommodore, Schumacher, joined in an attack by elements of II./JG 77 and ZG 76 on the RAF formation taking the southern route, as Schumacher recalled:

> It was madness! The Tommies were chased in all directions by our fighters. I also attacked an English bomber. He defended himself well and hit my machine on three occasions. One of the bullets, moreover, passed very close to my head. The bomber was finally in the centre of my sights. I fired at point-blank range, and continued to follow my victim. There were no more than several metres between the two of us—I had to pull away quickly. I was preparing for another attack after a wide turn when I saw the aircraft fall into the sea like a stone. My wingman immediately confirmed my victory.
>
> The combat had already taken us more than 30 kilometers [18 miles] to the west of Heligoland Island. And we were always on the tails of the English. We switched over during attacks, and chased them out as far as 150 kilometers [90 miles] before returning.[34]

His wingman, Oblt. Johann Fuhrmann of 10.(Nacht)/JG 26, was not so lucky. Fuhrmann was caught in the crossfire of several Wellington rear-

gunners and ditched, subsequently drowning. The southern Wellington formation then sustained severe losses in the course of a 30-minute combat with elements of I./ZG 76 and II./JG 77.

Aside from the other historically significant aspects of this battle, the number of future Luftwaffe luminaries taking part is noteworthy. Falck went on to become the "father of the German night-fighter force." Steinhoff would achieve 176 combat kills, and later head the postwar Bundesluftwaffe. Also making claims that day were Oblt. Gordon Gollob of I./ZG 76, who would score 150 kills and eventually replace Galland as General der Jagdflieger, and Leutnant (Lt.) Helmut Lent of the same unit would achieve fame as a night-fighter ace with 110 victories.

The German units involved claimed 38 Wellingtons; a number of these claims were not confirmed. In truth, 12 of the 22 RAF bombers had gone down, for a loss of only three German fighters (although many others were damaged). The British, although sobered by the losses, claimed 12 German fighters destroyed and another dozen severely damaged.

The ground crews arrive to recover 3./JG 1 Bf 109E-4 "yellow 3," which has formed a "pilot's monument" in the soft soil of De Kooi during the spring of 1941. (*Hess*)

Pilots of 3./JG 1 at readiness. Uffz. Hans Schubert's Bf 109E-4 "yellow 4" sits in front of a camouflaged hangar at De Kooi in the spring of 1941. (*Hess*)

The post-battle assessments were not long in coming. Initially, some senior Bomber Command leaders believed that the losses were due to poor formation discipline and leadership. Others maintained that technical fixes—self-sealing fuel tanks and beam guns—and tactical alterations might yet salvage the day-bomber concept. On December 22, No. 3 Group claimed that:

> There is every reason to believe that a very close formation of six Wellington aircraft will emerge from a long and heavy attack by enemy fighters with very few if any casualties to its own aircraft. A loose formation is however liable to suffer very heavy casualties under the same conditions.[35]

Within a few weeks of the battle, however, Ludlow-Hewitt began arguing for a shift to attacks under the cover of darkness.

The German assessments were obviously of a different tone entirely. Tactically, the Luftwaffe pilots noted the effectiveness of attacks from the beam, against which the Wellington was practically defenseless. In fact, some of the reports indicated that the British emphasis on staying rigidly in formation actually worked in the fighters' favor. A JG 1 after-action report noted:

The British seemed to regard a tightly closed formation as the best method of defense, but the greater speed of the Me 109 and Me 110 enabled them to select their position of attack. Rigid retention of course and formation considerably facilitated the attack . . . It was criminal folly on the part of the enemy to fly at 4,000 to 5,000 meters [13,000–16,500 ft.] in a cloudless sky with perfect visibility . . . After such losses it is assumed that the enemy will not give the Geschwader any more opportunities of practice-shooting at Wellingtons."[36]

Reports from Schumacher's command also tended to discount the effects of the Flak. A recent analysis is more generous: "By damaging bombers or loosening the bomber formations, the Flak was creating opportunities for the fighters to bring their attacks to bear . . ."[37]

At the same time that Schumacher's units were congratulating themselves on their success, commanders at every level in the German Army were analyzing their recent victory over the Poles. The operation had to all appearances been brilliantly successful—yet the officer corps was not satisfied. The Heer (German Army) embarked upon a rigorous analysis of the recent campaign, highlighting problems of leadership, tactics, command and control.[38] There is little evidence that the Luftwaffe took anything remotely resembling this approach following the victory at Heligoland Bight. The Luftwaffe General Staff's historian noted, "Unfortunately, this success was only propagandistically exploited in Germany . . . however, it had the most important operational [implications] for attacker and defender."[39]

Creating an Air Defense System

The personnel of JG 1 might be forgiven for failing to take full account of the lessons of their recent defensive success. The progress of the war from September 1939 through the summer of 1941, with few exceptions, seemed to validate the Luftwaffe's prewar focus on the offensive use of its fighter arm. Its forces overwhelmed the Polish Air Force within a few days, and created an umbrella of air power over the advancing German Army. In Scandinavia, use of (especially) the long-range Bf 110 helped the German forces pull off an improbable success against daunting British naval superiority. In the campaign in the west, the Luftwaffe again unfolded its battle plan like a script from the 1930s' doctrine manuals—gaining air superiority, supporting the Army, and striking deep behind enemy lines. The prewar idea that German air power would defend the homeland by driving the enemy away from the borders of the Reich seemed validated by the run of Blitz victories. German defenses were hardly tested in daylight during this time, yet even amidst a great deal of official neglect, the pieces of a centrally controlled air-defense system began to emerge.

Air defense, as described in the previous chapter, was the responsibility of the Luftgaukommandos (the air district commands), which controlled the Flak, the aircraft warning service, and any fighters assigned to air-defense duties. At the outbreak of the war, the prevailing wisdom in the Luftwaffe was that air defense was primarily a job for the Flak arm, with fighters playing a supporting role. Fighter and Flak forces were to be coordinated by the Luft-verteidigungskommandos. This did not always work out smoothly in practice. Grabmann relates the following revealing anecdote:

> The Commanding Officer of JG 3 . . . together with his units, was placed under Air Defense Command 2, Leipzig. On reporting to his new superior officer, a colonel of anti-aircraft artillery, the latter informed him quite frankly that he knew nothing of fighter operations and that it would be best for the wing commander to order the operations of his units as he considered wisest.[40]

Lack of common understanding between officers from the Flak and flying branches was to plague the Luftwaffe for its entire existence.

There were larger problems with the air-defense system as it existed in the fall of 1939. Its centerpiece was ostensibly Luftverteidigungszone West, which drew forces from participating Luftgaukommandos. These commands were designed to protect specific key objectives. Had the Allies launched a large-scale air offensive against (for example) the Ruhr, it would have been nearly impossible for the Luftwaffe defense commands to mass sufficient force to deal with the incursion. It would have proven very difficult to hand off control of fighter units from one Luftgau or air-defense command sector to the next, and there existed no higher headquarters capable of formulating a complete air situation picture. The weakness of the British and French air arms in the fall of 1939, however, ensured that this danger remained hypothetical.[41]

A September 21, 1939, directive from Luftwaffe Chief of Staff Hans Jeschonnek[42] clarified the fighter command situation somewhat. Fighters specifically earmarked for defensive tasks would remain under

Uffz. Hans Schubert of 3./JG 1 at cockpit readiness in his Bf 109E-4 "yellow 4." Its blue-gray fuselage mottle was the standard for the Jagdwaffe in 1941. (Hess)

the air-defense command, but all other fighter forces would come under the Luftflotten—"linked directly with the strategic [that is, offensive] concept for the continued conduct of air warfare." An official Luftwaffe publication of 1940 noted that fighters were assigned both offensive and defensive duties, but "these defensive tasks are carried out in an offensive manner."[43] New tactical manuals completed during the first year of the war reinforced this offensive emphasis.[44] This arrangement worked very well for operations near the front, but it soon became obvious that the Fliegerdivision and Fliegerkorps staffs had no experience with air-defense operations. Moreover, coordination between the Fliegerdivision and Flak arm took place only at air fleet level, making the conduct of combined arms operations extremely cumbersome.

An interim solution was the creation in late 1939 and early 1940 of the post of Jagdfliegerführer (Fighter Command Unit—Jafü). This command would be responsible for all fighter missions, whether on attack or defense. The first Jafü to be created was in Generaloberst (Genobst.) Albert Kesselring's Luftflotte 2 (Jafü 2, under Oberst Kurt-Bertram von Döring). In view of its special status, the fighter command in the Heligoland Bight area remained directly subordinate to Luftgaukommando XI instead of Luftflotte 2. In Genobst. Hugo Sperrle's[45] Luftflotte 3, the Jafü concept was slower to take root (he attempted to maintain separate "offensive" and "defensive" fighter commands), and Jafü 3 was not fully established until February 1940. Grabmann noted:

> That a command system so lacking in uniformity could continue to exist for such a relatively long time until the basic solution in the form of fighter commands was found was possible only because the small air activity of the western opponents did not make a quicker solution to the problem absolutely essential.[46]

These fighter commands in the early years gained much greater fame in an offensive, rather than a defensive role, conducting Luftwaffe fighter operations in the Battle of Britain during the summer of 1940.

With the fall of France, Luftverteidigungszone West was rendered irrelevant, and most of the fighter forces were moved forward to the Channel coast. In August 1940, the only fighter units assigned in a defensive role were Stab/JG 1, Stab/JG 77, II. and III./JG 77, and I./ZG 76.[47] After the Battle of Britain wound down in

the fall of 1940, some fighter units rotated back to the homeland, but they did not stay long; there were tasks awaiting them in the Mediterranean, the Balkans, and in Russia. These transfers left training units at home to cover air defense. The prevailing theory remained one of point defense—1940–1 instructions still spoke in terms of the 1936 idea of concentric "warning radii, operational radii, Flak zones" surrounding each defended target.[48]

Day-Fighter Air Defense Deployments, January 1, 1941[49]

Luftgaukommando	Unit	Defense Area
III–IV	I./JG 27	Berlin
XI	Stab/JG 1	Heligoland Bight
XI	I./JG 54	Heligoland Bight
XI	II./ZG 76	Heligoland Bight
VI	III./JG 3 (1 Schwarm)	Ruhr region
Holland	II./JG 52, I./JG 1	Holland

A True Air Defense Command

The command organization that eventually became Luftflotte Reich and presided over a fully centralized Reich air-defense effort had very humble beginnings. In August 1940, at the height of the Battle of Britain, a

Uffz. Heinrich Nöcker of 3./JG 1 stands beside the tail of his Bf 109E, on which have been painted bars for his first two victories, both RAF Blenheim light bombers downed on June 4, 1941. Such light forces were the principal targets for the defenders in the Reich during all of 1940–2. Nöcker was killed in action in North Africa in November 1942. (*Hess*)

handful of RAF bombers made a series of attacks on Berlin. Göring, who had famously pledged that that no such thing would ever take place, decided that the capital's air defenses needed attention. He turned to Generalleutnant (Genlt.) Hubert Weise, who had commanded I. Flakkorps during the French campaign. Weise was a skilled commander as well as a Flak pioneer from the secret Luftwaffe days, and energetically took over his new assignment, Luftgaukommando III, on September 27, 1940. Weise's command soon grew to encompass all air-defense forces not only of Berlin (Luftgau III) but also Dresden (Luftgau IV).[50] Weise established his headquarters at the Reichssportfeld in Berlin and set about improving both the tactical and technical aspects of homeland air defense.

Weise went about his task with a will and, spurred by the intensification of RAF night bombing activity, his authority continued to increase. On March 24, 1941, *Luftwaffenbefehlshaber Mitte* (Central Air Force Command—Lw Bfh Mitte) was created.[51] This new command, which was a unique creation existing somewhere between a Luftgau and a Luftflotte, gave

Oberst Werner "Vati" Mölders, the General der Jagdflieger, retrieves his ceremonial dagger from his Bf 108 Taifun on arrival at Jever to inspect JG 1 in 1941. Mölders was killed in a flying accident on November 22, 1941. (*Heinz Rose via Arno Rose*)

Weise operational control over all Luftwaffe defense formations in Luftgaue III, IV, VI, VII, XI, and XII/XIII.[52] In acknowledgement that Weise's command faced a threat that came primarily from the night attacks of RAF Bomber Command, the *Nachtjagddivision* (Night-Fighter Division) under Generalmajor (Genmaj.) Josef Kammhuber[53] became the main flying command under Lw Bfh Mitte. The Night-Fighter Division (later redesignated XII. Fliegerkorps) also assumed command over the day-fighter units formerly assigned to the various Luftgaukommandos. Kammhuber exercised overall operational control over the day fighters engaged in air defense through the Jafüs.[54] A March 1941 directive from the Luftwaffe Operations Staff clarified the role of the Jafüs within the new command:

> The Luftflotten and Lw Bfh Mitte are responsible for fighter defense in their command areas with the fighter forces assigned to them. As a rule they will delegate this responsibility to the Jafüs, which will subdivide the signal communications and aircraft reporting networks into defense sectors according to the requirements of their respective zones.[55]

Despite the illusion of centralization, Weise's new command retained something of a fragmented character. Weise had to share some Luftgau VII and XII/XIII forces with Sperrle in Luftflotte 3, and Kammhuber remained directly subordinate to Reichsmarschall Göring and frequently made use of the power this gave him.

Organizational reforms continued apace. In September 1941, the Luftverteidigungskommandos were redesignated as Flak divisions—since losing their fighters to the Jafü early in 1940 this had been essentially true anyway. In August 1941, Kammhuber took over the command of XII. Fliegerkorps, which included the Night-Fighter Division and the few day-fighter forces assigned to homeland defense. In recognition of the unique requirements of day-fighter operations, a new day-fighter command, Jafü Mitte, was created under General Werner Junck. Co-located with the night-fighter division at Zeist, Junck exercised operational control over the day-fighter forces of Jafü Deutsche Bucht, Jafü Holland-Ruhrgebiet, and Jafü Berlin, as well as aircraft from the schools and factory defense flights.[57] Junck reported directly to XII. Fliegerkorps. This

Command Structure, Lw Bfh Mitte, March 1941[56]

Luftwaffenbefehlshaber Mitte	Berlin-Reichssportfeld
Luftgau III	Berlin
Luftverteidigungskommando 1	Berlin
Flakbrigade II	Berlin
Luftgau IV	Dresden
Luftverteidigungskommando 2	Leipzig
Flakbrigade IV	Dessau
Luftgau VI	Münster
Luftverteidigungskommando 4	Ratingen (near Düsseldorf)
Luftverteidigungskommando 7	Cologne
Flakbrigade X	Bochum
Luftgau VII	Munich
Luftgau XI	Hamburg
Luftverteidigungskommando 3	Hamburg
Luftverteidigungskommando 8	Hannover
Flakbrigade VIII	Bremen
Luftgau XII/XIII	Wiesbaden
Luftverteidigungskommando 5	Frankfurt-am-Main
Nachtjagddivision	Zeist (near Utrecht)

arrangement continued to function until replaced by the Jagddivision command system in late 1942.

Daylight raids had all but ceased as RAF Bomber Command focused on building up the night offensive. In December 1941, "Whereas six regular groups were available for night-fighter defenses, daytime air-defense requirements had to be taken care of by only two regular groups [I./JG 3 and I./JG 1] and a number of provisional units of only limited combat effectiveness."[58] Without a doubt, night fighters and Flak bore the brunt of air defense in 1940–2.

During this time, day-fighter units in Germany faced incursions by reconnaissance planes and the occasional day raids on targets in Germany proper, such as the RAF raid on the Knapsack and Quadrath power stations near Cologne on August 12, 1941. Fifty-four Blenheims struck these targets in an effort to force the Luftwaffe command to recall fighters from the hard-pressed Eastern Front.[59] Throughout late 1941 and 1942, the two fighter wings of Luftflotte 3 on the Channel coast battled against "Circus" operations—shallow penetrations by heavily escorted RAF bombers—which posed no threat to the Reich territory proper. One aviation history footnote from this period deserves mention: the very limited use of the B-17C Fortress I by the RAF in daylight during the summer of 1941. The RAF was anxious to try out the new bomber, tiny formations of which did make several high-altitude daylight raids on German targets that summer.[60] The attacks achieved little. In General Hap Arnold's withering assessment, "In the RAF's hands in 1941, the long-awaited combat showing of the B-17 was a fiasco." He argued that they were used improperly and flown by poorly trained crews.[61] The British were equally unimpressed, but they blamed the technology. "On 6th December 1941 Sir Richard Peirse [who now led Bomber Command] reported that neither the Fortress I or II were suitable as day bombers. They should, he advised, be fitted with flame dampers and committed to the night offensive."[62] Bomber Command's verdict on the experiment echoed the lessons of Heligoland Bight: "Unsupported day attacks by heavies when faced by equal or slightly superior numbers of fighters are not a practical proposition."[63]

Oberst Werner "Vati" Mölders (*left*) inspects JG 1 at Jever in 1941. He is accompanied by an earlier General der Jagdflieger, Obst. Werner Junck. (*Heinz Rose via Arno Rose*)

General der Flakartillerie Hubert Weise, who commanded Luftwaffenbefehlshaber Mitte for most of its existence. Weise spent his entire career in the Flak arm, and his appointment to oversee Berlin's defenses in 1940 underscored the leading role played by ground-based air defenses in German airpower thinking. (*USAFHRA*)

The Luftwaffe seemed to have the daylight air-defense situation well in hand. This was fortunate for Germany, since in late 1941 the war began to turn against it on many levels. The failure of Operation Barbarossa to defeat the U.S.S.R. in four months revealed the bankruptcy of Göring's prediction to Adolf Galland and Werner Mölders in April 1941 that "It would be possible to throw all military power, vastly increased by the limitless strategic resources of the Soviet empire, into the battle against the western opponent." The strategy of concentrating the Luftwaffe's striking power on one front at a time was quickly unraveling.[64]

Generalfeldmarschall (GFM) Erhard Milch, brought in to assist Ernst Udet in managing aircraft

production, was forced to admit to the Reich Industrial Council on September 18, 1941, that he was increasing production of a number of obsolescent types, such as the He 111 bomber and Junkers (Ju) 87 Stuka dive bomber. He had no choice; the advanced follow-on designs to these types had failed to materialize, and the front line was demanding replacements. He put the matter starkly to the assembled industrialists:

We are simply faced with the question of whether we are to have no aircraft at all in 1943 or are to have large numbers of aircraft types which hitherto have proved adequate. For this reason I have recommended to the Reichsmarschall that in 1942–43 we should construct the tried and tested types in large numbers.[65]

Milch's program did include substantial numbers of the new Focke-Wulf (Fw) 190 fighter, but bomber and attack aircraft production still dominated. The problems ran deeper than the need to keep obsolescent aircraft types in production to keep up with the demands of the front line. A Lw Bfh Mitte

In 1941 the two *Kanalgeschwader*, JG 2 and JG 26, began equipping with the Fw 190, which would be the most effective weapon of the RLV in 1943–4. The first Staffel with the new fighter was 6./JG 26. This is the Fw 190A-1 of its Kapitän, Oblt. Walter Schneider, who led his Staffel into a hill during a bad-weather transfer flight on December 22, killing himself and four other pilots. (*Barbas*)

experience report covering the last quarter of 1941 contained a litany of complaints, including inadequate early-warning and direction-finding radar, the lack of a Zerstörer with all-weather capability, and the poor climbing power of the Bf 109.[66] The Luftwaffe's technical lead over its adversaries was slipping away.

On December 6, 1941, the German Army reeled back from the gates of Moscow under the hammer blows of a powerful Soviet counteroffensive. On December 11, 1941, Hitler declared war on the United States in the wake of the Japanese attack on Pearl Harbor (even though he was under no obligation to do so). A new enemy would soon be gathering across the Channel. The Bomber Offensive was about to become Combined.

A 6./JG 26 Fw 190A-1 upon arrival at Abbeville-Drucat in December 1941. The *erste Wart* (crew chief) stands on the wing; the *Waffen-Feldwebel* (chief armorer), on the ground. (*Naumann*)

A lineup of 4./JG 26 Fw 190A-1s on the Abbeville-Drucat apron in December 1941. Delivery of these fighters completed the re-equipment of II./JG 26. The conversion of the rest of JG 26 and all of JG 2 from Messerschmitts to the Focke-Wulf fighter followed quickly. (*Behrens*)

CHAPTER 3

AMERICA ENTERS THE WAR 1942

The New Enemy

The year 1942 was dominated by dramatic events in the east and in the Mediterranean, and marked the high water mark of German expansion. The battered German Army weathered the overly ambitious Soviet winter counteroffensive, and as spring arrived contemplated renewed offensive operations, albeit only in the southern sector of the vast Eastern Front. Fully half of the Luftwaffe was assigned to the eastern air fleets, much of it in support of Genobst. Erich von Manstein's successful conquest of the Crimean peninsula and the fortress of Sevastopol. General Wolfram von Richthofen's powerful Luftflotte 4, the Luftwaffe's premier tactical-support formation, then marshaled its combat power in support of the Army's drive towards the Volga and into the Caucasus. In the Mediterranean, Rommel prepared to renew his offensive against the British, which would eventually carry him almost to the gates of Alexandria. In the course of these operations, Fliegerführer Afrika provided air superiority and tactical support to Rommel's advance, while German air units based in Sicily attempted to neutralize the island stronghold of Malta.[1]

Reich air defense was viewed as a problem confined to the hours of darkness.[2] Air Chief Marshal Sir Arthur Harris took over at RAF Bomber Command in February, and almost immediately infused that organization with a new sense of purpose. Starting with raids on the port of Lübeck and the factory town of Rostock, Harris was determined to carry the war to Germany's cities in a systematic campaign. He mustered the whole of his force—including training units—for a spectacular 1,000-bomber raid on Cologne on the night of May 30/31.[3] The German air-defense system—oriented around radar, Flak, and ground-controlled night fighters—sought to respond effectively to this emerging threat. Weise's Flak-dominated Lw Bfh Mitte reorganized to deal better

GFM Erhard Milch. Effectively second-in-command of the Luftwaffe for much of the war, Milch's most significant position as regards the RLV was Generalluftzeugmeister, Director of the Office of Air Armament, in which he worked tirelessly to increase the production of fighters and strengthen the home defenses. (*Cranston*)

Generalleutnant Adolf Galland in one of his favorite service portraits, as a major in 1940. Galland was promoted from Kommodore of JG 26 to General der Jagdflieger at the end of 1941, and held this important staff position for three years. He attempted to defend the interests of the Jagdwaffe within the Luftwaffe high command, and was a consistent proponent of a strong RLV day-fighter component. (Galland)

with the increasing threat of the night area attacks.

With the Third Reich expanding on all fronts, the daylight defense of German airspace merited only a low priority. The RAF ventured into the daylight skies over Germany very infrequently, although at times Bomber Command could inflict a shock on the complacent German defenders. One raid that looms large in German accounts was the daring April 17, 1942, strike by 12 Lancasters from Nos. 44 and 97 Squadrons on the MAN diesel works at Augsburg, which was turning out engines for Admiral Karl Dönitz's U-boat fleet.[4] Although provided with cover from a diversionary raid and fighter sweep over northern France, the operation went wrong almost from the start. The diversion operation alerted the

coastal defense forces, and JG 2's fighters downed four Lancasters before they passed Paris.[5] After clearing the French coast and breaching the thin perimeter fighter defenses, the bombers were able to strike the target. Ultimately, the raid cost seven Lancasters and earned the mission commander, who returned in a badly damaged aircraft, the Victoria Cross. Despite optimistic British assessments, damage to the MAN works was insignificant. In the view of the chief of the Luftwaffe General Staff's historical section, the German leadership, flushed with victory, failed to draw the correct conclusions:

> [The] defense actions . . . were successful because of favorable circumstances: good weather conditions, lack of fighter escort, report in time by the German air warning system, and complete readiness for action of the defense units.
>
> Thus it was understandable that German Air Force command authorities fostered an erroneous opinion concerning the efficiency of German air-defense strength. It was thought that the *Alarmeinheiten* (interceptor units) set up by the fighter training schools could successfully deal with daylight operations in the inner German territory. Apparently, the High Command aimed to avoid any measure which would necessitate the building up of new formations, which would decrease the effective strength of units operating in the front areas.[6]

Reichsmarschall Göring made a most perceptive observation in a conference on May 16, 1942, noting that if enemy bomber units succeeded in penetrating beyond the German fighter defense belt at the Channel coast there was nothing left in Germany to oppose them.[7] Others quickly pointed out that the British, after the costly Augsburg attack, did not venture to repeat such daylight operations. Therefore, in the late summer of 1942 when the Luftwaffe home-defense force began to face the first daylight penetrations by the newly arrived USAAF, few senior commanders saw much cause for concern.

Plans drawn up by the United States armed forces before that nation's own entry into World War II always envisioned the use of Great Britain as the major staging area in any war against Germany. At the Arcadia Conference, held only weeks after Germany and Italy declared war on the United States following the Japanese attack on Pearl Harbor, the American and British political and military high commands confirmed

During 1942 the day-fighter units of Lw Bfh Mitte and
Luftflotte 3 converted almost entirely from Bf 109s to Fw 190s.
This uniquely marked Fw 190A-1 was passed down from
II./JG 26 to II./JG 1 and used in the latter's conversion training
at Abbeville. (*Rosch*)

a policy of "Germany first." This would govern Allied
strategy for the rest of the war. However, the immediate
need to reinforce the Pacific Theater, a lack of resources,
and disagreement within the Allied High Command as
to the proper strategy for the European Theater
prevented any appreciable build-up of American forces
in Great Britain during the first half of 1942.

The June arrival in England of the Eighth Air Force
headquarters under Major General (MGen.) Carl A.
Spaatz provided the Americans with at least a sense of
direction and the beginning of a timetable. The
Eighth Air Force was intended to be the major U.S. air
weapon in the war against Germany. Spaatz was
subordinate to MGen. Dwight D. Eisenhower, the
newly named commander of U.S. forces in the
European Theater of Operations (ETO), but would be
allowed to operate independently until the ground

forces had formulated a definite plan for the invasion
of Hitler's *Festung Europa*. Near-term, the air force
would have the sole responsibility for the offensive
against Germany. Spaatz was more than willing to take
on the job. His objectives were, first, to weaken
German military power by the destruction of its manufacturing facilities; and second, to gain air superiority
over Germany by defeating the Luftwaffe in the air.
His weapon of choice was to be the self-defending
daylight strategic bomber.

The bomber component of the Eighth Air Force,
Brigadier General (BGen.) Ira C. Eaker's 8th Bomber
Command, was to be equipped with two types of heavy
bomber. The model that was to predominate, the
Boeing B-17 Flying Fortress, became one of the classic
warplanes of World War II. The other, the
Consolidated B-24 Liberator, was a newer design than
the B-17, and its speed, range, and bomb load were
superior. But raw performance data were of little value
in the unforgiving ETO. The B-24 could not maintain
close formation at the typical bombing altitude of
25,000 feet (7,600 meters), and was forced to fly at
20,000–21,000 feet (6,000–6,400 meters), making it
more vulnerable to both fighters and Flak. The B-24
was also much less tolerant of battle damage than the
B-17. As a result, the composition of the 8th Bomber
Command stabilized at two-thirds B-17s and one-
third B-24s, and the last B-24 Groups to arrive in
Europe were sent to the lower-status Fifteenth Air
Force, flying from Italy.

The role envisaged for American fighters in early
Eighth Air Force plans is by no means clear. The
USAAF official history implies that the need for escort
fighters was always recognized,[8] but in fact American
doctrine did not call for fighter escorts, and the
bomber generals were slow to realize their importance.
It is certain that American plans called for unescorted
raids on Germany—the USAAF had no long-range
fighter.[9] The first two Eighth Air Force fighter groups
to reach England were equipped with the Lockheed
P-38 Lightning, which was an adequate mid-range
escort fighter, although it had been designed as an
interceptor. But these two groups left in November for
Operation Torch, the invasion of North Africa, and no
more P-38 groups saw action with the Eighth for a
year. The formation of new P-38 groups was delayed,
as all P-38 production was needed to make up combat
losses in the Mediterranean Theater. The next two
groups ordered to England had been equipped with
the Bell P-39 Airacobra. These aircraft were left in the

U.S.A., and the pilots re-equipped with Spitfires upon arrival in the United Kingdom. The official explanation was that flying P-39s across the Atlantic was deemed too risky; it is also undoubtedly true that the low-altitude, short-range Airacobra was totally unsuited for service in the ETO. These two groups were also sent to North Africa, leaving the Eighth Air Force with a single fighter unit, the Spitfire-equipped 4th Fighter Group, which was formed in September from the RAF's three Eagle Squadrons (which had American pilots who had volunteered to fight in the British forces before America entered the war). Escort for the first 8th Bomber Command missions was provided by the Eagles and by the numerous RAF Fighter Command Spitfire squadrons, whose radius of action was 280 km (175 miles), barely enough to cross the French, Belgian, or southern Dutch coasts from southern England.[10]

Sizing Up the Adversary

In 1942 the leaders of the Third Reich and the Luftwaffe's senior commanders tended to denigrate the combat capability of the USAAF. Hitler refused to accept reports suggesting that the United States' war industry was gearing up to produce thousands of first-rate aircraft, while Göring's flippant statement that the Americans could only manufacture refrigerators and razor blades has entered the folklore of the Second World War.[11] Historian Horst Boog has noted, "The two finally confirmed each other in their deprecatory attitude, as when, for instance, Hitler said

Göring had reassured him that the American Flying Fortress was of miserable quality."[12]

There was little excuse for this state of affairs. The capacity of the American aircraft industry was heavily documented in open source publications, and new types such as the B-17F and North American Mustang were widely depicted even in magazine advertisements and children's books and on cigarette cards. More to the point, the German military attaché in Washington, General Friedrich von Boetticher, produced a number of extremely detailed reports on four-engine bomber development, backed up by experts in the German aircraft industry and the War Economy and Armaments Office. Genobst. Hans Jeschonnek, the Luftwaffe Chief of Staff, was impressed by these reports, and in May 1942 sent Boetticher to meet with Hitler. After the attaché told Jeschonnek that Hitler had again dismissed the data, the General Staff Chief noted despairingly,

Boetticher, we are lost. For years I have, on the basis of your reports, forwarded demands to Göring and Hitler, but for years my requests for the expansion of the Luftwaffe have not been answered. We no longer have the air defense I requested and which is needed

Fw 190A-2 "black 5" at Katwijk in June. It was assigned to the 5./JG 1 Staffelkapitän, Oblt. Max Buchholz, and carried the Gruppe *Tatzelwurm* (dragon-worm) in the Staffel color, red; a tight white spiral on the spinner; and (unfortunately not visible here) a personal emblem, a large white bird, beneath the cockpit. (*Bundesarchiv 361-2193-32*)

for our German soil. Conflicting demands have been made by Hitler. We now no longer have any time . . . to provide ourselves with the weapons to fight the dreadful threat which you have predicted and reported to us. Then we will be covered from the air with an enemy screen which will paralyze our power to resist. They will be able to play with us![13]

It is difficult to reconcile Jeschonnek's public pronouncements with these privately expressed doubts. Not one month after the above exchange took place, the Chief of Staff interrupted an engineer's presentation on the growing threat from the USAAF heavy bomber force with the observation,

Every four-engine bomber the Allies build makes me happy, for we will bring these four-engine bombers down just like we brought down the two-engine ones, and the destruction of a four-engine bomber constitutes a much greater loss for the enemy.[14]

Most intimates of Jeschonnek believed he knew

A close-up view of the cowling and spinner of Oblt. Buchholz's Fw 190A-2. The *Tatzelwurm* was a creature from Nordic folklore. II./JG 1 kept the symbol when it was formed from I./JG 3 on January 15, 1942. (*Bundesarchiv 361-2193-33*)

better, and stated that privately he assessed the military situation with clarity, but he was unable to assert himself before Hitler or Göring. In the assessment of a Luftwaffe general who knew him well, Jeschonnek's tragic flaw was this inability to resist his masters, his "*Ja-Sagen* [obsequiousness]."[15] In the summer of 1942, therefore, official optimism won the day. The standard Reich Air Ministry aircraft recognition manual issued at that time contained data only on the old B-17C Fortress I, with five hand-held machine guns and indifferent performance.[16] More accurate information was available, but it was not disseminated with any real urgency.[17]

To be sure, such rosy prognostications did not survive the early combats with the Fortresses. Upon inspecting the wreckage of a downed B-17 at the Rechlin test establishment in October, Genmaj. Adolf

Galland, the General der Jagdflieger, commented that the aircraft united "every possible advantage in one bomber: first heavy armor; second enormous altitude; third colossal defensive armament; fourth great speed."[18] Despite his impressive-sounding title, Galland held a staff position, that of inspector-general, within the Luftwaffe General Staff. He could write technical regulations and evaluate new weapons, but his principal role was advisory. As one of his fellow inspectors noted, such a post was an "unenviable position, as one commands nothing."[19] He and Milch were the only high Luftwaffe officials arguing consistently for a strengthening of the day-fighter defenses as early as 1942.

Combat reports attesting to the quality of the American equipment and the difficulty of breaking up the formations soon reached the higher echelons. Although the senior leadership continued to underestimate the numerical output of American factories, the combat units and those who supported them began to develop tactics and technology to cope with the new threat, a process that would end only with the German collapse in May 1945.

The Defenses

The German fighter defense organization in 1942 was an uneasy amalgamation of a front-line air force, Luftflotte 3, and a Flak and night-fighter homeland defense command, Lw Bfh Mitte. GFM Sperrle's Luftflotte 3 in France, which had participated in the victorious western campaign and the Battle of Britain, was organized to function as a miniature air force in its own right, providing offensive air power across multiple roles in support of German grand strategy. It was intended "to serve not only the purposes of air defense, but also that of a base area for offensive strategic air warfare."[20] Its fighter units were the two well-known *Kanalgeschwader* (Channel wings), JG 26 and JG 2, stationed near the coast. Their original role was the traditional one, providing an umbrella above the German forces. During 1942 they covered the breakthrough of the German capital ships in the famed Channel Dash in February, and helped to repel the Anglo-Canadian landing at Dieppe in August.

In 1941 Luftflotte 3 had been forced to assemble an air-defense system to counter coastal raids by RAF fighters and light bombers. Its two Jagdgeschwader reported to separate fighter commands (Jafü). Interceptions could be controlled from the *Gefechtsstände* (command posts) of the Jafü, the Geschwader, or even the individual Gruppen. Other components of the defenses, for example the radar, the radio-intercept service, and the Flak, reported to headquarters spread from Paris to Berlin. Although badly fragmented, the system had nonetheless proved successful and, to most German air commanders, the western front seemed well in hand, despite the small forces stationed there.

Fw 190A "black 3" of 5./JG 1 preparing for takeoff from Katwijk in June. This airplane was assigned to Oberfähnrich Terborg. Its fuselage mottle is more pronounced than was typical for the period, and was probably applied in the unit. (*Bundesarchiv 361-2193-29*)

Lw Bfh Mitte was not dominated by the offensive mindset that pervaded Sperrle's force. Unfortunately, internecine rivalries and professional jealousies between the Flak and flying communities hindered command relationships within Lw Bfh Mitte. Interrogations of Luftwaffe commanders and postwar memoirs are filled with partisan commentary and scathing condemnations of the alleged ineffectiveness or shortsightedness of either the Flak or flying branches, depending on the source's perspective.[21] Commanded by a Flak officer and containing only a single Fliegerkorps, which was led by a night-fighter specialist, Lw Bfh Mitte remained a unique organization within the Luftwaffe. Its flying units were still grouped into a number of Jagddivision headquarters, under which local Jafü actually controlled the few day fighters assigned. In late 1942, therefore, Lw Bfh Mitte's day- and night-fighter defense units, still under XII. Fliegerkorps, came under the operational command of Jagddivision 1 (Deelen), Jagddivision 2 (Stade), Jagddivision 3 (Metz) which contained only night-fighter units, and (as of December 1942) Jagddivision 4 (Döberitz), also without assigned day-fighter units. To protect southern Germany, Jafü Süddeutschland at Schleissheim (near Munich) and Jafü Ostmark in Vienna were established; both of these drew their fighter strength from the single- and twin-engine fighter schools.[22] The Flak units were controlled by the ten Luftgau headquarters then assigned to Lw Bfh Mitte.[23]

The only day-fighter Geschwader in Lw Bfh Mitte was JG 1, whose four Gruppen were stationed along the North Sea coast from Norway to the Netherlands, assigned to Jagddivision 1 and Jagddivision 2. The only day fighters in the interior of the Reich were in schools or factory protection units.[24] The high command believed that "the allocation of daytime fighter forces to Jagddivision 3 was unnecessary because any enemy formation penetrating during daylight would have been intercepted either by the day-fighter defenses of Luftflotte 3 within France or by those of Lw Bfh Mitte stationed in Holland and Belgium."[25] The most obvious problem with this dual arrangement was that it violated the principles of unity of command and concentration of forces, Clausewitzian tenets long a staple of German operational art. The reasons for this are several. Sperrle, a field marshal and Luftflotte commander, refused to surrender scarce flying or Flak forces to Lw Bfh Mitte, or accept any diminution of his command's status. More fundamentally, front-line formations in the Luftwaffe, in keeping with the offensive thinking of the service, were always given priority.[26] Equipping

A Rotte of 11./JG 1 Fw 190As on alert at Deelen in June.
(*Güthenke via Burath*)

JG 2 *Richthofen* guarded the western half of Luftflotte 3's domain, including the important U-boat bases in Brittany. This is the very successful JG 2 Stabsschwarm, standing in front of "Rudi" Pflanz's Bf 109F. *From left:* Oblt. Erich Leie, Major Walter Oesau (Kommodore), Oblt. Rudolf Pflanz, Obfw. Günther Seeger. Note Oesau's autograph. (*Heinz Rose via Arno Rose*)

all four fighter divisions with day-fighter commands would deprive the front line of scarce air superiority fighters, as aircraft production was insufficient to support creation of new units. Thus did the Luftwaffe command endeavor to make a virtue out of a necessity.

This defensive organization was still weak, and possessed little real depth, but the centralization of the home-defense system was progressing in spite of the obstacles. Lw Bfh Mitte was bringing more and more of the Flak force under its control, and the expanding night-fighter organization brought with it a command structure capable of being used by day as well. Grabmann notes that "the outcome of the organizational changes thus introduced in 1942 . . . shows marked progress, in terms of clarity and simplification, over the system existing in 1941."[27]

Production and Pilot Training

Aircraft production and pilot training during 1942 seem woefully inadequate for a German Reich in the fourth year of an expanding global war, into which the economic power of the United States had just been thrown. Even if one considers that German strategic planning assumed the collapse of the U.S.S.R. by fall 1941, which would have permitted the return of fighter units to the west and south, the figures appear meager. And although the energetic Milch had replaced Udet as *Generalluftzeugmeister* (Director of the Office of Air Armament), his reforms (the so-called "Göring Program") would need time to take effect. Throughout 1942, the German aircraft industry produced a total of 2,647 Bf 109s and 1,850 Fw 190s,[28] as well as 853 Bf 110, Ju 88 and Me 210 twin-engine fighters.[29] These production numbers fed a front-line strength of

1,377 single-engine fighters (978 operational) on June 10, 1942, with barely 300 single-engine fighters serving with the RLV (Luftflotte 3 and Lw Bfh Mitte). On that date, 293 twin-engine day fighters were also in service (182 operational), none in the RLV.[30] The disposition of the operational fighter strength clearly demonstrates that the demands of the eastern and southern fronts took priority.

Hans Jeschonnek, the Chief of Staff, takes a (sometimes deserved) beating for the failures of the Luftwaffe in the Second World War. Many sources cite his March 21, 1942, statement to Milch that he "would not know what to do with more than 360 fighters per month!"[31] Yet in this instance Jeschonnek was merely reporting the situation as it stood. As a service chief, he was aware that priority in armaments production in 1942 went to Army weapons and ships for the burgeoning U-boat offensive, as the Wehrmacht attempted to complete the conquest of the U.S.S.R. and maintain pressure on Britain's Atlantic lifeline. As much as Milch and Galland disagreed with this policy, the Luftwaffe lacked the fuel, pilots and infrastructure in 1942 to capitalize on a huge increase in fighter production, even if the raw materials and skilled labor could have been made available on short notice.

In his memoirs Galland records a revealing conversation with Jeschonnek in early 1942. The General der Jagdflieger remonstrated to Jeschonnek that the Luftwaffe must not focus its efforts solely on the Eastern Front, but needed to prepare to resist the threat from the west. Jeschonnek's remarks illuminate the strategic dilemma the Luftwaffe faced, as Galland recalled:

Jeschonnek listened to me quietly and attentively. He did not dispute the validity of my argument, and to a certain extent he even agreed with me, but he thought that the fundamental problem of the war was a different one . . . the rapid annihilation of the [Soviet] enemy was now an essential prerequisite for the successful continuation of the war . . .

Jeschonnek spoke without vehemence, presumption or demagogy. Yet he was far from taking

JG 26 *Schlageter* and its Fw 190s helped defeat the RAF's Non-Stop Offensive, which culminated in the August 19 Dieppe raid. The unit was well positioned at its bases in Belgium and northeastern France to counter the early, tentative missions of the American Eighth Air Force. A 1./JG 26 Fw 190A-3, "white 5," is shown here landing at St. Omer. (*Meyer*)

things lightly. He was fully aware of the deathly crisis in which the Luftwaffe stood because of the war in the east; nor did he close his eyes to the potential of the Western Powers. But—and this was the crux of his argument—now that we were in this fatal struggle with the Soviet Union, we had to see it through . . .

The Chief of the General Staff had not weakened my argument; nor had he even tried to do so. But he had given me an insight into the problems of the war, and I could not deny the logic of his reasoning.[32]

Indeed, only a few months after his "360 fighters" comment, Jeschonnek was pushing for a production increase to 900 fighters and 500 bombers per month, in an effort to address the demands of both home defense and the fighting fronts, but actual output remained almost steady through 1942.[33] In 1943, the priorities would begin to change, and Speer's and Milch's production miracle would begin—but this lay in the future.

Pilot training remained virtually fixed at early war levels. The Luftwaffe flight schools turned out a total

This Fw 190A-3, "brown 12," saw long service in II./JG 26. Here it prepares to roll out under the close supervision of a large ground staff. (Petrick)

of 1,666 trained fighter pilots to front-line or replacement units throughout the whole of 1942, to offset a loss of 1,093 fighter pilots during that year.[34] On paper, this seems to indicate a surplus, and indeed on September 30, 1942, fighter personnel strength stood at 104 percent of authorized strength. Quality was another matter, however; the gaining units reported only 69 percent of their pilots (1,136 of 1,635) fit for duty; the rest were "not fully qualified for combat action."

A start was made during 1942 to increase the output of fighter pilots. In October the number of fighter-pilot schools was doubled, from five to ten. 1943 targets for day-fighter pilots (single-engine) were 274 per month, for a yearly total of 3,288.[35] Yet such expansion came at a cost.[36] Fuel shortages began to affect the training program as early as June 1942; Göring noted that if this kept up, the Luftwaffe would have more planes than trained pilots by 1943.[37] Measures to raise the fuel allocation to the training units were partially successful; in September 1942 the schools received 14,000 tons, in October 20,000; in November 22,000; while in December allocations fell to 19,000 tons.[38] With chronic fuel shortages, cutbacks to the duration of the courses were only a matter of time, and the quality of the newly trained pilots suffered.

The Reichsmarschall also took a dim view of the selection process. Early in 1943 he noted that "many promising young men were awaiting training, while 'idiots' were being trained" and that he was "at a loss to understand how some of these people were ever accepted." In spite of the difficulties, the training units made efforts to equip their graduates with the skills to meet the new threat. The syllabus of the *Ergänzungsjagdgruppen* (Advanced Fighter Training Groups) by mid-1942 included practice combats at 6,000 meters (20,000 ft.) as well as ground-controlled interceptions of incoming bomber formations.[39] Without these measures, and without Albert Speer's and Erhard Milch's concurrent efforts to raise fighter production, the German defensive successes of fall 1943 would not have been possible. Even then, the worsening situation at the front would siphon off a large percentage of the hard-won gains.

Early USAAF Attacks

The Luftwaffe leadership in Berlin knew that American airmen were beginning to arrive in the United Kingdom, and that USAAF doctrine called for high-altitude daylight strategic bombing. But in their minds this doctrine had already been discredited, by the failure of their own bomber force to defeat Britain in 1940 and by their fighters' success in fending off the RAF's small-scale daylight attacks on German targets over the past three years. The mere threat of an American bombing campaign did not warrant the reinforcement of Germany's day-fighter defenses. At this time these comprised three Jagdgeschwader, spread thinly in the coastal regions from Cherbourg along the English Channel and the North Sea coast to Denmark and southern Norway and partitioned between two independent operational commands. The authorized strength of the three Geschwader was 442 fighters; their operational strength on July 27, 1942, was 333. Almost all were Fw 190s, the nimble radial-engine fighter whose performance had shocked the RAF when it entered service on the *Kanalfront* in 1941.

As previously mentioned, the only day-fighter Geschwader in Lw Bfh Mitte was JG 1. Since the American forces did not cross the German border in 1942, JG 1 formations flying from Holland encountered them on only three occasions, and this Geschwader and Lw Bfh Mitte will not be mentioned again in this chapter. Most of the battle opportunities would fall to the two *Kanalgeschwader* of Sperrle's Luftflotte 3: Jagdgeschwader 2 *Richthofen* and Jagdgeschwader 26 *Schlageter*. These two Geschwader had been left on the Channel coast in mid-1941 when most

A lineup of 8./JG 26 Fw 190A-3s at Wevelghem, Belgium in late 1942. (*Meyer*)

of the Luftwaffe was transferred east to support the German invasion of the Soviet Union. Their job was to maintain air superiority over the western occupied zone (France and the Low Countries) against the fighters and light bombers of the RAF. They had performed this task with great success; they were now to face a different challenge.

In August the Fw 190s of Major Walter Oesau's JG 2 were all based in northwestern France, under the command and control of Jafü 3. The Stab and I./JG 2 were at Triqueville, II./JG 2 was at Beaumont-le-Roger, and III./JG 2 was at Cherbourg-Maupertus. Major Gerhard Schöpfel's JG 26 was under Jafü 2, and was disposed as follows: the Stab and I./JG 26 at St. Omer in the Pas de Calais; II./JG 26, known to Allied aircrew as the "Abbeville Boys," at Abbeville-Drucat on the lower Seine, and III./JG 26 at Wevelghem, in western Belgium. In addition to these Fw 190 units, there were two independent Staffeln, 11.(Höhen)/JG 2 and 11.(Höhen)/JG 26, which were equipped with the high-altitude Bf 109G-1. These were based at Ligescourt and Norrent-Fontes, nominally under JG 26.

A Schwarm of 8./JG 26 Fw 190s in flight, photographed by the Schwarmführer, Lt. Paul Galland, Adolf's youngest brother. Paul Galland was shot down and killed by Spitfires on October 31. (*Matthiesen via Petrick*)

The Eighth Air Force was committed to action while very weak in strength. Its units were inadequately trained and completely lacking in combat experience. Early raids barely crossed the coast, and were directed at airfields, railroad yards, and the few industrial targets within range of the bombers' Spitfire escort. The first heavy-bomber mission was flown on August 17, when 12 B-17s bombed the Rouen railroad yards. Close escort was provided by RAF Fighter Command's four Spitfire IX squadrons. Rear support was afforded by the Biggin Hill and Tangmere Spitfire V Wings. Only I./JG 2 and II./JG 26 made contact for the defenders. The Focke-Wulfs got close enough to draw fire from the B-17s, but did not close range immediately. The Abbeville controller ordered II./JG 26 to attack the formation on its return flight over the Channel. Nos. 401 and 402, the two Canadian squadrons on the right side of the escort screen, attacked the Focke-Wulfs and succeeded in keeping them away from the bombers, but lost two Spitfire IXs and their pilots; a third Spitfire crashed in England with a badly injured pilot. The German pilots misidentified the bombers as Stirlings or Halifaxes (RAF heavy bombers), and were impressed by their close formation and heavy defensive fire. The Gruppe was credited with downing four Spitfires, while sustaining no losses.[40]

After carrying out nine missions without the loss of a single bomber, 8th Bomber Command's attack on the Potez aircraft factory at Meaulte on September 6 cost two B-17s, victims of II./JG 2 and II./JG 26, which attacked the 30 Flying Fortresses continuously from the French coast in to the target. The close escort, four squadrons of Spitfire IXs, missed their rendezvous and apparently were never able to intervene. The high cover, No. 133 "Eagle" Squadron, was flying at 28,000 feet (8,500 meters) when it was bounced and dispersed by Focke-Wulfs attacking from above and behind. Three Spitfires failed to return. The bombers underwent repeated attacks by 45–50 Fw 190s and a few Bf 109s. Attacks came from all directions, and nearly all of the B-17s sustained damage. The honor of the Luftwaffe's first victory over an American heavy bomber went to

At this stage of the war the commanders of the Gruppen and Staffeln of the two *Kanalgeschwader* were all prewar professional officers who ran very efficient units. Karl Borris, seen here as a Hauptmann, joined III./JG 26 in 1940 and commanded I./JG 26 from June 23, 1943, until VE-Day. (*Meyer*)

Hptm. Conny Meyer, Kommandeur of II./JG 26. His target, a B-17F of the 97th Bombardment Group (Heavy) (shortened in this book to 97th Bomb Group), went down near Amiens. The Focke-Wulfs pursued the bombers back across the French coast. A B-17E of the 92nd Bomb Group succumbed to attacks by at least five fighters and crashed into the sea near Le Treport. II./JG 2 lost two Focke-Wulfs and one pilot in this battle, and was credited with downing two B-17s and two Spitfires. II./JG 26 came through the day unscathed; its claims for two B-17s and one Spitfire were also confirmed. The problem of excessive claims for heavy bombers, which bedeviled Luftwaffe strategists and statisticians every time more than one Jagdwaffe unit was involved in an interception, thus made a very early appearance: four victory claims were confirmed for the two lost bombers.

The credit for the day's success belonged primarily to the German radar and radio-intercept services and to the fighter-control organization, which were rapidly rising to the new challenge. Any major increase in activity on the American radio frequencies foretold a genuine raid; American strength was insufficient for diversions. German radar could pick up the high-altitude formations before they crossed the English coast, which had not been the case with the RAF's low-level offensive sweeps during the previous 18 months. Morale in the two Luftflotte 3 Jagdgeschwader, which had sagged in the previous weeks, climbed again, although the apparent low destructive capacity of their fighters' machine guns and cannon was frustrating. More effective weapons and ammunition were promised. General Galland established a test unit in Achmer, Erprobungskommando 25 (ErprKdo 25), and gave it the responsibility of developing *Sonderwaffen* (special weapons) to bring down American heavy bombers. Major Heinz Nacke and his men, aided by a number of civilian scientists and engineers, immediately began experiments with heavy-caliber cannon and air-to-air rockets.[41]

Several early raids were not intercepted at all, arousing the wrath of both Göring and Galland. Galland told his post-war interrogator that he was irritated by the timidity of the fighter pilots, who at first simply would not attack.[42] Concerned about the apparent decline in performance of JG 26, his former command, Galland made at least two personal visits to assure himself that his successor as Geschwader Kommodore, Major Gerhard Schöpfel, had the situation under control.[43]

In the meantime, the ability of the B-17s to absorb damage and keep flying was becoming legendary on both sides of the Channel. On one early raid, Oblt. Kurt Ruppert of 9./JG 26 repeatedly attacked an isolated B-17. Three engines were shot up; one fell off the plane and crashed into the Channel. Out of ammunition, Ruppert watched in amazement as the plane continued to fly on one engine, its crew throwing out equipment, guns and ammunition. The bomber succeeded in making it back to England, force-landing on the beach at Ramsgate.[44]

A typical interception in the fall of 1942 has been described by Johannes Naumann, at that time an Oberleutnant in II./JG 26. The Gruppe was ordered to attack the bombers on their return flight, as there was no chance of reaching them before the bomb run. The B-17s were flying in a staggered formation at about 8,000 meters (26,250 ft.). The Focke-Wulfs finally struggled up to 8,200 meters (26,900 ft.), only to see the American formation receding into the distance. The speed of the Fw 190s at that altitude was little greater than that of the bombers, and a stern chase closed the range only very slowly. Frustrated, Naumann opened fire with his MG 151/20 cannon at the extreme range of 700 meters (760 yards). By this time, half of the original formation of 24 fighters had dropped out of the chase for one reason or another. Suddenly there was a loud noise from in front of Naumann's feet—his engine had exploded, bringing his combat sortie to a sudden end. No bombers were downed; none had even suffered visible damage.[45]

Karl Borris, in 1942 the Kapitän of 8./JG 26, has described the emotional impact of the enemy bombers on the German pilots, who were now facing the most formidable challenge of their lives. The size of the heavy bombers and their formations, and their unprecedented defensive firepower, could not be described adequately to a green pilot; they had to be experienced at first hand. The classical stern attack, which was at first the only approved method, was frequently initiated and broken off too soon to cause damage. Range estimation proved difficult. The Revi gunsight was sized for attacks on fighters; the wings of a typical fighter filled its sighting circle at 100 meters' (110 yards') range. The bombers loomed huge in the Revi long before the German fighters reached effective range. The bomber gunners opened fire as soon as a target was seen, in order to disrupt or ward off attacks. The Americans' Browning .50-inch machine guns had a high muzzle velocity and a greater range than the German MG 151s and MG 17s. So the fighter pilots' cockpits were surrounded by red tracers "swarming like wasps" long before they themselves could open fire effectively; and because of the low closing speeds, this extremely uncomfortable situation could continue for several minutes. Some pilots, especially the younger ones, would break away before their own weapons were within effective range.[46]

October 9—Lille

This raid was the strongest American effort to date. Some 108 bombers were dispatched to attack the locomotive works, steel factory, and airfields in the Lille-Courtrai area; 36 squadrons of Spitfires and P-38s were assigned to support the bombers. There was no close escort, but rather two target support forces, plus two rear support forces and three diversionary forces. RAF Fighter Command's plan was far too complex; the Luftwaffe would conduct the coming battle as if there had been no Allied fighters in the air at all.[47]

The III./JG 26 airfield at Wevelghem was among the targets, and its Kommandeur, Hptm. Josef "Pips" Priller, led the German defensive effort. His three Staffeln had dispersed inland for the night, and had just landed back at Wevelghem and nearby Moorsele when the order was given to scramble. The Gruppe flew westward, straining for altitude. This was Priller's first sight of American heavy bombers from the air. He misjudged their size, and thus underestimated the altitude of the bombers. He had to repeat his attack orders three times, as he reached what he thought was the bombers' altitude only to see them still above him. The bombers flew in vics of three, but in no apparent overall formation; they reminded Lt. Otto "Stotto" Stammberger of a large swarm of bumblebees. (The size of the bomber force had been whittled to 69 by early returns, and the formation's integrity had been compromised.) The bombers passed by the fighters, which were still climbing through 8,000 meters (26,000 ft.). The bomber formation then made a sharp left turn south of Lille, allowing the Focke-Wulf pilots to reach attack position. Pairs of fighters attacked the individual vics from the rear. Hptm. Priller watched his target, a B-24 Liberator of the trailing 93rd Bomb Group, crash near Lille.[48]

Oblt. Ruppert led his 9./JG 26, a component of III./JG 26, against another formation of bombers, comprising B-17s from the 306th Bomb Group. He saw the contrails of the fighter escort, but they remained far above the fight. His pilots attacked the bombers from the rear, as briefed. Ruppert's target dropped away from the formation; he would be given credit for a *Herausschuss* or "shoot-out" for culling it from its formation. Lt. Stammberger attacked this Fortress, but saw that his fire was having no effect. He suddenly realized that he was firing from too great a range. Approaching closer, he saw strikes on the bomber's left wing. Still unmolested by the Allied fighters, he attacked the bomber repeatedly. By the third pass both left engines were blazing; he then fired at the right outboard engine as the bomber spiraled downward in broad left turns. According to bombardier Al LaChasse, who years later could still see "those yellow-nosed bastards as they almost flew into our nose," the pilot and copilot were already sprawled dead in their blood-spattered cockpit. LaChasse was one of three men to escape the spinning B-17.[49] Stammberger gave his full attention to the crash of the bomber east of Vendeville. When he again looked up, the sky was empty. Out of ammunition, he headed back to the 9. Staffel base at Moorsele. Stammberger was one of the few pilots to record personal comments in his logbook. He noted that evening that making four firing passes on a single bomber was "amateurish and stupid."[50]

7./JG 26, also from III./JG 26, made an effective attack, led by its Kapitän, Hptm. Klaus Mietusch. He identified his first target as an RAF Stirling; it was probably a 301st Bomb Group B-17 that made it back to England to crash-land. Mietusch made a second pass through the same formation and damaged another B-17, which became the first American bomber to ditch successfully in the Channel. Mietusch's claim for its destruction was not confirmed, because its ditching was not witnessed. Mietusch's wingman was hit by defensive fire in the first attack. He jumped from his plane, but was unable to open his parachute because of his wounds, and fell to his death. Another pilot of Mietusch's Staffel succeeded in shooting down a 92nd Bomb Group B-17 after repeated attacks from the rear and below (6 o'clock low, in the parlance of the American airmen).

The III./JG 26 toll of four bombers was the heaviest single-mission loss yet suffered by the Eighth Air Force. Many of the returning bombers had been damaged, and bombing accuracy was poor,

but the Americans proclaimed a decisive victory over the Luftwaffe. The gunners claimed 56 fighters destroyed, 26 probably destroyed, and 20 damaged (commonly abbreviated as 56–26–20 claims). Although Allied intelligence knew full well that the claims were greater than the total number of German interceptors airborne, and the total was subsequently lowered sharply, the original numbers were quoted by President Roosevelt himself in a radio broadcast, to the great amusement of the German pilots, who had suffered only one casualty.[51]

This raid on Lille marked the high point of the American effort in 1942. The two most experienced heavy bomb groups, the 97th and the 301st, plus four fighter groups, were withdrawn from combat in preparation for a move to North Africa. The new units arriving in England were very green, and had to be introduced to combat slowly. The first raid to exceed that of October 9 in strength was not mounted until April 17, 1943.

In mid-October the Eighth Air Force was ordered to destroy the five U-boat bases on the Bay of Biscay. General Eaker accepted the assignment with unseemly eagerness, given that he had no weapon that could penetrate the U boat pens' roofs of reinforced concrete 3.5 meters (11.5 ft.) thick. A totally unrewarding campaign began on October 21 with an attack on Lorient. Part of III./JG 2 had previously moved to Brest to provide cover for surfaced U-boats against the strike fighters of RAF Coastal Command, and was well positioned to attack the unescorted American bombers. Three 97th Bomb Group B-17s crashed immediately, and two more were scrapped after their return to England. The rest of III./JG 2 transferred to several bases in Brittany over the next few days to bulk up the defenses of the new American targets.[52]

The Allies landed in northwestern Africa on November 8 in Operation Torch. The Germans were forced to defend this new front with fighter units taken from western Europe. The only two Bf 109G-equipped Staffeln now in Luftflotte 3, the high-altitude 11.(Höhen)/JG 2 and 11.(Höhen)/JG 26, were ordered to Tunisia, along with the Fw 190-equipped II./JG 2. On November 9, a second Fw 190 Gruppe, I./JG 2, flew to Marseilles to support the German occupation of Vichy France and to guard against a possible invasion of southern France by the Allies. The aerial defense of the Channel coast was thus left to three Jagdgruppen, I./JG 26, II./JG 26, and III./JG 26, while III./JG 2 was the only unit available to defend Brittany and the submarine bases. To bolster the defenses of the Paris area, 9./JG 26 was detached from III./JG 26 and subordinated to III./JG 2. Lt. Stammberger, temporarily in command of the Staffel, led it to Beaumont-le-Roger, south of Le Havre, on November 27. Fortunately for the Luftwaffe, American strength in England was also at a low ebb, for the same reason—the need to supply the air forces in Africa with experienced units.

There was at this time no standard method of attacking the bombers. The most common direction was from the stern, where the fighters' classic pursuit curve positioned them. Luftflotte 3's fighter commanders spent hours in late 1942 discussing the best tactics to use against the heavies. Models were built, and attack angles were studied. Hptm. Egon Mayer is credited with suggesting that an attack from the front offered the best chance of destroying a bomber, or at least of killing its cockpit crew. It also appeared that the defensive armament of the bombers was weakest in the nose. Mayer, who had just replaced the less cerebral Major Hans "Assi" Hahn as Kommandeur of III./JG 2, was given permission by Jafü 3 to test his idea at the earliest opportunity. This came on November 23, when 36 unescorted B-17s and B-24s were reported headed for St. Nazaire. The bombers were greeted on their bomb run by Mayer's Focke-Wulfs, attacking from dead ahead in Ketten of three aircraft. Four B-17s tumbled from the formation, victims of the Luftwaffe's most successful single pass through the heavies to date. A fifth B-17 was scrapped after its return to England; Mayer's Gruppe was given credit for six victories, three by the innovative Hauptmann himself.

Adolf Galland, always ready to accept new ideas, was quick to give the new tactic his blessing. In a memo sent to all Luftwaffe fighter units he made the following points:

1. The diving attack from the front by Hptm. Mayer was very effective, and resulted in the immediate destruction of a B-17.
2. His Nos. 2 and 3 were seriously damaged when they pulled up behind the formation after the attack. This is not recommended.
3. Hptm. Mayer's second attack was also successful. In this case he dove in front of a bomber, pulled up to make his attack, and dove away in a tight bank, climbing back up ahead of the formation. He received no defensive fire.
4. General conclusions:
   a. Attacks from the rear on close formations are seldom successful and bring heavy losses. If it is necessary to attack from the rear, fire at engines and fuel tanks from a steep bank.
   b. Attacks from the side can be effective. These require training and a good firing angle.
   c. Frontal attacks at low speed from straight ahead, above, or below are the most effective of all attacks. Prerequisites for success are flying skill, good aim, and continuous fire up to the closest possible distance.

Klaus Mietusch, seen here as an Oberleutnant, joined III./JG 26 upon its establishment in 1939 and remained with it until his death as its Kommandeur on September 17, 1944. (*Meyer*)

d. Withdrawal is permitted only by a tight diving bank in the direction of flight of the attacked bomber. This maximizes the angular velocity and makes it impossible for the enemy gunners to draw the correct lead.

e. It is essential that the fighter units attack repeatedly in great strength and mass. The defensive fire will then be dispersed and the bomber formation can be split apart.[53]

December 20—Romilly-sur-Seine

On this date the 8th Bomber Command staged its largest raid since Lille. In all 101 B-17s and B-24s were dispatched to bomb the important Luftwaffe servicing base at Romilly-sur-Seine, 100 km (60

Johannes Naumann joined III./JG 26 as a Leutnant upon its establishment in 1939, transferred to II./JG 26, and rose to command it. He left the Geschwader after a 23 June 1944 injury and later commanded II./JG 6. (*Naumann*)

miles) southeast of Paris. Unfortunately for the Americans, their mission plan was a near-duplicate of one that had been used just the previous week, and the defenders were ready. RAF Fighter Command's four diversionary sweeps of the Pas de Calais brought up all of JG 26's fighters, which made desultory contact with one Spitfire wing, but were quickly ordered away, as the main Allied force had already been detected over the Channel, headed for Fécamp. Some JG 26 Focke-Wulfs landed for quick servicing, while most flew down the coast toward Dieppe. II./JG 26 and III./JG 26 were the first to arrive and paralleled the bomber formation until the Spitfire escort turned back. The fighters immediately hit the 91st Bomb Group from dead ahead. Two B-17s went down over Rouen. The 91st Group then endured one hour of continuous combat without further loss. The JG 2 and JG 26 Stab flights and the three JG 26 Gruppen attacked in relays until low fuel forced them to break off. 9./JG 26 scrambled from Beaumont-le-Roger, reached the bombers in the Paris region, and joined part of Hptm. Mayer's III./JG 2 in a successful head-on attack.

Lt. Stammberger saw one B-17 flip end-for-end before its tail section broke off and the bomber began its last dive. Stammberger's own target began shaking and shuddering under the fire of his guns. As he started a second head-on pass its crew began bailing out at short intervals; eventually there were nine parachutes hanging in the bright blue sky.[54]

4./JG 26, which had flown an early mission from Beaumont-le-Roger in response to the sweeps and had landed for refueling, was the last fresh formation to reach the bombers, and shot a B-17 into the Channel off Dieppe. The JG 2 Geschwaderstab flew a quick second sortie, Major Oesau downing his second B-17 of the day off Dieppe. JG 26 fighters on their second sortie began to arrive from the Pas de Calais just as the return escort was spotted over the Channel; after a few inconclusive engagements, both sides retired to their bases.

Six B-17s went down over France; 31 B-17s and B-24s returned to England with combat damage. Initial American claims of 53 German fighters destroyed were later reduced to 21. JG 2 claimed three B-17s and lost two pilots killed. JG 26 claimed five B-17s and lost one plane and pilot. Many fighters ran out of fuel in the prolonged engagement. Their pilots' radioed reports of forced landings were interpreted by Allied intelligence as evidence of widespread combat damage to the German formations, corroborating the bomber crews' claims; most of the German reports referred instead to routine dead stick landings. It is believed that only six Luftwaffe fighters were damaged beyond repair, while ten others survived their forced landings with slight to moderate damage.[55]

Lessons Learned

As winter set in, both sides worked feverishly on equipment and tactics. Armorers on every American bomber base in England improvised fittings in the noses of their B-17s and B-24s to accommodate various additional machine guns. New formations and tactical doctrines, most stemming from the fertile mind of the 305th Bomb Group commander, Colonel Curtis LeMay, were established throughout the Eighth Air Force. The staggered 18-plane combat box, known to the Germans as a *Pulk* (bunch), was but one of his ideas.

The Bf 109 and Fw 190 models reaching the Luftwaffe at the end of 1942 differed only in detail from those of 1941. Both fighter designs showed unmistakable signs of reaching maturity. Weights continued to rise, and engine power had to be increased to keep pace. Barred from major increases in engine compression ratios by Germany's chronic shortage of high-strength, high-temperature metal alloys and high-octane aviation fuel, engineers sought chemical additives to increase the energy of the detonations within the existing engines' cylinders. The Bf 109G-1's DB 605A engine had introduced nitrous oxide (GM-1) injection as a means of temporarily boosting engine power at altitude. The Bf 109G-4 was based on the G-1, but lacked the earlier fighter's complicated cockpit pressurization system, and was equipped with a new radio, the FuG 16Z, which had multiple channels and homing capabilities. The Fw 190A-3 had a new BMW 801D-2 engine with greater power than its predecessor. Cooling louvers cut into the cowling finally solved the Focke-Wulf fighter's overheating problem. The Fw 190A-3 was succeeded in late 1942 by the A-4, which had the FuG 16Z radio. While flying at their preferred altitudes, the Bf 109G-4 and Fw 190A-4 were equal in performance to the best RAF fighter, the Spitfire IX.

Most of the new fighters arriving at JG 2 and JG 26 bases at the end of 1942 were Bf 109s. Kurt Tank's Fw 190 was now in chronic short supply. Having overcome most of its original problems, it was now in great demand on all of the Luftwaffe's widespread combat fronts, for reconnaissance and ground-attack duties as well as in its original air-superiority role. If someone had to give them up, the two *Kanalgeschwader* were the most logical choices, as the performance of the Fw 190 dropped off markedly above 7,500 meters (25,000 ft.), which happened to be the altitude flown by the B-17 formations. On the other hand, Willi Messerschmitt's latest fighter, the Bf 109G-4, was in its element above 9,000 meters (30,000 ft.). By the spring of 1943, III./JG 26 was equipped exclusively with Messerschmitts, while I./JG 2 and II./JG 26 were flying a mixture of Messerschmitts and Focke-Wulfs. Mixed equipment did not prove satisfactory at the Gruppe level, and these two Gruppen were allowed to turn in their Messerschmitts for more Focke-Wulfs, remaining Fw 190 units until the war's end.

When II./JG 2 returned from North Africa it was re-equipped with Bf 109s. Each of the two *Kanalgeschwader* now had two Fw 190 Gruppen and one Bf 109 Gruppe. The Bf 109 was an excellent dogfighter, especially at high altitudes, and later played a useful role as high cover over Germany, taking on the Allied escort fighters while the Fw 190 units concentrated on the bombers. However, the fighters of Luftflotte 3 rarely had time to form up for such coordinated attacks, and the Bf 109 and Fw 190 Gruppen were forced to attack the bomber formations independently. The Fw 190A-4's armament mix of two MG 17 light machine guns, two MG FF 20-mm cannon, and two MG 151/20 20-mm cannon was considered effective against all targets. However, the Bf 109G-4's standard armament of two MG 17s and one MG 151/20 was too light to do much damage to B-17s and B-24s. In the next model of the Messerschmitt fighter to enter service, the Bf 109G-6, the MG 17s were replaced with heavier MG 131s. Plumbing for yet another chemical additive, MW 50 (methanol–water), was added to increase low-altitude performance, but most pilots noted instead the deterioration in maneuverability resulting from its increased weight. They gave it the derisory nickname "*Beule*" (boil) for the bulky fairings covering the MG 131 breeches.

The Bf 109 was always notorious for its fragile construction. All in all, the Fw 190 was a much more survivable aircraft, and was the mount preferred by most of the western *Jagdflieger* (fighter pilots) in 1942–3. Erich Schwarz, an experienced *Kanaljäger* (Channel fighter), quoted a favorite saying in JG 26: "When a Focke-Wulf crashed, Professor Tank made the broken parts thicker. When a Bf 109 crashed, Professor Messerschmitt made the parts that had held together thinner." In Schwarz's opinion, "The Bf 109 was a good airplane, but could not compare with the Fw 190. The Bf 109 had great success in the east, but the enemy there did not have the technically developed arsenal that we faced in the west."[56]

Otto "Stotto" Stammberger joined III./JG 26 in early 1941 as a Leutnant and was one of the most effective JG 26 bomber destroyers until severely injured on May 13, 1943; the injury eventually cost him his combat status. (*Stammberger*)

General Galland kept the pressure on Major Oesau and Major Schöpfel. Their percentage of successful interceptions had to be sharply increased; only then might the new threat be nipped in the bud. At year's end Galland was working on a set of detailed tactical regulations prescribing the methods of attack on heavy bombers. In his post-war interrogation he summarized their content as follows. Fighter units were to fly on a course parallel to and on one side of the bombers until about 5 km (3 miles) ahead of them. They were then to turn in by Schwärme and attack head-on. They were to aim at the bombers' cockpits, open fire at 800 meters (875 yards), and maintain a near-level course, passing above their target after ceasing fire. The second approved attack method was from the rear, which required concentrated attacks; the fighters were to attack by Schwärme in rapid succession and at high speed, and pass over the bombers after ceasing fire.[57]

In Galland's mind, one key to success with these tactics was for the fighters to maintain formation, or at least visual contact, in order to permit repeated concentrated attacks. Keeping position above the bombers was essential—and yet, from now until the end of the war, the German pilot's favorite method of ending an attack from either front or rear was with a split-S, which left him far beneath the attacked formation, and alone. Many pilots facing the hailstorm of defensive fire felt an irresistible urge to break off their attacks too soon. Although the bombers' guns did not bring down many German fighters, their streams of .50-inch tracers did in fact form an extremely effective defensive shield. Despite Galland's wishes, German formation attacks were rarely carried out exactly as prescribed. Some pilots would invariably break away prematurely, and the rest would pass through the bomber formation at whatever angle and orientation promised the best chance for survival. The formation leaders found it difficult to reassemble the scattered fighters, and each successive attack could be counted on for no greater than half the strength of the one preceding it.[58]

The Luftflotte 3 fighter commanders, apparently on their own initiative, were themselves working to improve the efficiency of their interceptions. Attack formations were to be increased in size, and tactics were to be modified. On December 20, most attacks had been made from dead ahead—12 o'clock level, as viewed from the bombers. The bombers were in effective firing range for only a fraction of a second at the closing speed of roughly 900 km/h (550 mph), and the flat angle of attack and the high altitude made range estimation extremely difficult. Pilots could not help but worry about the possibility of colliding with their target, and many broke off their attacks far too soon. JG 26 veteran Karl Borris has stated that, after experimentation, the optimum attack angle was found to be from dead ahead as before, but from ten degrees above the horizontal. A constant angle of fire could be maintained, similar to that practised often against ground targets. The proper lead was attained by keeping the Revi's crosshairs on the nose of the bomber. Distance estimation was simplified, and even the less experienced pilots could score hits. Thus was born the form of attack most feared by bomber crews—from 12 o'clock high.[59]

The year ended with the great German offensive aspirations in south Russia and the Mediterranean in tatters. A growing night-bomber offensive against the Reich's industrial and population centers demanded build-up of the integrated radar, Flak, and night-fighter defenses. Yet the upper Luftwaffe leadership still maintained that offensive air action was the best way to keep the Reich's enemies far from its borders. Bomber production continued at a high level throughout 1942, and Luftwaffe research and development teams pressed ahead with the next generation of offensive air armament.

A recent student of German air defenses has concluded, "By the end of 1942, the USAAF may have been in the war, but from a German perspective it appeared to make very little difference."[60] The Eighth Air Force had been blooded in combat, and the German fighter pilots and command staffs from Luftflotte 3 and Lw Bfh Mitte accorded the new enemy considerable respect. Yet the measures taken to strengthen the daylight defenses against this new threat remained piecemeal and counterproductive. The needs of the combat fronts took precedence; fighter deployments in Luftflotte 3 had to divide their efforts between air defense and a number of other operational tasks, and the few regular fighter units in the Reich territory had to be buttressed by training units. Yet the Reich itself

was virtually inviolate by day in 1942, and the existing defenses seemed to be holding their own against Anglo-American daylight strikes into the occupied western territories. Jeschonnek definitely summed up the prevailing wisdom when he told one of his staff officers, "Galland can take care of the [daylight] defense in the west with one wing."[61] 1943 would see this attitude put to a most severe test.

Erich Schwarz, seen here as an Oberfeldwebel, joined III./JG 26 in 1941 as an Unteroffizier after a full training course and served as a Schwarmführer in the mid-war period. He was severely injured on May 15, 1944, but returned to finish the war with the unit. (*Schwarz*)

CHAPTER 4

THE SLOW AMERICAN BUILD UP JANUARY–JUNE 1943

The Tide Ebbs: The War in Early 1943

The first months of 1943 were a grim time for the Third Reich and the Luftwaffe. The great German eastern offensive of summer 1942, launched with such high hopes, foundered in the streets of Stalingrad and, on February 2, 1943, the starving and disillusioned remnants of the Sixth Army—some 90,000 soldiers—capitulated. Army Group A had narrowly averted a potentially greater disaster in the Caucasus,

Obstlt. Dr. Erich Mix in the cockpit of his Bf 109F at Bergen aan Zee. At 43, Mix was one of the oldest fighter pilots in the Jagdwaffe when he took command of I./JG 1 in September 1941. He served as Kommodore from August 1942 until his relief by Major Hans Philipp in April 1943. Mix's airplane displays a large Geschwader emblem. (*Rosch*)

as von Manstein struggled to stabilize the collapsing southern sector of the Eastern Front. The Axis Mediterranean strategy, never well thought out to begin with, was also in jeopardy. The Torch landings in November 1942 came hard on the heels of Montgomery's victory at El Alamein, and the Axis forces in North Africa found themselves hard pressed between the British Eighth Army and the Anglo-American First Army, as the open spaces of the Western Desert gave way to the rugged hills of Tunisia. A reinvigorated RAF Bomber Command under the determined leadership of Air Chief Marshal Harris pressed home the night area offensive officially undertaken in February 1942, systematically striking the cities of the Ruhr industrial district beginning in March 1943. And on January 27, 1943, USAAF heavy bombers struck a target on German soil for the first time when 53 B-17s raided Wilhelmshaven. Both the Eighth Air Force commanders and the German defenders knew that this was only the beginning.

For the Luftwaffe, the reversal of fortune had been especially swift. Throughout most of 1942 it had been able to deal with its expanding commitments by effectively massing its limited combat power at the decisive point—if only at the expense of leaving large sectors almost devoid of operational units. Its air-defense forces in the west, both Flak and fighters, were able to cope with the shallow daylight penetrations of the USAAF, although the increasing weight of the RAF night offensive remained cause for concern. Most German air commanders believed that the technology, training and tactics of the Luftwaffe compared favorably with its RAF, USAAF and Red Air Force antagonists.

Events in late 1942 and early 1943 forced the Luftwaffe into a reactive posture from which, with few exceptions, it would not emerge for the duration of the war. Instead of supporting victorious German drives, the Luftwaffe's bomber, fighter and ground-attack units sought to buttress the faltering Axis position at the combat fronts. In the Mediterranean, Luftflotte 2 was expected to tie down Allied forces in North Africa, cover the sea approaches to Sicily, and generally shore up the southern front against an Anglo-American assault. In Russia, the crisis at Stalingrad ground down the combat units of the powerful Luftflotte 4, while the failed Stalingrad airlift damaged Göring's prestige—and by extension that of the entire Luftwaffe—in the eyes of Hitler. Incredibly, however, events on the Eastern Front in the spring of 1943 would stabilize to the point that the German high command could contemplate renewing the offensive in that decisive war theater. The OKH (Army High Command) began planning for a resumption of limited offensive operations against the Kursk salient. Although relatively modest in contrast to the titanic offensives of 1941 and 1942, the Zitadelle operation would occasion a massing of German air power and armor never again to be seen in that theater.[1]

This confluence of events was to have a decisive impact on the Reich's air defenses, and indeed on the entire German air war effort. Hitler, Göring, and the rest of the Reich's senior leadership remained determined to regain the initiative in the spring of 1943. While the OKH and army group staffs made preparations for a late spring 1943 riposte in the U.S.S.R. and the OKW (Armed Forces High Command) managed the crisis in North Africa and the Mediterranean, the German air commanders wrestled with the intractable problem of how best to employ the Luftwaffe during these critical months. In particular, Luftwaffe Chief of Staff Hans Jeschonnek

found himself in a most unenviable position. Although a belated convert to the need for strengthening the home fighter defenses, he also felt obligated to resume the offensive, and was determined that the Luftwaffe would participate fully in the coming operations. In March 1943, Hitler ordered renewed air attacks against Great Britain as a counter to Harris's offensive, and appointed the 29-year-old Oberst Dietrich Peltz[2] as *Angriffsführer England* (Attack Leader England). Jeschonnek, attempting to satisfy the conflicting demands, sought to strengthen the day and night defenses, while at the same time reconstituting the bomber force and maintaining powerful combat air fleets at the front. So untenable was his position that he sought command of one of those air fleets in an attempt to flee the growing nightmare at Luftwaffe headquarters. Hitler refused his request, and the young General Staff chief gamely pressed forward with an ambitious air strategy for 1943.

German Air Defenses in Early 1943

German documents from this period make reference to the *Reichsverteidigung* effort. This was not an organization *per se*, but was analogous to the British home defenses, which included flying units, anti-aircraft guns, civil defense, etc., all under separate commands. The role of the Luftwaffe in this effort was the *Reichsluftverteidigung* (aerial defense of the Reich), abbreviated RLV. Although Lw Bfh Mitte in Germany and Holland and Luftflotte 3 in France and Belgium were entirely independent organizations, their fighter units were all engaged in the air defense of the Reich, and it is useful for the purpose of this book to consider them all part of the Reichsluftverteidigung.

Jeschonnek hoped that the slowly growing day- and night-fighter defenses in Germany and occupied western Europe would stave off the Anglo-American threat while his plans to regain the initiative moved forward. As in 1942, the weight of those defensive tasks fell upon Lw Bfh Mitte and Luftflotte 3. The divided nature of the command reflected both the power of personalities and (more significantly) the influence of basic operational Luftwaffe doctrine. Luftflotte 3's GFM Hugo Sperrle was a powerful force

Obst. Walter Oesau, Kommodore of JG 2, prepares to lead a flight off Beaumont-le-Roger, France, in February. Oesau is in a Fw 190A-6 with the unusual staff marking of "green • – + –". In another unusual touch, the rest of his flight is in Bf 109s. (*Rosch*)

The Fw 190A-4 of the IV./JG 1 Adjutant, Lt. Eberhard Burath, after it crashed on takeoff from Deelen on March 11. Burath was not hurt. (*Burath*)

within the Luftwaffe and jealously guarded his prerogatives. In this case, however, his personal desires coincided with the basic principle underlying Luftwaffe organization: that the air force was best configured for offensive operations, with air defense an ancillary task.

Lw Bfh Mitte, headquartered at Berlin-Dahlem and under the command of General der Flakartillerie Hubert Weise, had overall responsibility for all flying and anti-aircraft forces based within the prewar borders of the Reich and earmarked for defense.[3] The flying units came directly under XII. Fliegerkorps, with four fighter divisions (Jagddivision 1 at Berlin, Jagddivision 2 at Stade, Jagddivision 3 at Deelen, and Jagddivision 4 at Döberitz).[4] Fighter divisions directed the combat operations of the day- and night-fighter units, and were also responsible for assembling operational and tactical information gleaned from the Luftwaffe listening and air reporting services into a complete "air situation" estimate.[5] The Jagdfliegerführer (Jafü), brigade-level staffs responsible for the actual conduct of day-fighter operations within the fighter division area, were located within the command posts of the fighter divisions. On April 1, 1943, the most important of these were Jafü Holland-Ruhrgebiet under Oberst Walter Grabmann and Jafü Deutsche Bucht under Genmaj. Walter Schwabedissen.[6]

Lw Bfh Mitte also had a number of subordinated Luftgaue (air force administrative areas). These Luftgaue, headquartered at Wiesbaden, Hamburg, Breslau, Munich, Münster, Berlin, Posen, and Königsberg, oversaw the powerful Flak forces defending German airspace.[7] Organizationally,

Weise's unique command ranked just below Luftflotte status.[8] Theoretically, this should have permitted the same powerful concentration of combat power that the Luftwaffe was able to bring to bear at the fighting fronts. In practice, the difficulty of fusing so many combat and service arms—many with their own traditions and cultures—proved problematical. Some of the aviators resented the primacy of the Flak arm in home air defense. Galland in particular complained about the prevailing view that the fighters' role was merely to "supplement" the Flak defenses.[9] In any case, the level of unity of effort produced by the arrangement was never completely satisfactory.

Moreover, Lw Bfh Mitte from its inception through much of 1943 was focused primarily on combating the RAF night area offensive. This emphasis explains much about the nature of the home-defense air command structure; it was devised for Flak-based defense augmented by night fighters, which accounts for the prominence of Flak and night-fighter personalities within the command staffs.[10] Some of its air commands had no dedicated first-line day-fighter assets. Jafü Süddeutschland, for example, had to draw from the day- and night-fighter replacement and training groups in order to participate in the daylight battles.[11] Part of the war diary for Jafü Süddeutschland's day-fighting activities for January–May 1943 has survived. It reveals a lengthy series of unsuccessful *Alarmstarts* (scrambles) against individual Mosquitoes, mostly by Bf 110s of Nachtjagdgeschwader (Night-Fighter Geschwader—NJG) 101 and Bf 109s of JG 104, both training units.[12] Behind the powerful front line represented by JG 1 in Holland and the Heligoland Bight region, much of the daylight defenses of Germany during this period were little advanced over what they had been in 1939–40. The Luftwaffe's swelling commitments forced the Luftwaffe leadership to bridge the gap on the cheap, with expedients such as tapping the operational training units, the use of night fighters in day operations, and other stopgaps.

The day defenses in the interior of Germany were at this time almost non-existent. The day-fighter operational-training Gruppen and factory-test units could each be called on to put up a Schwarm of their most experienced pilots in case of emergency. This expedient actually predated the establishment of Lw Bfh Mitte by a considerable margin. In 1940, several aircraft manufacturers created small factory-defense flights to provide on-the-spot air defense for the

sprawling industrial complexes. Originally these units came under Luftgau administration; later they would come under the regional Jagddivisionen. The organization of these *ad hoc* defensive units was apparently regularized in mid-January 1943. A document authorizing the establishment of *Industrieschutzstaffel* (Industry Protection Squadron) Messerschmitt at Regensburg, site of the main Bf 109 factory, has survived.[13] Its Staffelführer was to be a Luftwaffe Oberleutnant; his deputy, a civilian test pilot. It was to be subordinated for discipline to JG 104, an advanced-training unit at Fürth. It was to be responsible for defending a circular area 30 km (18 miles) around the factory. The order goes into great detail with respect to readiness states, Flak cooperation, and other matters, which was appropriate, as many of the test pilots were civilians with no recent military experience. Industrieschutzstaffeln were eventually established, originally in Schwarm strength as Industrieschutzschwärme, at the other factories producing day fighters: Focke-Wulf at Bremen and Marienburg, Fieseler at Kassel, AGO at Oschersleben (Fw 190s); and WNF at Wiener Neustadt, Arado at Warnemünde, and Erla at Leipzig (Bf 109s). The Focke-Wulf Schwarm at Bremen was heavily engaged during the April 17, 1943, raid, claiming several shared victories (*see below*).[14]

Obstlt. Dr. Erich Mix's JG 1 began the year as the only day-fighter Geschwader in Lw Bfh Mitte. It had four Gruppen instead of the standard three; these were stretched thinly along the North Sea coast. The Stab and I. Gruppe were at Jever on the north German coast with four Fw 190s, all of which were operational—abbreviated on the strength returns as 4 (4) Fw 190s—and 40 (27) Bf 109s. The II. Gruppe was at Woensdrecht in the Netherlands with 41 (40)

A Bf 109G-6 of 2./JG 27 taxies out for takeoff from Leeuwarden at the end of March. The I. Gruppe of JG 27 was the first fighter unit recalled from a peripheral theater (the Mediterranean) to bolster the defenses of the Reich. The airplane carries the well-known I./JG 27 emblem. Its other markings are standard for the Western theater: dark gray camouflage, yellow undercowl, and yellow rudder. (*Bundesarchiv 375-2706-19*)

Fw 190s; the III. Gruppe was based in western Denmark and southern Norway with 53 (48) Fw 190s; and the IV. Gruppe was at München-Gladbach with 41 (27) Fw 190s. The Geschwader saw some action against RAF Fighter Command and Coastal Command raids, but spent most of its time escorting convoys and flying patrols in anticipation of the arrival of the American heavy bombers.[15]

If Lw Bfh Mitte, the command specifically charged with home air defense, found it difficult to mass its forces against the mounting USAAF daylight offensive, the situation of Luftflotte 3 was even more constrained. Sperrle's air fleet faced a daunting array of tasks in the first half of 1943. Its bombers and fighter-bombers were ordered to prepare for a renewed bomber offensive against the British Isles. Its reconnaissance units were heavily committed to supporting the U-boat arm as the Battle of the Atlantic entered its most critical phase. And its fighter units, justifiably considered an elite force, continued to fulfill their role as guardians of the Channel coast, dealing with enemy fighter sweeps and reconnaissance flights, as well as providing escort for coastal convoys, reconnaissance missions, and air-sea rescue operations, while maintaining their readiness for the expected expansion of the American bomber offensive.

Fw 190A-4 "yellow 10" of 6./JG 1, photographed at Leeuwarden in late March or early April. A Bf 109G-4 of 2./JG 27 is visible in the background. (*Bundesarchiv 375-2706-17*)

The day-fighter defenses of Luftflotte 3 actually began 1943 at lower strength than the previous fall. Jafü 3 had one day-fighter wing, Obstlt. Walter Oesau's JG 2, with which to defend the Paris region and the U-boat bases on the western coast of France. But Oesau's Geschwader was at less than half strength. He commanded only a strengthened Stabsschwarm, with 14 (10) Fw 190A-4s and 6 (4) Bf 109G-1s; his III. Gruppe, with 49 (38) Fw 190A-4s; and one borrowed Staffel, 9./JG 26. The rest of the Geschwader had moved south in response to Operation Torch, the Allied invasion of Northwestern Africa. I./JG 2 returned from southern France in late January, but II./JG 2 remained in Tunisia until March. A high-altitude Staffel, 11.(Höhen)/JG 2, never returned from Africa, but was merged there into JG 53.[16]

On January 2, elements of JG 27, the famed *Afrikageschwader*, began arriving in Évreux. The wing had been withdrawn to Germany for rebuilding in late 1942, and I./JG 27 was deemed ready to re-enter combat. It was sent to Jafü 3 to help defend the Paris region. But the Gruppe was still far from full effectiveness, especially in its tough new operational environment.[17]

To the east of Jafü 3, the one day-fighter wing reporting to Jafü 2, Major Gerhard Schöpfel's Jagdgeschwader 26, was almost up to authorized strength as 1943 began. Its Stab had 5 (5) Fw 190A-4s; I. Gruppe 33 (26) Fw 190A-4s; II. Gruppe 33 (26) Fw 190A-4s and 11 (7) Bf 109G-4s; III. Gruppe, 35 (29) Fw 190A-4s and 3 (2) Bf 109G-1s and G-4s. The Geschwader lacked only its high-altitude Staffel, 11.(Höhen)/JG 26, which had been absorbed by JG 51 in Tunisia, and the Staffel that was on loan to JG 2.[18]

Shortly after New Year's Day Major Schöpfel was relieved of his command. His replacement was the 26-year-old Kommandeur of III./JG 26, Major Josef "Pips" Priller. General Galland had had doubts about Schöpfel ever since turning the Geschwader over to him at the end of 1941. In a post-war interview, Galland said, "I knew Schöpfel was not the right man ... He was a nice guy, but not a strong leader ... Priller was better. He was the aggressive type."[19] Priller's first major task as Kommodore would call on his administrative, rather than his combat skills. His entire Geschwader was to transfer to the northern sector of the Eastern Front over the next few months, in exchange for the Green Heart Geschwader, JG 54. The swap was to take place by Gruppen and Staffeln, staged to permit continuity of coverage on both fronts. Only the pilots, key staff members, and certain items of critical equipment were to move. Maintenance crews, aircraft, and all other equipment were to remain on their original bases. In late January I./JG 26 and 7./JG 26 left for the east by train.

Also in January Gen. Junck of Jagddivision 3, in command of the fighters of Luftflotte 3, ordered part of JG 26 to move to new bases, farther from the coast and less vulnerable to Allied attacks. The Geschwader headquarters transferred from St. Omer southeast to Lille-Vendeville, while the Abbeville Kids of II. Gruppe bade farewell to Abbeville-Drucat, the site of their greatest fame, and moved east to Vitry, near the industrial city of Douai. Both new fields were prewar French airbases with concrete runways, well suited to winter operations. III. Gruppe stayed at Wevelghem, in western Belgium near the French border. The six JG 26 fighter Staffeln left in the west were now concentrated in a small triangle in the industrial region along the French–Belgian border, athwart the most direct aerial route from England to the Ruhr.[20]

In early February, Major Reinhard Seiler's III./JG 54, with the Green Heart Geschwader's 7., 8., and 9. Staffeln, boarded trains in Smolensk and headed for the *Kanalfront*. They were followed soon afterward by Oblt. Graf Matuschka and his 4./JG 54. The pilots picked up new Bf 109Gs in Germany and flew them to Vendeville. Graf Matuschka's Staffel was subordinated to III./JG 26 in Wevelghem, where it replaced 7./JG 26 smoothly and without incident.[21]

Amalgamation of III./JG 54 into the western order of battle was another matter. The Gruppe was too large to merge into the flying organizations already present, and had to be trained to fight as a unit under the rigorous conditions of the western front. The Gruppe trained for a month, closely watched by Major

Priller, who took his responsibility for the new unit very seriously. He monitored their formation flights from the air, and several times bounced them from behind without being spotted. A disgusted Priller stubbornly refused to declare the Gruppe operational. In late March, III./JG 54 was detached from JG 26 and ordered to Oldenburg, near Bremen. From this location, it could assist JG 1 in defending northern Germany against the infrequent raids of the American 8th Bomber Command, while remaining outside the range of Allied fighters.[22]

Winter Doldrums

At the beginning of 1943 the Eighth Air Force could put no more than 100 bombers into the air for a mission. Reinforcements were withheld from General Eaker, now in command of the Eighth, and sent to his predecessor General Spaatz, who now led the American air units in northwestern Africa. The 8th Fighter Command contained only one group, the Spitfire-equipped 4th, which was subordinated to the RAF for operations. For the next four months the 8th Bomber Command would operate with only four groups of B-17s, the 91st, 303rd, 305th, and the 306th, wryly called "The Four Horsemen"; and two groups of B-24s, the 44th and 93rd, which were so understrength that they were asked to fly primarily diversions.[23]

The Americans' top priority targets were the U-boat bases in western France. Although both aerial reconnaissance and on-site inspections by intelligence agents confirmed that American bombs could not penetrate the roofs of the pens, the bomber commanders rationalized their continued efforts by claiming that the raids were destroying the ancillary facilities outside the pens themselves. But the German Navy had moved all of its shops and other installations within the pens as soon as the raids began. No submarine was ever damaged by the raids, which by all of the evidence had no effect at all on the U-boat campaign. The raids continued, however, for political reasons. On January 3, 85 B-17s and eight B-24s bombed St. Nazaire. Three B-17s were lost to Flak, and four were shot down by the fighters of JG 2, whose pilots received credit for downing 17. Over the next three weeks 8th Bomber Command flew only three missions, two to the U-boat bases and one to Lille. Eaker was under constant pressure from General Arnold in Washington to increase the number of missions flown and, preferably, to devote some of them

to targets in Germany. Eaker's staff concluded that they could no longer wait for delivery of the 300 bombers that theory suggested was the minimum requirement for a self-defending bomber force. Germany would be attacked with the forces on hand. The U-boat construction yards on the North Sea were chosen for attack. These were suitable industrial targets for the coming strategic campaign, while their destruction would aid in the top-priority struggle against the U-boats. They were coastal targets, and thus easy to find, and could be approached from the North Sea, reducing the unescorted bombers' vulnerability to the Luftwaffe's short-range single-engine interceptors.

January 27—Wilhelmshaven

This was the first day in 1943 that promised reasonably good weather over both the American bases and their prospective targets in northern Germany. A mission was ordered, and 64 B-17s and 27 B-24s were dispatched to Wilhelmshaven. JG 1 was given its first opportunity to intercept the heavies in strength. The 1st Bombardment Wing (abbreviated in this book as 1st Bomb Wing), containing the B-17s, flew its mission approximately as planned, although unexpected cloud cover over the target and poor radio communications caused the formations to split up, and damage to the

The Fw 190A-5 of Oblt. Rüdiger von Kirchmayr, Technischer Offizier of II./JG 1, in April. It carries the chevron-circle emblem of the TO, and a green *Tatzelwurm* on the cowling to designate the Gruppe Stab. An exhaust shield is barely visible above the black exhaust-masking paint, indicating that the plane was flown on night sorties by II./JG 300, which shared the Gruppe's Rheine base and aircraft. (*Rosch*)

targeted installations was negligible. The I./JG 1 base at Jever was directly below the B-17s as they approached from the North Sea, and the Gruppe apparently made a maximum-strength interception, but the light armament of their Bf 109G-1s had very little effect on the Fortresses. One B-17 finally went down, but three Messerschmitts and their pilots were shot down into the North Sea; the pilot of a fourth was able to bail out and come to earth without injury. The Luftwaffe credited the Messerschmitt pilots with four victories and scored the battle as a draw. The B-17 crewmen had in fact won a clear victory, somewhat obscured by their endemic over-claiming; they were credited with ten Luftwaffe fighters.[24]

The small B-24 formation got lost almost from takeoff and headed east across the North Sea far to the south of the ordered route. They crossed the coast of Holland near Woensdrecht, turned south, and wandered above the northern Netherlands before finally turning back north to the North Sea, where they jettisoned their bombs. II./JG 1 and IV./JG 1 scrambled from Woensdrecht and München-Gladbach and raced northward after this attractive target. The 5. and 6. Staffeln of II./JG 1 landed at Schiphol to refuel, which cost them the time necessary to make an interception. The 4. Staffel pressed on and was able to make one pass at the B-24s, which shot down one Focke-Wulf; its pilot was able to bail out with wounds. The German pilots in turn claimed two Liberators, but these claims apparently never made it to Berlin for confirmation. The 12. Staffel, part of IV./JG 1, made an effective interception as the B-24s withdrew over Terschelling. Two B-24s were claimed, and in fact two

went down, but the second was the direct result of the Staffel's only loss. B-24 gunners shot down a Focke-Wulf which then collided with a lower B-24, slicing off its tail. Neither the German pilot nor any of the American crewmen survived. The returning B-24 crews claimed 12 Luftwaffe fighters.[25]

The true losses in the day's fighting, six Luftwaffe fighters for three heavy bombers, clearly favored the Americans. The U.S. commanders, although doubting their own victory claims, were surprised at their own low losses. Flak downed no bombers, and a British observer who flew with them that day called the anti-aircraft fire "pathetic."[26] BGen. Haywood Hansell, commander of the 1st Bomb Wing, summarized the fighter opposition to his B-17s as follows: "The enemy's attacks were generally from the rear hemisphere and level or above. Their skill was lower than expected based on our experience over occupied France. More skillful attacks can be expected on the next raid in this area."[27]

Early Sparring Matches

For the next few months the 8th Bomber Command would divide its attention among the U-boat bases, industrial and transportation targets in northern France, and various targets in Germany, along the coast and extending inland as far as the Ruhr. The commanders on both sides sought to maximize the effectiveness of the small forces available to them. A bleak winter further complicated matters. On February 4, 65 B-17s were dispatched to Hamm; after circling over cloud-covered northern Germany for 90 minutes, 39 eventually found and bombed Emden. All 21 B-24s that took off returned early with mechanical difficulties from the extreme cold. In a prolonged battle with numerous fighters that attacked singly from all directions, the B-17 gunners shot down seven JG 1 airplanes,

The Fw 190A-5 of Hptm. Fritz Losigkeit, I./JG 1 Kommandeur, outside the JG 1 command tent at Deelen in early April. The tent had been brought from the Eastern Front by the new Kommodore, Hans Philipp, to show his pilots the rougher side of military service. (*Burath*)

After JG 1 was split into two two-Gruppe Geschwader, JG 1 and JG 11, on April 1, each had to establish a new III. Gruppe. The new III./JG 1 was activated at Leeuwarden on May 23. The Kommandeur, Major Karl-Heinz Leesmann, stands in front of his plane at the ceremony. He was killed on July 25. (*Petrick*)

killing five pilots. The leading 91st Bomb Group lost two B-17s to II./JG 1 Fw 190s before Emden was located. A 303rd Bomb Group B-17 turned back with frozen guns and was shot into the Zuider Zee by a swarm of JG 1 fighters. The 305th Bomb Group lost two B-17s, one apparently after colliding with a Fw 190. The second was shot down by a new weapon in the day battle: Bf 110 night fighters.

Eight IV./NJG 1 Bf 110s were ordered to scramble from Twente as the B-17s approached their base. The night-fighter crews were not trained in day tactics, but they made the only close-formation attacks reported by the returning Americans that day. The two Schwärme pressed their attacks to close range from the rear. They downed one B-17, while receiving credit for three, but all eight Bf 110s were damaged by defensive fire. Two were forced to make crash-landings. One of the successful pilots, a Schwarm-führer on this mission, was Oblt. Hans-Joachim Jabs, who later commented: "This was my only day victory in a night fighter. We flew these missions at no greater than Schwarm strength, and were ourselves never escorted. It was wasteful to use highly trained night-fighter crews in this role, and it was given up when U.S. escorts appeared."[28]

An American trip to the St. Nazaire U-boat base on February 16 was met by strengthened defenses.

Additional Flak batteries now surrounded the pens, and the Fw 190s available had nearly doubled with the return of I./JG 2 from southern France. Sixty-five of the 89 B-17s and B-24s dispatched dropped their bombs. Six B-17s were lost to Flak and/or fighters; the last downed was a 303rd Bomb Group cripple that was shot into the Channel by Bf 109s of Nahaufklärungs-gruppe 13 (NAGr 13), a tactical reconnaissance outfit. The rest were claimed by the Fw 190 pilots of I. and III./JG 2, and 9./JG 26, which was still on loan to JG 2 under the temporary command of Lt. Otto "Stotto" Stammberger. All units reported successful missions. The Jafü 3 controller had held his fighters away until the 11 escorting fighter squadrons turned back, and the return escort was late to arrive, giving the German pilots almost an hour in which to make their attacks with no hindrance except the bombers' gunners, who claimed 20 Focke-Wulfs. Only two I./JG 2 fighters, and no pilots, were in fact lost. Stammberger's Staffel, termed the "Vannes Staffel" in the 8th Bomber Command operations research summary,[29] reached the bombers as they flew north from the Bay of Biscay toward the target. The Staffel attacked continuously for the next 45 minutes, in head-on passes by one or two aircraft to very close range. One shell smashed Stammberger's canopy, and fragments hit his left hand, but he and his wingman teamed up to shoot down one B-17. Unteroffizier (Uffz.) Erich Schwarz downed another, as he recalled:

We scrambled from Vannes and reached the bombers in time to form up for a frontal attack. They were proceeding toward their target, and could not make even slight course changes without endangering their attack on the U-boat bunkers. They had to fly straight ahead. I chose as my target the highest-flying B-17 on the far right. They had recognized us, as the formation had pulled closer together to strengthen their defenses. As I approached to about 1,000 meters [1,100 yards], the pilot lost his nerve and pulled up into a steep climb, undoubtedly with the help of his copilot. This exposed the entire belly of his airplane. I followed this movement, and since a fighter is more maneuverable than a cumbersome B-17, my six weapons could scarcely miss. Although it was only a short volley, the B-17 could no longer hold its place in formation. I was impressed that a bomber had been capable of such a defensive maneuver at 7,000 meters [23,000 ft.].[30]

Stammberger's injuries were slight. The next day he and his Staffel were ordered to rejoin their parent Gruppe in Belgium. Stammberger stopped at Beaumont-le-Roger en route to receive a farewell commendation from Obstlt. Oesau.[31]

On March 4, the Eighth Air Force targeted Hamm once again. The 91st Bomb Group led the force of 71 B-17s across the North Sea; through the fortunes of

war the trailing three groups got separated, and the 16 B-17s of the 91st found themselves heading for the Ruhr alone. The first German fighter to attack was a lone Bf 110, 80 km (50 miles) inland; attacks by Bf 109s, Fw 190s and Bf 110s then began, continuing until the Dutch coast was crossed on the return flight. The single-engine fighters were from the I., II., and IV. Gruppen of JG 1. They succeeded in downing one 91st Group B-17 and one from the aborting 306th Bomb Group, while losing two of their number. These were surprisingly poor results against the small American formation. One B-17 pilot, Lt. Charles Giauque, recalled seeing no Luftwaffe fighters until the return flight; then, just before the Dutch border, a large number of Fw 190s arrived with a few Bf 110s, and attacked from all positions of the clock, from low to high, until the Channel was reached. The 110s "had never given a problem before, but on this mission they were as aggressive as the 190s."[32]

The Bf 110s were night fighters from the III. and IV. Gruppen of NJG 1, which put on a very creditable show. Lt. Dieter Schmidt-Barbo had been a pilot in III./NJG 1 since September 1941, but was still a "little bunny," a most inexperienced fellow (his words), especially in daylight. Schmidt-Barbo recalled:

At 1030 I am still in bed when I receive a phone call ... *"Ganze Gruppe Sitzbereitschaft!* [Entire Gruppe at cockpit readiness!]" I inform [my roommate], who replies, "What nonsense! We'll be too late, as usual!" I

Fw 190A-4 "white 4" of 1./JG 1 left the runway while landing on Schiphol on June 25. The aircraft of I./JG 1 now had unique checkered cowlings; each of its three Staffeln had its own color combination. (*Burath*)

check with the *Gefechtsstand* [command post], and am told, "The Amis will soon arrive over the airfield. Twenty bombers! End of message!"

I cycle across the field and meet [my Staffelkapitän] Hptm. Lütje . . . Four crews will be ready . . . Today I am to fly "Kurfürst-Siegfried", a Me 110G-4. I have a groundcrewman explain the counter for its two MG 151 machine cannon, and get strapped in . . . The Chief starts his engines . . . He taxies out, and I follow, struggling to stay out of his slipstream and dust cloud. We take off and I form up . . . of the second Rotte only one, Heinzelmann, has managed to take off.

We climb steadily. The radio is filled with loud chatter, but soon everything quiets down and we hear clear orders from ground control: set course for "Caesar." . . . "Mailcoach" [enemy course] 300 or 330 degrees. I fix my attention on the Chief, who suddenly waggles his wings and speeds up. Our course is northwest; we can already see the Zuider Zee. Suddenly, over the radio: "From Karin 1. Message understood. We can still see them." I ask Schönfeld (my *Bordfunker* [radio operator/gunner]), "Karin, that's we three, isn't it?" "Yes!" "But I can see nothing!" "Me neither!"

All at once I see them, to the right—a great heap of four-engine bombers, in close formation. The right outside Kette is streaming condensation trails. They are still 2,000 meters [6,500 ft.] above us. We continue climbing until we come level with what we now count as 16 bombers, and can see one of the brown Boeings is trailing. We can also see a single Me 110 attacking from the rear. A few single-engine fighters appear, and attack from the front in ones and twos. Some more Me 110s can be seen to the rear of the *Verband* [formation], which pulls closer together.

We three are now passing above the bombers, and a few take shots at us—I can see the strings of tracers. [From Lütje:] "*Wir greifen vor vorne an.* [We attack from the front.]" "*Viktor! Viktor!* [Understood!]" The weather is perfect—a little haze, but no clouds in which the Amis can hide.

We are now over the mouth of the Zuider Zee, near Texel. It is 1130. The Chief banks toward the formation. I turn with him, and see the Amis in front of my nose. The gunsight is on; I give the engines full throttle, find one in the Revi, and open fire. The guns roar and smoke; the tracers fly a little above my target. I drop the nose and press the button again. I am already past my bomber, but fire on the next one. Trash flies around my cockpit and into my eyes. This

time my tracers disappear into the fuselage and wing roots as I fly past. I can see nothing in front of me—what now? I see a Me 110 beneath me and fly to join him. Schönfeld gives the bombers a parting volley from his twin popguns. "Are you still alive?" "Yes." "Everything OK?" "Yes, engines are running OK, no hits I can see. Prima!"

I look around. We are now right beneath the *Verband*. One of the leaders is now diving away and heading for Texel Island. I don't see the Chief; the two Me 110s we are approaching have no flame-dampers, and are thus Leeuwardeners [from IV./NJG 1]. A bomber has crashed into the sea near Texel. Black smoke and white plumes of steam hang over the circles in the water. Another is hanging beneath the *Verband*, to my left. As I am deciding whether to go after him, a Me 110 dives past, at the same time as several Fw 190s. My help isn't necessary! The *Verband* has disappeared, as have the two Messerschmitts I was following. I re-establish connection with the Chief. He is landing in Bergen; we are to follow him in case something goes wrong. One of his engines has been damaged; not by enemy hits but by fuel pump failure. Engine change.

This was the only mission of the period in which our Gruppe came into contact with day bombers. We lost one crew; perhaps they were among the Me 110s attacking the *Verband* individually from the rear. This kind of flying was not a very promising profession. Attacking Fortress formations with our specially equipped, slow and clumsy aircraft was almost suicide. Only after the loss of Hptm. Ludwig Becker [holder of the Knights Cross with Oak Leaves] on February 26 did the higher-ups begin to realize this. Shortly thereafter we ceased to be called on to fly missions against the incoming day bombers.[33]

The night fighters succeeded in downing three 91st Bomb Group B-17s for the loss of one crew from each of the two Gruppen involved. The men of the 91st credited the survival of three-fourths of their number to their tight formation. The group was awarded a well-merited Distinguished Unit Citation for the mission.

The western *Jagdflieger* began to receive reinforcements. Hitler and thus Göring could not be persuaded to expand the fighter force or to give it higher priority than the bomber arm, which was offensive in nature and thus more to Hitler's liking. So any fighter unit added to the western order of battle had to come from another theater. The two *Kanalgeschwader* were especially hard pressed, as either the Americans or the

Royal Air Force could be counted on to appear over their territory on every flyable day. I./JG 27 saw its first combat from its new French base on March 8, but lost its Kommandeur to Spitfires on the 13th. I./JG 3 left Russia for Döberitz on the 10th to be rebuilt to establishment strength before moving to France. On the 15th II./JG 2 left North Africa to return to France. Its arrival at Poix would restore the *Richthofen* Geschwader to its full three-Gruppe establishment. III./JG 54 moved counter to this westward flow, transferring from the Channel coast to Oldenburg, from which it flew its first mission on March 29.

Major Günther Specht, II./JG 11 Kommandeur from May 1943, and JG 11 Kommodore from May 15, 1944, until his loss in Operation Bodenplatte on January 1, 1945. The inscription is to his former adjutant, Lt. Heinz Rose, who remained with II./JG 11, and reads, "Keep your head high, my dear Adju! Yours, . . ." Specht was awarded the Oak Leaves to his Knight's Cross after his death. His final victory total was 34, including 17 heavy bombers. He had entered active service with I./ZG 26 on December 3, 1939, as a Bf 109 pilot, and had lost his right eye to an RAF gunner over Heligoland. (*Heinz Rose via Arno Rose*)

Despite the extreme time pressure under which they operated, the Jafü 2 and Jafü 3 controllers and pilots continued to hone their skills against the *Viermots* (four-engine bombers). Combined missions by several fighter formations could now be controlled for the first time.

On March 8, a small B-24 force attacked Rouen as a diversion for a larger B-17 attack on Rennes in Brittany. The B-24s were escorted by no fewer than 16 RAF Spitfire squadrons, and supported by a 4th Fighter Group sweep. The controllers were able to get the JG 26 Stabsschwarm, II./JG 26, 12./JG 2 and part of I./JG 27 into position for a perfectly coordinated attack. Major Priller's Jafü 2 force and the Jafü 3 Messerschmitts held off all of the escorts, allowing Hptm. Wilhelm-Ferdinand "Wutz" Galland to lead his two dozen II./JG 26 Focke-Wulfs in a tight right bank into a head-on attack on the B-24s—*von Schnauze auf Schnauze*, or "snout to snout," in the German phrase. Their attack was devastating. The lead bomber burst into flames, followed by the No. 2 aircraft in the leading vee. The bomber formation fell apart completely; bombs were scattered over the French countryside as the aircraft sought to evade the German fighters. The two lead B-24s, from the 44th Bomb Group, crashed in France, while a 93rd Bomb Group aircraft crashed after reaching England. Major Priller shot down one of the escorting Spitfires, as did Lt. Eder of 12./JG 2. The Allied escorts shot down two 12./JG 2 aircraft, whose pilots bailed out, and one from 3./JG 27, whose pilot was killed.

Wutz Galland, a younger brother of the General der Jagdflieger, was showing great aptitude for leading bomber interceptions. The *Schlageter* fighters suffered no damage or loss. They were proudest, however, of having forced the bombers to turn back before reaching their target. This proved to be the only such triumph ever gained over the Eighth Air Force.[34]

Despite General Hansell's January prediction, the fighter organization in Germany could not yet come close to matching the performance of their brethren on the Channel. On March 18, 76 B-27s and 27 B-24s targeted the U-boat yards at Vegesack, near Bremen. The Bf 109s of I./JG 1 reached the bombers near Heligoland, and Lt. Heinz Knoke and his wingman Lt. Dieter Gerhardt each claimed a bomber after a quick head-on attack on the B-24 *Pulk*. Knoke's bomber exploded and was thus definitely destroyed, but it was also claimed by Oblt. Walter Borchers of 8./NJG 3, whose black Bf 110 was described accurately by bomber crewmen in their post-mission interrogations. Gerhardt's B-24 made it back to England, while the German pilot was shot down by his next target and was lost at sea.[35] Although the German attacks continued for almost two hours, they were weak in strength. Only I. and IV./JG 1, 2./JG 27 (temporarily reinforcing II./JG 1, which was itself diverted by an RAF light-bomber attack), and various night-fighter Schwärme made contact. The German pilots were credited with four B-17s and five B-24s, while losing two pilots and three aircraft. But the Americans lost only one B-24 and one B-17; a second crash-landed in England. This time BGen. Hansell reported the attacks on his 1st Bomb Wing (containing the B-17s) as follows:

> Sixty-one fighters of various types, including black night fighters, began attacking southwest of Heligoland and continued 80 miles [50 km] out to sea on withdrawal. There were a few coordinated attacks by Schwärme, but attacks were generally not pressed home. Only one B-17 was lost; the Wing's success could be attributed to a tight formation, a lack of stragglers, improved gunnery, and a lack of determination by the enemy.[36]

Two minor units established in the spring of 1943 require mention here. The presence of RAF Mosquitoes over the Reich at all hours of the day on reconnaissance and special-operations bombing missions was a personal humiliation for Reichsmarschall Göring, who ordered the formation of two anti-Mosquito units, JG 25 and JG 50, using stripped-down Bf 109s. Command was given to Obstlt. Herbert Ihlefeld and Major Hermann Graf,[37] two "heroes from the Eastern Front," in Galland's sarcastic words. Despite their impressive designation as fighter wings, these units were little more than glorified squadrons, and achieved little against the elusive RAF aircraft. Although creation of these units may have addressed the political embarrassment of the Luftwaffe's seeming impotence in the face of the Mosquito raids (and the units were given great play in German propaganda), Grabmann noted that: "The results they

achieved were entirely disproportionate to the expenditure required."[38]

This was a period of Jagdwaffe armament experiments, both official and unofficial. A popular example of the latter category was air-to-air bombing. Lt. Knoke of 2./JG 1 claimed to have conducted tests on his own initiative and settled on a 250-kg (550-pound) bomb with a 15-second fuse, released from 1,000 meters (3,000 ft.) above a bomber *Pulk*. He first dropped a bomb in combat on March 22, and reported that it exploded in the center of a vee of Fortresses, breaking the wing off one.[39] The only B-17 lost on this mission was in fact shot into the North Sea by a III./JG 1 Fw 190, but Knoke's supposed victory was acclaimed by the Luftwaffe high command, whose

Hptm. Heinz Knoke, in 1943 an inventive and articulate Staffelkapitän in I./JG 1 and II./JG 11. He later became Kommandeur of III./JG 1. This photograph was taken after an automobile accident during an October 1944 transfer left him too badly injured to continue flying. A dent in his forehead is readily visible. (*Heinz Rose via Arno Rose*)

radio messages were regularly intercepted and reported by Allied intelligence. Ironically, such intelligence reports did more to sensitize the Eighth Air Force to air-to-air bombing than the observations of its own aircrews. During the April 16 raid on Lorient, Luftflotte 3 sent 11 bomb-carrying fighters against the USAAF formation. Following attack procedures developed at the Luftwaffe's Rechlin experimental establishment, the bomb-laden fighters attacked the formation from above and behind, in a 30-degree dive. This attack had no effect, the bombs exploding some 100 meters (300 ft.) above and to the side of the American formation, and was apparently not observed by the bomber crews.[40] However, reports of aerial bombing attempts were common for the next year, long after the Luftwaffe had given up on the method due to the vulnerability of bomb-carrying fighters to the American escorts.

Air-to-air rockets were a weapon that required more engineering and a formal test program. Several Army rockets were modified for testing. On March 26, the first rockets were taken aloft from Tarnewitz by a Bf 109F. These were Rheinmetall-Borsig RZ 65 73-mm weapons in streamlined underwing fairings. A Messerschmitt fighter could carry eight without affecting its performance or stability. Unfortunately the speed and trajectory of the rockets were so poor that the fighter had to pull up at a steep angle before releasing them 300–500 meters (330–550 yards) from their target. This was unacceptable, and the rockets never saw service use, although ErprKdo 25 continued testing them for several months.[41] The WGr 21, a larger rocket converted from a 21-cm infantry mortar shell, offered more potential, but would require a period of development and testing.[42] Underwing cannon were a quicker and more conventional cure for the Bf 109's weak firepower, and these were being rushed into service.

On April 1, the number of day-fighter Geschwader in Lw Bfh Mitte was doubled by the simple expedient of splitting Jagdgeschwader 1 into two halves. The new unit, Jagdgeschwader 11, picked up III./JG 1 (as I./JG 11) at Husum and I./JG 1 (as II./JG 11) at Jever, and took over responsibility for the defense of southern Norway, western Denmark, and the northeastern sector of Germany's North Sea coast, reporting to the Jafü Deutsche Bucht in Jagddivision 2. Jagdgeschwader 1 retained IV./JG 1 (now I./JG 1) at Deelen and II./JG 1 at Woensdrecht, and defended the western half of its old sector, reporting to the Jafü

Holland-Ruhr in Jagddivision 1. JG 1 also received a new Kommodore. Obstlt. Hans Philipp, the popular and combat-proven Kommandeur of I./JG 54, replaced Obstlt. Dr. Erich Mix. Major Anton Mader transferred from II./JG 77 to become Kommodore of JG 11. New III. Gruppen were formed in both JG 1 and JG 11 in April and May to bring these Geschwader up to full three-Gruppe establishment.[43]

In mid-April Jagddivision 2 received a unique reinforcement, the Jagdstaffel Helgoland. Heligoland is a red rock rising from the middle of the Deutsche Bucht (German Bight), approximately equidistant (50–60 km/30–38 miles) from the East Frisian Islands, the Elbe Estuary, and the west coast of Schleswig-Holstein. In 1941 two short runways, 780 and 795 meters (850 and 870 yards) long, were built on a neighboring sand dune, Helgoland-Düne. The base was perfectly located to defend the German coast from Allied raids approaching from the North Sea, and was an important radar station and Flak site, but no operational fighter had the short-field performance necessary to use the airstrips.

Someone yet unidentified realized that such a fighter was indeed in existence—in storage. This was the Bf 109T "Toni," 70 of which had been built in 1941 for service aboard the aircraft carrier *Graf Zeppelin*. Completion of the carrier had been delayed indefinitely, and the aircraft were available for other duties. They were an extended-wing variant of the last Bf 109E-7s built, which meant that they had DB 601N engines, GM-1 (nitrous oxide) equipment for enhanced high-altitude performance, and an armament of two MG 17 machine guns and two MG FF 20-mm cannon, one more cannon than the standard front line Bf 109G-4. For naval service they carried low-frequency, long-range radios, which proved to be a boon for Allied intelligence, as their transmissions carried to England. Their extended wings, 1.21 meters (48 inches) longer than those of the Bf 109E, gave the Toni not only the necessary short takeoff run and low stalling speed, but outstanding high-altitude climb rate and maneuverability. The service life of this obsolescent design was thus extended for seven months, until American fighters began escorting their charges across the North Sea. The Bf 109T was too slow for combat with modern fighters, and the survivors were eventually forced to retreat to Norway, but the Staffel did an excellent job against 1943's unescorted raids. Jagdstaffel (JaSta) Helgoland was subordinated to II./JG 11 for discipline, but reported directly to the Jafü Deutsche Bucht for operations.[44]

Production, Training, Tactics, and Reforms

Aircraft production planning in early 1943 reflected the Luftwaffe leadership's desire to stay on the offensive. At a conference on February 22, 1943, between Göring and his senior staff (including Milch, Jeschonnek, Peltz, and Oberst Edgar Petersen, commanding the Rechlin test establishment), the emphasis was clearly on the problems of getting He 177, Ju 188 and Ju 288 bombers into mass production and ready for service at the front. Heavy fighter, ground-attack and multi-role aircraft such as the Dornier (Do) 335 also occupied a significant proportion of the group's attention. On the subject of fighter development and production, Göring noted that, "The Americans haven't so far produced a fighter that is worth writing home about."[45] Grabmann reported that as late as April 1943 Göring "flatly refused to acknowledge" the combat capabilities of the P-47, the fighter that was beginning to equip the 8th Fighter Command.[46] The Luftwaffe's senior operational as well as technical leadership seemed to believe that the existing fighter types were more than equal to the task of defending the Reich's daylight airspace.

Yet there was another side to the Reichsmarschall's perceptions of the Luftwaffe's engineering and technical prowess. On March 18, 1943, he summoned a mixture of senior officers, combat commanders, engineers and aircraft designers to his Karinhall residence for what became a five-hour harangue. Milch, who was present (along with Heinkel, Messerschmitt, Kammhuber, Peltz, and Luftwaffe signals chief General Wolfgang Martini) succinctly noted in his diary, "Major onslaught!"[47] In a virtuoso performance, captured in full by diligent stenographers, Göring lambasted his audience. Much of his ire was directed at the failure to produce acceptable electronic equipment and countermeasures for the battle against the RAF night offensive, but he also noted that the Bf 109 was nearing the end of its useful service life and there was no replacement on the horizon. He noted:

> Fun has been made of the enemy's backwardness and his slow four-engine crates, etc. Gentlemen, I would be extremely happy if you could reproduce one of these crates in the immediate future. I would then have at

least one aircraft with which something could be achieved. You know for a fact that in addition to night attacks the enemy does not hesitate for an instant to carry out daylight operations with these four-engine crates, which have excellent armament and terrific stability, and in spite of our so-called ultramodern fighters he gets through everywhere.[48]

In truth, as even the Reichsmarschall acknowledged, Milch and his staff were beginning to bring the morass that had characterized German aircraft procurement and production under Udet under control. Milch, in collaboration with Reichsminister for Armaments and War Production Albert Speer and the German aircraft manufacturers, was already rationalizing and increasing German air armaments production. Although Milch was unsuccessful up to July 1943 in gaining approval to shift production priorities from offensive to defensive weapons, his skill at raising overall production numbers obviously benefited the fighter force.[49] The Speer/Milch team could do little in the short run about the lag in technical development, however, and the huge defensive battles over the Reich in 1943 and early 1944 would be fought primarily by increased numbers of the old types—Bf 109, Fw 190, Bf 110, and Ju 88. The follow-on generation of advanced aircraft types—Me 410, Do 335, Ta 152, Me 262—would, for all of Milch's energy and Speer's ingenuity, be critically delayed.

Obstlt. Josef "Pips" Priller (*left*) in a tactical command post, probably at St. Pol. Priller spent months there in mid-1943 as an interim Jafü during the illness of the incumbent. Priller's primary position was JG 26 Kommodore; his need to do double duty was mute evidence of the scarcity of competent field-grade commanders in the Luftwaffe. (*Bundesarchiv 298-1751-13*)

It is worth noting that no apparent effort was made prior to mid-1943 to use Messerschmitt Bf 110 and Me 410 twin-engine day fighters for the daylight air-defense mission. The long-delayed Me 410 was just now entering service, but the Bf 110 had served since 1939 in a variety of roles including interceptor, long-range escort, air superiority fighter, light bomber, dive bomber, close air support, and reconnaissance. It was now the most numerous RLV night fighter. The few day models in service at this time were on the eastern and Mediterranean fronts, where they were treated as scarce commodities, transferred rapidly and often. When finally returned to the Reich the depleted Zerstörer units would require complete rebuilding, with new crews, tactics, and armament. The long range and heavy armament of the Bf 110 would make it a deadly weapon against unescorted USAAF bomber formations when it took on this role in late 1943, but these powerful bomber destroyers were unavailable for the day battle over Germany during a critical time.

The Luftwaffe's training program during 1943 seemed to be getting the job done, although signs of its later collapse were already evident for those who cared to see them. As early as February 24, Milch was forced to tell the Reichsmarschall that basic pilot training had been reduced from 72 to 52 weeks because of a shortage of aviation fuel.[50] (At the same time, units at the front were reporting the need to enforce stringent conservation measures for both 87-octane B4 and 94-octane C3 avgas). Luftwaffe training schools were plagued by shortages of Arado 96 trainers (only 40 percent of planned delivery actually occurred). The obvious remedy was to fall back on old Ar 66 and Gotha (Go) 145 trainers, but these were by then in high demand by the night harassing Staffeln operating in the east. A more serious shortcoming was the lack of fighter aircraft at the *Waffenschulen* (advanced schools). Establishment was 480 Bf 109s of all types, ranging from obsolete Bf 109Bs to new Bf 109Gs, but on April 1, there were only 298 Bf 109s in the advanced-training schools. But on the whole, General Werner Kreipe,[51] chief of Luftwaffe training, was satisfied with progress throughout 1943—"the needs of the front have been met."[52]

Despite Kreipe's optimistic assessment, it is clear that the German pilot-training establishment—which by early 1943 was supplying the needs of the reconstituted bomber arm, the expanding ground-attack units, and pilots from the Romanian and Hungarian satellite air arms, as well as the fighter force—was

already operating at near capacity. The real test would come the following year, when a sharp increase in Luftwaffe pilot losses coincided with a catastrophic fuel crisis.

Throughout the spring of 1943, the Luftwaffe staffs in the field, guided and assisted by the General der Jagdflieger's office and Galland, implemented tactical improvements in order to make their modest forces more effective. Recognizing that the greatest problem with the homeland air-defense system was lack of depth, Luftwaffe commanders in both the Luftflotte 3 and Lw Bfh Mitte areas began to develop and equip auxiliary airfields with ground personnel, fuel, spare parts and ammunition stocks. Fighter units of up to 30 aircraft could land in the course of a running air battle, rearm and refuel, and take off to engage the enemy bomber formation on its return leg. This capability would pay tremendous dividends during the great battles of summer and fall 1943.[53]

The Luftwaffe also benefited from an ability swiftly to digest and act upon lessons learned in the crucible of combat. With remarkable speed, a new manual dealing with fighter and Flak co-operation was ready by March 1943. It underscored the need for "close, personal liaison between the commanders of the day and night fighters, Flak, and the early-warning system," and called for "Flak mission commanders" at each Jagddivision headquarters. On the tactical level, the manual laid down six "rules" for cooperation between day fighters and the Flak batteries. Most involved the exchange of tactical information, and

A typical scene at Lw Bfh Mitte and Luftflotte 3 fighter airfields in the spring of 1943—shop talk while at readiness. An officer is demonstrating the proper method for attacking a B-24—from 12 o'clock high. (*Bundesarchiv 565-1406-30*)

minimizing confusion and accidents at the border between the fighter and Flak defensive zones.[54]

The pattern of American technical and tactical move followed by German riposte was already well established. Tactically, the Luftwaffe day-fighter arm responded to the challenge of the USAAF daylight raids with typical resourcefulness, creativity and innovation. The following months would see these innovations—which may fairly be described as a revolution in aerial tactics—come to fruition.

Arrival of the Thunderbolts

The 8th Bomber Command raided the Paris Renault factory on April 4, escorted to the limit of their range by 18 RAF Spitfire squadrons. JG 26 Focke-Wulfs shot down four B-17s before the escort could interfere. The next day 14 Spitfire squadrons escorted the B-17s all the way to Antwerp and back. The Jafü 2 controller guessed the target and put Major Priller and a small force of fighters in position to attack the arriving bombers head-on and break up their attack. Hptm. Wutz Galland then arrived with his II./JG 26 and made a head-on attack on the departing bombers, downing four. The Spitfires were too far above and behind the bombers to intervene. Although the RAF fighter pilots had better days, during which they did an outstanding job of shielding the bombers, the presence of the Spitfires actually simplified the job of the German defenders. The fighter controllers had learned to recognize the Spitfire escorts, which typically flew at 30,000 feet (9,100 meters), at least 5,000 feet (1,500 meters) above the bombers. Formations that high always gave away the presence of heavy bombers beneath them. The Luftwaffe fighter leaders had the option to attack the escort, wait until it turned back, or, as on the 4th and 5th, ignore them and attack the bombers before the escort could react.

The Americans waited impatiently for the 8th Fighter Command to become operational on its own equipment, the Republic P-47 Thunderbolt. Royal Air Force tactical doctrine called for "escort" to be flown high above the bombers, rather than within immediate supporting range. In part, this was nothing but the typical fighter pilot–bomber crew dispute as to what constituted effective escort, but the Americans suspected that their Allies preferred flying in the stratosphere because that is where their aircraft were most superior to those of the enemy. The advance notice the high-flying Spitfire formations gave the Germans was well-known from radio intercepts; American fighters would fly where they were ordered, which the bomber group commanders assumed would be within their own sight.

Three fighter groups were working up on the P-47, which had the distinction of being the heaviest single-engine fighter in the world. The 4th Fighter Group had been formed from the three RAF Eagle Squadrons; its pilots had absorbed RAF doctrine and slang, and were initially dubious about replacing their beloved Spitfires with these "bloody great milk bottles." The 78th Group also had shakedown problems with their new P-47s; the aircraft that they had trained on and brought to Europe, P-38 Lightnings, had been taken away from them to replace losses in North Africa. Only the 56th Group was entirely comfortable with their "Jugs"; they had been the first unit to receive them, while still in the U.S.A. The P-47 had excellent firepower in its eight .50-inch machine guns. Its supercharger gave it excellent high-altitude performance, and it was certainly expected to dive well, but the experienced RAF pilots serving liaison duties with the 56th gave it no chance at all as a dogfighter at medium or low altitudes.[55]

By early April, all three American units were ready to test their mounts in combat. Until auxiliary fuel tanks of acceptable design and quality were available, however, the range of their Thunderbolts was little greater than that of the Spitfires. The American fighter missions were thus limited initially to coastal sweeps similar to those flown by their British counterparts. They first made contact with the Jagdwaffe on April 15. On a sweep from Ostend to St. Omer 60 P-47s from all three groups were intercepted by 15 II./JG 1 Fw 190s scrambled from Woensdrecht. Several 4th Fighter Group pilots spotted the Focke-Wulfs some 6,000 feet (2,000 meters) below and dove on them. The German pilots evaded with an *Abschwung* (split-S), but Oberfeldwebel (Obfw.) Heesen's 4. Staffel Schwarm pulled up sharply as the P-47s shot past and dropped onto their tails, from which position Heesen shot down two of the Thunderbolts, although his claims were apparently not confirmed. The American pilots were credited with shooting down three Focke-Wulfs in the combat, but none were in fact lost; one did sustain 10 percent damage when landing at Woensdrecht, but whether this was the result of combat is unknown.[56]

Göring convened a conference at his headquarters the day after these first encounters between the Jagdwaffe and P-47s. Present were Galland, Grabmann, and personnel from JG 1. The problem was simple: how best to separate the USAAF escort fighters from their charges? The participants concluded that since the Fw 190A operated at a disadvantage at high altitude, the latest Bf 109G with the DB 605 engine would be handed the task of dealing with the escorts. The participants submitted the following recommendations:

1. Inclusion in each Jagdgeschwader of a specialized Gruppe as a "light fighter group" for high-altitude fighter action. This was to apply to all Geschwader under Lw Bfh Mitte.
2. These light Gruppen were to be stationed in the forward or outpost areas of the Reich air-defense system with the mission of attacking and containing enemy escort fighters when U.S. four-engine bombers penetrated with fighter escorts.
3. The operations of the "heavy fighter" Gruppen, stationed farther in the rear, were to be so conducted that they would only attack the bombers after the enemy escort fighters were engaged in combat.[57]

April 17—Bremen

American raids on the Reich could not yet be escorted, but Allied combat units supported every such mission indirectly with feints and diversions. Sometimes these worked; sometimes they did not. On this day they worked to perfection, keeping several of the best Jagdgruppen away from the bombers, which nevertheless suffered one of their most stinging defeats to date. The largest bomber force yet sent to a single target, 115 B-17s in six combat boxes, took off in the morning to bomb the Focke-Wulf factory in Bremen. The boxes flew in two new combat wing formations. Three 18-bomber boxes had previously flown in trail; from now on the second would fly above and behind, and the third would fly below and behind the lead box. Their course was due east across the North Sea, out of range of JG 26, which nevertheless was scrambled by the Jafü 2 controller on reports of numerous Allied formations over the Channel. The JG 26 fighters chased back and forth in response, but were not ordered to intercept, and no contact was made. The principal mission for the RAF was an afternoon raid on Abbeville by No. 2 Group light bombers, whose escorts occupied the attention of JG 2 and those JG 26 fighters that were eventually sent in their direction. The P-47 units swept along the Dutch coast in the early afternoon, and the Jafü Holland-

Ruhr scrambled 22 II./JG 1 Fw 190s from Woensdrecht, but was unable to put them into contact with any enemy. Jagddivision 1's other operational units, I./JG 1 at Deelen and 2./JG 27, flying from Leeuwarden in northern Holland, were loaned to Jagddivision 2 for use against the Bremen raiders.[58]

The Jafü Deutsche Bucht thus had these two borrowed units, plus all of its own—I. and II./JG 11, III./JG 54, JaSta Helgoland, NJG 1, NJG 3, and the Focke-Wulf Industrieschutzschwarm—available for use against the B-17s. The controller also had the advantage of reports from a *Fühlungshalter* aircraft, which reported the presence of the B-17s over the North Sea at 1145. Very little documentation has survived concerning these aircraft, which would play a very important role in the air defense of the Reich for the next year. At this early date they were probably drawn from operational night-fighter units, crewed by men with especially good navigational skills. The bomber crewmen soon came to hate their shadowers, which kept formation just out of range of the bombers' .50-inch machine guns.

Aided by his early warning, the Deutsche Bucht controller kept his fighters on the ground at full alert until the bombers were fully committed to crossing the German coast, and timed his interception to disrupt their bomb run. I./JG 1 scrambled from Deelen at 1220, but had a long way to travel, and did not make contact until after the bombing. I./JG 11 at Husum and II./JG 11 at Jever scrambled at 1230, and struck the bombers at about their Initial Point (IP), when they made their final course change before the bomb run. Lt. Knoke's 5./JG 11 (ex-2./JG 1) Schwarm dropped bombs, all of which missed, but the two Gruppen attacked the front half of the bomber stream continuously for nearly an hour, egged on by the controller to attack "at all costs," until they ran out of ammunition. JG 11 filed 13 victory claims, of which five were confirmed, while sustaining no combat losses. Three II. Gruppe Bf 109s were damaged in deadstick landings in the Frisians, out of fuel. When I./JG 1 reached the bombers, Major Fritz Losigkeit led it in a successful attack that claimed three B-17s (two were confirmed) for the loss of one pilot and two Fw 190s.

Major Reinhard Seiler led III./JG 54 up from Oldenburg at 1229 and contacted the bombers west of Wilhelmshaven at 1240, flying south-east at 7,000–

8,000 meters (23,000–26,000 ft.). This was the Gruppe's first contact with the American "furniture vans" since it had left Russia in early February, and according to Seiler the radio was filled with the pilots' "ooohs and aahs." Seiler planned a close-formation attack from the front, one line-abreast Staffel following the next. But the bombers' left turn at their IP for Bremen destroyed the plan, and Seiler ordered independent attacks by Staffeln. Seiler's own Stabs-schwarm was apparently the first to regain attack position, but not until the bombers had completed their bomb run. Seiler's head-on attack on one of the formation leaders damaged it and caused it to leave the formation. Seiler followed it and attacked alone from the rear, at close range, silencing the tail gunner and causing large parts to break off. His third attack caused seven or eight of the crew to bail out. He then ran out of ammunition, so he decided to follow the bomber down. He saw the pilot in the cockpit apparently attempting a crash landing, but the aircraft reared up while turning around a building and crashed vertically within the grounds of a barrel factory.[59]

Hptm. Hans-Ekkehard Bob, Kapitän of 9./JG 54, was behind Seiler's Schwarm on the initial approach, but got caught by the bombers' turn and had to make a long chase before regaining attack position. Bob recalled:

I started a new attack and approached the lead group of Fortresses from the front. I fired at the aircraft on the right of the leading element from 500 meters [550 yards], getting good hits on the cockpit and No. 2 engine. I approached too close, and when I tried to dive beneath the B-17, I rammed the bomber. I lost much of my fuselage, while the bomber lost a wing. My aircraft immediately began to spin, and of course did not respond to the controls. I immediately decided to bail out. I threw off the canopy, unbuckled my seat harness, and was instantly thrown out of the plane. I fell spinning for about 1,000 meters, to 5,000 meters [3,000 ft. to 16,000 ft.] , where I was able to open my parachute . . . It took about twenty minutes for me to reach the ground, carefully watching for obstacles . . . The final impact was so strong that I lost consciousness, and was dragged for several hundred meters across a field . . .

Meanwhile, the B-17 had been so badly hit that the entire crew had bailed out, and we all came down together south of the village of Grossköhren in

Oldenburg. I was captured by reserve soldiers along with the Americans . . . I was in shock and did not resist. Finally I opened my overalls, and one of the soldiers shouted, "That American has the Knight's Cross!" . . . I reported my experience to the mayor of the town and was given a big reception in the town hall. All of the inhabitants who had watched the battle celebrated my victory as if it was their own . . .[60]

Bob's claim was apparently never submitted for confirmation, despite all of his witnesses, but those of Seiler and two other Gruppe pilots were confirmed. Bob's Messerschmitt was the only loss for the Gruppe.

2./JG 27 was scrambled from Leeuwarden at 1239 and eventually reached the withdrawing B-17s north of Ameland. The Messerschmitt pilots received confirmation for one of their two B-17 claims, while suffering no casualties or reportable damage.

JaSta Helgoland scrambled its four operational Bf 109Ts from Düne at 1315 for their first operational mission and they were vectored to Langeoog. One Toni was hit in the Schwarm's first head-on pass; its pilot had to bail out into the North Sea, but his position was reported accurately and he was picked up by a Luftwaffe air-sea rescue aircraft. One Rotte continued to pursue the Boeings and caught two at low altitude; one had a burning engine. One German pilot reported low fuel and withdrew; the second, Uffz. Ewald Herhold, fired on the cripple until its wing broke off and the crew bailed out. The victorious pilot returned quickly to Heligoland and telephoned the location of the crash to the air-sea rescue station. A

A pair of 9./NJG 3 Bf 110G-4 night fighters patrol a bright sky over a solid German undercast. The time is probably mid-1943. The aircrews are undoubtedly watching the fighters swirling above with great caution. Night fighters formed a useful *ad hoc* supplement to the skimpy north German day-fighter force at this time. (*Bundesarchiv 659-6436-12*)

On their 1942 missions to France American heavy bombers proved how difficult they were to shoot down, and in early 1943 General Galland set up a test unit at Parchim, ErprKdo 25, to develop more effective weapons. Here four members of this unit converse with Galland (out of picture) before takeoff on a test of *schräge Musik* guns ("jazz music"— in this case a Fw 190 with three upward-firing recoilless 30-mm cannon, triggered by a selenium photocell). On the left is Oblt. Alois Höhn, who is already wearing his *Kombination* (flight suit). (*Höhn*)

He dove away, contacted a lower *Pulk*, and made a frontal attack on the low left bomber. He made four attacks on this airplane before it dropped from formation. Mehlhorn was then joined in the pursuit by various Bf 109s and Fw 190s until the B-17 crew bailed out. The bomber crashed at 1341. Mehlhorn made a quick landing at Jever, had his shot-through propeller replaced, and returned to Langenhagen in the evening.

Several lessons can be drawn from the Industrie-schutzschwarm report:

1. The attack method prescribed by the official directives—repeated frontal passes—was used correctly, even by this small, somewhat *ad hoc* unit.
2. Bombers flying in the least-well-protected parts of their formations—on the edges of the combat boxes, or lagging behind—were attacked preferentially.
3. As far as is known, neither Finke nor Mehlhorn received any official credit for their victories on this mission—they lacked friendly witnesses. Shared victories were always difficult to assess properly, especially when the claimants were from different units.

The last fighters in the air were the long-range Bf 110 night fighters, which were ordered to follow the withdrawing bombers out to sea in search of cripples. Three were shot down by pilots from NJG 1 and NJG 3, whose fighters sustained no known damage.[62] The Focke-Wulf factory was severely damaged in one of the most accurate American raids to date, losing 50 percent of its capacity and 30 burned-out Fw 190s. But this success came at the highest cost to date, 16 B-17s, 14 percent of the 115 dispatched. All 16 losses were sustained by the leading combat wing, comprising three combat boxes with B-17s from two groups, the 91st and the 306th. General Hansell's report blamed the losses on a 5-mile (8-km) gap between the first and second combat wings, which prevented "mutual support," and attributed the good fortune of the second formation to its close spacing, forming a "vertical wall" which discouraged head-on attacks. But this same "vertical wall" when tried on other missions led to more Flak damage and, by masking guns, greater vulnerability to fighters. A close examination of the loss records shows that many of the lost bombers were hit by Flak on the bomb run; the damaged planes that dropped

seaplane found an oil slick but no survivors. Herhold recruited the seaplane crew as victory claim witnesses on the basis of the slick, but his claim encountered bureaucratic difficulties and was apparently never confirmed.

The combat report of the Focke-Wulf Industrieschutzschwarm has survived, and provides many interesting details.[61] Obfw. Finke led the *Alarm* element up from from Hannover-Langenhagen at 1243; the Schwarm's other two Focke-Wulfs followed at 1245. The two pairs never met up, but flew separate missions. Finke sighted the incoming *Pulks* over Verden, climbed to 9,000 meters (29,500 ft.), and made an approved head-on attack at 1315. His wingman had to break off early with combat damage, but Finke continued to attack the first B-17 until its crew bailed out, and then further damaged two lagging B-17s until low fuel forced him to break off at 1332 and land on Jever. He was "helped" in all but his first pass by small numbers of Bf 109s and Bf 110s.

The leader of the Industrieschutzschwarm's second element, Uffz. Mehlhorn, lost his wingman early to engine and radio problems. His controller ordered him to fly toward Oldenburg, where he sighted the heavy bombers. He made a frontal attack on the high right B-17 in the high *Pulk*, forcing pieces to fly off.

out of formation made tempting targets themselves, and left holes in the combat boxes that increased the vulnerability of the remaining aircraft. The high losses of the first combat wing were thus the result of bad luck; the leading boxes just happened to be the day's "Flak magnets."[63] The effectiveness of the staggered 54-bomber combat wing in defense soon became clear, and it would become the standard formation used by the Eighth Air Force when enemy fighters were expected.[64]

The Race for Reinforcements

The Eighth Air Force was losing bombers faster than they could be replaced, and temporarily cut back the number of bomber missions, especially to high-risk areas such as the Heligoland Bight. The offensive was maintained by 8th Fighter Command Rodeos, the old RAF code name for fighter sweeps of the enemy coast. On April 29, all three groups—112 P-47s—flew the largest American fighter mission to date. The 56th Group saw all of the combat. Its sweep of the Dutch coast stirred up a hornets' nest. The low squadron was hit by pairs of JG 26 Focke-Wulfs that swept in from dead ahead, fired short, well-aimed bursts, and dove away. Two Thunderbolts and pilots were lost. No German fighter was hit in the brief encounter.

The immediate reaction of 8th Fighter Command was to increase the height of the P-47 sweeps to 30,000 feet (9,100 meters), well above the Fw 190's optimum altitude. These were usually ignored; for the next two weeks, the fighter sweeps provoked no German reaction at all. American bomber raids, of course, were a different story. Not only were they the German defenders' top priority, they were the only priority— when enemy bombers were airborne the fighters of Luftflotte 3 were at this time forbidden to attack enemy fighters, not even to clear away the escort to permit more effective attacks on the bombers. The performance of P-47s and Spitfires on short escort missions continued to improve. On May 4, they combined to keep the German fighters from approaching a formation of 79 B-17s, which bombed Antwerp without losing a single plane. That evening a disgusted Stotto Stammberger wrote in his logbook that the failure of his Geschwader had brought "a great salvo from Reichsmarschall Hermann Göring. We should be disbanded—our formation leaders should be arrested—we are all cowardly dogs!"[65]

A Luftflotte 3 Operations Staff report states that by April 1943 the main focus of its fighter operations was on engaging the mass raids by American bombers. Although the raids were few in number (in April, only three: Antwerp on April 4, Paris on April 5, and the U-boat pens at Lorient on April 16) they were seen as the most important and difficult defensive task. The fighter forces of Luftflotte 3 (now in Jafü 2, 3, 4 and Süd) flew a total of 3,758 sorties in that month (1,411 by Bf 109s and 2,347 by Fw 190s), claiming 16 *Viermots*, 11 medium bombers, and 50 fighters in the process, for a loss of 30 German fighters (17 Fw 190, 13 Bf 109).[66]

Lw Bfh Mitte continued its slow expansion in May, primarily by bringing in units from other theaters, but the formation of a few new units was permitted. The new III./JG 1 was moved to Leeuwarden as a "far-forward" defender of the Bight and the German interior. I./JG 3 completed its retraining and moved to München-Gladbach, where it joined Jagddivision 5, which was not yet under attack by day. I./JG 3 was among the first Jagdgruppen to receive Bf 109G-6/R6 "gunboats" with "*Gondeln*," underwing tubs each containing a single MG 151/20 cannon. The JG 3 Stab left Russia for München-Gladbach and Reich defense duty. Since the JG 3 Kommodore, Oberst Wolf-Dietrich Wilcke, was under a *Flugverbot* (flight prohibition), his Stabsschwarm did not receive any aircraft until October. May 23 brought the month's last reinforcement for Lw Bfh Mitte, when III./JG 26 left its familiar surroundings on the *Kanalfront* and joined Jagddivision 2 at Cuxhaven-Nordholz. A command change of some significance saw the fatherly, popular Major "Seppl" Seiler leave III./JG 54 and return to Russia; he was replaced by a younger pilot from JG 2, Hptm. Siegfried Schnell.

With the successful conclusion of the Allies' African campaign also in May 1943, the Americans again gave the Eighth Air Force top priority for reinforcements, which began arriving in England at an ever-increasing rate. The operational strength of 8th Bomber Command doubled on May 13 when the new 4th Bomb Wing (Provisional) entered combat with four new bomb groups. Its first mission was to bomb airfields in the Pas de Calais while the 1st Bomb Wing attacked the more important Potez repair facility at Meaulte. The 4th Wing was given another diversionary target on the 14th, but was welcomed to the "big leagues" on the 15th, joining the 1st Wing in a raid on Emden. The B-17s of the new groups had a greater fuel capacity than the earlier arrivals, and the 4th Wing was soon being assigned the longer-range, and thus more hazardous, missions.

Up to now the USAAF and RAF strategic bombers in England had operated under catch-phrases ("round-the-clock bombing") but no clear directive from the Combined Chiefs of Staff. Target priorities had been shifted with bewildering frequency. This changed in mid-May with the adoption of the Combined Bomber Offensive plan, code-named Operation Pointblank, which was to continue until the bombers were needed to soften up the German defenses in advance of the Allied invasion of the continent, the date for which had not yet been set. The target list had something to please everyone, except RAF Bomber Command's Air Marshal Bert Harris, who was allowed to pay it only lip service, and governed Eighth Air Force planning for the rest of 1943. In order, the top target priorities were: 1. Luftwaffe fighters; 2. submarine yards and pens; 3. the German aircraft industry; 4. anti-friction bearing factories; 5. petroleum refineries.[67]

On May 21, 8th Bomber Command dispatched nine B-17 groups to Wilhelmshaven and Emden. Bombing results were poor, and 12 bombers were lost to the same Deutsche Bucht units that had been encountered on April 17, plus a Schwarm from ErprKdo 25 that had been moved to Wittmundhafen for the operational testing of air-to-air rockets. The commander of this detachment, Hptm. Eduard Tratt, reportedly shot a B-17 from formation with his WGr 21s, the first victory for this powerful rocket that later in 1943 would become the weapon of choice for breaking up the bomber *Pulks*. The less-promising RZ 65 rockets were entrusted to Obergefreiter (Ogfr.) Heinrich Staniwoga, whose Bf 109F carried eight of them. He succeeded in damaging his target, and then decided to "capture" the B-17. Staniwoga recalled:

We flew wing-to-wing in the direction of Wittmun-dhafen. When the airfield came in sight I gave my "wingman" the sign to land with my hand, and he nodded his head. Shortly thereafter the Boeing opened its bomb bay doors and deposited its bombs on an open field. Perplexed, I would then have opened fire, but noticed that its landing gear had dropped—it must have been an emergency. I lowered my own gear and flaps and led him across the field to give him some protection from the Flak, in case someone had the dumb idea of opening fire. I landed and quickly turned right to clear the landing path—which was not at all necessary, because my "wingman" pulled up from 30 meters [100 ft.].

It attempted to escape at low altitude on three engines—its right outer engine was shut down. The Flak opened fire when it reached the edge of the airfield and peppered it with shells. What happened next I will never forget. The pilot pulled the Boeing up into a steep climb, entered a half-turn at 80–100m [260–330 ft.], and jumped out. The bomber spun out and crashed in flames. I did not visit the crash site, but recall that four or five crewmen were found in the wreckage.

It would interest me greatly to know if the pilot survived the war, and why he decided not to land . . . On his approach he had to have seen the Flak towers and the four-barreled railroad Flak, and knew that he had no chance to escape.[68]

Staniwoga's personal investigation after the war revealed that the B-17 *Abschuss* had been awarded to the Wittmundhafen light Flak. His own claim went nowhere; Tratt possibly penalized him for the poor judgment he had shown by landing in front of "his" B-17.

Bomber losses such as those of the 21st could only be stemmed by long-range escorts. The losses of 8th Bomber Command per mission were averaging 1.6 percent when escorted, 7 percent when not escorted. 8th Fighter Command had claimed only 15 enemy fighters shot down to date, 11 of these on short-range escort missions.[69] The P-47s still had no auxiliary fuel tanks; incredibly, these were only in fourth place on the Eighth Air Force's priority list of needed supplies.[70] There was an obvious disconnect between the men actually flying combat missions and the top Eighth Air Force commanders, who apparently still believed in the self-defending bomber. BGen. Frank 'Monk' Hunter of the 8th Fighter Command continued to order unopposed sweeps of the coast at 30,000 feet (9,100 meters), even though the Luftwaffe controllers always recognized them for what they were, and they served no useful purpose apart from improving the American pilots' formation flying.

The sweep flown on May 21 was one of the few to draw a response from Jafü 2, which scrambled 11./JG 26, a new Staffel that was functioning as an operational training unit, to hone its skills against the Thunderbolts. The 4th Fighter Group's 334th Squadron bounced a mixed formation of Fw 190s and Bf 109s crossing the coast and became involved in a tremendous dogfight off Ghent. Lt. Steve Pisanos was on his first P-47 mission and was flying as his squadron commander's wingman. He claimed the squadron's only victory (later downgraded to damaged), while three P-47s failed to return. He later wrote: "The German pilots were not high-quality (not 'Abbeville') because they didn't make sharp maneuvers—when bounced one should always turn into the opponent or throw the airplane into a violent, unpredictable maneuver."[71] This was an astute observation, because the German pilots were, in fact, trainees, but they had obviously been briefed on the best way to combat Thunderbolts. Their three victories had come at no cost to themselves.

Veteran Fw 190 pilot Oblt. Hans Hartigs summarized the tactics favored by JG 26 pilots against P-47s in a conversation recorded in late 1944 in a bugged POW holding cell in England:

> If attacked, we should draw the P-47s to a lower altitude (3,000 meters [10,000 ft.]) by diving, then turn about suddenly. The P-47s will overshoot; if they try to turn, they will lose speed and are vulnerable. The P-47 should zoom-climb and dive again. If we get into a turning combat, a P-47 can often get us on the first turn. If the Fw 190 climbs slightly in the turn (below 5,000 meters [16,500 ft.]), it will gain on the P-47.[72]

The 4th Fighter Group commander and squadron leaders were all ex-Eagle Squadron Spitfire pilots who despised the P-47. This hatred filtered down to the unit's pilots, with the result that the 4th was by far the least effective of the three original P-47 groups. Steve Pisanos was one of the few 4th Group pilots who liked the Thunderbolt. His scored five victories in the Jug, qualifying him as an ace. He has provided this useful summary of the tactics used by the early P-47 pilots:

> P-47 pilots avoided mixing it up with any German fighters at low altitude, unless of course you were chasing someone all the way down, because both the 109 and the 190 could outmaneuver the P-47 at low levels. We in the 4th preferred to deal with the German fighters at high altitude—bounce the enemy below, then zoom up to altitude again. The P-47 turned out to be a killer aircraft versus both the Me 109 and the Fw 190. The Germans used two maneuvers when bounced by P-47s at altitude, turning and climbing. Some might have dived for a short duration, but that was to build up some speed to zoom up again. Any pilot who attempted to get away from an attacking P-47 by going into a dive in a cloudless sky didn't live long enough to tell his comrades.[73]

A lucky one-wheel landing at Tarnewitz after a test of the *Bombenteppich* (bomb carpet) concept. A Schwarm of four He 177s was each to fire 33 21-cm rockets from beneath an American bomber formation. Some of the open rocket tubes are visible along the top edge of the fuselage. This weapon system was not adopted. (*Höhn*)

The barrel roll maneuver developed by 56th Fighter Group ace Robert Johnson should be mentioned in any discussion of P-47 tactics. When pursued from behind in a conventional turn, Johnson advised a P-47 pilot to counter by rolling opposite to the turn, which would usually put him on his opponent's tail. Skilful tactics, plus the rapid introduction of paddle-blade propellers and water-injected engines to improve the airplane's weaknesses in low-altitude climb rate and acceleration, made the Jug the equal of any Luftwaffe fighter, well suited for the forthcoming battle for air superiority over the Reich and the western occupied zone.

The fighter force based in the Reich proper continued to expand in June. The newly formed III./JG 11 was declared operational and moved to Oldenburg as part of Jagddivision 2. Another new unit was IV./JG 3, which began forming at Neubiberg at the start of the month. JG 3 was being given a fourth Gruppe, outside the normal table of organization. Although documentation is lacking, it appears that the intent was to make an enlarged JG 3 the core of an interior defense force, despite the preference of Hitler and Göring for a forward defense concentrated on the coast.

With the conclusion of the campaign in North Africa, the Allies launched an elaborate deception plan to mask the site of their next landing, which proved to be Sicily. The Stab and 1. and 2. Staffeln of I./JG 27 were ordered to leave Poix and transfer to

Marignane in southern France to help protect that region. 3./JG 27 was alone at Poix for no more than a week when I./JG 26 began arriving on the base from the U.S.S.R. Their transfer to the Eastern Front had proved temporary; their experience was badly needed back on their home grounds in the west.

The bomber strength of the Eighth Air Force was now growing rapidly. On June 11, seven bomb groups from the 1st Bomb Wing and three groups from the 4th were dispatched to bomb Bremen. Clouds over the target caused the combat boxes to divert to Wilhelmshaven, Cuxhaven, and other targets of opportunity. Eight B-17s were lost, and bombing results were poor.[74] The Jafü Deutsche Bucht scrambled seven Jagdgruppen and several independent Staffeln and Schwärme, for a total of 218 sorties. German pilots were awarded victory credits for at least 14 B-17s, while losing one killed and three injured. The effectiveness of their attacks on the unescorted bombers was obviously poor and would have to be improved. One possible solution was more destructive weapons. The ErprKdo 25 Schwarm at Wittmundhafen sortied again to test its rockets against the *Möbelwagen* (literally "furniture vans"—heavy bombers). Ogfr. Staniwoga was once more assigned the Bf 109F equipped with RZ 65 rockets, as he recalled:

> Today I attacked a *Pulk* alone from the rear at 8,000 meters [26,000 ft.]. It is better to say that I crept up on it. In order to use the RZ 65 successfully I had to match the speed of the *Pulk* exactly, maintain a distance of 500 meters [550 yards], and pull the nose of the Me up two rings on the Revi before firing. The unusual sight had to have made the American boys think that they were being attacked by a madman or a Sunday flyer.
>
> After I had my mill in position I fired a salvo and immediately sought to escape with an *Abschwung*, but lightning struck my Me. The stick was ripped from my hand, I heard a loud whistling noise, and a gray film clouded my eyes . . . My last thought before losing consciousness was, "I am blind." My memory is spotty, but the film cleared partially, I had my face close to the altimeter, which read 4,800 meters [15,700 ft.], and the whistling was still there. I then felt a strong jerk— and I was hanging in my parachute, surrounded by a pleasant quiet . . . I landed smoothly in a garden.[75]

The wreckage of Staniwoga's airplane was located and examined. Two unfired rockets had exploded in their tubes, probably hit by American machine-gun

fire, and had ripped one wing off the Messerschmitt. The lucky Heinrich Staniwoga was grounded for ten days for a slight wound, but he was not quite lucky enough to qualify for home leave. The career of the RZ 65 as an air-to-air weapon lasted only two more days.

The B-17s were again sent to Bremen on the 13th, but clouds caused the diversion of most bombers to Kiel and targets of opportunity. Once again results were poor, and the cost was high. The 1st Bomb Wing saw little opposition and lost only four B-17s, but the 4th Bomb Wing was attacked by an estimated 100 fighters from landfall to the targets and back out to sea, and lost 22 B-17s, 19 from the 94th and 95th Bomb Groups. The wing was led by its new commander, BGen. Nathan B. Forrest III, and crossed the coast in an experimental formation that he had devised. It proved to be fatally flawed. Many bombers could not fire directly ahead, which was the direction of most of the German attacks. General Forrest was in one of the 95th Bomb Group airplanes lost over the target; he was the highest-ranking USAAF officer killed in combat to date.[76]

The last two RZ 65-equipped Bf 109s were led on the 13th by the new leader of ErprKdo 25, Hptm. Horst Geyer. Galland had selected Geyer off his own staff to replace Major Nacke, a decorated Zerstörer pilot who left to take command of II./ZG1. Geyer's rocket salvo split apart a pair of straggling Fortresses, but apparently no claims were filed, and Geyer's report was sufficiently pessimistic that further trials were canceled.[77]

Hptm. Tratt, the top-scoring Zerstörer pilot, was also ordered away from ErprKdo 25; he took command of II./ZG 26, which was working up on Me 410s for the RLV. Skilled unit commanders were always in short supply in the Luftwaffe, and they were switched around frequently.

For the rest of June the Eighth Air Force confined itself mainly to French targets, in no discernable pattern. The bombers did make two more trips to Germany during the month. A mission to Hüls in the Rühr on the 22nd damaged that city's synthetic rubber industry so extensively that a follow-up raid could have stopped its rubber production entirely. A second raid never came, and the rubber industry, a true choke point in the German war machine, was let off the hook.[78] A tactical innovation worth noting was the presence of 11 YB-40s, including five in the leading combat box. The YB-40 "battle-cruiser" was a

The Luftwaffe made full use of its equipment, even failures. After its tests, the *schräge Musik* Fw 190 spent the rest of its days as an ordinary trainer at an operational training unit in southern France. An American soldier liberated this photograph at Bussac in 1944; the pilot remains unknown to the authors despite our efforts to identify him. (*Fletcher*)

B-17 modified to carry extra guns, ammunition, and armor in the place of bombs. The YB-40s could not keep up with standard B-17s once the latter had dropped their bombs, and themselves became good targets for the German interceptors. They did not remain on the front line for long, but bequeathed their nose armament (chin turrets with twin .50-inch machine guns) to the next standardized model Flying Fortress to come off the assembly lines, the B-17G. These turrets had an excellent field of fire, and every angle of approach to a B-17 would now be protected by at least one powered turret. The German head-on attacks would begin to lose some of their effectiveness.

Late June brought one noteworthy low-level command change in Lw Bfh Mitte. Hptm. Günther Specht replaced Major Anton Dickfeld as Kommandeur of II./JG 11. Dickfeld had been a successful fighter pilot in JG 52 on the Eastern Front and had commanded II./JG 2 in Tunisia. He had only been with JG 11 since mid-April, and had apparently made it known from the start that his stay would be brief. A committed Nazi with excellent connections,

he transferred to the RLM staff in Berlin, where he served as General for Luftwaffe Replacements and Inspector of the *Flieger-Hitlerjugend* (Flying Hitler Youth—FHJ) for the rest of the war. He was apparently responsible for the idea of a Jagdgeschwader *Hitlerjugend*, which would have taken young teenagers directly from glider training and put them into the cockpits of He 162 jet fighters.[79]

Günther Specht was "cut from a different cloth," in the German expression. His physical appearance was a startling contrast to the lanky, relaxed Dickfeld. The tightly wound Specht was the smallest man in the Gruppe. He had lost an eye to an RAF Wellington gunner in 1939, but could "see like a vulture" with his other eye, according to Heinz Knoke, one of his Staffel-kapitäne. The energetic Specht was a duty-conscious Prussian who held all of his men to his own high standards. He considered women an unnecessary diversion and would not allow them on the base. Knoke remembered one incident in which Specht's wife came to visit him but was held up at the guardroom. Specht asked Knoke to handle the call from the guard. Specht's message to his wife was to put herself on ice; he would have time for her after the war.[80] Specht led almost every Gruppe mission after he took command. He strove for perfection and wrote detailed, analytical mission reports for the benefit of his pilots and his superiors. Within a few months II./JG 11 had gained a reputation as (arguably) the best unit in the day RLV, and Specht became known as one of the most reliable formation leaders in the Jagdwaffe.

Throughout this period, Luftflotte 3 and Lw Bfh Mitte were waging related but separate defensive campaigns, with the inevitable inefficiency and wasteful duplication of effort. An obvious remedy was to centralize all of the western air-defense effort under a single command, but this was not to be. Proposals to reorganize the air-defense system into an integrated command structure dated back to Mölders's tenure as General der Jagdflieger in 1941, and Galland continued agitating for such measures through 1942. If recommendations from fighter commanders with first-hand experience of the growing Anglo-American air offensive fell on deaf ears, recommendations from more senior personnel, with access to intelligence appraisals of Allied intentions and industrial capabilities, might have more success. In March 1943, key personalities within the Luftwaffe leadership began to advance comprehensive proposals for a major shake-up. Kamm-huber, in his capacity as commander of XII.

Fliegerkorps, recommended a radical restructuring of the entire home-defense effort. He proposed greatly reinforcing the day- and night-fighter forces in the Reich and western occupied territories and combining them into a single *Jagdluftflotte* (Fighter Air Fleet) consisting of three Jagdkorps and nine Jagd-divisionen.[81] Weise, with whom Kammhuber enjoyed a good working relationship, endorsed the proposal, which also recommended strengthening and unifying the Flak defenses. Jeschonnek was quickly won over, and the proposal reached the Reichsmarschall later that spring. Göring, employing the divide and rule strategy that so often characterized the affairs of the Third Reich, instead ordered Kammhuber, Weise, and Galland to submit separate proposals for reorganization of the night-fighter, Flak, and day-fighter command structures. Ultimately, in a conference at the Führer's headquarters, Hitler decisively rejected Kammhuber's proposal. Hitler dismissed the night-fighter general's pessimistic statistics on Anglo-American aircraft production, and told him, "Once we have defeated Russia, then the night-fighter force can be built up. Until then your recommendation is rejected!"[82]

On June 29, 1943, Milch weighed into the debate with a proposal similar in most respects to Kammhuber's, but even more ambitious. He recommended creation of a single overall air command for the west, containing an integrated fighter-defense force, but also headquarters for conducting both the bomber campaign against the British Isles and the long-range air war out over the Atlantic. Göring rejected Milch's proposal; in fact there is some evidence that he never seriously examined it, since on July 3 he rebuked Milch publicly by stating: "You don't imagine that I actually read the rags you send me!"[83] A combination of factors—personal animosity, the high command's unfailingly offensive orientation, the command schism between Luftflotte 3 and the Reich territories, and disagreements between the various combat arms—ultimately prevented the Luftwaffe from meeting the gathering USAAF onslaught with a unified front.

As a result, the daytime defense of Germany and Occupied Europe remained an *ad hoc* affair throughout the decisive year 1943. It is difficult to disagree with the authors of the USAAF's Post-Hostilities Investigation of German Air Defenses, who concluded:

A loss of efficiency was caused by the Luftwaffe policy of unifying the air-defense effort on a mutual cooperation basis rather than on a unified command and staff basis, which failed to work well and resulted in operational friction and personal bickering between the young air commanders and the older Flak commanders which in time infected their subordinates. This system—based on elaborate rules for cooperation plus the High [Command] injunction to cooperate—lacked integrated air-defense staffs and competent air-defense commanders thoroughly familiar with the problems and operations of both arms, and resulted in much dissension and poor teamwork.[84]

The Balancing Act: The Relationship between the Air Fronts

The surviving Luftwaffe documentation on strength and dispositions is sometimes contradictory. Nevertheless, it is possible to speak with authority on the major trends of Luftwaffe deployments for the first half of 1943. Out of a total front-line established strength of 6,536 aircraft on May 31, 3,215 (49.2 percent) were on the *Ostfront* (Eastern Front) with Luftflotten 1, 4, 6 and the eastern portion of Luftflotte 5. A further 1,208 aircraft (18.5 percent) served in the Italian and southeastern fronts; Lw Bfh Mitte and Luftflotte 3 disposed of 998 and 864 aircraft respectively (28.5 percent). Comparison of total numbers of aircraft between Luftflotten may be somewhat misleading, as (for example) the eastern air fleets contained large numbers of night-harassing aircraft, battlefield reconnaissance airplanes, and Ju 87 dive bombers that had little utility in the west. If one restricts the discussion to single-engine fighters (Bf 109 and Fw 190, of which there were 1,624 at the front), the Ostfront had 447 (27.5 percent), the Mediterranean and southeast 377 (23 percent), Luftflotte 3 328 (20.2 percent), and Lw Bfh Mitte 296 (18.2 percent).[85] Serviceability was, of course, another matter; in the entire Jagdwaffe only 65 percent of these fighters were serviceable on that date.

The overall balance of forces among the war theaters raises another important issue. At what point did the home-defense effort really begin seriously to affect the combat strength of the Luftwaffe at the fronts? By the end of 1942, historian Horst Boog argues:

In the expectation of an Allied strategic bomber offensive against the centers of the Reich vital to the war effort, and of a landing on the mainland, the Luftwaffe . . . by perceptibly stripping the Eastern Front, had concentrated nearly 70 percent of its flying forces in the Mediterranean, the west, and the air defense of the Reich . . .[86]

This was certainly the conclusion reached by Allied intelligence as the Combined Bomber Offensive gathered momentum. A British Air Ministry assessment of Luftwaffe fighter defense in late 1943 concluded that the western front "has been substantially reinforced at the expense of the Russian and Mediterranean fronts."[87] Both accounts are essentially correct, but they do not capture the precise timing and sequencing of the shifting of German air priorities. Until the failure of the German Kursk offensive and the Allied invasion of Sicily, the forward deployed combat air fleets retained priority for fighter reinforcements. We might expect to see a wholesale pillaging of the Eastern Front of Bf 109 and Fw 190 groups throughout 1943 to reinforce the defense units of Lw Bfh Mitte and Luftflotte 3. Yet this did not take place in any appreciable way until the second half of the year. What expansion of the Reich day-fighter force that did take place during the pivotal months primarily involved the aforementioned reliance on factory defense flights, *Alarm* units run by the training schools, and a limited creation of new units.[88] The demands of the fighting fronts forced the Luftwaffe high command to maintain powerful single and twin-engine day-fighter forces on the periphery at the expense of a prompt reinforcement of the RLV. In particular, the build-up for the ill-fated Kursk operation called for the massing of over 1,000 first-line combat types, including nearly 350 Bf 109s and Fw 190s and 54 Bf 110s. The wholesale stripping of the fronts came after mid-1943—and by then it was too late.

On the eve of the big summer and fall 1943 air battles, the opposing air forces gathered strength, assessed the latest round of operational and tactical lessons, and prepared for the intensification of operations. In June 1943, Milch completed an inspection tour of the Reich's air defenses. On the subject of the day-fighter force, he approvingly noted:

The morale of the German fighter personnel is excellent, and under the circumstances imposed by their numerical weakness their performance deserves to be emphasized. The officers responsible for direction of fighter operations are fully capable to cope with their mission. The daytime fighter defense situation can be considered absolutely secure on the condition that adequately strong reinforcements are moved in.[89]

Milch added that the fighter defenses should be increased "until the Americans lose all pleasure in their handiwork."[90] Under his prodding, the defensive build-up was gathering momentum, but the pressures of the multi-front war in which the Luftwaffe was embroiled had delayed that expansion by at least six critical months. This lost opportunity was only one of many for the Luftwaffe, and it has received scant recognition in contrast to such dramatic episodes as the introduction of the Me 262 jet interceptor or the attempt to mass fighter reserves in 1944 for a "Great Blow." Yet the failure to reinforce the day-fighter defenses in early 1943 by a few hundred aircraft may have been the biggest missed opportunity of all. The greatest combat successes of the RLV were still to come, but its eventual defeat had already been assured.

The unknown instructor's Kommandeur was Major Hermann Graf, one of the best-known pilots of the Jagdwaffe. Graf's personal airplane was captured on the same roll of film as the *schräge Musik* Fw 190. His Fw 190A-5 was one of the most colorful fighters in the Luftwaffe, with red-over-yellow triangular markings and several personal emblems. As far as is known, it was never flown in combat. (*Fletcher*)

CHAPTER 5

HIGH TIDE FOR THE DEFENDERS
JULY–DECEMBER 1943

The Watershed: Summer 1943

Students of World War II have long debated the turning point of Hitler's war in Europe. They often nominate the halt before Moscow in December 1941, Hitler's subsequent declaration of war on the United States, or the twin disasters of El Alamein and Stalingrad as the decisive "hinge of fate." All these arguments have merit, yet for the war in the air the events of summer 1943 are no less a turning point. Until that time, the desire to mass air power in pursuit of conquest drove German air strategy, production, and technological development. After July 1943, defense of home air space became the Luftwaffe's overriding concern. Despite constant efforts to regain some offensive capability, the Luftwaffe and the RLV became ever more synonymous.

The last fight of the "old" Luftwaffe occurred during Operation Zitadelle, the summer offensive against the Kursk salient that began on July 5, 1943. For the final time in the war, the Luftwaffe threw entire air corps and air divisions—1,185 combat planes from VIII. Fliegerkorps (Luftflotte 4) and 730 from Flieger-division 1 (Luftflotte 6)—into a major offensive operation. After some initial success, German air strength ebbed as Luftwaffe reserves were depleted,

and the increasingly energetic Red Air Force gained the upper hand over the Kursk/Orel salient. For the rest of the year, the Red Army—supported by increasingly powerful and capable air armies—pushed the German Army back across the vast Eastern Front. In the Mediterranean, the Allied landing in Sicily on July 10, 1943, and the swift defeat of the Axis forces on that island further deepened the crisis.

Jeschonnek, the Luftwaffe Chief of Staff, clearly saw the handwriting on the wall. While mindful of the need to build up the home-defense force, he had staked virtually everything on achieving success in the east in 1943. With the failure of Zitadelle, the transfer of fighter aircraft from the *Ostfront* proceeded apace—in the opinion of Milch "absurdly late in the day, but at last it has been done." At the time of the Kursk offensive, there were 499 Fw 190 and Bf 109 fighters assigned to Eastern Front fighter units (392 operational). By August 31, only 313 remained (228 operational).[1] Beyond the decline in raw numbers, the method of employing the German fighter force had forever altered. No longer would hundreds of fighter aircraft be massed in order to gain air superiority over a key sector of the front. For the remainder of the war, with few exceptions, the fighter force concentrated in defense of the homeland, while a thin screen of overstretched Jagdgruppen held the line on the battlefronts. Milch noted, "My own attitude is this: I would tell the front that Germany itself is the real front line, and that the mass of fighters must go to home defence."[2]

Major Egon Mayer, JG 2 Kommodore, tries out the waist gun position on a crash-landed B-17. He was promoted from III./JG 2 Kommandeur in July, was the first German pilot to claim 100 victories over Western Europe on February 4, 1944, and was awarded the Swords to his Knights Cross with Oak Leaves after he was killed by P-47s on March 2, 1944. (*Bundesarchiv 377-2830-25*)

The second half of 1943 brought important gains in the strength, organization, tactics, technology and operational performance of the RLV. It would also bring one of the last major successes of German arms in the Second World War. By mid-1943 Germany was on the defensive everywhere after losing entire armies in the Stalingrad pocket and Tunisia. Although some fighting men on the Eastern Front were beginning to have their doubts, belief in the *Endsieg* or final German victory remained strong on the home front. The morale and combat efficiency of the units and pilots of the RLV peaked during the second half of 1943. All recognized that their task was hard and supremely dangerous, but vitally important if Germany was going to win the war. That said, their performance was uneven, and brought frequent reproaches from Reichsmarschall Göring and even from their own fighter general, Galland.

In an effort to reinforce the desired performance of the RLV pilots and, incidentally, boost their morale, the Luftwaffe instituted a points system for decorations. The pilots in the west had always felt some jealousy toward their fellow pilots on the Eastern Front, who had an easier time gaining aerial victories. Promotions and awards in the flying units were based strictly on success in combat. This basic principle could not be changed, but in recognition of the difficulty of the struggle against the heavy bombers, awards were now to be based on points earned as follows:

	Abschuss (shootdown)	Herausschuss (separation from formation)	Endgültige Vernichtung (final destruction)
Single-engine fighter	1	0	0
Twin-engine bomber	2	1	0.5
Four-engine bomber	3	2	1^3

The system recognized the fact that damaging a bomber sufficiently to separate it from its combat box was a significantly more difficult task than the final destruction of a damaged straggler. Decorations were therefore awarded after the following point totals had been reached:

Award	Points
Iron Cross 2nd Class	1
Iron Cross 1st Class	3
Honor Cup	10
German Cross in Gold	20
Knight's Cross	40

Despite the points system, medals remained much harder to obtain in the west than in the east. The Knight's Cross, which was worn on a ribbon around the neck, even in combat, was recognized in the Jagdwaffe as the sign of a true *Experte*. Glory-hungry pilots were said to have a "neck rash." If it was their luck to be assigned to the RLV, their necks in all likelihood continued to itch until their deaths. Surviving any pass through a massed phalanx of B-17s or B-24s was purely a matter of luck; and while a good Bf 109 or Fw 190 pilot could take on any opposing fighter one-on-one, most eventually succumbed to the odds of 10 or 20 to 1 that became the rule over western Europe.

It has been pointed out in many postwar references that the points system existed for the purpose of award qualification only. "Victory claims" and "points" were two distinct statistics. The requirements for the verification of victory claims remained unchanged; only the RLM in Berlin could confirm a claim, and this procedure could take more than a year. The RLM personnel clerks wrote the claims data in a large ledger in the order in which they were received, and added notes as the process continued. Claims verification ended abruptly in early February 1945, and the original ledgers apparently did not survive the war. They had fortunately been microfilmed in early

Fw 190A-6 "white 21" of the I./JG 2 Stabsschwarm, photographed in France in 1943. (*Rosch*)

January 1945, but the microfilm rolls themselves disappeared from public view until the 1990s, when they were made available to researchers in the German archives. They tell a fascinating tale of gamesmanship. In theory, a claim without a witness was only a "probable," which had no place in the system. In practice, some units habitually submitted unwitnessed claims, and some of these made it through the verification process, especially if made by successful pilots. In theory, the Luftwaffe did not accept shared claims. In practice, it happened. In theory, each "separation" claim should have matched up with a "final destruction." This rarely happened. Many pilots' "separation" claims were ultimately awarded as full victories; occasionally victories were awarded to other pilots who had claimed only the "final destruction" of the same aircraft.[4]

The daily OKW communiqués of this period habitually overstated American bomber losses by a factor of up to two. Defenders of the German fighter pilots have always maintained that these initial values were sharply reduced during the confirmation process. But the microfilms prove that this was not the case. Some 80–90 percent of the claims submitted to Berlin were eventually confirmed, or were "in order" for confirmation when the system broke down. Confirmed German claims for the destruction of heavy bombers are more difficult to reconcile with Allied losses than claims for any other aircraft type; it is probable that part of the explanation lies with the point system itself, and the rest lies with the *Ziffernkult*, or worship of numbers, promulgated by the Luftwaffe leadership.

The Bf 109G-6 "black 1"of Heinz Knoke, 5./JG 11 Staffel-kapitän, was equipped with WGr 21 rocket tubes in mid-1943. The airplane has a narrow red fuselage band, briefly the identification mark of RLV formation leaders. (*Knoke via Price*)

JG 26, Göring's and Galland's favorite fighter unit, and the most effective one in the eyes of Allied intelligence, remained on its exposed bases in Belgium and northeastern France unless its Gruppen were needed to fill temporary gaps in the Reich defensive line. Its personnel were under more stress than those of any other fighter unit. Their airfields were within easy range of Allied fighters and light bombers, and were subjected to frequent attacks. The pilots were expected to defend against these tactical raids while also forming the first line of defense against the heavy bombers. They were held at readiness throughout the daylight hours of every flyable day. Their interceptions of heavy bombers were frequently hurried, and tactics that worked well farther inland had to be rejected. Erich Schwarz, a pilot in 8./JG 26, shared some impressions of this period:

> Head-on attacks were a failure on the coast due to the lack of time to form up, as well as the brief firing time—only four rounds. The heavy bombers had not yet been fired on by Flak, and were in very close formations that we found impossible to penetrate after our own attacks. We tried dropping 250-kg bombs from above the formations. These were intended to be "superheavy Flak" and break up the *Pulks*, but I know of only two successful missions before the increased Allied escort and the slow climb and increased vulnerability of the bomb-carrying fighters put an end to their use. I was glad to see them go.[5]

Schwarz also described the physical effects on the pilots when full readiness was announced: everyone ran to empty their stomachs, bladders, and bowels, but even then could not relax. Only when in the cockpit did concentration on the mission rule out any other thoughts. After landing their bodies shook so much that they could not hold a cigarette without assistance. For decades after the war Schwarz had recurring nightmares in which he popped up through the cloud deck in his Focke-Wulf to see the silver bomber formations stretching to the horizon, gleaming in the sun.

July 24–30—Blitz Week

The weather over Germany stayed bad for the first three weeks of July. The Americans made one attempt to raid Hamburg and Hamm, but the bombers had to be recalled. Several missions were sent to familiar targets in France, facing their old opponents, JG 2 and

JG 26. The most noteworthy of these missions was mounted on the 14th. The targets were the airfields at Villacoublay, Le Bourget, and Amiens. In all 201 of the 279 bombers dispatched dropped their bombs. The raid on Villacoublay was an outstanding success; the hangars containing the Luftflotte 3 Fw 190 repair facility were destroyed, along with 70 Fw 190s, coming from every fighter, bomber, reconnaissance, headquarters, and operational training unit in France, according to the material loss list.[6]

The Amiens raiding force was smaller and somewhat earlier than the others, and served to shield the main force from the Jafü 2 fighters. The Amiens bombers were escorted by all three American P-47 groups; the target was well within their range. Jafü 2 scrambled its fighters from Lille, Vitry, and Poix as the Amiens force was crossing the French coast. The Poix fighters, Messerschmitts from 3./JG 27 and II./JG 2, were closest to the bombers' course, but apparently hung back until Major Wutz Galland arrived from Vitry with II./JG 26 and bullied them into attacking with a sarcastic radio message that was noted by the RAF radio monitors. P-47s were in the area, but did not intervene effectively for 20 minutes. Only one 381st Bomb Group B-17 went down, the victim of a 3./JG 27 Messerschmitt, but two more crash-landed in England, and an additional 34 were damaged by

fighters and/or Flak. Two of the Bf 109s were shot down; one pilot was killed and the other injured.[7]

In the meantime, Galland and his men took on the 78th Fighter Group off Hesdin. Galland was credited with two P-47s after prolonged dogfights, but both pilots survived. His first victim did not crash immediately, but staggered back toward England, its badly injured pilot holding the stick between his forearms. He decided not to crash-land because he could not buckle his harness, and so bailed out off the English coast, where he was quickly rescued. Galland's second opponent was also able to get close to England before bailing out into the Channel, and was rescued. The only 78th Group fatality was in the third P-47 to go down, which was hit in error by a B-17 gunner. The P-47 pilots managed but a single victory; a new replacement pilot in 5./JG 26 was shot down and bailed out into the Somme Estuary with slight injuries. He too was soon rescued.[8]

I./JG 2 Focke-Wulfs and II./JG 2 Messerschmitts arrived and took on some 4th Fighter Group P-47s and RAF Spitfires west of the Somme, near Le Tréport, but Major Egon Mayer, who had recently replaced Obstlt. Walter Oesau as JG 2 Kommordore, held most of his force over Évreux to await the arrival of the two B-17 formations that were headed for Paris—and the inevitable departure of the Allied

Heinz Knoke, 5./JG 11 Staffelkapitän, sits on a wheel of a Bf 109G-6 "gunboat" at Jever in the summer of 1943. The airplane is probably one of Knoke's; the narrow red band of a formation leader is visible around the rear fuselage. (*Knoke via Price*)

Bomb Group B-17 near Paris. The airfield Flak scored one success: a 303rd Bomb Group Fortress was hit and ditched successfully in the Channel. The 305th Bomb Group, leading the trailing combat wing, left the target area without major damage; then two Fw 190s appeared. Navigator Ed Burford recalled:

> Whoever it was gave a riveting display of aerobatics out in front of our entire 102nd Combat Wing before slashing in to fatally damage the leading ship of the 422nd Bomb Squadron in the low slot . . . The attack took place at 0818 near Etampes, southwest of Paris. After fires broke out between the #2 engine and the fuselage, and between the #3 and #4 engines, the ship nosed down in a spin—somehow seven men managed to hit the silk. I had never seen such a tremendous volume of tracer go after that one plane with a wingman in tow. Downright discouraging to hit nothing but air.[10]

The Fw 190 pilot was Major Egon Mayer himself. His second B-17 claim of the day, and the last one filed by the defenders, matches exactly the location and time of the 305th Bomb Group loss. He and his wingman were apparently the only two JG 2 pilots to reach the Villacoublay force. Mayer was not known as a showboating pilot, and one can only guess at the reason for his aerobatics. Exuberance at finding another unescorted *Pulk*, possibly—but it is more likely that his radio had failed, and he was trying to attract the attention of the rest of his men by the only method open to him.

The return flight of the Villacoublay force was an anticlimax. According to Burford, they had been ordered to descend to 14,000 feet (4,300 meters) to pick up an escort of clipped-wing, low-altitude Spitfires. The German fighters stayed away, but ground forces, including "four tanks lined up on a road," took potshots at the Fortresses all the way back across France. All of the bombers were holed, but none were lost.

During the last week of July the bad weather that had covered northwestern Europe for most of the previous three months suddenly cleared, allowing the Eighth Air Force a week of operations at the most intense level to date. The six days of missions on July 24-30 set new records for depth of penetration, weight of bombs dropped, and number of sorties flown. The targets chosen by MGen. Eaker and the new head of his 8th Bomber Command, MGen. Fred Anderson,

Lt. Eberhard Burath, I./JG 1 adjutant, is caught in a thoughtful mood at Schiphol in mid-1943. (*Burath*)

escorts. He then led a head-on attack on the 94th Bomb Group, which was leading the four 4th Bomb Wing groups in the Le Bourget force. Hptm. Georg-Peter Eder was leading the 12. Staffel in a Bf 109G-6/R6 "gunboat," which carried MG 151/20 cannon in underwing gondolas in addition to the standard armament of one MG 151/20 and two MG 17 machine guns in the nose. According to his combat report, he made an immediate head-on attack from 8,000 meters (26,000 ft.) altitude, aiming at the outer right B-17 in the lead *Pulk*. Pieces flew off and the Fortress sheered away from the formation. Eder followed up with a rear attack on the same plane from a distance of 800 meters (2,600 ft.) down to 200 meters (650 ft.), after which two men bailed out and the bomber crashed, witnessed by Eder's wingman. Mayer and his two Gruppen were credited with six B-17s from this *Pulk*; four in fact crashed.[9]

The Jafü 3 controller was forced to use training aircraft against the Villacoublay raiders; that was all he had left. A pilot from the JG 105 *Einsatzstaffel* (operational squadron) was able to bring down a 384th were all high priorities on the Combined Bomber Offensive's master plan. For the first time there was to be a degree of coordination with RAF Bomber Command. The campaign was not given a code name, but was known unofficially as Blitz Week.[11]

On the 24th the Eighth Air Force was sent to Norway for the first time. The primary targets were aluminum, magnesium, and nitrate plants under construction in Heroya. The defenses were taken completely by surprise. 10./JG 11, the only day-fighter Staffel in Norway, lost two pilots killed to B-17 defensive fire, while the only bomber to receive severe damage reached Sweden and internment.

The American bombing plan for the 25th was the most ambitious of the war to date. They were to follow up a massive night raid on Hamburg by RAF Bomber Command with a precision attack on two Hamburg targets by most of the 1st Bomb Wing. The rest of the wing would attack a Kiel U-boat yard, while the longer-range 4th Bomb Wing would bomb the Focke-Wulf factory at Warnemünde, near Rostock, the most distant target yet. More than 300 B-17s were to take part. The plan proved far too complex. The Kiel force aborted; one of the two Hamburg task forces assembled late, and in a strung-out, highly vulnerable formation. The lead crews arriving over Hamburg discovered that large fires set by the RAF the previous night were still burning, and they could not find their targets. Only Colonel LeMay's 4th Bomb Wing flew what could be called a successful mission, but they failed to bomb their primary target owing to cloud cover, and were forced to bomb their secondary target, Kiel.[12]

The German defenses also had their problems. The units in Jafü Holland-Ruhrgebiet were kept in their own areas to defend against what proved to be light-bomber raids, and the incoming raiders were thus faced only by Jafü Deutsche Bucht. Several of its units were scrambled after the early-arriving 4th Bomb Wing, which unexpectedly made a feint to the north, forcing the short-legged Bf 109s to return to base for refueling. Only two Gruppen were able to reach the large Hamburg force before its Initial Point. One was Major Specht's II./JG 11, which made two frontal attacks. The most notable success was gained by Lt. Wolfgang Gloerfeld, who was piloting an experimental Bf 109G "gunboat" with two 30-mm cannon in its underwing gondolas. His second attack knocked an entire stabilizer off of a 379th Bomb Group B-17. Gloerfeld then collided with the careering tailplane. He was able to bail out, but suffered a double skull

fracture and other broken bones that kept him out of combat until November. The B-17 did not crash immediately, and possibly even stayed in formation for a while. Two more Fortresses from the same unit were severely damaged in this attack; one eventually crashed, while the second reached England with a dead pilot. Specht's Gruppe returned to Jever to refuel and reload, but never reached the departing bomber formation. Its first mission, a "textbook attack," resulted in only three victory claims, and cost four injured pilots. Specht's report that evening was probably more caustic than usual. The three-gunned Bf 109Gs that were the main equipment of his Gruppe were virtually impotent against tight formations of B-17s.

The other Gruppe to make an early attack on the Hamburg force was Hptm. Mietusch's III./JG 26. Little is known about its engagement other than the score—three B-17s were confirmed destroyed for the loss of two Bf 109G-6s in forced landings and damage to a third. The claims cannot be matched with any American losses; again, the destructive power of the standard Messerschmitt fighter was not up to its task.[13]

The Deutsche Bucht controller was able to form up the rest of his units against the departing Hamburg force, aided by II./JG 1, which had transferred from Deelen to Jever, and III./JG 1, flying from its Leeuwarden base. Holland-based night fighters were able to reach the bombers as they returned across the North Sea. The 1st Bomb Wing lost a total of 15 B-17s on the mission, most after being damaged by the Hamburg Flak, the worst the Americans had yet seen. The well-flown 4th Bomb Wing lost only four bombers. The defenders lost seven fighters; one KIA (the III./JG 1 Gruppenkommandeur); five injured; and two prisoners, the crew of a ditched night fighter, who were rescued by a Royal Navy motor torpedo boat engaged in raiding the Dutch coast.

Air Chief Marshal Arthur Harris, the Commander-in-Chief of RAF Bomber Command, was all in favor of keeping the pressure on Hamburg, but decided that there was too much residual smoke even for area bombing, and sent his bombers to Essen on the night of the 25th/26th. The American bomber commanders decided to return to Hamburg on the 26th. The same six 1st Bomb Wing groups that had missed their targets in Hamburg on the 25th were to return and try again. The rest of the 1st Wing and the 4th Wing were dispatched to Hannover in another complex plan that

THE LUFTWAFFE OVER GERMANY

was intended to deceive and disperse the defenses, but did not go exactly as briefed. Some damage was done to the targets, but the Hannover force lost 16 B-17s, primarily to JG 1 Fw 190s. The Deutsche Bucht Bf 109s did not attack the Hamburg force aggressively, probably expecting the Hamburg Flak to break the *Pulks* up, as it had done the previous day. But the Flak was having an off day, and the Hamburg force lost only two bombers. Four German pilots were killed, and one injured, by fire from the B-17s.[14]

The weather over the continent deteriorated slightly, and the Americans stood down on the 27th. Air Marshal Harris, however, decided to resume the Battle of Hamburg that night. The British plan was little different from that of the 24th/25th, except that a larger percentage of incendiary bombs would be carried. The German night defenses were still in disarray from the introduction of Window, radar-jamming aluminum-coated paper strips, three nights previously, and losses were expected to be low. This indeed proved to be the case, and the resulting tight bomb pattern in a densely populated residential sector of the city, combined with low humidity at ground level, led to something unique—a firestorm, with extremely high temperatures and hurricane-strength winds. It consumed so much oxygen that most of its victims suffocated before they could burn (or melt). The death toll for this one night was estimated at 40,000, a new record for the area bombing campaign. After a follow-up night raid on the 29th/30th, approximately 1,200,000 people, two-thirds of the population, fled the city. It took five months for the city's industrial production to reach 80

percent of pre-raid levels, and full recovery was never attained.[15]

The Americans could not claim such a startling success for their efforts by day. Their plan was to knock out Germany's key war production plants, one at a time, and they had neither the desire nor the strength to destroy entire cities. Their current campaign resumed on the 28th with raids on two important Fw 190 factories. Some 182 1st Bomb Wing B-17s targeted Kassel, while 120 4th Bomb Wing B-17s headed toward Oschersleben. Few bombers attacked the briefed targets; 25 were lost or written-off after their return, and 118 were damaged. Both targets were far inland, and the Deutsche Bucht and Holland-Ruhrgebiet controllers were able to vector their Jagdgruppen for continuous attacks on the bomber stream on both the inbound and withdrawal phases of the mission. Specht's II./JG 11 made a very successful attack on the incoming 4th Bomb Wing. Its 5. Staffel dropped 250-kg (550-pound) bombs from above the formation, and Uffz. Jonny Fest scored a direct hit on a 385th Bomb Group Fortress that exploded and brought down two more B-17s. Fest was credited with three victories, the best result ever obtained by air-to-air bombing. The *Pulk* began to split up, and Oblt. Knoke quickly led the Staffel in an attack to close range. Knoke was flying a brand-new Bf 109G-6/U4 with a 30-mm engine cannon, which would prove to be a very effective weapon against heavy bombers. Knoke downed one B-17 and forced another from the formation, leaving its final destruction to his wingman. The Gruppe was credited with downing a total of 12 4th Bomb Wing B-17s, for

III./JG 26 was based at Cuxhaven-Nordholz May 23–August 13, far from its familiar surroundings on the *Kanal*, to reinforce the defenses of north Germany. Here Hptm. Mietusch leads the Gruppe in an *Alarmstart* on July 25. (*Möszner via Ivo de Jong*)

the loss of two Messerschmitts and injury to one pilot.[16]

This same B-17 formation was engaged by I./JG 1 on its withdrawal across Holland. The Gruppe adjutant, Eberhard Burath, recalled:

My Kommandeur told me beforehand that he wanted to observe a head-on attack from a distance, while I led the attack. We overtake a formation over northern Holland. He climbs to get in the right position. Now it is my turn. Far enough in front, about 3 km [1.9 miles], I tip my wing to signal the Gruppe, then make a 180-degree turn and head straight for the middle of the *Verband*. A quick glance over my shoulder, and it strikes me like a blow—I am alone! Far in front of the rest. Instead of splitting the defensive fire, the Amis can concentrate on me. I see the wall of tracers and shrink as small as I can behind my big radial engine. I find the B-17 I am headed toward in the Revi and squeeze the trigger briefly. Then "Ground floor and exit!" Split-S, smoke in the cockpit, electrical sparks—fortunately there is no fire. It is good that the Dutch have such beautiful farmland. I find a suitable landing site, but the bird doesn't want to settle in, and I overrun it and hit a dike almost head-on—but my wing catches first and spins me around 180 degrees. I have plowed up a potato field, and am showered with potatoes. Then the peaceful quiet after the storm—I thank my guardian angel, open the canopy, and climb out through the potatoes. My plane doesn't look too bad, except that it is 20 cm [8 in.] shorter than before.

I am soon fetched from the nearby village . . . Back at base I am not rebuked for my lone attack, which my comrades were unable to follow . . . Thus ended my role as Gruppenkommandeur.[17]

Burath had attacked the 95th Bomb Group, which lost three B-17s to fighters on the mission. His lagging comrades were credited with two victories and one *Herausschuss*. His vanishing Kommandeur's claim for a victory was not confirmed.

The day's most important technical development was American. Unwilling to wait for properly designed auxiliary tanks, which were caught in a bureaucratic SNAFU between Britain and the U.S.A., the 4th Fighter Group attached droppable ferry tanks to their P-47s, which enabled them to pick up the returning B-17s at Emmerich, on the Dutch–German border. Their surprise appearance broke up a promising attack on the withdrawing 1st Bomb Wing by I./JG 26

Lt. Heinz Rose of 4./JG 11 sits at cockpit readiness in his Bf 109G-1 "white 5" at Jever in July. The mechanic is waiting to finish strapping him in. Note the extended takeoff flaps and the large Geschwader emblem beneath the cockpit. (*Heinz Rose via Arno Rose*)

and I./JG 3. The ex-Eagles then had their best day to date, claiming nine victories for one loss, to Hptm. Rolf Hermichen of 3./JG 26. True German losses were apparently two JG 26 Fw 190s and four JG 3 Bf 109s. Each Gruppe claimed only one B-17. The day's battles had gone reasonably well for the defenders prior to the appearance of the Thunderbolts. Only two units from Jafü 2, Jafü Holland-Ruhrgebiet, and Jafü Deutsche Bucht failed to made contact: the JG 26 Geschwadergruppe (Priller's Stabsschwarm plus two Staffeln) and its powerful II. Gruppe were poorly directed and failed to find the bomber stream.

The 29th saw the Eighth Air Force attack the Kiel U-boat yards and a Heinkel aircraft factory in Warnemünde. The P-47s returned to their high-altitude sweeps, but the Luftwaffe's interceptions were generally from long range, and only ten B-17s went down. The day was only notable for a German innovation described in the bomber crew interrogations as "flaming baseballs." These were WGr 21 aerial rockets, which saw their first operational use on this day. These were converted from 21-cm mortar shells and carried in braced underwing "stovepipe" launchers. JG 1 and JG 11 had them on this occasion, and two Staffeln of III./JG 26 would have them within the week. While wildly inaccurate, they could be fired from well outside the range of the bombers' machine guns, and were intended to break up the bombers' tight formations, for which purpose a near miss was as good as a hit. The rockets carried 40.8 kg (90 pounds) of explosive, and were stabilized in flight by a spiral trajectory imparted by the grooved launch tube rather than by fins. The unwieldy launchers markedly reduced the performance of the fighters carrying them, but this had not been a great concern to the weapon designers, because the Allied escort fighters had previously lacked the range to reach Germany.[18]

Blitz Week ended on the 30th with a raid on two Kassel Fw 190 factories. All of the B-17s still operational, a total of 186, took part. The bombers' route took them through the heart of the Holland-Ruhrgebiet air defenses, and the bombers were ordered to fly in a single, long formation for mutual self-defense and to assist the escorts. The American intention was clear very early, and the German controllers located the entire strength of the 8th Bomber Command soon enough to concentrate fighters from four Jafü to intercept them. The German fighters flew an unprecedented 285 defensive sorties, including 40 second sorties. Jafü 3 sent JG 2

northeast, and Jafü Deutsche Bucht sent JG 11 southwest, in time to converge on the bombers' anticipated withdrawal course.

Early-morning raids on Woensdrecht and Schiphol by USAAF and RAF medium and light bombers prevented the use of I./JG 26 and III./JG 54 against the incoming heavies, and apparently only the JG 26 Geschwadergruppe from Lille and I./JG 3 from München-Gladbach intercepted the bombers before they reached Kassel. The JG 26 formation reached the bombers with too little altitude and turned to trail the bombers on their eastward course. They attacked near Antwerp, after the Spitfires turned back, and claimed six B-17s before they were ordered to land at Antwerp and elsewhere for servicing. Three of these victories were eventually confirmed; one Fw 190 was lost. I./JG 3 maintained contact for 30 minutes, and claimed two B-17s for the loss of two Bf 109s.

The controllers concentrated the defending fighters along the bombers' return route and planned a maximum-strength attack. By accident or design, the three P-47 groups were all assigned to withdrawal escort. All now had drop tanks, and on this day had abandoned high-altitude sweeps in favor of close defense of the American bombers. Twelve Jagdgruppen reached the withdrawing stream, but their attacks on the bombers were brought to an early halt by the arrival of the American escort above Bocholt, just inside Germany. The American fighters—107 P-47s from all three operational groups, the 4th, 56th, and 78th—found the bombers under attack by "150–200 German fighters," many of which turned their attention to the Thunderbolts after evading the Americans' initial attack. The result was the largest battle to date between American and German fighters. The escort units claimed 24–1–8 German fighters for the loss of seven Thunderbolts. The day's losses for the RLV totaled 14 dead and 12 injured pilots; 27 fighters were destroyed, and 13 damaged.[19]

The Luftwaffe air-defense commanders had to be bitterly disappointed at the day's results. The OKW communiqué claimed the destruction of 60 B-17s, but the true number was known to be much lower. (The actual loss was 17 B-17s destroyed or written off, plus 82 damaged.) The defending fighters had been

Hptm. Wilhelm-Ferdinand Galland, Kommandeur of II./JG 26. The second Galland brother to die in JG 26, "Wutz" was killed by P-47s escorting the Schweinfurt–Regensburg raid on August 17. (*Author's collection*)

brought together in greater numbers than ever before. Command and control procedures had worked well, and everything was in order for a smashing victory—which did not occur, owing to the untimely arrival of the Thunderbolts, which fought more aggressively than ever before. The future suddenly looked less promising.[20]

The leaders of the Eighth Air Force were well pleased with the results of Blitz Week, and basked in congratulatory messages from Washington and London. But the combat units themselves were worn down to ineffectiveness. Omitting the Norway mission from the calculations, the six raids had cost 8th Bomber Command 87 total losses—6.7 percent of the B-17s dispatched, 10.4 percent of those actually bombing, and 30 percent of the bombers needed for a full-scale mission. The Command stood down for the next 11 days. The major lesson of the week, according to Generals Eaker and Anderson, was their need for more bombers and fighters. The most important lesson to those doing the actual fighting, the importance of long-range escort, was apparently missed by these two gentlemen, who continued planning deep-penetration missions, well beyond the range of their P-47s.[21]

The Great Defensive Build-Up

Although Adolf Hitler was normally indifferent to civilian casualties, the lack of discipline shown by the Hamburgers after the firestorm shook him to the core. He told his military staff that the raids had had "a substantial effect on the *Volkssubstanz*," a word that can be loosely translated as the "people's Germanic essence," and that "absolute emphasis" was to be placed on the air defense of the Reich. GFM Erhard Milch immediately called a meeting of the "defensive clique" (Milch, Galland, and their staffs) to discuss how best to take advantage of the new national priority. Milch and his men were in fact far more worried about the growing day offensive than the night raids, but Hitler's outburst would give them the opportunity they had been looking for to strengthen the day forces. They could always argue that it had been the repetitive night–day–night nature of the Hamburg raids that had made them so damaging, even though that was not strictly true. And although the possibility of closer cooperation between the American and British strategic bomber forces was a constant worry for the German air-defense planners, it never came to pass.[22]

Milch, effectively second-in-command of the Luftwaffe, wore several hats, but in this instance his role as Generalluftzeugmeister (Chief of Air Armament) was most important. He began to plan for a significant increase in the production of Bf 109, Fw 190, and Me 410 day fighters, which were the only types immediately available. In 1942 Milch had canceled the Me 209, the Bf 109's planned successor, and the Me 210, the Me 410's predecessor, after the Messerschmitt firm had wasted an enormous quantity of resources on them. Milch was trying to accelerate the Me 262 program, with the enthusiastic support of General Galland, but the revolutionary jet fighter was probably a year away from front-line service. For now he would go with what he had.

An effective increase in the strength of the RLV required more than hardware. More pilots, more units, and a more effective organization were all needed. The chaotic Luftwaffe structure and the pervasive infighting in Berlin hindered a satisfactory resolution of the problems that Milch, Galland, and a few others could see. Resources were finite, and had to be won at the expense of the other arms of the Wehrmacht. Pilot training was already losing the battle for scarce fuel, and received only 40 percent of the requested amount for July. Increasing the number of combat personnel in the Jagdwaffe required the whole-hearted cooperation of Reichsmarschall Göring and his Chief of Staff, Genobst. Hans Jeschonnek, which was slow in coming. And the organization of the RLV was still fragmented and inefficient. Centralization was on the way, but no real progress would be made until the fall.[23]

Increasing the combat strength of the RLV could and did come in three ways: formation of new units, expanding the tables of organization of existing RLV units, and transferring units from other theaters. Of the three, the formation of new units was the most difficult. The Luftwaffe had only been in existence since 1935, and its corps of professional officers was extremely small. Good combat commanders and formation leaders were an ever-decreasing resource owing to combat losses, but good staff officers were just as important for an efficient combat unit, and these simply did not exist in the necessary numbers; neither did the combat-experienced Obersten and Generale needed for division-level command of a large number of Geschwader. Only two additional single-engine day-fighter units were made available to the RLV in the third quarter of 1943, and these were an unexpected gift. JG 25 and JG 50 had been unsuccessful at catching Mosquitoes, and were added to the strength of the conventional RLV order of battle. Although titled Jagdgeschwader, they were in reality only low-strength single Gruppen, but did contain a number of very experienced Eastern Front pilots.[24]

The only entirely new day-fighter unit to become operational in Germany in this period was IV./JG 3, but instead of joining the RLV it was transferred to Italy, apparently on the orders of Hitler, who was trying to encourage Mussolini to continue the struggle after Italy's formal surrender to the Allies in early September.[25]

A new night-fighter Geschwader that began forming in late June would ultimately play a prominent role in

Major Hermann Graf, one of the best-known RLV formation leaders. He was summoned from the Eastern Front in 1943 to command successively JG 50, JG 1, and JG 11, before returning to the east to finish the war as Kommodore of JG 52. (*Meyer*)

the day RLV, but in 1943 it was only a drain on the day fighters' resources. This unit was JG 300, which was the inspiration of Major Hajo Herrmann, a former bomber pilot. In early 1943 night fighters over the Reich were tightly controlled from the ground. Each ground controller could direct only one fighter at a time, and RAF Bomber Command had begun to swamp the system by increasing the density of its bomber streams. Herrmann advocated the use of single-engine fighters at night. These would not be controlled from the ground, but could locate targets with the aid of searchlights and burning cities. He was authorized to form a trials unit, which was forced into full operation prematurely by the RAF's introduction of Window, which blinded German airborne and ground radar and rendered ground control impotent. Herrmann's unit was expanded to full Geschwader strength and nicknamed the *Wilde Säue* (Wild Sows) because their wild chases across Germany resembled the aggressive behavior of sows defending their piglets. JG 300 was at first given no aircraft or ground crews, but only pilots, who lodged at the bases of day-fighter units and borrowed their aircraft for night missions. This was of course detrimental to the operational strength of the day units, especially as winter approached. The *Wilde Sau* pilots lost many more aircraft in landing accidents than in combat. Their principal fighter, the Bf 109, was difficult enough to land in clear daylight, though many pilots in fact preferred them to Fw 190s for night operations because of the ease with which Bf 109 landing gear sheared off in hard landings.[26]

In early 1943 General Galland had begun to argue for the expansion of the existing RLV day units. He first wanted to increase the number of Staffeln in each Gruppe from three to four, and then to increase the number of fighters in each Staffel from 12 to 16. The total establishment strength of a Jagdgeschwader would thus be increased from 124 to 208 fighters. This simple expedient would minimize the need for new staff officers and controllers, requiring "only" planes, pilots, ground crew, and a few Staffel-level combat leaders, but even this was not possible immediately owing to the demands of other fronts. The Mediterranean theater absorbed all "excess" fighter production for the first half of 1943; most of its units had to be rebuilt twice. And the last major German offensive on the Eastern Front, Operation Zitadelle, consumed much of the third-quarter production. As a result, only the two Luftflotte 3 Jagdgeschwader, JG 2 and JG 26, had been expanded to 12 Staffeln by the end of September. Galland hoped ultimately to add a fourth Gruppe to each RLV Geschwader, raising their establishment strength to 276 fighters.[27]

The reinforcement of the RLV with Jagdgruppen from the eastern and southern fronts was well under way when Milch received his green light to build up the defenses of the homeland. The four-Gruppe JG 3 was to form the heart of Jagddivision 5 in southern Germany, but would later move to Jagddivision 4, covering Berlin. All of the Gruppen of JG 27 would eventually return from the southern and southeastern fronts and be concentrated in Austria under Jafü Ostmark, which was later renamed Jagddivision 8. The Gruppen of JG 53 and JG 77 also came back from the south one at a time to rebuild, but were not fortunate enough to join the RLV as full Geschwader; instead they were farmed out to the Jagddivisionen as individual Gruppen. Most of the returning Gruppen had a difficult time in the RLV, losing the majority of their original pilots in a matter of weeks or months.[28] The history of II./JG 51 is somewhat anomalous. It relocated from Italy to München-Neubiberg in mid-August for rebuilding, and was thrown into action in October against the American deep-penetration raids. Its performance was outstanding; its reward was to be sent back to Italy. It would stay in the south and southeast for the rest of the war as an independent Gruppe.[29]

Three units that joined the RLV in the fall— Zerstörergeschwader 1 (ZG 1), ZG 26 and ZG 76—had a very checkered past. The twin-engine Bf 110 Zerstörer began the war as Göring's preferred escort fighter, but was found wanting in this role in the Battle of Britain. The units and aircraft were used as the basis of the early night-fighter force, losing their Zerstörer designations, but the units were later resurrected under their old names for naval escort and ground-support duties in areas in which the Luftwaffe still possessed a measure of air control. It was believed in Berlin that the heavy armament of the Bf 110 and its designated successor, the Me 410, would make them ideal bomber destroyers in areas free of escorts. Bf 110

night fighters had shown some promise in the role, even without crew training or tactical doctrine. In mid-1943 therefore the scattered Zerstörergruppen were recalled from the eastern and Mediterranean fronts and re-formed into RLV units. After a period of reorganization and renumbering ZG 26 became a full three-Gruppe Geschwader, with one Me 410 and two Bf 110 Gruppen, based around Hannover. ZG 76 was authorized two Bf 110 Gruppen, and after re-forming from training and reconnaissance units was based in southern Germany. ZG 1 had three Gruppen at this time. One, II./ZG 1, joined the RLV under this designation; it was sent to Austria with Bf 110s. Another, III./ZG 1, was renamed II./ZG 26; a new III./ZG 1 was formed in France, and joined I./ZG 1 flying Ju 88 maritime fighters out of bases on the western French coast.[30]

Heavy armament and long range were the major strengths that the Zerstörer brought to the RLV. Bf 110s and Me 410s could all carry four WGr 21 rocket tubes, and a bewildering variety of subtypes were produced with various combinations of 2-cm and 3-cm cannon. Hitler's favorite Me 410 weapon was the BK 5 5-cm cannon, developed from an army anti-tank gun. The cannon were produced in numbers, and equipped one entire Gruppe (II./ZG 26), but the recoil and feed mechanisms were not designed for the g-forces of aerial combat, and they could rarely get off more than one shot without jamming.[31]

One more twin-engine unit should be mentioned, although its stay in the RLV was brief. In May I. Gruppe of Kampfgeschwader 51 (I./KG 51), a conventional Ju 88 bomber unit, was transferred from Russia to Germany without aircraft, to be retrained as a Me 410 *Hornisse* bomber-destroyer unit. Fortunately for the pilots, there were no Me 410s immediately

Oblt. Alfred Grislawski, Kapitän of 1./JG 50, strikes the obligatory pose beside the tail of his Bf 109G-6 "white 10" at Wiesbaden-Erbenheim in the summer of 1943. The airplane has the full white empennage mandated for formation leaders at this time. This shows off his personalized rudder decoration, comprising his monogram and Knight's Cross, and notes his 112 victories. (*Grislawski*)

available, and they were given several months to learn the *Jägerart* (fighter pilots' ways) in Bf 110s. The aircraft they finally received were early Me 410A-1 *Schnellbombers* (fast bombers) with single-stage superchargers and maximum performance at only 3,000 meters (10,000 ft.), which left them completely unsuited for their planned role. Gruppenkommandeur Hptm. Klaus Häberlen's protest letters to Berlin went unacknowledged. The unit entered combat in September, with predictably mediocre results.[32]

Detailed orders of battle can be found in the Appendices, but it is useful at this point to insert a table giving the total day-fighter strength of the RLV by quarters since the end of 1942. Recall that we have defined the RLV as the force defending the Reich proper, at this time Luftwaffenbefehlshaber Mitte (Lw Bfh Mitte), plus the force based in the western occupied zone, Luftflotte 3. The growth of Lw Bfh Mitte was dramatic by any measure, but note the low number actually available for operations; on September 30, this was only 50 percent of establishment strength.

The small B-24 contingent had vanished from the 8th Bomber Command's order of battle in June. They had flown to North Africa to prepare for Operation Tidal Wave, a low-level raid on the refinery complex around Ploesti, Romania. The mission took place on August 1; the battered survivors made another contribution to the Combined Bomber Offensive on the 13th with a raid on the Wiener Neustadt Bf 109 factory in Austria, which was defended by only the four Bf 109s of the *Werkschutzschwarm* (factory protection flight). The B-24s were also used to bomb several Italian targets before returning to England.

The raid on the Bf 109 plant caused extensive damage, and reduced output for two months. A Second Front of the strategic air offensive had been

opened. The Luftwaffe High Command scrambled to set up defenses for Austria, Hungary, and Czechoslovakia. Jagdfliegerführer Ostmark (Jafü Ostmark) was established as the fighter-control organization. Its first operational unit was I./JG 27, which transferred from Münster to Markersdorf. III./JG 27 was rebuilding in Vienna, and was to be brought up to operational status as quickly as possible. Both JG 27 Gruppen were Bf 109 units. Similar hurried orders were passed to the Bf 110-equipped II./ZG 1, which was resting in Lorient after heavy duty on the Italian front.[34]

The B-17 units in England were given some time after Blitz Week to rest and regain their strength. They returned to Germany on August 12 with an ineffective raid on Bochum and Bonn that cost 25 bombers. Their missions on the 15th and 16th were short-range, fully escorted raids on Luftwaffe bases in France, Belgium, and Holland. B-17s hit Vlissingen, Amiens, Poix, Lille-Vendeville, Vitry, Le Bourget, and Abbeville, while the medium B-26s went after St. Omer, Woensdrecht, Abbeville, Bernay, Beaumont, and Conches. The Fortress crews had no way of knowing it, but the purpose of these missions was to weaken the outer ring of Luftwaffe defenses for another deep-penetration raid, the most ambitious of the war to date.[35]

Only half of the airfields bombed on the 15th and 16th housed fighters at that time. JG 2's bases were hit hard, but the JG 26 Stab at Lille-Vendeville was the only part of that Geschwader to be bombed, and it simply moved next door to the small, well-concealed Lille-Nord field and continued operations. The Luftwaffe defensive commanders had done a limited amount of unit shuffling to prepare for day raids on the Reich industrial heartland, especially the Ruhr, but were still constrained by the official doctrine of

Day-Fighter Strength of Lw Bfh Mitte and LF 3, by Quarters[33]

Date	Command	Establishment Strength	Aircraft on Hand	Serviceable Aircraft
31 Dec 1942	Lw Bfh Mitte	164	179	146
	Luftflotte 3	308	291	220
31 Mar 1943	Lw Bfh Mitte	260	185	138
	Luftflotte 3	213	269	209
30 Jun 1943	Lw Bfh Mitte	512	387	301
	Luftflotte 3	404	353	252
30 Sep 1943	Lw Bfh Mitte	1,000	815	533
	Luftflotte 3	416	289	179

A Bf 109G-6 "gunboat" at Wiesbaden-Erbenheim in the summer of 1943, one of several displaying *Stammkenn-zeichnungen* (factory delivery codes) rather than unit markings. It is known from logbook evidence that these airplanes were flown by I./JG 300 on night missions; JG 50 may also have flown them during the day. (*Bundesarchiv 650-5438-15*)

peripheral defense. III./JG 26 pulled back from Nordholz, but only to Amsterdam-Schiphol. This was another base near the coast, but it was beneath the direct route to the Ruhr.

August 17—Schweinfurt–Regensburg[36]

Schweinfurt, which contained much of the German ball-bearing industry, and Regensburg, the principal production site for Messerschmitt fighters, were two of the top targets on the Combined Bomber Offensive list. Both cities were far beyond the range of American escorts, but the Eighth Air Force was under pressure to show immediate results, and General Anderson's staff devised an ambitious plan to bomb both targets on a single day. In the final version, the smaller, newer 4th Bomb Wing would take off first and head to Regensburg on the most direct route, escorted as far as the German border by all of the available P-47s. After bombing, it would continue south over the Alps and land in North Africa. The larger, more experienced 1st Bomb Wing would follow 15 minutes later, bomb Schweinfurt, and return to England; these B-17s would be seen home by the entire escort force, flying its second sortie. It was expected that the novelty and complexity of the combined mission would confuse the German controllers and exhaust their pilots. The greatest flaw in the plan, apart from its dependence on perfect weather and exact timing, arose from the limited range of the bombers of the 1st Bomb Wing, which forced them to take the most direct route to the target and return; this was a near-duplicate of the route to Regensburg as far as Schweinfurt. The German controllers would have to deal with three bomber formations flying on the same route on the

same day, which would hardly stretch their capabilities. Plans to concentrate the defending fighters along any deep-penetration course had been drawn up in the previous months. German pilots were now given briefings and maps describing the airfields to look for at the end of long one-way combat flights, and these airfields had been equipped to service them. This would facilitate second sorties by fighters arriving in the battle zone from the most distant bases.[37]

The English weather turned what was already a questionable mission into a disaster. The weather over western Europe was perfect that morning—except over the B-17 bases, which were fogged in. Plans were hastily changed. The 4th Bomb Wing needed daylight to land on unfamiliar fields in North Africa, and could thus only wait an hour, but would take off then. The escort plan was apparently changed at this time; only two P-47 groups went with the 4th Wing, while the other two waited for the 1st. The 1st Bomb Wing, which was inadequately trained in bad-weather takeoffs, delayed its mission for 3½ hours, as long as it could wait and still return to England before darkness. However, this was still not enough time for the P-47 escorts to return from their first mission, refuel and reload, and thus escort of the large outbound Schweinfurt force was left to only two P-47 groups, plus the short-range RAF Spitfires. Two P-47 groups, the 56th and the new 353rd, managed to fly two missions, supporting the outbound Regensburg and the returning Schweinfurt forces. Most of the German Jagdgruppen would have little difficulty flying two or even three missions.

The pre-dawn radio testing at the B-17 bases gave the German fighter controllers ample warning of a full-strength deep-penetration raid. The Jafü Holland-Ruhrgebiet, Oberst Walter Grabmann, operating from a villa near Arnhem, brought his seven Jagdgruppen to full readiness at 0800. He scrambled Hptm. Karl Borris's I./JG 26 from Woensdrecht at 1048, just as the Regensburg force had finished crossing the English coast. Within five minutes it was apparent that the B-17s were headed directly for the Dutch coast, and Hptm. Klaus Mietusch's III./JG 26 was ordered to take off from Schiphol. Several Bf 110 night fighters from I./NJG 1 and II./NJG 1 scrambled, under orders to hunt down any stragglers. II./JG 1 was kept on the ground at Woensdrecht while the B-17s passed directly overhead, probably because less than half of the American bombers had as yet been located. Borris began climbing to the east to gain a good attack position; Mietusch's men would already have the morning sun at their backs when they reached the bombers.[38]

The oncoming bomber force comprised 146 B-17s in a long formation of three combat wings, with a small escort of two 353rd Fighter Group squadrons. Borris was waiting up-sun and slightly above the bombers as they approached, in perfect position for an immediate head-on bounce. The skimpy fighter escort was apparently concentrated around the first combat wing; no P-47 pilot saw the Focke-Wulfs as they swept around in a left turn and hurtled toward the second combat wing. After flying through it, they hit the trailing wing and then broke away in all directions. Borris's own target, the last aircraft in the 94th Bomb Group box, burst into flames, sheered from the formation and dove to earth—the first loss of the day for either side. Several B-17s in the rear combat wing began to smoke from damaged engines. One Focke-Wulf was hit and dropped away to make a forced landing on Venlo. No other German fighter was seriously damaged during this attack. Jörg Kiefner, at that time a new Leutnant in the 3. Staffel, recalled:

We popped up through a thin cloud layer, and suddenly spotted a large number of Messers, small brothers from our III. Gruppe. I was too inexperienced

to make much sense of it all. As we reached 8,000 meters [26,000 ft.], suddenly there they were—the *dicken Autos* ["fat cars," the Luftwaffe code for heavy bombers]. First, Flak bursts, and then a thick cluster of bombers, to our left below us. We closed up a little, maintained a parallel course far from the bombers—150!—passed them, and banked around for the attack—my second on heavy bombers. We came down on them from the front and slightly above. The huge airplanes were quickly distinguished as individual targets—we aimed at the fuselage and the right engines. We fired, then ripped through the entire bunch lightning-quick—a fantastic moment. Some of the monsters had caught fire. I dodged their huge, shark-like tails with their large black code letters.[39]

Borris did not attempt to re-form his Gruppe for a second pass, but was content to let his pilots search for stragglers while awaiting landing orders from the Jafü. Jörg Kiefner continued his story:

I quickly turned—there was my [Staffelkapitän] Hermichen. I joined up—he was already banking toward two lone Boeings that had been shot up (by us?) and were turning back toward England. Attack from low rear, press in, pull up—in front of me was the

Fw. Werner Möszner (9./JG 26) poses beside his Bf 109G-6 (16394) "yellow 12" at Nordholz in August. He was shot down by a B-17 gunner on August 19, suffered severe burns, and did not return to JG 26. (*Möszner via Ivo de Jong*)

Chief—he wasn't going to leave the Boeing. I pressed in close, firing below and beside him at our opponent, who now hung in the air in front of us as large as a barn door. The airplane was soon burning brightly from our fire, from the fuselage and the right engines. After pulling off to the right, we banked in again, in a school-book position to attack from the rear. "Cease firing!" from Hermichen over the radio. The bomber was burning brightly along its entire fuselage—5–6 crewmen had already bailed out. Now our Boeing dove nose-first toward the ground, where it crashed—an unforgettable sight. I closed up on Hermichen again; Peter Ahrens was also in the area, having shot down the second Boeing. It crashed in many pieces between Antwerp and our field at Woensdrecht. We crossed the field side-by-side, Hermichen and Ahrens waggling their wings. After one circle, we dropped our gear and landed. After reporting briefly to their ground crews, Hermichen and Ahrens headed for the *Gefechtsstand*, the former somewhat embarrassed. His crew chief had told him that his cannon still had the tape on them, and had not been fired. H. had already claimed his *Abschuss*, but immediately signed a combat report as a witness to a *Herausschuss* to Ahrens, and the *endgultige Vernichtung* to me, since I had flown and fired so close to him.

Mietusch's Gruppe was the next to attack. Upon its arrival it bored in on the rear of the bomber stream, which was totally unprotected by fighters. The Messerschmitts formed up, turned, and attacked the rear wing head-on. Only one bomber was forced from the formation by this initial attack, but the German pilots came back in repeatedly over the next 15 minutes. Mietusch's combat philosophy was unlike that of the cautious Borris; he had ordered his pilots to keep up the attack until forced by damage, low fuel, or low ammunition to break off. They concentrated on the rear two combat wings. Three more damaged Fortresses dropped back, but bomber fire hit and killed one Messerschmitt pilot and forced a second to belly-land with wounds. A third bailed out without injury after a spectacular cartwheel through the rear B-17 *Pulk*.

One of the four B-17s that had dropped back from the 4th Bomb Wing's rear box was shot down by Fw. Werner Kraft of the 9. Staffel, who pulled alongside the crippled bomber to look it over and was then shot down by the right waist gunner, Sgt. William Binnebose, who met Kraft that evening in a Belgian hospital.[40]

The other three damaged B-17s were shot down by JG 26 Focke-Wulfs and Messerschmitts and the lurking NJG 1 Bf 110s. A close examination of the claims microfilms shows how complicated the bookkeeping could become for even a relatively simple combat. Eight B-17s left the formation before the German border was reached. One of these was definitely shot down by Flak, according to the surviving crewmen. Of the other seven, I./JG 26 was credited with three full victories; III./JG 26 was credited with one, plus two more that were awarded "jointly with" NJG 1—although in theory the Luftwaffe did not accept joint claims—and NJG 1 crews were given full credit for three, although all of their victims had already left their formations and according to the rules should have been only "final destructions." The record is silent with respect to sharing any of these claims with JG 26.

The 56th Fighter Group relieved the 353rd on schedule; its pilots saw only one German fighter. The German controller had seen the new fighters coming, and whisked his own fighters away and back to their bases. When the last P-47 turned back at Eupen, the way was clear for new Jafü Holland-Ruhrgebiet fighter units to continue the attacks without hindrance. I. and III./JG 1 made contact at 1150, near Aschaffenburg. I./JG 1 claimed three full victories and three separations, for no losses. III./JG 1 claimed one final destruction, and lost one Bf 109. Next to arrive were the Messerschmitts of I./JG 3, which claimed three B-17s for the loss of two fighters. Oberst Grabmann's other two units, II./JG 1 and III./JG 3, were scrambled but failed to make contact, and landed at Woensdrecht to await the bombers' return.

As soon as it became apparent that the bombers were on course for a target in western or southern Germany, Jafü Holland-Ruhrgebiet requested support from Jafü Deutsche Bucht, Jafü 2, and Jafü 3. There was still no formal coordination of the defenses, but such help was rarely withheld. JG 11 was ordered southwest from its north German bases to the Netherlands; JG 2 moved east from its bases in western France. All were too late to intercept the incoming bombers, and landed to refuel on airfields near the assumed withdrawal route, which was usually close to the incoming route.

The bombers entered the territory of Jafü Süddeutschland, which had only one day-fighter unit, Major Hermann Graf's JG 50, under its command. The bombers came within 32 km (20 miles) of its base at Wiesbaden-Erbenheim; all of its 26 Bf 109s were scrambled, and were joined by the *Einsatzschwärme* (operational flights) of nearby operational training units. They began their head-on attacks at around noon, and continued until 1250, after the bombers had completed their final turn toward Regensburg at the Initial Point. Only now was the target known. The Regensburg Industrieschutzstaffel (factory protection squadron) quickly scrambled its 12 Bf 109s and downed one B-17 before the bomb run.[41] Graf's men and the training unit pilots were credited with eight bombers; their own losses on this mission are unknown. The last fighters ordered up were from NJG 101, a night-fighter training unit. They were ordered to search out stragglers, and did succeed in downing two—a third claim was not confirmed—but most orbited north of the city waiting for the B-17s to complete their bomb run and reassemble for the return trip to England.

The 4th Bomb Wing finished bombing at 1307 and then, much to the Germans' surprise, turned south, where no defenses existed. The Americans were now en route to North Africa, and had to contend only with their previous damage, navigational difficulties, and their fuel supplies. They lost a total of 24 B-17s; of this number, 14 were shot down over the continent, two force-landed in Switzerland, four crash-landed in southern Europe, and four ditched in the Mediterranean off Tunisia; 50 more were damaged. All of Colonel LeMay's bomb groups were awarded the Presidential Unit Citation for the mission, which was judged a success; reconnaissance photos showed that serious damage had been done to the Messerschmitt plant.

The Jafü 2 and Jafü Holland-Ruhrgebiet controllers were puzzled by the non-arrival of the larger part of the B-17 force; the two American bombardment wings had always in the past coordinated their attacks to split the defenses, and the earlier radio tests indicated that the other bombers were coming. But they could not worry about them now. The B-26 and RAF diversion raids that ordinarily preceded the heavy bombers were now reported in the Channel. The enemy was coming across at such widely spaced intervals that these secondary forces, which were usually ignored, could be attacked. Five Allied formations headed for the Pas de Calais, where the three Staffeln of the JG 26 Geschwadergruppe were waiting. The interception was not a success; only one Typhoon was shot down, for the loss of one Messerschmitt and one Focke-Wulf to the Spitfire

escorts. The Spitfires also encountered part of II./JG 2, probably en route to its base for the afternoon mission, and lost one pilot to the *Richthofen* fighters.[42]

Major Wutz Galland's II./JG 26 was based on several fields around Beauvais. The Gruppe was scrambled before noon, possibly just to clear their airfields in case of a B-26 attack. It was not vectored to a target, and landed 45 minutes later to prepare for future action. The Gruppe was next ordered to fly from Beauvais to Lille-Nord. The reason for this move is unknown. Lille-Nord was closer to the presumed path of the next heavy bomber raid, still assembling over England, but it was a tiny field that usually held only a single Staffel, and was already hosting the JG 26 Geschwadergruppe. II. Gruppe landed at 1430, shortly after the B-17s began crossing the English coast, but could not be refueled in time to play a role in the interception of the incoming Schweinfurt force.

Even without it, Oberst Grabmann was in good condition to meet the long-delayed second B-17 force—which was following exactly in the track of the first. Thirteen Gruppen of single-engine fighters had been assembled along the Regensburg bombers' assumed return route; it was the largest defensive force yet seen over Europe. Now the effort would not go to waste.

The first radar report of the 230 B-17s of the Schweinfurt force reached the controllers at 1426. This formation had a larger fighter escort than its predecessor. Eight squadrons of Spitfires would accompany the B-17s as far as Antwerp. There they were to be relieved by two groups of P-47s, which could stay with the bombers as far as Eupen, on the Belgian side of the German border. Woensdrecht was once again on the bombers' path. The Focke-Wulfs of II./JG 1 and I./JG 26 had been reinforced with the Messerschmitts of III./JG 3, flying their first RLV mission. The Messerschmitts began taking to the air at 1430, and were the first to contact the bombers. The controller's orders took them over the North Sea, directly beneath the Spitfires of No. 222 Squadron. These promptly attacked, downing three Messerschmitts and dispersing the German formation beyond recovery. Hptm. Walther Dahl, the Gruppenkommandeur, blamed the Jafü, but the error was at least partly due to the unit's own inexperience in the western cauldron.

Lt. Kiefner of I./JG 26 looked forward to his second mission of the day with great anticipation. He recalled,

The airfield was full of fighters—the *Beulen* [Bf 109G-6s] took off first, then the Focke-Wulfs. We were last. After a while we [the three planes of 3./JG 26] became the *Holzauge-Kette* [cover detachment] above the whole gigantic horde of 75 fighters. I'd never seen us so strong, and couldn't get over a feeling of perfect confidence and security.

Fw. Peter Ahrens was leading the 3. Staffel trio, and tried to reach the bombers before the Spitfires turned back. Jörg Kiefner continued,

We were at 5,000 meters [16,400 ft.] when the *dicken Autos* came into sight—well below them, and in no kind of attack position. To the right of us were about 180 bombers, like three tightly packed bunches of grapes. Yelling in the radio, "Watch out! Escort fighters around!" Peter [Ahrens] sheered off to the right, just under the lowest *Pulk*, in order to come up on the other side, to make an undisturbed attack on the big *Haufen* [heap of bombers]. We were now flying alongside the Boeings—a nerve-wracking experience. A glance up to the left, and I shouted over the radio, "*Aufpassen, Indianer!*" Three Spitfires were pointed at us. I shouted again, "Peter, they're coming down!" as he flick-rolled lightning-quick to his left. Münch followed. I banked to the left, too slowly—my crate was soon coming apart. I scarcely noticed a light blow to my left knee. My wings sprouted cauliflowers; both ailerons flopped up and down; I found myself in a flat spin, which my movement of the stick couldn't control. So out! If only it was so simple . . . I was plastered onto the right side of the cockpit, scarcely able to move my arms. Somehow I pulled the canopy lever and ripped off my harness. I was still in a damned spin. I was now at 1,500 meters [5,000 ft.]—With a last push I came

free, and seconds later the wonderful white cloud blossomed above me . . .

Kiefner's knee contained a .303-inch machine-gun bullet, and he had hit his head on his airplane's tail when bailing out. After landing, he was taken to an Antwerp hospital by two Belgian farmers. After a brief convalescence; a briefer home leave; a stop at Kurheim Florida, the fighter pilots' rest home; and a tour in an operational training unit; he returned to the Gruppe in late December.

The Spitfires turned back at Antwerp. One of the two P-47 groups, the 4th, missed rendezvous, and never reached its assigned position over the leading combat wings. The other unit, the 78th Fighter Group, carried out its escort of the rear B-17 wings exactly as ordered. It saw little combat, as the two Focke-Wulf Gruppen had already found the unprotected van of the bomber stream. They were able to prepare well-coordinated head-on attacks in the undisturbed air ahead of the formation. Once the cohesiveness of the leading wing had been broken, successive attacks sought it out as the least well-defended part of the bomber stream, in accord with the usual German pattern. Other preferred targets were bombers in the highest or lowest positions in the box formations, which were not as well covered by neighboring gunners. The American crews gave the name "coffin corner" to the low squadron position in a low box.

Borris's I./JG 26 stayed with the bombers far longer than on their earlier mission, and claimed four bombers before breaking away with low fuel; two claims were confirmed. Their only casualties were Kiefner and a brand-new pilot who flew as far as Koblenz before running out of fuel; he was killed attempting to make a dead-stick landing. II./JG 1 first attacked head-on by Schwärme in order of Staffeln, and then made repeated follow-up attacks. It claimed six B-17s downed and separated from formation;

General der Flieger Günther Korten. As Luftwaffe Chief of Staff, he presided over the dramatic increase in RLV fighter strength in 1943–4. A strong supporter of the "defensive clique," Korten worked with Milch and Galland to shore up the Reich's defenses while at the same time preserving the Luftwaffe's offensive striking power. Korten is shown here in command of Luftflotte 1 in Russia in mid-1943, shortly before being named to succeed Jeschonnek after the latter's August 1943 suicide. (*Author's collection*)

confirmed victories. One Messerschmitt was shot down, and three sustained damage, but none of their pilots was injured. Other units claiming victories were I. and III./JG 1; I./JG 3; Stab, I., II., and III./JG 11; JG 50; and NJG 101. The most successful were I./JG 11 and JG 50, each of which was awarded six victory confirmations. Several Staffeln carried underwing WGr 21 rockets, which were extremely tricky to use in the briefed head-on attacks. Oblt. Heinz Knoke led his 5./JG 11 in a head-on rocket attack on a low box—probably the 92nd Bomb Group—in a rear combat wing. Knoke was hit in the wing by defensive fire, causing one rocket to fire prematurely. He missed with the other, and dove away to examine his damage. The rest of his Staffel claimed two direct hits, but their targets did not leave their formations, and the claims were not filed.[43]

The fighter attacks slackened when the B-17s began their bomb run on Schweinfurt. JG 50, which was the single-engine unit closest to its home base, was probably the last to break contact. Bombs were dropped from 1559 to 1611. For a variety of reasons that need not be addressed here, no bomb group hit its target, even in conditions of cloudless skies and light Flak. Overall results were characterized as "very poor." Three B-17s from low groups were damaged sufficiently by the Flak to leave their formations; none reached England. The night fighters did an effective job of hunting down stragglers, receiving credit for five. A reconnaissance pilot joined the hunt, and was credited with one B-17.

The surviving bombers re-formed their defensive boxes and took up a return course to the north of their inbound route. The Americans credited this route with confusing the defenders; only a few fighters were seen by the bomber crews until they neared the Belgian border. In reality, the Germans were as exhausted as the Americans. Attacks by single-engine units flying their second or third sorties were weak in strength and tentative. I./JG 1 claimed three victories in this period; two were confirmed. I./JG 3 also claimed two. I./NJG 6 scrambled six Bf 110s from Mainz-Finthen, under orders to attack intact combat boxes rather than stragglers. One Kette made a formation attack on the trailing, low 303rd Bomb Group from 6 o'clock low, approaching to close range, as was customary when attacking RAF night bombers. They were sitting ducks for the B-17 tail and ball-turret gunners, who shot all three down; only two of the six crewmen survived. The other Kette approached the 379th Bomb Group more

Genmaj. Joseph "Beppo" Schmid, the underrated commander of I. Jagdkorps, the most important operational command in the RLV from its establishment in September. He worked tirelessly to enlarge, centralize, and improve the efficiency of the air defenses. (*Cranston*)

three claims were confirmed. It lost four Fw 190s in crashes or crash-landings; one pilot suffered serious injuries.

Oberst Grabmann timed the approach of most of his defenders so that they contacted the bombers immediately after the P-47s turned back at the German border, as expected. For the next two hours, the bombers were battered by fighters from ten Jagdgruppen, an intensity of attack far in excess of anything previously experienced. Mietusch's III./JG 26 is typical. It took off from Schiphol at 1439 under orders to head southeast, toward Germany. They reached the bomber stream near Aachen and stayed in contact for 30 minutes, claiming four gingerly; they shot down one previously damaged B-17, while losing none of their number.[44]

Formation leaders who had landed away from their own bases to refuel were under orders to improvise attack units from the pilots they found there. Oblt. Knoke had landed his damaged Bf 109 on Bonn-Hangelar, where it was diagnosed as having a cracked main wing spar. He gathered a small band of Bf 109 and Fw 190 pilots and led them up in his damaged fighter to find the bomber stream. He concentrated on stragglers, and the maneuvers of his crippled bird were cautious enough to be noticed by the crew of his target, a 305th Bomb Group B-17. He was able to shoot it down, but was himself hit; his engine quit at low altitude, and he was forced to make a crash-landing that according to Knoke left "nothing intact but the tail wheel." One of his sleeves was blood-soaked from a shrapnel wound, but he returned to Jever the following day in the Gruppe utility airplane.[45]

The controllers were counting heavily on the attack of the only fresh Gruppe left in the area, Wutz Galland's II./JG 26. At 1650 Galland led his three Staffeln up from Lille-Nord and flew southeast, along the reciprocal of the bombers' return course. Obstlt. Priller also scrambled with the JG 26 Stabsschwarm and the 8. Staffel, but Galland, who led the larger unit, probably held the tactical command. They met the bomber stream head-on, just east of the Belgian border, and attacked the third of the three combat wings. Priller's target began to burn. Galland then re-formed as much of his Gruppe as he could and led it toward the front of this half of the formation, for a second head-on attack.

At this moment the Germans were stunned by fighters attacking from their rear—from the direction of Germany. Colonel Hub Zemke had led his "Wolfpack," the P-47s of the 56th Fighter Group, farther east than they had ever flown before, 24 km (15 miles) beyond the German border. He had reached the rendezvous point exactly on time and course, but had then overflown the B-17 formation, unobserved by the German attackers, who were thus set up for a surprise attack. Wutz Galland disappeared after the initial Thunderbolt bounce; the screamed warning of his wingman, Uffz. Heinz Gomann, could not save him. Gomann's fighter was also hit. He managed to jump out, but got hung up on his plane's tail; he broke free just above the ground and was knocked out when he landed. After regaining con-

sciousness he found that he had suffered only "slight injuries," but was nevertheless granted three weeks' home leave to recover. A third member of Galland's Stabsschwarm was damaged on the same pass, and put down on Brussels-Evere; two more II./JG 26 pilots force-landed with damage. Galland's remains were discovered two months later, buried with the wreckage of his aircraft 3.5 meters (12 ft.) deep in the soft soil near Maastricht.[46]

One of the three JG 2 Gruppen reached the bomber stream at this time and made a successful attack. This was Hptm. Kurt Bühligen's II./JG 2, which was credited with four B-17s, one of them shared. However, Zemke's sudden arrival broke up the attacks of several more German formations that were forced to turn on the Thunderbolts. After the prolonged battle the 56th returned to England claiming 7–0–1 Fw 190s, 4–1–1 Bf 109s, and 5–0–7 twin-engine fighters, while losing three P-47s and pilots. The Focke-Wulfs were from I./JG 1 as well as II./JG 26. One Bf 109 was from JG 50. The twin-engine fighters were all Bf 110 night fighters from I./NJG 1., which lost four to the Thunderbolts and one to Spitfires. Two of the lost P-47s were engaged in an attack on the Bf 110s when they were bounced by III./JG 3 Bf 109s and shot down; Hptm. Dahl's pilots claimed three Thunderbolts, redeeming themselves after their failure against the Spitfires on their previous mission. The third P-47 lost was flying high cover when it was bounced from above and downed by a pair of German fighters that dove away.

When the 56th Group was relieved by the 353rd after the most successful escort mission to date by an American fighter group, there were no large Luftwaffe formations in the area; the remaining German fighters were scattered far and wide, searching for stragglers. Obfw. Adolf "Addi" Glunz of II./JG 26 was the last German pilot to make a successful attack on the bomber stream after the arrival of the escort. Calmly sticking to his orders despite the chaos around him, he maintained contact with the bombers, and finally shot down a 305th Bomb Group B-17 northwest of Diest, attacking "alone, head-on, and with a P-47 on his ass," in the words of Ed Burford, an admiring B-17 crewman.[47] Another II./JG 26 pilot and one from III./JG 3 downed straggling Fortresses near the coast, ending the day's confirmed victories against the *Viermots*.

As soon as the reconnaissance photographs were received on the evening of the 17th, Generals Eaker and Anderson knew that the Schweinfurt raid had been a failure. The excellent results at Regensburg were but small consolation for the loss of 60 B-17s, 16 percent of those dispatched. The losses could not be hidden from USAAF headquarters or the U.S. press, but the results of the bombing were exaggerated, and the poor operational plan that guaranteed the high losses was well disguised in the after-mission reports. No general lost his job as a result of the Schweinfurt–Regensburg mission. The lessons learned were mixed. Everyone who flew the mission stressed the importance of the escorts in reducing losses; the planners grasped only that Schweinfurt would have to be bombed again, soon, in another deep-penetration, unescorted mission.

The lessons learned by the defenders were also mixed. Based purely on the numbers, the fighters of the RLV had scored an outstanding success. The OKW communiqué claimed 101 heavy bombers and five fighters shot down. Claims for 87 bombers and seven fighters were ultimately confirmed, somewhat above the Allies' true losses, but close enough to prevent any misinterpretation of the results. As usual, performance of the various units making up the RLV varied widely. JG 26 had one of its best days of the war, with 15 confirmed B-17 and two confirmed fighter claims, against five pilots killed in action (KIA) and six wounded in action (WIA). JG 50, with less than one-third of the pilot establishment of JG 26, did almost as well, with 12 confirmed B-17 claims for the loss of two pilots killed. (Of course, Graf's unit had had the advantage of attacking unescorted formations.) Other units were entirely shut out. I./JG 2 and III./JG 2 reached the battle area in strength, but then disappeared. And Priller and Hptm. Förster of NJG 1 filed a formal complaint with the office of the General der Jagdflieger denouncing the pilots of III./JG 1 as *Leichenfledderei* ("corpse-looters") for failing to make a single concerted attack. After reaching the bomber stream, these pilots had immediately split up to look for stragglers. The difference between the good and the poor-performing units can be summarized as combat leadership and experience. Unfortunately for Germany, the RLV was always short of both.[48]

The defenders lost about 40 fighters on the 17th, nine of which were night fighters, which would soon be leaving the day order of battle, replaced by the Zerstörergeschwader equipped with twin-engine Bf 110 and Me 410 day fighters. These had powerful weapons that would increase the killing power of the

RLV. Their success would be dependent on the absence of American fighters. They could either stay outside the range of the P-47s or operate under an escort umbrella provided by single-engine German fighters. The Bf 109 and Fw 190 units being added to the RLV were intended as bomber destroyers; escort duties violated current doctrine, as did any mention of battling Allied fighters at the expense of maximum-strength attacks on the bomber stream. Future success of the Reich defenses was thus predicated on the assumption that USAAF escorts had already reached their maximum range. When Galland tried to tell Göring that Thunderbolts had crossed the German border on the 17th, the proof being several crashes near Aachen, Göring cursed the report as "*Hirngespinste schlapper Defaitisten*" ("rantings of a worn-out defeatist") and gave Galland an "order" that Allied fighters had never penetrated German airspace. A rational defensive strategy was impossible under such a commander-in-chief.[49]

Hitler and Göring appeared to find fault with the RLV for allowing any day bombers to reach southern Germany. The peripheral defense that these two men had ordered, and the weakness of the Luftwaffe fighter arm relative to the bomber arm, which had been mandated by the same men, certainly brought the fairness of such charges into question. The night after Schweinfurt–Regensburg, RAF Bomber Command made an extremely damaging raid on the rocket testing facility at Peenemünde, setting the V-2 project back by months. The following morning Hitler upbraided Jeschonnek for another failure. Jeschonnek committed suicide the same night, leaving behind a note reproaching Göring while praising the Führer. Jeschonnek's belief in an offensive strategy had been enthusiastic and unquestioning; he had helped to block every attempt to switch Luftwaffe priorities to the defense of the homeland. In an excellent example of the opportunism that was the rule among the upper command, Milch took the occasion of Jeschonnek's death to persuade Göring to increase the rate of return of fighter units from the land battle fronts to the Reich.[50]

Korten Takes the Helm

With Jeschonnek dead, the Luftwaffe would need a new Chief of Staff to guide it through its greatest crisis since the war began. An obvious choice was GFM Wolfram von Richthofen, one of the few senior Luftwaffe field commanders who still had Hitler's unqualified endorsement. Göring would never have tolerated such a strong-willed character in the key post, however, so the choice fell to a more congenial, highly capable yet less prominent air fleet commander, General der Flieger Günther Korten.[51]

Korten, like his predecessor, walked a tightrope. He was actively sympathetic to Milch and Galland, who maintained that the air defense of the homeland must have the highest priority. One Luftwaffe general recalled that Korten staunchly "stood by Galland although Galland at that time was *persona non grata*."[52] Korten and the "defensive clique" found unexpected allies in the Gauleiters, the powerful Nazi Party district governors, who wanted protection for their cities from the Anglo-American air assault. Yet, at the same time, Korten had to fulfill the wishes of the Reichsmarschall, who had promised Hitler a "new Luftwaffe" capable once again of carrying the fight to the enemy from a position of technological superiority.[53]

Korten did his best to meet the challenge. He put into place a complete restructuring of the Luftwaffe command the better to meet the demands of global war, and sought to streamline and reorient the Luftwaffe toward a few key missions.[54] Over the objections of the Army, he ordered the transfer of single- and twin-engine fighter units from the eastern and southern fronts and added them to the RLV. Himself a believer in the potential of strategic bombing, he concentrated the Luftwaffe's bomber forces into a single strong Fliegerkorps in each major war theater—Fliegerkorps IV in the east, Fliegerkorps IX in the west—and built up other bomber units for special tasks (anti-shipping, torpedo, and path-finder).[55] Finally, he greatly expanded the ground-attack arm on the Eastern Front, creating the post of *General der Schlachtflieger* (General of Ground-Attack Aviation) thereby rescuing tactical aviation from the clutches of the fighter and bomber inspectorates where it had been dying of neglect.[56]

Korten and his able Chief of Operations, General Karl Koller, a dour Bavarian who had risen from the ranks, were aware that time was their enemy. Yet Korten firmly believed that that "airpower [was] the solution to the puzzle" facing the Third Reich.[57] A strengthened and reorganized round-the-clock home-defense organization would deflect the USAAF and RAF Bomber Command from Germany's cities and vital production centers, allowing Speer's industrial miracle to proceed apace. Powerful attacks on Soviet

The Jagddivision 2 command bunker, code-named Sokrates. It was located at Schwarzenberg near Stade and played an important role in the defense of the Reich from its completion in mid-1943. Designed for Kammhuber's night-defense control system, Schmid considered it too large and unwieldy for the day defenses, but it remained in use into 1945. (*Cranston*)

war industry would ease the pressure on the German Army, while the revived ground-attack arm would restore the Army's confidence in the Luftwaffe. Korten and his staff briefed General Staff departments, operational commands, captains of industry, and Nazi Party agencies on the ambitious reforms—the coming "Russia Action," the intensification of the air war over the Atlantic, renewed strategic attacks on London, and the strengthening of the RLV.[58] Unlike Jeschonnek, Korten enjoyed the confidence and public backing of his chief; Göring in early September endorsed Korten's strategy almost verbatim.[59] Time would tell if Korten's plans, well thought out and energetically pursued, would prove more attainable than those of his predecessor.

Priorities, Production, Training

Göring's and Korten's "new Luftwaffe" was an ambitious project, and realizing the vision placed extraordinary demands on the German aircraft industry. In the last months of his tenure Jeschonnek had consented to an increase in day-fighter production, and Milch energetically pursued this goal. Yet at the same time the bomber arm required reconstitution, and was also demanding improved new types such as the Ju 188 and He 177 to carry out the offensive portions of the new strategy. Particularly after the Hamburg disaster in late July, prominent bomber commanders lobbied Göring for an expansion of their force. Bomber production remained high throughout 1943 and into 1944, consuming scare raw materials, factory floor space and skilled workers. Yet in spite of these distractions, the "defensive clique" made progress. In 1943 a total of

THE LUFTWAFFE OVER GERMANY

29,132 front-line aircraft became available from factories and repair establishments; 13,854 were single-engine fighters and twin-engine day and night fighters, 47.6 percent of total output. In 1942, fighters had made up only 31.7 percent of total output.[60] This represented a monumental shift in Luftwaffe operational thinking.

Just to keep pace with losses, the German aircraft industry faced a formidable challenge. Total fighter losses for 1943 were 8,286 single-engine fighters, 1,363 twin-engine day fighters, and 1,012 night fighters. Losses to the single-engine day-fighter forces had been especially heavy from July through September, when 2,804 fighters were lost.[61] Some of the fighter units in the Mediterranean lost their entire complement of aircraft twice over during the campaign, and the increasingly capable Soviet Air Force coupled with the primitive operating conditions of the Eastern Front ensured that Luftwaffe losses in that theater never slackened.[62]

There was a growing sense within the Luftwaffe leadership that the existing single-engine fighter types, the Bf 109 and Fw 190, were verging on obsolescence, although constant modifications and upgrades attempted to wring every last ounce of performance from the proven designs. Milch made it clear at an aircraft production conference on August 25 that numbers of aircraft, not technological superiority, were what mattered:

If we put twice as many fighters in the air, the number of successes will be at least twice as high. If we have four times as many fighters, the number of successes will be at least four times as high. But if we shoot down at least four times as many heavy bombers as now— and that is no astronomical figure, about 700 fighters would be required, which is less than one month's output—then I swear the daylight raids would have to stop.[63]

Galland, although he later became a staunch champion of advanced aviation technology, at this point agreed with Milch's logic. In response to a question from Hitler regarding what it would take to stop USAAF daylight penetrations, Galland stated:

To protect Germany we must have three to four times as many fighters as the enemy bombers. If the enemy escort strength continues to increase, the German side must have an [equal increase in] strength at least in order first to wage the battle for air superiority as the first condition for combat action against the bombers.[64]

Milch went on to note: "We must definitely decide on priorities. That means the 109, the 190 and the 110." Other more advanced types, such as the jet projects, would take a lower priority. The answer was clear; in the short term at least, quality had to give way to quantity.

Milch and Speer's achievements in obtaining the necessary production increases are well known, and remain one of the most remarkable economic and industrial accomplishments of the Second World War.[65] In 1943 German factories and repair facilities produced a total of 11,241 single-engine and 2,613 twin-engine fighters for the Luftwaffe. These figures included 8,497 Bf 109s, 2,744 Fw 190s, and 1,687 Bf 110s, 926 of which were day-fighter versions.[66] Their work, coupled with Korten's policies, was undoubtedly responsible for the steady increase in Lw Bfh Mitte's fighter strength in the second half of 1943.[67] Luftwaffe fighter strength in the combat units totaled 1,348 on December 31, 1942, and rose to 2,042 by September 30, with 916 assigned to Weise's command and 372 to Sperrle's.[68] On the surface, the production figures should have fueled an even greater surge in front-line strength, but combat attrition remained high throughout the second half of 1943, and much of the new output had to go to the front to replace combat losses. Some of the fighter production went to the training establishments or to equip the air arms of Germany's Eastern Front satellites. Other factors, such as lack of spare parts, low serviceability, and pilot output, placed a ceiling on RLV fighter force expansion. Nevertheless, Milch and Speer envisioned even more spectacular production increases for 1944.

The Luftwaffe fighter force's training situation mirrored that of aircraft production: an impressive surge in numbers masking weaknesses in quality and sustainability. German personnel losses in 1943 included 2,967 single-engine and 446 twin-engine day-fighter pilots. Predictably, the heaviest losses in single-engine fighter pilots (1,006) occurred during the same period as the heaviest aircraft losses—the third quarter of 1943. The fierce air battles in the Kursk/Orel sector of the U.S.S.R., the Sicily campaign, and the increasing tempo of home air-defense operations all took their toll.

The command and control side of the Jagddivision 2 command bunker (Sokrates), photographed from the 14 meter-high frosted-glass map that split the "Battle Opera House" down the middle. The two men in the center are at the desk of the division commander and his communications officer. The ground-to-air controllers will fill the two staggered rows in front. (*Cranston*)

Despite formidable obstacles, including a lack of fuel, a shortage of both basic training aircraft (Ar 96, Fw 58) and operational types for conversion training (Bf 109, Ju 88), the training establishments rose to the challenge. General Werner Kreipe, chief of Luftwaffe training, noted that although there were, for example, only 178 Bf 109 aircraft assigned to the fighter schools (against an establishment of 480) in October 1943, pilot output nevertheless increased. While only 1,662 single-engine fighter pilots were trained during 1942, 3,276 were turned out during 1943;[69] 371 Zerstörer pilots also completed training, as did 1,358 night-fighter pilots.[70] Kreipe attributed this success to, among other things, "the effective exploitation of aircraft and personnel to a degree hitherto deemed impossible. New records had been broken in aircraft hours."[71]

As we have seen, fuel shortages during early 1943 had already caused a reduction in training time for fighter pilots.[72] In 1943, single-engine day-fighter trainees were expected to have a total of 138 flight-training hours (88 in basic "A" and "B" schools, 50 in fighter schools). Forty-seven of these total hours consisted of blind-flying training. Zerstörer pilots received 204 flight-training hours, or almost as much as a night-fighter pilot (218). Successful trainees would then spend two to four months in one of the three advanced-fighter-training groups: Ergänzungs-gruppen Ost, West, or Süd.[73] By way of comparison, this was less than half of what USAAF or RAF pilots could expect to receive. USAAF fighter pilot trainees in 1943 could count on at least 200 hours of primary, basic and advanced flight training, followed by a much more rigorous program of transition, gunnery, and operational training.[74]

This output was enough to replace losses, and then some; it appealed to the statisticians of the Luftwaffe General Staff just as it fueled Kreipe's organizational pride.[75] Yet this achievement failed to fulfill the desires of Korten, Milch and Galland to increase the home-defense fighter strength. As Grabmann concluded:

> Numerically, the training output was amply large enough to meet the requirements for the replacement of losses in personnel for the single-engine and twin-engine day fighter forces, and for the twin-engine night fighter forces. However, the training output was not adequate to meet the cumulative requirements for increased authorized strengths, assignments to bring actual up to authorized figures, and assignments to newly activated units.[76]

The surge in fighter-pilot training Kreipe and his staff engineered during 1943 to make good the losses of Tunisia, Kursk, Sicily and the RLV was a remarkable feat, entirely comparable to the advances Milch was making in aircraft production. Kreipe claimed that, in 1943, "precautionary measures were taken which made it possible to make immediate allowances and modifications required by current conditions."[77] Yet the success masked the fact that the Luftwaffe's training establishments were only just keeping pace with losses. Their limited output precluded expansion, and the quality of aircrew they were supplying was dubious. Both the Luftwaffe fighter force's industrial base and its personnel supply rested on unstable foundations. As one Luftwaffe general said of Galland: "He could eradicate the mistakes of technical development of earlier years, or the defects in training, just as little as one can ask a man who is hanging from the gallows to take a deep breath."[78] Spring 1944 would bring these shortcomings into the glaring light of day.

Centralization of the Defenses

The weakened Eighth Air Force flew only six missions in the 19 days following Schweinfurt–Regensburg, all to targets in France and the Low Countries. Its next mission to Germany came on September 6. This was a disastrous deep-penetration raid on Stuttgart that cost 45 heavy bombers, plus ten write-offs. The more optimistic of the German defensive commanders were convinced that their continuing improvements in equipment, strength, tactics, and organization had checked the Americans; even so a fundamental reorganization of the day defenses was long overdue. The process began in early September, when Genmaj. Josef "Beppo"

Genlt. Walter Schwabedissen (*left*), Kommandeur of Jagddivision 2, greets Major Reimers, the Jever airfield commandant, after exiting his Fw 189 for an inspection of II./JG 11 in September. (*Heinz Rose via Arno Rose*)

Schmid relieved General der Flieger Kammhuber as commander of XII. Fliegerkorps, which had been nominally responsible for all defensive fighters in Germany since its formation in 1941. In practice, control of day-fighter operations had devolved to the Jafü staffs, while Kammhuber's XII. Fliegerkorps ran the night-fighter defense operations through the air division headquarters. Schmid immediately began advocating a similar centralization of the day fighters.

The RLV Jagddivision boundaries, as of September 14, are shown on page 119.[79] The formal unification of the RLV fighter command finally took place the next day, in the most significant Luftwaffe reorganization of the war. Schmid was named commander of the new I. Jagdkorps at Zeist.[80] His mission was "direction of day- and night-fighter forces and activities in the northern areas of Germany, Holland and northern Belgium." The new Korps became the principal operational flying command in Lw Bfh Mitte, controlling the day and night fighters based in the geographical areas of the three Jagddivisionen in northern and western Germany. Several of the Jagddivisionen were re-numbered at this time, apparently for geographic consistency. Jagddivision 4 in Berlin became Jagddivision 1; Jagddivision 2 in Hamburg-Stade was unchanged; Jagddivision 1 in Deelen became Jagddivision 3. In the south, Jagddivision 5, which continued to report directly to Lw Bfh Mitte, became Jagddivision 7.

The Jagdfliegerführer officers who had previously served as the tactical controllers lost that authority to the Jagddivisionen, and were phased out of existence entirely before the end of the year. As one former Jafü noted:

> The reason for this measure was the desire to establish clearly defined command responsibility for daytime and nighttime fighter operations. Since day and night operations were directed from one and the same centralized command post, so that overall responsibility rested with the division command anyhow, it had been found impossible to continue the system under which command authority had been divided between the Jagddivision commander and the Jafü concerned. If the Jagddivision commander was to perform his responsibilities to the fullest extent, it was essential for him to direct operations whenever enemy aircraft penetrated, whether during the day or at night.[81]

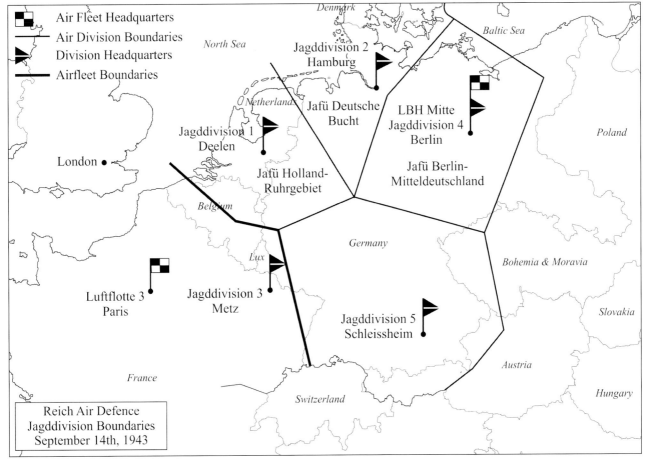

Air Fleet Headquarters
Air Division Boundaries
Division Headquarters
Airfleet Boundaries

Denmark
Baltic Sea
North Sea
Jagddivision 2
Hamburg
Netherlands
Jafü Deutsche
Bucht
LBH Mitte
Jagddivision 4
Berlin
Poland
Jagddivision 1
Deelen
Jafü Berlin-
Mitteldeutschland
London
Jafü Holland-
Ruhrgebiet
Belgium
Germany
Bohemia & Moravia
Lux
Luftflotte 3
Paris
Jagddivision 3
Metz
Jagddivision 5
Schleissheim
Slovakia
France
Austria
Hungary
Switzerland

Reich Air Defence
Jagddivision Boundaries
September 14th, 1943

Field Marshal Sperrle of Luftflotte 3 successfully resisted the trend toward defensive centralization. He retained full control of his fighters, arguing to Göring that his Luftflotte was an indivisible whole and that his fighter units fulfilled a vital offensive, as well as a defensive function. On September 15, they were put under a new II. Jagdkorps at Chantilly near Paris, which was given two Jagddivisionen: the 4th (ex-Jagddivision 3), headquartered at Metz, and the 5th (ex-Jafü West), based in Paris. All that Lw Bfh Mitte was able to wrest from Sperrle was control of the air-reporting and Flak assets of Luftgaue VII (Munich) and XII/XIII (Wiesbaden). On November 1, 1943, these air districts were transferred from Luftflotte 3 to Weise.[82] The line separating Luftflotte 3 from Lw Bfh Mitte ran through the middle of Belgium and then roughly along the French–German border. Eighth Air Force raids on Germany, especially to central and southern Germany, thus crossed the territories of both air fleets, and defensive command and control problems persisted; these ended only with the

expulsion of the Wehrmacht from the western occupied zone in 1944.

Several documents from late summer and fall 1943 describe the evolution of RLV defensive tactics. In August Galland distributed a brief memo to the Jagdfliegerführer giving Göring's edict to all single- and twin-engine fighter units engaging day-bomber formations:

1. Only bombers in formation are to be attacked, without regard for whether they are inbound or outbound.
2. Individual bombers are to be attacked only after the entire formation has been broken up or there is no other possibility of engagement.
3. Nebelwerfer-Flugzeuge [WGr 21 aircraft] are permitted to attack stragglers after successfully firing their rockets—no other exceptions allowed.
4. Formation leaders and pilots who violate these orders are subject to court-martial on the grounds of military disobedience with severe consequences to the security of the Reich.[83]

THE LUFTWAFFE OVER GERMANY

The August monthly report of XII. Fliegerkorps has survived, and contains a very important list of the month's tactical lessons for dealing with large-scale day incursions. The report is signed by Kammhuber, although it reads very much as if it had been written by Schmid. Its major points were:

1. In August the enemy clearly moved the *Schwerpunkt* [main focus] of his daylight attacks to targets in southern and southwestern Germany—these were escorted up to 200 km [125 miles] inland.
2. Attacks were made in close-formation waves, each of 70–80 bombers.
3. Our intention was to split up the lead formations with Zerstörer [a theoretical intention only; the Zerstörergeschwader did not join the RLV until September].
4. Attacks on four-engine aircraft from the front were again proven to be the most successful and suffered the fewest losses. On August 17:
   a) One Gruppe attacking from the front shot 18 enemy bombers from formation, losing two.
   b) Another Gruppe attacked from the rear and scored only one *Herausschuss*.
5. Defense against attacks on Germany requires long-ranging, centrally controlled fighters.
6. As in night fighting, day fighters must converge on a selected *Abschwerpunkt* [concentration point] in *Sternflugen* [literally star flights; rallies starting from divergent points].
7. The meager range of the defending fighters must be improved by accelerating the production of auxiliary tanks.
8. The introduction of *Fühlungshalter* must be accelerated. Me 210s and Ju 88s with crews with the best navigational training and complete communications equipment (FuG 16Y) are needed; the present use of Bf 110s with FuGX and Piel G-V is an emergency measure only.
9. The increased penetration depth of the heavy bombers, and the increasing range of their fighters, make it necessary to consider the entire Reich, including the western occupied region, as a single defensive zone.
10. The effectiveness of the defense must be increased. On August 17, one wave was followed by a second; of 500 aircraft, 80 were shot down, but this was insufficient to prevent the targets from being bombed.
11. Attacks in Geschwader strength led by a Kommodore are necessary to annihilate individual enemy formations; only this will break their willingness to attack.

12. The ability of the ground organization to service arriving fighters must be improved. There are difficulties in supplying ammunition to all airfields—for example, both electrical and mechanical feeds—also, there are insufficient personnel to belt the rounds. Critical airfields will be designated as *Jagdstützpunkte* [fighter support points]; all other airfields will at least be provided with fuel to facilitate flying to the next *Jagdstutzpunkt*.
13. Bf 110s fly too slowly and are too large to be anything but a stopgap. Bf 110 day missions are only successful against separated bombers.
14. Increasing attacks on airfields [now by heavy bombers as well as mediums and fighters] make it necessary to erect dispersals near all fields, which makes operations from coastal fields extraordinarily difficult, as there is insufficient time to make Gruppe takeoffs and climb to battle altitudes.
15. The fact that enemy formations are heavily escorted when they cross the coast, and the lack of time to assemble effective formations, make it necessary to move the main strength of the fighter defense farther inland, outside the range of enemy fighters. In many cases it is not tactically correct to oppose pure fighter sweeps in the coastal regions.
16. The Y-process for command and control [using the FuG 16ZY] works well, but a minimum of 12 aircraft per Gruppe need to be equipped with the apparatus.

The same report makes the following points with regard to day-fighter equipment:

1. Bf 109s and Fw 190s are being equipped with 21-cm Wurfgranaten [WGr 21s] as quickly as possible.
2. The MK 108 3-cm cannon in the Bf 109G-6/U-4 has proven itself; it has unequaled destructive capacity.
3. Drop tanks are available for Fw 190s and Bf 110s; equipment of Bf 109s has been delayed by supply problems.
4. The "Day and Night" Revi 16B gunsight in new Bf 109G-6s is unacceptable due to its lack of padding; until made removable for crash landings, aircraft have been re-equipped with the Revi 12D sight.
5. The Bf 109G-5/U-2 [high altitude fighter with GM-1 (nitrous oxide) injection] has proven unsuccessful: it is unstable in all flight attitudes; it gives off a light smoke trail at 10,000 meters [33,000 ft.]; its windshield (specially armored glass) ices up during dives; its pressure equipment, especially the compressor, is very unreliable and extremely difficult to obtain parts for;

servicing is extremely time-consuming; alarm takeoffs require three groundcrewmen per airplane.

The report also discusses air victory accounting. It is possible for modern historical studies to over-emphasize air victories and the *Ziffernkult* (cult of numbers), but a fair and accurate system was important, not only for morale, but to quantify the effectiveness of the defenses. The report claimed that the regulations in force were inadequate, and recommended this procedure:

1. On the day of the mission, the Gruppen-kommandeure should report claims to the Jafü as
   a) *sicher* [certain], those claims with unassailable witnesses.
   b) *wahrscheinlich* [probable], those sepa-rations from formation with no report of final destruction by other units, ground, etc.
2. The reports of the Gruppen shall be submitted to the Division as "provisional."
3. The Geschwaderkommodoren shall check the *Abschussmeldungen* [victory reports], especially for double claims; this will take several days.
4. The Jafü Ia's [operations officers] shall collect crash reports from the Luftgau Kommandos [Luftwaffe administrative area commands].
5. A *Kommission* will compare the victory reports to the crash sites, and should have a clear picture of the true numbers in 5–8 days. The *Kommission* must be of such a composition that its investigations are considered accurate by all sides.[84]

The number of claims by RLV pilots ultimately confirmed by the RLM was, and remained, higher than the number of crashes, despite the efforts of the *Abschuss-kommissionen*. These discrepancies grew in the following months as the scale of the battles grew larger and the number of units involved increased.

General Galland apparently attended this important XII. Fliegerkorps staff meeting, and incorporated its some of its conclusions in a tactical regulation that his office issued on September 3. While this document was only advisory, it is critical to an understanding of the leadership's expectations for the RLV during this period. Its key provisions were:

1. It is critical that a single attack wave is formed, with maximum strength. Timely cooperation with neighboring and rear Jagddivisionen is very important.
2. Attacks must be made by at least two Gruppen, led by the Kommodore on a single radio frequency.
3. Twin-engine *Fühlungshalter* aircraft are to be used to give running commentary on the strength, location, altitude, and course of the enemy formation.
4. Approach instructions to all aircraft without Y-Jägerleit apparatus to be by the new *Reichsjägerwelle* [running commentary; *see* Command and Control below for description].
5. After landing at a strange field the senior officer will immediately form all arriving fighters into a *Gefechtsgruppe* [battle group], independent of home unit, and bring it to a state of readiness as quickly as possible.
   a) Takeoff orders are to be given by the Jafü of the affected region, after it is informed of the unit's strength.
   b) If there is no communication with the Jafü the *Führer* [leader] of the *Gefechtsgruppe* is to take off on his own initiative.
   c) After takeoff he is to assume the name of the takeoff base as his call sign.
   d) The location of the enemy formation to be given over the *Reichsjägerwelle* in plain language.
   e) The *Gefechtsgruppe* is to be broken up on the order of the mission leader, and each pilot is then on his own to find his home unit.
6. Airfields in the Reich containing supply stock-piles are to be noted on the pilots' maps and marked so that they can be recognized from high altitudes.
7. Fighter leaders must keep in mind weather conditions and their influence on enemy activity in the various battle regions.
8. Each unit (Gruppe or Staffel) is primarily to attack one and the same bomber *Pulk*. If it jettisons its bombs or otherwise splits up, the next formation in sight is to be attacked.
9. Aircraft of all formation leaders, from Schwarm-führer up, are to have white rudders for identification. Isolated aircraft and Rotten are to form up immediately on these aircraft, independent of home unit.
10. The first attack has the goal of splitting up the enemy formation. Attacks are to be made from the most favorable position possible, by closed-up Schwärme with minimal spacing between Schwärme.
11. Withdrawal is to be in a predetermined direction, and the aircraft are to be re-formed as quickly as possible.

12. Effective now, attacks from the front are to be restricted to especially favorable conditions by Gruppen proven successful at carrying them out.

13. The standard attack will be from the rear, with a small angle of deflection.

14. The approach to effective firing range is to be monitored by all leaders.

15. Pilots who without sufficient reason do not approach to the ordered firing distance are to be brought before a court-martial for cowardice before the enemy.

16. Effective now, only bombers in formation are to be attacked (whether incoming or outgoing).

17. Only after the entire formation is split up, or there are no prospects for attacking it, may individual separated bombers be destroyed.

18. Nebelwerfer [WGr 21] aircraft are authorized to attack *Herausschüsse* after successfully discharging their mortars.

19. Industry flights, night fighters, and small *Einsatzeinheiten* [operational detachments] from the EJGrs are permitted to attack *Herausschüsse* if and only if there is no prospect of forming larger formations, either on the ground or in the air.

20. There are no further exceptions. Leaders and pilots who violate these instructions are to be brought before a court-martial for insubordination resulting in grave consequences for the security of the Reich.

21. In frontal attacks fire is to be opened no sooner than 800 meters [880 yards]; in attacks from the rear or other angles, from 400 m. [440 yds.].

22. The target of each attack is one aircraft—spraying the formation with fire never leads to success.

23. A fixed point of aim, not aiming with tracers or smoke trails, leads to victory.

24. All attacks at deflection angles greater than 30 degrees are ineffective.

25. The battle is to be continued in the strongest Flak, in Flak and balloon zones.

26. All possible means are to be used to prevent the bombers from dropping on their planned targets.[85]

Note Galland's negative attitude toward frontal attacks, in direct opposition to their enthusiastic endorsement by the I. Jagdkorps staff. Note also that none of his 26 points mentions the Allied fighter escort, evidence that its importance was still being underestimated by the Luftwaffe high command. This is extremely ironic in the case of Galland, whose brother had been killed by an American escort fighter only two weeks previously.

The rapid expansion of the American bomber force in England necessitated a new layer of administrative control. On September 13, three Bombardment Divisions (Bomb Divisions) were activated. The First absorbed the assets of the 1st Bomb Wing; the Second, the 2nd Bomb Wing; and the Third, the 4th Bomb Wing. Newly-arriving bomb groups were assigned to newly-constituted bomb wings within the divisions. After its heavy losses on the September 6 Stuttgart raid, the Eighth Air Force targeted only the western occupied zone for the next three weeks. On September 14, in the middle of this lull, Milch convened a large meeting to discuss the *Selbstopferung-vorschlag* (self-sacrifice proposal) of Oblt. Heinrich Lange, a noted combat glider pilot. Lange proposed using heavily armored BV 40 gliders to ram bombers and ships. The day's discussion also covered bomb-carrying fighters, aerial torpedoes launched from Me 410s with newly-developed ejection seats, and fighter-controlled drones. There was not much enthusiasm for the suicidal aspects of Lange's plan, and Galland was tasked with writing a counter proposal. This issued on September 22, and resulted in the last major innovation in RLV day-fighter tactics. Galland pointed out that if a heavily armed and armored fighter could approach a bomber closely enough to ram it, it had a very good chance of destroying it with gunfire, after which it could depart to fight another day. Ramming would be authorized as a last resort, in case of weapons failure. He proposed establishing a special Staffel, to be called a *Sturmstaffel* (assault squadron), to evaluate equipment and tactics. This was done; the three *Sturmgruppen* (assault groups) that were formed as a result of this successful experiment became the most important component of the day RLV in late 1944.[86]

The Americans did not target Germany from September 6 until the 27th, when four B-17Fs of the new Pathfinder Force (PFF) led an attack on Emden. The Pathfinders were equipped with H2S, a British radar device that was able to distinguish large geographic features such as coastlines, and permitted attacks on selected targets through cloud cover. PFF operations would play an ever more important role in the coming winter, allowing the Americans to keep their tally of bomber missions increasing, even though bombing through cloud was nothing more than area bombing, and thus the antithesis of the official pinpoint bombing strategy, which was never modified to reflect the realities of European weather.

American escort strength for the Emden raid was six P-47 groups, two more than had been available on August 17. All were now equipped with 75- or 108-U.S. gallon (284 and 409 liters respectively) pressurized drop tanks, and for the first time provided escort to a target in Germany, although this one was relatively close to England. Extending escort range was now an urgent priority for the Eighth Air Force. General Arnold in Washington made his desires clear by replacing the head of 8th Fighter Command with MGen. William Kepner, who had gained Arnold's notice as head of the Fourth Air Force on the U.S. west coast. Kepner had worked closely with the fighter manufacturers in California to increase the range of their products. Kepner was innovative, energetic, and aggressive, and proved to be a perfect fit in his new job. The days of the ineffective coastal fighter sweeps were long gone. The German defenders quickly noticed the new aggressiveness of the American fighters.[87]

The Emden raid was inconclusive; only one H2S unit functioned as planned, and the 246 B-17s out of 308 dispatched that dropped their bombs did not achieve a satisfactory concentration on the targeted dock area. The P-47 escort functioned well, and only seven B-17s were shot down, but the German defenders were hampered by bad weather.

October's first raid came on the 1st, from the south. The three Eighth Air Force B-24 groups had returned to North Africa in September to support the Allied landings in Italy, and were sent on this day to bomb the important Messerschmitt plant at Wiener Neustadt, while the B-17s of the Mediterranean Theater's Twelfth Air Force targeted Augsburg. The defenders in this area were still weak and inexperienced, but performed adequately against the unescorted bombers. III./JG 3 claimed seven heavy bombers, while I./JG 27 claimed six. I./KG 51 scrambled its Me 410s, and a number of school Bf 110s were also up, but apparently made no claims. American losses to all causes were seven B-24s and three B-17s. The Luftwaffe commanders could assume that attacks from the south would continue, and that the fighter force in Austria would somehow have to be strengthened. The "peripheral defense" of the north German coast once favored by Göring was gone; all regions of the German "fortress without a roof"[88] needed stronger air defenses.

The next day brought a repeat of the previous week's raid on Emden. Again the PFF equipment

Oberst Walter Grabmann (*left*), Jafü Holland-Ruhr, with Major Kurt Brändle, II./JG 3 Kommandeur, at Schiphol in September. Grabmann has just exited his Me 210, which is marked with his personal identification letter, "X." (*Crow*)

proved unreliable, and again bad weather hampered the defenses. Only one bomber was lost to fighter attack; the Luftwaffe pilots claimed nine, and were ultimately credited with at least three.

General Eaker was under constant pressure from General Arnold to show more results from his Eighth Air Force, which was the largest air fleet in the American inventory by a wide margin, and was still growing rapidly. Few of the Combined Bomber Offensive targets had as yet been hit hard by day. And the long European winter would soon arrive, which would further hamper operations. Eaker and his bomber commander, MGen. Fred Anderson, decided on a compressed series of maximum-strength missions to high-priority targets, most deep in Germany and thus far beyond the range of the available escorts.

The first such mission, on the 4th, was a successful

The famous ex-303rd Bomb Group *Wulf Hound*, the first crash-landed B-17 restored to flyable condition by the Luftwaffe, pays a visit to Jever sometime in 1943 with the *Zirkus Rosarius*, a special unit which flew captured Allied aircraft to operational fighter airfields to instruct the pilots on their flight characteristics and defensive capabilities. (*Heinz Rose via Arno Rose*)

raid on Frankfurt-am-Main. Some 130 B-17s of the 155 dispatched by the 1st Bomb Division hit their primaries, while 152 of the 168 3rd Bomb Division B-17s bombed several industrial targets in the Saar and the St. Dizier base of II./JG 27, which had just become operational in the RLV. Twelve B-17s were lost, and two more were written off on their return.

Success for the Americans meant a lack of success by the Luftwaffe. I., II., and III./JG 1, I. and II./JG 3, II./JG 27, and I. and II./ZG 76 were directed to the incoming B-17 stream. It is not known if single-engine escorts were planned for ZG 76 (known to be necessary since the Battle of Britain in 1940), but the

Bf 110s flew their mission alone, and after claiming four B-17s had the misfortune to run into the 56th Fighter Group and its P-47s near Düren. In the ensuing slaughter the newly reformed Geschwader lost 11 KIA (including the Kommandeure of both Gruppen), 7 WIA, and nine Bf 110s.

A diversion across the North Sea on the 4th by two B-24 groups that had just returned from North Africa was more successful than most such feints, in that it drew a major part of the defensive force in its direction. The Jagddivision 2 controller took the bait and ordered all of JG 11 and the Jagdstaffel Helgoland to scramble against the Liberators. I./JG 11 claimed five B-24s, but its Kommandeur was killed. Hptm. Specht led an attack unit consisting of his II. and III./JG 11 and JaSta Helgoland; this all-Bf 109 formation claimed six B-24s. True losses totaled four B-24s; 19 others reached England with combat damage. Specht returned to Marx complaining bitterly about the weak armament of the standard Bf 109, which allowed many of the damaged B-24s to escape. All attacks on the B-17s had ended before they reached their targets. No second sorties were flown, and no attacks were made on the withdrawing bombers. The combat units complained of hazy skies, but the truth remains obscure.

The October 1943 Air Defense Conference

At this critical stage of the fall daylight battles, the Reichsmarschall convened a major conference at Obersalzberg on October 7–8. Its main purpose was to "address issues across the entire spectrum of the Luftwaffe's air defenses."[89] Indeed, the conference ultimately covered everything from the effectiveness of the Flak forces to developments in anti-aircraft rocketry. Luminaries present included Milch, Weise, Kammhuber, Koller, Martini, and Galland. Göring had just returned from a tour of fighter bases, and he had received an angry missive from the Gauleiter of Frankfurt, who claimed that the day fighters had performed abysmally during the October 4 raid on that city. The Gauleiter had complained that the poor showing by Galland's fighters enabled the Americans to fly with impunity in "Nuremberg Party Rally" formations in the cloudless skies over the city and wreak havoc on the population.[90]

Göring used the conference to launch a scathing and sustained attack on fighter-pilot training, tactics, technology, and morale. He told the group, "I cannot have the German people say to me, 'We gave you billions, yet you cannot prevent this; of 300 bombers only 20 have been shot down," a state of affairs he referred to as a "scandal."[91] He had much to say about the weaknesses of German fighter technology, which only a few months earlier he had claimed was more than a match for the American. He noted that Werner Mölders, the great tactician who had been dead since 1941, had developed complex and individualistic fighter tactics that were "appropriate for the elite, but have proved disastrous and destructive for the majority." But he reserved his most withering criticism for what he saw as the decay in Luftwaffe pilot morale and fighting spirit. The Reichsmarschall announced that he would no longer wear his combat decorations until the German fighter force regained its élan. Milch stood up to the Reichsmarschall and stated that his criticism was unjust. Göring replied disdainfully, "They just have to close the enemy to 400 meters instead of 1,000; they just have to bring down 80 instead of 20. Then their low spirits will be gone, and I will doff my hat to them. But as for taking potshots at 2,000 meters . . ."[92]

Milch refused to accept that the Luftwaffe's problems stemmed exclusively from cowardice, and Göring agreed. He maintained that "worn out" veterans, some with the highest combat decorations, had poisoned the minds of the idealistic youth. "These young people come from training, they are relatively enthusiastic. They enter the Gruppe to which they are assigned, and there they are told: 'What tactics here? Make your escape.' What is a man given this advice to do?" The Reichsmarschall concluded his critique of Luftwaffe combat leadership with the observation that he would "prefer a young man without decorations to a halfhearted Staffel-kapitän who has won the Knight's Cross . . ."[93]

Göring managed to identify some genuine problems in Germany's air defense in the fall of 1943, even while glossing over his own substantial responsibility for this state of affairs.[94] As offensive as Göring's comments doubtless were to the fighter pilots, even their staunchest advocate acknowledged that Luftwaffe combat leadership and pilot morale were not above criticism. Galland, in replying to his chief's charges, promised:

The wing and higher commanders will be rechecked under these aspects, to determine their qualities of leadership and their degree of determination. Also I

have in mind a system that could be handled by wing commanders or by me personally. Under this system men would be placed in questionable groups to fly their missions with them, and determine what the group actually does, how it fights. These men would be what might be called flying commissars . . .

A second possibility to confirm in the case of the individual pilot whether he really makes a determined approach would be the installation of an automatic camera, something I have been asking for for longer than a year. The photos taken by such a camera could be developed immediately after action and would prove: this pilot approached at such and such an angle to within such and such a distance, or, this pilot fired his ammunition blindly into empty space . . .[95]

A number of specific initiatives emerged from this conference.[96] A written order dated October 7 made the following demands of the fighter units; they were apparently not enforced with any consistency:

1. Units are to be supervised by *Kommissare* [political officers].
2. Robot film cameras are to be used to confirm the course of fighter units.
3. Recording barographs are to be used to confirm the altitude reached.
4. Gruppenkommandeure are to report the performance of each pilot to the Jafü.

The Reichsmarschall also issued a set of orders to be read to the pilots by the unit commanders.

Hptm. Walther Dahl, Kommandeur of III./JG 3, strides forward to congratulate three 7./JG 3 pilots after their successful October 14 mission. Bf 109G-6 "white 6" bears full markings: the Geschwader emblem on the cowling, the Gruppe vertical bar, and a white comet denoting the Staffel. A WGr 21 mortar tube, standard equipment in this Staffel, can be seen beneath the wing. (*Bundesarchiv 652-5724-18*)

Unfortunately no written set of these orders is known, but this is how a former JG 1 pilot recalled them long after the war:

1. There are no weather conditions in which fighter units cannot take off and engage in combat.
2. Any fighter pilot returning to base with neither a combat victory nor combat damage will be court-martialed.
3. Any fighter pilot whose armament fails is expected to ram.[97]

The reactions of the combat leaders and pilots to these insulting directives can only be guessed at, but certainly varied widely. Obstlt. Hans Philipp, the highly successful and widely respected Kommodore of JG 1, allegedly told his officers that he would not be bound by such advice, adding somewhat obscurely, "I know what I have to do!"[98]

A requirement from Göring that German fighters rearm and refuel so as to engage deep USAAF penetrations two or possibly three times also became standing policy, and even Galland conceded it brought short-term benefits.[99] A general push for new tactics, technology, and innovation emerged from the lengthy conference minutes. This meeting is today chiefly remembered as an illustration of Göring's poor leadership style and the increasingly bad relations between the Reichsmarschall and his front-line commanders, especially the fighter pilots. Beyond the drama and the clash of strong personalities, however, the conference illustrates the dysfunctional nature of the Third Reich's leadership and the corrosive effect of Nazism on German military culture. It was in sad contrast to the manner in which the early Luftwaffe planners grappled with operational problems and defeat after World War I.

The next raid came on the 8th, even as the conferees droned on. The targets were shipyards and factories in Bremen and nearby Vegesack. The three bomb divisions flew on divergent courses before converging in the target area, which became clear soon enough for the German controllers to mount a fairly well-coordinated defense against the incoming formations. The fighters of Jagddivision 3 attacked the B-17s of the 1st Bomb Division, which approached due east across the Netherlands. The Jagddivision 2 fighters took on the B-24s of the 2nd Bomb Division and the B-17s of the 3rd, which took a more circuitous route across the North Sea before crossing the Dutch coast near Groningen.[100]

The 45 P-47s of the 4th Fighter Group provided the escort for the inbound 1st Bomb Division. While still over the Zuider Zee the formation was attacked by JG 3 Bf 109s, I. Gruppe from Bönninghardt and II. Gruppe from Schiphol. The Messerschmitts succeeded in drawing the Thunderbolts away from the bomber stream, setting it up for an attack by the better-armed Focke-Wulfs of JG 1, which were unaccountably late. The B-17s' respite was brief. They were hit hard in the target area by rocket-carrying ZG 26 Bf 110s, which had been briefed to remain near Bremen, well out of escort range. Only when the B-17s turned west on the reciprocal of their inbound course were they attacked by JG 1, which was flying as a fairly compact unit under the command of Obstlt. Philipp. The JG 1 pilots continued their attacks until Quakenbrück, where they were met by the 45 56th Fighter Group P-47s of the withdrawal escort. For the loss of one P-47, Colonel Zemke's pilots claimed five Fw 190s, one of which took Obstlt. Philipp to his death. Philipp, who wore the Knight's Cross with Oak Leaves and Swords, had been the second pilot to gain 200 aerial victories, and was by far the most successful RLV pilot to lose his life to date.

The 353rd Fighter Group picked up the 3rd Bomb Division when it crossed the Dutch coast, but could not stay long. As the fighters turned back the bomber stream was hit by the Stab flight and all three Gruppen of JG 11, which continued their attacks until the bombers reached Bremen. The other fighter units in the area—ErprKdo 25, III./JG 54, NJG 3, and the Bremen and Langenhagen Focke-Wulf factory protection Schwärme—also reached the bomber stream. The B-17s withdrew to the west along the track of the 1st Bomb Division, gaining the protection of the 56th Fighter Group, and the German attacks ended.

Schmid scored the day's efforts as a moderate success; the Americans lost 30 heavy bombers (plus two scrapped in England) and three P-47s, while the defenders lost 24 fighters, 21 KIA, and 12 WIA. The small size of his force had prevented him from inflicting more severe damage, although the Zerstörergeschwader had done well in its new role. In an unprecedented development, three pilots, Lt. Hans Ehlers, Lt. Erich Hondt, and Fw. Hans-Günther Reinhardt, brought down B-17s by ramming them. All three men survived with injuries. The ramming attacks were spontaneous or accidental rather than part of a tactical plan, but may have been inspired by Göring's exhortations. They were not repeated on this scale until the Third Reich's last desperate days.[101]

Philipp's replacement as JG 1 Kommodore was the only RLV pilot with more aerial victories than he: Obstlt. Hermann Graf, whose experimental JG 50 was due to be disbanded. Graf had been the first Luftwaffe pilot to reach 200 victories and wore the Wehrmacht's highest award for valor, the Knight's Cross with Oak Leaves, Swords and Diamonds. A media darling, Graf had become a quirky prima donna. He had a number of former professional soccer players assigned to him for personal duties, and brought this entourage with him to each new duty station. He claimed that he was thus saving German soccer for the postwar era, but his grandstanding did not sit well with many of his new subordinates in JG 1.[102]

On October 9, Eaker and Anderson took one of their greatest gambles yet, sending their entire bomber force to bomb targets in eastern Germany, entirely without fighter escort. The bombers were routed across the North Sea and Denmark before the bomb divisions split to bomb Anklam, Gdynia, Danzig and Marienburg. Schmid's short-legged Bf 109s and Fw 190s could not reach the incoming bombers, but staged forward to catch them on their return. The Bf 110s had ample endurance, but slow closing speed. And there were no day fighters based in eastern Germany. The bombers thus had a free ride until their bomb runs, which were quite successful—strike photos of the attack on the Marienburg Focke-Wulf plant were distributed widely as a classic example of precision bombing.

The return route of the bombers was obvious, and every I. Jagdkorps day- and night-fighter unit succeeded in making contact, aided by perfect, cloudless fall weather. Twenty-eight heavies were brought down; two more were scrapped after their return. German losses were ten fighters destroyed, 11 aircrewmen KIA or MIA, and 1 WIA.[103]

General Galland flew as a *Kommissar* to observe first-hand the much-maligned defensive forces. He and a wingman flew a courier plane to Staaken, scrambled into waiting Fw 190s, and, following the *Reichjägerwelle* (Reich Fighter Frequency) commentary, flew to the Frisian Islands to catch the departing Anklam raiders north of Heligoland. The pair were the first German aircraft to arrive. They flew in parallel with the heavy bombers until single- and twin-engine fighters arrived and began their attacks. Galland noted with disgust that the 21-cm rockets were fired from too great a distance, and that attacks on the bombers with guns were disorganized and broken off too soon. According to his memoirs, Galland made his own attack after his fighters left, and downed a B-17 on his second pass. He could not report it, as his flight plan did not call for combat. After thinking things over on his return flight, Galland concluded that the Luftwaffe pilots were exhausted after flying a long second sortie, and now that he knew from his own observation what requirements were reasonable, his arguments with Göring might carry more weight. However, he had to concede that Göring was right in many respects—*Viermotschreck* (fear of the heavy bombers) was a problem.[104]

Wielding the Sword: Command and Control[105]

A late 1943 tactical memorandum noted, "The prime condition for success against large Allied bomber formations is the concentration of fighters in considerable numbers and acting according to a single operational plan."[106] Achieving this "prime condition for success" was the goal of the Luftwaffe fighter-defense command and control system. As seen earlier, such a system was a stepchild in an air force that oriented itself almost exclusively towards the offensive. Nonetheless, Schmid and his staff developed an organization in a remarkably short time that, although far from perfect, proved operationally and tactically effective.

A Bf 110 or Ju 88 Fühlungshalter keeps formation with two B-17 *Pulks*. (*Price*)

A B-17 minus its entire tail section goes down behind a 385th Bomb Group B-17F. (*ww2images*)

While overall air-defense policy and guidance were set forth at Lw Bfh Mitte, operational authority for conduct of fighter operations rested with I. Jagdkorps. This headquarters was responsible for:

. . . providing fighter forces in time and space as well as for determining the *Abwehrschwerpunkt* [defensive point of main effort], on the basis of the air situation. It directs the operations of the controlling Jagddivision in each instance, and ensures the timely transfer of control to neighboring command areas.[107]

In broad outline, the Luftwaffe's fighter-control system first required the formulation of an overall *Luftlagebild* (air situation picture). Creating this picture was the responsibility of the I. Jagdkorps operations room. On Schmid's authority, the Korps operations room was reduced in size to a manageable level; he openly disdained the "Wagnerian opera house" atmosphere of the larger division operations rooms.[108] In this small venue, plotters assembled reports from the Jagddivision and other subordinate headquarters into a mosaic covering the whole of the Reich. Liaison officers from the Flak, the Y-service, intelligence, and meteorology were also present. The Jagdkorps operations room was connected via landline to all subordinate commands, through which *Aufträge* (battle directives) were communicated to the divisions.

The Jagddivision was responsible for "local centralized command and control of air defenses." Its major responsibilities were:

1. Assembly, evaluation and presentation of the regional air situation picture.

2. Tactical command and control of its subordinated formations. This included all measures that had to be taken prior to, and during, the battle to ensure the execution of the defensive plan and cooperation with the other combat arms.

The information that fed into the Korps and division headquarters came from a variety of sources. The four main sources of information were the *Flugmeldedienst* (Aircraft Reporting Service), which controlled the radar sites; ground observers and their associated communications signals links; the Radio Listening Service (Y-Service); and the *Fühlungshalter* (contact keeper) aircraft that actually accompanied the bomber formations.

Radar

The day-fighter organization benefited greatly from the sophisticated radar network built up over the preceding years to wage the battle against the RAF night offensive. By 1943, the Freya early warning sets, often paired with Würzburg installations which provided altitude readings, were augmented by a new generation of sophisticated radar equipment, notably Mammut and Wassermann, "the finest early warning radar to be produced by either side during the Second World War."[109] Radar sites supported the Jagdkorps and Division headquarters, as well as the Aircraft Reporting Service in the Reich territory which came under the Luftgaue—a "seam" in the command structure that Schmid constantly sought to address. Finally, the gunlaying radars (usually Würzburg) supporting the Flak batteries also shared their information with the Korps and Division—thereby providing "a very valuable augmentation of radar coverage."

RAF Bomber Command had employed Window jamming of German radar during the Hamburg operation in July with devastating effect. In time, USAAF bomber formations also began jamming the German early warning system.

The first case of American use of tinfoil on record is that of a daytime attack against Bremen on November 26, 1943. An aircraft radio jamming transmitter was operating at the same time, so that the Würzburg instruments were under two different types of interference simultaneously. This completely prevented altitude determination.[110]

German efforts to overcome Allied jamming marked the course of the day battle as well.

Ground observers

When German air defense was in its infancy in World War I, the humble ground observer with his steel helmet, binoculars, and telephone at the ready was the heart and soul of the aircraft warning service. While the "electric eye" had reduced his preeminence by 1943, he and his colleagues still had an important role to play. He could not be jammed, and the network of observers, arranged in a "checkerboard" fashion across the Reich territory, forwarded valuable information through channels. In addition to augmenting coverage where radar stations were few, the observers could positively identify aircraft types, and report on low-flying raiders, crashed aircraft, and parachuting airmen. In short, they provided a vital "man in the loop" and added important depth to the air situation picture.

Y-service (radio interception)

Although radar gets much attention from airpower enthusiasts, the true "early warning" came from the Luftwaffe's listening or intercept service, the *Funkhorchdienst* (usually referred to as the Y-Service or H-Dienst). This service remained under the control of General Wolfgang Martini, the *Generalnachrichtenführer der Luftwaffe* (Chief of Luftwaffe Signals) but was closely integrated into the activities of the fighter operations centers. Allied air operations on the scale of the 1943–5 raids inevitably generated a large volume of radio and radar emissions, much of which was intercepted, evaluated, and analyzed by the German listening service. It provided the Jagdkorps with important details such as the impending takeoff of Allied bombers, weather conditions over the British Isles, identification of units, and information on the course of incoming raids.[111]

Not only was it of invaluable assistance for identification, but it also permitted much greater conservation of force and energy than would otherwise have been possible. This information provided precious advance or early warning, as well as serving to clarify and speed the formation of an accurate air situation picture.[112]

The Y-Service worked hand in hand with the early-warning radar stations, informing them of a raid's likely approach route.[113]

Fühlungshalter

The Luftwaffe command and control system relied on information gleaned by "airborne observer posts," the *Fühlungshalter*. As we have seen, use of long-range aircraft for shadowing purposes was already part of Luftwaffe thinking before the war.[114] In 1943, the Jagddivisionen maintained special Staffeln of these aircraft. The shadowing aircraft only operated within the area of their own Division and usually took over the patrol from similar aircraft at the divisional boundary. Orders to these aircraft were issued by the operations officer at division. Once airborne, the aircraft flew under Y-Führung (*see below*). Their mission was to shadow the bomber formations and radio their size, course, altitude, and presence or absence of escorts to the ground controllers. All divisions used a common frequency for shadowing traffic so that a simultaneous exchange of information

Genmaj. Adolf Galland briefs Reichsmarschall Hermann Göring prior to an inspection of JG 1 and JG 11 at Deelen on October 23. (*Heinz Rose via Arno Rose*)

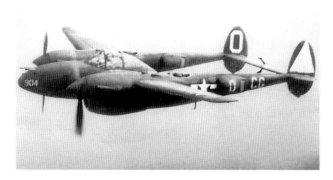

A P-38J of the 55th Fighter Group in flight over northern Europe in the winter of 1943–4. The 55th was the first Lightning group to reach full operational status with the Eighth Air Force. (*Gray*)

on enemy formations could take place between all the divisions in Germany.[115] By late summer 1943, *Fühlungshalter* were becoming a familiar sight to USAAF bomber crews on deep penetrations into Germany. Beirne Lay, an observer on the August 17, 1943, Regensburg mission, recounted one such encounter:

> For the first time I noticed an Me 110 sitting out of range on our level out to the right. He was to stay with us all the way to the target, apparently radioing our position and weak spots to fresh Staffeln waiting farther down the road.[116]

These shadowers had a powerful psychological effect on American bomber crews. Indeed, in Lay's postwar novel *Twelve O'Clock High*, a thinly disguised retelling of actual experiences, the "contact keeper" is embellished as a red Bf 110, with a fictionalized (and thoroughly unsportsmanlike) Wutz Galland at the controls.[117] The Allies believed that these aircraft issued orders directly to the formation leaders in the air, but this was not true; ground control received and re-transmitted their observations. Though an important cog in the command and control system, their numbers were few; no more than eight to ten *Fühlungshalter* aircraft were ever assigned to a Jagd-division. There is very little in the surviving records about these aircraft; however, the I. Jagdkorps war diary did record one pertinent order it received from Lw Bfh Mitte in November. Each Jagddivision was to form a "mixed Staffel" containing one Schwarm of Fühlungshaltern and one Schwarm of *Luftbeobachtern* (air observers), which served a similar function for the

night defenses. The aircraft were to carry a Flak officer as a third crewman. The most common night fighters, Ju 88Cs and Bf 110s, could not provide this man with adequate visibility, so the Ju 88A-4 bomber was recommended until the Ju 88H-2 or Ju 188 came into service. The aircraft were to have top-of-the-line radio equipment; those of Jagddivision 3 were to be equipped with captured American radios.[118]

Once the air situation picture was complete, it was necessary to scramble the fighters and vector them to the interception. This vital function took place one level below the Jagdkorps, in the Jagddivisionen. Each Jagddivision had its own complement of aircraft warning (radar and ground observer) regiments, battalions and companies. These fed up-to-the-minute information into the Jagddivision operations center, which in turn relayed the information to the *Luftnachrichten Jägerleit Abteilung* (fighter-control battalion). In 1943, German interceptors were controlled from the ground either by Y-Jägerleit apparatus, or by means of the *Reichsjägerwelle*, a comprehensive running commentary broadcast on a common radio frequency by I. Jagdkorps and used by all operational, training, and factory defense units. This was a report on the overall air situation that was broadcast on several transmitters throughout the Reich. Only formation leaders could receive transmissions from the Jagddivision ground controllers, but any pilot (and even civilians with the proper radio sets) could tune in the Reichsjägerwelle and receive basic information.

Y-Führung (Benito)

The Y system was the standard fighter-control system for day-fighter ground-controlled interception until augmented by the "Egon" radar guidance system in 1944. Often referred to by the Allies by the code name "Benito," the Y-system was operated by a fighter-control station which exchanged plotting information and instructions with the division Gefechtsstand (*see* page 132).[119] A typical Y-control site consisted of a plotting hut, a wooden direction finding (DF) tower, and a transmitter/antenna. The fighter-control station transmitted a carrier frequency of 3,000 cycles, which was picked up by a fighter equipped with a FuG 16ZY VHF set. The FuG 16ZY then retransmitted the signal (on a different, predetermined frequency) back to the fighter-control station, where the crew stationed in the DF tower determined the range and bearing of the fighter. A hut at the site was equipped with plotting tables on which information regarding the location and bearing of the friendly aircraft was combined with the most current information on enemy activity, obtained primarily from the Würzburg and Freya ground-control radars. The fighter-control station, acting in accordance with directives issued by the division Gefechtsstand, then transmitted course and range orders to the fighter leader. In a massed formation, only one aircraft could fly as the target aircraft; otherwise accuracy of plotting data would suffer. If this aircraft went out of action, another pre-designated aircraft served as its replacement. None of the other Y-equipped aircraft were permitted to switch on their sets. Since the information gathered by the Y-control station was shared with the Gefechtsstand, the division controller could also issue commands directly to the fighters. The Y-system's requirement for separate command and target aircraft was inherently clumsy, but made use of capabilities built into the standard FuG 16ZY transceiver, enabling the system to become operational very quickly.[120]

While the entire command and control system was designed to achieve unity of action through centralization of authority, the actual conduct of combat operations still depended on the initiative of individual commanders. As a fall 1943 Luftwaffe high command tactical instruction made clear, the principle of *Auftragstaktik* was essential:

> Against a large-scale raid all preparations must be made for double sorties. If returning fighters are unable to reach an airfield where a fighter unit is based, they must be directed to alternative airfields selected in advance. On landing at an airfield other than his own, the highest ranking fighter pilot should immediately collect all available aircraft, irrespective of the unit to which they belong, into a combat group; takeoff for this group is ordered by the officer commanding the Jagddivision concerned or, if communication is impossible, on the initiative of the Gruppenkommandeur.[121]

The technology may have been new, but the strengths of German command and control practices dated back to the early Prussian Army.

Finally, the command and control system, although centralized, was not excessively hierarchical. Information was shared widely. Divisions not only kept Jagdkorps and Lw Bfh Mitte apprised of developments, they also informed neighboring and

Uffz. Wolfgang Polster, an experienced III./JG 26 pilot, was loaned to II./JG 3, across Luftflotte boundaries, to help fill out the latter unit's ranks in late 1943 after its crippling casualties while flying from Schiphol. He poses here beside one of his temporary unit's Messerschmitts. (*Polster via Genth*)

subordinate commands at every level. If every command level was responsible for contributing to the overall air situation picture, they also reaped the benefits of truly decentralized execution. One perceptive postwar American analysis observed:

> This double flow served two purposes. First, it simplified and improved evaluation at all levels, assuring the ultimate formation of the simplest possible air situation picture. And second, it speeded up the interchange of basic but relevant intelligence; and assured the timely receipt by those actually engaged in combat, of the maximum pertinent information. The flow of information was not rapid by American standards, since it was consumed at all levels by the coordination, combination and evaluation processes. However, this feature produced a greatly simplified and coherent situation picture.[122]

In the second half of 1943, the Luftwaffe made tremendous strides toward constructing a modern and workable fighter-control system. Like so much German military innovation, its best features percolated up from below, and were recognized as superior practices and implemented by senior officers. Much work still needed to be done. In 1944 greater consolidation of Flak, fighter, and aircraft-warning forces would take place. The search for a true combined arms air-defense approach would continue.

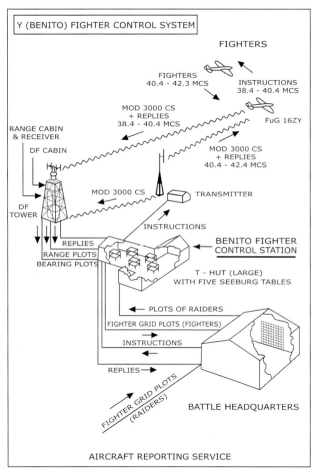

October 10—Münster[123]

The Eighth Air Force planners decided to keep the pressure on the Luftwaffe on October 10. A large high-pressure area was predicted to bring cloudless skies to Germany, permitting a broad choice of targets. A shallow-penetration raid to Münster was decided on, allowing escort to the target. The two B-17 bomb divisions would attack the city center in a single stream, while the weak B-24 division flew another diversion over the North Sea to pin the Jagddivision 2

fighters to their home areas. The aiming point for the B-17s would be Münster's distinctive cathedral in the heart of the city. This was the first time that the Eighth Air Force had specifically targeted civilians. The bomber crews were told that their target was nonetheless strategic; they would be attacking the employees of one of the largest railroad switching yards serving the Ruhr.[124]

The forecast of good weather was as significant to the German planners as it was to the Americans. On the assumption that the Eighth Air Force would return to Germany on the 10th, three Luftflotte 3 Jagd-gruppen were kept overnight on the Dutch bases to which they had moved on the 9th. In the early morning of the 10th, the large volume of radio traffic from the American bomber bases presaged a heavy raid. When the bombers did not take off in time for a deep penetration raid, Oberst Grabmann, the commander of Jagddivision 3 at Deelen, concluded that the bombers were coming to northwestern Germany, and began to deploy his forces accordingly. Before the bombers took off, I. and II./JG 26 had left Leeuwarden; I. Gruppe for Deelen, and II. Gruppe for the large permanent Luftwaffe base at Rheine. The skilled or lucky controller placed the latter Gruppe within 40 km (25 miles) of the 8th Bomber Command's target for the day, the center of Münster. Furthermore, the move was conducted in strict radio silence, and Allied intelligence never located the two Gruppen; the 8th Bomber Command mission report makes no mention of them. III./JG 26 was held at the small Dutch base of Eelde; again, the Americans had no knowledge of its presence.[125]

The 3rd Bomb Division began crossing the English coast at Felixstowe in early afternoon. It was followed 15 minutes later by the 1st Bomb Division, which was given most of the P-47 escort in the expectation that the 3rd Bomb Division would achieve surprise. A total of 274 B-17s and 216 P-47s was dispatched. At 1405, the Bf 109s of III./JG 26 took off from Eelde in far northern Holland; II./JG 3 scrambled from Schiphol three minutes later. It was still five minutes before the 3rd Bomb Division reached the Dutch coast. The direction of the attackers having been well established, the Fw 190s of I./JG 1 and I./JG 26 were ordered to take off from Deelen; a few minutes later II./JG 1 and II./JG 26 flew off the Rheine runway. These four Focke-Wulf Gruppen joined up in a single *Gefechts-verband* (battle formation). According to JG 26 veteran Heinz Gomann, this was the first and only time that

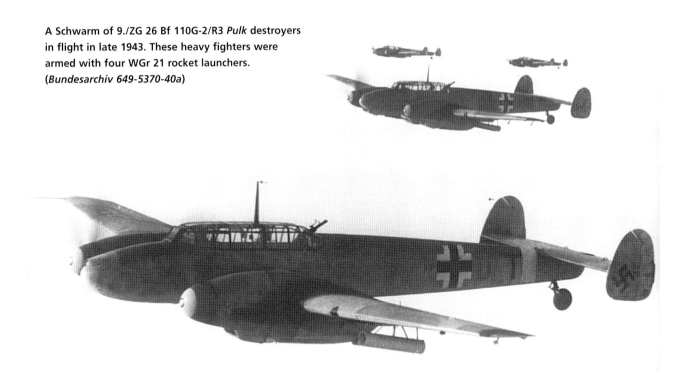

A Schwarm of 9./ZG 26 Bf 110G-2/R3 *Pulk* destroyers in flight in late 1943. These heavy fighters were armed with four WGr 21 rocket launchers. (*Bundesarchiv 649-5370-40a*)

his Gruppe was part of a force strong enough to carry out the old military aphorism, *Klotzen nicht Kleckern* ("Strike hard, don't mess around").[126]

The diversion by the 2nd Bomb Division B-24s accomplished nothing. The formation passed over a convoy that radioed its small strength back to land. Soon afterward the lead B-24 sustained an equipment malfunction and turned back, followed by the entire formation. The fighters of Jagddivision 2 were now freed up to join the battle farther south. At least 13 Jagdgruppen and Zerstörergruppen, approximately 350 fighters, would ultimately engage the Americans.

The fighters ordered up by Jagddivision 3 continued to concentrate along the track of the bombers, which was tracing a line due east across the Netherlands. A direct course to Münster had been ordered so that the escorting P-47s could stay with the bombers all the way to the target. II./JG 3 was the first Gruppe to reach the bombers. Its stern attack was easily driven off by the new 352nd Fighter Group, without damage to either side. However, the P-47s soon had to turn back, leaving the bombers totally without protection. The relief unit, the equally new 355th Fighter Group, was still fogbound in England. A careful American plan had once again been spoiled by the English weather. The patient leaders of the

six Jagdgruppen from JG 1 and JG 26 saw their opportunity and quickly took advantage of it. The onslaught began. The bomber crewmen in the leading 14th Bomb Wing's 390th, 95th, and 100th Groups saw an estimated 200 German fighters forming up to attack in the clear air ahead—the Jagddivision 3 commander obviously considered these units "proven successful" at head-on attacks, and thus exempt from Galland's directive of September 3 discouraging them.

The 14th Wing crossed Haltern, the Initial Point, nine minutes from Münster. Schwärme of Fw 190s began level attacks on the low 100th Bomb Group from dead ahead. The Focke-Wulfs closed to 45–70 meters (50–75 yards) before flicking over and diving away. Within seven minutes, the entire "Bloody Hundredth" formation had vanished. Six Fortresses had been destroyed; six others were turning back with smoking engines. All of these bombers were doomed; only one of the 13 B-17s dispatched by the group returned to England.

The Jagddivision 2 fighters now arrived in the combat area, and were directed to the head of the stream. Oblt. Heinz Knoke's 5./JG 11 Schwarm bounced some stray P-47s, and claimed two. These were apparently from the 352nd Fighter Group, which sustained the escort's only two losses: one P-47 failed to return, while the second crash-landed in England. The Kommodore of ZG 26, Major Karl Boehm-Tettelbach, led the Me 410s of III./ZG 1 and the Bf 110s of III./ZG 26 in rocket attacks on the rear of the shattered 14th Wing. Smaller units such as ErprKdo 25 also attacked the 3rd Division. The only target escort unit, the 4th Fighter Group, was with the trailing 1st Division. Lieutenant Colonel Don Blakeslee and his P-47s reached Haltern exactly on schedule, and began an incident-free escort of the 1st Division, which sustained only one loss on the mission. The main air battle was far ahead of them.

Attacks on the 3rd Division alternated between head-on passes by Fw 190s and Bf 109s and rocket barrages from the rear by Me 410s and Bf 110s. Most of the fighters broke away briefly when the bombers came within range of the Münster Flak defenses, which allowed the bombardiers to line up on their aiming point for this Sunday mission, the Münster cathedral, without hindrance. A few fighter pilots were so wrapped up in the battle, however, that they continued their attacks on the bombers over the city. Two 4./JG 26 Fw 190s had to dodge bombs dropped by the leading 95th Bomb Group before they reached position behind one of the *Pulk*'s last B-17s, which went down under their cannon fire.

Large-scale attacks resumed once the 3rd Division left the Flak area. Four more B-17s were ultimately lost by the 95th Group. Finally, as it appeared that the entire leading wing would be annihilated, the P-47s of the 56th Group arrived to begin their withdrawal escort. They sailed into the middle of the mêlée,

splitting up into flights of four to reach as many German attackers as possible. Lt. Robert Johnson's Thunderbolt was badly damaged by a Fw 190, but not until he had shot down two planes to become an ace. Major David Schilling, the deputy commander of the 56th, also downed his fifth German fighter on this mission. The last P-47 groups to arrive, the 78th and 353rd, found the large-scale attacks over, but Captain Walter Beckham of the 353rd did succeed in downing his fifth fighter to become an ace.

The German defenders had done well; they had destroyed 30 B-17s and 1 P-47 while losing 25 fighters and 12 crewmen. Nine of the German losses were twin-engine Zerstörer. It was obvious that these effective bomber destroyers would have to be shielded from the attentions of the American escorts if they were to remain a viable weapon. And the efforts of the Luftwaffe never seemed to be quite enough to attain its ultimate goal, which was to prevent accurate bombing. Concentration on a single bomber *Pulk* was an effective tactic that would be repeated, but on this day, even though the *Pulk* chosen for attack was leading the mission, and its near-destruction should have badly upset the bombing plan, the remaining bombers succeeded in making an effective attack on their target.

October 14—Second Schweinfurt

Although the 8th Bomber Command mission report tiptoed around the issues, the American commanders should have drawn the following lessons from the Münster mission:

1. The Luftwaffe air defenses were continuing to increase in strength and effectiveness.
2. In the absence of effective diversions, straight-line routing of the bomber stream allowed the defenders to concentrate in its path, facilitating mass attacks.
3. The rocket-firing twin-engine fighter was quickly becoming the most effective Luftwaffe weapon.
4. A realistic fighter-escort plan and an adequate number of fighters were necessary to minimize bomber losses.
5. Fighter escort all the way to the target was necessary to prevent disastrous bomber losses.

And yet, the next Eighth Air Force mission ignored all of these lessons. Based on favorable weather predictions over the continent, MGen. Anderson

The Bf 109G-6 in which Major Kurt Brändle, Kommandeur of II./JG 3, was killed on November 3. The white rudder that marks Brändle as a formation leader contrasts strongly with the machine's dark grey mottle. (Rosch)

scheduled a return trip to Schweinfurt on short notice, despite the knowledge that the fighter escort would be little stronger and no longer-legged than that on August 17. The new long-ranged P-38 Lightnings were not yet operational, and the P-47 units had run out of 108-gallon (409-liter) drop tanks, which were being manufactured (slowly) in England, and would have to revert to 75-gallon (284-liter) tanks. All three bomb divisions were scheduled to fly the mission; each would be escorted by a single P-47 group on penetration, and a single group on withdrawal. There would be no diversionary raids, though the courses of the three bomber formations would diverge slightly, in a weak attempt at deception.[127]

At daybreak on the 14th the American airfields were blanketed in chilly fall fog, but when the morning weather reconnaissance reported clear air over the continent, the crews were ordered to their planes. As the first of 291 B-17s took off, Oberst Grabmann in Deelen, expecting a full-strength deep-penetration raid from the volume of radio traffic and time of takeoff, put his own fighter units on alert, and 50 minutes before the bombers began crossing the English coast he was asking the neighboring Jagd-divisionen to bring their own fighters to full readiness. The poor weather over England prevented the B-17s from forming up properly and left the 1st Bomb Division in a very vulnerable formation, with the wrong bomb wing in the lead. The 305th Bomb Group could not find its own wing and joined another as a fourth group. A poor turn left it strung out for miles, and perfectly set up for destruction.

The small B-24 wing never did form up, and was finally ordered to fly a diversion in the North Sea, thus wasting one of the three airborne P-47 groups, which went with it. The B-17s and their own P-47s finally took up a course to the southeast—on a straight line toward Schweinfurt. The 1st Bomb Division was to the east of and slightly ahead of the 3rd, ensuring that it would receive most of the attacks from Jagddivision 3, based right in its path.

The first fighters to reach the bomber stream, the Bf 109s of I. and II./JG 3, attacked the P-47s between Woensdrecht and Antwerp. It is not known if Schmid authorized this attack on the escorts, a deviation from standard procedure, or if it was ordered on Grabmann's own initiative. Galland's continuing efforts to have these forward units tasked specifically with stripping the bombers of their escort had not previously found any favor in Berlin. Nevertheless, the

Beetle, a P-47D-5 landed at Caen by the 355th Fighter Group's 2Lt. William E. Roach on November 7, quickly became a fixture in the *Zirkus Rosarius*, and made familiarization flights to the RLV bases—here, the I./JG 1 base at Deelen—still in its colorful personal markings. (*Berger via Mombeek*)

353rd Fighter Group took the challenge well, shooting down seven Bf 109s while remaining fairly close to the bombers. The only P-47 lost all day belonged to the 353rd. It was claimed by a Messerschmitt pilot of I./JG 3 and a Focke-Wulf pilot of II./JG 26, one of the first Fw 190 units to reach the stream.

Grabmann had ordered the rest of his fighters to concentrate over Düren, near the limit of the escort fighters' range, rather than send them piecemeal at the bombers while they were still over the Netherlands. This force comprised all three Gruppen of JG 1 and two from JG 26, about 150 single-engine fighters. The moment the escort turned back near Aachen, the Fw 190s and Bf 109s began closing in. The four Focke-Wulf Gruppen attacked first—at 12 o'clock high, by Schwärme. Their prime targets, as always, were the bombers judged by the formation leaders to be the most vulnerable. These were most often those flying at the edges of the combat boxes. Today the 305th Bomb Group was in no recognizable formation, and drew attention from the start. It soon began to disintegrate; 13 of its 16 B-17s were lost prior to the bomb run.

Jagddivision 3 had no Zerstörer units under its direct command, but Grabmann's call for help was answered promptly, and every Bf 110 and Me 410 unit in Germany was ordered up; most of the day units reached the bombers well before they arrived at Schweinfurt, while most of the night units harried the withdrawing bombers. Crews from seven Zerstörer-gruppen and 11 Nachtjagdgruppen (night-fighter groups) ultimately filed victory claims.

On November 17 Genmaj. Galland flew to Achmer in his Fw 190A-6 to take part in an inspection by Reichsmarschall Göring. Here he is met by Hptm. Horst Geyer, the Kommandeur of ErprKdo 25. Galland's airplane carried a unique "double chevron + triangle + white 2" tactical marking. The "2" is masked here by Geyer. (*Smith*)

German tactics were a repeat of those found successful on the 10th. The twin-engine fighters made their first attacks from the rear, firing off their 21-cm rockets from 1,000 meters (1,100 yards), outside the range of the defensive gunners. The rockets destroyed a few bombers and damaged others, but their main purpose was to weaken the cohesiveness of the combat boxes. Some single-engine fighters carried rockets, usually in the ratio of one Staffel per Gruppe. The tactics of these mixed-weapon Gruppen varied according to whether Allied escorts were expected. Today, with no escorts, the rocket Staffeln attacked from the rear, while most of the other single-engine fighters attacked from the front by Schwärme, singling out those parts of the stream that were in the poorest formation. All of the German pilots were under orders to keep attacking until forced to withdraw by damage or shortage of fuel or ammunition. The better Jagd-gruppen could make repeated head-on attacks; most formation leaders settled for beam attacks, which were less hazardous to the German pilots, but were much less successful. The final destruction of damaged bombers that had left their formations was supposed to be left to the day and night twin-engine fighters, but single-engine pilots often made repeated attacks on bombers that they had already damaged, sometimes following them far enough to witness their crashes. Other single-engine pilots would disappear after their first closely monitored frontal pass on the close-packed bombers, and spend the rest of their mission seeking out stragglers. Göring and Galland cursed their inability to obtain uniformly heroic efforts from every pilot, but they were thwarted by human nature.

As the Jagddivision 3 fighters departed for their home bases, they were relieved by II. and III./JG 11, down from Jagddivision 2; II./JG 27, a Luftflotte 3 unit from St. Dizier; and Major Walther Dahl's III./JG 3, over whose Jagddivision 7 territory the bombers were now passing. The JG 11 pilots were at the limit of their range, and broke away to find landing sites after single passes. II./JG 27 did well in its first major RLV mission, claiming six bombers. Dahl's men stayed with the B-17s all the way to Schweinfurt and claimed the greatest success of any Jagdgruppe: 18 B-17s shot down or shot from their formations.

Jagddivision 7's other two fighter units also did well. With Graf's departure, command of JG 50 had passed temporarily to its senior pilot, Oblt. Alfred Grislawski, who downed two B-17s of the six credited to the unit. II./JG 51 had arrived at München-Neubiberg from Italy in mid-August for rebuilding and was kept for RLV duty. Its Kommandeur, Major Karl Rammelt, insisted on thorough training in formation tactics, even simulating attacks on bombers until a trainee collided with his target, a He 111. Today the Gruppe flew its first RLV mission, and attacked the B-17s before and after their bomb runs, claiming a total of four.

I./JG 27 flew west from Austria, made a hurried intermediate landing for fuel, and reached the bombers near their Initial Point, where they claimed six. Bf 110s and Ju 88s from all six night-fighter Geschwader joined the battle, as did the night fighters' operational-training unit. The result was the largest, and most successful, daylight operation ever flown by the twin-engine fighters. Two more Jagddivision 2 day-fighter units, the independent III./JG 54 and JG 25, reached the bombers just after bombs away and remained with the stream as long as possible, claiming four B-17s.

The only Kampfgruppe (bomber group) in the RLV, I./KG 51, had no success. Its Kommandeur, Major Klaus Häberlen, had been relieved three days previously after a public confrontation with Reichsmarschall Göring during a unit inspection. Its altitude-challenged Me 410A-1s scrambled from Hörsching, reportedly contacted the heavies after bombing, fired rockets and closed with the formation, but could claim no victories. This proved to be the unit's last RLV mission. It was withdrawn from the order of battle to retrain for bombing missions against England.

The clouds that had so disrupted the Americans' formations over England in the morning grew thicker during the day. None of the USAAF or RAF withdrawal escorts could get off their bases. The B-17s were only saved from annihilation by the movement of the front across the Channel. None of the Jagddivision 3 units was able to fly a second mission, owing at least in part to the worsening weather. III./JG 26 had been held in reserve at Lille-Vendeville, and when it finally got the order to scramble it was apparently not given a vector from which it could locate the bombers. The bombers' return route took them down the course of the Somme River to the Channel. The numerous JG 2 fighters in the area should have had it easy against the unescorted, disorganized bomber formations, but could claim only nine B-17s; the rest managed to escape in the towering cumulus formations.

In all, 60 B-17s were destroyed by the Luftwaffe in 3 hours and 14 minutes of continuous attacks; seven more bombers were scrapped in England. Every Luftwaffe fighter unit in western Europe was ultimately employed—833 combat sorties were flown. The Germans lost only 38 fighters. The OKW announced that 121 American aircraft had been brought down. The true losses were only half that, but it was obvious to both sides that the defenders had won a stunning victory. Although they had not prevented the bombing, which was much more accurate than that of August 17, dispersal of the ball-bearing industry was already under way, and would be complete before the Americans again turned their attention to Schweinfurt. Albert Speer, the German production czar, stated after the war that no weapon was ever held back from reaching the front owing to a lack of ball bearings.[128]

The Americans' Fall Crisis

The second week in October brought a turning point in the daylight bombing campaign. Four full-strength missions in seven days—to Bremen, Marienburg, Münster and Schweinfurt—had cost the Eighth Air Force 148 heavy bombers, 50 per cent of its average daily operational strength. The American doctrine of unescorted daylight bombing was well and truly dead. No more deep-penetration raids would be made into Germany until the bombers could be escorted all the

way to the target. The operational training of the first two groups of truly long-range American fighters, P-38 Lightnings with twin 150-gallon (568-liter) drop tanks, was rushed to completion.[129] The big Lockheed fighter was returning to the ETO after a year's absence.

The RLV organization continued to be tweaked in the second half of October. XII. Fliegerkorps was disbanded, and Schmid was given command of all day- and night-fighter units in the I. Jagdkorps area of responsibility, which still did not include southern Germany or Austria. The boundaries between Schmid's three Jagddivisionen, Jagddivision 7 and its subordinated Jafü Ostmark, and Luftflotte 3 in the west were redrawn. III./ZG 1 was renamed II./ZG 26, making Jagddivision 2's ZG 26 a full three-Gruppe Geschwader. Jagddivision 7's ZG 76 had only two active Gruppen; formation of a third was delayed until overwhelmed by events. II./ZG 1 remained in Austria as the lone representative of its Geschwader in the RLV.

By November the best of the Jafü commanders had taken over the Jagddivisionen. In I. Jagdkorps these were: the 1., under Oberst Günther Lützow[130] at Berlin-Döberitz; the 2., under Genmaj. Max Ibel at Hamburg-Stade, and the 3., under Oberst Walter Grabmann at Arnhem-Deelen. Thus, as Grabmann noted, "A complete change of command personnel took place within the space of two months in all fighter divisions and fighter commands."[131] The 7. Jagddivision, under Genmaj. Joachim-Friedrich Huth at München-Schleissheim, reported directly to Weise in Berlin, with Jafü Ostmark in Vienna reporting to Huth. Jafü Ostmark eventually became the 8. Jagddivision, and Schmid gained control of it and the 7. in the spring of 1944. Another sticking point for Schmid was that the Aircraft Reporting Service (including the Flak radar stations) in the Reich territory remained under the Luftgaue and therefore Lw Bfh Mitte; Schmid had direct control only over those radar and reporting stations directly assigned to the Jagdkorps or Jagddivisionen.

An RLV formation leaders' school was formed at the end of October and attached to I./JG 27 in Austria. It offered a six-week course to teach successful young combat pilots the bare essentials of how to lead fighter formations against the heavy bombers. Course work and formation flights stressed moderate speeds and gentle changes in course and altitude. The key ingredients of successful leadership, situational awareness and good judgment, could not be taught.

THE LUFTWAFFE OVER GERMANY

B-24Ds of the 376th Bomb Group fly over the Alps in a formation loose enough to suggest that they are on a return flight, probably from one of the first missions from Italy to the Reich. The Liberators were based in the Mediterranean Theater from June 1942 to VE-Day, serving successively in the Ninth, Twelfth, and Fifteenth Air Forces. (Hess)

The students were scrambled by Jafü Ostmark against raids on Austria, but apparently they flew without their instructors, and separately from I./JG 27. Some of the survivors complained that their training was thus more theoretical than practical.[132]

Oberst Hajo Herrmann's single-engine night-fighter unit, JG 300, had gained enough success to be expanded to a full Jagddivision, containing two new Geschwader, JG 301 and JG 302. The three *Wilde Sau* Geschwader were not immediately assigned their own aircraft, but borrowed fighters from the day units on their bases, to the detriment of the serviceability of those units.

Galland's experimental assault-fighter unit, Sturmstaffel 1, was formed at Achmer and subordinated to Hptm. Horst Geyer's ErprKdo 25. The Staffel was to be operational by December and undergo a six-month trial. Command was awarded to Major Hans-Günther von Kornatzki, a professional officer with a mediocre combat record but excellent political connections—he had married one of Göring's secretaries. Kornatzki had been an outspoken proponent of ramming tactics while serving a brief tour on Galland's staff. He now began visiting operational and training day-fighter units, explaining the purpose

of the new unit and asking for volunteers. Enough pilots responded to fill the unit's table of organization, despite Kornatzki's insistence that they sign an oath pledging to ram a bomber on every mission on which it proved impossible to down a bomber by conventional means. All of the pilots were enthusiastic about the home-defense mission; some, but by no means all, also had disciplinary problems that satisfactory service in the new unit might help to clear up.[133]

ErprKdo 25 was the only operational unit in the small department commanded by the General der Jagdflieger, and Genmaj. Galland kept a close eye on it. In addition to the Sturmstaffel, it contained a Staffel devoted to weapons development for single-engine fighters, a similar Staffel for twin-engine fighters, and Erprobungskommando 16, a small test unit for the revolutionary new Me 163 Komet, the world's first rocket-propelled fighter.

The weakened Eighth Air Force flew only one mission in the second half of October. Düren was an important industrial target in the Ruhr that was close enough to England for full escort and the use of a new British navigation aid, Oboe. The raid was flown on the 20th. The target was covered in clouds, the Oboe failed, and the bombing was poor. From the point of view of the air-defense tacticians, however, the Americans won a victory. The first of the new P-38 groups flew its first mission, an easy section of the withdrawal leg. The P-47s provided adequate escort to the short-range target. The fighters of Jagddivision 3 were hampered severely by bad weather, and lost 16 of their number, while only nine B-17s failed to return to England. Three days later Jagddivision 3's day-fighter pilots were ordered to fly to Deelen for a review by Göring. After presenting medals to the assembled pilots, Göring gave a long speech excoriating them for their poor performance and accusing them once again of cowardice before the enemy. This was only nine days after their best performance of the war. A stunned Milch, who was present, recorded the speech. He may have intended to use it against Göring at some future date, but it went no farther than his diary.[134]

A new version of an American fighter that had seen some service in other theaters, but was still little known in the ETO, began arriving in England. The P-51 Mustang was an exceptionally clean single-engine fighter from North American Aviation that had previously been limited to low altitudes by its engine. The version of the P-51 now in production, the P-51B, had a Rolls-Royce Merlin engine with a two-stage mechanical supercharger that gave it excellent high-altitude performance. The new plane would prove to be in most respects the best fighter of the war, and was certainly the longest-ranged to see service in Europe. But some of the USAAF brass still considered it a low-altitude fighter based on its origins, and the first units to receive it were scheduled to join the tactical Ninth Air Force when they reached England. MGen. Eaker proved how out of touch he was when he agreed with the commander of the Ninth that "to simplify maintenance and repair" all new P-51 units would go to the Ninth, while the Eighth took the new P-47 units. The immediate reaction of the short-fused General Arnold when he learned of this agreement is unrecorded; he did succeed in having it rescinded. Arnold made a gutsy move on October 29 that demonstrated the urgency with which he viewed the Eighth Air Force's need for long-range escorts: he ordered that all P-38 and P-51 production for the next three months was to be withheld from all other theaters and sent to the Eighth.[135]

November began with a major strategic move by the USAAF. A new air force, the Fifteenth, was established in Italy and absorbed the few heavy-bomber units in the Mediterranean Theater. Previous raids on Axis industry by these bombers had been successful, with the exception of the low-altitude Ploesti attack, and it was apparent that the German defenses in southern Germany and Austria were still weak. A build-up of the strategic bombing force in Italy to the point that the Reich could be attacked from there with regularity would further stretch the forces of the RLV and, by taking advantage of the (supposedly) better Italian weather, allow missions to be mounted on days that the Eighth in England was grounded. Another reason was probably to find a more congenial home for the new B-24 groups that were being declared battle-ready in the U.S. on a weekly basis. The B-24 was always outshone in England by the more-glamorous B-17, but was associated with heroic battles in the south. Airbase construction in England was barely keeping up with demand, and the Eighth Air Force's command and control structure was stretched to the utmost. A number of new B-24 groups that were scheduled to join the Eighth were thus sent to the Fifteenth, reducing the final establishment strength that had been planned for the Eighth.[136]

The Fifteenth Air Force flew its first mission on November 2. A total of 112 B-17s and B-24s made a very successful attack on the Messerschmitt factory complex in Wiener Neustadt; 11 bombers failed to return to Italy. Three Jagdgruppen—I./JG 27, II./JG 51, and II./JG 53—and the factory protection Schwarm claimed victories. Göring and Galland were dissatisfied with the defensive effort, and flew to Austria a few days later to chew out the Gruppen-kommandeure.[137]

The Eighth Air Force returned to Germany on November 3 with a raid on Wilhelmshaven. Its only operational P-38 unit, the 55th Fighter Group, provided the target escort, and was praised by the bomber crews for an effective job. Most of the defenders were hampered by poor weather. II./JG 3 from Schiphol again made an early interception of the escort. The Messerschmitts bounced the 4th Fighter Group over the Zuider Zee; the Thunderbolt formation was 'hopelessly broken up," in the words of the American mission report, and returned to England without meeting the bombers. Jagddivision 3 frequently ordered its "light" Bf 109 Gruppen, I. and II./JG 3 and III./JG 1, to concentrate on the escorts, despite Berlin's ambivalence on this tactic. The principal problem for the Germans was a lack of numbers. One Jagdgruppe had taken one American group out of the battle on the 3rd, but the other seven escort groups carried out their assigned missions according to plan.[138]

II./JG 3 was the most successful of the three Jagd-division 3 light Gruppen against Allied fighters, but paid a heavy price. The Gruppe was frequently forced into the air to defend its Schiphol base, which was a prime target for Allied medium bombers. On the very afternoon of its successful mission against the 4th Fighter Group the Gruppe was scrambled against such a raid, and its Kommandeur, Major Kurt Brändle, a holder of the Knight's Cross with Oak Leaves, was shot down and killed by Spitfires. The cumulative casualties of the Gruppe were so high that it had to borrow experienced Bf 109 pilots from a nearby Luftflotte 3 unit, III./JG 26, to fill out its formations, while Schmid and his staff debated when to withdraw the Gruppe for rebuilding.[139]

The Eighth Air Force flew eight escorted raids to close-range German targets in November. Average mission strength had increased only to 380 bombers by the end of the month, and the number of fighter groups remained at eight. The RLV responded using its previous tactics, while its commanders met to plan its future course of action. Genobst. Weise chaired an important meeting at his Berlin-Dahlem headquarters that was attended by Genlt. Schmid, the Divisionkommandeure, and representatives from Galland's office.[140] The problems posed by the American escorts were now foremost on their minds. Weise pointed out that the escorts had reached Wilhelmshaven, and could thus be expected on the arc Bremen–Bielefeld–Koblenz. The "heavy" fighters (all of the Zerstörer, all Fw 190s, and Bf 109s with gun tubs or rockets) were having trouble penetrating the escort to reach the bombers. What to do? The answers he got were all variations on two themes: increase the number of light Gruppen and make all attacks with the strongest force possible. Oberst Grabmann, whose Jagddivision 3 usually formed the first line of defense, offered the following suggestions for his own division:

1. All five of his Bf 109 Gruppen should be assigned to tie up the escort. [This implied that all would be converted to light Gruppen by the removal of gun tubs and rockets.]
2. The two forward-most Gruppen [I. and II./JG 3] should take the shortest course to the enemy and attack early; the rest would assemble as large a force as possible before attacking the escort.
3. All of his Fw 190 Gruppen should be treated as heavy formations and directed to the bomber formations that the light units had stripped of their escort.

It was decided that Grabmann's coastal Gruppen should be withdrawn inland, and that two of Jagddivision 2's ZG 26 Gruppen should remain near Hannover, "outside the range of escorts," while its other Gruppe should move to Grove in Denmark to attack unescorted bomber formations crossing Jutland.

Weise ended the conference by issuing two orders:

1. The Jagddivisionen were to work out a way to attack the escort with the strongest force possible, so that the Zerstören should have a chance to attack unescorted *Pulks*.
2. If the heavy bombers penetrated beyond the range of their escort, the tactics hitherto practised would be applied.

But the outspoken and pessimistic Schmid had the last word, pointing out with total accuracy that the large formations that Weise was calling for could not be assembled in time, and that in any case the day-

fighter force was too small to attack both heavy bombers and fighters.

The two senior RLV Jagdgeschwader received new commanders in mid-month. Major Anton Mader of JG 11 had a public falling-out with Genmaj. Ibel of Jagddivision 2 and was sent to take command of JG 54 in Russia. His replacement was Obstlt. Hermann Graf, who had only recently taken over JG 1. Graf was allowed to take his soccer team to JG 11, along with a number of pilots who had previously served with him in JG 52, JG 50, and JG 1. His replacement at JG 1, Oberst Walter Oesau, refused to release the best of these men, Hptm. Alfred Grislawski, whom he retained as Kapitän of 1./JG 1. Oesau was a highly respected professional officer who had been ordered to give up command of JG 2 after being awarded the Knight's Cross with Oak Leaves and Swords, but circumstances now forced him to return to a combat unit, as had happened previously with Graf.

Air activity over the Reich remained at desultory levels through December. The Eighth Air Force flew to France on three days, and to Germany on seven. All but one of the raids on Germany were to the Ruhr, Emden, or Bremen, well within P-47 range. But on the 13th the bombers penetrated all the way to Kiel in bad weather, escorted over the target by P-38s from the 55th Fighter Group and P-51s from the 354th Fighter Group, the latter unit borrowed from the tactical Ninth Air Force. This mission by the "Pioneer Mustang Group" was not especially successful—one Mustang being lost for the probable destruction of one Bf 110—and the presence of the new fighter was apparently not even reported to I. Jagdkorps. Within a few months the Mustang would become well known to every member of the RLV.

Although the serviceability of the RLV units improved during the quarter owing to the low rate of operations, GFM Milch's plans for a dramatic expansion of the day defenses came to little. The six Luftflotte 3 Jagdgruppen were expanded from three to four Staffeln at the beginning of October, but there were not enough fighters available to allow the Lw Bfh Mitte Jagdgruppen to be enlarged. The number of units stationed in the Reich actually decreased in December, when JG 50 and its less-successful twin, JG 25, were disbanded and II./JG 51 transferred from Munich to Italy to defend the north Italian industrial region. This Gruppe was probably intended to placate Mussolini, and was a late replacement for IV./JG 3, which had returned from Italy to Munich in September, without aircraft. Re-equipment of IV./JG 3 went slowly at first, but was rushed to completion when it was ordered to replace II./JG 3 as a Jagd-division 3 front-line unit. The latter Gruppe was still at Schiphol. It had lost yet another highly decorated Kommandeur, Hptm. Wilhelm Lemke, on the 4th, when he and his Schwarm were scrambled late to oppose a sweep by 352nd Fighter Group Thunderbolts, which killed Lemke and two of his men without loss to themselves. On the 13th the Gruppe was surprised on the ground at Schiphol by Ninth Air Force B-26s, and nearly destroyed. Its shattered remnants joined III./JG 1 at Volkel, while IV./JG 3 prepared to move to Grimberghen, which was slightly farther from the North Sea coast than Schiphol.

A late-year reinforcement of the day RLV came about by somewhat devious means. By December, I./JG 300 was fully equipped with its own Bf 109s at Bonn-Hangelar. On December 16, apparently without advance notice, Hptm. Gerhard Stamp was ordered to lead his Gruppe in an interception of an Eighth Air Force day raid on Bremen, although the Gruppe had been on readiness all of the previous night. Stamp was able to get eight of his Messerschmitts off the ground and lead them to the B-17 armada between Bremen and Oldenburg. Their rear attack claimed one bomber, but only two Messerschmitts returned to Bonn. All eight were damaged to some degree, though only one pilot was killed, and one was injured. The experiment was judged a success. The *Wilde Sau* pilots would soon find themselves regularly called on to fly day missions. Their success rate at night had dropped with winter, but their blind-flying skills were very useful for bad-weather day missions.[141]

During what the official USAAF historians termed the "Autumn Crisis," General Arnold and his sub-ordinates in Washington and London sought to preserve the essential place they had claimed for the strategic bomber in the European war. The primary role that the Combined Bomber Offensive had assigned the Eighth Air Force was the fatal weakening of the Luftwaffe prior to the Allied invasion of France, now scheduled for May 1944. The commanders of the American strategic air forces had planned to destroy the Luftwaffe by bombing the factories producing its weapons. However, the RLV was still growing slowly in strength and effectiveness despite the bombing and the continued high claims by the bombers' gunners for the destruction of fighters. American plans to

The new kid in the European Theater—a 354th Fighter Group P-51B at a base in England in the fall of 1943. It displays white identification bands intended to reduce confusion with the Bf 109. (*ww2images*)

attain air superiority underwent a radical change at the end of 1943. All prewar theories were discarded. Arnold took command of the Eighth Air Force away from his good friend Eaker and gave him a new high-level position in the Mediterranean Theater. Eisenhower, the new Supreme Commander of the European Theater, relocated from the Mediterranean to England, bringing with him his own air team of generals and air marshals. These men had learned the hard way that the way to defeat the Luftwaffe was in the air. Their ideas were quickly put into practice. Aided by several groups of P-51s, the fighter that Arnold had had to force on Eaker, they were fatally to weaken the RLV and the Luftwaffe in ample time to control the skies over the invasion beaches.[142]

On the Receiving End: USAAF Perspectives

Completing the story of Luftwaffe's defensive success of fall 1943 requires a look at how it appeared from the other side of the hill. Without a doubt, most USAAF leaders recognized that the Luftwaffe day-fighter force had fought them to a standstill. In the wake of the Second Schweinfurt disaster, Hap Arnold remarked that the "cornered wolf fights hardest."[143] Those closer to the sharp end were even more unstinting in their acknowledgement of the Jagdwaffe's combat prowess. Beirne Lay, after the August 17 Regensburg mission, wrote of "the largest and most savage fighter resistance of any war in history . . . a hailstorm of individual fighter attacks that were to engulf us all the way to the target in such a blizzard of bullets and shells that a chronological account is difficult."[144]

This is an impressionistic account, to be sure—but it is backed up by reams of statistical evidence and operational analysis. In November 1943, the 3rd Bomb Division completed a study of over 2,500 separate encounters with German fighters.[145] Its purpose was straightforward: "By knowing and understanding the standard maneuvers of enemy fighters new crews can profit more from the lessons learned by experienced crews in the past." The report gave full credit to the pilots of the RLV, as it spoke of the danger of "sending out green crews to meet the best fighter pilots in the entire Luftwaffe." It further noted, "The Hun is an opportunist and is quick to change his approach if he can get in a better shot."

The report identified 11 distinct tactics that had been observed during the summer and fall of 1943. Some were assessed as more dangerous and effective than others, and each analysis contained tactical lessons and recommendations for countermeasures. First on the list were rocket attacks from the rear by single- and/or twin-engine fighters in line abreast, while conventionally armed aircraft pressed the attack and picked off damaged or isolated aircraft. The "tactics lesson" grimly noted, "The straggler's number is up. Keep in formation at all costs after explosion of rocket projectiles."

Rated next in effectiveness were massed head-on attacks, described as follows: "Two thousand yards [1,800 meters] on either side of the B-17 formation, and 500 yards [450 m.] above, two columns of up to 18 fighters each overtake the formation, and execute a series of alternating diving attacks from 11 and 12 o'clock high in groups of two or three planes at a time." Schmid's staff would have liked to take credit for two-column attacks, but such tactical concentrations were attained only rarely, and often fortuitously. The more common single-column head-on attack did not make the USAAF list.

Although some of the attack methods on the list are easily matched to actual RLV tactics, others are obviously the result of the list-maker's attempt to categorize the bewildering array of approaches flown by the German fighters, especially when alone or in small formations. The Americans credited the RLV with the frequent use of lone decoy fighters; most of these were in fact piloted by men who were unwilling to close with the bomber formations. In general, the

American analysis confirmed what many German tacticians had already surmised: the effectiveness of the 21-cm rockets, the value of massed, coordinated attacks, and the wide disparities in pilot skill within the Jagdwaffe.

USAAF combat reports often provide glimpses of Luftwaffe experiments and innovations. On the December 11, 1943, Emden mission, *Lemon Drop*, a B-24D of the 44th Bomb Group, was attacked head-on by an Fw 190 which appeared to be trailing a length of steel cable. The cable struck the nose of the bomber, wounding several crewmen, and an explosion blew in the rear bomb bay. The damaged plane returned to base with the cable still entangled in the shattered nose.[146] This was the first confirmed instance of "cable bombing." German accounts describe ErprGr 25 experimenting with

. . . 10-kg [22-pound] bombs slung on cables about 90 meters [300 ft.] long and hung singly on Fw 190s. Tactics were to attack from the front and exit flat over the bombers. Tested in combat with two unconfirmed victories. Experiments stopped because the bomb tended to trail behind the Fw 190 rather than hang down, because the bomb swung too much, and because the aircraft had to come very close to the bomber to achieve victories.[147]

While use of the cumbersome technique was not widespread, it continued to figure in Eighth Air Force combat reports well into 1944, with cable-swinging Bf 109s, Ju 88s and Fw 190s attacking and occasionally damaging USAAF bombers.[148] Another obscure technique involved the dropping of steel nets, intended to foul aircraft engines—at least one bomber brought the evidence home with it.

American combat reports also contain their share of implausible observations. Nonexistent (He 113) or improbable (Ju 87, He 111, Fw 189) aircraft are sometimes reported as engaging the bomber formations.[149] Attacks by German-flown Allied aircraft were reported throughout the war. Some accounts defy explanation: "An unidentified enemy aircraft dropped several 'square objects the size of a stabilizer' to the left and high above the bombers . . . but no results were observed."[150] Perhaps the most extraordinary combat report was submitted after the October 14 Schweinfurt raid. It stated: "50 radio directed FW 190s and a few ME 109s encountered. No pilots were in these A/C. Personnel are positive. A/C possibly controlled by

ME 110/Ju 88/ME 210 . . ."[151] The unit intelligence officer forwarded it with a cover letter stating there was no evidence that the Luftwaffe—innovative though it may have been—possessed any such remote-controlled aircraft. And there the matter rests.

Thus ended the watershed year 1943. In one of the first postwar histories of the Luftwaffe, the British Air Ministry's analysts concluded:

From early in 1943 until the Allied landings in Normandy on 6th June 1944, the combined Anglo-American air attack on the Reich was the dominating factor in the air war. It resulted . . . in the reduction of the German Air Force in the Mediterranean to a size at which their influence over the course of operations became negligible. It resulted in the transfer from Russia to Germany of single-engined and twin-engined fighter units at the very moment when the growing superiority of the Soviet Air Force required a strengthening of German fighter opposition. And, above all else, it enforced a change-over from bomber to fighter, from offensive to defensive equipment,

which irrevocably altered the whole composition and character of the German Air Force.[152]

The fall of 1943 was also the high water mark for the Luftwaffe defenders. And—apart from the night-fighter arm, whose greatest victory, the Battle of Berlin, was yet to come—the day-fighter forces of Lw Bfh Mitte were one of the last major branches of the German military to achieve such a substantial victory. The U-boat arm had been broken in May 1943 in the Battle of the Atlantic; the Panzer arm was shattered at Kursk in July. The *Afrika Korps* was in Allied POW cages, the Mediterranean was an Allied lake, and the German Army was everywhere in retreat.

Young German pilot trainees at a fighter *Vorschule* (primary flight school) pose on an Ar 96 trainer, probably during the winter of 1943–4. These men would receive less than half the flying training hours of their American antagonists. The Luftwaffe's pilot training establishment produced sufficient numbers of pilots through mid-1944, but quality was always a problem. Few of these pilots survived their first five missions. (*ww2images*)

CHAPTER 6

THE AIR WAR IS LOST
JANUARY–APRIL 1944

Optimism Fades in the New Year

The defensive victories of fall 1943 seemed to bode well for Korten's plans to reinvigorate German air strategy, and there was some optimism that the "new Luftwaffe" might yet appear. At this critical stage of the war, nearly every center of power in the Third Reich—Hitler, Propaganda Minister Joseph Goebbels, the Gauleiters, the Armaments Ministry—had awakened to the threat from the third dimension. Korten's Chief of Operations, Koller, spoke for the Luftwaffe senior leadership on March 21, 1944, when he noted,

> I have instructions from General Korten to state this here. There is definitely no other single factor which can play a more decisive role towards victory or defeat than that of air armament. Air power will be the determining weapon in the last phase of this war. Neither tanks nor submarines will play as decisive a

role. If this is denied today all I can say is, history will prove me right.[1]

1944 would indeed see the climax of the air war in Europe, and some of its most dramatic episodes.

The Luftwaffe began the year with a major organizational improvement. Korten and Koller noted to their dismay that the Luftwaffe was still organized as it had been in peacetime—with a bloated command structure in which Reichsmarschall Göring, the *Oberbefehlshaber der Luftwaffe* (Supreme Commander of the Luftwaffe, ObdL) and his Reich Air Ministry (RLM) oversaw the entire scope of aviation activities in Germany, both military and civilian. The Luftwaffe had nothing comparable to the Army and Navy High Commands. In February 1944, Korten and Koller were successful in putting the Luftwaffe command onto a true wartime footing. In Koller's words, "We tried to split up the vast organisation of ObdL, to group all the

Oberst Walter Grabmann (*far right*), Kommandeur of Jagddivision 3, inspects the men of Sturmstaffel 1 on the rain-slick Dortmund apron in January. Recognizable in the ranks are: Hptm. Günther Wrobel (*2nd from left*), Obfw. Erich Kaiser (*4th left*), Obfw. Emil Demuth (*6th left*), Obfw. Gerhard Vivroux (*far right*). (*Smith*)

parts which were necessary to the conduct of the war under a military command, and to detach them from the unessential sections of the Air Ministry."[2] On February 5, 1944, the *Oberkommando der Luftwaffe* (Luftwaffe High Command, OKL) was created, encompassing the general staff, the operations staff, the weapons inspectorates (including Galland's GdJ), the quartermaster branch, and signals. Training, administration, civil defense, and technical development remained under the RLM.[3] Given the problems facing the Luftwaffe, it is difficult to concur with Koller's claim that training was "unessential," but the new organization did prove more efficient and endured to the end of the war.

The multi-front challenges facing the German air arm were formidable. At a conference in February 1944, Milch spoke of two main points of effort by the enemy—the air war against the Reich (which he regarded as the most important) and the Eastern Front. He noted that the war in Italy was of secondary importance, but warned his audience that Germany would no doubt face another enemy landing somewhere on the European continent that spring.[4]

Faced with four looming threats, maintaining a strong "offensive defensive" orientation would prove a pipe dream. Only in the east did Korten's plans for an offensive build-up make any headway. Over the objections of the Army High Command (OKH), the Luftwaffe assembled a powerful force of 300–400 bombers under IV. Fliegerkorps for an attack against Soviet war industry. Yet before this attack could be launched, Soviet gains in the spring of 1944 captured key airfields and placed the most lucrative Soviet targets out of range of He 111 bombers. IV. Fliegerkorps resumed its earlier role as a railroad interdiction force.

Despite Korten's efforts, the war in the east remained overwhelmingly an army-support struggle in 1944, with some 60–80 percent of the Luftwaffe's effort going to the direct assistance of the hard-pressed ground forces. The now largely Fw 190-equipped *Schlachtgruppen* (ground-attack groups) did yeoman service, while at the same time siphoning off a significant proportion of German fighter production. The few fighter units left on the *Ostfront* faced a resurgent Red Air Force, employing aggressive and sophisticated combat tactics.[5] With only 289 serviceable fighters in the theater at the end of March 1944, the eastern Luftflotten gradually yielded air superiority to "Stalin's Falcons."[6]

Nowhere did the Luftwaffe's longstanding policy of "attack as the best defense" misfire so badly as in the west.[7] The strengthened bomber force of Luftflotte 3 carried out its long-delayed major assault on London, Operation Steinbock (Ibex), from January through May 1944. IX. Fliegerkorps lost nearly 300 bombers and their irreplaceable crews to little purpose other than keeping the offensive dream alive and fulfilling the Führer's desire for reprisals.[8] One of the reasons Sperrle had defended his prerogatives so strongly was to ensure that Luftflotte 3 could conduct such offensive operations; the bankruptcy of this policy was now evident. After the failure of Steinbock, only the V-weapon campaign would continue the offensive against the British Isles. Things were only slightly better in Italy, where the Luftwaffe achieved some local successes in support of Kesselring's defensive campaign.[9] Here the Luftwaffe was simply a small cog in a delaying action, in what was rapidly becoming a backwater theater that continued to wear down German air strength on the periphery.[10]

As early as December 1943, Göring and the Operations Staff began working on a detailed scheme, code-named Dr. Gustav West (for *Drohende Gefahr West*—Imminent Danger West—abbreviated DGW), to reinforce Luftflotte 3 and its II. Jagdkorps with fighter units from the RLV and elsewhere in the event of an Allied landing.[11] The German high command could

Ogfr. Gerhard Vivroux's Sturmstaffel 1 Fw 190A-6 runs up its engine at Dortmund in January. The fighter carries the unit's lightning bolt and gauntlet badge on the cowling, and black–white–black identification bands on the rear fuselage. It has been fitted with armored glass on the canopy quarter and side panels. (*Smith*)

never be certain of the location of the Anglo-American assault, and as a result developed contingency plans for meeting landings everywhere from Scandinavia to the south of France to the Balkans. Yet a landing somewhere on the Channel coast in northern France seemed the most likely scenario, and the Luftwaffe was prepared to counter it quickly. In its earliest incarnations, DGW foresaw the immediate transfer of ten Jagdgruppen, four Zerstörergruppen, and six Nachtjagdgruppen from the RLV, as well as assorted bomber, ground-attack, reconnaissance, and fighter units from other theaters, to new bases in France and the Low Countries.[12] Like the Luftwaffe of old, it would meet the invasion with an overwhelming concentration of forces, even if it meant virtually denuding the Reich defense organization.

A 389th Bomb Group B-24 in its final dive over southwestern Germany, its bomb bay in flames. It was hit by fighters while returning from Ludwigshafen on January 7. (*ww2images*)

As important as were these challenges, Milch correctly identified the Allied strategic air offensive as the most immediate threat facing Germany at the beginning of 1944. The RAF night offensive was reaching a crescendo with the Battle of Berlin, Air Chief Marshal Harris's attempt to "wreck Berlin from end to end." Harris's winter campaign ended with a severe check for his command. Although the German night-fighter force seemed to have weathered the winter crisis, the damage Bomber Command was causing to large sections of the German war economy—and the enormous drain of resources in defending against it—was cause for concern at the highest levels of German leadership. An even more direct threat to the survival of the Luftwaffe was encapsulated in Hap Arnold's Christmas greeting to the commanding generals of the Eighth and Fifteenth Air Forces on December 27, 1943. He concluded with a statement of air strategy remarkable for its clarity: "My personal message to you—this is a MUST—is to '*Destroy the Enemy Air Force wherever you find them, in the air, on the ground, and in the factories*.'"[13] The German defenders were equally determined to stop the USAAF—and their effort would be waged in the air, on the ground, and in the factories as well.

The Formation of Luftflotte Reich

The advocates of a defensive build-up received a belated vindication of their efforts in January. In a long-overdue recognition of the importance of the command, Luftwaffenbefehlshaber Mitte was renamed Luftflotte Reich, giving it an organizational status equivalent to that of the Luftflotten at the combat fronts. Command was taken from Weise, a Flak general, and given to an experienced aviation commander, Genobst. Hans-Jürgen Stumpff, who was summoned from Luftflotte 5 in Norway. His new headquarters was located in Berlin-Wannsee. Some saw Weise's demotion as a result of his "unfairly" being held accountable for the shortcomings of the Flak arm in Reich defense.[14] Stumpff was undoubtedly qualified for his new job, but several insiders claimed that the reason it was given to him was political; the Luftwaffe was so hated in Germany that the regional Gauleiters would have complained to Hitler if an aviation general already serving in the RLV had been given the job. Politics aside, Grabmann believed that Stumpff's appointment was simply an acknowledgment that Reich defense required "a commander versed in the direction of both air and anti-aircraft artillery operations and experienced in the execution of both offensive and defensive air missions." The effectiveness of the Flak was still compromised by Window jamming, and the fall battles had underscored the importance of the day-fighter force, so the appointment of a flying commander seemed prudent. Stumpff would command Luftflotte Reich to the end of the war, and would have the thankless task of surrendering the remnants of the Reich to the Allies.[15]

The roles of the command organizations were still evolving, and depended as much on the personalities of their commanding officers as on any real attempt to achieve unity of effort. Luftflotte Reich provided overall direction, and much later unified the day- and night-fighter forces, the Aircraft Reporting Service, and the Flak commands under a single headquarters. I. Jagdkorps (in Luftflotte Reich) and II. Jagdkorps (in Luftflotte 3) coordinated and supervised most of the day-fighter forces, but Jagddivision 7 in south Germany and Austria continued to report directly to Luftflotte Reich. Schmid continued trying to increase the role of his I. Jagdkorps. In a January 24 letter to the RLM, routed through Luftflotte Reich, he wrote:

> In order to assure successful air-defense measures within the territory of the Reich, the following conditions must be met:
> 1. One central agency should be given the responsibility of preparing the "situation picture."
> 3. All of the reporting agencies engaged in RLV activity (radio reconnaissance, radar, and ground reporting stations) should report to a single central agency and should be made subordinate to this agency.
> 3. A central commanding unit should be set up to direct the commitment of day- and night-fighter units in home air-defense activity.

In a history Schmid wrote for the USAAF after the war he added, "This suggestion, a repetition of one made by the I. Jagdkorps headquarters [i.e., Schmid himself] . . . 11 December 1943 . . . was not carried out until 31 March 1944."[16]

The main function of the Jagddivision headquarters was the control of aerial operations. In 1944 this control became tighter, and the formations they controlled in the air, called *Gefechtsverbände* (battle formations), became larger, typically of Geschwader strength or greater. The *Gefechtsverbände* were commanded while in the air by senior officers,

preferably Kommodoren or Kommandeure. For the first time since the Battle of Britain, the Jagdgeschwader became a tactical unit. Jagdgruppen, which had previously tended to operate alone, were in several cases relocated closer to the bases of their home Geschwader staff flights, which were to command the *Gefechtsverbände*. In early 1944, the *Gefechtsverbände* were intended to be:

Gefechtsverband	Area of Operation	Controlling HQ
JG 1	Netherlands	Jagddivision 3 (JD 3)
JG 3	Rhineland	Jagddivision 3 (JD 3)
JG 11	Northern Germany	Jagddivision 2 (JD 2)
JG 27	Austria	Jafü Ostmark
JG zbV	Southwestern Germany	Jagddivision 7 (JD 7)[17]

Note that JD 3, over which most Eighth Air Force raids on Germany passed, controlled two *Gefechtsverbände*, while JD 1 in Berlin, which was not yet threatened by day, had none. Also note the JG zbV, or *Jagdgeschwader zur besondere Verwendung*. This was not a full Geschwader, but a fighter staff established "for special use," in this case the command of a *Gefechtsverband* comprising several independent Jagdgruppen based in the area of JD 7. There were no "regular" Jagdgeschwader staffs available for this duty. Formation of the JG zbV staff was delayed, and it did not come into existence until mid-April.

Of the two Zerstörergeschwader, ZG 26 was assigned to Jagddivision 2, while ZG 76 was in Jagddivision 7. At the end of 1943 the bases of both Geschwader were out of range of most American escort fighters. Their Bf 110s and Me 410s were to operate in Geschwader strength if possible, but formating with the single-engine *Gefechtsverbände* proved problematic owing to different cruising speeds. Special mixed units were formed several months later, when the need for continuous escort of the twin-engine bomber destroyers became obvious.

Gefechtsverbände were an expedient necessitated by the Allied escort, and had many problems, as pointed out by Galland:

1. The time required for assembly reduced the time available for combat.
2. They were very unwieldy to command and maneuver in the air.
3. It was very hard for inexperienced pilots to stay with the formation.[18]

Not mentioned by Galland, but equally important, was the shortage of competent *Verbandsführer* (formation leaders). A school was now training junior officers to lead Schwärme and Staffeln in the RLV, but men with the experience, combat skills, and situational awareness to command *Gefechtsverbände* of up to 200 fighters in the air were very rare, and were an ever-dwindling resource.

In an early post-war interrogation Galland provided a brutally frank assessment of command and control by the Jagddivisionen:

1. There was a definite geographic bias. They controlled their own units even when these crossed boundaries, but had to give them up when out of radio and radar range—this never went smoothly.

2. The commanders were World War I veterans; their chiefs of staff were General Staff officers—good men, but not operational pilots.

3. There were no deputy commanders. This post should have existed, and been filled with fighter pilots, but there were not enough of them.

4. The fighters were controlled in the air by Jägerleitoffiziere (JLO)—one for each airborne Gruppe. These men were either war-weary pilots or very good signals officers—they tended to play "board games," and couldn't think in 3-D to give their own forces the tactical advantage.

5. The radio-intercept service belonged to Gen.

Bf 109G-6 "yellow 1" of 5./JG 302, photographed at the beginning of 1944, while the unit was still flying night missions. Its rippled skin is very noticeable in the sun's glare. (*Sinnecker*)

Martini, the chief Luftwaffe signals officer, and could only be controlled at the Luftflotte level—thus airborne "tricks" by JLOs [for which the RAF was famous] were not possible.

6. The Jagdkorps, Jagddivisionen, Luftflotte Reich, Göring, Galland, and the high command staff were on a single phone circuit—all (but Galland) could issue orders; "Göring's were frequently silly."

7. The Fühlungshalter aircraft had to be withdrawn in early 1944 because of the Allied escorts. This left the JLOs in the dark as to weather, clouds, altitudes, escort, etc.

8. The formation leaders were not given enough freedom to use their own initiative [a consistent complaint of Galland since 1940].[19]

The Flak units remained under the Luftgaukommandos to the end of the war. In early 1944, however, the position of *Flakeinsatzführer* was established in order to further the "effective operational employment of the combined arms." More than a simple liaison officer, this Flak commander could issue orders to anti-aircraft batteries as well as exchange information with the fighter commanders. His headquarters was co-located with the Jagddivision headquarters, and he worked "in closest cooperation" with the Jagddivision commander. The Luftwaffe operations staff noted that this arrangement produced excellent results, as the Flakeinsatzführer was often able to bridge the gap separating the fighter and Flak forces and ensure effective cooperation between them.[20] Fighter control steadily improved as the latest Mammut and Wassermann radar sets became available in increasing numbers.[21] 1944 also witnessed the development of new early-warning radar and fighter-control techniques, including the Jagdschloss panoramic radar and the Freya-Egon-Gerät radar-control procedure.[22] Through painful evolution, and despite formidable technical and bureaucratic obstacles, a modern, fully integrated air-defense system was taking shape.

The tactics, ground organization, and command and control procedures of the RLV were evolving rapidly. In contrast, the aerial equipment itself was stagnating. The day units of the RLV were equipped with two types of single-engine fighters and two types of twin-engine "destroyers." All were adequate against unescorted bombers, but except when piloted by the ever-scarce *Experten*, all had problems with the

American escorts. There was no chance of replacing any of them in the first half of 1944. The oldest design, the Messerschmitt Bf 109, was now represented by the Bf 109G-6, which would prove to be the model produced in the greatest quantity. Its 1,475-hp DB 605A in-line engine provided a top speed of 621 km/h at 6,900 meters (386 mph at 22,600 ft.). Its standard armament of one MG 151/20 cannon and two MG 131 heavy machine guns was adequate against Allied fighters, but was too light to pose much of a threat to B-17s or B-24s. Increased firepower was available in the form of rocket launchers or MG 151/20 cannons in underwing gondolas, at a dramatic cost in maneuverability and speed. During the spring the unburdened versions were given to "light" Gruppen, which had the task of battling escorts, while the others were given to "heavy" Gruppen. A variety of Bf 109 models with improved performance, especially at high altitude, were in the pipeline. They were equipped with new engines and/or enlarged superchargers and showed efforts to clean up what had become a very cluttered design.

The most versatile of Luftflotte Reich's fighter types was the Focke-Wulf 190. Their usefulness on the combat fronts kept them in short supply in the Reich. The type was considered easy to fly and very resistant to combat damage, and was always popular with its pilots. The version in service at the start of the year was the Fw 190A-6. This had a 1,700-hp BMW 801D radial engine which gave the plane a top speed of 652 km/h at 6,300 meters (405 mph at 20,700 ft.), but its rated power decreased sharply above that altitude. The fighter's armament of four MG 151/20 wing cannon and two MG 17 machine guns provided ample destructive power against Allied aircraft. Early in the year the Luftflotte 3 Focke-Wulf Gruppen received some Fw 190A-7s, which had improved internal equipment and 12.7-mm MG 131s in place of the rifle-caliber MG 17 cowling machine guns. This model was quickly supplanted on the production lines by the similar Fw 190A-8, which was the variant built in the greatest numbers and was standardized for the RLV. It had proved impossible to boost the power of the BMW 801D, and the increased weight of the new models degraded performance. A new engine was needed. Two in-line engines were being tested, but the aircraft intended to use them, the Fw 190D and Ta 152, would not be available until late in 1944.

Of the two destroyer types, the Bf 110 was obsolete and due to be phased out of production, but its

Bf 109G-6 "white 6" of 7./JG 1, at Leeuwarden, Holland, in early 1944. It carries the "winged red 1" Geschwader emblem introduced by Obstlt. Oesau in late 1943 and a rust-red RLV fuselage band. (*Crow*)

successor, the Me 410A-2, had problems of its own. It was superior to the Bf 110 only in raw speed, 624 km/h at 6,700 meters (388 mph at 22,000 ft.) compared to 550 km/h at 6,980 meters (342 mph at 23,000 ft.). It was inferior in maneuverability, and very important to the crews, it was very difficult to exit in emergencies. Plans to re-equip the Bf 110 Gruppen with Me 410s had to be delayed because of the high loss rate of the latter type in the few Gruppen which had them. The only replacement planned for the Me 410 was the tandem-engine Do 335, which at this stage of the war was little more than a fantasy.[23]

The War of Attrition

The American strategic air forces in Europe also underwent a major reorganization in January. Unlike that of the RLV, which was to a large degree cosmetic and driven by personalities, that of the USAAF coincided with a major change in strategy.

The relief of the commander of the Eighth Air Force, Lieutenant General (LGen.) Eaker, and his departure for the Mediterranean Theater coincided with the arrival in England of the newly named Supreme Commander of the European Theater of Operations, Gen. Dwight D. "Ike" Eisenhower, and his staff. One member of the staff, LGen. Carl "Tooey" Spaatz, was given command of a new organization, the U.S. Strategic Air Forces in Europe (USSTAF), which was to coordinate the American strategic forces deployed against Germany from both England and Italy. His deputy commander for operations was MGen. Fred Anderson, who was to control the day-today employment of these forces. He had previously led the 8th Bomber Command, which was abolished. Command of the Eighth Air Force, now stripped of its principal operational command, was given to MGen. James H. Doolittle.

Jimmy Doolittle, America's first genuine World War II air hero, had been jumped two grades in rank for planning and leading the famous Tokyo raid in April 1942, and had been sent to North Africa at the end of 1942, apparently for his publicity value. Eisenhower, then the Mediterranean Theater commander, resented the brash parvenu at first, but came to admire him for his intelligence, energy, and flexibility, and wanted him on his team in England. But the Air Force hierarchy was never fond of Doolittle, the only reservist ever to rise to three-star rank or command a numbered U.S. air force. This may be an overly cynical interpretation of Arnold's motives, but his decision to reduce the size of the Eighth Air Force commander's job may have come from a distrust of Doolittle's basic competence. On paper Doolittle had little to do except address the Eighth's organizational and personnel issues and follow Anderson's orders with respect to combat operations. Doolittle may have been expected to excel as a "front man" for America's strategic air forces—he attracted good press wherever he went—while the "real" war was conducted behind the scenes by the bomber generals, the dour Spaatz and the invisible Anderson.

However, after less than a month at the helm of the Eighth, Doolittle made a command decision that drastically altered the course of the air war over Europe and ensured the success of Operation Pointblank, the Allied campaign to gain air superiority prior to D-Day. Unlike Arnold, Spaatz, Eaker, and Anderson, Doolittle was not a "bomber man"—in fact, his early active service had been in fighters—and, lacking their preconceptions, was able to separate the objective of Operation Pointblank from their preferred means, strategic bombing.

To Doolittle, the goal of destroying the Luftwaffe fighter force was all-important; the means were irrelevant. An early visit to MGen. Kepner at 8th Fighter Command convinced Doolittle that the bomber commanders had held Kepner's fighters on too tight a leash. On January 21, Doolittle announced at his staff meeting:

> The fighter role of protecting the bomber formations should not be minimized, but our fighter aircraft should be encouraged to meet the enemy and destroy him rather than be content to keep him away.

The German fighter force was to be destroyed by attrition—worn down in the air.[24]

Doolittle's decision to "free the fighters" was in his opinion his most critical of the war. Kepner and his

The Bf 109G-6 *Kanonenboot* (gunboat) of the I./JG 27 Kommandeur, Hptm. Ludwig Franzisket, in early 1944. Markings of interest include the green JG 27 fuselage band, Kommandeur chevrons, the Gruppe emblem, a yellow cowling underside, and the white rudder that denoted a formation leader at this time. (*Bundesarchiv 662-6659-38*)

pilots were, of course, overjoyed, while the bomber commanders were anything but. According to Doolittle:

> As soon as my decision was announced to the bomb groups, their commanders descended on me . . . to tell me, in polite terms, of course, that I was a "killer" and a "murderer" . . . There was no compromise as far as I was concerned, and many bomber crews remained very unhappy. Some still are.[25]

Typical winter weather reduced the level of aerial operations in January. The Eighth Air Force flew seven raids to Germany; the Fifteenth Air Force, now under the command of LGen. Nathan Twining, three. New bomber groups continued to arrive in England and Italy; the Eighth Air Force now had 25 B-17 and B-24 groups in operation. The pipeline was also full of fighters, most of them still the range-limited P-47s. 8th Fighter Command now had nine P-47 groups and two P-38 groups, plus one Ninth Air Force P-51 group that was on indefinite loan. On January 4, a small force of B-17s was sent to bomb Münster, escorted by all of the P-47s. The bulk of the bomber force left 20 minutes later on a straight-line course for Kiel. They flew most of the mission without escort, but were met in the target area by the three long-range escort groups (two P-38 and one P-51). The RLV day fighters were hampered somewhat by bad weather at their bases, and the defensive effort as a whole was unsuccessful. The night fighters of NJG 3 and NJG 5 were less challenged by the weather, and flew one of their best day missions against the withdrawing Kiel raiders. Lt. Peter Spoden of II./NJG 5 recalled:

> Our tactics had been worked out beforehand—using our Lichtenstein radar to determine range, we were to attack from the rear to break up the formations; singles were then to be shot down with guns.
>
> I led a Schwarm of four Bf 110s from Parchim to attack the withdrawing B-17s over the North Sea. We were to meet a Schwarm from Schwerin but didn't see it or any other fighters. There were no plans for aerial cooperation; we had only lousy HF radios for air-to-air communication. We were to attack from the rear in line abreast, firing our *Dödels* [WGr 21 rockets] from 2 km. [1.25 miles]. I was hit by defensive fire at 3 km [1.8 miles], and ordered rockets fired from 2.5 km. [1.5 miles]. I couldn't fire my own rockets due to a bad electrical circuit. I pulled away after an engine quit,

hosing the *Verband* with my guns as I left. Two of my Bf 110s crash-landed; I was able to force-land at Parchim, the only member of my Schwarm to return to base. This was dangerous business, and limited to the more expendable crews—those with more than ten victories were forbidden to fly them.

> I learned after the war that my fire had shot an engine out of a B-17; it had to force-land in the North Sea off England.[26]

Kiel was targeted again on the 5th, once more with a small force and a target escort comprising the three long-range fighter groups. The rest of the bomber force and the P-47s were split among targets from Bordeaux to Eberfeld. Anderson picked a single target for the 7th, the Ludwigshafen chemical complex. The plants were strung along the Rhine River and made an easy target for identification by H2X, the American version of British H2S airborne radar. With 11 fighter groups available to protect a single continuous bomber stream, few Luftwaffe fighters were able to penetrate to the bombers, and only 12 bombers were lost to all causes.

Also on the 7th, the Fifteenth Air Force targeted Wiener Neustadt. The bombers turned back early, but the P-38s of the 1st and 14th Fighter Groups continued to the target, where the 14th Group downed a II./ZG 1 Bf 110 without loss. The 1st Group was met by the Bf 109s of Major Gerhard Michalski's II./JG 53. After a 30-minute battle that concluded at low level over Yugoslavia, the German pilots returned to base claiming 15 victories for no combat losses; one Bf 109 was destroyed and four were damaged in dead-stick landings forced by fuel exhaustion. Michalski stated in his report that his opponents had flown like cavemen. The German pilots had indeed done extremely well; six 1st Fighter Group P-38s were in fact shot down. The Americans claimed 1–1–6 Bf 109s and 3–0–0 Fw 190s, but there were no Focke-Wulfs in the area.

On the 11th Doolittle approved a maximum-strength mission against Oschersleben, Halberstadt and Brunswick. Bad weather over England caused difficulties in forming up, but Germany was clear, and the forecast was for England to clear before the bombers' return. However, the weather got worse over the bases, and Doolittle ordered a recall as the leading bomber wings were already crossing into Germany. The result for the Americans was disastrous. Some bomber wings turned back, while others proceeded to their targets. Most of the escort fighters either turned

THE LUFTWAFFE OVER GERMANY

back or missed rendezvous. Oberst Grabmann had his forward units up early; they began attacking the bombers over the Zuider Zee. The Fühlungshalter aircraft were quick to report the escort gaps, and Jagddivisionen 1, 2, 3, and 4 (the last-named from Luftflotte 3) threw their fighters at them by Gruppen; no attempts were made to form *Gefechtsverbände*.

Major James H. Howard, the leader of the 354th Fighter Group on this mission, found himself entirely alone after dispatching his P-51 squadrons to various parts of the bomber stream and then getting separated from the other three members of his flight. He observed one B-17 combat box under constant attack and spent 30 minutes diving on the German fighters to break up their attacks. After the mission B-17 crews from the 401st Bomb Group tracked down Howard's unit from his airplane's code letters and recommended him for the Medal of Honor, the highest American award for valor. Howard became the only fighter pilot in the European theater to receive this award.[27]

Most of the RLV units flew successful missions. Sturmstaffel 1 scrambled from Rheine in its Fw 190A-6s for the first test of its novel *Sturmtaktik* (assault tactics). Although it took off with I./JG 1, it soon separated, and attacked the stream alone from dead astern to very close range. Three B-17s dropped from formation as a result of their 20-mm cannon fire. The Staffel suffered no casualties on this mission, which was considered an unqualified success.[28]

I./JG 1 made a frontal attack, which was still the norm for single-engine RLV fighters, but other Gruppen had developed their own tactics. Despite Genmaj. Galland's belief that formation leaders were not given enough freedom, they were in fact on their own once the enemy was sighted, and some had worked out novel ways to get at the bombers. Oblt. Eberhard Burath of II./JG 1 recalled that on this day his Gruppe used Hptm. Walter Hoeckner's unique *Schlangenbiss* ("snakebite") tactic—a wave attack from low rear. The Gruppe claimed ten B-17s shot down and one more shot from formation, for the loss of one pilot and two Fw 190s.[29]

I./JG 302, a *Wilde Sau* Gruppe that normally flew Bf 109s at night, made an attack that downed one B-17 for the cost of three fighters. The use of the *Wilde Sau* fighters by day would become more common in the coming month, and these Gruppen would soon join the table of organization of the RLV day fighters, classed as "bad weather" fighters.

Jagddivision 4 scrambled several Jagdgruppen against the withdrawing bombers. Hptm. Karl Borris's I./JG 26 located a small unescorted *Pulk* north of Nordhorn. It contained the 19 B-17s of the 306th Bomb Group, all alone in their combat box. Borris led a close-formation frontal attack, rolled through the formation, and returned to attack from the rear. In seven minutes, eight B-17s had dropped from their formation, resulting in eight German victory claims. Five crashed in Europe, while two were scrapped in England; the eighth reached base with severe damage. Defensive fire brought down three Fw 190s, but no German pilot was injured.[30]

The returning Americans reported "the heaviest opposition since Schweinfurt." Their estimate of the number of German fighters they had seen was high. I. Jagdkorps reported only 239 sorties, 207 with enemy contact, but they were certainly effective. A total of 60 bombers went down (matching Schweinfurt), and five more were scrapped in England; 592 American escorts took off for the mission, and claimed 31–12–16 German fighters, for a loss of 5–3–6. The German fighters were punished by both bombers and escorts, and lost 53 aircraft destroyed and 31 damaged beyond economical repair (abbreviated as 53–31), 38 KIA, and 22 WIA.

In mid-January Major Heinz Bär[31] joined II./JG 1 for duty as an ordinary pilot. Bär was one of the Luftwaffe's top-scoring *Experten*, and a holder of the Knight's Cross with Oak Leaves and Swords, but had

When the Zerstörergeschwader were re-formed in the fall of 1943 and added to the strength of the RLV, the Bf 110G-equipped II./ZG 1 joined JG 27 in Austria. Here is a Gruppe airplane on the I./JG 27 flight line at Fels-am-Wagram in early 1944. Behind it is a 3./JG 27 Bf 109G-6, "yellow 9." *(Bundesarchiv 658-6395-7a)*

been relieved of duty with JG 77 in Italy for insubordination. His Kommodore, Obstlt. Johannes Steinhoff,[32] did not courtmartial him, but had him sent to an operational training unit, Jagdgruppe Süd. His combat skills were too great to overlook, however, and he was soon ordered to JG 1, where Oberst Oesau welcomed him with the warning that he had had to assure the OKL that Bär was not to be given any command responsibilities. On the surface Bär accepted this insult with good humor, but commented to others that, in the air, he was "Kommodore of his own crate." Oesau soon found ways to use Bär's skills as a formation leader.[33]

On the 24th the target for the Eighth Air Force was Frankfurt. As on the 11th, the weather over their bases worsened after takeoff and Doolittle recalled the bombers while they could still land safely. This time the recall came before German fighter attacks began, and bomber losses were very light. Doolittle was nevertheless issued both an oral and a written reprimand by Spaatz for issuing the recalls on the 11th and the 24th. Operation Pointblank was falling behind schedule, and the tension within the USAAF high command was building. An increased loss rate due to weather would have to be accepted.[34]

The mission of the 24th is notable as the first application of MGen. Kepner's new escort directive. Continuous close escort was no longer to be practised; fighter groups were now to provide "area coverage"; that is, they were to patrol specific areas along the bomber track. One squadron of each group was designated a "bouncing squadron," which was free to pursue any approaching Luftwaffe fighter formations well beyond the visual range of the heavy bombers. The escorts' new aggressiveness had an immediate impact on the RLV pilots and commanders. Many survivors can recall the exact month that the American pilots began chasing them all the way to the ground, without suspecting that it was the result of a deliberate high-level change in policy.[35]

The Eighth Air Force returned to Brunswick and Frankfurt before the end of the month, while the Fifteenth made a successful attack on the fighter base at Udine that forced the main regional fighter headquarters to relocate from northern Italy to southern Austria. The month of January was summed up succinctly in the history that Beppo Schmid wrote for the USAAF, using some statistics provided by the Americans. Highlights are reprinted below—note that he frequently referred to himself in the third person:

1. Following a suggestion made by the I. Jagdkorps commander in December, the geographical concentration of day fighters was carried out in northwestern Germany, eastern Holland, and the area between Bremen and Hannover. The corresponding organizational changes were made for almost all units.
2. The technique of combat by mixed units in close formation proved effective when weather conditions were favorable. Assembly was rarely possible in poor weather.
3. The technique of attack from the front, which had proved to be most generally successful, had not yet been mastered by all fighter units.
4. There was no numerical reinforcement of the RLV day-fighter units, although they were requested by the I. Jagdkorps commander in December.
5. The use of day fighters by the Herrmann-Jäger [Wilde Sau night fighters], and the high losses of the latter during January 44, hurt the operations of the day-fighter forces.
6. Supply of replacement day fighters was, for the most part, satisfactory.
7. The "total striking power" of I. Jagdkorps fighters was greater in January than in late 1943. The successes on January 11 did much to increase the confidence of the command and the line units in an ultimately successful defense, although the tactical and numerical superiority of the American fighter units had not yet been fully demonstrated.
8. During January, the average daily operational strengths of I. Jagdkorps were: 400 single-engine fighters, 80 twin-engine fighters, and 100 night fighters available for day use.
9. January sorties by I. Jagdkorps = 2,306; losses = 122, or 5.3 percent.
10. January sorties vs. Reich by USAAF = 7,158; losses to fighters = 179, or 2.5 percent.[36]

The American strategic forces continued to struggle against the weather in February. The Eighth Air Force flew five missions to the Reich between the 1st and the 19th; the Fifteenth flew none. Genmaj. Schmid kept up his cries for reinforcements for I. Jagdkorps, but got none; the only Jagdgruppe to join the RLV in February was I./JG 5, most recently in Bulgaria, but it went to Genmaj. Huth's Jagddivision 7 in southern Germany. One new fighter Staffel was established, 1./JG 400, under Major Wolfgang Späte. It was not an operational unit, but a re-designated testing unit,

A large part of the JG 27 command staff, photographed on Sicily in July 1943. Its Gruppen began returning to the Reich in early 1944 from various Mediterranean bases for service in the RLV. *From left:* Major Gustav Rödel, Kommodore; Hptm. Werner Schroer, II./JG 27 Kommandeur; Major Rudolf Sinner, IV./JG 27 Kommandeur. (*Crow*)

ErprKdo 16, and had the job of bringing the rocket-propelled Me 163 into service. The Komet was the most revolutionary fighter to see combat in World War II, but was not the war-winner that some hoped for. Its service introduction would be prolonged, and painful.

On the 3rd the Eighth dropped a number of bombs in the general area of Wilhelmshaven and Emden. Losses were very low; few RLV fighters could get off the ground. The next day brought a mission to Frankfurt. Losses increased to 20–3 and 1–1 escorts, but could have been worse. Only 124 defensive sorties were flown, and the only units to contact the enemy were two JG 26 Gruppen from Jagddivision 4. The blame lay with the German controllers. Frankfurt was in the area defended by Jagddivision 7, whose controllers were unable to put their own fighters into contact with the bomber stream and were slow to request aid from I. Jagdkorps. I./JG 26 did very well, considering the odds it was up against. It scrambled against the withdrawing stream and made contact near Brussels. Its quick attack downed three B-17s before the arrival of 352nd Fighter Group P-47s forced the Fw 190s into a defensive circle, from which two were shot down with minor injuries to their pilots. The Gruppe scored a fourth B-17 victory a half hour after this combat, when a straggling bomber was located and shot down.[37]

II./JG 26 did not have the luck of its sister Gruppe. An early scramble shot down a B-24 aborting from the inbound stream, but a full-strength Gruppe mission against the withdrawing stream never reached the bombers. It was attacked in turn by P-38s of the withdrawing target escort and 56th Fighter Group P-47s of the reception escort, which shot down two Gruppe Fw 190s, killing one pilot and injuring the other.

Genmaj. Schmid was summoned to Berlin to explain the command failures of the 4th. He placed the blame squarely on Jagddivision 7, and recommended (again) that it be put under his command, but the time was apparently still not right.[38]

The Eighth Air Force B-17s flew to Frankfurt again on February 8, while the B-24s attacked V-1 sites in the Pas de Calais. (The Allies still knew few details of the V-1, but they were suspected to be among Hitler's "revenge weapons," and a campaign against them was necessary. It was, however, a diversion from Pointblank, and was usually conducted in marginal weather.) Bombing accuracy through the overcast was poor everywhere. The German defenses were more effective than on the 4th, and most of the single engine units of Jagddivision 3 and Luftflotte 3 made contact; 13–2 B-17s were lost from all causes. The fighter command organization of Luftflotte 3 had undergone restructuring paralleling that of Luftflotte Reich. Its new II. Jagdkorps commanded two Divisionen: Jagddivision 4, which had only one day Jagdgeschwader, JG 26; and Jagddivision 5, whose lone Jagdgeschwader was JG 2.

Miserable weather did not prevent the Americans from sending a small force of bombers to Brunswick on the 10th. Three 3rd Bomb Division combat wings—169 B-17s—were to have been escorted by 12 fighter groups. However, weather-induced takeoff delays on the fighter airfields caused a 20-minute gap in the escort coverage that Schmid's controllers were quick to take advantage of. The three north German *Gefechtsverbände* all made successful attacks. Some 30 B-17s were lost or scrapped, 17.8 percent of those taking off; 11 escorts were lost. In all 42 of the 292 Luftwaffe fighters to scramble were shot down, a 14.4 percent loss; 30 German pilots were killed, and 19 were injured.[39]

The B-17s' target for the 11th was once again Frankfurt. Its location along the Main River made it a recognizable target (in theory) for the pathfinder

B-17s. The bomber stream's path was smothered by 606 escort fighters from 13 fighter groups, and the German fighters found it almost impossible to get through to the B-17s, which sustained losses of only 5–3. Vicious dogfights were responsible for most of the 17 KIA and 10 WIA reported by the Luftwaffe. The 8th Fighter Command lost 13 fighters, eight of them 20th Fighter Group P-38s.

Ultra, the Allied code-breaking organization, picked up a message from the RLM congratulating II./JG 3, I. and II./JG 11, and I. and II./ZG 26 for their performance in defense of Frankfurt. Ironically, these Gruppen claimed only one B-17, their principal target, and ten fighters. The message was obviously sent primarily to boost the morale of the hard-pressed pilots, especially those of ZG 26, who for the first time on this day formed an escorted *Gefechtsverband* successfully and flew as far as Frankfurt. This piece of data was noted by another Allied intelligence group, this one responsible for monitoring radio messages to and from the airborne fighters.[40]

The 11th brought the first Me 410 combat sortie for Fw. Fritz Buchholz, who had just joined II./ZG 26 after service as a Ju 52 copilot and instructor. II./ZG 26 was the only Me 410 Gruppe now in the RLV, and was considered a "suicide command" by its pilots. Its aircraft were armed at this time with four WGr 21 rockets and four 20-mm cannon. The rear gunner and his two 13-mm machine guns had been removed to save weight, at a disastrous cost to the morale of the pilots, who missed the extra eyes, the defensive weapons, and, although few would admit it, the companionship in the air. The mission was led by the Kommandeur, Hptm. Eduard Tratt, the top-scoring Zerstörer pilot of the war. Fritz Buchholz recalled:

Twelve of us took off. I was #12. We met a number of Bf 110s and took up a course to the southwest, trailing long condensation plumes. Hptm. Tratt, probably afraid that he would be too late to catch the "Fat Cars," sped up and left the 110s behind. Eight of our 410s dropped out for various reasons, and I moved up to #4. I had no radio contact, and concentrated only on keeping formation while awaiting whatever was to come. A sudden vibration of the starboard engine got my attention, and I went spiraling down, trailing white smoke . . . The snowscape below gave me nothing to orient myself by, but I "bought a ticket" by spotting the Bad Kreuznach train station and followed the rails to the Wiesbaden airfield on one engine and one red

light. My crate was soon serviceable. Flight control did not want me to take off . . . My instrument rating and my last piece of chocolate helped me secure permission . . . I was soon swallowed up in the dark, and the Mittelland Canal became my savior . . . In a two-seater with a radio operator this flight would have been easy, but this was criminal . . . I found the rail line to Hildesheim. Hptm. Tratt was back with two or three claims for Lightnings. His wingman had bellied in at Hanau.[41]

Genmaj. Schmid inspected six of his Jagdgruppen on the following day. He reported his findings to Genobst. Stumpff:

1. The morale and military attitude of the flying crews is excellent—in units commanded by superior officers, it is better than excellent.
2. Crews are, however, inexperienced in flight technique as well as tactics, leading to high losses.
3. I suggest that training continue after crews reach their units, until they are actually needed for commitment.
4. The Staffelkapitäne, as deputies of their Kommandeure, should be given continuous training in the exercise of command authority, even to the extent of granting them greater initiative in the accomplishment of actual missions.
5. Personnel officers must be extremely careful to select only the best-qualified men to fill these [leadership] positions—and not pay excess attention to length of service, as bureaucrats do.
6. A way must be found to meet the [enemy] fighters effectively.[42]

The last point had to have been a cry of desperation, as Schmid knew that his command lacked the numbers and skills necessary to defeat the escorts, and time was running out. He was reduced to shuffling his units around. Major Specht's II./JG 11 was integrated in a permanent *Gefechtsverband* with ZG 26, as its escort unit. It was replaced in the JG 11 (JD 2) *Gefechtsverband* by II./JG 3. The JG 1 (JD 3) *Gefechtsverband* now had I. and II./JG 1, IV./JG 3, and Sturmstaffel 1 as its "heavy" units, to be escorted by the "light" I./JG 3. III./JG 1 at Volkel was to be the "forward" unit, attacking the American escorts early to force them to drop their tanks. Jagddivision 3 had never been given the requested reinforcements for this last-described task, which the American "bouncing squadrons" would now make obsolete.

February 20–25—Big Week

In November 1943 the Eighth Air Force staff had formulated an ambitious plan called Operation Argument as part of the ongoing Pointblank campaign. Argument was to be a series of closely spaced attacks on German fighter production—specifically, a dozen factories producing Bf 109, Bf 110, Me 410, Ju 88, and Fw 190 fighters or their components. The plans were passed up to USSTAF at its formation, in the expectation that coordinated attacks by the Eighth and Fifteenth Air Forces would be possible. At least six successive clear days were needed. On February 19, the Eighth Air Force weather office forecast clearing conditions and a week of good weather, although LGen. Doolittle's weather scouts reported thick cloud cover and icing conditions over the continent. After heated discussions with Anderson and Doolittle, Spaatz ordered the start of what became known as "Big Week." The Fifteenth Air Force was needed to support the Anzio beachhead in Italy, so the Eighth would begin Argument alone.[43]

The operational plan for February 20 was complex. A small task force of six combat wings took off at 0930 and headed northeast toward Denmark, outside the range of the German radars on the coasts of Holland and northwestern Germany. It then split to bomb targets in northern Germany and East Prussia. Both forces returned on a reciprocal course, two hours apart because of the distances to their targets.

The main shield for the unescorted northern task force was to be provided by the main force of 12 combat wings, which left England two wings abreast two hours later and headed due east, thus pointed at Berlin. It split into seven parts when approaching its targets, but remained concentrated in time and space to the greatest extent possible to ease the burden on the escort, which was provided by 835 fighters from 15 fighter groups. All rallied southeast of Kassel and returned south of the Ruhr in two compact forces.

For once a complicated Eighth Air Force operation was carried out exactly as planned. The I. Jagdkorps controllers missed the northern force, which carried out its mission almost untouched, losing only 6–1 B-17s. Berlin was assumed to be the target of the large southern force, but its split precluded attempts to form a large Gefechtsverband. The southern return route also proved deceptive. Allied radio intercepts indicated an unprecedented degree of disorganization and confusion on the part of the German controllers. The southern force lost 15–4 bombers and only three escorts.[44]

USSTAF considered the day a great success, despite the fact that many targets had been bombed through thick cloud with "unobserved results." The post-mission report claimed that it was a "landmark in the history of aerial warfare." The USSTAF post-war summary of the strategic campaign reconstructed the mission from the (notional) viewpoint of the I. Jagdkorps controllers. It was claimed to represent a typical mission, but was far from it; it was probably the best use of misdirection in the strategic air war.[45]

The defenders lost 44 KIA, 29 WIA, and 74–29 aircraft. All of the *Wilde Sau* Gruppen were scrambled against this maximum-strength raid. At least one, I./JG 300, had practised daylight formations sufficiently to attempt a mass head-on attack, but their successes were few. The Zerstörer units suffered severe losses. III./ZG 26 lost 10 KIA, 7 WIA, and 10–3 Bf 110s when it was attacked out of the sun by 56th Fighter Group P-47s while forming up to attack the van of the southern stream. The most successful Jagdgruppen were Hptm. Rudolf Klemm's III./JG 54, with seven confirmed B-17 claims, and Hptm. Rolf Hermichen's I./JG 11, which filed claims for 13 B-17s and B-24s, 11 of which were confirmed. Hermichen himself was credited with four B-24s, in one of the best missions ever flown by an RLV pilot.

Unit histories and pilot logbooks confirm the confusion of the day. The experience of 3./JG 11's Fw. Heinz Hanke is perhaps representative. He has provided the following extensive account:

> Our Gruppe of 40 Fw 190s made a *Blitzverlegung* [rapid transfer] from our Husum base [south of Denmark] to Oldenburg [west of Bremen]. The morning was hazy with blue skies above, but fog then moved in and covered the airfield, and our Kommodore ordered the quickest possible takeoff. The entire Geschwader took off successfully and assembled at 8,300 meters [27,000 ft.] over the North Sea. The controller reported that the American bombers had split into three waves, two crossing the Dutch coast while the third "circled over the German Bight." We were led northeast toward Denmark, exactly retracing our route earlier that morning. After 75 minutes the aircraft in the rear of the formation began reporting low fuel. The cloud deck below us was

A Schwarm of 6./ZG 76 Bf 110G-2s peels off during a flight over an undercast southern Germany in the winter of 1943–4. (*Bundesarchiv 663-6734-22a*)

now solid, and pilots began to break away to seek a landing ground. Finally there were only seven left. As my Fw 190 had the red cowling stripe of a Schwarmführer, I gathered the six around me, three to either side. We flew north; I was hoping to spot Husum or Neumünster through the clouds and land to refuel.

Suddenly I spotted a formation of 200–300 B-17s to the east at 6,000 meters [20,000 ft.]. I ordered my comrades, "Attack from the front!" But the hellish defensive fire made me change my orders to a *freie Jagd* [free hunt], every man for himself . . . The B-17s dove from 6,000 to 4,500 meters [15,000 ft.] to gain speed. My red fuel lamp blinked, then glowed steadily—eight minutes of fuel. I climbed slightly, then dove to attack the rear B-17 at a speed of 700 km/h [435 mph]. I was buffeted in the slipstream but fired all six guns from 200 meters. My barrage hit the cockpit and then moved back to the tail. It was a good job—the cockpit exploded, parts dropped off the fuselage, and the left wing and its two engines burst into flames. I saw five men bail out. But when I again glanced forward I got a terrible shock. My speed had carried me into the middle of the formation. The blood drained from my face as I half-rolled to dive away—but it was already too late. My aircraft was hit, and strong oil fumes and aluminum shards filled my cockpit. At this moment my controls went out . . .[46]

After the usual difficulties Hanke succeeded in bailing out, striking the tail with his shoulder and ankle, and landed on the Danish island of Fünen, covered in oil and in great pain. Coincidentally, the other six members of his flight all force-landed on the same island. Hanke did not encounter them, but did meet the crew of the 100th Bomb Group B-17 that he had shot down. Ironically, the bomber had passed directly over Hanke's Husum base that morning en route to bomb Tutow, after Hanke had flown south. He managed to carry on a conversation with one man, who gave him his flight jacket decorated with the B-17's name, *Miss Behavin*, and 18 mission bombs. The jacket later burned in an air raid, but after the war Hanke tried to locate the man, remembering only that his jacket had the name "Mark" in it, and that he was from Minneapolis. In 1976 *Miss Behavin*'s copilot, Orlin Markussen, responded, and the two men became close friends.

Heinz Hanke attached a 3./JG 11 pilot roster to his letter. Of the 29 men who served with him, 23 were killed in action, one committed suicide, and two remained missing. The three survivors were all injured; Hanke listed himself as 70 percent disabled. A 90 percent pilot fatality rate was fairly typical of RLV units.

The Eighth Air Force adopted a simpler operational plan on the 21st. Its 15 combat wings (861 bombers) headed for Germany in a single stream, splitting up to attack targets in the Brunswick area. Heavy cloud restricted visibility, and few primaries were hit; most of the groups bombed airfields. The day proved to be just another minor battle in the war of attrition. Fifteen fighter groups (679 fighters) provided the new, looser escort, and claimed 33 German fighters for losses of 5–3. I. Jagdkorps and Jagddivision 4 fighters flew 331 defensive sorties, but in small units rather than *Gefechtsverbände*—weather was blamed for the failure to form the latter—and few holes in the escort were found. The RLV forces lost 24 KIA, 7 WIA, and 30 fighters. American bomber losses from all causes were 16–7.[47]

On the 22nd the Fifteenth Air Force was temporarily relieved of its tactical responsibilities in Italy and allowed to rejoin the strategic air war. Its 204 B-24s and B-17s were assigned targets in the large Regensburg Messerschmitt factory complex. This air force's three P-38 groups and one P-47 group flew escort missions, but either the plan or its implementation was faulty. The bombers were entirely without escort for most of the mission. Jagddivision 7 was needed to oppose an Eighth Air Force raid, and the aerial defense of

6./JG 3 Bf 109G-6s prepare to taxi out for a mission from Rotenburg in February 1944. The aircraft bear subdued markings. Note that the tops of the white Geschwader fuselage bands are overpainted with gray camouflage. (*Crow*)

Regensburg was left to Jafü Ostmark alone. All of its Gruppen made contact after the bomb runs, two only after long stern chases. The German fighters shot down 14 B-24s and two B-17s, while losing eight of their number to the bombers' gunners. There were apparently no encounters with American fighters.[48]

I./JG 27 was one of the principal Jafü Ostmark Jagdgruppen. It scrambled from Fels-am-Wagram along with eight fighters of the formation leaders' school and was ordered to fly to Vienna below a 200–300 meter [650–1,000 ft.] cloud deck, climb through it, assemble, and fly to the area of Linz, where the controller directed it to the enemy formation. Contact was made an hour after takeoff. The Gruppe overtook the last B-24 formation, turned in from 6–7 km (approx. 4 miles), but instead of the customary direct head-on attack, attacked in a pursuit curve from *seitlich vorne*, angling from the front. Oblt. Fritz Engau, flying in the rear with the school fighters, thought that this was nonsense, as it exposed the attackers to fire from many more bombers. Engau's two-second burst of fire at a B-24 on the edge of the formation had no effect; he made a second fruitless pass before breaking off with low fuel. Engau was an experienced night-fighter pilot who had been reassigned to day fighters after an injury had cost him his night vision. He was outspoken in his criticism of the formation leaders' school—its lack of cooperation with I./JG 27, its host unit, especially irritated him—but he was lucky to receive the training, and after graduation became a stalwart Staffelkapitän and formation leader in I./JG 11. The JG 27 Gruppe claimed three B-24s and two *Herausschüsse*, while losing 2 KIA and 1 WIA. The school pilots claimed one B-24, without loss.[49]

On the 22nd the Eighth Air Force dispatched 799 bombers against a variety of targets, but once again weather disrupted Allied plans. A small diversionary force sent to Denmark was properly identified as non-threatening, and the north German Jagdgruppen flew south to join the main battle. The 2nd and 3rd Bomb Divisions were recalled before bombing, and only 99 1st Division B-17s were able to bomb their primary targets. The bomb groups scattered over Germany were vulnerable to attack, and 41–4 bombers, most from the 1st Division, failed to return. The 16 escort groups found no shortage of targets, and claimed 59–7–26 German fighters for the loss of 11–1; actual German losses were 48 single-engine and 16 twin-engine fighters. Once again III./ZG 26 was the hardest hit, losing 4 KIA, 3 WIA, and eight Bf 110s. II./ZG 26 lost only one Me 410, but it was piloted by its Gruppenkommandeur, Hptm. Eduard Tratt, who was killed in a lone attack on a bomber *Pulk*. Tratt was the Luftwaffe's most famous and successful Zerstörer pilot, with 38 victories. He was awarded the Oak Leaves to his Knight's Cross after his death.

The Eighth Air Force did not attempt to fly on the 23rd. The Fifteenth sent its bombers to Austria, but the entire B-17 wing and many of the B-24s and P-38s returned early because of the weather. Only 81 B-24s bombed their primary target at Steyr, but succeeded in destroying 10 percent of the Reich production capacity for aircraft ball-bearings. The mission plan again called for the P-38s to escort the bombers' withdrawal, while the penetration and target legs were unescorted. The bomber wing that reached Steyr was severely punished, losing 16 B-24s after a 30-minute Luftwaffe attack that started before the bomb run and ended only after the arrival of the P-38s.

Two Jafü Ostmark and one Jagddivision 7 formation reached the bombers. According to the bomber crews, the II./ZG 1 Bf 110s fired two rockets apiece from 1,000 yards [900 meters] dead astern, and then attacked with their guns in shallow dives. They were finally driven off by 14th Fighter Group P-38s, which shot down two; these were the day's only successes for the American escorts. The four B-24 claims by Bf 110 crews were all confirmed.

Hptm. Ludwig Franzisket's I./JG 27 scrambled from Fels-am-Wagram and flew west, while Major Walther Dahl led the 24 Bf 109Gs of his III./JG 3 east from Leipheim. Both Jagdgruppen reached the bombers at noon, and immediately joined battle. They attacked the B-24s aggressively, singly from all angles, as described by the bomber crews. Pilots from I./JG 27 and the formation leaders' school claimed 14 B-24s shot down or driven from their formations; nine of these claims are known to have been confirmed. III./JG 3 claimed 15 B-24s, but only four were confirmed. Dahl allowed many claims to be filed without crash witnesses. This boosted the Gruppe statistics for the daily OKW press release, but the RLM clerks had a special rubber stamp for claims filed without a witness—*ohne Zeugen!*—and these were almost never confirmed. The 17 B-24 claims that were confirmed match up very well with the 16 actual losses.

III./JG 3 lost 2 KIA, 1 WIA, and five Bf 109s to the bomber gunners, while I./JG 27 lost 1 KIA, 1 WIA, and four Bf 109s. Both Gruppen were forced to turn their attention to the P-38s when they arrived, and claimed the destruction of seven. None of these claims was

confirmed, and all of the P-38 fighters in fact returned to Italy. The only P-38 claim to be confirmed was by a pilot from FLÜG 1, a ferry unit. His victim was in fact an F-5B, a photo-reconnaissance version of the P-38.[50]

On the 23rd Schmid hosted a meeting at his I. Jagdkorps headquarters, attended by his Jagddivision and Geschwader commanders and Galland.[51] Schmid announced a major reorganization of his Jagddivisionen, effective immediately. Their day units would now comprise:

JD 1: JG 3 (4 Gruppen), ZG 26, 3 Gruppen of JG 300 and JG 302

JD 2: JG 11 (3 Gruppen), III./JG 54

JD 3: JG 1 (3 Gruppen), I./JG 300

Noteworthy are the strengthening of Jagddivision 1 and the listing of the *Wilde Sau* Gruppen as day units. In the postwar history written for the USAAF, Schmid takes credit for recognizing that the purpose of the current USAAF campaign was to secure air supremacy as a prelude to a large-scale invasion. Bolstering Jagddivision 1 would help protect the important aviation industry targets in the Hannover and Magdeburg areas, as well as Berlin.

The Luftwaffe High Command and the RLV commanders were still debating the problem of the American escorts. Schmid announced a policy change on this issue:

> At the suggestion of the General der Jagdflieger [Galland], the Reichsmarschall [Göring] has agreed that one Gruppe from each Jagddivision shall be designated for combat with the escort, which will be attacked by small groups of two or three aircraft plunging down on them from above. The Bf 109s employed for this purpose will be equipped with light armament and with automatic ammunition loaders.

These Gruppen were known as *Höhengruppen* (high-altitude Gruppen) and were to be equipped with Bf 109G-5s and G-6s with GM-1 equipment. These were to be replaced as soon as possible by Bf 109G-6/AS high-altitude fighters with new DB 605AS engines. Each Jagddivision was to get one Höhengruppe: I./JG 3 in JD 1, II./JG 11 in JD 2, and III./JG 1 in JD 3. The tactics recommended above were unrealistic and were seldom employed. The

Höhengruppe formation leaders always tried to attack in the greatest strength possible, rather than in driblets.

A sore point with Göring was the small number of second sorties flown by the RLV units. In large part this was an organizational problem, which Schmid addressed on the 23rd as follows:

> As many fighters as possible will make second sorties versus the withdrawing heavy bombers. This has too often been impossible owing to landing on the wrong airfields. From now on, specific airfields will be designated as fighter fields. They will be fully stocked, whereas other airfields will have only fuel supplies. If a fighter lands on the latter, the pilot must refuel immediately and take off for the nearest fighter field.

The weather over central Europe was clear on the 24th. The Eighth Air Force mounted a complex full-strength three-stream attack on Schweinfurt, Gotha, and Rostock. The Fifteenth Air Force sent its B-17 command, the 5th Bomb Wing, to Steyr. The Fifteenth, which was short of fighters, used the same escort plan that had worked poorly on the two previous missions—the B-17s were escorted on withdrawal only. The Jafü Ostmark controllers recognized the target early and got all three of their Gruppen—I./JG 27, II./JG 53, and II./ZG 1—to the B-17s 160 km (100 miles) from Steyr. Jagddivision 7

was again called on, and its III./JG 3 and II./ZG 76 arrived as the target was being bombed. All of the approximately 120 fighters concentrated on the 2nd Bomb Group at the rear of the stream; its 33 B-17s were flying in two "waves," roughly equivalent to Eighth Air Force combat boxes. Attacks were primarily by Schwärme, from 4 to 8 o'clock high, level, and low, and were pressed aggressively to 50 meters' [150 ft.] range. The rear B-17 formation was chosen first to minimize defensive fire, and became an even more desirable target as it began to break up. A total of 14–1 B-17s were lost from the 2nd Group, plus three from the 301st, before the P-38s arrived to disperse the attacks, which had lasted a full hour. The P-47s of the 325th Group came close to Steyr, but were at the extreme limit of their range, and had no influence on the battle. The P-38s claimed two Bf 109s and six twin-engine fighters, while losing two of their own. The German pilots claimed 23 B-17s, of which 13 are known to have been confirmed, and both of the P-38s, while losing ten aircraft.[52]

The Eighth Air Force plan for the 24th attempted to duplicate the success of the 20th. The 1st and 2nd Bomb Divisions would fly directly east from England toward the German heartland, while the 3rd Division

An imposing array of 381st Bomb Group B-17s. This group was the subject of some of the best Eighth Air Force formation shots; this one was taken in early 1944. (*ww2images*)

flew east-northeast without escort, crossed Schleswig-Holstein, and attacked targets on the Baltic Sea coast. The southern shield again worked effectively, aided by the fact that the RLV had no day units based in eastern Germany. The 3rd Division was opposed only by the two Staffeln in Denmark, 10. and 11./JG 11, and night fighters from NJG 5 and NJG 6, and lost only five B-17s.[53]

The main force was led by the B-24s of the 2nd Bomb Division, which bombed Gotha while the trailing B-17-equipped 1st Bomb Division split off to the south and bombed Schweinfurt. Eighteen fighter groups provided escort, but they were not enough, as strong tailwinds put the bombers ahead of schedule and caused gaps in the coverage. The B-24s proved especially vulnerable; they flew the mission between 16,000 and 21,500 feet [4,900–6,600 meters], well below the B-17s and below the critical altitude of the Fw 190s. Jagddivision 3 requested help early, and Jagddivision 4 from Luftflotte 3 scrambled all three of its Jagdgruppen and sent them northeast, where they met the bomber stream near the Dutch–German border. The attack of I./JG 26 on the leading 2nd Bomb Division was broken up by P-47s, but II. and III./JG 26 found that the 40th Combat Wing, leading the 1st Bomb Division, was unescorted, and the Focke-Wulfs and Messerschmitts were able to make repeated head-on attacks, re-forming in the undefended air ahead of the division. Five B-17s went down before the 78th Fighter Group's P-47s arrived to find the bombers far ahead of schedule. One squadron raced ahead and interrupted an attack by III./JG 26, some of whose pilots foolishly attempted to escape by diving. The Thunderbolts caught them easily and shot down four, killing all of the pilots.

The JG 1 *Gefechtsverband* was directed to the B-24s, and reached them well before Gotha. Although the bombers were escorted by P-47s, Major Bär led II./JG 1 in a diving attack out of the sun through the escorts and shot down four B-24s; I./JG 1 made a more conventional head-on attack and claimed five.

The JG 11 *Gefechtsverband*, augmented by II./JG 3, arrived as the B-24s were realigning their formations for their bomb run, and Major Graf led an immediate attack that claimed 24 B-24s. The other two JG 3 Gruppen apparently arrived next, led by their Kommodore, Obstlt. Wilcke, and eventually every day-fighter unit in I. and II. Jagdkorps was involved.

Very few German fighters were able to land on their own bases, and the new directive on assembly airfields

was put to the test. The senior pilot to put down at each of these designated fields was to lead the other pilots who had landed with serviceable aircraft on a second sortie against the withdrawing bombers, despite the mixture of units and equipment. There is little documentation of these missions, but it is known that Oberst Oesau of JG 1 and Hptm. Borris of I./JG 26 led two of these improvised formations on successful missions on this day.

The day's effort for the RLV forces totaled 479 sorties; 31 aircrew were KIA, 14 were WIA, and 46 aircraft, 9.6 percent of those to sortie, were lost. The Eighth Air Force lost 33–1 B-24s, 16–1 B-17s, and 10 escorts. In all, 505 bombers had taken off that morning; 451 were credited with flying the mission. The 11.3 percent bomber loss was high, but bearable, given the importance of Argument. American escort sorties totaled 767; their losses were negligible.

The German and American meteorologists all predicted clear weather over southern Germany for the 25th. The RLV commanders and controllers expected a major USSTAF raid on that region, and began concentrating their day-fighter units early. The American planners did not disappoint them, sending the Eighth Air Force on a maximum-strength raid to Regensburg, Augsburg, Stuttgart, and Fürth, while the much smaller Fifteenth Air Force bombed Regensburg an hour before the Eighth arrived. Again, the Fifteenth provided no escort for the penetration or target legs of the mission. The bombers' route and the absence of escorts were noted soon after takeoff, telegraphing their probable destination. Two Jagd-gruppen in northern Italy, I./JG 53 and I./JG 77, were ordered to intercept, and claimed eight B-24s and three B-17s for the loss of four Bf 109s. Jafü Ostmark ordered II./JG 53 to head south, and the Bf 109s met the bombers over the Alps, claiming seven B-24s for the loss of three fighters. The other Austrian units— I./JG 27, the formation leaders' school, and II./ZG 1— met the unescorted bombers near Klagenfurt, and also reported numerous shootdowns. The Jagd-division 7 units, III./JG 3, II./JG 27, and parts of ZG 76, were well positioned, and their attacks on the unescorted Fifteenth Air Force bombers achieved great success at low cost. The German fighters disappeared when the escorts finally arrived; the P-38 pilots were able to claim only one victory, for the loss of three of their own. The Fifteenth's bomber losses for the day totaled 19 B-17s and 21 B-24s, about one-fourth of those targeting Regensburg, and it was

GFM Erhard Milch, the Luftwaffe's Chief of Air Armament and inspector-general for much of the war. Former director of the German state airline Lufthansa, Milch possessed a superior understanding of aviation technology and industrial matters. He recognized much earlier than most of the senior Nazi leadership the need to increase fighter production, and was instrumental in creating the Fighter Staff in the wake of "Big Week." *(Authors' collection)*

Jagddivision 2 to keep JG 11 on the ground until the stream's direction was known. When the B-24s finally turned back, it was too late to employ JG 11 against the main raid, farther south. The other successful diversion was an unexpected bonus. Every Eighth Air Force mission was accompanied by medium-bomber raids on coastal targets. These were usually ignored by the German controllers, but on this day Jagddivision 4 sent its strongest Gruppe, I./JG 26, to intercept a formation of medium bombers. They downed four B-26s, but played no role in the day's main battle. Jagddivision 4's other Gruppen, II. and III./JG 26, were directed toward the incoming heavy bombers, but they were at such low strength that they were ordered to parallel the stream and attack only unescorted *Pulks*. II./JG 26 eventually brought down two B-17s, but lost its formation leader and one other pilot to 4th Fighter Group P-47s. Hptm. Mietusch and his III./JG 26 were more successful, patrolling the area above Saarbrücken for more than an hour and eventually bringing down five B-17s without loss.

The defensive effort against the Eighth by I. Jagdkorps and Jagddivision 7 was definitely hampered by the absence of JG 11 and the need for Jagddivision 7 to service its fighters after their successful mission against the Fifteenth. The only full-strength *Gefechtsverband* used was that of JG 1, under the direct command of Oberst Oesau. The defenders scrambled 490 fighters, including night fighters and fighter school operational flights, but their success did not come close to matching that of the previous day. The Eighth Air Force hit all of its primary targets, with reportedly excellent results, while losing 31–3 heavy bombers and 3–2 fighters. The day's casualties in the RLV units totaled 19 KIA, 20 WIA, and 48 aircraft.

The weather over Europe now changed for the worse, and Spaatz brought Big Week and Operation Argument to an end. Both sides needed a pause. The Fifteenth Air Force, as noted, was out of the battle. It had lost 90 bombers, 14.6 percent of those to sortie, in striking contrast to the Eighth, which lost 157 bombers (4.8 percent), and RAF Bomber Command, which lost 131 bombers (5.7 percent) during this week. The operational strength of the Eighth Air Force bomber units had dropped from 75 percent of establishment strength at the start of the week to 54 percent; the strength of its fighter units had dropped from 72 percent of establishment to 65 percent.[55] The RLV had lost 355 fighters, and its serviceability hovered at about 50 percent. But more serious was its

forced to end its participation in deep-penetration raids on the Reich until it could obtain more long-range escort units.[54]

Although their probable targets were suspected by the RLV commanders, the Eighth Air Force bombers benefited by the success of two diversionary raids. A new B-24 group was sent across the North Sea accompanied by Mandrel aircraft, which simulated larger formations on German radar. I. Jagdkorps, suspecting another raid on eastern Germany, ordered loss of pilots—almost 100 were killed during the week.[56]

Spaatz and Anderson proclaimed a great victory, based on intelligence estimates of the damage done to the major aviation industry production sites. But the USSTAF operational planners overestimated the destructive power of American bombs, mostly of only 500 pounds (225 kg), and underestimated the recuperative power of German industry, with its unlimited supply of forced labor. The production of fighters dropped off briefly, but then increased, and did not reach a peak until the fall of 1944. Nevertheless, Big Week was a major Allied victory, even though no single battle with the drama of a Schweinfurt had been fought. Aerial superiority had passed irrevocably to the Allies. The message of Big Week was crystal-clear to the American planners: Allied fighters could dominate the air over any part of Europe, by their mere appearance. The German fighter force remained a formidable foe, but the era of maximum defensive effort against every American bombing raid was over. The hit-and-run tactics that the "forward" units of Jagddivision 3 and Jagddivision 4 had found necessary for their personal survival now became the unofficial policy of the entire Jagdwaffe.

The Fighter Staff and the Aircraft Production Miracle

Out of the rubble of the German aircraft industry produced by Big Week emerged the most significant reform in the German wartime aircraft industry, the creation of the *Jägerstab* (Fighter Staff). Prior to early 1944, aircraft production was strictly a Luftwaffe matter, overseen by Milch's Generalluftzeugmeister (GL) office. Albert Speer had worked wonders with German war production since taking office in early 1942 but had made few inroads with the Luftwaffe, as Göring jealously guarded his empire against encroachment by the Armaments Minister. The fact that Milch and Speer enjoyed a good personal relationship and worked together effectively on the Central Planning resource allocation committee eased matters somewhat, but problems with raw material and labor supply continued to hamper German aircraft production. Speer's altruism and warm feelings for Milch went only so far, and he understandably gave precedence to those sectors of the armaments industry that were part of his own empire.

The crisis of Big Week made both Milch and Speer realize that half measures and interagency

Albert Speer (*3rd left*), the youthful Minister of Armaments and War Production, enjoys Christmas dinner with Luftwaffe officers in 1943. Speer worked effectively with Milch in greatly increasing the output of fighter aircraft, eventually absorbing all Luftwaffe production into his industrial empire. Under Speer's energetic and ruthless direction, fighter production peaked in September 1944. (*Authors' collection*)

cooperation would not suffice. Speer assessed that fully 75 percent of the airframe and component assembly plants had sustained major damage by the end of February; damage to machine tools in these industries was nearly 30 percent.[57] Milch and Speer were united in their belief that an "umbrella of fighter aircraft over the Reich" was a necessity. Speer had earlier set up "special staffs" or "miniature ministries" with sweeping powers to deal with emergencies in ball-bearing production and in the Ruhr industries. The Fighter Staff was an extension of this idea, and it required an extraordinary move: Milch ceded much of his authority over aircraft production to the Armaments Ministry. He told his staff at the GL, "As the officer responsible for supplying the Luftwaffe with aircraft, I therefore consider that decisive measures must be taken as we can no longer continue by normal means."[58] Speer and Milch were the directors, but actual executive control of the new agency went to Karl-Otto Saur, Speer's "pushing, ruthless subordinate."[59] Speer declared that the staff's mission was "to bring about the repair or transfer of damaged factories through the exercise of direct command authority, untrammeled by bureaucracy."[60] It would soon exceed this mandate. Milch and Speer worked out the organizational details in late February and, bypassing Göring, took the proposal directly to Hitler. In a moment of black comedy, Hitler initially objected to the term "Jägerstab," fearing that the public would mistake it for an agency providing assistance to hunters in a time of national emergency.[61] He formally approved the creation of the new staff on March 5, 1944. One sure indicator of the seriousness of the situation was that Hitler gave repair of damaged aircraft factories priority over aid to the bombed-out civilian population.[62]

The Jägerstab was consciously modeled after the Armaments Ministry—it had a broad-based membership with small working groups that maximized efficiency. It brought together representatives from the aircraft industry, Armaments Ministry officials, and key Luftwaffe personnel. Galland was a regular attendee, and consistently represented the front-line perspective. In fact, of his many duties, liaison with the Jägerstab may have been Galland's most important and influential task, as it brought him into direct contact with the overlords of the German war economy. Every major aircraft factory sent a representative to the staff; at the same time, a staff "watchdog" was sent to each plant. Many of its committee chairmen wielded special plenipotentiary powers that enabled them to cut through red tape (of which there was never a shortage in the Third Reich), requisition materials, and reduce production bottlenecks. Efficiency was the watchword. When the Jägerstab meetings began to attract large numbers of hangers-on, Saur ruthlessly trimmed the membership down to the essential players.[63]

The Jägerstab's first task was the physical repair and reconstruction of bombed plants; access to the Speer Ministry's resources greatly assisted this herculean effort. Teams from the staff conducted "flying visits" to bomb-damaged sites to oversee repair efforts. Members of the Fighter Staff also addressed the workers of the hardest-hit factories. On one such visit, noted fighter ace Oberst Hannes Trautloft, the Inspector of Day Fighters, joined Saur on the Erla factory podium on March 14, 1944. Trautloft conveyed an unvarnished picture to the assembled workers of the desperate situation facing the Reich's defenders, while Saur outlined the role they could play in giving the fighter squadrons the aircraft necessary to do the job, including working a 72-hour work week and Sunday shifts.[64] Industrialists came to dread the midnight appearances of the "Saur Train," carrying the Fighter Staff chief to conduct compliance inspections and deliver morale-bolstering harangues. The Fighter Staff conference minutes are remarkable documents, with the caustic Saur exhorting, needling, and cajoling his diverse group to new heights of performance.[65]

Beyond physical repair, the Jägerstab sought to put the entire aircraft industry onto a more secure footing. An obvious antidote to bombing was to disperse the factories, but Speer was not in favor of wholesale dispersal of aircraft manufacturing, as doing so would have reduced output and sacrificed economies of scale. Instead, the Jägerstab favored a more limited process known as "decentralization," an attempt to wean the industry from over-reliance on single factories. Saur came to believe this practice to be ineffective, and championed the construction of enormous bombproof factories and exploitation of existing mines and caverns. This undertaking brought the Speer Ministry into uncomfortable proximity to the SS, whose slave labor empire had created many such facilities. While protection of the plants was an important goal of the staff, it ultimately took a back seat to the push to increase output. Saur favored a policy of "rationalization," by the Luftwaffe's own definition "the systematic savings of materials and manpower in order to achieve the highest quantities of output."[66] There was a constant tug of war between dispersal/decentralization and rationalization, as the most efficient plants were almost by definition centralized and therefore vulnerable.[67] Finally, the staff took direct control of aircraft production, initially following the Luftwaffe's "225" program but by July issuing its own production plan, "226." Selection of types and production priorities, formerly the prerogative of the Luftwaffe, passed to the Jägerstab and the Speer Ministry.

There are no doubts about the success of the Fighter Staff in boosting production to levels undreamed of even in 1943. British Air Ministry analysts freely admitted: "The achievement of the Jägerstab in attaining its objective was astonishing and beyond all expectation; it completely defeated the aim of the Allied attacks to knock out aircraft production."[68] Placing the aircraft industry directly under the Speer Ministry unleashed hitherto-untapped financial reserves, innovative planning, rationalization and management techniques, extra rations for workers, and scarce raw materials. Earlier in the war, seven factories managed a Messerschmitt 109 production of just 180 per month; under the

Speer Ministry this figure rose to 1,000 per month by May 1944 in just three large, efficient plants (Regensburg, Leipzig-Erla, and Wiener Neustadt).[69] Although production figures for German aircraft often disagree, owing to the various accounting methods used by different agencies, the following Speer Ministry figures—covering Bf 109, Fw 190, Me 110, Ju 88, Me 410, He 219 and the very first Me 262 production—indicate the scope of the accomplishments of German industry and the Fighter Staff.

Fighter Production

(Speer Ministry figures, compiled October 18, 1944)[70]

Date	New Production	Repaired	Total
1943			
July–Dec (monthly avg)	1,369	521	1,890
1944			
January	1,340	419	1,759
February	1,323	430	1,753
March	1,830	546	2,376
April	2,034	669	2,703
May	2,377	647	3,024
June	2,760	834	3,594
July	3,115	935	4,050
August	3,051	922	3,973
September	3,538	776	4,314

Part of the fighter staff's rationalization drive focused on a drastic reduction in the number of aircraft types and models in production. By one count, German aircraft industry manufactured nearly 200 different models and sub-types in January 1944; Saur's team eventually reduced this to a more manageable 20.[71] Even more dramatically, the number of basic aircraft types slated for mass production starting in spring 1944 fell from 42 to 20 to 9 to 5.[72] Among the casualties were the Ta 154 and He 219 night fighters, the Do 24 flying boat, the Bf 110, Ju 88/188, He 111, Me 410—even Bf 109 production was slated to wind down in early 1945.[73] In July 1944, the only types envisioned to remain in mass production by mid-1945 were the Ta 152 fighter

(a vastly improved Fw 190 with an inline engine), the Me 262 turbojet, the Do 335 tandem-engine heavy fighter, the Ju 388 bomber/recce plane/night fighter, and the Ar 234 turbojet reconnaissance bomber.[74] Göring, Korten, Koller, and even Milch fought at first to keep some bomber production going, but after mid-1944 bomber production (with the exception of the Ar 234 and Ju 388) virtually ceased. Göring predictably grumbled that it was "no trick" to increase fighter output at the expense of bombers. It is more remarkable that level-headed professional officers like Koller refused to abandon the Luftwaffe's offensive roots even at this desperate juncture of the war.[75]

The need to rationalize also brought into sharper focus the debate between quality and quantity. As Saur himself noted, "The character of air combat is being transformed to an ever-increasing extent from encounters between bombers and fighters to encounters between opposing fighters. We can win this struggle only if we have aircraft of superior quality."[76] Although the July 1944 production decision certainly featured technically advanced designs, the 1944 surge consisted of huge increases in production of proven types. In May 1944, for example, of 2,377 new aircraft, there were 999 Bf 109, 723 Fw 190, 208 Ju 88, 157 Bf 110, 108 Me 410, 16 He 219—and only seven Me 262. Of the mass-produced aircraft, only the latest Bf 109G-6, G-10 and G-14 models with the DB 605AS engine, which gave them a service ceiling of 11,500 meters (38,000 ft.), could be considered short-term qualitative improvements.[77] On May 11, 1944, Galland told his Jägerstab audience:

> I have now visited the units committed as "high-altitude fighters," which have the mission of combating the enemy fighter escorts. These units say, "It is a real pleasure; we fly at altitudes of 10,000, 10,500, and sometimes of 11,500 meters [33,000, 34,500, 38,000 ft.], and the enemy climbs as high as 9,000 meters [30,000 ft.]; we dive down in Schwarm formation at the enemy pair, shoot down one plane, and before they can even look around, we are already back above them."[78]

This modest success aside, most Luftwaffe commanders recognized that the production gains were providing the squadrons with obsolescent aircraft through the end of 1944. "Priority was given to numerical output"—in early 1944 there was no alternative.[79]

On March 6, Lt. Hans Berger (1./JG 1, *nearest camera*) took off from Twente to intercept the first large-scale American raid on Berlin. He shot down a B-17; his Fw 190A-7 "white 3" was hit, but he was able to return to base. His mechanic Konrad "Kari" Ell stands beside him near the damaged rudder of his aircraft. (*Berger via Mombeek*)

It was fortunate for the Luftwaffe that the Fighter Staff achieved the production figures it did, for at times it seemed that the Jagdwaffe's own pilots sought to undo all its hard work. On April 18, 1944, Saur noted at a Fighter Staff conference:

> Here is a very unpleasant report which states that of 20 aircraft picked up by the ferrying service, eight were destroyed on take-off as a result of burst tires. This is due to the transfer of experienced pilots and their replacement by inexperienced newcomers who have not yet flown the 109.[80]

Saur's anecdote, in microcosm, illustrates the severe consequences for German air strength brought about by the steady decline in training standards. Although the Luftwaffe's training establishments managed to turn out sufficient numbers of pilots from the A and B schools, the number of flying hours on operational-type aircraft was reduced to a bare 25 by the beginning of 1944.[81] During the month of February 1944 alone, the Luftwaffe lost over 1,300 aircraft destroyed or damaged in non-combat accidents, which killed 406 and wounded 227 personnel. The Luftwaffe's quarter-master general meticulously broke down the causes:

> ... 33.1 percent, pilot error during landing; 9.7 percent, taxiing damage; 9.9 percent, flying into bad weather areas despite correct weather data; 6.6 percent, bad runway conditions; 6.3 percent, pilot's errors during take-offs; 6.1 percent, collisions on the ground; 3.7 percent, lack of fuel; 3.1 percent, got lost; 2.1 percent, collisions in the air; 1.3 percent, paid no attention to safety regulations ...[82]

Even before the fuel famine caused by the USAAF attacks on the synthetic oil plants beginning in May 1944, the Luftwaffe's training program failed to provide the squadrons with sufficiently trained pilots.

The Fighter Staff was officially dissolved in August 1944, as Speer's Ministry took charge of the entire German war economy. The next month saw the peak of German fighter production for the entire war. Undoubtedly, the Jagerstab kept the German fighter force in the fight through 1944, despite the heaviest Anglo-American bombing. The Germans were keeping pace in the numbers game, although the incredible rate of combat attrition, coupled with declining pilot quality, fuel shortages, and the number of aircraft destroyed in accidents or by Allied bombing prevented the front-line Jagdgruppen from reaping the full benefits.

In recounting this tale of aircraft production feats against formidable odds, one final fact must be driven home. In May 1944, 7,130,000 foreign workers (civilian and prisoners of war) toiled in all aspects of the German economy.[83] The production miracle rested on the backs of millions of slave laborers as much as on the organizational brilliance of Albert Speer and the dedicated functionaries of the Fighter Staff. As historian Alan Clark told us over 40 years ago:

> It is all the more important to remember that just as the Nazi state rested on a basis of total brutality and corruption, so the actual weapons ... came from the darkened sheds of Krupp and Daimler-Benz, where slave labor toiled eighteen hours a day; cowering

under the lash, sleeping six to a "dog kennel" eight feet square, starving or freezing to death at the whim of their guards.[84]

After Big Week, the principal focus of USSTAF mission planning changed from evasion—circuitous routing, diversions, and other measures—to confrontation. The bombers would now be sent directly toward critical targets to provoke the maximum possible response from the RLV, so that the German fighter force could be totally neutralized in advance of D-Day. The day of "bombers as bait" had arrived. The critical target most obvious to both sides, of course, was "Big B," Berlin, and plans were made for a maximum-strength raid as soon as weather permitted.[85]

Genmaj. Schmid summed up the German position at the end of February in the history he wrote for the USAAF. The benefit of hindsight cannot be ignored, but his summary was based primarily on a contemporaneous document, the I. Jagdkorps war diary:

1. American offensive activity increased appreciably during the month, beginning 20 February. The chief target was apparently the installations of the German aircraft industry. Effectiveness was greater than heretofore, and the operations of aircraft plants were disrupted to such an extent that systematic supply to the air-defense forces was impossible.
2. The U.S. tactic of flying several missions on the same day dissipated the air defenses.
3. The U.S. attacked targets throughout the Reich, including southern Germany and Austria. The decentralized command organization of the German defenses proved a decided disadvantage. JD 7 and Jafü Ostmark forces stayed in their areas, subject only to instructions by Luftflotte Reich.
4. Missions assigned by ObdL [Göring]:
   a. I. JK: defense of northern sector, central Germany, coastal areas, and Berlin area.
   b. JD 7: defense of southern Germany, especially the industrial areas of Frankfurt, Mannheim, Stuttgart, Nuremberg, Munich, and Augsburg.
   c. Jafü Ostmark: defense of vital Austrian installations, especially in Vienna, Steyr, Wiener Neustadt, and Linz.
5. Our forces were inadequate to fulfill the mission.
6. In number as well as technical performance, the daytime fighter units assigned to the RLV are inferior to the American fighter forces. In spite of their demonstrated courage and their willingness to make every sacrifice for their country, our forces are in the long run fighting a hopeless battle.
7. In the interest of the overall conduct of the war, the Luftwaffe must face the fact that its most important mission is the prevention of American daytime attacks on the Reich. The Me 262 is badly needed by the fighter units.
8. During February, the average daily operational strengths of I. Jagdkorps were: 350 single-engine fighters, 100 twin-engine fighters, and 50 night fighters available for day use.
9. February sorties by I. Jagdkorps = 2,861; losses = 299, or 10.3 percent.
10. February sorties vs. Reich by the Eighth AF = 10,452; losses to fighters = 310, or 2.9 percent.[86]

Schmid's mention of the Me 262 may have been a post-war insertion, prompted by the well-known stories of the program delays supposedly caused by Hitler. In reality, the fighter was not ready for production in February 1944. While its airframe was sound, its Jumo 004B jet engines were still breaking down on the test stands after running for no more than five hours.

Many RLV units were pulled back to new bases at the end of February and early March. The aim was to reduce their vulnerability and permit better concentration in defense of targets in the Reich heartland. Three of the JG 3 Gruppen were now in the Salzwedel–Burg–Gardelegen area, forming the basis of a new Jagddivision 1 *Gefechtsverband*. Sturmstaffel 1 moved to Gardelegen, sharing the base with the Stab of JG 3. II./JG 5 was ordered to leave the Eastern Front and relocate in Jagddivision 1, possibly as a substitute for III./JG 3, which remained in Jagddivision 7. JG 1, while remaining in Jagddivision 3, withdrew entirely from Holland, concentrating in the Rheine–Twente–München-Gladbach area. I. Jagdkorps would no longer attempt a "forward defense," which was left to the few fighters of II. Jagdkorps, primarily the three JG 26 Gruppen. Jafü Ostmark received the strongest reinforcements. Three full Gruppen, I./JG 5 and III. and IV./JG 27, moved from the Balkans to Austria for a brief period for refitting, and stayed in Austria when they joined the Luftflotte Reich order of battle.

The first Eighth Air Force trips to Germany after Big Week were to the oft-visited targets of Brunswick,

THE LUFTWAFFE OVER GERMANY

Frankfurt, Wilhelmshaven, and the Ruhr. These attracted little attention from Luftflotte Reich. The two Jagdgeschwader of II. Jagdkorps were the principal defenders on March 2, and were severely punished. The JG 2 Kommodore, Obstlt. Egon Mayer, was among the 11 killed and missing from JG 2 and JG 26. Mayer, a holder of the Knight's Cross with Oak Leaves and Swords, had been the first Luftwaffe pilot to claim 100 victories in the west. The originator of the head-on attack had claimed 25 heavy bombers at the time of his death, the most of any German pilot. In all probability he was a victim of the 365th Fighter Group, a brand-new Ninth Air Force ground-attack outfit that saw its first air combat on this day, claiming 6–2 Fw 190s for the loss of one P-47. The green 365th flew a perfect

Lt. Günther Wolf, a pilot in III./NJG 5. On March 6, he flew one of the last missions by night fighters against USAAF heavy bombers. He was shot down by a Mustang, but made a successful belly-landing in a cultivated field near Berlin. (*Wolf***)**

escort mission; German experience was proving no match for American numbers and training.[87]

The Eighth Air Force first targeted Berlin on March 3, but the mission was abandoned when dense clouds with tops above 28,000 feet (8,500 meters) were encountered. Another attempt on the 4th resulted in another recall. One combat wing of the 3rd Bomb Division failed to hear the signal and proceeded to Berlin, which it bombed through a solid undercast. The new Jagddivision 1 *Gefechtsverband*—Obstlt. Wolf-Dietrich Wilcke's Stab and three Gruppen of JG 3, plus Sturmstaffel 1—was able to form up despite the weather and catch the withdrawing bombers, claiming eight B-17s and three escorts.

March 6—Berlin[88]

The weather finally cleared on the 6th, and Doolittle succeeded in getting his full bomber force to "Big B." His 730 bombers were escorted by 644 fighters from the Eighth and Ninth Air Forces and the RAF. Many fighter groups flew two missions, boosting the fighter sortie total to 943. In accord with the new policy of "confrontation," the path of the bomber stream was directly east from England toward Berlin, with a few minor course changes to avoid known Flak concentrations. The target was apparent in I. Jagdkorps headquarters soon after takeoff, and Genmaj. Schmid ordered all of his fighters to concentrate along the approach path. The boundaries of the RLV commands at this time are shown on the theater map, and in greater detail on page 169.[89] Schmid requested reinforcement from II. Jagdkorps and Jagddivision 7 early, and it was granted. A total of 463 defensive sorties was flown, of which 332 were credited with *Feindberührung*, or enemy contact.

The bombers began leaving the English coast at 1000, and were crossing the Zuider Zee by 1130 in a stream 150 km (94 miles) long. The B-17s of the 1st Bomb Division led in five combat boxes, staggered two abreast. The B-17s of the 3rd Bomb Division followed, its six combat boxes also staggered two abreast. The three combat boxes of the B-24-equipped 2nd Bomb Division brought up the rear, in trail. The new RLV tactical doctrine no longer required the II. Jagdkorps fighters to sortie against the incoming stream; they were to wait for the course of the returning bombers to be determined and fly a single concentrated mission against them. But the Jafü 4 controller made one major error, by scrambling Hptm. Klaus Mietusch and his III./JG 26 against some medium bombers

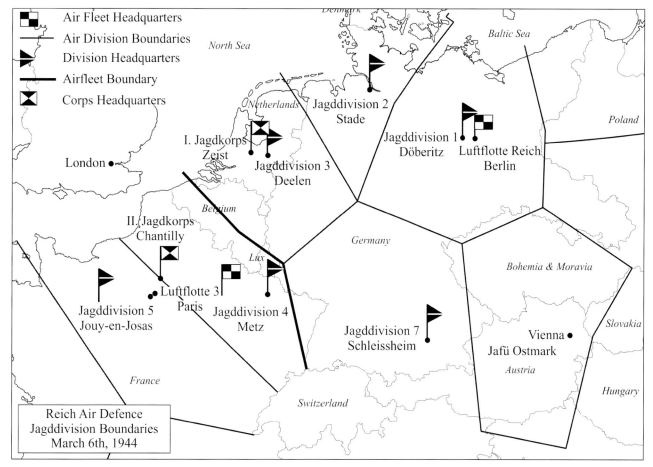

Reich Air Defence
Jagddivision Boundaries
March 6th, 1944

attacking the Poix airfield. Mietusch downed one of the escorting Typhoons, but was forced to land his Gruppe on Vitry, a Fw 190 base that apparently could not service his Bf 109s, and was unable to take part in the later mission against the returning heavies.[90]

II. Jagdkorps sent most of its fighters to Biblis and Wiesbaden-Erbenheim, both Jagddivision 7 fighter bases. These were to the south of the bombers' track, and this choice may have been intended as a blocking move in case the stream made an unexpected turn in that direction. This was not likely, given the weather conditions over southern Germany, but most of the fighters of JG 2 and JG 26 were now well within range of the bomber stream, whatever its ultimate course.

Although the bombers passed directly across the northern half of Jagddivision 3 territory, Oberst Grabmann did not order his *Gefechtsverband* to form up for an attack. Oberst Oesau had only his JG 1 Stabsschwarm and two Fw 190 Gruppen available— III./JG 1 was for some reason not operational—and it was decided that his fighters should join the JD 2

Gefechtsverband, which was assembling over Lake Steinhuder. This formation was led by Hptm. Rolf Hermichen, one of the best RLV combat commanders, and ultimately totaled 107 Bf 109s and Fw 190s from the Stab and three Gruppen of JG 11; III./JG 54; and the Stab and two Gruppen of JG 1. A smooth rendezvous was achieved, and after a short jog to the northwest the Jagddivision 2 controller at Stade ordered Hermichen to turn due west on a collision course with the American bombers, which were now 190 km (120 miles) away.

The bomber stream had by now split into two parts. Owing to a radar malfunction in the leading B-17 that its navigator did not catch, the entire 1st Bomb Division and half of the 3rd Division veered slowly to the right from the planned course. The rear half of the 3rd Division, led by the 13th Combat Wing, did not see the unplanned turn and continued on course, followed by the 2nd Division. Most of the escorts were with the van; only eight 56th Fighter Group P-47s stayed in the immediate vicinity of the 13th Wing.

Major Heinz Bär was given command of II./JG 1 after the death of Hptm. Segatz on March 8. He is seen briefing his pilots at Rheine. *From left:* Oblt. von Kirchmayr, Oblt. Burath, unknown, Lt. Schwarz, Lt. Wegner, Lt. Deppe, Lt. Terborg, Obfw. Bach, Obfw. Schuhmacher, Obfw. Niedereichhoolz, Fw. Sauer, Fw. Fuchs, and Uffz. Zinkl. (*Burath*)

A few minutes before noon Hermichen ordered his Gruppe to spread out into attack formation and drop auxiliary tanks. He checked his gunsight and primed his guns, in preparation for the one-second firing run to come. He aimed at the low box of the 13th Wing, which contained 16 100th Bomb Group B-17s, and a minute later picked a specific target. The Fw 190 pilots echeloned back to both sides conformed to his slight movements and prepared to fire on their own targets, if they happened to line up on any. Behind and above the Focke-Wulfs came the Messerschmitts of Hptm. Rudolph Sinner's III./JG 54. Sinner chose a box slightly higher than Hermichen's for his own Gruppe. Behind Sinner came Hptm. Toni Hackl with III./JG 11, Oberst Oesau with the Stabsschwarm and I. Gruppe of JG 1, and Major Bär with II./JG 1. Above them all and upsun flew Major Specht's II./JG 11, the high cover, moving to head off the only American escorts Specht saw, several flights of 78th Group P-47s that had turned back from the front half of the stream.

Just at noon Hermichen shouted "*Hinein!*" ("Get in there!"); three seconds later, he opened fire. The most concentrated attack in the history of the RLV began, carried out by the cream of I. Jagdkorps. Ten B-17s went down on the first attack. After passing through the *Pulk*, Hermichen reversed course sharply to return to the van for another head-on attack. Sinner was surprised at this, as he would have preferred to continue to the rear and attack the following *Pulk*.

There were no firm rules covering subsequent attacks, which as a result were carried out from multiple directions, by single aircraft and pairs. Most pilots were able to expend most of their ammunition on the bombers and leave the area before P-47s from the 56th and 78th Fighter Groups were able to drive the rest away. When the battle ended at about 1225, 20 bombers had been shot down, one was headed to Sweden, and others had turned back with damage. All of these B-17s were from the 13th Combat Wing, which lost 25–1 during the mission. Three P-47s also went down at this time, while Hermichen's *Verband* lost about 12 fighters.

The experience of Fw. Fritz Ungar of III./JG 54 can be taken as typical. Ungar recalled:

I saw strikes in the #2 engine of my B-17 and saw parts fly off. There was no time to rejoice. I was now inside the enemy formation trying to get through without ramming anyone. No one fired at me then; they were too concerned about hitting each other. When we emerged behind the *Verband* things got really hot. The tail gunners of some 30 bombers were letting fly at us with everything they had. Together with part of our Gruppe I pulled sharply up to the left and high, out to one side. Glancing back I saw the Fortress I had hit pull up and go down to the right, smoking heavily.

Just then I came under attack by a P-47. I dove for a nearby cloud and reached it without being hit. But when I pulled out of my dive at 2,000 meters a P-47 was waiting for me. My Messerschmitt was hit with a loud bang and a sharp pain shot through my foot. I looked back to see the P-47 banking away, much to my relief. I could see the blood from my foot running over the floor of my cockpit and looked for a suitable field to belly-land in before I fainted for loss of blood. A jolt, a quick spin as fighter turned around, and everything became still . . .[91]

After the war Fritz Ungar was able to identify his opponents as the 56th Fighter Group's Captain Walker Mahurin and his wingman Lt. Barney Casteel.

The American mission commander in the leading 1st Bomb Division B-17 caught his navigation error, turned north, and led his part of the formation back into place and onto the correct course by 1230. At this time the Jagddivision 1 *Gefechtsverband* was assembling over Magdeburg. It was led by Major Hans Kogler with seven cannon-armed Bf 110s of his III./ZG 26. Next came ten Me 410s of II./ZG 26, each with four 21-cm rockets, followed by 24 rocket-armed Bf 110s from ZG 76, up from Jagddivision 7. Next came 55 Bf 109s from JG 3 and ten from JG 302 and various Industrieschwärme. I./JG 3 had the mission of high cover for the formation. The other single-engine pilots were told to protect the Zerstörer until the bombers were attacked; then it was every pilot for himself. The main formation was to make a standard frontal attack. Associated with the *Verband* but flying separate from it were seven Sturmstaffel 1 Fw 190s, which were to make stern attacks from close range. Kogler's *Verband* had a total of 41 Zerstörer and 72 single-engine fighters, somewhat stronger than Hermichen's force. Also up from the Berlin area were several single-engine fighters from various factory units, 16 NJG 5 and test unit Bf 110 night fighters with orders to pick off stragglers, and at least five Fw 190 Fühlungshalter aircraft, which were beginning to replace the twin-engine models previously used.

The Jagddivision 1 controller directed Kogler on what was thought to be a head-on approach, but when Kogler made visual contact the stream had unexpectedly turned slightly to the south for the approach to their targets, which were all just south of Berlin. He could not turn his heavy twin-engine fighters sufficiently, and the Zerstörer had to attack from a slight angle; the Bf 109s following were apparently able to swing farther and attack as briefed. Kogler began his attack on the leading combat boxes at about 1240 over the town of Tangerhütte, just as Sturmstaffel 1 began making stern attacks on the same formation. The P-51 escorts in the area, of which there were many, spotted the Zerstörer and went after them, ignoring the Fw 190s of the Sturmstaffel, which made repeated passes and eventually downed six 91st Bomb Group B-17s. One of these was the first ramming victory for the Staffel. Fw. Hermann Wahlfeldt decided to ram when he ran out of ammunition. He sliced off the right stabilizer of his target with his left wing; he was able to bail out normally, while only two gunners were able to escape the spinning B-17.[92]

Rocket attacks by the Zerstörer had been difficult enough from dead astern, and were now to be made from the front to reduce the heavy fighters' vulnerability. Judging distance in an oblique attack such as those made on this day was impossible, and according to the bomber crews no B-17 was hit by a rocket. However, the Zerstörer made effective use of their heavy cannon armament, and shot a number of B-17s into flames; ten victory claims were confirmed. Most of the Bf 110s and Me 410s were quickly under attack by P-51s from

Hptm. Rolf Hermichen, the I./JG 11 Kommandeur, is hoisted from his airplane, a brand-new Fw 190A-7, after a successful March mission from Rotenburg. The Focke-Wulf appears to be painted in an overall *Hellgrau* (light gray) scheme, common for Bf 109 high-altitude fighters but not Fw 190s. (*Bundesarchiv 676-7973A-18*)

the 4th Fighter Group, the 1st Bomb Division's assigned escort, which had remained upsun until Kogler had committed his force. Mustangs from the 357th Group were also present, but by accident; their assigned 2nd Bomb Division was late for rendezvous, and the eager pilots had rushed to the "sound of the guns." Kogler's escort Gruppe, I./JG 3, was totally ineffective in protecting its charges, and claimed no victories. Kogler lost 16 of the 41 Bf 110s and Me 410s that were engaged, as well as five Bf 109s and two Fw 190s. In this battle eight 1st Bomb Division B-17s were lost to gunfire, and three to collisions, while several were damaged sufficiently to drop from formation. Four P-51s were also lost in this area.

Fighter attacks tapered off after 25 minutes, as the leading bombers reached their IP south of Berlin. Most of their small briefed targets were covered in cloud, and most bombs were thus salvoed on residential districts—a pure *Terrorangriff* or terror attack, as the Germans called it. The feared German Flak added its share of damage to the American bombers, which rallied west of Berlin and took up a course that was the reciprocal of the approach flight. Their formation was now different; the three divisions now flew side-by-side rather than in trail, reducing the length of the stream for the benefit of the escorts.

Few fighters from either side penetrated the Berlin Flak zone deliberately; four that did were night fighters from III./NJG 5, one of which was piloted by Lt. Günther Wolf. Wolf recalled:

> We were in no formation, led by no one! We had no orders, only "tips" to attack stragglers and stay away from compact formations, which was only common sense. We caught sight of the enemy bomber formation and, keeping a wary eye for enemy fighters, wondered how we were going to tackle them. Then we saw a straggler all alone below the formation. Not a word was said on the radio, but all four Messerschmitts swung after what looked like an easy target.
>
> I closed on my prey from behind. Suddenly, when I was at about 600 meters [660 yards], just outside firing range, my airplane shuddered under an impact of bullets. The canopy was smashed and glass flew in all directions. I never saw what hit us.[93]

Wolf's right engine burst into flames, streaming black oil and smoke. He ordered his gunner to bail out, but his gunner told him that his chute had been ruined by gunfire. Wolf had to make a crash landing. He entered a steep diving turn while throttling back. His opponent, a 357th Fighter Group P-51 pilot, thought the Bf 110 was out of control and claimed it as destroyed. At the last moment Wolf pulled up and made a belly landing in a field northeast of Berlin. Many of his comrades were not as lucky; 11 of the 16 night fighters sent up were shot down and eight crewmen were killed.

The prowling 357th Group Mustangs were now seeking out German fighters attempting to return to base after completing their attacks. Oblt. Gerhard Loos of III./JG 54, a Knight's Cross holder with 92 victories, was caught at low altitude and shot down. Loos succeeded in bailing out, but his parachute harness ripped apart and he fell to his death.[94]

The withdrawal leg of a mission to the Reich was frequently uneventful for American bombers, or at least for those that were not straggling from battle damage. The RLV always had trouble mounting successful second sorties. But along the route on this day were many units that had not been employed previously: II. and III./JG 2, I. and II./JG 26, and I./JG 300. There was also more time than usual to service airplanes that had already flown a first mission. More than 100 fighters were ordered up against the returning bombers. Most were sent to the Lingen area near the Dutch–German border in an attempt to achieve a tactical concentration, although nothing like a unified attack could be hoped for. The only known attack by a complete unit was by ten Bf 109s of I./JG 300. Tactical command was given to Oblt. Waldemar Grafe, the only experienced day-fighter pilot among the ten. Grafe led his Messerschmitts 1,000 meters (3,300 ft.) above the bomber stream and pushed over in a vertical dive from out of the sun. Hurtling through the formation, his inexperienced pilots succeeded in damaging several B-17s in their surprise bounce and pulled out of their dives below the bombers; only then were they seen by the escorts.

Most of the other German fighters had great difficulty in evading the escort to get at the bombers, and attacked in ones and twos. Some experienced pilots were able to use the compact bomber formation to their advantage, striking quickly from the gaps between the bomb divisions and eluding the P-47s of the withdrawal escort by dodging between the combat boxes, but most could not evade the Thunderbolts. Fw. Gerd Wiegand of 4./JG 26 recalled:

> I scrambled from Biblis at 1330 with Obfw. Heitmann as my wingman. We climbed to 9,000 meters [29,500 ft.] and after dodging a Flak barrage contacted B-24s over Dortmund. I positioned us for an attack on a lower-flying formation of P-47s from out of the sun, but Heitmann suddenly dove away to make a lone attack on the bombers. *Diziplinlosigkeit*! [Lack of discipline!] I then dove on the Thunderbolts alone, attacking head-on and escaping in a vertical dive. I don't know if I hit any of them. By now I was low on fuel, so I landed at Rheine.[95]

Hans Heitmann's lone attack resulted in a claim for a B-17, but he was then shot down and badly wounded. He did not fly again until March 1945.[96]

The raid cost the Eighth Air Force 69–6 bombers, the heaviest numerical loss of any mission of the war, and 11–3 escorts. The bomber loss rate of 10.2

percent was high, but acceptable at this stage of the war. The new large-formation tactics of the RLV had their greatest success on this day, but at a cost of 64 aircraft (19.2 percent of those credited with sorties), and aircrew losses of 8 KIA, 36 MIA, and 23 WIA. (All crewmen not reporting in by day's end were considered MIA, or more accurately "not yet returned." Nearly all of these men were in fact dead.)

USSTAF intelligence was quick to pick up on the new German tactics. Employment of the *Gefechts-verband* was noted in May 1944:

> Only one tactic has been developed since the basic 13 tactics or diagrams [identified in fall 1943] which has caused concern to the operations officers of this division. This is the MASS ATTACK FROM HEAD ON. As many as 60 fighters have participated in one of these attacks . . .[97]

By August, through crew combat reports, Ultra intercepts, and POW interrogation,[98] most of the details of *Gefechtsverband* attacks, including the use of Höhengruppen and ground-control procedures, were accurately summarized in intelligence appraisals.[99] As always, the most compelling accounts are those of the airmen themselves. Bert Stiles, a 23-year-old B-17 copilot, wrote this account of an encounter with a *Gefechtsverband* on a Berlin mission in spring 1944:

> I was still wondering what nationality that big mob was. It didn't take long to queue up. They trailed off out at 2 o'clock and came swinging in.
>
> "Here they come," I yelled thickly.
>
> Sam was flying. The RPM was okay. The engines were doing all right. All I had to do was sit there and watch them come slow rolling through us. There was an endless stream of 109s and 190s. Some went high and some went low, and half a dozen more came streaming through us. I don't know whether I was scared or not. Mostly I was numb. A 190 rolled over, came straight at us, everything opened up. His gun ports were blinking yellow flashes. He couldn't have missed us by more than a few inches. Maybe our top turret threw a burst in him. Anyway, he lived one-tenth of a second more, before he crashed into a Fort in the group behind us. All our guns were firing. The whole ship seemed to shake apart . . . The 190s knocked a whole squadron out behind us.[100]

The daylight bombing of Berlin was certainly a propaganda disaster for the Third Reich, and caused many of its citizens (quietly) to begin questioning the course of the war. It is of interest that the daily Wehrmacht communiqué singled out Major Kogler for praise as the "leader of a *Zerstörerverband* that especially distinguished itself," despite its crippling casualties. The heavy fighters had been touted as wonder weapons in their new role as bomber destroyers, and their extreme vulnerability was being kept from Hitler and the German public.[101]

The Wastage Continues

The Eighth returned to Berlin on March 8. On this day 623 bombers from all three bomb divisions targeted the Erkner ball-bearing factory. Bombing conditions were good, and serious damage was both claimed and attained. Fortunately for the German war effort, the dispersal of ball-bearing production was already well under way. The defensive effort was only

An informal portrait of Major Walther Dahl, Kommandeur of III./JG 3, taken at Leipheim shortly after he was awarded the Knight's Cross on March 11. One of the most successful RLV formation leaders, Dahl commanded JG 300 for five months. He was then relieved by Göring, but continued flying missions with JG 300 for two more months before joining the OKL staff. (*Bundesarchiv 666-6893-23a*)

slightly less than that of the 6th, 378 sorties being flown, and was effective in two major combats. Only Jagddivision 1 formed its *Gefechtsverband*, and this contained only seven Zerstörer. But other units sent up against the incoming bomber stream formed an even larger concentration, even if it was not formally called a *Gefechtsverband*. Schmid knew full well what the day's target would be, and asked Luftflotte 3's Jagddivision 4 to send its fighters north at 1000, a full hour before the B-17s and B-24s started leaving England. The bombers' course was a duplicate of that of the 6th, due east across Holland and northern Germany. II., III., and 4./JG 26 (4./JG 26 normally ooperated independently) landed at Rheine with a total of 49 fighters. They took off at noon and flew to Steinhuder Lake, a distinctive landmark west of Hannover. Here they rendezvoused with five Jagdgruppen of JG 1 and JG 11. They succeeded for once in overwhelming the escorts, which on this part of the route were the P-47s of the 56th and 353rd Fighter Groups. JG 26 Bf 109s and Fw 190s formed up ahead of the 45th Combat Wing, which was leading the 3rd Bomb Division and had already lost cohesion owing to early returns. This time the Focke-Wulfs attacked in trail, in closely spaced strings of 10–12 aircraft. The B-17 gunners found this confusing; targets were difficult to select, and no JG 26 aircraft was seriously damaged by return fire. Eight 45th Wing B-17s crashed between Steinhuder Lake and Brunswick, all victims of JG 26. 4./JG 26 got into a scuffle with a flight of 56th Fighter Group Thunderbolts. Gerd Wiegand, now a Fähnrich-Feldwebel or officer candidate, shot down a P-47, but was shot down in turn by another, and suffered injuries that kept him

A lineup of III./JG 27 Bf 109G-6s at Wien-Seyring in March. The Gruppe was rebuilding there before beginning operations with the RLV. (Schroer via Price)

out of combat for three months. The more persistent pilots from this first formation continued to nibble at the bombers until the Jagddivision 1 *Verband* took up the fight. For the day the Eighth lost 37–3 bombers and 18–16 fighters; the RLV lost 42 fighters and 3 KIA, 26 MIA, and 9 WIA among the aircrew.[102]

One pilot, Uffz. Gerhard Kroll of III./JG 54, flew his first mission on the 8th, and shared his experiences with the authors. Kroll recalled:

I was naturally very excited. We were stationed in Lüneburg and flying Bf 109Gs. Flight order was as usual Stab, 7., 8., and 9. Staffeln. Being one of the newest members of the 9. Staffel my place was at the end of the whole formation. I didn't see much until we were on top of the bombers . . . I learned later that we made contact west of Nienburg in Westfalia. I don't know if there were more bombers than those I saw right in front of me . . . Lucky for us there were no escort fighters. Attack was made head-on from above. This was fine for the 7. and all right for the 8., but because of our closing speed the 9. Staffel had to make our attacks almost straight down. I didn't even try to shoot, but witnessed the victory of my Schwarmführer over a B-17 . . . One thick tracer from his engine-mounted 30-mm cannon vanished in the left wing root and the whole left wing broke off at the fuselage. All of the Messerschmitts continued their dive below the bombers, then climbed again for a second attack from the rear. When I passed the rear of the B-17 formation I saw a straggler . . . It looked so good to me that I left my Staffel and turned on the B-17. This was a clear violation of orders. However, with my speed from the dive I gained fast on the B-17 from behind and below. And then I pressed the buttons. Thick black smoke came from the right inboard engine. I kept firing and got closer and closer—too close. I believe I caught something from the tail gunner. All of a sudden my plane tumbled down and I saw only light and dark patches move across the canopy. I failed to regain control and it was clear I had to bail out . . .[103]

Kroll's inexperience resulted in more problems than usual with the bailout procedure; he hit the ground at a 45-degree angle and sprained his left ankle. After convincing the nearby villagers that he was a German pilot and not an American *Terrorflieger*, he was shown every courtesy and told that six parachutes from "his" Fortress had been seen. He reached Lüneburg that evening by train, was given the usual "birthday party" for his survival, an Iron Cross Second Class for his victory, and several days of light duty to heal his ankle. Unfortunately for Kroll the villagers did not prove to be adequate witnesses, and his claim was never filed; that of his Schwarmführer was filed and confirmed as the only Gruppe victory this day.

Another battle in the ongoing Luftwaffe turf war was fought on the 8th. A new RLV command, *Jagdabschnitt Mittelrhein* (Fighter Sector Central Rhine) was established in Darmstadt to command the air defenses of the Frankfurt basin–central Rhine region, under Jagddivision 3. Its territory was carved out of Jagddivision 7. The RLV history written after the war for the USAAF gave three reasons for setting up yet another headquarters. Coincidentally, this section was written by Walter Grabmann, the commander of Jagddivision 3 during this period:

1. Forward defenses needed to be withdrawn from their "outposts" to allow time to assemble in large Gefechtsverbände.
2. The region was being attacked or crossed frequently by U.S. formations. Passing control from Jagddivision 3 to Jagddivision 7 was inefficient, leading to inconsistencies.
3. I. Jagdkorps radio and intelligence personnel were "far more experienced" than those of Jagddivision 7, which was still directly under Luftflotte Reich.[104]

The USAAF returned to Berlin on the 9th. The bombers took the same route as the two previous raids, with no attempts at deception. The RLV commanders chose not to respond to this obvious provocation, and kept their fighters on the ground, using bad weather as a convenient excuse. They had already lost the propaganda battle for Berlin, and the value of Berlin's industrial targets was ruled insufficient to risk the dwindling fighter force further.[105]

The Eighth Air Force returned to Münster on the 11th, and Brunswick on the 15th; the German reaction was muted. On their mission on the 15th II./JG 11 was overwhelmed, losing 6 KIA, 2 WIA, and eight Bf 109s. Major Specht announced the same evening that his Gruppe would be taken off operations for six weeks to rest and rebuild. I. Jagdkorps moved its headquarters from Zeist in Holland to Brunswick as the RLV continued pulling its forces back from the borders of the Reich to the heartland. A mid-level promotion of some significance saw Major Heinz Bär

take command of II./JG 1. According to Gruppe survivors, "morale soared." He had been the *de facto* leader of the Gruppe for some time, and was considered by his pilots to be the best officer in the entire Geschwader. His formal rehabilitation from the previous year's demotion was now complete.[106]

The Eighth Air Force's next deep-penetration raid targeted Augsburg and Friedrichshafen on the 16th. All bombing was done through cloud, and was largely ineffective, but the RLV commanders put up a full-strength defense, despite low clouds and snow flurries that greatly hampered takeoffs and assembly. The Americans lost 23–1 bombers and 10–2 escorts; the Germans lost 46–14 of the 266 fighters credited with sorties, 9 KIA, 38 MIA, and 29 WIA. The day marked the beginning of the end of the Bf 110 Zerstörer as a first-line weapon in the RLV. ZG 76 was caught by 354th Fighter Group Mustangs as it formed up to attack the bomber stream. Its Bf 109 escorts disappeared, and the P-51s made short work of the lumbering Bf 110s, shooting down 23 of the 77 airborne. III./ZG 76, a new unit which had just been declared operational, never flew another mission, and was soon disbanded. Bases farther to the rear were sought out for the six remaining Zerstörergruppen; in the future they were to be used only against unescorted bomber formations, which were rare, and becoming rarer. Walter Grabmann remarked in a post-war report that crew morale remained "noteworthy," based on the superior firepower of their twin-engine fighters and the psychological advantage of a two-man crew.[107]

I./JG 5 was now fully operational in Jagddivision 7, flying from Herzogenaurach. The Gruppe was part of JG 5, the *Eismeer* (Arctic Ocean) Geschwader, and had been formed in Norway, but had been moved to the Balkans in one of the Luftwaffe's frequent unit shuffles before joining the RLV.[108] The Gruppe was ordered to scramble 24 Bf 109Gs at noon to attack the bombers withdrawing from Augsburg. Lt. Heinrich Freiherr von Podewils flew as wingman to his Gruppenkommandeur, Major Erich Gerlitz, and recalled:

Our takeoff was delayed for 30 minutes by a snowstorm that blew over, leaving clear skies. Six Schwärme, all with belly tanks, scrambled from our very short field. We climbed to 7,000 meters [23,000 ft.], and caught the last *Pulk* of 40 departing heavies at 6,000 meters [20,000 ft.]. We overtook them and made a close-formation attack from the front. Our closing speed was 700 km/h + 350 km/h = 1,050 km/h [650 mph]. We dove straight through so as not to provide the rear gunners with a target. As Gerlitz pulled up, his gear dropped. I told him, and his gear went back up. We prepared our next attack. Fighters were seen at 10,000 meters [33,000 ft.], but were assumed our own. The Gruppe made two more attacks before the fighters came down—P-47s! Gerlitz dove away, and I had to follow. A P-47 got on Gerlitz's tail; I tried to reach him, but was myself taken under fire from the rear. My seat armor and engine were hit. I cut my throttle; the P-47 sailed past, its pilot staring. My engine now seized up. I was over Ulm at 1,000 meters [3,300 ft.], with no good place to bail out. I rode my crate down. Trees tore both wings off, and the fuselage overturned. I was knocked out, but suffered only surface facial wounds. I reached base the next morning with three other pilots, after much drinking of home-brewed Schnapps on the train. Major Gerlitz had been shot down and killed; he had tried to bail out too low, and his chute didn't open.[109]

Podewils's Gruppe lost two pilots killed and five injured on this mission. Five Bf 109s were shot down, and another ten were damaged.

Luftflotte Reich underwent another organizational change on the 16th. Jagddivision 30, the special head-quarters set up to control the *Wilde Sau* single-engine night fighters, was disbanded. The *Wilde Sau* units had not been able to maintain their early success rate; losses had been very high during the winter of 1943–4. They were now in the day-fighter order of battle, as bad weather specialists. The reinforcement was welcome. Many *Wilde Sau* pilots had followed their commander, Major Hajo Herrmann, from the bomber

2./JG 1 Fw 190A-7 "black 3" prepares to take off in March from its snowy Twente airfield, carrying a 300-liter (79 U.S. gallon) drop tank. It has black–white Gruppe bands on the cowling and a rust-red RLV fuselage band. (Rosch)

arm, and were fully instrument-qualified; all had had more instrument training than the typical day-fighter pilot. Herrmann, a Hitler favorite, had to remain in the public's eye, and was immediately given another high-profile command, replacing Oberst Lützow at Jagddivision 1. Lützow, a highly respected fighter commander, was placed in the *Führerreserve* (General Reserve) until another position could be found for an officer of his demonstrated talents.[110]

The Fifteenth Air Force flew to the Reich on March 17 for the first time since February 25. Some 192 bombers dropped on Vienna through solid cloud. The German defenders were unable to respond. The Hungarian Air Force scrambled 16 Bf 109s and 11 Me 210s which were ordered to intercept an unescorted B-24 formation over Lake Balaton. One Bf 109 flight made contact, but in the first documented air battle between the Hungarians and the Fifteenth Air Force was able to claim only two damaged Liberators for the loss of 2–2 fighters.[111]

On the 18th the Eighth Air Force sent its three bomb divisions to south-central Germany to bomb aviation targets at Munich, Friedrichshafen, and Oberpfaffenhofen. The Fifteenth attacked Udine, an airfield in northern Italy; this was far enough north to fix most of the Jafü Ostmark fighters near their bases until it was too late to take part in the interception of the Eighth Air Force. The defensive strategy of I. Jagdkorps was somewhat unusual. The fighters of Jagddivision 1 were not employed at all; those of Jagddivisionen 2 and 3 did not attempt to attack the incoming stream, but flew south to refuel and attack the withdrawing bombers. The Jagddivision 7 controllers were apparently overwhelmed, and only 152 of the 353 fighters that sortied made contact. The Americans reported that most attacks were made half-heartedly in the face of the heavy escort. The 14th Combat Wing of the 2nd Bomb Division apparently took a wrong turn leaving Friedrichshafen, and wound up flying alone, and unescorted. The JG 11 *Verband* was quick on the scene; its Schwärme made head-on passes on the hapless B-24s, then turned, made rear passes on the same wing, turned again, and repeated the process. Some 55th Fighter Group P-38s arrived, but the Bf 109s and Fw 190s avoided them by staying on the opposite side of the bomber formation. The JG 11 pilots returned to Erbenheim claiming the destruction of 19 B-24s; they suffered no casualties or reportable damage.

Over Strasbourg the attack on the 14th Combat Wing was taken up by II. and III./JG 2. The *Richthofen* pilots had their best results against the heavy bombers in some time, claiming seven B-24s, plus four B-17s and two P-51s, for the loss of two fighters.

The Eighth Air Force returned to England short 43 bombers; four more were scrapped. In all, 22 of the losses were from the 14th Combat Wing: eight from the 44th Bomb Group and 14 from the 392nd. Sixteen of the missing airplanes had headed for Switzerland, where three were shot down by the Swiss defenses and the other 13 made forced landings, their crews going into internment. This mass defection is a good indication of the amount of stress faced by the American bomber crews. They were told that the Luftwaffe was being annihilated; however, the number of missions required before rotation to the States had just been increased, and their own fighters seemed to be fewer than before, or at least not as visible. The odds of surviving their tours of duty still seemed poor.[112]

Seldom did weather conditions allow USSTAF to use both of its air forces against the Reich on the same day. It was the turn of the Fifteenth on March 19. En route to Austria its small bomber force was attacked by the one Italian and two German fighter Gruppen of Jafü Oberitalien in northern Italy, and then faced the newly reinforced Jafü Ostmark. A formation of 92 B-24s was met coming off its Graz target by 87 JG 27 Bf 109s, led by their Geschwaderkommodore, Obstlt. Gustav Rödel. III. and IV./JG 27 were flying their first RLV mission, and their pilots attacked the unescorted B-24s enthusiastically from all directions (except head-on, never a popular option in JG 27). The Geschwader lost six pilots and ten Bf 109s to the B-24 gunners, but returned to base claiming 27 B-24s shot down; 21 claims were eventually confirmed. American losses to all causes totaled six B-17s and 12 B-24s, eight from the 454th Bomb Group. This was bad enough, and could be attributed to a shortage of escorts. The one P-47 and three P-38 groups of the Fifteenth were insufficient to protect the bomber force after it had split up to bomb multiple targets. The Fifteenth Air Force commanders pleaded with USSTAF headquarters and Washington for some P-51 groups but, as always, their needs took second priority to those of the Eighth.[113]

The Fifteenth Air Force did not return to the Reich until April 2. Conditions were more favorable for the Eighth, which flew five missions to Germany between March 20 and 29. Only one met significant resistance

in the air. The RLV fighters were grounded on most days by low cloud decks over their bases. Instrument-rated instructors and *Wilde Sau* pilots were sent to the bases of the Luftflotte Reich day fighters to give the pilots quick courses in instrument flying, but their competence never rose sufficiently to allow formation takeoffs through cloud.

A raid on Brunswick and Münster on the 23rd met significant opposition. Strong tailwinds brought the 3rd Bomb Division to the rendezvous point with its penetration escorts 30 minutes ahead of schedule, and the division flew the entire mission to Brunswick without escort. This gave I. Jagdkorps the opportunity for an effective interception. Nine Jagdgruppen of Jagddivisionen 1, 2, and 3 were scrambled and sent to the Brunswick area. The first and last combat wings in the 3rd Bomb Division stream were attacked by successive waves of fighters for 15 minutes, making good use of cloud and contrails, and lost 16–1 B-17s. Mustangs of the 354th Fighter Group were the first to respond to the B-17 leader's call for help, and downed five fighters, including that of the JG 3 Kommodore, Oberst Wolf-Dietrich Wilcke, who was killed. Wilcke, nicknamed *Fürst* ("Prince") for his aristocratic manner, wore the Knight's Cross with Oak Leaves and Swords for his 192 victories, and had been a highly respected fighter commander since before the war.[114]

Two Jagdgruppen, II. and IV./JG 3, and one independent Jagdstaffel, Sturmstaffel 1, were vectored west to meet the 1st Bomb Division, which was bombing Münster. They concentrated on a single bomb group, the 92nd, which was flying high position in its combat wing and was apparently enough out of position to attract attention. Five of the six B-17s lost by the division were from the 92nd. The JG 3 Gruppen made close-formation frontal attacks, while the nine Fw 190s of the Sturmstaffel, led on this occasion by Major von Kornatzki, attacked the same group from the rear. Uffz. Willi Maximowitz was being chased through the *Pulk* by a 55th Fighter Group P-38 and decided to ram a B-17. He raised his right wing and clipped 1.5 meters (5 ft.) off the left horizontal stabilizer of his target with his own left wing, which sheared off. Maximowitz then bailed out with little trouble. He was credited with a *Rammabschuss* (ramming shoot-down) and was allowed to paint a coveted skull-and-crossbones on his rudder to celebrate it, but the B-17 returned to England without much difficulty. After leaving the bombers the

Sturmstaffel ran afoul of marauding 4th Fighter Group Mustangs, which were sweeping across north-central Germany after missing their rendezvous with the 3rd Bomb Division, and lost three Fw 190s with their pilots. The 4th Group went on to fly a very successful mission, claiming 13 single-engine fighters without loss. The day's losses totaled 28–1 bombers and 4–1 fighters for the Eighth Air Force; 31 fighters and 6 KIA, 12 MIA, and 6 WIA for the RLV.[115]

No twin-engine fighters were seen by the Americans on the 23rd; they had retired from the north European battlefield. By month's end ZG 26 had relocated at Königsberg in East Prussia. In the words of the III./ZG 26 war diary, its mission would now be "to battle enemy formations that penetrate east of Berlin without fighter escort."[116]

There were two major command changes on March 31, one on each side. The Combined Bomber Offensive officially came to an end, and the Eighth Air Force was taken from USSTAF and put under SHAEF control to prepare for the invasion. But Eisenhower, Spaatz, and Doolittle respected one another's judgement and ability, and when Spaatz told Ike that he would like the Eighth to continue the strategic

The Wunstorf flight line of II./JG 11 on a day in March, as viewed from the command post. On the far right, the 4./JG 11 Kapitän, Oblt. Sommer, hustles into the building. The subject of the discussion in the center is unknown, but probably involves the Kommodore, Major Graf. Noteworthy are the winch-equipped munitions truck (*far left*), the drop tank, the takeoff signals box, and the Kommandeur's staff car. (*Heinz Rose via Arno Rose*)

bombing offensive until specifically needed for tactical purposes, Eisenhower gave his permission.[117]

Göring issued an order on this day that, as of 2100 hours, Jagddivision 7, including Jafü Ostmark, would be subordinated to I. Jagdkorps. Schmid had gotten his wish. Operational command of the Reich air defenses was now vested in a single headquarters, his. He calculated the effective date of the reorganization to be April 1, so that highlight was omitted from this March summary in his postwar history for the USAAF:

1. American operations versus the Reich were characterized by a strong increase in escort strength.
2. American losses during Big Week had no effect whatsoever on American air operations.
3. American air forces captured air supremacy over the entire Reich except the far east.
4. Bombing of Berlin and Munich meant the complete collapse of German air power.
5. No systematic American plan could be discerned. The successful attack on aircraft factories was discontinued.
6. There was no sign of close cooperation between U.S. forces in England and Italy; attacks on the same cities by the USAAF (day) and RAF (night) were discontinued.
7. Of 15 major raids from England and three from Italy, weather allowed visual bombing on only three; limited visual on three, and instrument bombing on four.
8. The few attacks on airfields in the occupied territories were ineffective.
9. American approach and attack tactics were simple and straightforward and caused no particular problems for the German defenses.
10. American escort was organized to give continuous protection over entire flights.
11. No increase in I. Jagdkorps strength was possible. Fighter production was far behind schedule because of the successful February attacks.
12. Striking power of the RLV day-fighter units remained unbroken. Whenever weather permitted concentrated employment of all available forces in close-combat formation in a single area, success was obtained in bringing down enemy aircraft and keeping our own losses low—for example, over Berlin on March 6 and 8.
13. Jagddivision 7 and Jafü Ostmark forces were even weaker than those of I. Jagdkorps.

Organization of Day Fighter Defenses, April 1944

Command	Commander	Headquarters
LUFTFLOTTE REICH	*Genobst. Stumpff*	*Berlin-Wannsee*
I. Jagdkorps	*Genlt. Schmid*	*Brunswick*
Jagddivision 1	*Oberst Herrmann*	*Döberitz*
Jafü Ostpreussen	Oberst Nordmann	Neuhausen
Jafü Schlesien	Oberst Witt	Cosel
Jagddivision 2	*Genmaj. Ibel*	*Stade*
Jagdabschnittsfü Dänemark	Oberst Schalk	Grove
Jagddivision 3	*Oberst Grabmann*	*Deelen*
Jagdabschnittsfü Mittelrhein	Oberst Trübenbach	Darmstadt
Jagddivision 7	*Genmaj. Huth*	*Schleissheim*
Jafü Ostmark	Oberst Handrick	Wien-Cobenzl
Jagdabschnittsfü Ungarn	Obstlt. Neumann	Budapest
LUFTFLOTTE 3	*GFM Sperrle*	*Paris*
II. Jagdkorps	*Genmaj. Junck*	*Chantilly*
Jagddivision 4	*Oberst Vieck*	*Metz*
Jafü 4	Oberst von Bülow	St. Pol-Brias
Jagddivision 5	*Genmaj. Hentschel*	*Jouy-en-Josas*
Jafü 5	Oberst Gollob	Bernay
Jafü Bretagne	Oberst Mix	Rennes
Jafü Südfrankreich	Oberst Vollbracht	Aix

14. An RLV strength of 1,000–1,200 day fighters would have altered the situation.

15. The strength ratio [Eighth AF to I. JK?] was 7.5 U.S. heavy bombers: 4 U.S. fighters: 1 Luftwaffe fighter.

16. General Galland flew defensive sorties, became convinced of U.S. superiority, and attempted to speed up production of superior aircraft (Me 262 & Me 163).

17. During March, the average daily operational strengths of I. Jagdkorps were 300 single-engine day fighters, 60 twin-engine day fighters, and 50 night fighters available for day use.

18. March sorties by I. Jagdkorps = 2,226; losses = 240, or 10.9 percent.

19. March sorties versus Reich by Eighth Air Force = 16,612; losses to fighters = 302, or 1.8 percent.[118]

The day-fighter defenses of the Reich and the western occupied zone had now reached their penultimate state of organization, as tabulated above. *Jagdabschnittsführer* (Jagdabschnittsfü—Fighter Sector Leaders) controlled smaller forces than did Jagdfliegerführer, sometimes single Staffeln. Jafü 1, Jafü 2, and Jafü 3 had by now been disbanded, their functions having been taken over by their parent Jagddivisionen. The last major change would come on June 15, when Jafü Ostmark was renamed Jagddivision 8 and left Jagddivision 7.[119]

Seven Jagdgruppen from the three *Wilde Sau* Geschwader (JG 300, JG 301, JG 302) were merged smoothly into the day order of battle. According to Willi Reschke, an experienced *Wilde Sau* pilot, this was ". . . a period of great day success . . . The combination of bomber pilots experienced in night and formation flying and aggressive young fighter pilots (most at this time with some bad-weather training) gave good results—each learned from the other."[120]

Sturmstaffel 1 received new aircraft in April—special-build Fw 190A-8/R2 *Sturmböcke* ("assault billy goats" or "battering rams"), which were up-armored and up-armed for the sole purpose of attacking the bomber *Pulks*. The *Sturmbock* was 180 kg (400 pounds) heavier than the standard Fw 190A-8, with external armor plate bolted around the cockpit and the gun troughs and laminated 30-mm-thick glass panels on the front and sides of the canopy. The outer-wing 20-mm cannon were replaced by 30-mm MK 108s firing high explosive shells called *Minengranate*. Only 55 rounds of ammunition could be carried for each cannon, enough for five seconds of fire. The Staffel's standard rear attack to close range was deemed to be ideal for maximizing the destructive effect of these weapons.[121]

On April 2, the Fifteenth Air Force bombed two major targets in Steyr, Austria: a ball-bearing factory and an aircraft assembly plant. The Fifteenth still had only three P-38 groups and one P-47 group for escort, but this time staged them better to support the penetration leg of the mission. This undoubtedly saved many bombers, because Jafü Oberitalien and Jagddivision 7 responded early, and with maximum force, aided by the presence of a Fühlungshalter airplane from Osoppo and a straight-line course to Steyr by the bombers. The one Italian and two German Bf 109 Gruppen based in northern Italy attacked the stream and claimed 11 bombers, but were then driven off by the P-38s and P-47s. Jagddivision 7 called on Jagddivision 3 and was able to form nine Jagdgruppen and three Zerstörergruppen into three *Gefechtsverbände*, which attacked before, over, and after the target area. The Bf 110s had one of their last truly successful days in the RLV; 62 took off, and all made contact, attacking both the B-17 and the B-24 streams from the rear, with rockets. Claims by the twin-engine crews totaled five B-17s, three B-24s, and one P-38, for the loss of eight, most to 14th Fighter Group P-38s. The 312 single-engine fighters also attacked primarily from the rear—a preferred mode in Jagddivision 7—and claimed 11 B-17s and 31 B-24s (not all filed or confirmed), plus three P-38s and one P-47 from the inevitable dogfights, for the loss of about seven Bf 109s. True American losses were eight B-17s and 20 B-24s, while all P-38s and P-47s apparently made it back to Italy.[122]

On the 3rd the Fifteenth Air Force shifted its attention to a new target: Budapest, the capital of Hungary. While three Jafü Ostmark JG 27 Gruppen made an interception, the fighters from the rest of Jagddivision 7 could only reach a target so far from their bases if given ample warning, which they did not

receive on this day. The JG 27 formation claimed four B-17s, one B-24, and one P-38, while losing no Bf 109s. Two squadrons of Hungarian Bf 109Gs and one of Me 210 night fighters were based near their capital and were ordered up. The Hungarian pilots had some success, claiming four B-17s and one B-24 for the loss of one pilot, but it was obvious that Luftflotte Reich would have to be stretched further to provide protection to yet another target. The Fifteenth Air Force lost four B-17s and one B-24; its P-38s claimed three single-engine and four twin-engine fighters. The next week III./JG 27 was ordered to transfer from Austria to an airfield south of Budapest.[123]

The next major raid on the Reich came on the 8th, when the Eighth Air Force sent its three bomb divisions to bomb north German airfields and aviation industry targets around Brunswick. Schmid had no answer to the American fighters sweeping ahead of the bomber stream—estimated by the Germans to number 600—but ordered the battle formations of Jagddivisionen 1, 2, and 3, the latter augmented by three Jagddivision 7 Gruppen, to concentrate in specified areas near Brunswick to attack the bombers in the target area and on withdrawal. Only the 2nd Bomb Division penetrated as far as Brunswick, and its B-24s received the undivided attention of 250 Bf 109s and Fw 190s, which for once were able to overwhelm the escort.

The three German battle formations all reached the B-24s at about the same time, short of the target, and their leaders chose different parts of the stream to attack. The *Verbände* of both Jagddivision 3, primarily JG 1 Fw 190s, and Jagddivision 2, mainly JG 11 Fw 190s, made successful head-on attacks. Fritz Engau, at that time the Staffelkapitän of 2./JG 11, recalled that the formation was led by his Gruppenkommandeur, Hptm. Rolf Hermichen, who had devised a special formation for his own Gruppe, a double arrowhead. The fighters of the 1. Staffel, the Stabsschwarm, and the 3. Staffel formed a single vee, with Hermichen himself at the point. Engau's 2. Staffel, also in a vee, trailed as the rearguard, but was expected to follow the others through the bombers, so was forced to fly at a lower altitude—in a "very vulnerable" position—so that their gunfire would not hit the leading vee. Hermichen led the *Verband* in a conventional approach, paralleling the bombers on the side of the stream away from the high escort of P-51s, who would not dive through the bombers to get at them. When far enough ahead, Hermichen turned the formation around and led it through the bombers from dead ahead. He had ordered his Gruppe to pass through the first *Pulk*, turn right and climb steeply to reform for a second pass, but this was the opportunity that the 357th Fighter Group P-51s were waiting for, and the Focke-Wulfs were hit from all sides; six were shot down. The Kapitän of the 1st Staffel, Oblt. Josef Zwernemann, a Knight's Cross holder, shot down one P-51 but was then shot down himself. He bailed out successfully, but several Gruppe pilots then saw a P-51 with red-and-yellow nose markings shoot him as he hung in his parachute.[124]

The planned route of the B-24 division was north of Brunswick, where it was to turn southeast and then southwest, to approach the city from the east. The leading 14th Combat Wing had made its first turn early, before the appearance of German fighters, while the three trailing wings remained on course. The 14th Wing missed Brunswick altogether, and as its commander searched for a suitable target of opportunity for his now unescorted bombers, the exposed nature of the wing was quickly reported by a shadowing Me 410 Fühlungshalter. The Jagddivision 1 formation was put on a direct course for a close-formation head-on attack. The JG 3 Bf 109 Gruppen were first to attack the *Pulk*, followed quickly by 14 Sturmstaffel 1 Fw 190s, whose leader did not attempt to circle behind the bombers for a conventional *Sturm* attack, but seized the opportunity and headed right in. Eleven B-24s dropped from the formation of the leading bomb group, the 44th, either crashing immediately or on the return flight; this was the war's highest single-day loss for the group. The Bf 109s and Fw 190s then tried to evade the P-51s, which were quickly on the scene.[125]

Attacks on the strung-out 2nd Bomb Division continued as it withdrew toward Holland, but petered out as the escorts were able to concentrate around it. Jagddivision 4 ordered 69 JG 26 fighters to fly northeast to the Venlo area to attack the bombers, but they ran into a buzzsaw. Most were fully engaged by the escorts. Oblt. Karl Willius, the Kapitän of 2./JG 26 and one of the best of the Geschwader's younger pilots, shot down a straggling 44th Bomb Group B-24, but was himself shot down and killed by a flight of 361st Fighter Group P-47s. Willius was awarded a posthumous Knight's Cross; his body remained buried in a Dutch polder with his Fw 190 until 1967.[126]

The day was costly for both sides. The 2nd Bomb Division lost 30–2 B-24s, most to fighter attack, while only four B-17s were lost, none to fighters. American

Hptm. Hermann Staiger. An outstanding formation leader, Staiger joined JG 26 as a Staffelkapitän after a long tour as an instructor, and served as interim commander of both I./JG 26 and III./JG 26. He transferred to II./JG 1 for a permanent posting as its Kommandeur, and finished the war in jets, attempting to bring II./JG 7 up to operational status. (*Vanoverbeke*)

fighter losses were higher than usual, at 23–2, and were attributed to the airfield Flak, which was growing stronger, and the fierce combats around the 2nd Division. The sources reporting German casualties conflict, but at least 40 RLV pilots were killed, and about 70 fighters were lost.[127]

Although all of the 1st and 2nd Bomb Division B-17s attacked airfields on the 8th, the damage they caused was played down by the I. Jagdkorps war diary, which gave the American fighters' strafing runs most of the credit for destroying 72 aircraft and damaging 45 on the fields, while blocking four airstrips with debris.[128]

The following day the Eighth Air Force sent all of its bomb divisions to bomb aviation industry targets in Poland and East Prussia. These long-range missions were previously the specialty of the 3rd Bomb Division, which from its inception had B-17s equipped with long-range "Tokyo Tanks." All bombers now had the range required, and made the long approach flight across the North Sea and Denmark before turning southeast to their targets. The RLV met the challenge fairly well, in that Jagddivisionen 1 and 2 were able to attack the penetration leg of the attack. The withdrawal leg was flown across north-central Germany, but was escorted by 14 USAAF groups and several squadrons of RAF Mustangs, and was left alone. The Eighth lost 32 bombers; another ten sought refuge in Sweden. American escort losses totaled 10–4. The RLV forces lost 12 KIA, 5 WIA, and 24 fighters.

The lightly escorted attack on East Prussia should have given ZG 26 a good opportunity to prove its relevance from its lonely Königsberg base. II./ZG 26 did in fact make an attack, and claimed three B-17s while losing two Me 410s. I./ZG 26 was not operational, and III./ZG 26 flew a mission that Americans would describe as a total foulup. According to its war diary, the Gruppe had received word the previous night that it should install rocket launch tubes on all its aircraft in preparation for ground-attack missions during a brief transfer to the Eastern Front. The next morning it was given ten minutes to remove the tubes for a mission in the RLV. Eighteen Bf 110s were scrambled and led past the incoming bombers without being ordered to attack. They flew around until their fuel ran low, and were then ordered to land on an airfield that had none of the B4 fuel that their engines required, taking them out of commission for the rest of the day. The diarist resisted making any editorial comments.[129]

On April 11, the Eighth Air Force tested its dominance by scheduling raids on six separate aviation targets located deep in central and eastern Germany. Again I. Jagdkorps rose to the challenge. The Eighth Air Force Narrative of Operations paid the Luftwaffe a rare compliment by stating:

> The enemy contrived one of his most severe and well-coordinated defenses, marked by the skillful handling of a considerable number of twin-engine day fighters in the Stettin area and single-engine fighters in the Hannover–Oschersleben area.

Sixty-four bombers failed to return to England—nine of these landed in Sweden—and 16 escort fighters were lost.[130]

The 3rd Bomb Division took the northern route across the North Sea and Denmark alone, while the 1st and 2nd Divisions flew the well-traveled "bomber *Autobahn*" (so-called by the RLV pilots) due east from England across the Zuider Zee, then to Osnabrück,

Major Günther Specht, the II./JG 11 Kommandeur, shows off his new Bf 109G/AS to Professor Kurt Tank at Wunstorf in April. Both are wearing flight suits; Specht is in prestigious Luftwaffe leather. The Fw 190 designer served as leader of the Focke-Wulf factory defense flight at nearby Bremen; his reaction to this product of Willi Messerschmitt's bureau is unknown. (*Bundesarchiv 676-7975A-22*)

Hannover, and Brunswick, passing very near most of the Jagddivision 1, 2, and 3 bases. Some wings skirted Berlin to the south and proceeded farther east to bomb Cottbus and Sorau. I. Jagdkorps called on 18 Jagdgruppen, 2 Zerstörergruppen, and 2 Nachtjagdgruppen for a total of 432 defensive sorties against 917 bombers (828 effective) and 819 escorts.[131]

The presence of so many separate bomber formations reduced the escort density everywhere. Anderson and Doolittle probably believed that their advance fighter sweeps would disrupt the takeoff and assembly of the German fighters, but this did not happen. The Messerschmitts and Focke-Wulfs were up early, and proceeded to their assembly points and the various bomber streams before they were seen by the escorts. The JD 3 *Verband* (JG 1) formed up over Lippspringe and waited for the arrival of three JD 7 Gruppen, which were unable to make contact with the Jagddivision 3 controller and had to fly the mission by the *Reichsjägerwelle*. Two of these Gruppen, II./JG 27 and II./JG 53, tagged along with JD 3, but the third, III./JG 3, encountered B-24s and made an independent attack. The JD 3 *Verband* then rendezvoused with the JD 1 fighters (JG 3) and was directed to the incoming 1st Bomb Division, which it caught during a gap in escort support. Each Gruppe made a head-on attack before 357th Fighter Group P-51s arrived. The leading 40th Combat Wing lost 12 B-17s, most at this time. After bombing Cottbus and Sorau the division did not withdraw via the "bomber *Autobahn*," but turned due north to the coast and followed the 3rd Division west across the Baltic Sea, Denmark, and the North Sea. The 4th Fighter Group accompanied them from the target all the way to Kiel and broke up the only attack attempted during this phase, by ZG 26 Bf 110s and Me 410s. The 1st Division's losses for the day totaled 19–3.[132]

The JD 2 *Verband*, containing JG 11 Fw 190s and JG 302 Bf 109s, assembled without difficulty and was directed to the 2nd Bomb Division, which it contacted near Osnabrück. Major Toni Hackl, the *Verbandsführer*, led a frontal attack on the 14th Combat Wing, flying second in the stream, and then dispersed with the arrival of P-47s and P-51s. Sturmstaffel 1 made a rear attack on one of the B-24 wings at the same time. The Staffel had taken off from Salzwedel with IV./JG 3 as usual but had not made rendezvous with the Jagddivision 1 *Verband* and had attached itself to Hackl's force. Their one-minute *Sturmangriff* (assault attack) forced five B-24s from their formation; follow-up attacks claimed another two, plus one P-47, before the pilots returned to Salzwedel to prepare for another sortie. Two B-24s were seen by the Americans to explode with "bright white flashes," which were attributed to new German rockets, but were probably the result of 30-mm cannon fire. The B-24s experienced their last fighter attacks in the area of their targets at Oschersleben and Bernburg. Their return to England along the "bomber *Autobahn*" was unmolested. The 2nd Division's losses totaled 12–1.[133]

The unescorted 3rd Bomb Division, flying the northern route, saw its first German fighters at the Danish coast, where the two Denmark-based JG 11 Staffeln put in an appearance and brought down a 96th Bomb Group B-17. The next attacks came over the Baltic Sea, where two ZG 26 Gruppen were up in force and waiting. II./ZG 26's Me 410s attacked from the rear, with rockets, while III./ZG 26's Bf 110s, which no longer carried rockets on RLV missions, made four

frontal attacks with their guns. The Zerstörer returned to Königsberg after expending their ammunition, reporting the destruction of 16 B-17s; the 96th Group alone lost nine aircraft in the Baltic, while a tenth found refuge in Sweden.[134]

The 3rd Division could not reach its briefed targets around Posen because of adverse weather, and sought suitable targets of opportunity at Stettin and Rostock. Fighters landing after their combats with the 1st and 2nd Bomb Divisions were serviced as quickly as possible and sent north after the still-unescorted 3rd. Over 50 Bf 109s and Fw 190s from seven Gruppen reached the B-17s in the Rostock area. Their aggressive head-on attacks brought down a number of Fortresses; eight B-17s succeeded in reaching Sweden. The 3rd Division lost a total of 33–1 of the 302 B-17s that it dispatched on this mission.

The luck of the Zerstörer crews ran out on their second sortie from Königsberg. They encountered the escorted 1st Division, rather than the unescorted 3rd, and were treated roughly by 4th Fighter Group Mustangs. ZG 26 lost 16 crewmen KIA, 3 WIA, eight Me 410s and three Bf 110s during the day, most on this second sortie.[135]

Schmid and his men considered the 11th a great success, qualified as always by the fact that the defenses failed to keep any bomber formations away from their targets. The day's losses totaled 38 KIA, 15 WIA, and 57 fighters. The performance of IV./JG 3 stood out; its pilots claimed 16 B-17s and one P-38 on the day's first mission, and eight B-17s on the second, for the loss of two of their own Messerschmitts. Göring and Galland took note; the Gruppe would be given greater opportunities to show its prowess in the near future.[136]

On the 12th USSTAF attempted a rare combined mission. The Fifteenth Air Force carried out a successful raid on aircraft industry targets in the Vienna area, while the Eighth Air Force bombers took off for Schweinfurt, but returned early because of weather conditions. The fighters of the Eighth continued with their sweeps and airfield attacks, but the I. Jagdkorps war diary claimed that these were successfully beaten off by the defenses. The Fifteenth Air Force attack was another matter. It caused severe damage for the cost of only seven bombers to all causes, whereas the 190 Jagddivision 7 fighters that scrambled lost 21 of their number, primarily to the four Fifteenth Air Force fighter groups, which were obviously gaining in effectiveness.[137]

Another combined mission on the 13th was carried

Major Hans Kogler, Kommandeur of III./ZG 26, inspects one of the B-17s downed by his Me 410 Zerstörer unit on April 11. (*ww2images*)

out as planned. The Fifteenth Air Force returned to Budapest, with different results from the 3rd. Eighteen bombers failed to return. III./JG 3 from Jagddivision 7, the two JG 27 Gruppen in Jafü Ostmark, and all of Jagdabschnitt Ungarn—III./JG 27 and five Hungarian units: three Bf 109G squadrons, the Me 210 night-fighter squadron, and a new Me 210 squadron formed from the Hungarian Air Force experimental unit—made interceptions. The two Me 210 squadrons lost 13 to the escorts. The type was immediately withdrawn from the day-fighter order of battle, and the crews began retraining for the ground-attack role.[138]

The targets for the Eighth Air Force bombers on the 13th were well-known (and hated) by the American crews: Schweinfurt, Oberpfaffenhofen, and Augsburg. The mission report claimed that the 1st and 3rd Bomb Divisions experienced the heaviest fighter attacks since January 11, but no details stand out. The Eighth Air Force lost 38–3 bombers, including 13 interned in Switzerland, and 9–2 fighters; the Germans lost 34 fighters defending against the Eighth.[139]

On the 15th Galland visited IV./JG 3 at Salzwedel and announced that in recognition of its superior performance in the RLV since returning from Italy the previous fall, it was to become the first Gruppe to adopt *Sturm* tactics. The Gruppe was immediately renamed IV.(Sturm)/JG 3, and would soon be withdrawn from combat for its pilots to train on Fw 190s for their new role. The pilots were given the option to transfer to another unit; none apparently did. The ramming oath was produced at this time, and most pilots signed it, although at least one refused. He remained an active

member of the unit, and was evidently treated no differently from those who signed.[140]

Adolf Hitler had belatedly become convinced of the importance of air defense, and on the 19th met with his fighter production staff and Organisation Todt, which built major projects, to order fighter production to be increased and new, dispersed factories to be built, underground if possible. Hitler wanted to see 2,000 operational fighters in the RLV. Nothing was said about expanding the training establishment, the responsibility of a different organization, and although the fighter inventory approached Hitler's desired number in late 1944, there were not enough qualified pilots to fly them.[141]

In mid-April the Jagdgeschwader zur besondere Verwendung (JG zbV) was finally established in Kassel. This was a fighter staff tasked with leading a Jagd-division 7 Gefechtsverband comprising five "orphan" Jagdgruppen based in southwestern Germany: III./JG 3, I./JG 5, II./JG 27, II./JG 53, and III./JG 54. Its first Kommodore was Major Gerhard Michalski, who relinquished command of II./JG 53.

Another organizational change of some significance saw Major Günther Specht leave II./JG 11 to become a "Kommodore-in-training" on the JG 11 Stab. His replacement was one of the best of the endless stream of *Experten* spawned by JG 52 on the Eastern Front, Major Günther Rall.[142] II./JG 11 was still rebuilding at Eschborn, and Rall would thus be given a chance to become acclimated to conditions over the Reich at the same time as his new men.

In the absence of any new operational plan from SHAEF, LGen. Spaatz kept ordering the Eighth Air Force to targets in the Reich, in order to keep the pressure on the Luftwaffe fighters. The pattern established on the first Berlin raid continued: the Gefechtsverbände could punish any portion of the bomber stream caught without escort, or with so few escorts that they could be overwhelmed. But the size of the Luftflotte Reich fighter force was stagnant, while the Eighth Air Force was not only continuing to add new P-38 and P-51 groups, it was converting its P-47 groups to P-51s at the rate of two per month. Soon the Mustangs would be doing the overwhelming.

A raid to Hamm on the 22nd fit the pattern, with two highlights worth noting. After landing from the II./JG 1 intercept mission, Major Heinz Bär scrambled quickly with his wingman to pursue a smoking 458th Bomb Group B-24 that had passed right over his airfield. The victory was easy—the bombers' gunners had already bailed out—and Bär returned to Störmede to receive the congratulations of his men for his 200th air victory.[143]

The day's other highlight for the German defenders came after the raid itself ended, and proved to be unique. II./KG 51 specialized in night hit-and-run raids on England in Ju 88s. It contained one Staffel of Me 410s to fend off RAF night fighters. The American bombers took off late on the 22nd, and it became apparent to the Luftwaffe controllers that the last of them, B-24s of the 2nd Air Division, would not reach England until after dark. Someone authorized Hptm. Dietrich Puttfarken and his Me 410 Staffel to follow the B-24s back to their bases and attack them as they landed. This was a classic "intruder" mission, forbidden to the Luftwaffe since 1941, when Hitler and Göring decreed that it was preferable for night fighters to down their opponents over the Reich, so that the civilian population could see them fall. Puttfarken and his men performed their unaccustomed duty well, so well that accurate figures on American losses are impossible to obtain. One source estimates the number of B-24s shot down or destroyed after landing to be 14. Personnel casualties on the ground, including many attributable to "friendly fire," were apparently never tabulated. Only two Me 410s failed to return from the mission; one of them was piloted by Puttfarken, who remains missing. The Eighth Air Force drew the proper lesson and never again scheduled such a late mission; the Luftwaffe reverted to its earlier practice and never again followed the American bombers back to England.[144]

The Fifteenth Air Force flew a maximum-strength mission on the 23rd, sending 434 bombers to four aviation targets in Austria. Jagddivision 7 responded with all available fighters, even calling on Jafü Schlesien to scramble Fw 190s from Schlachtgeschwader 152 (SG 152), a ground-attack training unit. Only 11 bombers were recorded as lost. Credit was given to effective escort, which benefited from the presence of a new group, the 31st, which introduced the Merlin-engine P-51 to the Mediterranean Theater. This group had flown short-range Spitfires with the Twelfth Air Force since the invasion of northwestern Africa in November 1942, and welcomed the chance to take the war to the enemy. It claimed 15 German and Italian fighters on this day, for the loss of four Mustangs.[145]

Jagddivision 7 was also benefiting from a welcome reinforcement—III./JG 26 of Luftflotte 3's Jagddivision 4, which had been ordered to southern

A 1944 lineup of II./ZG 26 Me 410s. Worth noting are the horizontal II. Gruppe bar and the rust-red RLV band. Zerstörer were seldom photographed in these typical *Jäger* markings. (*Petrick*)

Germany on April 14, to bolster the defenses in anticipation of a major American raid on Munich, the birthplace of the Nazi Party, on April 20, Hitler's birthday. The raid had not come, but III./JG 26 had stayed, and could put up 30 Bf 109s from Neubiberg. The JG 26 Gruppe was intimately acquainted with Mustangs, and claimed two of them on the 23rd, in addition to one B-24 and two B-17s, for the loss of one Bf 109 and its pilot.[146]

The Eighth Air Force raided aviation targets in the Munich and Friedrichshafen areas on the 24th. It dispatched 754 heavy bombers with an escort of 22 fighter groups. Resistance in the target area was surprisingly heavy (owing in part to the unexpected presence of III./JG 26), and 40 bombers and 17 fighters failed to return to England. The crews of 13 B-17s and one B-24 chose to fly to Switzerland for internment.[147]

Hptm. Hermann Staiger led III./JG 26 up from Neubiberg on the 24th and climbed toward Ulm, where they met III./JG 3 from Wörishofen at 7,000 meters (23,000 ft.). Staiger led the combined formation toward the position reported by the Jagddivision 7 controller, who was female, and thus a great novelty to the JG 26 pilots; GFM Sperrle barely tolerated the presence of servicewomen in Luftflotte 3 and did not allow them to fill positions of such responsibility. The B-17 stream was observed to have a strong P-51 escort. Staiger led the Bf 109s upsun and stayed there, waiting for the escorts to leave. They did not, but the B-17 formation soon split, and Staiger found that two combat wings had been left unescorted. These contained the 108 Fortresses bound for Oberpfaffenhofen. The German fighters were well positioned, and Staiger quickly led his 30 Bf 109s in a textbook attack from 12 o'clock high. Staiger's own fighter was a Bf 109G-6/U4 with a 30-mm MK 108 cannon in its nose, and he used it to good effect, shooting down three B-17s and forcing two more from their formations, to be shot down by two young pilots in the Gruppe. The German fighters attacked repeatedly, retiring only when they had exhausted their ammunition. The final score for the Gruppe totaled 17 B-17s, not all confirmed. Their initial head-on attack succeeded in breaking up the American combat box; thus separated, the B-17s were fairly easy targets. III./JG 3 also claimed nine B-17s. The Oberpfaffenhofen force lost 26 of the 1st Bomb Division's total of 27 losses.

The frantic calls of the bomber pilots soon brought 355th Fighter Group P-51s to the rescue. III./JG 26 pilots shot down two of the Mustangs, and completed

A Me 410 of ZG 1, the *Wespengeschwader* (Wasp Wing). Its forward-firing armament comprises four MG 151/20 machine cannon and four MG 17 machine guns. (*Price*)

the mission without a single loss. III./JG 3 was not as fortunate, claiming the third 355th Group fighter to go down, but losing three pilots killed and two injured, and seven of the total of 20 fighters claimed by the 355th this day. IV./JG 3 reached the Oberpfaffenhofen force a few minutes after the Jagddivision 7 fighters, and made a steep diving frontal attack to avoid the escorts that were by now present. Repeated firing passes resulted in claims for 15 B-17s, for the loss of three Bf 109s and two pilots. The day's successes were somewhat Pyrrhic for Luftflotte Reich, which lost 39 pilots KIA, 12 WIA, and 60 fighters.[148]

Heavy cloud cover over the continent on the 29th led MGen. Anderson to adopt a plan that unintentionally simplified the job of the defenders. The center of Berlin was chosen as the target of the entire force. Because of the shortage of pathfinder aircraft, the 12 combat wings of the three bomb divisions flew the mission in trail; the stream took 38 minutes to cross Berlin. Once Schmid's fighters got off the ground and assembled, it was impossible not to find the stream, and his shadowing aircraft and experienced controllers were able to locate the inevitable thin spots in the escort screen and direct the *Gefechtsverbände* to them. In all 271 Bf 109s and Fw 190s made contact. The battle formations of the three north German Jagddivisionen all made effective attacks, most notably on the 3rd Division's 4A Combat Wing, which deviated from its ordered course, and the trailing 2nd Division, which seemed to be the second option of all of the attackers. The escorts spent much of their time chasing back and forth along the bomber stream seeking the elusive German fighters. A total of 63–2 bombers and 13–1 escorts were lost; I. Jagdkorps lost only 12 KIA, 5 WIA, and 21 fighters. Once again the Eighth Air Force summary report had to pay tribute to the defenders, stating:

> The enemy's plan succeeded. He showed great skill in handling his force of approximately 400 aircraft. He refused to engage unless assured of substantial numerical superiority and rapidly exploited weakness or gaps in the fighter escort. His effort paid high dividends at a relatively low cost.[149]

The end of April found the USSTAF war on the Luftwaffe to be hurting both sides. The Eighth Air Force sustained the greatest bomber loss of any month of the war, about 25 percent of the force. The Americans knew that they were winning the production war, and were confident that they would win the war of attrition, no matter how bloody it was proving to be. The German position can best be summarized by Josef Schmid's post-war history, which stated that, in April:

1. American supremacy over the Reich was consolidated. Fighters began strafing attacks on airfields within Germany, whereas there were few attacks on airfields by heavy bombers.
2. American fighters destroyed several hundred aircraft on the ground; an equal number were damaged.
3. Luftwaffe striking power was only slightly impaired by airfield attacks.
4. The freedom of action of the U.S. fighters had grave consequences for the RLV: single fighters could not escape; assembly and even landing operations were interfered with.
5. American fighters were released from rigid escort, and were now in their proper role on freie Jagden [free hunts].
6. Escorts sometimes left the heavy bombers unprotected, allowing decimating surprise attacks.
7. Emphasis of U.S. attacks returned to the aircraft industry. Attacks in good weather caused heavy damage. The planned RLV reinforcement to 2,000 fighters was impossible.
8. Heavy bombers in England began attacks on transportation targets in northwestern Germany.
9. Coordination between U.K. and Italian operations was obtained on only three days.
10. Missions from Italy extended to Austria, Hungary, Yugoslavia, and Romania—one-third of all heavy bomber sorties, excluding France—causing dispersion of RLV forces.
11. Instrument bombing was required on only two days—all others were visual.
12. On April 1, I. Jagdkorps assumed responsibility for the Greater Reich, including Austria and Hungary, and was assigned JD 1, JD 2, JD 3, and JD 7 [which included Jafü Ostmark].
13. Reorganization of Luftflotte Reich was effective 2100 hours 31 Mar 44 (LF Reich Order 1921/44).
14. II. Jagdkorps fighters were to be committed only against raids crossing southwestern Belgium and France. They were no longer to be sent for long distances over the Reich.
15. Advantages of the new command organization:
    a. Single command staff for entire RLV;
    b. Uniform interpretation of the air situation while conducting fighter operations over the Reich; c. Better possibility of concentrating forces in the air.

A Hungarian Me 210 after it was belly-landed by Helmut Zittier. Zittier, a successful Zerstörer pilot, was assigned to the Hungarian factory as a test pilot, a move which he felt saved his life. The Hungarian Me 210s flew only a handful of missions in the RLV before the survivors were retrained for ground-attack duties on the Eastern Front. (*Zittier*)

16. The commanding general of I. Jagdkorps [Schmid] could not get permission from ObdL. [Göring] to concentrate all day fighters within one area. Göring demanded that all parts of the Reich be protected for economic reasons and reasons of internal politics.
17. I. Jagdkorps day fighters were thus deployed [approximately] as follows:
    1 Jagdgeschwader, 1 Zerstörergeschwader: area between Hannover & Berlin [JG 3, ZG 26];
    1 Jagdgeschwader: northern Germany [JG 11];
    2 Jagdgruppen: area of Frankfurt [JG 1];
    2 Jagdgruppen: Bavaria [II./JG 53, III./JG 54];
    1 Jagdgeschwader, 1 Zerstörergeschwader: area of Vienna [JG 27, ZG 76].
18. Dispersion of bases seldom allowed critical mass to be attained in the air.
19. Good weather allowed a more favorable strength balance in April than March:
    March sortie ratios: total USAAF/RLV = 7.5:1;
    USAAF fighter/RLV = 3.5:1;
    April sortie ratios: total USAAF/RLV = 4.5:1;
    USAAF fighter/RLV = 2.2:1.
20. Operations versus raids from Italy were hindered by the incomplete observation and plotting system in the south and poor communication with Luftflotte 2 in Italy. Interceptions were usually poorly organized and late. The situation was improved by the energy and initiative of Oberst Handrick, Jafü Ostmark. There was a workable warning and control system by the end of April.

21. American freie Jagden hampered assembly, which had to find areas away from the probable U.S. operating zone. The time available for combat was thus limited.

22. U.S. freie Jagden added to the strain on RLV aircrews. Inexperienced pilots suffered Jäger-schreck [fear of fighters] owing to the realization of their own vulnerability when forced to fly alone due to weather or damage. This led to premature bailouts.

23. Zerstörer could no longer be employed in areas in which U.S. fighters operated.

24. The operational strength of the RLV day fighters decreased due to the build-up of pre-D-Day reserves.

25. During April, the average daily operational strengths of I. JK were: 400 single engine fighters, 100 twin-engine fighters.

26. April sorties by I. JK = 4,522; losses = 395, or 8.8 percent.

27. April sorties versus Reich by USSTAF = 20,337; losses to fighters = 514, or 2.5 percent.[150]

In assessing the results of the first four months of 1944, we return once more to the main conference

The pilots of Sturmstaffel 1 pose for photographs at Salzwedel in late April, shortly before the Staffel was disbanded. *From left:* Oblt. Othmar Zehart, Lt. Hans-Georg Elser, Lt. Siegfried Müller, Lt. Rudolf Metz, Major Hans-Günter von Kornatzki, Lt. Werner Gerth, Fw. Kurt Röhrich, Lt. Richard Franz, Gefr. Wolfgang Kosse, Obfw. Gerhard Marburg, Fw. Werner Peinemann, Uffz. Willi Maximowitz, Fw. Josef Groten, Uffz. Oskar Bösch, Uffz. Helmut Keune. Only four of these men survived the war. *(Bösch)*

room of the Fighter Staff, the nexus between economic, strategic, technological, and operational decision-making affecting the Third Reich's air war. On April 27, 1944, a familiar figure rose to deliver a sobering report on the state of the Jagdwaffe. While paying full tribute to the exertions of Saur's staff, Galland did not mince words regarding Germany's air situation:

I need not say much about the situation of the Luftwaffe. Unfortunately you too are living with it every day. The problem with which the Americans have confronted the fighter arm—and I am intentionally dealing only with the question of day fighters at this point—is quite simply the problem of air superiority. The situation is already beginning to be characterized by enemy air supremacy.

The numerical ratios in daytime combat at present fluctuate between approximately 6:1 and 8:1 in favor of the enemy. The enemy's standard of training is astonishingly high. The technical capabilities of his aircraft are so manifest that we are obliged to say that something must be done immediately.

It is very unfortunate that the Jägerstab's efforts to increase aircraft production must be carried out under the pressure of bombing and very heavy losses. I am convinced that the Jägerstab will meet with success if its present efforts are maintained. It must succeed. It is the only chance; I might even say that it is the last chance . . .

In the last four months our day-fighter forces have lost well over 1,000 pilots,[151] including many of our best Geschwader, Gruppe and Staffel commanders. We are having great difficulty in closing this gap, not in a numerical sense, but with experienced leaders . . .

What measures must now be taken to get out of this predicament?

First of all the numerical balance must be redressed . . . industry must produce a guaranteed number of aircraft, which will enable the air arm to be built up, beginning with basic training followed by reinforcement of operational formations . . .

Secondly, as we are numerically inferior and will always remain so . . . the technical performance of aircraft must be improved. I wish to emphasize that the improved performance which we require can be provided immediately by the AS engine or later by the jet engine . . .

I believe that a great deal can be achieved with a small number of technically far superior aircraft such as the [Me] 262 or the [Me] 163 . . . With the aid of these two components, quantity and quality, the operational effectiveness of formations is bound to increase and the standard of training will consequently be similarly affected. I do not expect that we will achieve parity with the enemy, but merely that a reasonable ratio will once again be reached.

If this numerical ratio and the experience of recent attacks are examined, it must be admitted that by day we have never, or hardly ever, succeeded in preventing the main enemy force from reaching the target or effectively upset their bomb-aiming over the target. If we allow this defense mechanism to run constantly at full speed and assume that enemy attacks continue to be directed against industry, the enemy will doubtless achieve two objectives: he will destroy further factories and he will also destroy us in the air. In order therefore to provide not only for the task of defending the Reich but also for the other tasks which will fall to the Luftwaffe in the event of an invasion, we must adopt a more economical policy with regard to the operational employment of our formations . . .

In each of the last ten daylight attacks we have lost on average over 50 aircraft and 40 pilots, that is 500 aircraft and 400 pilots in ten major operations. In view of the present state of training and the rate of these losses, formations cannot be supplied with fresh pilots. This is simply not possible. Replacements can be found in a purely numerical sense, but this will not give us organized formations. I again request that while the efforts to provide the required number of aircraft are extremely welcome, it must be made absolutely clear that performance is at least of equal importance. Even if their number is limited, we need high-performance aircraft to restore the feeling of superiority in the Luftwaffe.

To quote an example: I would at this moment rather have one 262 in action than five 109s. I used to say three 109s, but the situation develops and changes.[152]

In this single short report, Galland identified with great clarity the major issues facing the Luftwaffe in April 1944. It was reeling under the impact of numerical and technical inferiority, a pilot training crisis, and the hemorrhaging of seasoned personnel. All of these were clearly spelled out by the General der Jagdflieger to his hushed audience. Yet Galland offered a ray of hope: a strategy of husbanding resources, and gradually integrating superior designs into the production plans in order to restore the Luftwaffe's combat edge. Many historians have argued persuasively that these were vain hopes, that in fact "the battle for air superiority had

been lost because the battle of production had been lost in 1940, 1941 and 1942—not 1944."[153]

Some other Luftwaffe generals admitted what Galland did not. Writing immediately after the war in 1945, one of them noted:

The air war over the Reich territory was lost by the fighter arm because its inner strength had been exhausted. In fact it was already exhausted when the decisive battle began. It had never been strong enough to carry out the many missions expected of it.[154]

By April 1944 the Luftwaffe's air war was indeed lost. But it would go on for another terrible year.

One of the last photographs taken of Oberst Walter Oesau, Kommodore of JG 1, prior to his death in combat on May 11. He is seen on a visit to I./JG 1 at Lippspringe. (*Berger via Mombeek*)

CHAPTER 7

THE OIL CAMPAIGN
MAY–AUGUST 1944

A New Priority Target for the USAAF

Allied strategic air war planners had always considered Germany's petroleum supply to be a weak link in that country's war economy. In 1938 fully two-thirds of Germany's oil had been imported. With the approach of war drastic measures had been taken to reduce consumption, and a huge industry had been developed to produce synthetic oil from coal by hydrogenation processes. All of the Luftwaffe's aviation fuel was produced from coal by I. G. Farben's Fischer-Tropsch process. Many small synthesis plants were built, most of them near Germany's major coal deposits in the Ruhr, in central Germany near Leipzig, and in Silesia. They were not designed to be resistant to air attack. Many were part of integrated chemical production complexes with above-ground reactors, piping, and storage facilities which were themselves very vulnerable to bombing. The natural crude oil which was available to Germany from oil fields in Hungary and Romania was unsuitable for the production of high-octane gasoline, and was used for other purposes. Conversion of this crude oil to usable products took place in large conventional refineries which were also susceptible to bombing and could not be "hardened" or dispersed.[1]

The USSTAF could spare no resources for these tempting targets until the late spring of 1944, and was then faced with conflicting priorities. Its two air forces, the Eighth and the Fifteenth, were still fully engaged in Operation Pointblank, the neutralization of the Luftwaffe, when the Combined Bomber Offensive ended on April 1 and command passed from the Combined Chiefs of Staff to General Eisenhower, the supreme Allied commander in Europe. Eisenhower's staff was planning to use the Eighth Air Force, RAF Bomber Command, and the tactical air forces of both Allies to bomb the rail yards of the western occupied zone and western Germany continuously up to the day

of the invasion of France (Overlord). Both General Spaatz and Air Chief Marshal Harris opposed this Transportation Plan in favor of their own, competing, air plans.

Harris argued that his Bomber Command could not hit such small targets as rail yards. His nominal superior, Air Chief Marshal Portal, and Prime Minister Churchill expressed a concern for French civilian casualties, and Harris was allowed to continue his own campaign, which had the objective of shattering German industrial capacity and morale by turning the cities of Germany into mountains of rubble.

Spaatz's arguments in favor of an oil campaign did not benefit from any high-level support among his own superiors in Washington, who said that it was Eisenhower's decision. Spaatz argued that his force could, indeed, hit railroad yards, but that these could be repaired so quickly that a prolonged campaign was a waste of resources; a few intense attacks just prior to D-Day would serve the same purpose, and would leave him free in the interim to attack other targets. He believed that the Luftwaffe was not yet defeated, and that, whereas attacks on rail yards would not provoke the Luftwaffe to respond, attacks on petroleum targets most certainly would. Spaatz apparently had to threaten to resign, but Eisenhower ultimately gave him the opportunity to prove the thesis that oil attacks would bring the Luftwaffe up, and authorized the Eighth Air Force to use two good-weather days for attacks on synthetic oil works in Germany.[2]

Spaatz planned to use the Fifteenth Air Force to attack the Hungarian and Romanian refineries, which could not be reached from England, but the target list which the Fifteenth received from Eisenhower's headquarters made no mention of oil targets. By a fortuitous coincidence most of the Romanian rail yards which were on the list were near refineries, and the inevitable bomb misses could be counted on to damage oil targets "by accident." So both of Spaatz's air forces were ready at the start of May to begin the oil campaign; one as part of a planned experiment, and the other by subterfuge.

The Luftwaffe High Command faced two major challenges in early May: bolstering the strength of the day-fighter units in Luftflotte Reich while at the same time preparing for the Allied invasion, which was expected in the very near future. Luftflotte 3 would command the air defenses against the Allied landing, wherever it took place, and was responsible for building and stocking airfields to handle the reinforcements which would stream from the Reich to France as soon as the invasion began. The two experienced II. Jagdkorps Geschwader, JG 2 and JG 26, were expected to form the main defense, and were sent to southern France one Gruppe at a time for rest and recuperation and to be built up to establishment strength.[3]

Several new weapons began arriving in the RLV in small numbers. Two revolutionary new fighters, the jet-propelled Me 262 and the rocket-powered Me 163, were available in sufficient quantities to allow service evaluation. Service test squadrons ErprKdo 262 and 1./JG 400 were established to introduce the Me 262 and Me 163 to combat and develop tactics for their use. The newly designated Sturmgruppe, IV.(Sturm)/JG 3, began receiving aircraft for its new mission: the Fw 190A-8/R2 *Sturmbock* (assault battering ram), which had proven itself in Sturmstaffel 1. Its two 30-mm cannon were extremely effective versus bombers; only three hits were required to bring down a B-17, while a single hit could often crumple a B-24. The assault fighters had proven almost invulnerable to bomber fire, but were so slow and unwieldy that they were prime targets for American fighters and, like the twin-engine Zerstörer, required escort by conventional fighters to fulfill their own mission. The Sturmgruppe was to attack the bomber formations in close formation from the rear, the tactic developed by Sturmstaffel 1, but in May, while training in its new aircraft as conditions permitted, the Gruppe continued flying combat missions in its Bf 109s, typically making frontal attacks as part of the JG 3 *Gefechtsverband*.[4]

Sturmstaffel 1 was disbanded on May 8; its personnel were absorbed in the new Sturmgruppe. When the new Gruppenkommandeur, Hptm. Wilhelm Moritz, learned that neither Major von Kornatzki nor his deputy had ever attempted to ram a bomber, and

that neither were currently flying missions, he called General Galland and had both men transferred from his Gruppe. Moritz let it be known that although his pilots had been asked to sign the *Rammjäger* oath, he considered the standard Wehrmacht oath of service to be adequate. He held his men to very high standards of duty, up to but not including suicidal zeal.

While waiting for the propitious moment to begin execution of the Oil Plan, Doolittle's Eighth Air Force flew missions of three types: continued attacks on sensitive German targets such as Berlin, continued attacks on the V-1 launch sites in France (Operation

Major Anton "Toni" Hackl, one of the few consistently successful RLV formation leaders, was moved frequently to fill critical vacancies, and commanded III./JG 11, JG 76, II./JG 26, JG 300, and JG 11 in succession. (*Cranston*)

Crossbow), and attacks on French and Belgian rail yards and airfields, as part of the Transportation Plan. As Spaatz had predicted, few of these missions drew a significant response from Luftflotte Reich or Luftflotte 3. A full-strength raid on Berlin and Brunswick on the 8th was the first in May to bring the Luftwaffe up in force. The three bomb divisions flew due east from England in a single stream; 807 bombers took part, escorted by 20 fighter groups. Over Germany the 2nd Bomb Division B-24s turned southeast to bomb Brunswick aircraft factories, while the B-17s of the 1st

Lt. Willi Unger. One of the Luftwaffe's most gifted assault pilots, Unger spent three years in the Luftwaffe as a mechanic before beginning flight training. He joined 12.(Sturm)/JG 3 in January 1944 and began scoring immediately. After shooting down 22 aircraft, including 19 heavy bombers, in 59 combat flights, he was awarded the Knight's Cross and commissioned as a Leutnant before transferring to jets in March 1945. (Unger)

and 3rd Divisions continued east to Berlin. Weather conditions over Germany reduced the number of areas suitable for the formation of the RLV Gefechts-verbände, but did not unduly hinder operations. JD 7 and the two Zerstörergeschwader did not take part, but the Bf 109s and Fw 190s of Jagddivisionen 1, 2, and 3 flew 400 sorties. The JD 2 Gefechtsverband (primarily JG 11) was directed to the heavily escorted Berlin stream and had a rough mission. The JD 3 Gefechts-verband (JG 1) and the JD 1 Gefechtsverband (JG 3), on the other hand, were directed to weak spots in the southern stream, and were more successful. The most conspicuous bomber formation in the sky contained the B-17s of the 45th Combat Wing, which had lost its parent 3rd Bomb Division and, without escort, had tacked onto the 2nd Division B-24 stream. It lost 13 B-17s, most to Oberst Oesau's JG 1. Major Friedrich-Karl Müller's JG 3 was led to the van of the 2nd Division stream and met it head-on. Ten B-24s of the leading 2nd Combat Wing went down.[5]

Sturmstaffel 1 flew its last mission. It took off with the JG 3 Verband but remained some distance away from it, and when the B-24s were spotted was able to circle behind the leading Pulk and attack it from the rear. Oskar Bösch recalled:

After sighting inbound B-24s we positioned ourselves 1,000 meters [3,300 ft.] above and behind one Pulk. My engine was hit by Flak while forming up, and oil was flowing over my left wing root. I reported the damage, but decided to make one attack before my engine seized and forced me to bail out—the weather was too bad to force-land. I attacked in a high-speed sideslip, firing from 400 meters [440 yards]. I flew through the formation without receiving any fire, and hit several more heavies before running out of ammo. I decided to ram by hitting the left aileron of a B-24 with my right wing tip. I lost control due to wake turbulence and regained control in a vertical dive in front of the Pulk. My plane was shredded by gunfire. The heavies continued firing and hitting my 190. After the firing stopped I jettisoned the canopy, unbuckled, pushed the stick forward and was catapulted into the cold air. I pulled the cord after falling for two minutes in cloud. I landed near Goslar with frostbitten nose and ears, bleeding from a head wound. I was taken to a military hospital, where the wound was found to be a shrapnel graze. I was given one week's leave.[6]

The mission on the 8th cost Doolittle 36–8 bombers and 13–2 fighters, while I. Jagdkorps lost 32 fighters.

The next USSTAF raid on a strategic target was flown on the 10th by MGen. Nathan Twining's Fifteenth Air Force. Four hundred B-17s and B-24s were dispatched to bomb the important Wiener Neustadt Bf 109 plant. Escort was provided by one P-47, three P-38, and two P-51 groups; enough to give some coverage to the penetration, target, and withdrawal phases of the mission, but not enough to offer complete protection. The Fifteenth Air Force consistently lost more bombers on a percentage basis than did the Eighth, its larger cousin to the north. The bombers of the Fifteenth flew in smaller formations than the Eighth, and their fields of defensive fire were thus less dense.

The Kommandeure of the southern Jagdgruppen preferred rear attacks, even though they were all flying the relatively vulnerable Bf 109, but took advantage of sun and formation gaps to make quick strikes from all directions—the day's Fifteenth Air Force mission report referred to attacks by "experienced and aggressive" German pilots from all angles, high, level and low, some pressed to 100–150 meters/yards. The Messerschmitt factory was hit, but at a cost of 28 bombers, 7 percent of those dispatched. Three American fighters were lost; the German defenders, who succeeded in avoiding most of the escorts, lost only nine fighters.

The German fighters were obviously up on the 10th in sufficient time to make effective interceptions. The credit for this is owed in part to timely reports from the Fühlungshalter. The aircraft types used for this mission had first been changed from night fighters to Me 410s, for more speed, but by May 1944 every twin-engine Luftwaffe aircraft in service was vulnerable to Allied fighters. The logical next step was to use single-engine fighters as formation keepers. The authors were fortunate to locate a pilot who flew a Bf 109 in this service. Uffz. Berthold Wendler had joined III./JG 3 in April after completing fighter training. After a month in Major Dahl's Gruppe, he and three other NCO pilots were told that they had been ordered to Fühlungshalter duty, and would be flying from Italy. He reached his new base on May 8, and was possibly one of the pilots who helped locate the Fifteenth Air Force stream on the 10th. Bertl Wendler recalled:

The fast Allied advance and the use of Window had made ground tracking from Italy impossible. Fast aircraft and experienced pilots were needed to follow

Fw. Oskar Bösch. A highly motivated assault pilot, Bösch volunteered for the Sturmstaffel directly from flight training and ended the war in IV.(Sturm)/JG 3. (*Bösch*)

the course of the Fifteenth Air Force bombers. We reported directly to Jafü Süd, Oberst Maltzahn. We flew as *Rotten* [pairs] 1–2 km to the side or 2–3 km above the bombers, trying to keep the sun to our backs. Ground control located our aircraft by our FuG 16ZY [homing radio] transmissions. We only used our voice radios to report strength. The closest controller was on Monte Vente Padua, who passed the information to *Adler 1* on the highest Austrian mountain, then to *Minotaur* at Schleissheim. We avoided the escorts, and left the bombers immediately on the approach of *kleine Brüder* [small brothers—our own fighters], who would have attacked us. Two of us were based at Udine, the other two at Ferrara. Both were JG 77 bases, whose pilots didn't trust us—they thought we were NSFOs [political officers].[7]

On the 11th the Eighth Air Force flew two missions to numerous French and Belgian rail yards and airfields, in support of the Transportation Plan. I. and II. Jagdkorps scrambled 148 fighters, but the German-based units remained airborne only until it was obvious that no deep raids were intended, and most were then ordered to land. A few pilots, however, tangled with the leading bombers and their escorts. One such pilot was Oberst Walter Oesau, the JG 1 Kommodore, who led a pair of Bf 109s in an attack on a flight of P-38s. The Lightnings turned into the attack, out-turned the Messerschmitts, and after the American leader, Captain "Pappy" Doyle, fired a single high-deflection burst at the leading Bf 109, broke away and resumed their escort. Doyle filed no claim until his combat film was developed, and then put in for one "damaged" Messerschmitt. Oesau had in fact been killed by a 20-mm shell, and his fighter crashed to the ground west of St. Vith. Doyle's victory had been scored during the 474th Fighter Group's first contact with the Luftwaffe; it had only been operational for two weeks. Oesau, on the other hand, was a career officer with 125 aerial victories and he was the holder of the Knights Cross with Oak Leaves and Swords. Oesau was a highly respected combat leader, and although men in his unit claim that he was by this time at the end of his physical and intellectual powers, his loss was impossible to fill, as it represented yet another reduction in the small number of successful RLV formation leaders. Major Bär, the Kommandeur of II./JG 1, was named interim Kommodore, but was quickly replaced by Obstlt. Herbert Ihlefeld, who was already on the Geschwader staff. Ihlefeld retained his position until VE-Day. It is said that orders for Oesau to cease operational flying and report for duty on the staff of the General der Jagdflieger arrived the day he was killed.[8]

May 12—The First Attacks on the German Petroleum Industry

On the evening of the 11th the USSTAF weather staff predicted that a high pressure area would ensure clear conditions over all of western and central Europe on the following day. This was the opportunity Spaatz

Fw. Berthold Wendler, a fighter pilot with a very broad résumé: in his one year's combat service he flew with two high-altitude Bf 109 Gruppen and a unique single-engine Fühlungshalter detachment. When the fuel shortage curtailed his flying he volunteered for the ramming unit Sonderkommando Elbe, and having survived its only mission, he volunteered for another special operation, Bienenstock (Beehive); the war ended before it could be carried out. (*Wendler*)

and Anderson had been waiting for, and orders were cut for Doolittle's Eighth to make a full-strength attack the next day on the concentration of synthetic oil installations in central Germany. The day that Albert Speer and Germany's war economists had dreaded had arrived.

Beginning at 1030 on the 12th, 886 B-17s and B-24s began crossing the English coast in a single stream, headed southeast. In the lead were five combat wings of the 3rd Bomb Division, headed for the most distant targets, the refinery at Brux and an aircraft factory at Chemnitz. They were followed by six 1st Bomb Division combat wings, whose targets were the refineries at Merseburg-Leuna and Lützkendorf, and four 2nd Division wings, which were to bomb the Böhlen and Zeitz refineries. The stream maintained a steady course until south of Koblenz, when it turned due east. After passing Frankfurt, it split up to head for its various targets. Escort was provided by 876 fighters in 22 group formations.[9]

I. and II. Jagdkorps began ordering units to readiness before the American bombers reached the Belgian coast. II. Jagdkorps, whose I. and III./JG 26 were based nearest to the projected course, ordered these two Gruppen to move inland to await further developments—hitting the full-strength incoming stream head-on was no longer considered a worthwhile proposition. I. Jagdkorps ordered all of its controllers except Jafü Ostmark to scramble their fighters, which were to assemble in their usual *Gefechts-verbände* and head to Frankfurt. Jafü Ostmark first ordered its Gruppen toward an incoming Fifteenth Air Force formation, but when that went elsewhere, these fighters also headed for Frankfurt. The RLV controllers succeeded for the first time in concentrating all of their day fighters in a single combat area. In all, 22 Jagdgruppen containing 475 single-engine

fighters and three Zerstörergruppen with 40 twin-engine fighters sortied; this was the maximum defensive effort of the entire strategic air war. Unfortunately for the defenders, they found the bomber stream to be highly concentrated and generally well-escorted. The German pilots were fought out before the stream broke up into smaller, more vulnerable units, and their exhaustion was so great that only 51 could fly second sorties against the withdrawing bombers.[10]

The first fighters to reach the bombers were the three Gruppen of JG 1, flying as the JD 3 *Gefechts-verband*. They sighted the stream before it made its turn to the east south of Koblenz, but were attacked by the P-47s of the 78th Fighter Group. The formation's Bf 109 Gruppe, III./JG 1, took on the Thunderbolts, as briefed, while the two Fw 190 Gruppen apparently

Uffz. Willi Maximowitz of 11.(Sturm)/JG 3 taxies his Fw 190A-8/R2 "black 8" into its revetment at Dreux during the one week that IV.(Sturm)/JG 3 spent on the *Invasionsfront*. It was June 13 before Berlin came to its senses and returned the newly designated, newly equipped Sturmgruppe to Germany and the RLV. The Gruppe's black cowling and wavy IV. Gruppe bar, the Geschwader emblem and white fuselage band, and this model's 30-mm MK 108 outer wing cannon can be seen. (*Bundesarchiv 493-3362-4a*)

proceeded west to seek out an unescorted part of the stream. II./JG 1 made a head-on attack on the B-24s in the trailing 2nd Division, claiming five; these were to be the only single-engine German fighters seen all day by the B-24 crews. I./JG 1 did not make an attack, but returned to Rotenburg to prepare for a second mission.[11]

Jagdabschnitt Mittelrhein controlled two Jagdgruppen, II./JG 27 and II./JG 53, as *Gefechtsverband Dachs* (Badger). They were under orders to rendezvous with JG 1, but were attacked by Mustangs while still climbing and, after breaking free, caught the bomber stream over the Taunus Mountains and attacked it in small formations. Both Gruppen reported successful attacks, but sustained heavy losses, a total of 11 Bf 109s.[12]

The JD 1 *Gefechtsverband* was led by the JG 3 Kommodore, Major Friedrich-Karl Müller, and comprised his Stabsschwarm, I., II., and IV.(Sturm) /JG 3, all in Bf 109s except for the former Sturmstaffel, which had retained its Fw 190s when transferring to the Sturmgruppe. Müller was directed to the front of the stream, and reached the leading combat boxes of the 3rd Bomb Division just west of Frankfurt at the same time as Major Anton Hackl's JD 2 *Gefechtsverband*, which contained the Fw 190s of I. and III./JG 11, escorted by the Bf 109s of II./JG 11. The last-named Gruppe peeled off to look for escorts, whose absence was puzzling, while the other five Gruppen made devastating head-on attacks on the

45th and 4th Combat Wings. They were able to make repeated firing passes by Gruppen to close range. The 3rd Division lost 41 B-17s on the mission, nearly all during this 15-minute attack, which did not end until the 4th and 357th Fighter Groups arrived to take over the escort from the missing 355th Group, which had inexplicably been escorting part of the 1st Bomb Division farther back in the column. The bomb groups hardest hit were the 96th, with 12 losses, and the 452nd with 14, on what would be its hardest mission of the war.[13]

In mid-April II./JG 11 had received a new Kommandeur, Major Günther Rall, from the Eastern Front. He had no experience against the USAAF, but was an incredibly skilled fighter pilot—in fact, he is the third-highest scoring in history—and it was obviously felt that he would do well in his new command, which had the primary mission of dogfighting the U.S. escorts. The Gruppe did find some escorts: P-47s of Colonel Hub Zemke's 56th Group, which were flying a scheduled sweep but were too far in front to support the bombers. Zemke was trying a new tactic, the "Zemke Fan," which scattered independent flights in front of the bomber stream,

Bf 109G-6 "yellow 4" of 9./JG 1 taxies out for takeoff from La Fère, France, in July 1944. Although photographed on the *Invasionsfront*, the airplane displays the camouflage and markings it brought with it from the RLV. (*Bundesarchiv 677-8004-6*)

A III./JG 3 Bf 109G-6 after crash-landing on the *Invasionsfront*. It carries an interesting set of markings. The Geschwader emblem and vertical bar identify the unit. The dark band around the rear fuselage is probably rust-red, a Reich theater marking, although by this time each Jagdgeschwader in the RLV had received its own color—that of JG 3 was white. (*Mol*)

sweeping a large volume of sky to maximize the chance of finding German fighters. The flaw in this plan was that flights of four P-47s were themselves in danger if they happened to encounter a large formation of Messerschmitts, which is just what happened.[14]

The day's mission found Rall leading his Gruppe at 11,000 meters (36,000 ft.), without pressurization or cabin heating, and 3,000 meters (10,000 ft.) above the Fw 190s. Rall dove onto a formation of P-47s and shot down one of Zemke's two wingmen (Zemke's flight was missing a plane). Zemke and his other wingman dove away, and another flight attacked Rall, who dove all-out from 8,000 meters (26,000 ft.) to tree-top level. He reached 1,000 km/h (620 mph) and saw paint peeling from his wings. Rall knew he could not out-dive P-47s, but he had no option. He was being attacked by four in line abreast, and could not turn into either pair without being attacked by the other. He took some hits in his engine and radiator, and at some point his thumb was shot off; he was wearing gloves, and did not learn the extent of his injury until later. He felt no pain at the time. After cleaning the ice off his windshield with his good hand, Rall zoom-climbed to 2,500 meters (8,200 ft.) and attempted to bail out. He was upside down and was pushed back into the plane, but eventually got out. He was able to reach the chute handle and pulled it at about 500 meters (1,600 ft.). Only then did his thumb start hurting—badly. His descent was smooth. He landed in a tree on a steep slope, hit the release, dropped to the ground, and rolled down a forested hill into a gully, without further

injury. This was a "lucky" landing, because Rall had broken his back three times in Russia and had been warned not to bail out again. He started walking through the forest and was eventually found by some farmers, who took him to their village, gave him juice and cigarettes, and entertained him royally. The region was on alarm status and there was no road traffic. An ambulance arrived after an hour and took him to Nassau hospital, which was waiting to operate on him. He had left his glove on all this time (he still has the glove), but the thumb was hanging on only by a thread of skin and could not be saved. He developed an infection and stayed in the hospital for some time, eventually leaving with the wound still open. He returned to operations in 1945 as Kommodore of JG 300, but never flew another combat mission. His Gruppe did its duty on May 12, but at high cost. The other three members of his Stabsschwarm were all shot down; the Gruppe's losses totaled 2 KIA, 5 WIA, and 11 Bf 109s, for claims of Rall's P-47 and two P-51s.

Two more German formations arrived before the bombers had passed through the Frankfurt gauntlet, but all gaps in the escort coverage were now closed. The JD 7 *Gefechtsverband*, which contained only two Bf 109 Gruppen, III./JG 3 and I./JG 5, never reached the bombers at all, but was driven to ground by American fighters with heavy losses. I./JG 5 did claim three P-47s; their opponents were probably from the 56th Group.[15]

The Jafü Ostmark *Verband*—Obstlt. Gustav Rödel and his JG 27 Stabsschwarm, I and III./JG 27, all in Bf 109s—reached the bomber stream east of

Frankfurt. They found a heavily escorted bomber formation, and after "bitter air battles" claimed 24 B-17s and two P-51s for losses of 3 KIA, 7 WIA, and 14 Bf 109s. These attacks came just as those of the JD 1 and JD 2 *Verbände* ended, and many of their victims had probably already been damaged.

There was only one interception in any of the target areas. ZG 26 scrambled all 40 of its Me 410s from Königsberg and flew to Dresden to await developments. It was well-placed to attack some unescorted bombers heading for Chemnitz, a target of opportunity, and claimed three B-17s and two B-24s for the loss of four Me 410s and most of their crews, all to bomber gunfire. ErprKdo 25 suffered its last casualties of the war when this experimental unit lost one of its Me 410s, possibly in this same attack.

Aided by good weather and the absence of aerial defenders over the targets, the bombardiers had an exceptionally good day. The post-mission evaluation that evening rated results at three of the refineries as "very good," at one as "good," and at only one as "fair." Aerial opposition on the return trip was relatively weak. Only one full-strength Gruppe from II. Jagdkorps, Major Klaus Mietusch's III./JG 26, made an attack. I./JG 26 sortied, but failed to make contact. Mietusch was able to locate the chewed-up 45th Combat Wing over the Ardennes, and downed another 452nd Bomb Group B-17, while claiming two more shot from formation; he lost one pilot. The 51 I. Jagdkorps pilots who flew second sorties operated in small, improvised formations and looked primarily for stragglers. The USAAF lost a total of 46–9 bombers and 7–0 escorts on the mission; the Luftwaffe lost 28 KIA, 26 WIA, and 60 fighters. None of the German

Hungarian groundcrewmen take a break from servicing a Bf 109G-6 of Jagdgruppe 101, the famous "Red Pumas." (*Bundesarchiv 503-241-6a*)

formation leaders were fatalities, but two were lost for the duration of the war, nonetheless—Major Rall, as mentioned above, and Hptm. Rolf Hermichen, the Kommandeur of I./JG 11 and a frequent leader of the JD 2 battle formation. After Hermichen was shot down and bailed out, apparently without injury, he was immediately relieved of command and ordered to a staff position at Jagddivision 2 headquarters. He was never restored to combat status.[16]

May 12, 1944, can fairly be called the worst single day of the war for Germany. Other days brought dramatic battlefield defeats, and terrible casualties, but never ended without leaving the possibility of a reversal of fortune. This was not true of this day, which was the true tipping point, leading irrevocably to Germany's final defeat. Albert Speer recorded in his diary that, "On this day the technological war was decided." Five synthetic oil refineries, all absolutely crucial to the successful prosecution of the war, were reached and heavily bombed. The RLV put up its largest day-fighter force ever; I. Jagdkorps' command and control procedures worked perfectly; and the bombers still could not be stopped. All the Americans had to do was keep up the campaign they had now begun, and German defeat was inevitable. On May 19, Speer commented to Hitler at Obersalzberg:

> The enemy has struck us at one of our weakest points. If they persist at it this time, then we will soon no longer have any fuel production worth mentioning. Our one hope is that the other side has an air force general staff as scatterbrained as ours![17]

The May 12 raid was even more successful than the staff of USSTAF had hoped. An Ultra intercept confirmed a cutback in non-operational flying as a direct consequence of the reduction in supply of aviation fuel. The stocks which had been built up in anticipation of the Allied invasion immediately began to fall. The "Bomber Barons" at last had a target to justify the enormous investment which had been made in the strategic bombing force. Support for the Normandy invasion required a large effort by USSTAF for the next two months, but by July 21, according to Speer, 98 percent of all of Germany's aircraft fuel plants were out of operation. The German powers of recovery were, as usual, remarkable, but monthly production of aviation fuel dropped from *c.* 180,000 tons in March 1944 to *c.* 20,000 tons in November; inventory dropped from *c.* 575,000 tons in March to *c.* 175,000 tons in November.[18]

The USSTAF scheduled an immediate follow-up to the successful May 12 attack. Refineries in Poland were targeted on the 13th, but the weather did not cooperate, and targets of opportunity were bombed. The Wehrmacht struggled to bolster the defenses of the oil targets. Confidence in the fighter arm reached a new low. An Ultra intercept on the 14th recorded a call for the transfer of Luftwaffe Flak units from the Eastern Front, where they were valuable anti-tank resources, to the refineries. On the 15th Galland and Schmid met with Göring to discuss means of strengthening the fighter defenses. A condensed list of recommendations is presented below. Where known to the authors, the action taken is shown in brackets.

1. Galland proposed that two Jagdgruppen transfer from the Eastern Front to Luftflotte Reich [Göring agreed; II./JG 5 and IV./JG 54 were transferred.]
2. Galland proposed that II./Schlachtgeschwader 2 become a fighter unit and transfer to the RLV force. [Göring disagreed. Qualified Schlachtgeschwader (ground-attack) pilots were to be allowed to transfer individually.]
3. Galland proposed that two *Wilde Sau* Geschwader Stäbe and three Gruppen be dissolved to economize in unit commanders, with their resources to be divided among the remaining six Gruppen. [Göring agreed.]
4. Galland proposed that Luftflotte 3 give up its Jagdgruppen to the RLV force. [Göring disagreed.]
5. Galland proposed that any Gruppenkommandeur off duty for more than 14 days should be replaced. [Göring disagreed—cases were to be settled individually; time was to be four weeks. Galland was to form a reserve of supernumerary commanders in the form of a "course."]
6. Galland proposed the continual withdrawal of one Jagdgruppe per Jagddivision for a period of up to four weeks for training. [Göring agreed, and ordered all Jagdgruppen to find their own practice ranges.]
7. Göring wanted one of the remaining *Wilde Sau* Jagdgruppen subordinated to each of the two Zerstörergeschwader for escort duty. [This was done in the case of one Gruppe.]
8. Göring allowed II./ZG 26 to remain the only Zerstörer unit with 5-cm cannon "for the time being." [This was a "politically favored" weapon that was not proving itself in service.]
9. Göring wanted the Zerstörer units to remain in the RLV for now. He flatly rejected sending them to other theaters because of their "inferiority to enemy fighters" [*sic!*].

10. Schmid proposed placing the Flak Operations Director on the staff of I. Jagdkorps. [Göring ordered a conference of the Flak and fighter commanders.]
11. Schmid proposed taking the Flak Operations Commanders out from under the Luftgaue, and placing them in the Jagddivisionen. [This was eventually done.]
12. Schmid proposed subordinating Jafü Ostmark directly to I. Jagdkorps, renaming it "Jagddivision 8." [Göring eventually agreed.]
13. Schmid proposed moving the Jagddivision 7 fighters from Munich and Frankfurt to Ansbach-Bernberg to permit the formation of compact *Gefechtsverbände* of 4–5 Jagdgruppen. [Göring agreed.]
14. Schmid proposed moving II./JG 27 from Jagddivision 7 to Jafü Ostmark to rebuild and rejoin its own Geschwader. [Göring agreed.]
15. With Galland's concurrence, Schmid proposed disbanding the fighter commander's course at I./JG 27. [Göring agreed.]
16. Schmid proposed that some complete Jagdgruppen remain in Germany after the Invasion. [Göring decided to retain the previous plan: certain "third Gruppen" were to stay, after surrendering their serviceable aircraft and fit pilots.]
17. Göring ordered more training of airfield staffs in the firing of anti-aircraft weapons.
18. Göring stated that he would propose to the Führer that American and British aircrew who fired indiscriminately at towns, civilian trains, or parachuting airmen were to be executed on the spot.
19. General Kreipe, the Director of Training, requested 60,000 metric tons of fuel per month for aircrew training. [Göring cut this to 50,000.][19]

Galland had another concern which was even more serious, if that were possible: fighter pilot losses in the RLV were now exceeding the supply from the training schools. His recommendations for making up the shortfall included returning all fit fighter pilots serving in staff positions to operational posts, making 80–100 instructors available for combat duty, and transferring some qualified night-fighter pilots to day units.

Technical innovations were in the pipeline, but would not be available in time to aid in the current crisis. Hptm. Werner Thierfelder, the Kommandeur of ErprKdo 262, had the personnel for a full Gruppe— III./ZG 26 had simply been redesignated—but very few Me 262s. He sent some of his pilots and ground crews to the Messerschmitt factory at Leipheim to assist in modifying and test flying the new fighters.[20]

Major Wolfgang Späte's 1./JG 400 had its few Me 163s ready for service. Späte himself flew the first tentative operational sortie on the 13th in a bright red machine; its color was probably intended to buck up the spirits of his own men as much as to strike fear into the hearts of the enemy. The rocket-engine fighter was still killing its own pilots with regularity. Späte's reward for thus tempting the fates was to be sent back to his home Geschwader, JG 54, before the end of May.

A third new weapon which was nearing service in May was the *Krebsgerät* (Crab Apparatus), the last incarnation of the WGr 21 rocket, which had originally entered service as an infantry mortar shell. A single *Krebsgerät* tube was placed beneath the fuselage of a Fw 190, its rocket facing to the rear. It was to be fired after the fighter passed through a heavy bomber formation, as a parting shot. Tests in the spring by ErprKdo 25 were favorable, and Galland authorized equipping 20 Fw 190A-8s of a single Sturmstaffel for service evaluation. 12.(Sturm)/JG 3 was chosen, and the rocket tubes were installed while the Staffel was converting from Bf 109s. But the *Krebsgerät* had originally been intended for fighters attacking from the front. The Sturmjäger attacked from the rear, with very low closing speed. To fire their rockets, they had to maintain their course and speed as they slowly pulled away, directly in front of the bombers. Firing was completely blind, as the Fw 190 pilots had no vision to the rear. As can be imagined, the *Krebsgerät* was extremely unpopular with its pilots, and its service use did not last a month.[21]

The Fifteenth Air Force made its first authorized attack on the Ploesti refinery complex on May 18. Most of the 700 bombers turned back owing to heavy cloud, but the raid served as a warning to the overstretched Luftwaffe, which was forced to react to yet another Allied threat. A Jagdgruppe was moved to Romania from Italy, and plans were made to employ the closest Eastern Front Jagdgruppen as heavy bomber interceptors. The Ploesti campaign is unfortunately outside the scope of this book, and will be mentioned only as it impacts the air campaign over the Reich proper.[22]

On May 20, Major Anton Hackl, the Kommandeur of III./JG 11, radioed a report to the General der Jagdflieger which was intercepted, decoded by Ultra, and read with interest at the highest levels of USSTAF. Hackl's thoughts had probably been solicited by Galland. The report claimed:

Bf 109G-14 "white 16" of 1./JG 301. Lt. Horst Prenzel flew it across the Channel to England on July 21, 1944, and surrendered. (*Rosch*)

1. The aim of all fighter forces operating versus bombers, when the target is known, should be either to attack as late as possible [before bombing], causing the bombers to jettison; or as early as possible, to permit multiple, staged attacks, thus splitting the Allied fighters.

2. On second sorties, auxiliary tanks should be retained as long as possible, to challenge Allied formations as deep as possible inside the Reich, taking advantage of weaker escort (less bold, relief not arriving, etc.).

3. After the Allied formations are thus broken up, rear attacks are then possible, so that even poor gunners have to get a victory or be suspected of cowardice. Experience shows that only old pilots get victories in frontal attacks—and also get hit. Young pilots do not approach correctly or go in near enough.

4. Every pilot, even with no ammunition, must attack with the formation as long as the Kommandeur does, to split up the defense and prevent our own pilots from refusing combat.

5. It is proposed that young pilots with a few victories be rotated in continually from the Russian front, so that the east will become a battle school for the west.[23]

The JG zbV Geschwader Stab, which had been established in April to command the Jagddivision 7 *Gefechtsverband*, was apparently given a broader role on May 20. It moved from Kassel to Ansbach, as part of the consolidation Schmid had proposed on May 15, and also received a new Kommodore to replace Major Gerhard Michalski, who had been injured in combat on May 1. Galland gave the command to Major Walther Dahl, telling him that the OKL intended for it to stay in the Reich after the Allied invasion and command all of the remaining RLV day units;

according to the current plan, these would comprise five *Wilde Sau* Jagdgruppen.[24]

While waiting for the perfect day for its second attack on the oil industry, the Eighth Air Force returned to important, but not critical, strategic objectives when not given Transportation Plan targets. Attackers and defenders fell into somewhat of a routine. Berlin and Brunswick were visited on May 19, Kiel, on the 22nd. The 24th brought a rare full-strength combined raid; the Eighth returned to Berlin, while the Fifteenth bombed Wiener Neustadt and other Austrian aviation targets. I. Jagdkorps was losing fighters at a rate of about 10 percent per mission. Eighth Air Force bomber losses had dropped to 2 percent per mission; those of the Fifteenth were somewhat greater, but not high enough to hamper operations. The trend obviously presaged disaster for Germany.[25]

Weather conditions on May 28 were adequate for another Eighth Air Force attack on oil targets in central Germany. A single stream of 1,341 bombers formed up and headed due east across the Zuider Zee toward Berlin, on the "bomber *Autobahn*." The assembly of this stream over the English coast was always fraught with problems. The 94th Combat Wing of the 1st Bomb Division had to dodge an oncoming wing of B-24s and lost its place in line. It finally squeezed in between two 3rd Bomb Division boxes, but was left without escort when it turned for its own target, with devastating consequences. North of Brunswick the stream split up according to plan; the individual combat wings headed for the refineries at Ruhland, Magdeburg, Lützkendorf, Zeitz, and Merseburg-Leuna; the Junkers factory at Dessau; and a large armor depot at Königsborn. Twenty-eight fighter groups from the 8th and 9th Fighter Commands were intended to provide ample escort for all bomber formations that were on course and close to on time.[26]

I. Jagdkorps ordered all of its Jagddivisionen to scramble their fighters and rendezvous near Magdeburg. The Allied radio-intercept service heard one controller order his formation leader to attack not the first, but the succeeding waves. Oblt. Rüdiger von Kirchmayr, the Kapitän of 5./JG 1, was leading the JD 3 *Verband*, which contained the three JG 1 Gruppen. The JD 2 *Verband* (three JG 11 Gruppen), the JD 1 *Verband* (three JG 3 Gruppen), and the JD 7 *Verband* (I./JG 5, II./JG 53 and III./JG 54) arrived on time and fell in behind JG 1. Contact with the bomber stream

came immediately. True to orders, Kirchmayr passed the leading 1st Bomb Division and led his main formation in a close-formation head-on attack on the 13th Combat Wing, in the van of the 3rd Division, while the three Höhengruppen, III./JG 1, I./JG 3, and II./JG 11, stayed above to fend off the Mustangs.

Kirchmayr led his nine Jagdgruppen—probably 180 Fw 190s and Bf 109s—directly at the leading 390th Bomb Group. Many B-17s fell away after the blistering attack, but only six crashed. Others which were credited to the German pilots as having been shot from their formation were able to limp back to England, as they were not attacked again. The 357th Fighter Group, which was responsible for the entire 3rd Division stream and some of whose pilots may have become confused when the 94th Wing pulled out from behind the 13th Wing to make its lone run, quickly concentrated at the head of the 3rd Bomb Division, where some of the Mustangs climbed to attack the high-altitude Bf 109s, while the rest went after the German fighters in the bomber stream. The 354th Fighter Group was just arriving for its escort shift, and the 4th Fighter Group, up ahead with the 1st Bomb Division, reversed course and came back to help. The three groups claimed 33 single-engine fighters for the loss of two P-51s to German fighters. Kirchmayr's pilots had to fight off other Mustang and Lightning units before regaining their bases. The 12 Jagdgruppen lost 13 KIA, 13 WIA, and 37 fighters on this mission. No second sorties were possible.

The Jafü Ostmark *Verband*, comprising the Stab and three Bf 109 Gruppen of JG 27, reached Magdeburg a few minutes after Kirchmayr's fighters, and were directed to the choicest target in the area: the 50 B-17s of the 94th Combat Wing, heading for Dessau entirely alone. JG 27 did not normally employ a set formation to attack bombers, but tried to take advantage of the specific combat situation. Based on the sketchy records available, the Gruppen split up and attacked by Staffeln, some from the front and some from the rear. IV./JG 27 was assigned the high-altitude protection role, but the absence of American fighters allowed it to participate in the bomber attacks. There were some Höhenjäger from the other units in the general area, and they apparently took on the first P-51s to respond to the B-17 commander's call for help. The JG 27 pilots were given the luxury of making multiple attacks, and nearly all of the B-17s they damaged actually went down. Many bombers jettisoned their bombs in open fields to gain speed.

When the Initial Point for the Dessau bomb run was reached, the lead bombardier could not see the target through the smoke and haze, and the formation leader ordered the shattered formation to head for Leipzig, its secondary target. There the six B-17s still carrying bombs dropped them, with poor results. When the 94th Wing finally reached England, it was short 15 B-17s.

In its isolated battle JG 27 claimed 16 B-17s shot down or shot from formation, plus one P-51 shot down. Its losses were relatively light: 4 KIA, 2 WIA, and seven Bf 109s. It was given credit for driving the B-17s away from their target, a very rare accomplishment, and close to the literal truth.[27] The mission flown by Lt. Alexander Ottnad was typical. He was piloting a Bf 109G-6/U4 "gunboat" with a 30-mm engine cannon and 20-mm cannon under the wings. His combat report reads:

I took off from Götzendorf at 1244 hours as leader of 8./JG 27. At 1410 we sighted two waves of escorted B-17s between Dessau and Magdeburg, flying at 8,500 meters [28,000 ft.]. Our Gruppe attacked from the front. I targeted the enemy aircraft flying third from the right. Firing from 400 down to 200 meters [1,300–650 ft.], I observed hits in the nose and the right wing. When I broke off my attack I was hit in the engine and fuselage. The Fortress was going straight down, its right wing on fire. I bailed out because my airplane was smoking heavily. The B-17 should have crashed south-southwest of Zerbst at 1428 hours. Fw. Franz Büsen is my witness.[28]

Although there was no witness to the actual crash of the B-17, a 401st Bomb Group B-17 did crash at the time and place of Ottnad's claim, and was probably his victim.

Eighth Air Force losses totaled 32–1 bombers and 14–3 fighters. I. Jagdkorps lost 18 KIA, 13 WIA, and 52 fighters. (II. Jagdkorps' fighters were not used; they were being rested for the imminent Allied invasion.) Of the day's oil targets, only Zeitz was hit hard, and the USSTAF could not claim a success comparable to that of the 12th. For the defenders, the pattern was clear. Their equipment, tactics, and control procedures were sufficient to allow them to punish any bomber formation caught without escort. But bombers which were fully shielded by escorts were invulnerable to attack, and in fact on the 28th most bomber crewmen never saw a German fighter.[29]

Kurheim Florida, the fighter pilots' convalescent home in Bad Wiessee. "Flown-out" and badly injured pilots were sent here to regain their strength. Lt. Heinz Rose (4./JG 11) suffered severe head injuries on November 13, 1943, and spent time here in July and August 1944. (*Heinz Rose via Arno Rose*)

The USSTAF mounted another combined attack on the 29th. The Fifteenth Air Force damaged the Wiener Neustadt Messerschmitt factory severely for the loss of only 18 bombers, five of these to fighters. II./ZG 1 lost 17 KIA, 7 WIA, and 13 Bf 110s to 31st and 52nd Fighter Group P-51s, and was effectively wiped off the Jafü Ostmark organization chart.

The Eighth Air Force attempted to split the northern defenses by sending its B-17s to attack aviation targets in central Germany while its B-24s flew in a separate stream along the Baltic coast, bombing the Pölitz refinery and Tutow aviation targets. The tactic was not especially effective; the German response was late but severe. Seventeen 2nd Bomb Division B-24s were lost, most over the Baltic to an attack by the JD 1 *Verband*, which was led by the JG 3 Stabsschwarm and contained II./JG 3, IV.(Sturm)/JG 3, the three Gruppen of JG 11, and the three Gruppen of ZG 26. The JG 3 Kommodore, Obstlt. Friedrich-Karl Müller, turned back early, stalled out over the Salzwedel airfield, and crashed to his death from 15 meters (50 ft.) altitude. It was the consensus of his men that he was completely exhausted after having led every Geschwader mission for the previous two months. His replacement was Major Heinz Bär.

The RLV fighters left in central Germany, reinforced by the Einsatzstaffel of the training unit

I./JGr Ost, flew a successful mission against the Eighth Air Force B-17s, 17 of which failed to return to England. Norbert Hannig, an instructor in I./JGr Ost at Liegnitz, has stated that the Einsatzstaffel included six instructors, with six of the more experienced pupils as wingmen. They attacked the B-17s by independent Schwärme before being dispersed by P-51s. Claims for three B-17s and one P-51 were confirmed, but at severe cost. One Fw 190A-6 returned early with a bad engine; two made it back with combat damage. Five crash-landed with wounded or dying pilots; the other four pilots baled out, but two were shot and killed in their parachutes. The day's lessons were quickly added to the curriculum. The official purpose of the Gruppe was to train replacement pilots for the *Ostfront*; half of the course was now to be devoted to RLV tactics. The operational Staffel would no longer attack bombers by Schwärme, but in frontal attacks in a double arrowhead, mimicking the front-line units.[30]

The last three strategic missions by the USSTAF prior to the invasion of Normandy on June 6 were flown by the Fifteenth Air Force: a return to Wiener Neustadt on May 30, a return to Ploesti on May 31, and the first shuttle mission to the Soviet Union on June 2. The target of this last mission was a relatively innocuous Hungarian rail yard. Shuttle missions, code-named Operation Frantic, were begun with high hopes. Both the Eighth and the Fifteenth Air Forces were to attack eastern targets which were normally beyond their range before landing at airfields which had been prepared in the Soviet Union after long and hard negotiations. But the Americans could not overcome Soviet distrust, and only a few missions were flown before a disastrous failure in June soured the Americans on the whole idea; the missions petered out in mid-September.[31]

Galland and Milch believed fervently that given enough time, the Me 262 could regain air superiority for Germany. The timing and extent of Hitler's interference with the Me 262 program are subjects of controversy, but one date is fixed. The ErprKdo 262 war diary has the following entry for May 31:

> The General der Jagdflieger, Genmaj. Galland, announces that by order of the Führer the Me 262 is to be used as a bomber. Hptm. Thierfelder is to receive a Gruppe of pilots from KG 51 to train at Lechfeld and with industry. The III./ZG 26 flight leaders and ground crews are to stay; the ordinary pilots from III./ZG 26 are to transfer to other Gruppen.[32]

The plan to re-equip the outmatched day-fighter units of the RLV with the revolutionary Me 262 was, for the moment at least, stymied.

Walter Grabmann, in a postwar history written for the USAAF, had the following comments on the Luftflotte Reich order of battle at the end of May:

1. Totals in operational units = 587 single-engine fighters, of which 333, or 57 percent, were effective; 8 (2 effective) Me 163s; 126 twin-engine fighters, of which 53 (42 percent) were effective.
2. The Höhengruppen now had Bf 109s equipped with DB 605AS engines and a ceiling of 11,500 meters [38,000 ft.]. Their mission was to dive on the escorts and decoy them away from the bombers.
3. The Einsatzstaffeln of fighter schools were committed only against reconnaissance aircraft and separated and/or damaged heavy bombers.
4. Jagddivision 7 received Fühlungshalter support: Luftbeobachterstaffel 7 detachments were committed as contact aircraft to establish routes of Fifteenth Air Force formations coming from Italy.
5. Eighth Air Force raids now consisted of 800–1,000 heavy bombers escorted by 1,000 fighters. Attacks on northern and central Germany could be met by at most 246 single-engine plus 55 twin-engine fighters.
6. The decision taken in 1943 to increase the establishment of Jagdgruppen to 68 fighters could not be realized. The 18 Jagdgruppen averaged 31 aircraft per Gruppe; only two had as many as 40, the old establishment.

Grabmann summarized the state of the RLV at May's end in these bleak words:

1. Increasing enemy strength was not balanced by increased German commitment.
2. Enemy losses were too small to be a deterrent.
3. German losses were at the highest level which could be tolerated for any length of time.[33]

Galland's 1943 plan to grow the Jagdwaffe by expanding the establishment strength of each Staffel (to 16 aircraft), of each Gruppe (to four Staffeln), and eventually of each Geschwader (to four Gruppen) had had the advantage of putting more planes in the air while minimizing the need for trained officers for leadership and staff positions. The two Luftflotte 3 Jagdgeschwader had been enlarged, but the process had then stalled. It was proving impossible to keep the

RLV battle formations up to strength. In late May the RLM took the drastic step of ordering 11 Jagd-gruppen from the eastern and southern fronts to surrender one complete Jagdstaffel each—one third of their combat strength—to the RLV. Most Kommodoren took their orders literally and sent off entire Staffeln; Obstlt. Steinhoff in Italy was able to get away with releasing the "equivalents" of two Staffeln from I./JG 77 and II./JG 77. Several of the transferred Staffeln—notably 2./JG 51, 12./JG 51, 4./JG 52, and 2./JG 54—provided much-needed boosts to their new Jagdgruppen; the others were quickly chewed up with no noticeable effect on the efficiency of their new host units.[34]

German Training and Tactics in Response to the Oil Campaign

The attacks on the synthetic oil plants not only crippled the Luftwaffe's front-line forces; they also effectively destroyed those forces' ability to regenerate themselves. Luftwaffe aircrew training, which had been living hand to mouth ever since 1942, finally disintegrated under the hammer blows of the oil offensive, the depredations of USAAF fighters, and its own leadership's poor management. From spring 1944 on, the Luftwaffe's training establishment desperately attempted to fill the cockpits of the fighter planes pouring from Speer's factories. The fighters were needed to protect the petroleum industry, whose output was critical for training new pilots, as well as for the continuation of Hitler's war. By the end of the year, the vicious circle had closed.

In April 1944, Göring assembled his senior staff and issued a clarion call for the "mass production" of fighter pilots, exhorting Kreipe's office to build up fighter pilot strength rapidly in an effort to match the achievements of the Jägerstab:

I now give the order, which shall be carried out under all circumstances, even though those at the front howl and wail, and even though training [duration] has to be cut down temporarily to reach the target: 2,000 as quickly as possible, then 2,500, then 3,000 and from that point the normal output. Then we shall have a further discussion to see how the enemy is faring . . . The military people are always talking of concentration of effort without having the faintest idea of its meaning . . .[35]

Göring demanded not just increased output, but better quality. In March 1944, he mandated better

blind-flying training for fighter and Zerstörer crews in the RLV. He noted that it was intolerable that the enemy, with his superior training, was able to locate and attack German targets in bad weather while the RLV defenders remained grounded.[36]

Kreipe's organization attempted to fulfill its master's wishes. New recruits streamed into the training schools. On June 29, 1944, the Reichs-marschall, over Koller's strong protests, finally decreed that all bomber production and bomber pilot training cease, except for the jets and a handful of Ju 388s and Ju 188 pathfinders. "The use of all facilities thus released [was earmarked] for the production of fighter aircraft and the training of fighter pilots"—and hundreds of highly trained bomber pilots became available for fighter conversion.[37] The training course was reduced yet again, and further cuts were soon to follow. The 1944 "mass production program" fighter course consisted of the following stages:[38]

A School
Stage 1: 2 hours glider instruction;
Stage 2: *Motor-Auswahl:* 30 hours initial powered instruction, primary training;
Stage 3: *Luftwaffenführerschein:* 20 hours elementary instruction in aerobatics, formation flying, etc., usually on the Bücker 181.

Fighter School
Vorschule: 26 hours on trainer types (Arado 96);
Endschule: 14 hours on earlier model operational types;
Ergänzungsjagdgruppe: 20 hours on Bf 109 or Fw 190;
Total: 8 months, 111 flying hours.[39]

This was barely half the flying hours a 1942 German trainee would have received. By late fall, some German fighter pilots were arriving at their units with only 6–10 flying hours on operational-type aircraft.[40] Blind flying and gunnery training were notable weaknesses in this program. Nevertheless, Kreipe believed that, if he received sufficient fuel allocations (60–80,000 tons/month) through the summer and fall of 1944, his organization could turn out 1,200 trained fighter pilots each month, as well as 250 ground-attack, 40 bomber, 75 jet bomber (Me 262/Ar 234), 64 recce, and 40 night-fighter pilots.[41]

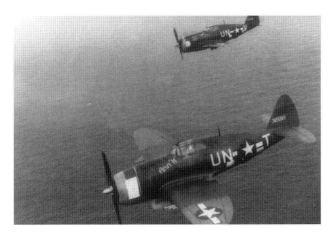

Ann K and *Pat*, a pair of well-worn 56th Fighter Group P-47Ds, return to base at low altitude over the Channel after a summer 1944 mission. The black and white invasion stripes visible beneath the rear fuselage date the photo as after D-Day. (*ww2images*)

Nothing worked according to plan. Kreipe's demands for fuel were never met; his schools received only 13,500 tons in July, 13,400 tons in August, and 6,300 tons in September. The mass call for volunteers and transfers largely succeeded, but there were far too many for the fuel-starved schools to handle. As a temporary expedient, the primary schools were temporarily shut down, with all fuel allocations going to the fighter schools. This allowed fighter pilot output to remain high for a time, as the windfall from the bomber force converted to fighters and the previous months' output from the primary schools passed through the fighter schools and operational training unit programs. They were, however, living on borrowed time. Bad weather and a chronic shortage of modern fighter types at the schools created further difficulties. By fall 1944, truly bizarre expedients were finding favor. Allied intelligence noted a captured German document which called for the "remustering of flying personnel" from infantry divisions—anyone with a pilot, observer, or glider pilot certificate was to be transferred to the advanced training establishments at once.[42] With the bomber arm virtually dismantled, Luftwaffe personnel officers shifted their attention to the transport and ferrying units. A general staff recommendation in September 1944 offered an idiotic burst of optimism:

> The possibility exists that there may not be such a large drain on the reserves as might be expected, in view of the recent contraction of the front, the smaller operating area and the fewer forces and missions required. Many corps and division staffs may be dissolved, thereby freeing up large numbers of pilots.[43]

The fuel crisis was bad enough, and the troubles facing the training establishments were multiplying. In April and May 1944, the Luftwaffe operations staff noted an alarming rise in losses of training, courier and transport aircraft operating in previously safe havens in eastern and southern Germany. In those two months, the Luftwaffe lost 35 and 32 such aircraft respectively, some as far east as Dresden and as far south as the Swiss frontier. Allied fighter aircraft ranging at will over the Reich territory greatly reduced the Luftwaffe's ability to train new pilots to replace the spiraling losses of the previous months. Many gun camera films from USAAF Mustangs and Thunderbolts show attacks on aircraft, frequently misidentified as "Me-109s," that are in fact Arado 96 trainers, usually with a dazed student pilot at the controls.

In order to cope with this situation, the Training Branch of the Operations Staff issued a series of emergency instructions. Non-combat flights were to take place only during the dawn and dusk hours. Crew vigilance was emphasized ("Daydreaming leads to death"). The Luftwaffe expanded its aircraft warning system, and devised a series of radio and visual signals to alert pilots to incursions by enemy fighters. Even courier aircraft were to carry armament. If attacked, poorly armed aircraft were to take evasive action and dive quickly to ground level. If necessary, the pilot was to belly-land the aircraft and take cover in order to avoid being strafed, since by this time crews were far more valuable than aircraft.[44]

The commencement of "aerial guerrilla warfare" by USAAF escort fighters meant that not only the training facilities, but the whole of the Luftwaffe's ground organization and supporting infrastructure was vulnerable. American escort fighters, at first on an individual basis but by late spring 1944 as a concerted policy, began strafing German airfields and ground installations on their homeward flights.[45] The Germans were initially successful in their efforts to combat this menace. Airfield commands adopted a number of passive measures, including construction of revetments, increased use of camouflage and smoke screens, and burying vital communications and

P-51Ds of the 357th Fighter Group fly over England in loose formation in July. The aircraft display black and white invasion stripes, and are painted overall in dark green paint from British stocks, a practice unique to this group. (*Permann*)

electrical cables serving the command posts and radar installations.[46] Deep slit trenches appeared on airfields, with fuel and ammunition stored in tunnels. Posting of additional lookouts and the reorganized Flugmeldedienst provided crucial early warning.[47] In the final months of the war, some German fighter units operated off stretches of *Autobahn*, sheltering their aircraft beneath the overpasses.

The single most effective countermeasure the Luftwaffe took in this regard was equipping airfields with additional Flak protection. While it was difficult to protect airfields against high-altitude carpet bombing by AAF heavies, the Germans took strong counter-measures against a more common threat, Thunderbolts, Mustangs and Lightnings carrying out strafing attacks from altitudes as low as 3 meters (10 ft.). Luftwaffe operational directives noted, "Only the effect of fire from Flak weapons concentrated at key points provides adequate protection against attacks at low and very low levels."[48] Accordingly, local Flak commanders employed every available weapon—even machine guns and cannon removed from grounded aircraft—and turned airfields into deadly "Flak traps."

Most of the damage to USAAF fighters involved in strafing attacks was caused by light cannon (20-mm quadruple and 37-mm) and multiple machine gun (13-mm and 7.9-mm) positions. In many cases the American pilots pressed home attacks against German aircraft grounded with empty tanks, or even abandoned

and derelict aircraft left in position to invite attention. The Luftwaffe operations staff noted with satisfaction the testimony of captured USAAF pilots, who spoke of the dangers of strafing work.[49] Many an ace fighter pilot of the Eighth Air Force wound up in a German Stalag as a result of ground strafing operations. Yet for the Luftwaffe's fighter force, this was cold comfort. By late 1944, the Flak had "assumed the dominant role in the Reich's air defenses."[50]

How did the collapse of the training program play out at the sharp end? Throughout the war, the Luftwaffe attempted to develop new tactics and improve its combat performance. Yet by 1944 the reduced state of pilot training was evident to all. A July 15, 1944, Operations Staff tactical assessment is revealing:

If the formation leader discovers during the head-on attack that the bomber formation is unprotected or poorly protected by fighters, he should lead the unit after the first pass by Staffel formation into an attack from behind. By this means, the more poorly trained pilots may be given the opportunity to score victories as a result of the slower closure speed and greater time for firing . . .[51]

It is difficult to imagine Luftwaffe directives from 1939–42 explicitly referring to "poorly trained pilots." One Luftwaffe general was even more pessimistic:

During aerial combat, the unit's cohesion was quickly lost, and it had to reassemble and take up a new offensive position. This was hardly ever accomplished, as such maneuvers presupposed a superior state of training, which was particularly lacking. The Jagdgruppen Kommandeure often stated that they would rather attack a superior enemy with four or six of their best pilots than take an entire Gruppe of 25–30 aircraft into the air because most pilots were too poorly trained to maintain contact . . .[52]

It is noteworthy that just as effective tactics were perfected, the human material was inadequate to execute them properly.

Let us leave the final verdict on the Luftwaffe's training debacle to a veteran 4./JG 26 Staffelkapitän, Hans Hartigs, as recorded by his Allied interrogators in late 1944:

His opinion was that the training of fighter pilots today is pitiful; he complained that pupils arrived from different schools having been taught by different methods according to personal choice of the instructors; he complained that blind-flying instruction was totally inadequate for interception in cloud and indeed that the majority of new pilots were afraid of cloud flying. He stated that in his Staffel he had no pilot to whom he could entrust the leadership of a section of four. The seasoned veteran summed up, "Things are not what they were in my days."[53]

The Invasion Front

Both Allied and German leaders were fully aware of the significance of the looming cross-Channel invasion. Göring bluntly told his operations staff, "Defense against this landing attempt is decisive for the outcome of the war."[54] The Luftwaffe command, despite the fearful losses its day-fighter units had sustained in the first months of 1944, still believed that it could mount a successful aerial response. While the withdrawal of units for rebuilding had temporarily reduced the strength of Luftflotte 3's fighter units in northern France to only about 125 serviceable aircraft by late May, the Luftwaffe high command had refined a complex scheme for reinforcing the invasion sector quickly once the Allies launched Overlord.[55] They recognized that the enemy's invasion attempt had to be defeated during its initial stages. The Reichsmarschall's directives stated, "The concentrated employment of all flying units in the first hours of a landing may be decisive for the outcome of the entire enterprise."[56] Indeed the Luftwaffe intended to throw the whole of its forces—bomber, ground attack, Zerstörer, and fighter—into the battle over the invasion beaches, as at Dieppe nearly two years before. Initially, it planned to employ its fighters primarily in an escort and air superiority role.[57]

As the invasion approached, it became clear that the available ground-attack strength was insufficient, and the fighters would have to function in a dual role, as both pure fighters and fighter-bombers. In May 1944, the Training Branch of the operations staff initiated a crash program to train fighter pilots in the nuances of ground-attack tactics and procedures. It sought to impart, in a very short time, skills that had long since vanished from the syllabus of the Luftwaffe fighter training schools. These included complex air-ground liaison and recognition procedures, the effective use of the Revi C/12 D gun sight for bomb dropping, and a grasp of basic land warfare tactics.[58] As many fighter aircraft as possible were to be

equipped with ETC centreline bomb racks so that they could participate directly in the ground battle. Overall, the Luftwaffe command hoped to contest air superiority successfully with the Allied air forces in the first days, thereby freeing up the whole of the force to repel the invasion.

Nor were the logistical underpinnings of this undertaking neglected. The Luftwaffe command took note of the experiences gained during the months preceding the invasion in preparing for battle against the Allied air forces. Luftwaffe units in France in early 1944 reported increasing enemy fighter and fighter-bomber attacks, augmented by medium and heavy bomber strikes, against airfields, transportation centers, rail communications, and radar and signals installations.[59] After these experiences, the Luftflotte 3 ground organization was to have implemented sophisticated techniques of camouflage, concealment, dispersal, and mobility as a means of reducing losses of material and personnel to air attack. Staging fields for the units transiting from the Reich had been selected months in advance. The arriving RLV units would escort Ju 52 transports flying in the ground personnel and spare parts.[60] Optimism may not have been high, but the Luftflotte 3 staff believed its augmented forces would play a significant part in combating the Anglo-American landing.

At dawn on June 6 the Western Allies began the long-anticipated invasion of France, storming the beaches of Normandy under the protection of naval gunfire after a night in which three divisions of para-troopers and glider-borne infantry dropped in the rear of the coastal defenses. The long-standing plan of the RLM to reinforce the fighter force in France with units from the home-defense forces should have gone into effect immediately. Upon receipt of the code words "Dr. Gustav West" 17 RLV Jagdgruppen were to tank up and take off for prepared fields in France. By afternoon the fighters were to have been attacking the beachheads in full force, helping the Army drive the invaders back into the sea. The expectation was that this would be a short campaign—the Wehrmacht's specialty. Nothing happened according to plan; the Luftwaffe failed yet another critical mission. The reasons for the failure are many, and start with a delay in issuing the order to execute. The initial reports from Normandy were confusing, and the Allied deception campaign put enough doubt into the Luftwaffe High Command as to the principal landing site that they waited for confirmation—and Hitler's approval. The code words were finally passed to the Jagdgruppen at about 0830. The morning weather was bad on their home bases, delaying takeoffs in most cases until afternoon. The transfer flights required refueling stops, and the designated intermediate fields were not prepared for the masses of fighters which descended on them. Servicing the aircraft and organizing the final leg of the transfer caused further delays.

As night fell, small numbers of RLV fighters began arriving at their assigned bases. Many dropped out en route; 15 I./JG 27 Bf 109s crash-landed after their pilots got lost and ran out of fuel. The night of June 6/7 was a *Horrornacht*, a *Katastrophe*, in the words of the unit leaders. Almost without exception, their new French bases were nothing but emergency fields. They were unprepared for permanent occupation, lacking such essentials as control rooms, quarters, fuel, communications equipment, and adequately camouflaged dispersals. The alibi the Luftflotte 3 staff gave to the inevitable RLM investigators was a lack of manpower for construction work. A spring inspection trip by an influential Berlin general such as Galland could have called attention to the deficiencies, but this was apparently not done.[61]

No RLV fighter played any role in the fighting on D-Day (a term not yet known to the Germans, of course). The effort by II. Jagdkorps totaled 121 combat sorties, all by the *Kanalgeschwader*, JG 2 and JG 26. The ground support command, II. Fliegerkorps, reported 51 sorties, all by SG 4, which was already in France. According to one source, the Eighth Air Force and the two tactical air forces, the Ninth Air Force (U.S.) and Second Tactical Air Force (RAF), flew 14,000 combat sorties on June 6.[62]

By the evening of June 7, only the five *Wilde Sau* Gruppen and five Zerstörergruppen remained operational in Germany. The 17 RLV Jagdgruppen now in France would have contributed a force of 900 aircraft to the defenses, had they been at full strength. However, most were at half strength or less and, owing to the disorganization resulting from the rapid move and the chaotic state of most French airfields, only 289 were reported operational in the strength return radioed to the RLM on the night of June 7. Although the RLM fed reinforcements to France for more than two months, this figure never grew appreciably. Most of the German fighters were destroyed on the ground. The new bases were located very quickly by the Allies; the complaints radioed by the arriving RLV formation leaders were intercepted and decoded by the Ultra organization, which distributed an accurate order of battle of the expanded Luftflotte 3 on June 8. The vital importance of ground dispersal and camouflage, which was second nature to the two *Kanalgeschwader*, had to be learned by the new arrivals through bitter experience. Allied tactical fighters were overhead from dawn until dusk, searching for suspicious movements on the ground; taxiing aircraft were always favorite targets. The pilots of the new units had to service their own aircraft and manhandle them into and from cover until their ground crews made their laborious way from the Reich by motor vehicles or night flights in Ju 52s. Several Gruppen suffered so badly that they could put up only a handful of aircraft for operations. III./JG 1 never became operational at all; it was sent back to Germany on June 14 for rebuilding.[63]

Had the RLV Jagdgruppen arrived on the *Invasionsfront* (Invasion Front) on D-Day and ready for operations, they would possibly have had an impact on the course of the invasion. As it was, they could never concentrate in sufficient strength to have an appreciable effect on events on the ground. About half of the new fighter units were assigned to II. Fliegerkorps, the ground-attack command which had established a fully staffed headquarters in France in advance of the invasion. The combat experience of most of the pilots arriving from Germany was limited to bomber interception, and they proved totally ineffective in their new role as fighter-bomber pilots. On June 12, the Ultra organization decoded an order calling for all Jagdgruppen in France to remove their bomb racks and keep them off until further notice. This was clear evidence that the Luftwaffe's defense plan had collapsed, and that in the future the Allied ground forces would have to contend with nothing more dangerous from the German fighters than cannon fire and an occasional WGr 21 rocket. The commanding general and staff of II. Fliegerkorps were soon sent back to Germany. Its Jagdgruppen were given to II. Jagdkorps' Jagddivision 5, which already commanded the other fighter units nearest the invasion zone. The 20 Jagdgruppen ultimately under Jagddivision 5's direction overstrained its control apparatus, and most fighter missions during the invasion period had to be conducted as *freie Jagden*, uncontrolled sweeps, which was an inefficient use of already insufficient resources.[64]

German commanders quickly realized that the active and passive measures for contesting Allied air superiority were not equal to the tasks facing them in Normandy. Luftwaffe airfields in northern France had to deal with conditions far worse than those in the Reich territory. As a result, the Luftwaffe high command emphasized that "the flying forces and the ground organization are a single weapon," and sought to instill "warlike deportment" even in the personnel manning second-line airfields.[65] The existing air-raid-warning service was greatly strengthened, since Allied fighter-bomber attacks often occurred with little or no warning. Camouflage and concealment were raised almost to art forms, with aircraft removed from camouflage immediately before a sortie and replaced there almost the moment the propeller stopped turning. Anti-aircraft defense and other measures came under the direction of a *Führer der Flugplatzverteidigung* (Airfield Defense Commander), responsible for training, implementation of new defense measures, and the actual conduct of operations if the base came under attack.

By early August 1944, II. Jagdkorps had withdrawn its fighter forces from its airfields to the north and northwest of Paris, since Allied fighters often intercepted German aircraft shortly after takeoff. The chief of staff of II. Jagdkorps, Oberst Martin Mettig, recalled:

> It soon became evident that the Lille area was too near the front line. Fighter units operating in this area had to take off as soon as a report of enemy aircraft was received through the aircraft warning service if they were not to run the risk of being pinned to the ground by enemy fighter squadrons, waiting over the airfields at an altitude of 2,000–3,000 meters [6,500–10,000 ft.], ready to attack from an advantageous position any aircraft taxiing to take off or actually taking off.[66]

The new bases, located east of Paris, while marginally less vulnerable to direct attack by Allied aircraft, compelled the Luftwaffe to fly greater distances, using precious fuel and decreasing operational loiter times. The hope of using the Luftflotte 3 and RLV fighter forces as ground-attack aircraft having quickly proved vain, the missions of the fighters were limited to providing a modicum of air cover over key German ground deployments and hunting Allied spotting aircraft that were registering the fire of land and naval artillery against the hard-pressed infantry fighting in the *bocage* country. Mettig bitterly noted, "Our own fighter force became the

A 491st Bomb Group B-24J in flight under the protection of friendly escorts. (*ww2images*)

universal scapegoat, and was blamed for every setback and loss."

The day fighters left in the Reich were spread very thinly. Jagddivision 2 lost all of its day fighters, as did Jagddivision 3, after a few weeks of flux. The majority of the active units were concentrated around Nuremberg in Jagddivision 7. Major Gerhard Schöpfel took over the JG zbV Stab from Major Walther Dahl, who became Kommodore of JG 300 and served as the JD 7 *Gefechtsverband* leader. Dahl's fighter units were I. and II./JG 300, and I./JG 301. III./JG 300 was still based south of Berlin in Jagddivision 1, flying *Wilde Sau* night missions in defense of that city, but it was also charged with flying day escort for ZG 26, a mission for which it was completely unsuited. Schöpfel's JG zbV Stab, shortly renamed Stab/JG 4, was not to participate in combat operations, but was to supervise the units and pilots shuttling back and forth from the *Invasionsfront*. Schöpfel had a number of units to administer. Two Gruppen, III./JG 11 and II./JG 27, served as assembly Gruppen for Fw 190 and Bf 109 pilots, respectively. III./JG 1 soon returned from France for rebuilding; IV./JG 54 and II./JG 5, which had just joined the RLV from the Eastern Front, were still training. II./ZG 76 was also reforming, alone, at Prague. The other Zerstörer units were all operational, but had to be employed with caution. The ZG 26 Stab, I. and II./ZG 26 remained isolated at Königsberg, in East Prussia, while the ZG 76 Stab, II./ZG 1, and I./ZG 76 were based in the Vienna area as part of Jagddivision 8. The only single-engine fighter Gruppe in Jagddivision 8 was I./JG 302, which had recently transferred to Vienna-Götzendorf from the Berlin area. Its role had changed from night fighting to day-bomber interception. It was now a "heavy Gruppe," with three Staffeln in Bf 109G-6/U4 "gunboats" with 30-mm engine cannon and 20-mm cannon in underwing tubs, and a new 4. Staffel, formerly 12./JG 51, that flew standard Bf 109Gs as high cover. One more fighter Gruppe was available to Jagddivision 8 to oppose flights over Hungarian airspace. This was the Bf 109-equipped Hungarian Jagdgruppe 101, the "Red Pumas," based at Budapest.

The next major change in the RLV order of battle came on June 14, when IV.(Sturm)/JG 3 left the *Invasionsfront* and joined Jagddivision 8. Sending the specialized Sturmgruppe to France had been a big mistake, quickly realized. It had been assigned to II. Fliegerkorps, and the pilots had flown their lumbering "battering rams" on several bombing missions—obviously very prudently, as they had suffered no losses. Major Dahl wanted the Sturm-gruppe for his own Jagddivision 7 *Gefechtsverband* in exchange for I./JG 301, which he had already been ordered to send to France. His entreaties had the desired result and, by June 21, IV.(Sturm)/JG 3 had relocated to Ansbach, as part of Jagddivision 7.[67]

The Luftwaffe High Command's plan for the future employment of its fighter force was in reality nothing but a wish. If the invasion were repulsed, the RLV fighters would return to Germany. If the Allies succeeded in retaining their foothold in France, then the Eighth Air Force would at least be fully employed on tactical duties for some time, allowing the few fighters in the Reich to be concentrated against the Fifteenth Air Force coming from Italy. The USSTAF staff, however, had other plans. The Eighth Air Force was able to send a small number of B-17s to Hannover

oil targets on June 15, to show the minuscule RLV force in northern Germany that it had not been forgotten. In the meantime, despite its broad geographic responsibilities, Twining's Fifteenth scheduled a number of trips to the Reich. A raid on Munich on the 9th met unexpectedly strong resistance. Italian fighters and the three Luftwaffe Jagdgruppen still based in northern Italy attacked the north-bound stream, stripping away much of the escort. I./JG 302, flying its first mission as a day RLV unit, made a close-formation attack on the bomber stream west of Vienna while 4./JG 302 sparred with the escorting P-51s. The ex-*Wilde Sau* pilots flew a very successful mission, claiming six B-24s shot down, 10 B-24s shot from formation, and one P-51 downed, for no losses. American losses to all causes equaled 16 B-24s, one B-17, and one P-47.[68]

The Fifteenth returned to Munich on the 13th, visited a number of central European oil targets on the 14th, and bombed refineries in Vienna and Bratislava on the 16th. The Axis fighters in Italy did not make an appearance on this day, and the American escort reached the target areas at full strength. The B-24s bombing Bratislava lost only three to the Pumas and II./ZG 76. A Slovak Bf 109 squadron scrambled, but apparently circled Bratislava, their capital, without attacking the bombers. The Pumas, however, scored heavily against the escort, claiming one P-51 and seven P-38s. The defenders from Vienna, comprising I./JG 300, I./JG 302, II./ZG 1, and I./ZG 76, claimed 20 B-24s, one P-38, and two P-51s. American losses totaled nine B-24s, 2 B-17s, seven P-38s, and one P-51. American fighters claimed 40 victories; the Axis lost at least 16 German and Hungarian fighters.[69]

The Eighth Air Force returned to strategic bombing in full force on the 18th, with a raid by 1,378 bombers on targets in Hamburg, Hannover, and Bremen. No Luftwaffe fighters were seen; all were grounded by bad weather, and the 11 bomber losses were all credited to the Flak. Two days later the Eighth put up 1,965 bombers and 1,111 fighters against oil and industrial targets in Germany and Poland. The 167 airborne defenders performed as well as possible against this armada, although only 53 single-engine and 62 twin-engine fighters made contact. The key, as always, was to concentrate on that part of the bomber stream

Fw 190A-8 "white 21" of II./JG 6 at Königsberg-Neumark during the unit's conversion from the Me 410. (*Buchholz via Price*).

where the escort protection was weakest. Ferreting out these weak spots was, as ever, the job of the Fühlungshalter aircraft.

The three bomb divisions left England and headed east across the North Sea in separate formations. I. Jagdkorps ordered its fighters to concentrate in two areas: I. and II./JG 300 rendezvoused near Magdeburg, while III./JG 300 and I. and II./ZG 26 assembled over the Muritz See. The 3rd Bomb Division turned south first, to hit targets in central Germany. The Magdeburg formation attacked them, but succeeded in downing only two B-17s for the loss of six planes, while claiming six B-17s and two P-51s. The 1st and 2nd Bomb Divisions crossed Schleswig-Holstein, and the 1st turned back to hit targets in the Hamburg area in the rear; these B-17s encountered no Luftwaffe aircraft. The B-24s of the 2nd Bomb Division were left alone over the Baltic in a strung-out formation, with only one P-51 group nearby. When the leading 44th Bomb Group turned south toward its target, Pölitz, the 492nd Bomb Group, which was echeloned to the left of the 44th, could not keep up, and its formation spread further. III./JG 300 then attacked the rear box in the stream, drawing the escort, which downed 13 of the Messerschmitts. The 492nd was now completely exposed, however, and was set upon by the Me 410s of ZG 26, which made repeated attacks from front and rear. Thirteen B-24s went down or broke from formation to head for sanctuary in Sweden before the relief group of P-51s finally arrived to punish the Me 410s; 12 of these were shot down or crash-landed back at their Königsberg base. The enthusiastic German pilots claimed 39 B-24s and five P-51s, triple the true loss of 13 and two. Most of the claims were confirmed. The rules were obviously bent slightly; the crash sites of aircraft attacked over water could not be located and matched with the claims, as was the standard practice. The only other RLV unit within range of the bomber force, II./ZG 76, flew north from Prague, but was hit by the P-51s before reaching the bombers and lost three Me 410s with their crews.[70]

The Eighth Air Force mounted another full-strength mission to Germany on the 21st. This became known as the "Poltava Mission." The bombers executed a very complex flight plan in which Berlin was attacked from all directions. This mass of bombers effectively screened an attack on the Ruhland oil installation south of Berlin by two wings of 3rd Bomb Division B-17s that proceeded east to Russia after

bombing. I. Jagdkorps had very little success, downing only 14 bombers and no fighters, but fighters from the Eastern Front had a very significant role in the mission and consequent Allied strategy. The *Ostfront* Gruppen I. and III./JG 51 were flying a practice mission over Poland when Major Fritz Losigkeit received the surprising order to attack an approaching heavy bomber formation. Losigkeit, an experienced RLV pilot now serving as JG 51 Kommodore, succeeded in forming his fighters up and made a frontal attack on the B-17s, downing one before it began "raining Mustangs," in Losigkeit's words. One of the P-51s was shot down in the ensuing dogfights and crash-landed on the edge of the Bobruisk airfield. A mission map was found inside the cockpit—destination Poltava, a previously unknown airfield built specifically for the American Frantic missions. In addition, in one of the few recorded cases in which the Luftwaffe's trouble-ridden He 177 four-engine bomber operated as a makeshift Fühlungshalter, a machine of the long-range recce unit 2./(F) 100 tailed the Fortresses to their Poltava base and photographed it. Luftflotte 6 had the information within hours. IV. Fliegerkorps, which had been attacking Soviet marshalling yards since March, was swiftly redirected against this new target. KG 4's pathfinders illuminated the field, and 180 He 111s and Ju 88s attacked with great effect. Some 43 B-17s and 15 P-51s were destroyed on the ground.[71] Recriminations between the Allies were bitter; the Soviets had insisted on defending the field themselves, despite American offers to do so, but had provided no night protection at all. American enthusiasm for these shuttle flights waned, never to be restored.[72]

The Eighth Air Force restricted itself to French targets for the next few days, while the Fifteenth paid two visits to Ploesti. The Soviets had begun their summer offensive, Operation Bagration, which crushed Army Group Center and pushed the front line out of the Soviet Union and roughly back to the prewar borders. On the 23rd III./JG 11, which was off operations at Reinsehlen, received orders to transfer to the east immediately to reinforce Luftflotte 6. II./JG 5 would take over its role as an assembly Gruppe. III./JG 11 had always been a home-defense unit, and few of its personnel had any direct knowledge of the Eastern Front. The Luftwaffe fighter force has frequently been called a "fire brigade" for the frequency with which its units were called on to change missions and fronts to meet emergencies. But that term implies a definite plan, purposefulness on the part of the Luftwaffe High Command which just was not there. The sudden uprooting of unprepared units such as III./JG 11 was no more than a panicky reaction to events. Simply put, the Luftwaffe was too small for the missions assigned it.[73]

June 26—Vienna

The Fifteenth Air Force scheduled a major mission to Reich oil targets on the 26th. A total of 677 B-17s and B-24s took off to bomb six refineries, hydrogenation plants, and oil depots in the Vienna area. From Vienna, Oberst Gotthardt Handrick, the commander of Jagddivision 8 (code-named Rosenkavalier), coordinated a defensive force comprising his own German fighters, those of two Axis allies, Slovakia and Hungary, and those of neighboring Jagddivision 7. The bombers flew north-northeast from Foggia, Italy, across the Adriatic, Yugoslavia, and Hungary. The stream apparently made a slight left turn at Lake Balaton, a favorite landmark, and turned hard left near Bratislava. The combat wings then separated, the leading 304th Wing attacking Moosbierbaum west of Vienna while the others bombed several targets nearer to the city. The Pumas were the first to strike, as the stream passed over their Veszprém base. The Hungarian pilots claimed three B-24s, one P-38 and one P-51, but lost three killed. The stream next clipped a corner of Slovakia, whose armed forces were under great pressure from Germany to increase their efforts in defense of their own country (which was in fact secretly negotiating with the Allies), and its most combat-worthy squadron was ordered to scramble its eight Bf 109G-6s. They claimed one B-24, probably from the 459th Bomb Group, but were savagely mauled by the 52nd and 82nd Fighter Group escorts, which killed three pilots while shooting down four Messerschmitts and forcing three more to crash-land. II./ZG 76 Me 410s flew south from Prague and attacked the stream near Bratislava. They lost four Zerstörer, while claiming four B-24s, 2 P-51s, and 1 P-38. They also drew the escort fighters to themselves, facilitating the attacks of the remaining German force.[74]

Handrick had split these fighters into two *Gefechts-verbände*. The first, containing I. and II./JG 300, and II./ZG 1, was directed toward the Moosbierbaum bombers, while the second, with I./JG 302 and I./ZG 76, was ordered to attack the main stream in the Vienna area. The turn of the 304th Wing at the Initial

The Fw 190A-8/R2 *Sturmbock* of Hptm. Wilhelm Moritz, Kommandeur of IV.(Sturm)/JG 3, in the fall of 1944. Notable markings are the spiral spinner, black cowl, black wavy line (Gruppe identification) on a white Geschwader band, and the double chevron identification marking of a Gruppen-kommandeur. (*Smith*)

Point for its bomb run to Moosbierbaum left one section of the 455th Bomb Group far out on the right flank. This was the opportunity for which the 27 Bf 110 crews of II./ZG 1 had waited for months. A quick head-on attack on the section brought several B-24s down and started others smoking. The Zerstörer then broke away to try to avoid the escorts, just as the 61 JG 300 Messerschmitts and Focke-Wulfs began an attack from 12 o'clock high. Ignoring both the escorts and the target-area Flak, they continued their attacks from all directions to close range, colliding with one B-24. The 455th Group lost ten B-24s in these attacks, in its worst day of the war; the other three groups in the wing lost eight. II./ZG 1 claimed four B-24s in its quick attack, while losing 5 KIA, 2 WIA, and four Bf 110s. The two JG 300 Gruppen claimed 28 B-24s downed or shot from formation, while losing 5 KIA, 2 WIA, and nine fighters.[75]

The main bomber stream was protected by most of the escorts, and proved a difficult target for the other German force. I./ZG 76 claimed three B-24s in the target area, but lost eight Zerstörer to defensive fire. I./JG 302 attacked the wing targeting Floridsdorf, and claimed three B-24s downed or shot from formation (two probably from the 485th Bomb Group), and two P-51s, while losing three fighters and their pilots. The Allied radio-intercept service next heard Rosen-kavalier order all fighters still airborne to assemble over the Neusiedler See to await the withdrawing bombers. This was done, and five B-17s, three B-24s, and one P-51 were claimed in this area. The last shot at the bomber stream was taken by II./JG 77 from northern Italy, which claimed one of the returning B-24s.[76]

Rosenkavalier could claim a tactical success on the 26th. The full-strength defensive effort scrambled 117 twin-engine plus 203 single-engine fighters from three nations; 72 plus 168 made contact; 44 Axis fighters were lost on operations; American losses to all causes totaled three B-17s, 35 B-24s, and six fighters.[77]

RLV successes during the following week were scant. A Fifteenth Air Force raid on Budapest on the 27th was out of range of Jagddivision 7, and the German and Hungarian fighters in Jagddivision 8 (the Slovaks were permanently off operations) were ineffectual. Jagddivision 7 did a poor job on the 29th, putting up only 72 single-engine and 37 twin-engine fighters against a full-strength Eighth Air Force raid on the Böhlen refinery and other oil and aircraft industry targets in the Leipzig area. Only seven victory claims were filed by German fighters. On the following day the two Jagddivision 8 Zerstörergruppen flew one of their last successful missions. A major raid to the Blechhammer refinery complex was foiled by the weather. The bomb wings split to look for targets of opportunity, and II./ZG 1 and I./ZG 76 took advantage of cloud cover over Lake Balaton to shoot down four B-24s from the 460th Bomb Group and two from the 465th, the only bombers lost on the mission. The Hungarians were also present, and apparently claimed the same bombers. Fighters from the Croatian Air Force put in a rare appearance, but lost five of their six planes. The Germans lost one Bf 110, one Me 410, and one I./JG 302 Bf 109; the Hungarians, several Bf 109s.[78]

Fighter units shuttled in and out of I. Jagdkorps in late June and early July. These did not represent true reinforcements, which were almost impossible to find. On June 27, III./JG 53 moved permanently from the Italian Front to the Reich, but required training and re-equipment before joining the RLV order of battle. The ex-RLV Jagdgruppen on the Invasionsfront were being worn down so quickly and completely that the plan to keep them up to strength with individual reinforcements drawn from two assembly Gruppen in the Reich was scrapped. The new plan called for entire Gruppen to return to the Reich from France to be rested, re-equipped, and restored to strength before being sent back to the Invasionsfront meat grinder. The I./JG 3 air echelon moved from France to Germany on June 27 for this purpose, followed in the next three weeks by six more Jagdgruppen. The two assembly Gruppen were given new roles. II./JG 27 received new Bf 109G-6/AS fighters and returned to RLV operations as the high-altitude Gruppe in Jagddivision 8, while II./JG 5 was sent to France, where nine of its pilots were killed in its first five missions. This luckless Gruppe returned to the Reich permanently on July 1. III./JG 1, the first Gruppe to return from France to rebuild, was sent back on July 5, but most of its new pilots were either hastily converted bomber pilots or ill with malaria, and expectations for its performance were not high.[79]

The size of the Luftflotte Reich day-fighter force had peaked in early 1944. The following table shows the dramatic drop in strength after D-Day, when most RLV units were shifted to Luftflotte 3. Only operational units are tallied; units in the Reich for rehabilitation are not included. The Invasionsfront was a bottomless sump for Luftwaffe aircraft (and aircrew); note that Luftflotte 3 had only 37 percent of its establishment strength in fighters on June 30, and only 49 percent of these were operational.

Day-Fighter Strength of Luftflotte Reich and Luftflotte 3, by Quarters[80]

Date	Command	Establishment Strength	Aircraft on Hand	Operational Aircraft
Dec 31, 1943	Luftflotte Reich	1,108	758	548
	Luftflotte 3	388	237	148
Mar 31, 1944	Luftflotte Reich	1,308	949	643
	Luftflotte 3	364	134	92
Jun 30, 1944	Luftflotte Reich	684	471	254
	Luftflotte 3	1,208	444	216

On July 2, a major Fifteenth Air Force attack on Budapest posed another severe test for Jagddivision 8. The bombers flew straight north from Italy in a single stream. Rosenkavalier attempted to assemble all of his fighters into a single Gefechtsverband comprising 28 II./JG 27 Bf 109s, 39 I./JG 302 Bf 109s, 20 Hungarian Bf 109s, 22 II./ZG 1 Bf 110s, and 20 I./ZG 76 Me 410s. The stream's turn east toward Budapest caught the defenders by surprise, and apparently the Axis battle formation never formed up. Few attacks were made on the bombers prior to the bombing, which according to the RLM report did severe damage to the Budapest refineries. Most Gruppen were ordered south to Lake Balaton to await the withdrawing bomber stream.

They were apparently left on their own to get at the bombers through gaps in the escort screen, which was denser than usual owing to the presence of two Eighth Air Force fighter groups which were basing temporarily in Italy as part of Operation Frantic.[81]

The fortunes of the intercepting Gruppen varied widely. II./JG 27, now tasked as a high-altitude escort Höhengruppe, had no one to escort, and attacked a B-24 wing, claiming one bomber before the escorts arrived. Eight Messerschmitts were shot down, killing five pilots and injuring two. II./ZG 1 lost one Bf 110, and made no claims. I./ZG 76 reported excellent results. Concentrating on the single B-17 combat wing as part of it split off to seek a secondary target, the pilots filed claims for 13 B-17s shot down, for the loss of only one Me 410. Only four B-17s failed to return to Italy, however.

The Messerschmitt pilots of I./JG 302 made a successful interception in the face of heavy opposition, and suffered very high casualties. Uffz. Willi Reschke was a new pilot who was flying his third combat mission. He reported:

> The Gruppe scrambled from Vienna-Götzendorf at 0927 . . . Our takeoff orders from Rosenkavalier came late; our formation was not the best, and a report of *Indianer* (enemy fighters) unnerved our pilots. One 4. Staffel escort fighter suddenly dove to the ground, probably from oxygen failure. The Gruppe saw smoke from Budapest, and reached the heavy bombers after they had bombed and were turning south. The P-51 escorts were few more in number than our 4. Staffel, which attacked them. The rest of us formed an *Angriffskeil* [attack wedge] behind a B-24 *Pulk*, and attacked from 500 meters [1,600 ft.] above. I hit a B-24 in the wing; it eventually dove and broke up. The 4. Staffel was still holding off the P-51s; this allowed the Gruppe to make a second attack. I fired at a B-24, hitting it in the rear fuselage and working forward. The bomber did a split-S and crashed. I was hit in the radiator and needed to land quickly. I couldn't find an airfield, but made a smooth belly landing in a clover field. I was taken to Budapest, there to be knocked unconscious by a mob before being rescued by the SS. I was taken to a hospital and returned to base by train the same day. My Kommandeur reported the mob action, and RLV pilots were soon given yellow armbands saying "Deutsche Luftwaffe."[82]

Reschke was awarded the Iron Cross 2nd Class for his two victories. The Gruppe claimed 19 B-24s

downed or shot from formation and two P-51s in this engagement, plus a B-17 in a second sortie. The Gruppe lost 10 KIA, 1 WIA, and 10 Bf 109s. Their target was the 304th Bomb Wing, which was escorted by the 52nd Fighter Group. Five 456th Bomb Group B-24s were lost to the Messerschmitts' rear attacks, some of which were pressed to 180 meters' (200 yards') range. One 52nd Group Mustang was lost; the other Gruppe claim for a P-51 matches a loss by the 4th Fighter Group. The 52nd Group pilots claimed seven Bf 109s and four Fw 190s, although there were no Focke-Wulf fighters airborne in the theater.

The Hungarian Air Force scrambled all three of its fighter squadrons to defend its capital city. They were led by their Gruppenkommandeur, Major Aladár Heppes, the "Old Puma." They too missed the battle group rendezvous and flew an independent mission. They claimed seven bombers, which match no known losses but were possibly B-24s which had been shot from formation by I./JG 302, and were then bounced by Mustangs from the Eighth Air Force's 4th Fighter Group, which was flying a sweep from Italy. Dogfights were the Hungarians' preferred mode of fighting, and they showed much more skill than the Americans expected. The Pumas lost 3 KIA, 1 WIA, and four Bf 109Gs in the battle. The Americans returned to Foggia less four P-51s; two more made it back with severe damage and seriously wounded pilots. Two of the missing pilots were captured, while two were killed. One of the latter was Captain Ralph Hofer, a well-known ace who proved to be the highest-scoring Eighth Air Force pilot killed in aerial combat during the entire war. As one Fifteenth Air Force Mustang pilot gleefully noted in an interview, the cocky ex-Eagle Squadron boys of the 4th Group had gotten the "living shit" kicked out of them.[83]

The battle on July 2 brought down 15 American bombers and eight P-51s, at a cost of 20 German and four Hungarian fighters. It demonstrated once again that the fighters of the RLV, even when they fought bravely and well, could not prevent the destruction of Germany's critical defense industries. The leadership scrambled to find answers. On the 3rd the Emergency Fighter Program was promulgated. The production of all aircraft but jets, single-engine fighters, and modern twin-engine fighters was to stop forthwith; capacity thus gained was to be used for fighters. But the key shortages were not in fighter aircraft, but in pilots and fuel. Bomber Gruppen began disbanding for both reasons; their pilots were quickly sent to operational training units for a few hours of conversion training before joining the fighter Gruppen. And Ultra intercepted an interesting message ordering all transport units to give up a specific number of pilots to the fighter arm; the records of those pilots who passed up the opportunity to volunteer were so to indicate. Another message made the same request of certain operational bomber units. Ultra also picked up an order by Göring restricting flying by fighter unit commanders and staff officers to especially important operations, "owing to intolerable losses." Several messages on the effects of the fuel shortage were also intercepted; one cut back on test flights at the factories and transit depots, while a second restricted courier flights within the Reich to the communications flights of Hitler, Göring, and the Wehrmacht High Command.[84]

A Fw 190A-8/R2 *Sturmbock* with no visible unit or individual markings. The aircraft was in fact assigned to Lt. Oskar "Ossi" Romm, Kapitän of 15.(Sturm)/JG 3, and was probably photographed revving up at Schongau in August. (*Rosch*)

July 7—Leipzig: The Sturmgruppe Sees Action

A favorable weather forecast for July 7 allowed the USSTAF to order the Eighth and Fifteenth Air Forces to fly a rare joint mission. Both air fleets targeted oil targets. This was a day that Genmaj. Schmid had been dreading. He had to split his meager forces, sending Jagddivision 8 against the Fifteenth, and Jagddivisionen 1 and 7 against the Eighth. However, he did have a new weapon ready to deploy. The first Sturmgruppe, Hptm. Wilhelm Moritz's IV.(Sturm)/JG 3, was fully operational and would fly as part of Major Walther Dahl's Jagddivision 7 battle formation. MGen. Anderson's plan for the Eighth was excessively complex for this stage of the campaign. The two B-17 divisions, the 1st and 3rd, were to head directly toward Berlin to draw most of the defenders before turning sharply south for the refineries and armament industry targets in central Germany. The B-24-equipped 2nd Division, with fewer escorts, would turn southeast, cross the B-17 stream, and take a more direct path to its targets, which were in the same area. Schmid quickly deduced the target area and ordered all of his fighters to concentrate near Leipzig. The B-17s were running late and low, and the B-24 formation was disrupted somewhat while passing through them. The 3rd Division was a full 30 minutes late and was ignored totally by the controllers, somewhat simplifying their job. They could order attacks on the 1st Division's tight boxes of B-17s or the 2nd Division's looser formations of B-24s. The choice was obvious; all fighters were directed toward the B-24s. The orders were even more specific; an airborne radio intercept operator heard the Jagddivision 1 controller order his fighters to concentrate on the third wing in the stream, which was less heavily escorted than the van. These orders were carried out, and this formation, the 14th Combat Wing, was soon under heavy attack.[85]

Once they approached the stream, the German formations operated independently; it was up to the leader of each to find a way past the escorts to get at the bombers. The largest formation comprised 42 ZG 26 Me 410s escorted by 37 III./JG 300 Bf 109s. Approaching from the northeast, it attracted most of the P-38s and P 51s. The *Wilde Sau* fighters did their best to defend the vulnerable Me 410s, but claimed only one P-51 while losing 4 KIA, 3 WIA, and 13 Bf 109s. One flight from this Bf 109 Gruppe did reach the B-24s, and claimed two. The Zerstörer, always favorite targets of the American fighters, did as well as could be expected. Captain James Morris, the leading ace of the P-38-equipped 20th Fighter Group, was shot down by the crossfire put up by the rear gunners of a flight which he was chasing. A 4th Fighter Group P-51 collided with a Me 410, and both went down. ZG 26 lost a total of 5 KIA, 4 WIA, and eight Me 410s, while claiming four B-24s.[86]

The second formation contained only a single Gruppe, II./JG 5, which had scrambled from Salzwedel on its first major RLV mission. It was overwhelmed by the escorts, and lost 2 KIA, 4 WIA, and ten Bf 109s for claims of one B-24 and one P-51.[87]

The fighters from Jagddivision 7, approaching from the southeast, obviously benefited from all of the activity on the northern side of the stream. The formation comprised 26 Fw 190s of the Stab and II./JG 300, 32 I./JG 300 Bf 109s, and 44 IV.(Sturm)/ JG 3 Fw 190 assault fighters, all led by Major Walther Dahl, according to his own account. The Sturmgruppe Kommandeur, Hptm. Wilhelm Moritz, later stated emphatically that his Gruppe never formed up with the JG 300 fighters; Moritz observed them taking fire from the Leipzig Flak and deliberately kept his distance. The escort Gruppe, I./JG 300, was split up badly by the Flak, "spreading like the blades of a fan," according to Lt. Günther Sinnecker, but resumed formation just in time to be hit by the American fighters. They fulfilled their protection mission well, although this was perhaps inadvertent. The Gruppe lost 2 KIA, 6 WIA, and nine Bf 109s, while claiming five bombers and two P-51s. In the meantime Dahl's Stabsschwarm and II./JG 300 found an unprotected B-24 *Pulk* and made repeated attacks, resulting in claims for 28 B-24s, of which at least 21 were confirmed. The mode of these attacks is uncertain; Dahl claims in his memoir to have attacked from the rear, but his JG 300 pilots had never been trained in this tactic.[88]

There is no doubt as to the method of attack of Moritz's men, or the identity of their targets. The 492nd Bomb Group, flying the high right position in the 14th Combat Wing, should have been well shielded by the group behind it, but a series of mishaps, including the loss of one B-24 by collision, had left the 492nd straggling and exposed, as on June

Fw. Oskar Bösch of IV.(Sturm)/JG 3 prepares to board his Fw 190A-8/R2 "black 14" *Sturmbock* at Schongau in August. (*Bösch*)

20. Moritz sighted the B-24s flying at 6,500 meters (21,000 ft.) near Oschersleben and positioned his 44 pilots directly behind them for the first Gruppe-strength *Sturmangriff*. Most of the attackers formed up in close formation in a shallow vee, with Moritz at the point. He ordered tanks dropped, and assigned targets to individual Staffeln, with each to adjust its altitude as needed during the run-in from 1,000 meters (3,300 ft.) to firing range, which took about 1½ minutes. Firing began at Moritz's order, "*Pauke, Pauke!*" ("Beat the kettledrums!") The 2-cm cannon were generally fired at 400 meters (1,300 ft.), the 3-cm at 200 meters. Ammunition—especially the 3-cm—was typically consumed in this first pass, which was broken off at 100 meters by an *Abschwung* (split-S) in the direction chosen by each pilot, who was free to make a second pass or take evasive action, as warranted.

The Gruppe had its own protection Staffel, 2./JG 51, which had been part of I./JG 51 on the Eastern Front until the previous month, when it was separated from its Gruppe and ordered to join the RLV. Its orders were to fly in a separate vee 1,500 meters behind and above the main formation, to ward off the escorts. However, on this occasion there were no escorts in the immediate area, and it followed the main formation in a pass through the bombers.

Moritz's three-minute attack was devastating. The air thickened with exploding B-24s. Eleven 492nd Group Liberators went down, including the entire low squadron. The rest of the 14th Combat Wing did not escape unscathed; the 44th Group lost three, and the 392nd five B-24s. Most of the Fw 190s made it through the bomber formation without serious damage—the up-armored *Sturmböcke* were very resistant from the front to the bombers' .50-inch machine-gun fire—and the pilots returned to Illesheim to celebrate their victory. Casualties were taken, of course; four Fw 190s were shot down on the trip back, killing two pilots and injuring a third, and the 12. Staffel Kapitän and his wingman were shot down and killed by P-51s while attempting to land. The 12. Staffel was still equipped with the drag-producing *Krebsgerät*, which could not be jettisoned in such emergencies. Since no tactics had been developed for rear attacks using the rockets, and the pilots had been unable to fire them on the mission, Moritz now ordered the removal of the rocket tubes.

The number of bomber carcasses in the Bernberg–Halberstadt–Oschersleben area provided mute evidence of the Sturmgruppe's success. Genmaj. Galland, accompanied by a bevy of photographers and correspondents, hurried to Illesheim to congratulate the pilots and commanders on this rare victory. To the great dismay of Moritz and his pilots, Major Dahl horned in on the festivities, and most of the news reports gave primary credit to Dahl, who in reality had played no role in the development of assault unit equipment or tactics. Although Dahl had had a successful career as a fighter pilot and formation leader, he decided to make assault tactics his principal claim to fame, even titling his memoir *Rammjäger* ("Ram Fighter"), a term which was never used by the Sturmgruppe members themselves.

Galland knew where the truth lay, and upon his return to Berlin recommended the immediate formation of two more Sturmgruppen. He told his post-war interrogators that if not for the D-Day invasion, each of the RLV Jagdgeschwader would have contained a Sturmgruppe by mid-September, for a total of about nine. He also went on record as opposing the tactics ordered for battle formations containing Sturmgruppen. All of the Bf 109 escort Gruppen flew close to the Fw 190 assault Gruppe, which held tight formation until reaching the bombers. If the escort crust was penetrated by the American fighters, the *Sturmböcke* became easy targets. Galland would have freed one escort Gruppe from the formation, allowing it to roam and head off the American fighters. Freedom of action was always important to the old fighter pilot Galland.[89]

The pilots of the first Sturmgruppe now considered themselves an elite unit, and painted white eyes on the fronts of their leather flight jackets, to show the look of fear in the eyes of the bomber tail gunners as the *Sturmböcke* approached.[90] Of their 32 B-24 claims on the 7th, at least 27 were ultimately confirmed. Adding those of JG 300 and ZG 26 gives a total of 51 confirmed claims for B-24s, 2½ times the actual number lost, which was 20. This degree of overclaiming was common for RLV units during the last year of the war; historians cannot fully explain it, but simply must accept it.

The Americans had followed the earlier Sturmstaffel experiment with interest through Ultra intercepts, and had been expecting a larger assault formation—a Sturmgruppe—to appear on the I. Jagdkorps order of battle. Their reaction to the "*Blitzluftschlacht* [lightning air battle] over Ochsersleben," as it was called in the German press, took three forms:

1. Escort flight plans were changed to give more coverage to the rear of the combat wings;
2. Allied propaganda broadcasts threatened Major Dahl and "his" Sturmgruppe with imminent destruction, "in the air or on the ground";
3. The hapless 492nd Bomb Group was disbanded, the only Eighth Air Force group ever to suffer this ignominy.

This last was not simply a case of punishing an innocent victim; the group lagged the rest of the 2nd Bomb Division in a number of statistical parameters, and was obviously suffering from poor leadership and training.

The other RLV battle on the 7th, against the Fifteenth Air Force coming up from Italy, was almost anticlimactic. The day's main targets were the hydrogenation plants at Odertal and Blechhammer, in the southeastern tip of Silesia. The five Jagddivision 8 Gruppen were up in time, but Rosenkavalier was apparently surprised when the bomber stream, flying west of Budapest, continued due north. I./JG 302, II./ZG 1 and I./ZG 76 made stern attacks on the passing bombers, claiming a few, before all fighters were ordered to land and refuel. When the target became obvious, Jafü Oberschlesien ordered every fighter in its area to scramble and proceed to Blechhammer. These fighters were all from the operational training unit Jagdgruppe Ost, which ordered up both its instructors and its trainees—a total of 17 Fw 190s and 24 Bf 109s. They provided the only aerial defense in the target area, and claimed four B-24s and one P-51 at a cost of 1 KIA and 3 WIA, all in Bf 109s.[91]

The number of Jagddivision 8 fighters able to fly second sorties against the withdrawing bombers was pathetically small. The two Zerstörergruppen were not ordered up. II./JG 27 scrambled four Bf 109s, and lost one KIA for no successes. Twelve I./JG 302 pilots took off, apparently found an unprotected B-24 *Pulk*, and claimed six bombers for the loss of 1 KIA, 1 WIA, and four Bf 109s. Ten Hungarian fighters likewise made a quick attack on some unescorted B-24s, claiming four for the loss of one Messerschmitt, before the P-38s drove them off. One P-38 went down, as did one Puma. The Americans lost nine B-17s, 15 B-24s, and three fighters on the mission from all causes. The Axis lost only nine fighters, but failed to prevent significant damage to two of their most important oil installations.

The development of the effective new *Sturmtaktik* (assault tactic) is yet another example of the General Staff ethos which still pervaded the Luftwaffe in 1944. When something worked, details of the procedures were disseminated throughout the force in a swift and realistic "lesson learned" process. On August 25, 1944, the *Sturmangriff* was the first item highlighted in the Luftwaffe Operations Staff's "Tactical Instructions," a monthly synopsis of combat experience. It noted concisely,

> The Sturm-Jagdgruppe consists of 3 Staffeln, each with an established strength of 16 aircraft and pilots. The aircraft—Fw 190A-7 and A-8—are equipped with special armor for the assault attack. The MG 131 machine guns are removed, and the aircraft are armed with 2 MK 108 and 2 MG 151.
>
> Task of the Sturm-Jagdgruppe is the unconditional destruction of enemy bomber formations in the defense of the Reich, regardless of whether or not they are escorted by fighters. As a last resort, the enemy is to be destroyed via a ramming attack.
>
> The assault fighters are always assembled into task forces and employed against the enemy. The battle formation is the tightly closed-up Staffel wedge. *The assault attack will be carried out in close formation from behind with as near as possible a 0-degree angle of approach,* so as to divide the defense, shatter the enemy's morale, enhance our own *Angriffsschwung* [spirit of attack], and provide better protection against enemy fighters.
>
> The assault fighter unit will take its place in the *Gefechtsverband* so that it may be protected by high-altitude fighter Gruppen and other fighter Gruppen.
>
> The basic principle for the Sturmgruppe is: *"For every assault fighter which encounters the enemy, a sure kill."* [emphasis in original][92]

The Sturmgruppe tactics must be considered one of the few real Luftwaffe success stories of the 1944 air battles over Germany. At a time when most of its weaponry was obsolescent, and its pilot training standards declining, the RLV was still able to field a number of these high-morale units, which were used with deadly effect against USAAF bomber formations. It remains one of the most remarkable innovations of the 1939–45 air war.

Word of this attack method spread quickly from USSTAF intelligence to its operational units. "The tactics employed by the Luftwaffe were new; the results, successful. These tactics have been nicknamed 'Company Front.'"[93]

> In waves of as many as 30 single-engined e/a [enemy aircraft], in line abreast as in a "company front" formation, attacks are made from the rear of bomber formations. The first wave is succeeded by one or more waves of like or similar composition. Sometimes the attacks are made from a position higher than that of the bombers, sometimes from a lower position, and sometimes from a position on a level with the bombers. The methods of breakaway vary, but usually the e/a on or nearest the ends of each wave or "front" will break away right, or left, as the case may be, while those in or nearest the center will split-S out of the attack or will execute a climb over or a dive under the bombers. Most of the attacks have been pressed close home. The e/a's have been reported to open fire from 600 to 1,000 yards [550–900 meters].[94]

At the same time, American bomber units filed disquieting reports of "unusual battle damage." One account noted:

> The wings of several B-17s were reported to bow or to become bulged upon being hit by projectiles . . . In the case of Aircraft No. 43-38199, the projectile went through the wing into the engine and upon the explosion the engine caught afire. The nose fuze and shoulder of the projectile found in the engine . . . represented tangible evidence of guns larger in caliber than 20-mm . . .[95]

The terribly destructive effects of the 30-mm MK 108 cannon were a cautionary reminder that the Luftwaffe still had some fight in it.

Motivation and Morale

The deterioration of the war situation led a group of German Army officers to attempt to assassinate Hitler in mid-July. His survival led to a fearsome purge of the officer corps, and a heightening of the ideological fervor both on the home front and throughout the Wehrmacht. Luftwaffe participation in the plot was insignificant, which saved its personnel from the bloodbath, but not from new programs designed to bolster morale while keeping tabs on loyalty to the Nazi Party.

While sparing Hitler, the bomb blast killed General Korten, the Luftwaffe Chief of Staff. Much of his "New

Luftwaffe" was by then a shambles, but the "defensive clique" lost its most powerful friend at court. (Milch had been dismissed the month before.) Koller filled the post until a successor could be selected; he could do little to fend off Hitler's recriminations. On August 8, he recorded:

> At every conference the Führer goes on for hours on end about the Luftwaffe. He strongly reproaches the Luftwaffe. The reasons are our lack of aircraft, technological shortcomings, and noncompletion of the replacement squadrons in the Reich, the Me 262, etc. How am I to know what claims the Reichsmarschall and General Korten made or undo the wrongs committed from 1939 to 1942 through the total absence of any planning? It's a hard lot to have to answer to these errors.[96]

To add insult to injury, Göring bypassed Koller and named General Werner Kreipe, the *General der Fliegerausbildung* (Inspector of Luftwaffe Training), to the post of General Staff chief. Kreipe's tenure was brief and most inauspicious. He lasted only until September 21, when Hitler banned the mild-mannered "Fräulein" Kreipe from headquarters.

From the summer of 1944 on, the war was obviously lost, yet the Luftwaffe's fighter force continued the unequal struggle. That Luftwaffe day-fighter pilots fought to the end is beyond dispute; even after the surrender in May 1945 some 40 trainee pilots and instructors attempted to carry out a last-ditch sabotage mission against the Allied occupiers.[97] Many explanations have been offered to explain this tenacity: Nazi indoctrination, nationalism, youthful idealism, or a simple love of flying. That the senior Luftwaffe leadership was thoroughly Nazified is beyond dispute; Göring was the "Second Man" in the Third Reich, while Jeschonnek and Milch worked eagerly to further Hitler's designs. Schmid was literally "present at the creation"—he marched in the Beer Hall Putsch as a young cadet in 1923. Wever, the first Chief of the Luftwaffe General Staff, had asserted, "Our officer corps will be National Socialist, or it will not be at all."[98] Senior commanders, including Sperrle, Milch, and Richthofen, accepted enormous bribes from the Führer to ensure their loyalty.[99] Luftwaffe adjutant Nicolaus von Below recalls serving as Hitler's errand boy in July 1943, bringing Sperrle a check for 50,000 RM while the latter was summering near Biarritz.[100] But what accounts for the tenacity of

Fw 190A-8 "yellow 17" of 12.(Sturm)/JG 3, with rearward-firing 21-cm *Krebsgerät* (crab apparatus) rocket-launcher tube. The pilot is Willi Unger. (*Crow*)

the rank and file?

Recent scholarship on the German Army has noted that German combat morale remained high even though normal "primary group" cohesion was destroyed by high casualty rates. Omer Bartov, in his pioneering study of German Army combat motivation, notes that the military reverses and "demodernization" of the German Army in the last years of the war, coupled with intensified National Socialist indoctrination of the combat troops, generated a new level of fanaticism among German soldiers.[101] While the living and combat conditions of German airmen defending the Reich territory were not as desperate as those faced by the Army in the east, the RLV went through this process as well, as the Luftwaffe became progressively outclassed technically.

The top leadership certainly took explicit measures to ensure political conformity in the face of the deteriorating war situation. Earlier in the war, Luftwaffe morale issues were the responsibility of the *Wehrbetreuung* (Wb) organization. Its official charter was "to sustain the fighting efficiency of units by the creation and fostering of off-duty interests." Wb walked a fine line between simple entertainment and outright political and military indoctrination. Its programs included reading material, films, lecture series, games, a "Luftwaffe Comradeship Hour" radio show, cabaret and theatrical productions, vocational training, and the provision of musical instruments. Mercifully, the instructions required that "musical instruments . . .

should [only] be distributed to personnel who can actually play them . . ."[102]

Alongside the benign activities of the Wb lurked the efforts of National Socialist political officers and propagandists, especially after July 20. Well before this, however, Göring had charged the chief of the Luftwaffe personnel office with overseeing National Socialist indoctrination. The Wb organization was placed under the *NS-Führungsstab* (Nazi Party Leadership Staff), which oversaw large numbers of *NS-Führungsoffiziere* (Nazi Leadership Officers, NSFO) akin to the commissars of the Red Army.[103] The NSFO were assigned to the combat units, and took part in every facet of unit activities while advising the commander on ideological matters. Reading material and lectures assumed an overtly political character. Nor was this simply higher headquarters window dressing; the operations staff as well as unit commanders participated. Just as commanders were responsible for providing off-duty amusement and vocational training, so did they develop leadership principles and indoctrination programs for ensuring firm commitment to the National Socialist cause during a difficult time in the life of the German nation.[104] The Luftwaffe operations staff in August 1944 noted that the hard fighting at the fronts as well as "the crisis in the homeland" demanded that commanders set an example of the "National Socialist world-view," since only this would provide the necessary "inner strength to vanquish the enemy."[105] This only intensified as the end approached. A March 13, 1945, directive to the NSFOs portrayed the struggle in the harshest terms: "The enemy intends to promote the biological annihilation of the German people . . ."[106]

How far this penetrated the average unit is difficult to answer. Surviving pilots, in memoirs or postwar interviews, understandably tend to distance themselves from the regime. Many go out of their way to emphasize their "apolitical" backgrounds.[107] Some Allied interrogators tend to confirm this. One report noted, "The flying personnel, though educated almost completely within the years of the Nazi regime, were not very politically minded. Furthermore, there is, in their minds, no substantial substitute for the system which has done them no apparent harm." Yet other Luftwaffe personnel acknowledged their support for the regime. One officer recalled:

We really believed in him. Hitler did a lot for me. I had a wonderful youth. We were young, we were so much

indoctrinated by propaganda, by the years of victory reports. Afterwards, people said, "How could you have believed in this man?" Yet we did—totally.[108]

Another officer, a successful pilot on both the Eastern Front and in the RLV, admitted, "Ours was the age group [the propaganda] was aimed at, and we gladly answered the call. We also suffered the consequences."[109] The link between the Hitler Youth and gliding fed naturally into the Luftwaffe recruiting machine, providing a large pool of thoroughly indoctrinated young recruits. As late as November 1944, 86,000 Hitler Youth of the 1928 class sought entry into the Luftwaffe; only those who were physically fit for aircrew duty were accepted, and even then the training organization could no longer keep pace.[110]

Many pilot accounts emphasize a more apolitical patriotism, and especially a desire to defend their homeland against the ruinous Allied air offensive. Despite Propaganda Minister Josef Goebbels's rhetoric about *Terrorflieger* and *Luftgangster*, the battle over the Reich lacked the ideological and racial dimension of the struggle on the Eastern Front. There was little serious attempt to dehumanize the airmen of the Western Allies. The nature of air combat bred a certain detachment which was impossible in close ground combat. Yet the destruction of German cities and the heavy casualties among the civilian population proved a powerful motivating factor for German pilots, even those who might have become disillusioned with the regime. Heinz Bär, for example, noted in a September 1945 interrogation that many Sturmgruppe pilots volunteered for the difficult and dangerous task primarily because "their homes had been destroyed" and family members killed in the bombing.[111]

Some Luftwaffe pilots sought simpler inducements. Napoleon once remarked on the power of bits of ribbon to motivate combat soldiers, and this was certainly true of the Jagdwaffe throughout the war. As noted earlier, there were well-established procedures for awarding decorations to fighter pilots, and it is clear that the Luftwaffe leadership was aware of their effectiveness as a motivational tool. An inkling into what was important may be gained by examining some of the publications issued to Luftwaffe personnel by the Luftwaffe High Command. Typical of these was the *Frontnachrichtenblatt der Luftwaffe*, produced by the intelligence branch of the ObdL Operations Staff. In addition to the expected information on new Allied aircraft types, the newsletter contained lists and photographs of recent *Ritterkreuz* (Knight's Cross) recipients, with a summary of their deeds and the Reichsmarschall's congratulatory messages to the lucky winners.[112] Galland agreed with this philosophy, remarking shortly after the war that "the fighter arm continued to be stimulated by the race for decorations," although he also noted that "stiffened requirements" to avoid debasing the highest medals were implemented "just as the air war became much harder for the fighters."[113]

So what, then, motivated thousands of young pilots to climb into their cockpits and engage in deadly combat with a technically and numerically superior adversary? As with most important historical questions, an easy answer is elusive. Some insight may be gleaned from several interrogation reports of captured German fighter pilots late in the war:

> The impression generally gained by interrogators is that the morale of fighter pilots is still good and that it shows little or no weakening since D-Day. Pilots realise, of course, the immense Allied air superiority, but they are nevertheless fully prepared, if ordered to do so, to join in combat against odds.
>
> The feeling that Germany is beaten and that further resistance is hopeless does not readily penetrate the minds of fighter pilots. Firstly, they live under reasonably comfortable conditions and escape much of the grimness of the front line, and secondly they are youngsters who usually treat flying as an exciting sport and do not often stop to think why they are fighting . . .
>
> There is considerable belief in the promises made by Generalmajor Galland that the tables will soon be turned by the appearance of jet-propelled aircraft . . .
>
> On the other side of the scale, the more experienced pilots feel that the newcomers of to-day are not as good as those of yesterday; equally, owing to losses . . . there is a growing shortage of section, flight and squadron commanders, and newcomers tend to have insufficient confidence in their leaders. There is, therefore, some lack of mutual confidence amongst pilots in a unit.[114]

Another appraisal noted succinctly that German pilot morale "was based on a mixture of the following factors: the natural discipline of nearly all Germans, youthful spirit, love of flying, patriotism, and a general ignorance of the real facts of the war."[115] Even their bitterest opponents testify that they fought well, long after any real hope of victory was gone.

The authors of a recent history of JG 300 interviewed several surviving pilots on their motivations and morale during the fall of 1944. Most were quartered with farm families near their airfields. Although their hosts offered them full breakfasts, one pilot recalled that if the day dawned clear, his stomach immediately tightened, and all he could manage was coffee and a small glass of

Uffz. Paul Lixfeld of 6.(Sturm)/JG 300 stands in front of his Fw 190A-8/R2 "yellow 12," nicknamed *Muschi*. His airplane carries the *Wilde Sau* emblem, the rust-red RLV band, and peeling dark camouflage. (*Rosch*)

schnapps. Another would throw up at the first sight of sunshine. Once on the field, everyone awaited the order to go to cockpit readiness, at which time a deathly silence descended over the entire airfield. All of the pilots knew the odds against them. One said that of the four pilots in his Schwarm, he calculated that, "One would not come back, and would end the day either in a hospital bed or mangled in the shattered wreckage of his Focke-Wulf." But the green flare signaling takeoff was awaited eagerly—for the pilots, fear was instantly replaced by concentration. Any of them could have flown west and deserted, but did not. They attempted to fulfill their missions from a sense of duty, a desire to defend their homes, and strong bonds with their comrades.[116]

The Decline Continues

On July 8, the Fifteenth Air Force made a full-strength attack on oil targets and airfields in the Vienna area. The five Jagddivision 8 Gruppen made independent interceptions, with varying results. The 82nd Fighter Group had flown directly to Vienna and was positioned well above the bomber stream when its leader spotted the 16 I./ZG 76 Me 410s climbing to attack. He left one of his squadrons as high cover and led a devastating bounce with the other two. Nine Me 410s were shot down. The Me 410 was notoriously difficult to bail out of, and 13 crewmen were killed; only five survived, two with injuries. The Zerstörergruppe had to be withdrawn from combat; it was replaced at Vienna-Seyring the next day by its sister Gruppe II./ZG 76, which flew down from Prague.[117]

The Fifteenth Air Force directed its attention toward Ploesti during the following week, using for the first time the blind-bombing equipment which had been available to the Eighth for months. The senior air force concentrated on Munich for three straight days. All bombing was through cloud, and most of the I. Jagdkorps stayed on the ground. The Fifteenth split its effort on the 14th, sending half its bombers to Ploesti and the other half to Budapest oil targets. Very few Jagddivision 8 fighters could reach the bombers, but several notable battles with the escorts took place. Six Lightnings failed to return to Italy. II./JG 27 claimed three, for a loss of two Bf 109s; II./ZG 1 claimed four, while losing a single Bf 110; the Hungarians claimed two, for no losses.

Mid-July brought several organizational changes to the RLV. A second Sturmgruppe was formed at Salzwedel by redesignating I./ZG 1 as II.(Sturm)/JG 4. Command was given to Major Hans-Günther von Kornatzki, who had five ex-Sturmstaffel 1 pilots join him to serve as an experienced nucleus, while the rest, former twin-engine pilots, were learning the fine art of assault fighting in Fw 190A-8/R2s. A conventional Bf 109 Gruppe, III./JG 4, was formed from III./ZG 1 at the same time. The two ZG 1 Gruppen had previously flown Ju 88s in France; their principal mission had been protection patrols over the U-boats as they entered and left the Brittany submarine pens. It would obviously take some time to make effective single-engine fighter units from this starting material, but JG 4 was now (on paper) a full three-Gruppe Geschwader, and would eventually join I. Jagdkorps as such. Stab/JG 4 was at present administering the *Invasionsfront* fighter units which were off operations

in Germany while rebuilding; I./JG 4 was a Bf 109 unit in Italy. Other changes saw III./JG 11 return to Germany from its brief sojourn in Russia, while I./ZG 76 transferred from Vienna to Malacky in Slovakia and began receiving Bf 109s, another clear indication that the death knell had sounded for the once-proud Zerstörer force.[118]

On July 16, the USSTAF sent its two air forces to Munich and Vienna, and successfully split the defenses, which were ineffective against both. The Americans repeated the tactic on July 18. The Eighth Air Force flew to north Germany and bombed a Kiel refinery and the Peenemünde rocket experimental station without seeing a German fighter. The Fifteenth Air Force targeted the Manzell Dornier factory near Friedrichshafen, but bad weather caused most of the formation to abandon the mission or search for alternate targets. Weather also caused problems for the defense, but IV.(Sturm)/JG 3 flew a successful, although expensive, mission against the Fifteenth. The JG 300 Stab and the Sturmgruppe had just transferred to Memmingen, near Munich, at the insistence of Major Dahl, who had taken the Allied radio threats to destroy him very seriously. Major Moritz led 45 Fw 190s off the ground and was directed to a *Pulk* of B-17s which was flying entirely alone. Moritz came in too low and overshot his target, but his deputy was at the right altitude to lead a devastating stern attack on the 26 B-17s of the 483rd Bomb Group, which had split up their tight combat box and re-formed in trail to bomb their chosen target of opportunity—Memmingen airfield. Fourteen B-17s went down before a dozen 1st Fighter Group P-38s arrived and drove off the Sturmjäger, who lost 7 KIA, 5 WIA, and 12 Fw 190s. The surviving B-17s exacted their revenge with their bombs, which killed 170 personnel, injured 140, and destroyed three hangars, two workshops, the ready room, a barracks, and 50 aircraft on Memmingen. The members of the Sturmgruppe were convinced that the Allies knew of their base move and had targeted them deliberately. This is unlikely, but their location was made clear to the Allies that same evening, when their radioed casualty report was intercepted and decoded by the Ultra organization.[119]

ErprKdo 262 was putting the few available Me 262 fighters through their paces at Lechfeld. The program suffered a severe blow on the 18th when the unit commander, Hptm. Wilhelm Thierfelder, was killed in a Me 262 crash. He took off alone to attack an approaching Fifteenth Air Force bomber formation, and did not return. German sources state that he was shot down in a battle with "15 Mustangs," but no American pilot filed a claim, and Thierfelder's crash may have been the result of a mechanical failure. His replacement, Hptm. Horst Geyer, had served as Kommandeur of ErprKdo 25, and had the technical qualifications for his new job, but did not arrive at Lechfeld until August 5. This delay in filling what should have been a top-priority position is puzzling, but may be indicative of the confused status of the Me 262 program at this time. Hitler's order that the Me 262 was to be employed exclusively as a *Blitzbomber* ("fast bomber") was still in force. However, like all of the experimental fighter units, ErprKdo 262 was under the direct command of the General der Jagdflieger, Genmaj. Galland, who continued testing his few Me 262s as fighters, but could not allow them to attract undue attention at the Führer's headquarters. In late July the fighters were allowed to sortie singly against Allied photo-reconnaissance aircraft. The first Me 262 victory claim was filed on July 26, but the targeted RAF Mosquito escaped with structural damage sustained during violent evasive maneuvers.[120]

The Luftwaffe's second revolutionary fighter, the Me 163, was finally declared ready for operations in July. A two-Staffel Jagdgruppe, I./JG 400, was formed at Venlo under Hptm. Robert Olejnik. The rocket fighter's short range made it a true point-defense interceptor, and a base was prepared at Brandis, near Leipzig's oil installations. The 1. Staffel had moved by July 25, and the first mission by the new unit was flown on July 28. One pair of Me 163s sparred with some P-51s in the rear of a bomber wing, and broke off with no damage to either side. The P-51s were led by the commander of the 359th Fighter Group, Colonel Avelin Tacon, whose report on the flight characteristics of the rocket fighter was so detailed that MGen. Kepner used it as the basis of an immediate order to the 8th Fighter Command: his fighters were to resume close escort of the bombers, after months of loose escort and sweeps. The "jets" would probably be seen first as contrails at 30,000 feet (9,000 meters) or above, approaching the rear of the bombers. They could be expected especially in the Munich and Leipzig areas. This last bit of information was not from Tacon, but came from Ultra. That ever-helpful organization had intercepted a communication from Jagddivision 1 to its units which described the Me 163

exactly, and stated that with immediate effect the fighters would be operating against Allied raids within 100 km (60 miles) of Leipzig.[121]

During July 19–31 the Fifteenth Air Force flew seven missions to the Reich; the Eighth Air Force, five. On the ten days on which they took off to intercept, the average number of RLV fighters to make contact with enemy aircraft was 75. More bombers were lost to Flak than to fighters, and fewer than 2 percent of the bombers dispatched per mission were being lost. The defensive effort of July 25 was noteworthy in that it was probably the last successful bomber interception by Me 410s. The day's target for the Fifteenth Air Force was the Hermann Göring Panzer factory in Linz. As always, a successful interception required finding an unescorted bomber formation. The day's victim was the 461st Bomb Group, which had just opened its bomb bay doors at the Initial Point when it was attacked from 12 o'clock low by a formation of Me 410s. According to the American survivors, the Zerstörer lobbed rockets (or 30-mm shells) into the open bomb bays. This attack was quickly followed up by a rear attack by single-engine fighters. According to the Americans themselves, the B-24 formation split apart and the bomb run was aborted. Twelve B-24s crashed before reaching Italy, and three more were destroyed in crash landings on their base. The victorious single-engine units are known: I. and II./JG 300, and I./JG 302, escorted by II./JG 27. But an intriguing mystery remains: the identity of the Me 410 Gruppe. The presence of one Zerstörergruppe in the battle is confirmed by Allied radio intercepts, but none reported any combat losses. It was almost certainly II./ZG 76, the last Gruppe still operational on Me 410s. But RLM documents clearly state that no twin-engine fighters made contact with the enemy during the Linz raid, and the Gruppe did not file any claims in Berlin for victories on July 25.

The checkered history of the Luftwaffe heavy fighter force thus came to an anticlimactic end. By the end of July most of the Zerstörer units were off operations—reclassified as single-engine fighter units, and training on Bf 109s. The Stab, I., and II. Gruppen of ZG 26, still at Königsberg, became Stab/JG 6, I./JG 6, and II./JG 6. The Stab and I. Gruppe of ZG 76 moved from Austria to Hungary and became Stab and I./JG 76; II./ZG 1 joined them as III./JG 76. The last Me 410 Gruppe, II./ZG 76, kept its twin-engine fighters until January 1945, but did not return to operations until re-equipped with Fw 190s.

On August 1, the operational day-fighter strength of Luftflotte Reich comprised seven single-engine Jagdgruppen. Each now had four Staffeln, expanded in theory to the new establishment strength of 16 aircraft per Staffel. There was an ample supply of new aircraft. However, replacement pilots were either *Nachwuchs* (new growth) trainees or were drawn from disbanded bomber and transport units. In either case, their skills as fighter pilots were minimal, and the fuel shortage prevented much training, even in the combat units. I./JG 77 arrived from Italy for service in the RLV, but would require time to re-equip and train. An eighth combat Gruppe was added to the RLV order of battle on August 4 by the simple redesignation of ErprKdo 25 as Jagdgruppe 10.[122]

On August 3, a raid by the Fifteenth Air Force on targets in the Friedrichshafen area resulted in another noteworthy but expensive success for the senior Sturmgruppe. Jagddivision 7 formed a battle formation from two Gruppen: 19 IV.(Sturm)/JG 3 Fw 190s from Schongau, escorted by 17 I./JG 300 Bf 109s from Bad Wörishofen. A third Gruppe, III./JG 53, sortied on its first RLV mission, but was set upon by P-51s before reaching the bombers. Major Moritz, leading the *Gefechtsverband*, did not reach the bomber stream until it had finished bombing and re-formed for its return to Italy. He unerringly headed for the weakest link of the chain. The 465th Bomb Group was flying in two boxes. Countrary to orders, the second had dropped back to cover a straggling B-24, and was now 24 km (15 miles) behind the main formation, and unescorted. Moritz led the Sturm-gruppe in a surprise attack from the low rear, out of the undercast. The *Sturmböcke* made a single pass and then broke in all directions, as was their custom. The I./JG 300 Bf 109s apparently followed the Fw 190s through the bombers, but made no claims, and were out of position when 325th Fighter Group Mustangs responded to the bombers' calls for help. They fell on the Focke-Wulfs, shooting down nine, as well as two Messerschmitts. Seven German pilots were killed. Their single pass had brought down eight of the fragile B-24s, however.[123] Fw. Willi Unger recalled:

Each Staffel put up one Schwarm. I led the 12. Staffel Schwarm in an attack on a small *Pulk* of nine B-24s to the right and above the main formation. I damaged the mid B-24 in the rear vee, which sheered away, burning. I overflew the next bombers and attacked the left B-24 of the leading vee. Three engines caught fire and two men bailed out, but I was hit in the engine by the rear gunner. My canopy oiled up, and I bailed out without hesitation. I left the airplane cleanly and dropped 2,000 meters [6,500 ft.] before opening my chute as I entered a cloud. I left the cloud near the ground and landed uninjured in a valley of the Lechtaler Alps. I hiked out, found a hunter in a hut, was led to a village, borrowed a car, and returned to Schongau at about midnight, reporting back to Moritz "from an Edelweiss picking expedition."[124]

The experience of the RLV on August 4 fit into what would become the common pattern. The Eighth Air Force bombed Hamburg and Peenemünde. The Jagd-division 8 fighters in Austria were completely out of range. The heavy *Sturmböcke* of IV.(Sturm)/JG 3 scrambled from Schongau, but ran low on fuel and had to return to base. The five Jagdgruppen that did approach the bombers were savaged by the escorts and lost 29 fighters. The German pilots claimed victories over seven escorts and four B-17s, but of the 19 escorts and 24 bombers lost or scrapped on return to England, the USAAF credited only two fighters and one bomber to German fighters. Over-claiming was not limited to one side, of course; the American escorts received credit for downing 68 German fighters.[125]

Performance against the Eighth Air Force was at about the same level on the 5th, but deteriorated on the 6th to a total *Fehlschlag* (disaster): 198 defenders scrambled, 128 made contact, and 30 were shot down, for nine victory claims, all by JG 300. The German fighters flew in two *Gefechtsverbände*. One comprised the Stab and the three Gruppen of JG 300; the other was a mixed unit of I./JG 3, II./JG 5, and II./JG 27, led by Major Gerhard Schöpfel, the JG 4 Kommodore, and his Stabsschwarm. This was probably Schöpfel's first combat mission in a year and a half. Mustangs apparently dispersed his whole formation. Schöpfel's Messerschmitt was hit in the engine by one of them; he attempted to bail out, only to find that his canopy was stuck. When it broke free, he catapulted out, breaking his shoulder on the tail. He was able to open his parachute at 200–300 meters, and fortunately landed in a cultivated field, preventing further injury. His shoulder required hospitalization, and he was replaced as JG 4 Kommodore by Obstlt. Gerhard Michalski.[126]

On the 7th it was the turn of the southern defenders to suffer a *Fehlschlag*. The Fifteenth Air

Force's target was Blechhammer. Jagddivision 8 was able to position its three German Jagdgruppen and the Hungarian Pumas over Lake Balaton to intercept the incoming stream. Two famous Eastern Front Jagdgruppen, II. and III./JG 52, were nearby owing to the approach of the battle lines from the east, and they were also scrambled. But the Americans knew that Lake Balaton was a favorite rendezvous point, and always covered it well with sweeping fighters. Accordingly 31st Fighter Group P-51s fell on the Axis fighters, forcing most of them to scatter. The Hungarians claimed one B-24 and three P-51s, but lost 2 KIA, including Lt. László Molnár, their leading ace; 1 WIA; and eight Bf 109s. II./JG 52 claimed one B-24; III./JG 52 claimed one P-51 while losing 2 KIA, 1 WIA, and three Bf 109s. II./JG 27 and I./JG 302 evaded the escorts and returned to base to prepare for a second sortie against the withdrawing bombers. Interceptions in the target area were left to the operational training unit Jagdgruppe Ost, which claimed two B-24s for the loss of three fighters. The two Gruppen which attacked the withdrawing stream found no soft spots in the escort. I./JG 302 claimed

one B-17 and one B-24 for the loss of 1 KIA, 3 WIA, and four Bf 109s to 325th Group P-51s; II./JG 27 claimed one B-17 and one P-38 for the loss of 1 KIA, 1 severely WIA, and two Bf 109s to 14th Group P-38s. For 12 victory claims, the Axis had lost 20 fighters.[127]

The Reich air defenses can be said to have reached a critical state by mid-August, matching Germany's overall war situation. The Soviet summer offensive had been a smashing success, and the Red Army was nearing the eastern borders of Germany and Romania. The Western Allies had broken out of Normandy and were racing across northern France. They had also invaded southern France, which would force the Germans out of that country entirely while simplifying Allied lines of supply. Good news for the RLV was hard to find. On the positive side, ErprKdo 262 shot down a No. 540 Sqd. RAF reconnaissance Mosquito on August 8, and a 303rd Bomb Group B-17 on August 15, the first heavy bomber

Oblt. Fritz Müller stands on the wing of an early production Me 262A (WNr. 170059) newly delivered to ErprKdo 262 at Leipheim. (*ww2images*)

victory for the Me 262. One potential reinforcement for the RLV was I./JG 4, which arrived from Italy, leaving that front with a single Jagdgruppe.[128] As of August 9 there were two operational Sturmgruppen; Major Dahl obtained up-armored Fw 190A-8s for his II./JG 300, and without a day off operations it entered the RLV order of battle as II.(Sturm)/JG 300. The third Sturmgruppe, II.(Sturm)/JG 4, was still training.

There was much more bad news for the defenders. The Luftwaffe fuel situation was so tight that defensive fighter operations were the only flights allowed to continue without restriction. Weather and other reconnaissance was cut back, and bombers were limited to "decisive missions." The restrictions affected the highly successful *Fühlungshalterschwarm* (contact-keeping flight) of Bf 109s in Italy; it was disbanded and its pilots were ordered to Hptm. Gerhard Stamp's I./JG 300 at Bad Wörishofen. They were given a warm welcome, as they had as much experience as any NCO pilot in the Gruppe. Kommando Schenck flew to France to begin Me 262 bomber operations; this was bad news to Galland and the RLV commanders, who considered this a criminal misuse of the precious jets. Possibly the worst news was a *Hitler Befehl* (Hitler Order) that rebuilt *Invasionsfront* Jagdgruppen would have to return to the western front cauldron rather than remain in the Reich. Furthermore, JG 6 and JG 76, the two new Jagdgeschwader created from the old Zerstörergruppen, were also to be sent to France, as was I./JG 4, newly arrived from Italy. The operational strength of the RLV was thus doomed to remain below the level needed to have any effect whatsoever on the American bombing campaign.[129]

USSTAF operations during the second week of August continued much as before. After a trip to Budapest on the 9th, the Fifteenth Air Force returned to Ploesti. The Eighth divided its attention between oil and aviation industry targets in Germany and airfields in Germany and the Low Countries. The only noteworthy defense was put up on the 15th, when Major Dahl led a *Gefechtsverband* comprising his JG 300 Stabsschwarm, I./JG300 high-altitude escorts, and both active Sturmgruppen, II.(Sturm)/JG 300 and IV.(Sturm)/JG 3, in an effective attack on the 1st Bomb Division as it withdrew from Wiesbaden. The 303rd Bomb Group was subjected to a classic rear *Sturmangriff*, which downed eight B-17s immediately; a ninth was finished off by a Me 262 as it attempted the return flight alone. I./JG 300 kept most of the Mustangs away from the *Sturmböcke*, and Dahl's force

lost only 5 KIA, 2 WIA, and ten fighters. A second battle formation, containing II./JG 5 and III./JG 53, reached the bombers and claimed eight B-24s (the 466th Bomb Group lost four to their attacks), but had no high-altitude protection and lost ten Bf 109s to the American fighters. Major Dahl claimed initially that his force had downed 83 B-17s and 18 escorts, which if true would have made him the new savior of Germany. True Eighth Air Force losses to all causes totaled 13 B-17s, five B-24s, and five escort fighters.[130]

A full-scale mission by the Eighth Air Force to the central German oil installations on August 16 was resisted by 121 I. Jagdkorps fighters, among them the entire operational strength of I./JG 400: five Me 163s. These attacked the rear of two 1st Bomb Division combat wings singly or in pairs. The 305th Bomb Group was the first target. The B-17 gunners found that they could not track the rocket fighters, but one tail gunner had a zero-deflection shot and downed Fw. Strasnicky, who was able to bail out without injury. Lt. Hartmut Ryll shot up two B-17s, but was then shot down and killed by a 359th Fighter Group Mustang. One of Ryll's claims was upgraded to a destroyed, but the B-17 was able to limp back to England with severe damage. News of the blazing speed of the new fighters spread quickly around the Eighth Air Force bases; the American unit commanders were just as quick to point out that the fighters had proved to be vulnerable. Allied intelligence knew from Ultra that the Me 163s were very few in number, but had to protect their precious source, and thus could not disseminate this news widely.[131]

The Fifteenth Air Force made three final raids on Ploesti, ending on the 19th. The Red Army was only a few days away from the refineries, which were now heaps of twisted steel scrap. Postwar historians have speculated that the excess destruction was part of a deliberate attempt to retard the U.S.S.R.'s postwar recovery, but the real answer probably lies in the law of military momentum: once started, a campaign is almost impossible to halt. Now that the Ploesti campaign had ended successfully, General Twining was able to pay more attention to strategic targets in the Greater German Reich and its remaining Axis allies, Hungary and Slovakia. The Fifteenth flew missions every day from the 20th to the 29th. The Eighth was grounded for much of this period owing to bad weather over England and northern Europe. This allowed Schmid to give his undivided attention, and most of his skimpy forces, to defending the south. The new Fifteenth Air Force campaign got off to a flying start on the 20th. Targets in Bohemia-Moravia, Hungary, and Poland were bombed for the loss of only three bombers. Of the 224 German and Hungarian fighters to scramble, only 22 made contact. These were the Bf 109s of I./JG 302, which lost its Gruppen-kommandeur and one Staffelkapitän to bomber gunfire. The record is maddeningly silent on the reason for the poor performance of the Pumagruppe and the other Jagddivision 8 fighters on this mission.[132]

After a small-scale mission to Hungary on the 21st which drew little resistance, the Fifteenth flew in full strength on the 22nd to bomb the oil refineries at Blechhammer, Odertal, and Vienna, and the under-ground oil storage facility at Lobau. With no immediate threat from the Eighth Air Force, Jagd-divisionen 1 and 7 moved some Gruppen to Silesia and others to Austria. The Fifteenth was therefore opposed by nine RLV Jagdgruppen, Jagdgruppe Ost, and the Hungarian fighters, which were now down to the strength of a single Staffel. Jagddivision 8 directed an attack by the Austria-based fighters on the incoming stream, and a second mission on the withdrawing bombers. Jafü Schlesien attempted to control an unprecedented five Gruppen in the Silesian target area. Few holes in the escort coverage were found, but very hard fighting brought fairly good results, indicating the crucial importance of defensive numbers. The Fifteenth lost at least 22 bombers and four escorts to all causes; the Axis lost about 16 fighters.[133]

The Fifteenth Air Force returned to Blechhammer, Odertal, and Vienna on the 23rd. The defenses were much weakened after their efforts the previous day, but did put up 96 fighters. IV.(Sturm)/JG 3 was presented with an attack opportunity when the leader of the 451st Bomb Group formation decided to proceed alone to a secondary target after losing the rest of his wing. A classic close-formation rear *Sturmangriff* shot down eight B-24s and damaged eight others. In the absence of escorts, such attacks were always successful, even when weighed against losses to bomber gunfire, which were exceptionally heavy on this occasion owing to the close range to which the attacks were pressed; the Sturmgruppe lost 5 KIA and six Fw 190s.[134]

Romania surrendered unconditionally to the Soviet Union on the 23rd. The German High Command

thought that the Wehrmacht would remain in the country as occupiers, as had happened in Italy the previous year. But on the 24th Genlt. Alfred Gerstenberg ordered the Romanian royal palace bombed, to strike at the heart of "treasonous elements." Romania promptly declared war on Germany, trapping most of the Wehrmacht forces, including the personnel of the three Jagdgruppen which had been defending Ploesti until the previous week. One of these Gruppen had to be disbanded; cadres of the other two escaped to Hungary, where they were rebuilt, but never again reached their previous levels of performance.[135]

A break in the weather over northern Europe on the 24th allowed the Eighth Air Force to join the Fifteenth in attacks on oil installations and aircraft factories. Battles raged across the North German Plain to Stettin, northeast of Berlin, and south across the Czech provinces of Bohemia and Moravia. The German controllers did a fairly effective job of directing their small forces, although only 99 of the 222 fighters to take off made contact with the enemy. III./JG 53 had one of its best days, claiming seven B-17s over Lüneburg for the loss of four Bf 109s. The Eighth Air Force lost 26–5 bombers and 4–3 fighters to all causes; the Fifteenth lost 13 bombers. The losses of the RLV force totaled 19 fighters.[136]

I./JG 400 Me 163s were again up in force on the 24th. Their pilots had no time to search for weak spots in the bomber streams; their goal was simply to find something to attack during the few minutes that they were airborne. Eight pilots flew, some on several sorties. Lt. Hans Bott made his first three combat flights. Bott recalled:

My first mission was without result. The second was flown in the last operational Me 163 left on the flight line. It was the only Me 163 with two 20-mm MG 151 cannons instead of the usual 30-mm MK 108s. It also had a faulty fuel pressure gauge. I was directed to a B-17 *Pulk* 20 km [12 miles] away, approaching Leipzig. I climbed at 800–900 km/h [500–560 mph], made a wide approach curve, and fired from 1,000 meters [1,100 yards]. The B-17 exploded. I landed after seven minutes in the air. Since I was Officer of the Day, I ordered myself up on a third sortie versus a single unidentified aircraft. I navigated by my own "sun compass." [His gyrocompass had failed; it was notorious for tumbling during turns.] The airplane proved to be a Fw 190 with an unserviceable radio. Hptm. Olejnik chewed me out for not shooting it down.[137]

Me 163 pilots claimed four B-17s, which match known losses. Bott's and one other were from the 92nd Bomb Group; the others were from the 305th and 457th Bomb Groups. Unknown at the time, of course, the day proved to be the high point of the Me 163's combat career.[138]

The two USSTAF air forces flew another joint mission on the 25th. I. Jagdkorps countered neither with much effectiveness. The day's worst news for the RLV commanders came from the *Invasionsfront*. JG 6 and JG 76 had been sent to France over Galland's strong objections. Two of the new Jagdgruppen saw action for the first time. III./JG 76 lost 11 KIA, including its Gruppenkommandeur, and one WIA. II./JG 6 lost 19 KIA and 4 WIA; its Gruppen-kommandeur was then relieved. Fw. Fritz Buchholz, a pilot with the latter unit, attributed its poor

performance to the battle fatigue of the former Zerstörer pilots and their basic unfamiliarity with the Fw 190A and single-engine fighter tactics. Acording to his *Flugbuch* (logbook) Buchholz had made three familiarization flights in a Bf 108 followed by 18 in a Fw 190 before coming to France; none was devoted to developing tactical skills. Another bit of bad news came from I./JG 4, which had been ordered to France on short notice. On the transfer flight Major Walter Hoeckner, its Gruppenkommandeur and a successful RLV formation leader, was killed when the engine of his fighter caught fire.[139]

Flights over the Reich were hampered for the next few days by bad weather, although missions were flown by both USSTAF air forces. The next RLV mission showing a modicum of success came on August 29. The Eighth Air Force was grounded, and the Jagd-

Me 262A-1 "white 10" of ErprKdo 262, taking off for a practice flight from Lechfeld. (*Price*)

division 7 fighters were able to help Jagddivision 8 defend against a Fifteenth Air Force raid on several targets in Bohemia-Moravia and Hungary. Rosen-kavalier attempted to form a single battle formation from his disparate forces, which on this day comprised six high-altitude protection Gruppen, two Sturm-gruppen, and one conventional bomber interception Gruppe. The airborne strength of the nine Gruppen totaled only 89 fighters; I./JG 302 was down to its last three fighters. Although Willi Reschke of I./JG 302 claims that there was "no one in charge" of the formation, and that there was no radio communica-tion between fighters of the different Divisionen, everyone played their roles well. A contact-keeper in a Fw 190 reported that the B-17s were in poor formation. The 2nd Bomb Group was in fact lagging behind the rest of the 5th Bomb Wing, and vulnerable. The protection Gruppen climbed to counter the escorts while the other fighters practised their accustomed roles: the two Sturmgruppen made close-formation attacks from the rear, while the three I./JG 302 Messerschmitts attacked the flanks from out of the undercast. The escorting 31st Fighter Group Mustangs were apparently sweeping too far ahead of the B-17 wing to intervene, so the protection fighters were able to join in the attacks on the bombers. A high-altitude haze added to the confusion of the crews of the trailing bomber squadron as it was hit simultan-eously by about 60 German fighters. All seven B-17s of this squadron went down quickly, together with two B-17s which had fallen back from their own squadrons and a B-24 with mechanical problems which had joined the B-17 stream for protection. German casualties were amazingly light—one KIA and four fighters shot down. One fighter crash-landed success-fully after sustaining severe damage; it was piloted by Uffz. Reschke, who shot a B-17 out of formation but was then hit in the tail by fire from one of his own fighters. He crash-landed in a field, and on his return to Mörtitz was told that his Gruppe had been ordered to Alperstedt to disband—a sad end for a unit which had been the bulwark of Jagddivision 8 for several critical months.[140]

At the end of August Germany's military position was so desperate that the few clear-thinkers in Berlin thought it doubtful that the Third Reich would survive the year. The Luftwaffe was held in low esteem throughout Germany, and for good reason— it had lost its ability to influence events. Other than the night harassing units, only the fighter arm and (on the Eastern Front only) the ground-attack arm remained fully functional. The 12 Jagdgruppen remaining on the *Ostfront* could still win their jousting matches with Soviet fighters, but that was no real help to the beleaguered German Army. The huge ground staff of Luftflotte 3 was leading a disgraceful retreat from France, well ahead of the Army. The only commander it had known, GFM Sperrle, was relieved as soon as he reached Germany, and never received another assignment. The Luftwaffe units in Romania were trying to escape the Red Army as it surged toward the Hungarian border. Luftwaffe strength in Italy was down to one Jagd-gruppe and one Jagdgeschwader Stab, and they were packing up in anticipation of a return to the Reich. The night fighters of the RLV could still on occasion knock down significant numbers of RAF bombers, but could not stop the wholesale destruction of German cities. The RLV day fighters were shooting down fewer than 2 percent of the American bombers that formed an aluminum curtain over the daytime Reich. The quantitative inferiority of the Luftwaffe fighter force had been established years before. There were still hopes that qualitative superiority could be regained. But of the dozens of technically innovative Luftwaffe weapons programs, only the Me 262 offered any chance of reversing Germany's fortunes. And the Me 262 program was still mired in politics. Although Genmaj. Galland had only a staff position, he at least had a recovery plan, and expressed it forcefully. The Me 262 would have to be given the predominant role in the fighter defenses; this would require Hitler's concurrence. And the con-ventional fighter units, especially those now streaming back from France, would have to be rebuilt and retrained with the best equipment available, which would mean withholding them from operations for several months. Time would tell whether Hitler and the High Command had the patience for such a program.

CHAPTER 8

THE "BIG BLOW" THAT NEVER FELL SEPTEMBER–DECEMBER 1944

The Struggle to Rebuild the Defenses

As the Allied armies approached the German borders, the Third Reich gained a reprieve from a frequently under-appreciated source—logistics. The offensives of both the Soviets and the Anglo-Americans ground to a halt when their armies ran out of supplies: most critically, gasoline and diesel fuel. The Red Army's summer offensive, Operation Bagration, had advanced the central portion of the Eastern Front 750 km (450 miles), to the Vistula River. Stalin and the Soviet high command were willing to pause in the center while straightening the line with offensives through the Baltic States in the north and the Balkans in the south. East Prussia was directly threatened, but the Red Army was still far from the major German population and industrial centers. These were already menaced by the armies of the Western Allies. But the forced pause of the latter roughly along the western German border allowed the Wehrmacht to improve the old frontier defenses, the *Westwall*, enough to make them impervious to attack in a fall or winter campaign. Morale in the German high command and in the armies defending the Western Front improved. The men on the Eastern Front could only prepare their winter defenses and hope for the best. 1945 would be another year. Wonder weapons were promised, and the Anglo-American alliance with the Russians could always split apart.

Genmaj. Josef "Beppo" Schmid, the commanding general of I. Jagdkorps, pays a morale-boosting visit to II./JG 27 and the Stab of JG 11 at Finsterwalde in early September. (*Bundesarchiv 680-8264-4*)

The commanders of the Luftwaffe knew that there were no wonder weapons, and that only the weapons already in or entering service would be of use in turning the tide of the war. The new generation of aircraft was clearly superior to anything the Allies had. The limitations of the first to reach service, the rocket-powered Me 163, were now clear, but it was hoped that the jet-propelled Me 262 would restore air superiority over the Reich. The twin-jet Ar 234, a true bomber and reconnaissance aircraft, was entering service and would relieve pressure on the Me 262 to fill those roles. Two other novel designs, the Do 335 and Ju 287, could be useful, but Albert Speer, now in full control of all of Germany's war production, ruthlessly canceled other experimental projects as well as production contracts for now-superfluous aircraft types and attempted to set realistic goals. Production efforts focused on the jets and two tried-and-true conventional fighters, the Bf 109 and the Fw 190. The program begun by Karl-Otto Saur and the Fighter Staff to decentralize fighter production and move several large factories underground into unused iron mines proceeded with amazing speed, with the aid of slave labor, and September was the peak month of the war for fighter production, with 4,103 being built, and 3,013 accepted by the Luftwaffe.[1]

These thousands of new fighters needed pilots and fuel. Luftwaffe administrative staffs and training units were given a shaking out for experienced combat pilots who could be returned to front-line duty. Bomber, transport, and reconnaissance pilots from disbanded units were given short fighter-conversion courses and sent to the Jagdgruppen, but most of the new fighter pilots were *Nachwuchs* trainees, mostly 18–20 years old, who were sent from the training schools to the combat units with as few as 110 total flying hours, in some cases only 6–10 of them in front-line fighters.[2] The best aspect of their training was that the standard fighter course now included rudimentary blind-flying instruction and familiarization with the FuG 16ZY navigation aid.

The most critical problem for Albert Speer and the German defenses was fuel. The recuperative powers of German industry were enormous, and production facilities which appeared from the air to be nothing but a mass of smoking wreckage could usually be restored to partial service in a few weeks. New hydrogenation plants under construction were now smaller, better camouflaged, and separated from the highly visible and vulnerable chemical production plants and petroleum refineries. Jet fuel was essentially kerosene, and was easier to produce than conventional high-octane aviation fuel. But the constant pounding by Allied bombers did not allow the restoration of any fuel reserve. The RLV needed to halt the bombing at least temporarily to allow German industry some time for recovery.

Two of the more creative Luftwaffe fighter generals made highly classified proposals for one-time operations intended to cause such high casualties that the Americans would curtail their strategic bombing campaign to prepare counter-measures, as had happened after the second Schweinfurt raid in October 1943. The better-received proposal was that of Genmaj. Galland. He called it *der grosse Schlag* ("The Big Blow"), a greater-than-maximum effort against the bombers, using every fighter that could get off the ground. I. Jagdkorps was to put up 2,000 day fighters in 11 battle formations. Luftflotte 3 would employ 150 of its fighters, both early and late in the mission. One hundred night fighters would patrol the flanks to down damaged bombers before they could reach Sweden or Switzerland. Five hundred fighters would fly second sorties. It was hoped that 400–500 bombers could be downed for a loss of 400 fighters and 100–150 pilots. Galland's office drew up the plan in detail, but the OKL Operations Staff never blessed it with a true code name. Much of the benefit of the operation would come from the shock effect on the Americans of an interception force ten times larger than anything seen since D-Day. The units back from the *Invasionsfront* were not to rejoin the RLV order of battle in a piecemeal fashion, but would have to be husbanded until the right moment. Galland's authority extended to operational training, and he kept the rebuilding Jagdgruppen under his tight control. That this was permitted implies that he had at least the tacit approval of the Luftwaffe Chief of Staff, General der Flieger Kreipe. The principal flaw in Galland's plan was its excessive optimism. It expected too much of the pilots, whose mean level of skill had dropped markedly in the previous year. Also, Allied order-of-battle intelligence was far better than the Germans ever suspected, and the USSTAF commanders would know immediately that the Big Blow was a one-shot operation, never to be repeated, and need not affect future plans. But the RLV commanders at least had a definite goal to work toward.[3]

The second plan was much more radical. It was proposed by Oberst Hajo Herrmann, who was now in command of Jagddivision 1. He took the ramming concept of von Kornatzki to the next level: a full air fleet of suicide fighters. His proposal was titled, "Mathematical Justification for Suicide Missions," and cold-bloodedly set out to prove the relative efficiency of suicidal ramming missions over conventional fighter interceptions. The bases for comparison were the expenditure of aircraft and the consumption of that most precious of commodities, aviation fuel. Both training and operational losses were factored in, as was the ratio of successful to unsuccessful combat sorties. To bring down a bomber by conventional means required 65 tons of fuel, 3 aircraft, and 0.8 fatalities. The downing of a bomber by a *SO-Mann* (*Selbstopfer-Mann* or suicide pilot), considering that he would be only half-trained, would require only 3 tons of fuel, 1.2–1.4 aircraft, and 1.2 fatalities. Herrmann sent the only copy of his proposal to Kreipe, who probably did not immediately forward it to Göring and Hitler—Hitler's aversion to suicide tactics was widely known—but its time would come. Soon after sending off his proposal Herrmann was relieved by Schmid, and spent a brief time in exile in the *Führerreserve* before joining the staff of II. Jagdkorps.[4]

The tactics of the previous weeks would continue for the short term while Galland supervised the training of his reserve. Jagddivision 1 in Berlin took command of all the RLV day fighters, which were now concentrated to defend the critical oil targets in central Germany. Attacking bombers was the primary task of the two, soon to be three, operational Sturmgruppen, each escorted by one or more conventional fighter Gruppen. In the future the ex-*Wilde Sau* Geschwader JG 300 and JG 301 would form the core of the RLV day force, flying when the rest of I. Jagdkorps was grounded. JG 301 would give up all of its Bf 109s for Fw 190A-8/R11s and Fw 190A-9/R11s, which were fully equipped for operations in poor weather. It was intended to build both Geschwader up to the new establishment strength of four Gruppen, each of four 16-fighter Staffeln. They contained enough instrument-rated pilots to be considered bad-weather units and were expected to operate in bad (in effect typical German) weather conditions.

New pilot Robert Jung finished blind-flying school and reported to I./JG 300, which he thought was a night-fighter unit, only to find that it was now on day operations. He recalled that the ex-*Wilde Sau* pilots prayed for clouds, "the salvation of the RLV pilot." The role of Jung's Gruppe was high-altitude protection for the bomber destroyers. He received a brand-new Bf 109G-14/AS, which was operational up to 11,000 meters (36,000 ft.).[5]

The sole surviving Gruppe from JG 302, I./JG 302, was not disbanded as its pilots had feared, but was simply redesignated III./JG 301. Willi Reschke recalled that its 22 pilots remained in their old Staffeln. The Gruppe was to retain its old role as a bomber-killing unit. It exchanged its Bf 109G-6s for Fw 190A-8s, which were much better for this purpose, and began brief conversion training at Alperstedt. Most of the unit's replacement pilots were retrained reconnaissance or bomber pilots or former primary instructors who found it hard to adapt to the rougher flying required for survival in a fighter. In recognition of this weakness, training was under the supervision of Lt. Karl Gratz, a Knight's Cross holder from JG 52, the world's most successful unit in fighter-to-fighter combat.[6]

The slowdown in ground fighting at the start of September was matched for a few days by a lack of air activity over the Reich. The Eighth Air Force was hampered by bad weather. The Fifteenth was flying two types of mission: repatriation flights of Allied POWs from Romania to Italy, and tactical missions over the Balkans to interdict the line of retreat of the German Army, at the request of the Soviets. The RLV did not contest the next five missions by the Eighth Air Force, all attempts to bomb west German targets through cloud. The Fifteenth returned to strategic bombing on September 10 with a raid on Vienna that the Luftwaffe also ignored. Jagddivision 8 in the south now had only one day-fighter unit, the Hungarian Pumas, which could be hazarded against a complete heavy bomber armada only under exceptionally favorable circumstances. The German day fighters in the RLV were now concentrated and organized to defend only the most important strategic targets in the greater German Reich: the oil installations in central Germany.

September 11—Petroleum Targets

A slight improvement in the weather forecast for the 11th encouraged the Eighth Air Force planners to schedule a full-scale attack on central Germany. The targets were primarily synthetic oil plants, but included military vehicle factories and one ordnance depot. The three bomb divisions put up 1,131 bombers in 23 combat wings. The 15 Eighth Air Force fighter groups sortied 715 P-38s, P-47s and P-51s, all as close or medium escort; sweeps were temporarily out of favor owing to the perceived danger from jets. The bomber stream crossed the Belgian coast on a southeasterly course before turning east toward the target zone. Genmaj. Schmid was able to scramble all 12 of his Jagdgruppen—355 fighters—and attempted to form them into three *Gefechtsverbände*, each anchored by a Sturmgruppe. The result was the heaviest air fighting over the Reich since D-Day.[7]

For reasons probably related to weather, only two battle formations assembled; other Gruppen had to make their attacks alone. The largest formation was led by Major Dahl, and contained his Stab, I., and II.(Sturm)/JG 300, IV.(Sturm)/JG 3, I./JG 76, and possibly other units. They were vectored to the 1st Bomb Division stream after the three bomb divisions split up, but were sighted and attacked by P-51s while still out of range of the bombers. The JG 300 Stabsschwarm and IV.(Sturm)/JG 3 evaded the escorts and searched for an unescorted B-17 box. Major Dahl and his flight of four Bf 109s claimed two B-17s shot down and one shot from formation (all by Dahl) and returned without loss. The Sturmgruppe found the 92nd Bomb Group circling Merseburg for a second run on their target. Just before bomb release the bombers were hit by a terrific Flak barrage that loosened their formation. The Fw 190 pilots formed their assault wedge and blasted the rear of the box. Eight B-17s went down immediately; four more crashed or crash-landed behind Allied lines. The

Sturmgruppe made its customary single pass and attempted to leave the area before the arrival of the escorts. Most pilots made it back to Schafstädt; seven of the *Sturmböcke* were shot down, with a loss of 3 KIA and 1 WIA.[8]

II.(Sturm)/JG 300 was dispersed completely by the Mustangs; few pilots reached the bombers, and only one claimed a victory: Lt. Walfeld rammed a B-24 when his guns jammed, after which he bailed out successfully. The Gruppe's other pilots were forced to dogfight the P-51s in their clumsy *Sturmböcke*. The survivors returned to Bindersleben claiming nine Mustangs, but were missing 13 Fw 190s; ten pilots were killed and two injured. One of their two high-altitude protection Gruppen, I./JG 300, was totally ineffective, losing six Bf 109s, one KIA and one WIA for no claims. The other Gruppe, I./JG 76, was more successful, claiming five P-51s, but lost 7 KIA, 7 WIA, and 13 Bf 109s.

The second battle formation to assemble on the 11th was formed around II.(Sturm)/JG 4 and III./JG 4, both flying their first RLV missions. They were not led by their own Major von Kornatzki, but by Major Specht and his JG 11 Stabsschwarm. Kornatzki did, however, give his men a rousing patriotic speech before they boarded their planes. Through luck, good ground control or Specht's skill the formation located a bare spot in the 3rd Bomb Division's escort coverage. The P-51s were concentrated at the rear of the stream. Far ahead of them, the low box of the second combat wing was invitingly far behind the rest of its formation. This box contained 34 B-17s of the 100th Bomb Group. The Germans punished the "Bloody Hundredth" yet again for its poor formation flying. Specht stayed above with his Schwarm and most of III./JG 4 to head off the Mustangs, while the Sturmgruppe wheeled around behind the B-17s to make the attack it had been practicing. This Gruppe employed three broad vees, stepped up to the rear. The trailing Staffel formed a rearguard against surprise escort attacks, but was briefed to attack the bombers if the situation allowed it. One III./JG 4 Staffel was in the right position for a quick frontal pass, and carried it out. Single passes by this Staffel and the Sturmgruppe were enough. Eleven 100th Bomb Group B-17s fell to earth; three more crashed in France or in England. One 95th Bomb Group B-17 was caught in the crossfire and also went down. The first escorts to come to the bombers' aid were 14 P-51s of the 339th Fighter Group's 504th Squadron. They

attacked both the Fw 190s and Bf 109s and quickly claimed 15 without loss, for which the unit was awarded the Distinguished Unit Citation. The JG 4 pilots had to fight their way through more escorts before reaching base. They ended the day with losses of 21 KIA, 9 WIA, and 42 fighters; a 50 percent loss on their first mission. The only P-51 lost by the 339th Fighter Group was damaged while strafing an airfield and was then shot down by a nearby ErprKdo 262 Me 262. The American pilot survived as a POW.[9]

All of the operational I. Jagdkorps Gruppen were up on this day. Mission details for several units (I./JG 3, JGr 10, II./JG 27) remain sketchy. III./JG 300 is known to have missed rendezvous with its *Gefechtsverband* and tried to attack the bombers alone. III./JG 53 also made a solitary attack, and was moderately successful; it penetrated the 2nd Bomb Division stream and downed three 392nd Bomb

The 20-year-old Fahnenjunker-Unteroffizier Robert Jung as a new I./JG 300 pilot in the fall of 1944. (*Jung*)

Group B-24s before being dispersed by 355th Fighter Group P-51s. This Gruppe lost three killed—one by collision with a Mustang—two injured, and six Bf 109s. I./JG 400 flew a full-strength mission with seven Me 163s, and claimed one success, a B-17 that was shot down near the rocket fighters' Brandis base. Several II. Jagdkorps Gruppen (including II./JG 2, I./JG 11, III./JG 26, III./JG 76, I./JG 77) were also ordered to intercept the bomber stream; they had little or no success.

The events of the 11th demonstrated the utter inadequacy of conventional RLV tactics and equipment. The USAAF lost 46 bombers and 25 fighters to all causes. The Luftwaffe lost approximately 60 pilots killed and 25 injured on this full-strength mission. Of the 305 fighters to make contact with the enemy, about 110 were destroyed—a calamitous 36 percent loss rate.

Favorable weather conditions on the 12th allowed the Eighth Air Force to repeat the previous day's attacks on the central German oil targets. This was the area that I. Jagdkorps was best prepared to defend, and again Genmaj. Schmid ordered a full-strength mission—but only 190 fighters could take part, owing to the previous day's losses. The three bomb divisions headed east across Heligoland, then turned southeast toward Brunswick. Schmid formed his fighters into three battle formations, which were intended to hit the bombers inbound, in the target area, and on withdrawal.

The first group of fighters contained II.(Sturm)/JG 4 as the striking force, escorted by III./JG 4 and I./JG 76. Major von Kornatzki led the formation. They met the incoming 1st Bomb Division stream near Magdeburg. Kornatzki's Sturmgruppe, one Staffel of III./JG 4, and all of I./JG 76 were able to make one pass through the B-17s before the arrival of Mustangs. Von Kornatzki's Focke-Wulf was hit by bomber fire; he attempted a quick forced landing, but hit power lines and was killed in the resulting crash. His formation claimed 27 B-17s and two P-51s, but lost 16 KIA, 4 WIA, 13 Bf 109s, and seven Fw 190s. Its most likely target was the 351st Bomb Group, which lost nine B-17s.[10]

The second I. Jagdkorps *Gefechtsverband* was led by Major Dahl and the JG 300 Stabsschwarm, and contained all three JG 300 Gruppen, I. and IV.(Sturm)/ JG 3, II./JG 27, and III./JG 53. A seven-Gruppe formation was too large to be controlled by one man, but might have been ordered simply because of Dahl's reputation and influence. Inevitably, it broke up before reaching the bombers, but the result was two successful attacks. IV.(Sturm)/JG 3 approached the 1st Bomb Division stream north of Berlin and found a promising target. The leader of the 306th Bomb Group had seen that the boxes ahead of him were being slammed by Flak and slipped to the left. This put the group on a collision course with a neighboring combat box; the resulting confusion gave the lurking Sturmgruppe an attack opportunity that it was quick

Two crew chiefs and a darkly mottled I./JG 300 Bf 109G-6 in the fall of 1944. The aircraft number "yellow 2" is the only visible marking; even the national insignia is obscured. (*Jung*)

to take advantage of. Five B-17s went down under the pounding of 30-mm shells; a sixth crash-landed on the English coast; three more were shot down by the Flak. The senior Sturmgruppe lost 3 KIA, 2 WIA, and seven Fw 190s. Prior to the mission several American crewmen had questioned the routing of the stream so close to the Berlin Flak, when Berlin was not a target, only to be told that this was to "draw up the Luftwaffe." The tactic had worked.[11]

Dahl led the rest of his formation toward the 3rd Bomb Division stream, but did not reach it until the combat wings had separated and bombed their individual targets. Dahl chose to attack the bombers leaving Magdeburg. The specific box targeted contained the 493rd Bomb Group, which was flying its first mission in B-17s after converting from B-24s. As Dahl's Sturmgruppe, II.(Sturm)/JG 300, was circling for its stern attack, Hptm. Alfred Grislawski, now commanding III./JG 53, led it in an immediate frontal pass. Eight B-17s went down under the two-direction attack; three more crash-landed in France or England.[12]

II. Jagdkorps supplied three Gruppen of its tactical Fw 190s, I./JG 2, I./JG 11, and I./JG 77, for the third battle formation. It was ordered to attack the withdrawing bombers, but while the Fw 190s were still heading for the stream they were bounced north of Frankfurt by two P-51 flights from the 354th Fighter Group, the "Pioneer Mustang Group." Ironically, these were also tactical fighters, assigned to the Ninth Air Force. The Mustang pilots summoned one more squadron for help; these were sufficient, although some 4th Fighter Group pilots on withdrawal escort saw the battle and joined in. The result was a disaster for II. Jagdkorps: 29 Fw 190s were shot down, carrying 14 pilots to their deaths; 13 pilots survived with injuries. The 354th Group claimed 25 Fw 190s destroyed; the 4th Group claimed the other four. Two Mustangs went down, but both pilots survived.[13]

Of the 147 I. Jagdkorps and II. Jagdkorps fighters to contact Eighth Air Force (and 354th Fighter Group) aircraft on the 12th, approximately 76 were shot down, a loss of 52 percent of the force. Forty-two pilots were killed, and 14 were injured. Losses to the Eighth from all causes totaled 40 bombers and 16 fighters. The Fifteenth Air Force was also up on the 12th, and made a successful attack on a Munich jet engine factory, but the RLV made no attempt to intercept the southern intruders.

On the 13th the USSTAF carried out yet another punishing blow on the oil industry. The combined mission saw the Fifteenth Air Force bomb the Odertal and Blechhammer refineries without aerial opposition, while the Eighth returned to its central German targets. Schmid chose to confront the latter attack, but only 137 fighters scrambled, and of these, only 63 made contact. Dahl's force, as usual the largest, was misdirected into a large force of Mustangs and dispersed. Of the 22 bombers lost by the Eighth, no more than six could be credited to German fighters. The Americans' three-day concerted attack on the oil industry brought production rates and inventories of aviation fuel to their lowest levels of the war at the same time that the efficiency of the RLV had sunk to its nadir.[14]

A meeting of the principal RLV fighter commanders and staff and the RLM staff, including Göring, took place at Hitler's headquarters on September 15. The accounts available from participants differ, but the air of unreality that now enveloped Hitler and his staff is unmistakable. While waiting for the Führer the air commanders bickered about the proper ratio of high-altitude Gruppen to Sturmgruppen. Göring spent the time briefing a new member of the OKW liaison staff, Obstlt. Karl Boehm-Tettelbach, on a planned private meeting with Hitler. The Führer's favorite bomber destroyer, the Me 410 equipped with a 5-cm cannon, had proven to be a highly vulnerable crew-killer and had been removed from RLV service in July. No-one had yet told Hitler. Boehm-Tettelbach, until recently the Kommodore of ZG 26, the only Geschwader equipped with this model, was given the job. Apparently Hitler took the news well. The meeting ended with an unexpected bonus; Hitler rescinded his order that the Me 262 was to be used only as a bomber. The Me 262 would be given a chance to prove itself in the defense of the Reich.[15]

Market-Garden and its Aftermath

Operation Market-Garden was a bold attempt by the Western Allies to end the war in the fall of 1944, before bad weather ended the campaign season and allowed the Germans to strengthen their frontier defenses. Field Marshal Montgomery proposed to use three airborne divisions to liberate a narrow corridor 50 miles (80 km) deep into the Netherlands, jumping three broad rivers, including two downstream branches of the Rhine. One British armored corps would speed up a single highway for 100 miles (160 km) to the Zuider Zee, relieving the airborne troops as it passed them. This advance would cut off the German forces in the Netherlands, outflank the frontier defenses, and directly threaten the Ruhr and, beyond that, Berlin. General Eisenhower was startled that the conservative Montgomery had suggested such an unconventional operation, but gave his approval, prompted in part by his desire to showcase the elite airborne divisions. Plans were finalized in great haste; the drop took place on the morning of September 17, and took the Wehrmacht totally by surprise.[16] The potential threat was obvious, and the Luftwaffe was ordered to make every effort to stop Allied aerial reinforcements and resupply missions. II. Jagdkorps commanded the tactical fighters on the Western Front, but was overstretched covering the entire line, and needed help. Ten Jagdgruppen were moved into northwestern Germany from the Reich interior and placed under Genmaj. Grabmann's Jagddivision 3, which received day fighters for the first time since D-Day. The Jagdgruppen were assigned to three permanent battle formations, which were commanded by Major Michalski (JG 4 Kommodore), Major Specht (JG 11 Kommodore), and Major Späte (IV./JG 54 Kommandeur). The Gruppen were a mixture of operational RLV units and formations rebuilding as part of Galland's reserve. The "Big Blow" would have to be postponed until the present crisis was resolved.[17]

The September 18 orders for Jagddivision 3 read, "Day fighters attack Allied transports and bomber formations over Holland in closest collaboration with II. Jagdkorps. Destroy Allied gliders and transports and shoot up landed parachutists. Times of dropping assumed to be morning and evening." Jagddivision 3 flew tactical missions for the next two weeks, along with the fighters of Genlt. Alfred Buelowius's II. Jagdkorps. Aerial claims for the campaign totaled 96 for Jagddivision 3, including 15 transports and bombers used as glider tugs, against 109 losses. The full-time tactical fighters of II. Jagdkorps claimed 113 aircraft, including 20 transports, against 83 losses.[18]

The German Army and Waffen-SS responded quickly and effectively to the initial threat from the airdrop. Two SS armored divisions were present in the northernmost landing area, apparently unsuspected by Allied intelligence. Soon they not only trapped the lightly armed British 1st Airborne Division in Arnhem, on the north side of the lower Rhine, but also stopped the British ground forces tasked with relieving it. The 1st Airborne Division was ordered to withdraw on September 25, but only a few men made it across the Rhine to Allied lines. The operation cost

the Allies 11,850 casualties and, although it pushed the front lines 105 km (65 miles) into the Netherlands, across the Maas and the Waal rivers, it failed in all of its major objectives, and lost the Allies any chance to win the war in 1944.[19]

During the two weeks of Market-Garden the RLV was weaker than at any time since immediately after D-Day. The only operational day-fighter units were concentrated in Jagddivision 1, and comprised JG 300 and its three Gruppen; II./JG 3; IV.(Sturm)/JG 3; JGr 10; and I./JG 400. They were not challenged for a few days, as the Eighth Air Force flew only small missions, dropping supplies to Warsaw insurgents and bombing low-priority targets in western Germany. Most of the 8th Fighter Command was employed flying patrols over the Allied bridgehead in Holland and escorting supply missions. The large Second Tactical Air Force (RAF) Spitfire contingent had been neglected in the hasty Allied planning, and it was a week before they were brought forward to take over the defensive patrols.

On September 22, Luftflotte 3 was redesignated Luftwaffenkommando West (LwKdo West) and was subordinated initially to Luftflotte Reich. For the first time in the war the Western Front and Reich air defenses were to answer to one commander. However, Field Marshal Gerd von Rundstedt, recently reinstated as C-in-C West, objected, arguing that he needed tactical air support for his defensive efforts. Hitler appeased him by making LwKdo West directly responsible to Göring.[20] Although the Reichsmarschall probably exerted little operational control, the perpetuation of a divided command was still seen as "unsound" by many experienced RLV commanders.[21] It was not until December 1, 1944, that Stumpff's Luftflotte Reich gained direct control of LwKdo West. II. Jagdkorps and its commander, Genlt. Buelowius, reported to Genlt. Alexander Holle at LwKdo West. Schmid, now a Generalleutnant, remained in command of I. Jagdkorps and continued to report directly to Stumpff. The harmful division in air-defense command between Front and Homeland would bedevil the Luftwaffe almost to the end of its days.[22]

The next step in the slow process of bringing the Me 262 fighter into service took place on September 26. III./ZG 26, which had provided most of the support personnel to ErprKdo 262, was named as the first Me 262 Jagdgruppe, and given the new designation III./JG 6. As Kommandeur, Galland nominated one of the most successful pilots on the Eastern Front, the 23-year-old Major Walter Nowotny,[23] a holder of the Knight's Cross with Oak Leaves, Swords, and Diamonds for his 256 aerial victories, all scored in the east. Because the unit was to operate independently, and (probably) for publicity purposes, the new unit was soon renamed Kommando Nowotny. The establishment strength of the Achmer-based Gruppe was to be 52 fighters. The experience of the first jet-bomber unit, I./KG 51, had shown that takeoffs and landings were the most vulnerable parts of jet missions, and the jet fighters were to be protected by a Flak belt and standing patrols of Fw 190D-9s, the newest version of the Focke-Wulf fighter, which were just being brought into service by III./JG 54. These orders were apparently a surprise to III./JG 54, which could only make two Staffeln operational, and this only by robbing the other two Staffeln of their few experienced pilots. The assets of ErprKdo 262 still at Lechfeld were used to form an Ergänzungsjagdgruppe, III./EJG 2, which was to provide jet conversion training for pilots of conventional fighters.

After a full two-week pause, the RLV was ordered up in force on September 27 against an Eighth Air Force raid on small hydrogenation plants along the Rhine. Schmid apparently expected a raid on the more vital central German oil targets and scrambled 121 fighters, which assembled in a single battle formation.

Unable to see their targets, the bombers dropped on Cologne, Ludwigshafen, and Kassel through cloud and turned back. The operational plan called for the 2nd Bomb Division to fall in behind the 3rd Division and fly the reciprocal of the latter unit's incoming route. However, one B-24 group, the 445th, was badly out of position. It had turned 30 degrees north of course on the approach to Kassel and confused Göttingen for the correct target, but bombed only open fields. It then made the correct turns for the withdrawal course, but 16 km (10 miles) to the east of it, out of sight of any other Americans. They were in between the oncoming German fighters—the three Sturmgruppen, covered by the Stab and I. Gruppe of JG 300—and the escorted bomber columns. The Jagddivision 1 controller positioned the Sturmgruppen for an immediate attack. The Focke-Wulf pilots had already aligned themselves in their assault wedges and bored in in quick succession—IV.(Sturm)/JG 3, followed by II.(Sturm)/JG 4 and II.(Sturm)/JG 300. B-24s began bursting into flames or exploding. Within five minutes, the Liberator formation had been reduced to seven airplanes; 25 crashed immediately, while five more dropped back to crash- or force-land in France or England, saved from total destruction by the lack of German pursuit. The bomber commander's frantic calls for help were answered by the 361st Fighter Group's 376th Squadron, 160 km (100 miles) away with the 1st Bomb

A Bf 109G-14 *Begleitjäger* (high altitude escort fighter) "white 7" of III./JG 3. (*Romm via Price*)

Division. The Mustangs arrived just as IV.(Sturm)/JG 3 was completing an atypical second pass, and split into flights to chase the *Sturmböcke*, which now scattered in all directions. I./JG 300 attempted to intervene, but without success. Its two P-51 claims were not confirmed, and the Mustang squadron lost only one, in a collision with an Fw 190. The RLV force lost 18 KIA and 8 WIA, 25 Fw 190s and five Bf 109s, but had one of its better days. The 445th Bomb Group, on the other hand, had suffered the greatest single-mission loss of any Eighth Air Force group in the war—28 bombers.[24]

An Eighth Air Force raid on the central German oil targets the next day brought up the same RLV units as on the 27th, following the same tactical plan. The number of German fighters up was reduced to 96 by the previous day's losses. The 12 combat wings of the 1st Bomb Division led the stream. Major Dahl saw a temporary break in escort coverage and led an attack on the closest escorts while the three Sturmgruppen made conventional stern attacks on the rear bomb groups of the rear combat wings. Eleven B-17s went down from the 303rd Bomb Group, and seven from the 457th, before P-51s and P-38s were able to drive off the Fw 190s. Nine Focke-Wulfs were claimed by the 479th Group. These were the last victories by Eighth Air Force P-38s. The other three Eighth Air Force Lightning groups had already converted to Mustangs,

A lineup of II.(Sturm)/JG 300 Fw 190A-8/R2 and A-7 fighters at Holzkirchen in August. No personal markings or Geschwader bands can be seen; the aircraft numbers and horizontal II. Gruppe bars are the only identification codes carried. (*Price*)

and the 479th would soon join them. The surviving 303rd Bomb Group crews complained bitterly that they had been attacked despite being in perfect formation, which was supposed to keep the German fighters away. Such were the fortunes of war; Major Dahl had seen a fleeting opportunity, and had taken advantage of it.[25]

I./JG 400 scrambled six Me 163s on the 28th. Tactics for the rocket fighters were being standardized. The hope of achieving concentration was abandoned. Ground control was so difficult that an individual controller was assigned to each pilot and attempted to stay in contact for the entire mission. After takeoff the fighter climbed at 50 degrees to a position 3,000 meters [10,000ft.] above the bomber stream. The pilot then cut off his power and made a gliding attack, resuming power to dive away. Tight turns were used to evade pursuing American fighters. The Me 163 pilot had to be extremely careful with his eight-minute fuel supply. If Brandis was no longer in sight, he had to retain enough fuel to find a suitable field in which to belly-land the fighter, which had no landing gear. The day's efforts were duly observed by the American bomber and fighter crews, but only one Komet was able to approach to firing range in its high-speed glide. However, the pilot's attempt at a dive-and-zoom attack failed when his two 30-mm cannon jammed—the low-precision, slow-firing MK 108 cannon was a poor weapon choice for the fast fighter, which badly needed upward-firing cannon or rocket armament, both of which had been promised.[26]

The shortage of aviation fuel had nearly strangled the German pilot training program. The amount of fuel allotted to the training schools in June was 50,000 tons; in October, 7,000 tons. Disbanded bomber units continued to be a good source of trained pilots for the Jagdgruppen during the fall. New fighter units were also established by redesignating bomber units, absorbing not only their pilots but their ground staffs. Jagdgeschwader 7, with a Stab and two Jagdgruppen, had been formed in August from KG 1, but made little progress toward operational readiness, apparently due to indecision as to its equipment and role. The redesignation of bomber units as fighter units displeased the former bomber pilots who now carried great influence within the OKL, and the next such change was handled differently. On October 1, KG 54 was renamed Kampfgeschwader (Jagd) 54 [KG(J) 54]. It was to remain a bomber wing, but would be re-equipped with fighters and operate in a conventional fighter role. The unit would continue to be supervised by the General of the Bomber Arm, Genmaj. Dietrich Peltz, and would be subordinated for operations to IX. Fliegerkorps rather than I. Jagdkorps. Furthermore, it was to be the first complete Geschwader equipped with Me 262 fighters. The hard-pressed fighter units were to be left out in the cold, and the fighters' champion, Genmaj. Galland, could do nothing but stamp his feet in the snow. The petty rivalries that had riven the Luftwaffe since its foundation had produced one of their most insidious results. The arguments used to justify moving bomber pilots into Me 262 fighters—twin-engine experience and instrument training—had some validity, but ignored certain basic differences between fighter and bomber pilots: the latter tended to be older, more conservative, slower to react, and unwilling or unable to throw their airplanes around in the sky in the barely controlled manner necessary for survival when facing ten or twenty Allied fighters. Leaving bomber-as-fighter units in the bomber chain of command was a terrible insult to the commanders who had built the RLV into a formidable combined-arms force in a very short time, and against heavy internal and external opposition.[27]

The first Me 262 fighter unit of Gruppe strength, Kommando Nowotny, began operations from Achmer on October 3 with about 40 Me 262A-1as. The unit accomplished little during the month, claiming to be hampered by poor serviceability and bad weather. It was apparently subordinated to the tactical II. Jagdkorps for operations rather than I. Jagdkorps, but as an experimental fighter unit it reported administratively to Galland. The Gruppe obviously did not receive the high-level supervision that its importance warranted. No tactical regulations were developed for the potentially revolutionary new weapon; Nowotny apparently considered the Me 262 to be just another fighter.

The *ad hoc* Jagddivision 3 tactical force supporting the Arnhem defense was disbanded on October 2. All of its units returned to their previous Jagddivisionen. Several RLV fighter units changed bases in early October to accommodate them. JG 300 was concentrated around Jüterbog, just south of Berlin, the better to defend both Berlin and the critical central German oil targets. III./JG 300, the last of the original *Wilde Sau* units on night duty, joined its home Geschwader for the first time and was designated a high-altitude cover Gruppe. At the emphatic request of Major Bär,

IV.(Sturm)/JG 3 left Dahl's JG 300, moved to Schafstädt and rejoined JG 3, becoming the Geschwader's only operational Gruppe; the other three were all rebuilding.

The next Eighth Air Force mission to be intercepted in force came on October 6; this was a full-strength strike on 11 oil facilities and other north German industrial targets. The tactical plan of late September was repeated by I. Jagdkorps. The three Sturmgruppen formed the heart of the intercepting force. IV.(Sturm)/JG 3 was directed to the 1st Bomb Division stream northeast of Berlin, but had no high-altitude cover and was dispersed by the P-51s before contacting the bombers. II.(Sturm)/JG 4, with its escorting III./JG 4, and II.(Sturm)/JG 300, with Dahl's Stabsschwarm and III./JG 300, reached the rear of the 3rd Bomb Division stream near Brandenburg and made successful assault attacks which downed 15 B-17s: 11 from the 385th, three from the 94th, and one from the 447th Bomb Group. German losses were relatively light, 12 Fw 190s and five Bf 190s, or 22 percent of those making contact, but they had accounted for only 1.25 percent of the bombers which penetrated Reich airspace.[28]

On 7th the Eighth Air Force dispatched even more bombers, 1,422, to attack oil and other industrial targets in central and northeastern Germany. I. Jagdkorps ordered up its 113 defenders, 80 of which made contact. Seven Jagdgruppen containing Fw 190A *Sturmböcke* and Bf 109G escorts formed a single battle formation and caught a 3rd Bomb Division combat wing in poor formation near Leipzig. Twelve B-17s from the 94th and 95th Bomb Groups went down after a single assault attack from the rear. The German fighters then scattered; 16 were shot down by bomber or escort fire, with the loss of nine dead and three injured pilots.[29]

The rocket and jet fighters were up on this date in their greatest numbers yet. I./JG 400 scrambled five Me 163s from Brandis against the oncoming 3rd Bomb Division. One 95th Bomb Group B-17 was shot down by Fw. Siegfried Schubert, possibly after it had been damaged in the assault fighter attack. The rocket fighters kept scrambling in small numbers for as long as the Fortresses remained within range. Lt. Hans Bott, Fw. Rudolf Zimmermann, and Fw. Schubert prepared for a second sortie. Schubert's takeoff run ended when his trolley apparently lost a wheel in the soft earth; his plane flipped over and exploded, leaving nothing but a crater. Bott and Zimmermann took off successfully; after expending his fuel and making one firing pass on a Fortress Zimmermann was chased to ground by 364th Fighter Group Mustangs, but survived. The Gruppe suffered a second fatality when a pilot lost control of his apparently damaged plane while landing at Brandis; it cartwheeled and broke up. The Gruppe's one success had thus cost it three Me 163s and two dead pilots.[30]

Major Nowotny led his Me 262s up from Achmer, but he lost an engine soon after takeoff and had to return. The rest of the flight was directed to attack the 2nd Bomb Division near Magdeburg. The tactics the jets were to follow in bomber attacks were still in a state of flux. Me 262 pilots had earlier been forbidden to attack heavy bombers at all, due to the lack of armor protection for their jet engines and large (2,500-liter/660-gal.) fuel tanks. The jet pilots' orders for the day are unknown. The returning pilots claimed three B-24s, but the American mission report noted that although Me 262s had been sighted, none closed to firing range. Two jet fighters were apparently lost on this mission under unclear circumstances; their pilots survived. Two more were shot down by a 361st Fighter Group pilot as they were taking off from Achmer; one of the jet pilots was killed. For the day Nowotny's unit thus lost four jets, and one pilot, for three victory claims.[31]

III./JG 301, formerly I./JG 302, had exchanged its Bf 109s for Fw 190s and was ready to return to action as a "heavy" Gruppe. It was to specialize in rear attacks on bomber formations, but in conventional fighters rather than the up-armored *Sturmböcke*. It had moved into Stendal, a new airfield with extensive facilities, which was good for morale. It gave up its successful Gruppenkommandeur, Hptm. Heinrich Wurzer, in exchange for Hptm. Wilhelm Fulda, a Knight's Cross holder. This might have been considered an even swap by the High Command, but Fulda had won his decoration as a glider pilot in the 1941 Greek campaign. He had been in the *Wilde Sau* organization for a year with nothing to show for it, according to unit veteran Willi Reschke, who considered the change of commanders a "bad sign."[32]

The RLV ignored the next two Eighth Air Force raids. The American planners of the October 12 mission were limited to targets in northwestern Germany by a large weather front covering the rest of the country. To keep the pressure on the Luftwaffe, 12 bomber wings were sent to attack four airfields and

the Bremen Focke-Wulf plant, escorted by a small force of 11 fighter groups. The fighters of I. Jagdkorps were grounded by the weather, but the airfields of the northern units of II. Jagdkorps were clear, and Genlt. Buelowius was told that his tactical fighters would form the German defense. Of the three northern Jagdgeschwader, only JG 26 was able to assemble; Obstlt. Josef "Pips" Priller's 57 fighters would be up against 552 bombers and 514 P-47s and P-51s. Priller's Stabsschwarm and three Gruppen scrambled from their bases near the German border and climbed to 6,700 meters (22,000 ft.), course northeast. The Allied radio intercept operators listened in fascination as Priller cursed his pilots by name, trying to get them into formation. The units gradually drifted apart in the clouds; II. and III./JG 26 pulled ahead of the Stabsschwarm and I./JG 26. Over Hannover Priller's remaining force was attacked from above by a number of P-47s and P-51s, and his fighters were dispersed. After combats ranging down to ground level, the Focke-Wulfs landed where they could. I./JG 26 lost three pilots to Thunderbolts from the 56th and 78th Fighter Groups, while filing no victory claims. Priller shot down an isolated 357th Fighter Group P-51 south of Wunstorf for his 101st (and last) victory. The name of the captured American pilot appeared on Priller's claim documents; this identification was easy for the interrogators to make, because Priller was the only German pilot to claim a victory over Germany.[33]

After losing the rest of the Geschwader formation, II./JG 26 succeeded in locating the bomber stream and an apparently unescorted B-17 combat box. They were just forming up to attack it when they were hit by 364th Fighter Group P-51s. The mostly green German

A Me 163 Komet accelerates across Bad Zwischenahn airfield on takeoff. (*Price*)

pilots could do nothing but dive away, and were easy prey for the experienced Americans, who shot down five of the Focke-Wulfs. The end result of the III./JG 26 mission was the same. They flew the farthest, to Bremervörde west of Hamburg, before running afoul of the omnipresent Mustangs and losing five Bf 109s. Two pilots were killed, and a third was seriously burned. No victories were claimed. The Mustangs were from a single flight of the 357th Fighter Group's 363rd Squadron, led by Lt. Charles "Chuck" Yeager. They claimed eight Messerschmitts; five were credited to Yeager, giving him the coveted status of ace-in-a-day—an early accomplishment of note in his long and distinguished aviation career.

Ultra intercepts for this period imply (indirectly) that the use of JG 26 on a bomber intercept mission was a test for General Galland's Big Blow, which was to employ II. Jagdkorps as well as I. Jagdkorps. The test had failed. The Allied intelligence report summarized German efforts as follows: "The tactical fighters proved themselves incapable of making an effective assembly and inexperienced in attacking escorted formations. This may be classed as one of the GAF's [German Air Force's] poorer shows."[34]

No attempt was made to intercept an Eighth Air Force raid for the rest of October. Bad weather and the fuel shortage prevented Jagddivision 1 from either putting up an effective defense or training its inexperienced pilots for the Big Blow. The Market-Garden diversion had left Jagddivision 8 in the south with only the Hungarian fighters under its command. Two low-strength Luftwaffe Jagdgruppen were added by the end of September, but there were still so few fighters in the south that they were not ordered up against most full-strength Fifteenth Air Force missions. Conditions seemed right on October 16 for an interception of the Fifteenth by most of the RLV fighters in north Germany; these were scrambled and sent south. The result was the least effective RLV mission to date. The Fifteenth split into individual group formations and attacked numerous targets in Germany, Austria, and Bohemia-Moravia. Each of the small boxes seemed to be fully escorted, and the controllers could not locate any suitable targets for the 223 fighters which eventually made contact. Only a single victory was claimed, a P-51 over Prague, while 16 Messerschmitts and Focke-Wulfs were shot down by 31st and 325th Fighter Group Mustangs. Jagddivision 8 sent up 17 fighters the next day against a Fifteenth Air Force raid on

Vienna, and then joined Jagddivision 1 on the sidelines for the rest of October.[35]

Luftflotte Reich continued to shuffle its fighter resources. Most of its Jagdgeschwader were expanded to the new four-Gruppe establishment. JG 27 had had four Gruppen for some time, but these had never operated together under a single command. After the present round of re-equipment, which saw III./JG 27 receive 75 Bf 109K-4s, the last model of the venerable fighter to enter service, the entire Geschwader was assigned to Jagddivision 1 and moved to bases south of Berlin. It was an unusual Geschwader for the RLV in that it had only Bf 109s, "light" fighters, rather than a mixture of Bf 109 high-altitude fighters and Fw 190 bomber destroyers. The Geschwader was apparently to operate as a battle formation and would thus be expected to attack primarily bombers. Its effectiveness in this role was yet to be determined.[36]

The Luftwaffe radio messages decoded by the Ultra organization during this period included, in addition to the usual accurate order-of-battle information, numerous snippets related to *grosse Schlag* moves and planning and ever-more-stringent restrictions on fuel consumption. On October 30, LwKdo West issued the following orders:

1. No operation is justified unless the weather and other prerequisites for conduct of operations promise absolutely certain success.
2. Training flights, even within the front-line units, are forbidden with immediate effect, unless special quotas of fuel are allotted for special retraining.
3. All [non-operational] flights except those for operational transfers, workshop, or ferrying purposes are forbidden.[37]

Kommando Nowotny's first three weeks of operations were conspicuously unsuccessful. Ten Me 262s were destroyed or damaged, for few victory claims. The unit's reports blamed design flaws in the engines and landing gear. Willy Messerschmitt dispatched test pilot Fritz Wendel to Achmer with a design team to investigate the charges. Wendel's blistering report placed the blame for the unit's problems squarely on Nowotny, and, by implication, his superiors. Some points made by Wendel:

1. The unit flew only three missions during October 3–24. The very first had been marred by confusion; takeoffs had been delayed until Allied

fighters were directly over the airfield, costing the unit four fighters.

2. Major Nowotny was a successful eastern pilot but was unfamiliar with the situation in the west, and "at age 23 is not the superior leader personality needed to guarantee success of this vital operation."

3. The pilots and leaders held contradictory views with respect to the correct tactical use of the Me 262. "Clear tactical objectives and pilot instructions are lacking."

4. Too little training was taking place. No single-engine training or intensive theoretical instruction was attempted—both of these could have saved airplanes. Poor weather could have been used for classroom training, but was not.

5. Inadequate effort was being made to find and eliminate the true weak points of the airplane. Nowotny had decided that the starter button was in the wrong place, and wanted Messerschmitt to move it from the side console to the main panel.

6. The technical officers were incompetent. The Gruppe technical officer was not an engineer. One Staffel technical officer was a 19-year-old novice who had already destroyed two aircraft through pilot error.[38]

The Kommando Nowotny experiment was further proof to the bomber clique in the OKL that the fighter organization was no longer competent to manage the air defenses. On October 24, four more Kampfgeschwader were redesignated Kampfgeschwader (Jagd) prior to reequipping with fighters. Several would receive Me 262s; all were to be subordinated for operations to IX. Fliegerkorps rather than the principal defensive fighter command, I. Jagdkorps.

In late 1944 the Luftwaffe General Staff continued to address the air-defense crisis and attempted to come up with eleventh-hour operational and tactical remedies. These proposals, contained in studies originating in both the OKL operations staff and the General Staff's 8. Abteilung (Military Science Branch), provided a candid assessment of the state of the RLV. They noted the overpowering numerical superiority of the USAAF and RAF, and the great—and still growing—imbalance in pilot skill and training standards. Somewhat unhelpfully, one of the proposals recommended that the inexperienced pilots "attempt to counterbalance this obvious disadvantage by greater enthusiasm and courage."[39] The studies faulted Luftwaffe senior leadership for both underestimating the industrial might of the Allied nations and neglecting the need for air-defense measures earlier in the war. The failure to streamline aircraft production until 1944 was also highlighted. In spite of the impressive production surge achieved by Saur's Jägerstab, the best the RLV forces could hope for was to meet the enemy "with temporary and local concentrations of power."[40]

The engine of a Fw 190A-8/R2 *Sturmbock* is tested by II.(Sturm)/JG 300 mechanics at Löbnitz in October. JG 300 favored the generic rust-red RLV fuselage band over its own blue–white–blue bands, which were applied only near the end of the war. (*ww2images*)

The causes for this situation were many, but the proposed remedies were few. Other than modest organizational reforms and increased use of radio countermeasures, improved fighter-control techniques, and blind-flying aids, only the rapid introduction of technically superior interceptor aircraft, possessing great speed, superior climbing capability, and powerful armament, had any real hope of redressing the balance.

These were not merely studies drafted by staff officers; the agencies actively solicited suggestions from front-line veterans. Some of these experienced commanders were posted to the staff while recovering from wounds; others submitted proposals through various official channels.

One of the more elaborate proposals came from the Kommandeur of I./JG 300, Hptm. Gerhard Stamp.[41] Stamp was a highly decorated Ju 88 bomber and *Wilde Sau* pilot. He argued that the philosophy of meeting the enemy with masses of conventional fighters as envisioned by the planners of the Big Blow would not produce the desired results, or at best would achieve only a temporary success. He foresaw a continued war of attrition, which would heavily favor the Allied air forces. Stamp maintained that sufficient numbers of technically superior aircraft—in other words the Me 262—were necessary to redress the balance. He argued:

> The operational aim would be to intercept the bomber formations and their escorting fighters at or before the German frontier and force them to jettison their auxiliary tanks. The Luftwaffe would thus regain not only technical but also moral superiority during the combat. The enemy would be forced to keep in closer formation, the fighters would have to give up their free lance tactics in which they range over nearly the whole German front, and the bombers would have to keep closer together on account of their weaker escort. They would, therefore, make a better target for our defenses.
>
> Assuming that one of our new fighters [Me 262] could replace about five of the older types, it follows that 20 high-speed fighters would release 100 other fighters to attack the bombers. The losses in high-speed fighters would be bearable, as owing to its superior speed the aircraft would only be vulnerable during take-off and landing. After achieving air supremacy over Germany, we can then begin to attack the enemy air forces at assembly points and on their

landing grounds. Surprise attacks against assembling bomber formations would also force the enemy to use a part of his fighter strength for protection, thus weakening his fighter effort at the front and on escort duty.[42]

Stamp's suggestion, although containing a fair measure of wishful thinking, did suggest a method for effectively integrating the few Me 262s trickling into operational service into an overall Reich air defense scheme. Just as German Panzer and mechanized forces had in earlier years punched holes for the largely horse-drawn German infantry, so might the latest products of the German aviation industry clear the way for the Bf 109s and Fw 190s and allow them to operate effectively once again.

Command and Control: Late War Developments

Even as the Luftwaffe as a whole withered on the vine, the RLV command and control system continued to improve. It had come a long way from its improvised beginnings in the first years of the war. By the fall of 1944, the formerly patchwork organization reached its pinnacle as a centralized combined-arms force.[43] Under Stumpff's command Luftflotte Reich had evolved into a highly effective headquarters. Its internal boundaries are shown on page 244;[44] eastern and western boundaries were no longer applicable. While sensibly leaving the details of the command of fighter operations to the staff at I. Jagdkorps, Stumpff maintained effective control of unit dispositions, relocating them as necessary to deal with enemy moves. He issued overall directives for fighter operations, "supervised the operations, and intervened when necessary."[45] The large signals staff of the air fleet oversaw the expansion of the Air Reporting Service and the fighter-control system, determining the locations of radar sites and fighter-control stations to ensure fully integrated coverage of the Reich territory.[46] This overall direction facilitated the efficient employment of the combined fighter and Flak forces. When it finally absorbed LwKdo West, it ceased being a purely defensive command, and took over control of the tactical formations supporting the Army on the western front as well.[47] This expansion of Luftflotte Reich's role would have unintended and fateful consequences during the Battle of the Bulge.

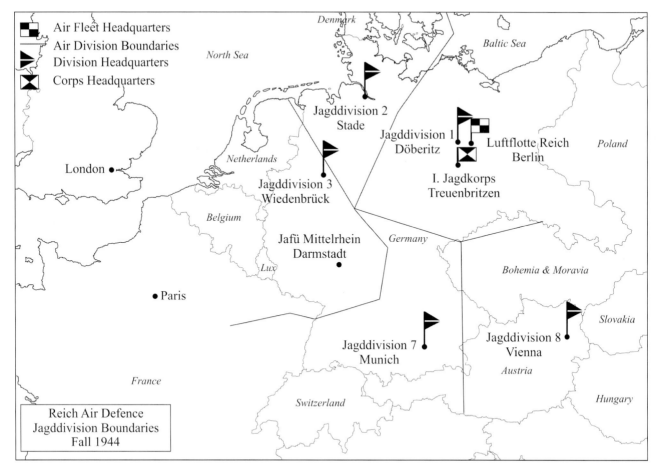

Air Fleet Headquarters
Air Division Boundaries
Division Headquarters
Corps Headquarters

Denmark
Baltic Sea
North Sea
Jagddivision 2
Stade
Jagddivision 1
Döberitz
Luftflotte Reich
Berlin
Poland
Netherlands
London
Jagddivision 3
Wiedenbrück
I. Jagdkorps
Treuenbritzen
Belgium
Jafü Mittelrhein
Darmstadt
Germany
Lux
Bohemia & Moravia
Paris
Jagddivision 7
Munich
Jagddivision 8
Vienna
Slovakia
Austria
France
Switzerland
Hungary

Reich Air Defence
Jagddivision Boundaries
Fall 1944

Schmid's I. Jagdkorps suffered from no such division of responsibility. It fused its five Jagddivision commands into a unified day and night defensive fighter force. Its guiding principle remained, in Schmid's words, "to lead the biggest possible number of our own aircraft against the enemy, under the most favorable conditions for battle . . . this is only possible with an energetic and centralized command."[48] Since taking command in September 1943, Schmid had worked tirelessly to bring this about, and his efforts were finally bearing fruit. The RLV could never match the USAAF in total numbers of combat aircraft, but with proper command and control, enough combat power could be brought to bear at the *Schwerpunkt* to make a local success possible.

Full control of the Aircraft Reporting Service at last rested with the Jagdkorps and Jagddivision commands; this was the realization of Schmid's long struggle to gain sole authority over the operational air situation picture. The Luftgaukommandos still retained command and control over the Flak, civil

defense, and navigational aids (although the night-fighter beacons were under Jagddivision control), and therefore remained important partners in air defense to the end of the war. The methods for assembling the air situation picture were nominally the same as in 1943. These involved bringing together information gleaned from radar stations, ground observers, contact-keeper aircraft, and the Y-service, but the changing nature of the air war and the march of aviation technology had increased the importance of some components while downgrading others.

The loss of the forward radar belt in the occupied western territories hindered the German early-warning system and made the Reich more vulnerable to surprise attacks. Despite this major setback, radar remained the most important component of the Flugmeldedienst. German radar technology had continued to evolve, and by 1944 comprised a mixture of proven technology and highly advanced new types. Radar sites were designated as *1., 2., und 3. Ordnung* (1st, 2nd and 3rd order) positions, classified according to their location, equipment and ability to control day and night fighters and Flak. The radar devices themselves were classified as *Suchgeräte* (search apparatus) and *Führungsgeräte* (control apparatus).[49] The long-range search radars included Mammut, a vastly improved Freya set with a maximum range of 300 km (185 miles). More sophisticated still was the potent Wassermann "M," with a 210-km (130-mile) range, height-finding capability, and a 360-degree scanning field. Medium range sets included the venerable Freya and the improved Freya-Fahrstuhl, the Jagdschloss, and the Würzburg-R.

The most impressive Axis radar development of the entire war was the new Jagdschloss set. Equipped with a revolutionary panoramic display, it could be used for medium-range early warning and ground-controlled interception. Like any piece of new technology, however, the complicated Jagdschloss had its teething troubles, and poorly trained operators limited the effectiveness of the *c.* 100 sets that had entered service by war's end. Schmid spoke of the "tragedy" of Jagdschloss, and it joined the Me 262 and the Type XXI U-boat in the dismal pantheon of "too little, too late" Third Reich miracle weapons.

Short-range radar sets, usually Würzburg A, C or D, with only a 40-km (25-mile) maximum range, provided final course and altitude information as the enemy formation approached the target. Many of the early-warning radar sets, including some models of Freya and Jagdschloss, were also used for fighter control. The information they provided on German fighter activities also contributed to building the overall air situation picture.

The radar sites and co-located aircraft spotting, reporting and fighter control were incorporated into aircraft reporting companies (heavy, medium, or light). From three to six companies made up an aircraft reporting battalion, and three to five battalions formed an aircraft reporting regiment. These formations ultimately reported to the chief signals officer of the fighter division. At the Jagd-division Gefechtsstand, all of this information was assembled and made available to the users. Schmid continued his efforts to simplify the working of the command posts. Accordingly, their "size, method of construction, and internal facilities depended on the tactical requirements and the principles of command, and battle tactics in air defense." Fulfilling these requirements with the existing technical means in the simplest and most efficient manner possible was "the

Uffz. Ernst Schröder stands on the wing of his 5.(Sturm)/ JG 300 Fw 190A-8 "red 19" at Löbnitz in the fall. The airplane carries the coat of arms of Schröder's hometown, Cologne, and the motto *"Kölle alaaf!"*—dialect for "Cologne lives!" (*Schröder*)

highest goal of the Gefechtsstand technology."[50] Complex technological gadgetry and visual displays would not pass muster if they did not contribute to simple and efficient operation.

The Luftwaffe's radio- and radar-intercept service (Y-service) also retained its importance in the final stages of the war. Although the loss of the forward intercept stations caused persistent problems, the Y-service was still able to acquire vital information on American intentions. Schmid recalled: "The badly disciplined R/T traffic of the U.S. bomber units facilitated the plotting of the courses and the early identification of the target in case of bad weather. Thus, messages such as 'Crossing the enemy coast' or 'No clouds over target' could be picked up again and again."[51] Increased USAAF use of electronic target-finding aids, including the H2X radar (known to the Germans as "Rotterdam"), provided additional opportunities for

381st Bomb Group B-17Gs cruise in a clear area between cloud layers en route to a target in late 1944. (*ww2images*)

the radar-intercept service. To the end of the war, the Luftwaffe signals branch retained tight control over the process. A Luftwaffe manual summed up, "Radio interception is an important command tool! Information thus gleaned must be handled with special security precautions. Incautious and careless handling may cause this most valuable source of intelligence to dry up. *Beware of enemy deception measures!*"[52]

As radar and signals intelligence increased in importance, other arms of the Aircraft Reporting Service declined in relative significance. The ground observers still earned their keep, standing watch in those few areas in the shrinking Reich not covered by radar or where terrain features limited radar's effectiveness. In keeping with the "total war" philosophy, customs officials, railroad personnel, police, and other civilians were expected to function as observers. The Fühlungshalter aircraft had largely faded from the scene, but many Luftwaffe commanders believed that superior radar coverage lessened their importance. They are still mentioned in fall 1944 manuals, but these documents stress that owing to the strong USAAF fighter presence, Fühlungshalter operations were to be restricted to periods of bad weather. In an attempt to bridge the gap, the Aircraft Reporting Service began to rely on reports from German fighter formations concerning strength, altitude, and course of enemy formations, and especially the fighter escort. Luftwaffe instructions continued: "It has proven a useful method to assign to the *Rottenflieger* [wingman] of the commander of the *Gefechtsverband* the task of

sending these reports. After sighting the enemy, he switches to a previously determined frequency and transmits his observations, in a running commentary, to the division Gefechtsstand."[53]

In 1944, *Jägerführung* (fighter ground-control) procedures also continued to improve. The overall operational principles remained unchanged: "It is the responsibility of the commanding Jagddivision concerned to direct the fighter forces into battle in a concentrated striking force against the enemy formations. The attack objective of the fighter aircraft, in this case, is the bomber formation. Simultaneous enemy fighter sweeps cannot, as a rule, be engaged by air action."[54] Coverage improved as more and more fighter-direction sites were built. Normally positioned alongside the radar sites, these control detachments reported air activity to the Jagddivision headquarters while vectoring the fighter formations under their control against the main enemy threats identified by the Jagddivision command.[55]

The primary fighter-control technique remained Y-Führung (Y-Control, known to the Allies as "Benito") using the airborne FuG 16ZY transceiver.[56] The method is described in detail in Chapter 5. It had a 100–250 km (60–155 mile) range, depending on the altitude of the formation being controlled. Schmid thought that Y-control was an effective system, despite its cumbersome aspects. In a statement shortly after the war he observed:

Y-control nearly always created difficulties when passing day-fighter units from one division area to another; such difficulties mostly occurred through faulty tuning-in. This kind of control moreover required understanding and careful training of unit commanders and crews. Where these conditions were met, Y-control was a quite safe means of control, limited though it was on account of the few frequencies available. Even in the last phase of the war enemy jamming of Y lines was rarely effective.[57]

In mid-1944, Y-control was augmented by a new procedure, EGON (sometimes referred to as Freya-EGON or "Erstling Long Range Control Procedure"). In contrast to Y-control, EGON was the essence of simplicity (*see opposite*).[58] EGON was an ingenious combination of the FuG 25a Erstling IFF (Identification Friend or Foe) device and a Freya radar fitted with the Gemse IFF receiver array. As the radar set tracked the German fighter, the IFF receiver detected the IFF signal from the FuG 25a. Bearing and range information were then sent to a display in the control hut. It was possible to exert control by using only the IFF signal, although in practice the Freya range return (Tube I) and the IFF range information (Tubes II and III) were cross-checked for greater accuracy.[59] The controller would then guide the fighter to the enemy formation in the same manner as with the Y-system. EGON had a range of up to 240 km (150 miles), and it had several advantages over Y-control. Its multiple frequencies made it less susceptible to jamming and made controlling several formations an easier task.[60] A shortage of Freya sets and a desire to have a common system for both day and night fighters (which Göring in 1942 had determined would be Y-control) delayed its introduction into general use. In this case, perhaps the "good" was the enemy of the "best." Galland definitely preferred the EGON system, as did most of the day-fighter unit commanders.[61] The two procedures coexisted in action, although the Y-system remained the more common. Special control detachments, designated *Funkleittrupps* (Y) and *Funkmessleittrupps* (Egon) operated the systems at the warning and control sites.

Three other control measures deserve mention:

1. The crudest system was the *UKW-Peil-Führung*, a VHF system which provided a very approximate means (within a square kilometer) of locating a friendly aircraft. "Tornado" ground stations triangulated on a brief direction-finding transmission from a FuG 16 and reported the information to the Gefechtsstand.[62]
2. High hopes were placed on the very advanced FuG 120 *Bernhardine* night-fighter control system which was test flown in day fighters, but Allied bombing of the German electronics industry prevented its actual use in combat.[63]
3. And finally, the *Reichsjägerwelle* running commentary, provided by Jagdkorps headquarters, remained available for all to use.

Fighter controllers in 1944 underwent extensive training, which totaled 275 hours of theoretical and practical instruction. Trainees mastered the fine points of radar (75 hours), radio (42 hours), the reporting system (16 hours), navigation (23 hours) and airborne aids and monitoring service (11 hours). They were also schooled in friendly and enemy battle tactics (34 hours). A final 74-hour course in "Fighter Control—Theory and Practice" concluded the instruction.[64] There was, of course, no substitute for experience, and the chief controller at Jagddivision level was ideally a veteran combat pilot, often recovering from wounds. The Luftwaffe personnel system attempted to provide controllers and at the same time fulfill the myriad other demands for battle-hardened officers.

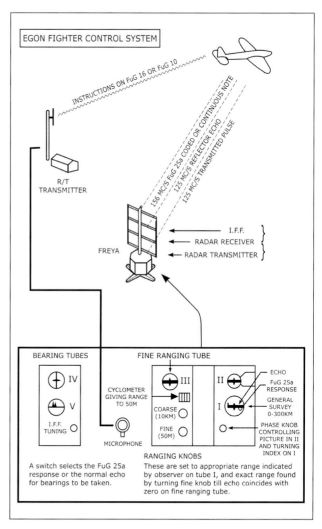

As the effectiveness of the German fighter force declined, the Flak arm assumed greater prominence, although officially the principles of an integrated air-defense concept were never abandoned. A Luftwaffe Flak manual of September 1944 still maintained that "Flak and fighters carry the brunt of the burden in combat . . . the main effort of the fighter is made on the approaching formation before bomb release and on bombers returning to base. The Flak is concerned with the direct protection of the objective."[65] The Luftwaffe Operations Staff concurred in yielding the airspace over the target to the Flak; its tactical instructions acknowledged:

> The anti-aircraft fire control methods previously employed have proven a failure. Uncertainty regarding our own air operations has frequently led to the Flak ceasing fire too early. In this manner, neither the Flak nor the fighter defenses may be used to fullest effect over the target.
>
> In the case of Flak concentrations around individual objectives ... the only way to ensure maximum effectiveness is for every weapon to fire without any restrictions whatsoever. They should "free fire" at all altitudes without regard for our own fighters, by day and night. The fighter defenses are best employed away from the objective, particularly along the incoming and outbound flight paths of the enemy bomber formation.[66]

Although some Luftwaffe leaders continued to maintain that the RLV fighter force was "still the most effective defensive measure at the present time," the emphasis placed on the Flak arm in the fall of 1944 was undoubtedly warranted. During the series of attacks against the vital Leuna hydrogenation complex, for example, 59 USAAF heavy bombers were lost to the Flak against only 13 to the fighters. Moreover, the heavy Flak defenses noticeably reduced bombing accuracy.[67]

To ensure the necessary cooperation and removal of conflicts, the position of *Flakeinsatzführer* (Flak Operations Commander) had been created at Jagddivision level and had proven its worth in the conduct of operations. This commander provided a link between the Jagddivision's aircraft-reporting and fighter-control functions and the Flakartillerie and the civil defense organization in the Luftgaukommandos.[68] And just as their predecessors in World War I had done, RLV fighter pilots continued to home on the puffs of exploding Flak shells which led them to USAAF bomber formations—another demonstration of the "low tech" yet effective nature of German tactics. Although the command and control seam between Flak and flying communities never completely disappeared, and friendly-fire incidents would continue to occur, this was an aspect of Reich air defense in which real progress had been made since

the beginning of the war.

The systems worked well enough, but there were always attempts to improve upon them. In September 1944 Genlt. Kurt Kleinrath, the commander of Jagddivision 1, made a proposal for a further simplification of the command structure.[69] He called for a division of the Reich territory, with a single Jagdkorps HQ, containing two Jagddivisionen—West and East— to which would be assigned generals in command of Flak and ground services, dispensing with the Luftgaukommandos entirely. In a similar vein, the Luftwaffe General Staff's Military Science Department proposed in November that all fighter and Flak forces be merged into a single "Air Defense Corps." This Corps headquarters would unify 4–5 fighter divisions, and a general in command of several Flak divisions, all under a single corps commander:

> The fighter divisions would also be responsible for their ground organization, supplies, and signals communications. For this purpose there would be at each headquarters a senior officer for ground organization, a senior supply officer and a senior signals officer. These senior officers are at the same time formation commanders and are all stationed at the Division Gefechtsstand. Thus, command centers would be created which would be directly responsible for operations, and unity of command would thus be assured.

This proposal would also have downgraded the importance of the Luftgaukommandos, which were to be left only with civil defense, administration, and ground organization and supply not related to the RLV effort. It offered the clear advantage of dramatically streamlined command and communications channels.[70]

Despite their evident merits, none of these more radical proposals found favor. The increasing prestige of the Flak arm, and the Führer's known bias in favor of that branch, may account for the refusal to consider reducing the importance of the powerful Flak fiefdoms, the Luftgaukommandos. The chaos of the Kreipe–Koller interregnum, and Hitler's complete disdain for the "flying Luftwaffe" certainly worked against the possibility of any internal RLV reorganization gathering momentum. So in the end, I. Jagdkorps carried on through the fall as the main operational command for the air defense of the Reich, coordinating its efforts through Luftflotte Reich and the liaison channels with the Flak.

The final stages of the evolution of the RLV command and control system highlight the best and worst aspects of the German military tradition. At the operational level, the Germans developed sound basic principles for defensive air operations and energetically developed the necessary supporting tactics, technology and organizations. These measures were "taken under great strain and at the cost of enormous sacrifices." Many of the problems under which the Luftwaffe leadership labored, however, were of its own making. The Luftwaffe command was still held captive by its offensive fixation. The bomber arm retained tremendous influence within the Luftwaffe even as its squadrons melted away. Even some of the most clearheaded proposals for reorganizing the air defenses saw this as only a prelude to a return to offensive action. And finally, just as the improved measures were ready for action, Allied superiority and the deteriorating war situation rendered them ineffective. Yet it is worth remembering that this organization to the very last remained able to strike hard blows against USAAF formations. One B-24 navigator interviewed by the authors recalled his missions in the late fall of 1944:

> You'd fly several missions and never see a German fighter. We knew they were low on gasoline and were conserving their forces. Then, without warning, they'd throw everything they had against you . . . and a good part of the Group wouldn't come back.[71]

November 2—Merseburg-Leuna

November was the peak month of the American air offensive against German oil production, although most bombs had to be dropped through the pervasive fall undercast. The Eighth Air Force flew 13 missions against petroleum facilities; the Fifteenth Air Force, 12. Production dropped to 31 percent of the monthly average in the spring of 1944. Most of the plants still operating were tiny benzol plants, making oil substitutes from coke oven byproducts. November was one of the least effective months for the RLV, which was hampered by bad weather and low fuel supplies. During the month only four Eighth Air Force missions and one Fifteenth Air Force mission were intercepted.[72]

The first defensive effort in November came on the 2nd. The Eighth Air Force sent 1,174 B-17s and B-24s to bomb the Merseburg-Leuna oil installations and

Walter Nowotny, photographed as an Oberleutnant while in JG 54 on the Eastern Front in 1943. He was brought to the Reich to lead Kommando *Nowotny*, the unit charged with bringing the Me 262 into full operational service. (*Crow*)

several other targets in central Germany, escorted by 968 P-47s and P-51s from 15 fighter groups. The straight-line course chosen by the USSTAF planners was probably meant to challenge the defenders, who responded by flying the most sorties since D-Day. The weather was sufficiently clear to permit takeoffs and landings, but interfered with assembly and the search for the bombers; of the 490 fighters to take off, only 305 were able to make contact.

The 4th Fighter Group screened ahead of the leading 3rd Bomb Division, anticipating that the Me 163s would be up from Brandis. I./JG 400 in fact made a maximum-strength effort (five Me 163s), and

Hauptmann Wilhelm Fulda, phographed during a visit to a glider unit on a training field near Aschaffenburg, Germany, in early 1944. Originally a glider pilot, Fulda joined the *Wilde Sau* night fighters, and commanded in succession II./JG 301, I./JG 302, and I./JG 400. (*Crow*)

the alert bomber gunners and Mustang pilots shot down four of them, killing three pilots. The survivors made no claims. Hurt by shortages of rocket fuel and trained pilots, the Luftwaffe's only operational Me 163 Gruppe was unable to fly another mission in this strength for four months.[73]

Kommando Nowotny scrambled at least six Me 262s from Achmer. These were directed to the bombers nearest them, 2nd Bomb Division B-24s, whose target was the Bielefeld viaduct. Some of the jets were carrying two bulky launch tubes for WGr 21 rockets beneath their noses. Several rockets were launched at B-24s without hitting anything; one jet then damaged a 56th Fighter Group P-47 with 30-mm cannon fire before it pulled away from the Americans.[74]

I. Jagdkorps ordered its conventional fighters to

assemble in three battle formations, formed around JG 3, JG 4, and JG 27. The JG 3 formation was led by Major Bär in his Stabsschwarm and contained that Geschwader's I. and II. Gruppen as high-altitude protection for the IV., the Sturmgruppe. The protective screen soon engaged Mustangs, and Major Moritz was left alone to find a suitable target for his *Sturmböcke*. An opportunity quickly presented itself in the form of 36 91st Bomb Group B-17s, flying at the rear of the 1st Bomb Division stream. The bomb group had already had a bad mission. It had been hit hard by Flak before the target, losing one B-17, and had dropped its bombs in open country before apparently making the wrong turn at the target. The division's fighter escorts were at the front of the stream, and Moritz's men were able to make a classic *Sturmangriff* on the 91st before the return of the Mustangs. Twelve B-17s went down under a hail of 30-mm cannon fire. The *Sturmböcke* were then severely punished by the P-51s, losing ten pilots killed, five badly injured, and 21 Fw 190s; the survivors landed on airfields throughout central Germany.[75]

The rest of JG 3 had little to show for its own sacrifice. The two Bf 109 Gruppen claimed two P-51s and two B-17s, but lost 16 KIA, 5 WIA (3 severely), and 30 fighters. Two pilots were inadvertently responsible for a disaster to another Gruppe. JG 300 and JG 301 had been left on the ground for this mission, even though the Merseburg raiders passed directly over their airfields south of Berlin. Two JG 3 Bf 109s attempted to land on Borkheide, the I./JG 300 base, after evading Mustangs. The technical officer of I./JG 300 fired two red flares to indicate "no fuel." The flares attracted the attention of Mustang pilots from the 355th Fighter Group, who then saw and shot down the two JG 3 Bf 109s, spotted the dispersed I./JG 300 Bf 109s, and dropped to ground level to strafe. According to one source, 26 Bf 109s were destroyed and ten more damaged on the field, temporarily erasing the Gruppe from the RLV order of battle.[76]

The JG 4 *Gefechtsverband* was able to give its Sturmgruppe, II.(Sturm)/JG 4, the opportunity to make a successful assault attack. Major Michalski led all four Gruppen of his Geschwader toward the Merseburg raiders. He was as lucky as JG 3's Major Moritz, and spotted a single B-17 group far out of position. The 457th Bomb Group had been blown 56 km (35 miles) north of its course by high winds. They were flying over a solid undercast and the leader did not suspect his error because his radar was malfunctioning. How they lost the rest of their combat wing is not addressed in the group records, but the 457th bombed a secondary target and was striving to regain the security of the escorted stream when it was hit by Major Schröder's II.(Sturm)/JG 4 from the rear by that unit's favored "attack arrows" while IV./JG 4 Bf 109s made frontal attacks on the unescorted bombers. Nine B-17s went down in the first pass; the American survivors felt that the rest of the 35 Fortresses would have met the same fate if not for the timely appearance of some Mustangs, which fell on the *Sturmböcke* and shot down nine of them, killing six of their pilots and wounding the other three. The rest of the Geschwader came off relatively lightly, losing 8 KIA, 3 WIA, and eight Bf 109s while claiming several B-17s.[77]

JG 27 flew its first RLV mission as a full Geschwader, with results that ensured that it was also its last. The Stabsschwarm and four Gruppen of the all-Bf 109 "light" Geschwader scrambled at noon and were directed to the Merseburg bomber stream. Just as the formation reached the van of the 1st Bomb Division to begin a head-on attack, it was set upon by some 352nd Group Mustangs, specifically those of Major George Preddy and his 328th Fighter Squadron. After a 20-minute combat the Americans claimed 25 Messerschmitts, a record for a single squadron mission, for the loss of one pilot shot down and taken prisoner. JG 27 was then attacked by other P-51 units; its casualty toll at the end of the day was 27 KIA, 12 WIA, and 50 Bf 109s, for six P-51 claims. This was the most costly day in the distinguished history of the *Afrika* Geschwader, which had to stand down until other employment could be found for it.[78]

I. Jagdkorps' maximum strength effort cost it 133 of the 305 fighters that made contact, a staggering 44 percent loss. Seventy-three pilots were killed or remained missing; 32 others were injured. The USAAF historians stated that the large number of aggressive German fighters made a "deep impression" on the American commanders. The impression left on Adolf Hitler by the performance of his fighters was at least as deep, and of greater consequence for the course of the war. Neither Göring nor Koller was present at the Führer conference on November 6, so it fell to Genmaj. Eckhard Christian, chief of the Luftwaffe operations staff, to defend the performance of the RLV day fighters on the 2nd. The unconfirmed victory claims as of that date totaled 30 for the Flak and 52 for the 305 fighters which had made contact.

Thirty of these 52 claims were attributed to the 61 assault fighters. Hitler was concerned about the other 244 fighters, which had downed only 22, and refused to listen to any discussion of their role in neutralizing the American escorts. He stated that he had confidence in both the pilots and their equipment, and was at a loss for an explanation. After some quick math, he concluded, "If I deploy 2,600, I have the possibility of shooting down 200. In other words, the hope of decimating the enemy with a mass deployment is not realistic. So it is insanity to go on producing the aircraft, just to give the Luftwaffe a chance to operate with numbers!" Galland, who was not there, did not know it, but his Big Blow died at this moment.[79]

Word of Hitler's latest expression of dissatisfaction with the fighter force quickly reached Göring. He summoned the RLV fighter commanders to a meeting at his Berlin-Wannsee headquarters the very next day. There he excoriated his fighter pilots once again, in a 3½-hour tirade that was then sent to the combat units as a wire recording. No improvement in pilot performance can be correlated with this speech.[80]

Genmaj. Galland visited Kommando Nowotny at Achmer on November 7 and 8 to observe operations for himself and discuss the unit's problems. An Eighth Air Force bomber stream passed nearby on the morning of the 8th on another trip to Merseburg-Leuna. The weather was so bad that Schmid did not order an interception by his conventional forces, but Nowotny's men were ordered to scramble, probably for Galland's benefit. Of the first four Me 262s to take off, two, including Nowotny's, returned immediately with engine and landing-gear problems. A few minutes later Nowotny led three fighters up on a second sortie. By this time the area was swarming with American fighters, which a few III./JG 54 Fw 190D-9s were attempting to keep away from Achmer. One jet pilot, Oblt. Franz Schall, shot down a 357th Group P-51 and two 356th Group P-47s, one with the assistance of a Focke-Wulf, before he was forced to take to his parachute. The second jet pilot was also hit by a Mustang and bailed out successfully. Major Nowotny was then heard to say either "It is burning" or "I am burning," before plunging vertically through the overcast in his airplane and crashing to his death one kilometer away from the airfield. Shortly after his return to Berlin Galland ordered his only jet fighter unit withdrawn from operations; it was to transfer to Lechfeld in Bavaria for more training. Only four of its original 30 Me 262s remained operational. Its poor performance was yet another blot on Galland's fading reputation. The decision to place the unproven Nowotny in command of the unit, which was compounded by the failure to provide him with adequate supervision and technical assistance, has to rank as one of Galland's worst of the war.[81]

The pilots and ground staff of Kommando Nowotny reached Lechfeld on about November 14. The unit was kept off operations for the training it had previously missed. On the 19th Kommando Nowotny was disbanded and reconstituted as III./JG 7. Major Erich Hohagen, a very experienced western front pilot, was named its first Kommandeur.

On November 15, Genmaj. Dietrich Peltz replaced Genlt. Buelowius as commander of II. Jagdkorps. The appointment of a bomber pilot to one of the highest positions in the fighter chain of command was another sign of the power of the OKL bomber clique, and was a blow to the morale of the fighter commanders, if not yet to that of the lower-ranking pilots.[82]

Two entire Geschwader left the RLV on the 19th. JG 27 was moved to northwestern Germany and assigned a single mission: protection of the jet bases in the area, from which now operated the Me 262 bombers of I./KG 51 and the Ar 234 reconnaissance aircraft of Kommando Sperling. The jet fighters which could have used the cover over Achmer earlier in the month were now far away in Bavaria. The second Geschwader, JG 4, was ordered to transfer to LwKdo West bases in the Frankfurt-Darmstadt area. Its pilots were told that they were now to specialize in hunting Allied fighter-bombers, which was in fact the top priority mission of all of LwKdo West's established fighter units. The Geschwader's short tour in the RLV thus came to an abrupt end.[83]

Although III./JG 7 was off operations for training, III./EJG 2, the Me 262 conversion training unit which shared its Lechfeld base, flew occasional small-scale combat missions in the same manner as its predecessor, ErprKdo 262. According to his logbook, Major Rudolf Sinner contacted 30 Fifteenth Air Force bombers and 40 escorts near Munich on the 16th and attacked them, but without result.[84]

Genmaj. Galland was informed on November 20 that all RLV day-fighter units except JG 300 and JG 301 were soon to be transferred to the west for offensive operations. *Der grosse Schlag* was thus canceled. In his memoirs Galland expressed the opinion that he had been "set up," that the High

Command had never been serious about the operation. Considering the low opinion of the fighter force then current in both Hitler's OKW and Göring's OKL, this is in all likelihood true.[85]

Although the weather was typically bad on the 21st, Genlt. Schmid decided to defend against major raids on oil targets in Merseburg and Hamburg. The result was a *Fehlschlag*. Cloud cover at high altitude was nearly continuous, and it was raining on most bases. Schmid apparently waited to issue his takeoff orders in hopes that either the rain would abate or the bombers would turn back. Neither took place, and his fighters did not take off until after the targets had been bombed. Most were attacked by the escorts as they attempted to form up or as they broke through the overcast. I./JG 1 lost 15 KIA, 5 WIA, and 27 Fw 190s on its first mission since its return to the RLV. III./JG 4 lost 1 KIA, 3 WIA, and eight Bf 109s on its last mission in the RLV, after which it filed JG 4's last two heavy bomber claims. Of the two bad-weather Geschwader, JG 300 was dispersed by the escorts and made only weak attacks on the bombers. JG 301 flew its first mission since re-equipping with Fw 190s. When III./JG 301 reached the bombers, Hptm. Fulda led the Gruppe in a quick frontal attack from too great an angle; Obfw. Reschke and a few other pilots broke away and made their more customary rear attacks. Although the German pilots filed a large number of claims, only five B-17s and four P-51s were lost to the RLV fighter force, which itself lost 40 KIA, 22 WIA, and 61 fighters.[86]

Genmaj. Galland continued to tinker with the organization of JG 7, which was destined to become the only jet fighter Geschwader in the traditional fighter chain of command. On November 24, he obtained a full Gruppe of trained fighter pilots for it by the expedient of renaming II./JG 3 as I./JG 7. For the post of Kommandeur he was able to obtain Hptm. Theodor Weissenberger, a mature Eastern Front unit commander with an outstanding record in the west since taking command of I./JG 5 in June and bringing it to the *Invasionsfront*. His task was to get his Bf 109 pilots qualified on the Me 262 as quickly as possible. The old I./JG 7, which was having a hard time converting its ex-bomber pilots to conventional fighters, was renamed II./JG 7; the old II./JG 7 became II./JG 3. Galland named Oberst Johannes Steinhoff as Kommodore of the all-jet Geschwader. Steinhoff wore the Knight's Cross with Oak Leaves and Swords, and had commanded JG 77 on the Mediterranean Front for 19 months. Steinhoff made his first jet flight on November 25, and took command on December 1.[87]

On November 26, the Eighth Air Force executed a maximum-strength attack on several targets in the Hannover area. The most important of these was the Misburg hydrogenation plant, which was assigned to the B-17s of the 1st Bomb Division and the B-24s of the 2nd Division. Although the persistent cloud cover prevented visual bombing, the I. Jagdkorps airfields were clear at ground level, and Schmid broke with recent practice by getting his fighters up early against this relatively short-penetration raid. The old rendezvous point of Dummer Lake was used for the formation of a strong Gefechtsverband which was able to attack the incoming stream prior to bombing. The formation was led by the JG 1 Kommodore, Obstlt. Herbert Ihlefeld, and contained I. and II./JG 1, with III./JG 6 as high-altitude cover. Ihlefeld reached a temporarily unescorted 1st Bomb Division combat wing as it was approaching its target, the Altenbeken railroad viaduct, and led a quick head-on attack which downed three 91st Bomb Group B-17s and knocked a fourth from formation. P-51s and P-47s from the 356th Fighter Group were quick to respond to the bombers' calls for help, and chased off the German fighters. JG 1 lost 12 KIA, 3 WIA, and 15 Fw 190s. III./JG 6 lost 6 KIA, 6 WIA, and 12 Bf 109s. The JG 6 Kommodore, Obstlt. Johann Kogler, claimed that the Messerschmitts were rendered defenseless by iced-up canopies; the Gruppe had failed to install its deicing equipment. The pilots of the 356th Group were grateful for any opportunity; it was the most successful mission of the war for this lowest-scoring of the 15 Eighth Air Force fighter groups, with 24 confirmed claims and no losses.[88]

The next battle formation to reach the bombers was that of JG 301, led by Obstlt. Fritz Aufhammer and his Stabsschwarm and containing all three of its Gruppen, now equipped completely with bad-weather Fw 190s. Their target was the 2nd Bomb Division B-24 stream, now approaching the Initial Point for Misburg. Since they were planning a rear attack, the fighters headed for the end of the stream, and found an ideal target. The last combat wing was spread out owing to a delayed turn over the North Sea; its trailing group, the 491st, had no escort. (The American mission report claims that the escort had been drawn away by a Luftwaffe "bait unit," but this cannot be verified.) The Geschwader dropped from the clouds in its first-ever close-formation stern attack. Although its aircraft

lacked the armor and 30-mm cannon of the Sturmböcke, the unit's attack was just as successful as those of the elite Sturmgruppen; its two passes downed 16 491st Group B-24s, plus five from the 445th Group, next ahead in the stream. The attacks were pressed so closely that several Fw 190s were shot down by B-24 gunners. A handful of Mustangs from the 2nd Scouting Force were the first to respond to the bombers' distress calls, followed by three full groups, the 339th, 355th, and 361st. The Focke-Wulfs, most of whose pilots had no dogfighting experience, were slaughtered; the 361st Group had its most successful day of the war. The Geschwader lost 26 KIA, 13 WIA, and 35 Fw 190s; half of the rebuilt unit's strength was gone after its first two missions.[89]

Taking advantage of the relatively good weather, the tactical II. Jagdkorps ordered some of its fighters up against the withdrawing bomber stream. The four JG 27 Jagdgruppen, whose holiday from attacking bombers had not lasted long, and IV./JG 54, which had never before flown a mission against heavy bombers, formed up over Osnabrück and were directed to the 1st Division B-17s departing Misburg. They were driven off by the Mustangs with heavy losses of aircraft (32 Bf 109s and four Fw 190s), but only moderate losses of personnel (13 KIA and 7 WIA) —the JG 27 pilots had apparently become adept at rapid bailouts from their Messerschmitts.[90]

Each defensive mission by the RLV was becoming more expensive. That of the 26th cost it 60 KIA, 32 WIA, and 119 aircraft. The sacrifice had netted 25 USAAF bombers and six fighters; a few more Allied aircraft crash-landed for unknown reasons. The American escort fighter force was now being directed by a Microwave Early Warning (MEW) station in the Netherlands which had been converted from defensive to offensive purposes, and could only rarely be surprised. The jet fighters, which by this time should have formed the heart of the RLV force, were literally on the sidelines. III./EJG 2 at Lechfeld was allowed to attack reconnaissance aircraft, and became quite good at it. Today Obfw. Buchner and Major Sinner each downed a 7th PRG F-5 (photo-reconnaissance P-38), while Lt. Müller damaged a No. 80 Squadron (SAAF) Mosquito, which returned to Italy on one engine.[91]

Apparently not fully satisfied with conventional tactics, the USSTAF planners ordered a spoof raid for the 27th. Ten fighter groups simulated a bomber mission to central Germany. One group carried bombs; it and four others designated as strafers flew the usual course to Merseburg at the bombers' accustomed altitude, while the other five groups flew high cover. All flew above the undercast. At I. Jagdkorps headquarters, Genmaj. Schmid was apparently forced to make his decisions based on radar images alone, and was fooled completely. Since most of his airfields were clear, he ordered a maximum-strength interception. As the fighters of JG 1 and JG 3 came up through the overcast, their leaders saw only sweeping Mustangs, and quickly ordered their men to withdraw, which they did, suffering only light losses. JG 300 and JG 301 were not so fortunate. The six Gruppen to get airborne were ordered to form a single battle formation, and became a huge, irresistible target for the Mustang pilots. The fighter group carrying bombs dropped them on targets of opportunity; the strafers abandoned their mission; and all piled on the hapless Luftwaffe pilots. The two Geschwader lost 27 KIA, 8 WIA, and 39 fighters.[92]

In the meantime, lightly escorted Eighth Air Force bombers attacked rail targets in southwestern Germany, completely unmolested by the Luftwaffe. Since weather conditions favored an interception, II. Jagdkorps ordered many of its fighters up against the heavy bombers as they withdrew. IV./JG 54, I. and III./JG 26, and JG 27's four Gruppen were unable to get through the escort screen, however, and lost 10 KIA, 6 WIA, and 19 fighters. The American losses to conventional German aircraft totaled six fighters, and no bombers. In the meantime the Bavarian sideshow produced one success—a III./EJG 2 Me 262 downed a No. 683 Sqd. RAF reconnaissance Spitfire. Schmid's decision to intercept the fighter sweep is a clear indication that he lacked the information from Fühlungshalter aircraft that had been so valuable earlier in the year. Although documentation has not been found, it is probable that the contact-keeper

Gefr. Wilhelm Mittag poses in front of a Fw 190A-8 used by his operational training unit, JGr Süd, in late 1944. The unit had displaced from southern France to Zeltweg, in Steiermark, Austria. The training units had plenty of first-line operational aircraft, but very little fuel to fly them. (*Mittag*)

squadrons had by this time been disbanded.

November ended with another full-scale Eighth Air Force attack on Merseburg and other oil targets in central Germany. Only JG 300 was ordered up on the 30th, in generally miserable weather. I./JG 300 lost three Bf 109s and II./JG 300 one Fw 190, all with their pilots, to the Mustangs, without reaching the bombers. The 41 bombers lost on this mission, or scrapped after it, were downed by Flak, collision, or mechanical failure. The Luftwaffe's Flak arm had been concentrated around Germany's high-priority targets and was now a far greater danger to the bombers than was its fighter arm.[93] Major Dahl remained on the ground at Jüterbog-Damm with III./JG 300, awaiting Reichsmarschall Göring's arrival to present him with the Oak Leaves to his Knight's Cross. The two men exchanged words; Göring relieved Dahl of his command and took his Oak Leaves back to Berlin. Two conflicting versions of their argument are known; whichever is true, the eventual result was the loss to the RLV of a major personality and one of its best combat leaders. In the short term, however, little changed; Dahl continued to lead JG 300 missions for the next two months, claiming nine victories over American and Soviet aircraft, most witnessed by his favorite wingman Walter Loos, while his interim successor as Kommodore, Major Kurd Peters, ran the Geschwader from the ground. Dahl did not report to his next posting, on the staff of the General der Jagdflieger, until the following February, and even that did not ground him; he claimed 13 more victories before the end of the war, his last, a P-51, on April 26.[94]

Although Galland's fighter office recognized that the Me 163 was a technical dead end, and its production was reduced to 50 per month, the resources already invested appeared to support the formation of a full Geschwader, to be based at Brandis with the operational I./JG 400. Major Wolfgang Späte was named JG 400 Kommodore in December. II. and III. Gruppen were authorized. Each was to have three Staffeln of 12 aircraft. This was a totally unrealistic goal; I./JG 400 struggled constantly to find enough rocket fuel to fly missions at all.

The last major victory by a Sturmgruppe was secured on December 2. The Eighth Air Force returned to Bingen and other rail yards in southwestern Germany, but bad weather caused one division to abort and the 2nd Bomb Division to lose cohesion. JG 1, JG 3, and JG 301 were ordered to scramble, form battle formations and intercept.

Aufhammer's JG 301 was unable to assemble. Ihlefeld's JG 1 was recalled because of the weather. Bär's JG 3 was directed precisely to the B-24 stream by Y-Führung, and as I./JG 3 and III./JG 3 fought off the escorts, IV./(Sturm)/JG 3 made a close-formation Sturmangriff which downed nine B-24s, six from the 392nd Bomb Group. JG 3 then paid the price. The Geschwader lost 16 KIA, 7 WIA, and 25 fighters; their tormentors, primarily 56th Fighter Group Thunderbolts, lost one P-47 and pilot. In the south, III./JG 7 was allowed to join III./EJG 2 in the war on Allied reconnaissance aircraft, and shot down one Lightning.[95]

The principal target for the Eighth Air Force on December 5 was the Tegel munitions factory in Berlin, which was assigned to the 1st and 3rd Bomb Divisions. The 2nd was ordered to bomb the Munich rail yards, and was not expected to draw any opposition. The defenders would be split even further by a RAF Bomber Command day raid on the Soest rail yards. The RLV made a valiant attempt to defend Berlin with JG 1, JG 300, and JG 301, but could not reach the bombers. The JG 1 Stabsschwarm and three Gruppen formed up as a battle formation for the second time since D-Day. III./JG 1, the high protection Gruppe, was ordered to an altitude 1,000 meters (3,300 ft.) below the P-51s, but still so high that iced canopies caused many pilots to withdraw early. The rest offered little challenge to the Mustangs, which penetrated the Bf 109 formation easily and fell on the two Fw 190 Gruppen before they could reach attack position. JG 1 lost 25 KIA, 14 WIA, and 37 fighters on its worst day of the war, and the senior RLV Geschwader was forced to withdraw to the sidelines yet again to rebuild its strength.[96]

Fj.-Uffz. (Officer Cadet) Willi Andiel was a new pilot in III./JG 1 who flew his first combat mission on this day. He recalled:

I was given the aircraft "white 14," a Bf 109G-14/AS, and assigned to fly as #2 to Lt. Holz. As it turned out, after the four Staffeln took off and assembled over the field to climb away to the southwest, I found myself to be the very last aircraft in the whole formation. This looked pretty good, seeing all the others flying in front, but it was also the most vulnerable place to be in an attack by enemy fighters, so I kept scanning the sky continuously . . . At 4,000 meters [13,000 ft.] I put on my oxygen mask. As we reached about 5,000 meters [16,000 ft.] I spotted a formation of planes with their vapor trails bending in our direction, so I alerted the formation, and the leader immediately ordered us to drop our tanks. I switched to main tank, watched the fuel flow stop, and pulled the release. I could see all the others dropping their tanks, but to my horror they all pulled away from me—I couldn't keep up even with full throttle.

About 60 Mustangs charged into our formation, and as I was a sitting duck, four attacked me. I immediately went into a sharp right-hand climbing turn. One of them followed, trying to out-maneuver me, while the other three tried to get me by climbing away and then swooping down on me. This went on for what I thought was ages. As I was constantly on full power, my cooling flaps opened and slowed me down. I decided at this point to try to break off before one of them got lucky. The one behind me had just stopped firing (if you get shot at from behind, you can see the rounds which miss you) when I flipped my plane over the right wing, hoping to reach the clouds 3,000 meters [10,000 ft.] below. Luckily I was able to put a little distance between the Mustang and myself, and by diving and sideslipping I made it into the cloud cover. Safe, I thought—but not so! Ice began to build up. I had to drop below the clouds. Coming into clear air at 1,500 meters [5,000 ft.], I saw to my surprise that the Mustang was waiting for me; coming straight at me just below the clouds. I had him in my sights and pulled the trigger for the machine guns and pressed the button to fire the cannon. In a fraction of a second he passed over my head into cloud and was gone.

I now had to find an airfield—I was short of fuel! After dogfighting for 20 minutes, I had no idea where I was, so I headed northeast, found a railroad line, followed it to a station and "took a ticket" [dropping low to read the name of the station]. After finding my position on the chart, I headed to the closest airfield, after climbing to just below the clouds. Reaching the field, I descended to circuit height and lowered the gear. At this moment the engine hesitated and stopped. I tried to retract the wheels by pumping furiously on the hand pump, but could not make it . . . I had to belly-land in a weed patch 150 meters [500 ft.] short of the strip . . . On touchdown my left wing hit a tree stump, the plane dug into the mud, the cabin filled with fumes, and I got out very quickly! The damage to the plane was 85 percent . . . For myself, nothing but a stiff neck for a couple of days from watching the Mustang behind me! Ironically, people on the ground observed my belly tank hanging at a

Oberst Johannes Steinhoff, the first Kommodore of JG 7, photographed as a Hauptmann and Kommandeur of II./JG 52 on the Eastern Front. (*Crow*)

strange angle under the plane, and we found it on the ground just before the point of touchdown. In the afternoon I made it back to my base by rail, carrying my parachute and radio over my shoulder. The mission had cost my Staffel three casualties, not including my wreck.[97]

JG 301 had no better luck in reaching the B-17s, and also suffered from the Mustangs. Two Gruppen of JG 27 were sent up after the RAF Lancasters bombing Soest, but could not get past the swarms of RAF Spitfires and Mustangs. For the day the RLV force lost 44 KIA, 16 WIA, and 77 fighters. The Eighth Air Force lost no bombers, and 11 fighters, to the Luftwaffe; the RAF lost no bombers, and one Spitfire.[98]

The three Gruppen of KG(J) 54 in southwestern

Germany inched toward full operational status. Individual pilots were allowed to shadow Fifteenth Air Force bomber streams, which were otherwise unopposed in the air, and joined III./JG 7 and III./EJG 2 in attacks on reconnaissance aircraft, at first without success. There were still no jet fighters in northern Germany, although Eighth Air Force fighter pilots reported seeing Me 262s on almost every December mission, and shot a few of them down. In fact these were bombers from I./KG 51, not fighters. Most of these encounters were inadvertent, but a few of the jet pilots obviously enjoyed taunting the Americans by making quick individual attacks on the bombers and pulling away from the approaching fighters. These attacks were in no way controlled by the RLV organization, and are thus outside the scope of this history.[99]

The Allied bombing plan for December 12 was similar to that of the 5th: Eighth Air Force B-17s would bomb Merseburg-Leuna, diverting the RLV fighters from the B-24s, which would bomb western rail targets, and part of RAF Bomber Command, which would bomb a major steel plant at Witten, in the Ruhr. Schmid, however, ignored the Americans altogether, and directed two Jagdgruppen to the RAF Lancaster formation. The sight of RAF bombers was the answer to every RLV pilot's prayers. The armor and armament of Lancasters were much poorer than those of B-17s and B-24s; they did not fly in close formation; and their escorts from RAF Fighter Command, while skilled in dogfighting, were not trained in the escort role, and frequently left stretches of the bomber stream unprotected. Both of Schmid's Gruppen made successful attacks. I./JG 3 scrambled from Paderborn, assembled below the clouds, and after skillful direction, pulled up through the clouds within sight of the 140 Lancasters. Their head-on attacks resulted in claims for 13 bombers before RAF Mustangs arrived to shoot down four Messerschmitts and their pilots for the loss of one of their own. This proved to be the last RLV mission for I./JG 3.[100]

Hptm. Hanns-Heinz Dudeck led the 20 Bf 109G-14s of his IV./JG 27 up from Achmer and immediately entered the solid overcast. He had drilled his green pilots in climbing through cloud, which they did successfully on this day. They then formed a stepped-up line of Schwärme at 6,000 meters [19,000 ft.] and headed south-southwest. Dudeck's radio went out, but he reached the Ruhr by dead reckoning, and quickly spotted the contrails of unescorted bombers,

obviously RAF because of their poor formation. His Gruppe attacked "as trained for day missions," even without radio instructions. The mode of attack preferred by JG 27 since their days in Austria had been by Schwärme from all directions, and this is exactly what they did this time, although this was the first bomber interception for nearly all of the pilots. The leader of each Schwarm picked a different compass quadrant from which to attack. Dudeck himself attacked the leading bombers from the rear and flamed his target while keeping an eye on several approaching Mustangs. He then moved farther back in the formation and made a second attack before leading his own Schwarm in a shallow dive into cloud as more Mustangs arrived. The Gruppe returned to Achmer to claim eight Lancasters and one Mustang for the loss of one Messerschmitt, whose pilot survived. The RAF lost a total of eight Lancasters and one Mustang, while missing the targeted steel mill altogether. Dudeck was taken prisoner on January 1, 1945. He took tremendous pride in this mission, and described it to his Allied interrogators in great detail.[101]

The warning that Galland had been given on November 20, that all of the conventional RLV Jagd-geschwader except JG 300 and JG 301 would move west for offensive operations, came to pass on December 14–17, when JG 1, JG 3, and JG 11 flew to bases near the border and transferred to Jagddivision 3 or II. Jagdkorps, never to return to the RLV. IV.(Sturm)/JG 3 had been the most successful unit in the RLV since its return from the *Invasionsfront*. claiming 270 heavy bombers for the loss of 76 killed or missing and 44 injured pilots. Major Moritz, the man who had built it, had left already left its Störmede base. Major Bär had relieved Moritz on the 5th and sent him to an operational training unit as an act of mercy. Moritz was obviously at the end of his nerves and strength, and had begun to question orders; Bär's action saved him from an almost inevitable visit by a courtmartial judge.[102]

The Battle of the Ardennes

The fighter reinforcements were needed for Hitler's last great offensive in the west, Operation *Wacht am Rhein* (Watch on the Rhine), the Battle of the Ardennes, known to the Allies as the Battle of the Bulge. Although Allied intelligence knew that German armies were shifting positions and concentrating behind the Ardennes forest, and had exact knowledge of every westward transfer of a fighter unit—the Luftwaffe sent and confirmed all such information by radio—somehow the pieces were not assembled properly, and the German offensive on the morning of December 16 achieved complete tactical surprise. The II. Jagdkorps contribution was to have been a massed dawn attack on Allied tactical airfields on the first day of the offensive. This attack, code-named Operation *Bodenplatte* (Baseplate), had been finalized by General Peltz and his staff and fighter unit commanders at a conference in Altenkirchen on December 14, but intriguing details—the use of night fighters as guide aircraft, special pyrotechnic signals, and other techniques—had been picked up by Ultra weeks earlier. Bodenplatte was delayed repeatedly by exceptionally bad weather which grounded the air forces of both sides. Bad weather may have disappointed Peltz, but was welcomed by the German ground forces, which were thus able to move freely during the daylight hours, unseen and unattacked by Allied aircraft.[103]

General Schmid's I. Jagdkorps commanded the few conventional fighters still available for the defense of the Reich. Jagddivision 1 controlled the two former *Wilde Sau* Geschwader, which were based south and west of Berlin for the defense of northern and central Germany. JG 300 was headquartered at Jüterbog; JG 301, at Stendal. III./JG 7 was to transfer to Brandenburg-Briest and join Jagddivision 1 when it returned to operations. It moved in late December, but flew no missions until January. Jagddivision 8 was responsible for defending the south and southeast, but controlled only the Hungarian fighters, which had flown their last organized mission against the Fifteenth Air Force on November 7. They were now under orders from their own government to ignore the strategic bombers and assist the German and Hungarian armies in their fight against the advancing Red Army.[104]

The sleet and fog blanketing northwestern Europe on the 17th grounded the Eighth Air Force and much of the Luftwaffe, but JG 300, a bad-weather wing, was still able to take off. It was scrambled and ordered to form up and fly in an unusual direction—southeast, to the Silesian oil installations at Blechhammer and Odertal. The USSTAF had ordered the Fifteenth Air Force to fly another mission to these critical targets. The Italy-based bomber crews had not seen a Luftwaffe fighter in two months, and the 49th Bomb Wing was taken completely by surprise when the

JG 300 Sturmgruppe suddenly burst from the clouds in wedge formation, prepared for an assault attack. The Geschwader, led on this occasion by Lt. Klaus Bretschneider, the Kapitän of 5.(Sturm)/JG 300, had managed to stay in formation in the clouds until an unescorted bomber wing was located. The Sturmgruppe flew a complete circle and attacked the rear of the 461st Bomb Group, flying in the high rear position, while III./JG 300 attacked from the flanks. Nine 461st B-24s went down immediately; a tenth ditched on the return flight. The attacks proceeded forward in the bomber stream, and brought down two B-24s from the 484th Group, two from the 464th, one from the 451st, and probably several of the five others which did not return from the mission. Lightnings of the 14th Fighter Group and Mustangs from the 52nd and 325th Groups quickly reached the B-24s and drove off the German fighters, at the cost of three Lightnings and two Mustangs. The Stab and four Gruppen of JG 300, the only Geschwader involved in this interception, lost 19 KIA, including the Kommandeur of the new IV./JG 300; 6 WIA; and 36 fighters.[105]

Uffz. Ernst Schröder led a Schwarm of four 5.(Sturm)/JG 300 Fw 190s on the mission, and has provided this account:

> After an hour of standing around Löbnitz, my airplane is still unserviceable. A red flare goes up; cockpit readiness! My Staffel comrades climb into their cockpits and strap in. Every loudspeaker on the field then broadcasts a message for me to report to the Stab dispersal area; "Blue 13" is ready for me. I grab my parachute and run a couple of hundred meters to the plane, which had once belonged to Obstlt. Dahl, our previous Kommodore.
>
> The green flare for takeoff soars into the sky just as I reach the plane. I buckle on my chute and strap in with the aid of the mechanics. I am last to take off, and have no time to adjust the seat and rudder pedals, which were positioned for the shorter Dahl. I thus have to fly the mission with my knees bent back almost double. Lt. Bretschneider has taken off first, and climbs away in a broad sweep so that everyone can join up. At 1,500 meters [5,000 ft.] I catch the rear plane and then pick my way through the heap looking for my leaderless Schwarm. I find them and am in position by the time we reach Wittenberg on the Elbe, the assembly point for the whole Geschwader, which is marked by colored smoke rounds fired by the Flak.

Messerschmitts from our escorting Gruppen approach from the right and below. After two orbits at 2,500 meters [8,000 ft.] the formation is complete: 30 Sturmgruppe Fw 190s escorted by 50–60 Bf 109s. While we fly just beneath the clouds we are ordered by the Jagddivision 1 controller at Döberitz to climb away to the southeast. We are told over the radio about the locations of American bomber formations coming up from Italy. We climb through 4,000 meters [13,000 ft.] and put on our oxygen masks.

Bretschneider leads us around most of the towering cloud formations, but through some of the smaller ones, but we stick together. I look around my cockpit and discover that I am flying the most heavily armed fighter in the Gruppe, with the full original *Sturmbock* armament of two 30-mm cannon, two 20-mm cannon, and two 12.7-mm machine guns; most of the others have been lightened by removing or substituting some of the guns. The task of my Schwarm is to fly high cover for the Gruppe, to fend off the first escorts; the heavy "dungheap" I am flying will not make the job any easier. My usual airplane is a standard Fw 190A-8 with no extra guns or armor.

After a long flight in peaceful silence, we are given the position of the oncoming enemy bombers. The radio then crackles with an impatient series of course changes. The controller tells us that the *dicken Autos* should be in sight. But—nothing. We switch on our guns and gunsights. Suddenly, from Bretschneider: "*Viktor, Viktor von Specht Anton. Ich sehe dicke Autos! Wir machen Pauke-Pauke!*" ["Roger, Roger from Woodpecker Leader. I see the bombers. We are attacking!"]

I pull my Schwarm up about 100 meters [330 ft.] above the Gruppe for a better overall view. I see the contrails of only a few escorts above the bombers. We drop our tanks on orders. Bretschneider swings us onto a reciprocal course to the bombers. The first *Pulk* of red-tailed B-24s passes us. As the second approaches, Bretschneider begins a fairly tight right turn to slot us in between the second and third *Pulks*, which are passing from our left to our right. I remain on course for a last look around and then join my comrades. We rapidly overhaul the second *Pulk*. The few P-38s overhead do not come down; perhaps they are calling for reinforcements. From my high position I have a perfect view of the unfolding drama. First the B-24 tail gunners open fire, filling the sky with tracer. The *Sturmböcke* bore in at full throttle, weaving slightly to throw off the gunners' aim. At 300 meters [1,000 ft.]

the main force opens fire with their cannon. The explosive shells streak toward their targets, and within seconds two bombers have turned into fireballs. Others quickly catch fire. My radio becomes an incoherent babble of shouts and cries. My Schwarm comes down last. I line up on my target, press the firing button at 300 meters, and—nothing! Damn! I close to 30 meters [100 ft.], swearing and flipping all the circuit breakers. Nothing works. I look around to see a sky full of falling debris and parachutes. I give up, and break away in a steep dive. A few months earlier, I would have been expected to ram a bomber. But in December 1944 we are so short of pilots that this is no longer required. I shall face no repercussions for my action.

I land at Liegnitz in Silesia, having been in the air for two hours. After refueling, I return to Löbnitz, land, and taxi to the Stab dispersal. I begin shouting at the first mechanic to reach me about the failure of my guns. He reaches into the cockpit and calmly points to an extra safety switch, still set on "safe." A special feature of Dahl's crate, one I had never seen before. Upon reflection, I am pleased for the sake of the ten American airmen that my guns had not worked.[106]

For the next several days the Eighth Air Force was directed against tactical targets in western Germany whenever it could get off the ground. Two Jagdgruppen were ordered to intercept heavy bombers in the Bonn area on the 18th, but unsurprisingly could not get through the P-51 escort screen. The Fifteenth continued its campaign against strategic targets in central Europe, once again without aerial opposition.

The weather over western Europe cleared on the 23rd, in time for a small tactical raid by the heavy bombers and a maximum defensive effort by the strengthened II. Jagdkorps. The Eighth Air Force heavy bombers were well-protected by their experienced escorts and were scarcely molested. Some RAF Bomber Command heavies, and the Ninth Air Force mediums, were not as fortunate. A small force of 27 Lancasters and 3 Mosquitoes, all from No. 8 Pathfinder Group, was sent to bomb a Cologne rail yard through what was expected to be cloud. The cloud cleared, leaving the bombers in a strung-out formation, and unescorted. Major Toni Hackl, who now commanded II./JG 26, was leading its new Fw 190D-9 "long noses" on a sweep of the Ardennes. They had engaged some P-51s when he received word of the tempting target. He broke free with five of his men and headed toward Cologne. He quickly downed the leading Lancaster and one of the Mosquitoes; his five pilots downed five more Lancasters. His fighters were not touched by British return fire, never saw an escort, and broke away only when out of ammunition. The pilot of the leading Lancaster was awarded a posthumous Victoria Cross.[107]

II. Jagdkorps directed the rest of its fighters to Ninth Air Force B-26 formations making a maximum-strength raid on communications centers supporting the German offensive. The result, according to the official USAAF history, was the "most furious aerial opposition ever encountered by the medium bombers." Thirty-eight B-26s were lost. Claims by the exuberant German pilots were so high that it is impossible to sort out their individual targets. The attack by IV.(Sturm)/JG 3 stood out; the unit was able to form a close-formation Sturmgruppe wedge and decimate a B-26 box in a stern attack.[108]

The weather over northwestern Europe stayed good on the 24th, allowing the Eighth Air Force to fly its greatest strike of the war—2,700 sorties—against German communications centers and airfields. The 3rd Bomb Division's leading 4th Combat Wing was attacked over Liége by IV.(Sturm)/JG 3, which shot down three 487th Bomb Group B-17s and collided with two others. One of the lost B-17s was piloted by the wing commander, BGen. Fred Castle, who was awarded a posthumous Medal of Honor for the mission.[109]

Two other Jagdgruppen, II.(Sturm)/JG 300 and III./JG 301, attempted to attack the 2nd and 1st Bomb Divisions in the Magdeburg–Brunswick area. Lt. Bretschneider was leading the JG 300 formation again, despite his low rank, and had reached firing position on a B-24 box when his Gruppe was caught in a timed barrage of 88-mm Flak. He was killed when his Focke-Wulf was hit and exploded; two B-24s and several more Fw 190s were also hit and went down. The rest of the Gruppe was then dispersed by P-51s. III./JG 301 claimed a successful attack on B-17s, but the American unit involved cannot be determined. The other Luftwaffe fighter units in the west were fully occupied over the Bulge, attempting to shield their Army from Allied tactical aircraft. For the day I. Jagdkorps and II. Jagdkorps lost 68 pilots killed and 19 injured.[110]

The Eighth Air Force's 1st Bomb Division stood down on Christmas Day; the 2nd and 3rd Divisions targeted communications centers and rail bridges west of the Rhine. The I. Jagdkorps fighters did not fly. II. Jagdkorps attempted to assemble a battle formation comprising the Stab and three Gruppen of JG 1, plus IV.(Sturm)/JG 3—all of them experienced RLV units—to oppose the bombers. The Gefechtsverband could not be formed. Every Gruppe but one was broken up by the P-51 escorts; I./JG 1 reached the 2nd Bomb Division stream unmolested, downed three 389th Bomb Group B-24s, and returned to Twente short only three Fw 190s, all of whose pilots survived. IV.(Sturm)/JG 3 apparently shot down a single 467th Group B-24, but was punished badly by 479th Group Mustangs, losing eight Fw 190s and seven pilots. Again most of the day's aerial activity was over the Bulge, on tactical missions; II. Jagdkorps lost a total of 49 pilots KIA and 13 WIA.[111]

Whenever possible for the next five days, the Eighth Air Force bombers attacked German communications targets and rail yards behind the Ardennes battlefront, taking off for some missions through freezing rain. I. Jagdkorps was not ordered to intercept the heavies until the 31st, when, with the ground situation stabilized, the Eighth Air Force returned to its strategic campaign, sending 2,100 fighters and bombers to a variety of targets, including the Hamburg-Harburg refineries and the Misburg hydrogenation plant. JG 300 and JG 301 scrambled in full force against the 3rd Bomb Division, which was making the deepest penetration. Both Geschwader succeeded in finding small openings in the escort screen. The "Bloody 100th" Group was scourged once again, losing seven B-17s to the fighters, three to collision, two to Flak, and one to an internal fire. The 452nd Bomb Group was also hit by the Focke-Wulfs, and lost five B-17s. The P-51s then arrived to inflict typical punishment on the German fighters, which lost 24 KIA and 10 WIA on the mission.[112]

The following table shows the strength of I. Jagdkorps (containing the RLV fighters) and II. Jagdkorps (containing the western front tactical fighters) at the end of the last two quarters of 1944. These totals include some units that were rebuilding and not operational. These were intended to be activated for Galland's Big Blow against the Eighth Air Force, but most were instead ordered to II. Jagdkorps for the Ardennes battle.

Day-Fighter Strength of I. Jagdkorps and II. Jagdkorps, by Quarters[113]

Date	Command/ Aircraft type	Establishment Strength	Aircraft on Hand	Operational Aircraft
September 30, 1944				
	I. Jagdkorps			
	Me 163s	68	23	14
	Me 262s	52	23	22
	prop fighters	2,088	1,244	829
	II. Jagdkorps	904	307	219
December 31, 1944				
	I. Jagdkorps			
	Me 163s	52	45	22
	Me 262s	84	91	12
	prop fighters	672	473	264
	II. Jagdkorps	2,352	1,208	842

The German winter offensive had stalled, and on the 31st the top priority missions for all of the II. Jagdkorps fighters were within the Bulge. They had flown a few offensive ground-support missions over the Ardennes to aid the leading armor units and the fighting around Bastogne, but their most valuable service was on anti-Jabo patrols, searching for the deadly Allied fighter-bombers. This was very dangerous work, because once the Allied fighters dropped their ordnance they were equal in performance to the German fighters, and nearly always outnumbered them. During December 16–31, II. Jagdkorps lost 400 pilots killed or missing. Despite these losses and the stagnant ground situation, the II. Jagdkorps unit commanders received coded radio messages on the afternoon of the 31st announcing that Operation Bodenplatte would be carried out on the next day and authorizing the briefing of the pilots. The coded attack time came through later. The targeted airfields would be all be hit at 0920 hours. Although it no longer made any military sense, General Peltz had gotten his wish, and 34 Jagdgruppen—the largest force of German fighters ever to take to the air—would take off at dawn on a mission which would seal the fate of the German fighter force.[114]

B-24s of the Fifteenth Air Force's 460th Bomb Group on a December 11 mission to oil targets in Vienna. The loose formation is fairly typical for Liberators of either strategic air force. (Hess)

CHAPTER 9

THE FINAL DESPERATE EXPEDIENTS
JANUARY–MAY 1945

Bodenplatte and the Battle in Berlin

Nine hundred fighters and fighter-bombers—the full remaining strength of the expanded II. Jagdkorps—took off after dawn on New Years' morning and flew at low altitude to their targets, 16 USAAF and RAF tactical airfields in the Netherlands, Belgium, and eastern France. Genmaj. Peltz's planners had made a real effort to take into account the limited skills of their fighter pilots, but the operation was much too ambitious for that stage of the war, and was doomed from the start. Lack of night-flying skills delayed takeoffs until there was some daylight. Although they achieved complete tactical surprise, their targeted airfields were well into their daily routines; the ground defenses were manned, although at low strength, and some Allied squadrons were already airborne. Guide aircraft (night fighters) were assigned to each formation, but their navigational skills proved inadequate. Of the 34 Gruppen, ten never found their assigned targets at all; their missions were total failures. Nine Gruppen made ineffective, low-strength attacks on their targets. Two Gruppen made successful approaches to their assigned airfield, only to find that it was non-operational. Only one-third of the force, or 11 Gruppen, made completely successful attacks—on time, in strength, and with surprise, against airfields that contained the desired targets, Allied tactical aircraft. And even in these cases, the German success was much less than it should have been, and much less than the German pilots themselves believed it to have been. As long-distance fuel tanks had to be carried instead of bombs, attacks were confined to strafing. And as most fighter pilots had had no training in attacking ground targets, their fire was for the most part inaccurate.

Operation Bodenplatte weakened the Jagdwaffe past any last hope of rebuilding. It had sacrificed itself in a single grand, insanely futile gesture. Three hundred of the nine hundred fighters failed to return to their bases. Pilots made their way back individually over the next few days, but a total of 214 were killed, taken prisoner, or remained missing. Counted among the casualties were 19 irreplaceable formation leaders: one ground-attack and two fighter Kommodoren, including the incomparable Major Specht; six Gruppen-kommandeure; and ten Staffelkapitäne.

In their embarrassment at having been taken completely by surprise, the Allied air commanders failed to compile a comprehensive list of their losses, but about three hundred RAF and USAAF aircraft were destroyed or damaged beyond repair. Few Allied pilots were lost, however, and all units were back up to strength in aircraft within a week. The effect of the German fighter pilots' self-sacrifice on the course of the war was thus non-existent. An OKL intelligence appreciation concluded that the attack had had no effect on Allied operations other than to move up the takeoff time of their early-morning patrols.[1]

Bodenplatte had no impact on the career of its commander and chief advocate, Dietrich Peltz, despite its disastrous failure. Reichsmarschall Göring had decided to reorganize the RLV and fighter staff and replace the most outspoken fighter commanders with bomber men, of whom Peltz was the most prominent. In mid-December Galland had been told by the Luftwaffe Chief of Staff, General Koller,[2] that Hitler and Göring wanted him removed from office, but that his successor had not yet been determined. Galland, who had recently been promoted to Generalleutnant, had then gone on leave, not suspecting the extent of the efforts being made to discredit him by opponents inside and outside the Luftwaffe. Both the Gestapo and the SS began investigations and interrogations, concentrating on Galland's circle of off-duty acquaintances. It was Himmler's intention, with Göring's apparent concurrence, to have him arrested for

Generalleutnant Karl Koller, the Luftwaffe's last Chief of Staff. The RLV was a totally spent force by the time he received this appointment in November 1944. (*Cranston*)

commanders. On January 13, Günther Lützow and Hannes Trautloft met with the Luftflotte 6 commander, General Robert Ritter von Greim,[4] who was close to Hitler but had no role in the fighter defenses and thus could be considered neutral, to explain the situation and ask for advice on approaching Hitler directly. Greim declined to get involved. Someone informed Göring, who called a meeting of the "mutineers" and all available fighter commanders (excluding Galland) for the 19th. The pilots chose Lützow as their spokesman, and he read a paper citing their chief complaints. These can be summarized as follows:

1. The dismissal of Gen. Galland is incomprehensible to the troops. He is recognized as the outstanding Fighter Arm personality and leader and—despite the hard demands he made on those under him—remains close to their hearts.
2. The frequent accusations of cowardice directed at the fighter pilots by Göring are rejected; their casualties are as high as those of any other arm of the Wehrmacht.
3. Gen. Peltz, although held in personal and professional respect, can never gain the confidence of the Fighter Arm, because:
   a. At this time of national crisis he has withheld the IX. Fliegerkorps from action with excessive training requirements, while the poorly trained *Jagdflieger* are thrown heedlessly into combat.
   b. He is no fighter pilot.
   c. He is responsible for the operation of January 1, 1945, and the wastage since the beginning of the Ardennes Offensive on December 17, 1944, which has cost: 2 Geschwaderkommodoren, 14 Gruppenkommandeure, and 64 Staffelkapitäne. In the opinion of the Fighter Arm, these losses are attributable primarily to errors in leadership.[5]

treason. Himmler's interest evidently stemmed from his desire to see a dedicated Nazi, Oberst Gordon Gollob, take over the position of General der Jagdflieger. Göring did not like Gollob, but a single suggestion by Hitler was ultimately enough to get Gollob the job.[3]

Göring's opinion of Galland turned from grudging respect to hatred as a result of the so-called "Fighter Pilots' Mutiny," in which Galland's name figured prominently, although he was apparently not directly involved. The rumor of Galland's forced relief was the ultimate indignity for most of the senior fighter

Göring stalked from the room after threatening to have Lützow court-martialed and shot. Cooler heads prevailed, and before day's end Lützow received his punishment: banishment from the Reich. He was given the post of Jafü Italien (Fighter Leader Italy), which was a deliberate insult, since there were no Luftwaffe fighters left in Italy to lead. Galland was reached at his Berlin quarters and told to get out of town; he went to an estate in the Harz Mountains. The insurrection had absolutely no effect on the conduct of

A 384th Bomb Group B-17 drops a load of M-17A1 incendiary clusters through the undercast late in the war; someone is about to get a nasty surprise. (*ww2images*)

the war. Göring proceeded with his plans to reorganize the entire Jagdwaffe. Gollob became General der Jagdflieger on January 23, and celebrated by throwing himself a banquet. According to the testimony available (all by friends of Galland), Gollob then spent two weeks searching the files for documents that would incriminate his predecessor. The fighter inspectorate accomplished little for the rest of the war; the staff had no respect for Gollob, and would work only under direct orders.[6]

In the meantime, the war went on. The Eighth Air Force celebrated New Year's Day by returning to the strategic air war with a raid on oil installations in northern and central Germany. The 8th Fighter Command had been abolished, and one of its three five-group fighter wings had been assigned to each bomb division, which were renamed air divisions. JG 300, JG 301, and the two operational Gruppen of JG 7 were scrambled, but only one 1st Air Division B-17 formation encountered Luftwaffe aircraft; most were dispersed by the escorts. The unlucky B-17 force comprised 12 B-17s flying 80 km (50 miles) ahead of the main formation and tasked with screening it from radar by dropping Window. The three JG 301 Gruppen made a well-coordinated attack; I./JG 301 drew the P-51 escort away to the north, whereupon the other two Gruppen attacked the B-17s from the rear, and downed two B-17s from the 92nd and four from the 305th Bomb Group. Willi Reschke was shot down by a bomber gunner, bailed out, and returned to Stendal severely bruised. He noted that the perfectly set-up attack should have downed all 12 bombers, but many of the inexperienced German pilots lacked the

required skills. The small RLV force lost about 30 fighters, in exchange for the six B-17s, plus a single 364th Group P-51 downed by a II./JG 301 Fw 190.[7]

The Eighth Air Force bombed communications targets in western Germany every day for the next two weeks without opposition from the RLV. Its three operational Geschwader were held back in the Berlin area to defend the critical oil targets. The Jagd-gruppen earlier transferred to II. Jagdkorps for the Ardennes offensive were withheld from operations as they struggled to rebound from the Bodenplatte disaster. The Ultra organization picked up several revealing messages during this fortnight: operational flights over enemy lines were forbidden, as were combat flights by the Geschwader Kommodoren. The Luftwaffe High Command ordered an emergency measure necessitated by the high casualties to day-fighter formation leaders: all officers suitable to serve as Gruppenkommandeure or Staffelkapitäne after short training were to be reported by name to Berlin; and non-commissioned pilots were to be considered for promotion to Staffelkapitäne based solely on a high number of aerial victories. One Jagddivision 3 message puzzled the Allied intelligence officers: a Schwarm-sized test ordered by II. Jagdkorps was modified to increase the size of the Schwarm to six aircraft. This was clarified by a later message from Jagddivision 1 asking the opinion of all its units on a proposal to make the Kette the basic fighter unit. This was obviously Peltz's doing; he was proposing to replace the tactical unit of the Jagdwaffe since 1938, the Rotte comprising an element leader and his wingman, with the bombers' Kette of three aircraft.[8] The Schwarm, comprising two elements, would thus increase from four to six aircraft. Most if not all of the jet units did adopt the Kette as their combat element. Whether this was by directive is unknown, but the mutual protection of the leader–wingman team was not as important for the fast jets as the enhanced firepower of a three-airplane attacking unit.

The Soviets began their winter offensive on January 12. It quickly replaced the Ardennes and the western front as the chief preoccupation of Hitler and the German high command, and with good reason; the Red Army advanced from the Vistula River to the Oder, well within Germany proper, in two weeks. Twenty fighter Gruppen were withdrawn from the west and sent east to counter the Soviet juggernaut. These included all of the Gruppen of JG 1, JG 3, and JG 11, the most senior of the home-defense Geschwader.

These never returned to the RLV, which soldiered on with the two former *Wilde Sau* Geschwader, JG 300 and JG 301, and the jet and rocket units as its sole day-fighter components. When JG 3 moved to the Eastern Front, Major Bär requested an opportunity to fly jets, and left JG 3 to take command of the operational jet training Gruppe, III./EJG 2.[9]

January 14 was a rare cloudless winter day over western Europe. The Eighth Air Force took advantage of the unlimited visibility to send two of its air divisions to bomb oil targets in central Germany; the small synthetic petroleum plants were hard to hit under most weather conditions, and were rebuilt as quickly as they were destroyed. This attack on the most important strategic targets remaining to Germany brought a full-scale response from the RLV. Many II. Jagdkorps fighters also became involved, but mostly as unwilling participants, attacked on their tactical missions by the 761 Eighth Air Force fighters flying sweeps and escorts along the route of the bombers. JG 26, a representative tactical Jagd-geschwader, suffered its most costly day of the war. Its three Gruppen claimed two Eighth Air Force P-51s in addition to three Spitfires and two P-47s, their usual tactical targets, but lost 13 KIA and 3 WIA. IV./JG 54, an independent Jagdgruppe operating in the west, lost eight killed, including two Staffelkapitäne, and was never rebuilt—the survivors eventually served as the cadre for a new II./JG 7, in an ultimately unsuc-cessful attempt to bring the jet-fighter Geschwader up to full three-Gruppe strength.[10]

The RLV ground commander of the day—probably Beppo Schmid at I. Jagdkorps—made an attempt to coordinate his forces. III./JG 7 was ordered to draw off the escorts to allow the Fw 190s of II.(Sturm)/JG 300 and JG 301 to reach the bombers. Few of the jets were seen by the Americans, but the new tactic was evaluated correctly by the Eighth Air Force—it had been expected for some time—and was noted in its mission report. Of the two conventional Geschwader, JG 301 was met head-on by P-51s while still climbing and was unable to reach the bombers in strength. Willi Reschke implies in his memoir that poor ground direction was responsible for their bad tactical position, but it is probable that the absence of clouds—the "savior of the RLV pilot"—made their detection inevitable.[11]

JG 300 was able to make a successful attack, but paid an extremely heavy price. Its Sturmgruppe was directed to a weak spot in the 3rd Air Division stream.

The 390th Bomb Group had fallen 16 km (10 miles) behind the other two groups in its combat wing, and was temporarily unescorted. The Fw 190s made an assault attack on the rear of the group and downed nine B-17s, including all eight in the low squadron. Only one pass was possible before the *Sturmböcke* were hit by the Mustangs of the 357th Fighter Group's 362nd Squadron. That group's other two squadrons stayed high to take on JG 300's three Bf 109 Gruppen. The slaughter was on. The Messerschmitts downed three P-51s, but in only ten minutes the Geschwader lost 32 KIA, 7 WIA, and 56 aircraft, a near-exact match for the 357th's 56.5 confirmed claims. This was the highest single-day claims total for any Eighth Air Force group, and won the 357th its second Distinguished Unit Citation.[12]

Most of the JG 300 pilots had never been involved in a dogfight before. Many had barely mastered straight-and-level flight. The previous fall's supply of experienced bomber and transport pilots had dried up, and the replacements now arriving in the units were 18–20-year-olds with an average of 120 flying hours, as few as ten in fighters. Many were Fähnriche or Oberfähnriche (officer cadets), a dead giveaway that they had been chosen for pilot training and commissions based on their standing in the Hitler Youth rather than any inherent flying or leadership skills. The experienced JG 300 pilots called the new men *Kanonenfutter* (cannon fodder). Most showed false reactions, or none at all, in combat situations, and had to be closely led. One exception was Oberfähnrich Heinz-Günter Kuring, one of six Sturmgruppe pilots to survive bailouts. Kuring recalled:

> We scrambled at 1100 on a clear, sunny day and climbed to the northwest. I flew as Obfw. Löfgen's wingman in the Stabsschwarm. The radio was silent, but I saw contrails near Berlin. We banked toward a 15 B-17 *Pulk* from above, and lined up with full throttle and MW-50. We attacked on "*Pauke-Pauke.*" The B-17s fired rockets, which exploded at 1,000 meters [1,100 yards]. I opened fire at 600 meters [650 yards] without result, and fired again at 300 meters [330 yards], flaming the two left engines and fuel tank. I passed over the B-17 at 5 meters [16 ft.], saw another to the right above, pulled up and rammed it. I could see nothing, but the wind told me the canopy was gone. I released my harness and fell out, falling horizontally as trained before opening my chute. I shared the air with about 20 chutes, including Uffz. Erhard with a

shot-up knee. A farmer took Erhard to the doctor in a horse cart; I went to Berlin by train. I visited my mother and then returned to the station and rode to the Bitterfeld station. I waited at the *Fallschirmecke* [parachute corner] with three other pilots, was picked up at 1930 and driven back to Löbnitz.[13]

The permanently shrunken RLV could never accomplish any more than it did on the 14th unless and until the Me 262s entered the battle in force. The conventional RLV fighters shot down the nine B-17s and three P-51s previously mentioned, plus two 56th Fighter Group P-47s, while losing 55 pilots KIA and 15 WIA. II. Jagdkorps lost 52 KIA and 17 WIA, not just to the Eighth Air Force escorts, but also to their more frequent opponents: Allied tactical fighters, anti-aircraft fire, and other battlefield hazards. The 107 fatalities made this one of the worst days of the war for the Jagdwaffe.[14]

The RLV fighters were not ordered up again against the Eighth Air Force until February 9. Fifteenth Air Force P-51s from the 325th Fighter Group did encounter four JG 301 Fw 190s on January 20, shooting all of them down, but these Focke-Wulfs were not on a bomber intercept mission. The entire Geschwader had been ordered cast to fly fighter-bomber missions against the Red Army, and the four fighters were caught by surprise while on their transfer flight. They were the only Luftwaffe fighters seen by the Fifteenth Air Force during February. III./JG 301 stayed in the east for only a few days before coming back for re-equipment with the Ta 152, the last piston-engine Luftwaffe fighter design to enter service. The pilots were very enthusiastic about Tank's fighter, which reached an altitude of 13,200 meters (43,300 ft.) and a clocked speed of 820–830 km/h (490–500 mph) in the unit, and had the ability to "turn around its own tail" without buffeting or stalling, unlike the Fw 190A. But only a handful of them ever reached the Gruppe. The rest of JG 301 remained on the Eastern Front for a few more days, but their inexperience in ground-attack tactics led to higher losses than they had been suffering in the RLV, and they too returned to the Reich.[15]

On January 21, Major Theodor Weissenberger replaced Oberst Steinhoff as JG 7 Kommodore. Steinhoff's many friends have claimed that this was in retaliation for his role in the "mutiny," but his logbook shows that he was flying very seldom, and he was obviously having difficulty mastering the Me 262.

Gollob stated that Steinhoff was not punished for the revolt, in which his role had been less prominent than he later claimed, but that he was infecting the unit with his sloth and negative attitude. Steinhoff had led JG 77 in the long retreat from North Africa to Sicily and up the Italian boot, and was obviously exhausted. The unit's performance improved quickly and dramatically under the energetic Weissenberger. The ever-objective Messerschmitt envoy Fritz Wendel stated that its training now showed evidence of real planning, and for the first time incorporated ground control, navigation aids, and formation flying.[16]

Göring carried out his threat to reorganize the fighter defenses on January 26. I. Jagdkorps was disbanded, and its role in commanding the Reich day fighters was given to IX. Fliegerkorps (Jagd), under Genmaj. Peltz. Three Reich Jagddivisionen were retained to control the night fighters. A new unit, Fliegerdivision 9 (Jagd), was established to finish the job of converting bomber pilots to fighter pilots for the Kampfgeschwader (Jagd). This command was awarded to Oberst Hajo Herrmann; this non-combat job gave his fertile mind ample time to devise new operational plans. The rest of the fighter organization did not go untouched; II. Jagdkorps was also disbanded, and three new Fliegerdivisionen, 14, 15, and 16, were established to command all of the units on the western front—mostly fighter Gruppen, but including reconnaissance and night ground-assault units—under LwKdo West, command of which was given to Beppo Schmid.[17]

Some notes from a General der Jagdflieger conference on January 29 have survived, and demonstrate the paucity of choices available to the new incumbent, Oberst Gollob. Production of Me 262s was still going strong, with 700 planned for February, although 60 percent of the inventory of wing spars had been lost in Silesia. However, of the 681 produced "theoretically" [sic] in December, only 186 had reached the operational units. (The document notes that the production total included subassemblies scattered throughout the Reich.) JG 7 would be operational in full strength by the end of March. The first of the converted bomber units, KG(J) 54, would "probably" be operational on Me 262s by the end of February, but prospects for the other five Kampfgeschwader (Jagd) trailed off into March and April, and one would instead become a Mistel (composite "flying bomb") unit. With respect to other fighter types, JG 400 was to "use up" its remaining

Oblt. Gerhard Stamp was awarded his Knight's Cross as a Ju 88 bomber pilot before volunteering for the *Wilde Sau* night fighters in August 1943. Always a popular leader, he commanded I./JG 300 as it converted to the day-fighter mission and became an escort unit for the JG 300 Sturm-gruppe. After recovering from a late 1944 injury he led a unit charged with developing weapons for the Me 262. (*Wendler*)

Me 163s and convert to a new single-engine jet fighter, the He 162. This prediction, like most of those expressed in the conference, failed to come to pass.[18]

The internecine struggles within the Luftwaffe turned even uglier at the end of January, when Galland returned to Berlin from his leave. His automobile was confiscated, and he was placed under house arrest. His allies within the service were scattered, and it was up to his personal friends to console him. Since many of these were in the enter-tainment business and were already under surveillance by the Gestapo, this did not help his status with Himmler or Göring.[19]

The RLV's most humiliating defeat of the war came on February 3, when Peltz kept most of his fighters on the ground during the Eighth Air Force's most destructive raid on the Berlin city center. A few jet fighters were seen, but according to the Americans

these did not attack as the B-17s of the 1st and 3rd Air Divisions pummeled the government quarter. Fires raged over an area of 5 square kilometers (2 sq. miles). The Air Ministry was hit with eight high-explosive bombs. Probably not by coincidence, two of the Luftwaffe data ledgers most useful to the historian, containing its aerial victory claims and combat losses, end suddenly on about this date. The Armed Forces High Command (OKW) headquarters, the Reich Chancellery, the Propaganda Ministry, and the Gestapo headquarters were also hit. The rest of the Eighth Air Force bombers, 2nd Air Division B-24s, paid a return visit to the Magdeburg synthetic oil plant, also unopposed in the air. The bombers did not return to England unscathed, however; 36 were lost, most to the highly concentrated Flak, and a few to the usual operational causes: collision and mechanical failure.[20]

The last weapons testing and evaluation unit established by Galland before his departure from the RLM was Kommando Stamp, which was given the job of perfecting weapons systems and tactics for Me 262 bomber interceptors. Some time was wasted on bomb-dropping schemes, which should have been discredited long before. On February 3, the unit was disbanded and its commander, Major Gerhard Stamp, took his aircraft and pilots to JG 7, where he formed a Stabsstaffel (staff squadron) in which he had a free hand to continue testing. Air-to-air rockets were the most promising weapons available. At first Stamp had only old WGr 21s to test, but newer, smaller R4Ms, which were already being produced as anti-tank weapons, would be delivered for air-to-air testing within a month.[21]

The Technological "Marvels" of 1945

The aircraft available to the RLV in the final stage of the war were a curious mixture of old warhorses, remarkable emerging technology, and products of bitter-end Nazi fanaticism and self-delusion. Under the firm guidance of Milch, Speer and Saur in 1944, the German aircraft industry, which had produced a bewildering variety of types and subtypes through 1943, was planning to begin 1945 with only five major types in production: the Me 262, the Do 335, the Ta 152, the Ar 234, and the Ju 388.[22] After the years of waste and inefficiency, such a ruthless streamlining of the Luftwaffe's material position represented a con-siderable accomplishment. The technically superior turbojet Me 262 would bear the brunt of the day-fighter defense duties, augmented by what was perhaps the ultimate piston-engine fighter of the war, Kurt Tank's Ta 152. The Do 335 tandem-piston-engine heavy fighter would provide the all-weather capability the Luftwaffe fighter force sorely lacked. The Ar 234 reconnaissance bomber might allow the Luftwaffe to retain a modicum of offensive power, as would the final development of the Ju 88, the Ju 388. The latter was also developed as a high performance night-fighter. A rejuvenated Luftwaffe built around these five aircraft, the few remaining optimists believed, might yet stave off complete collapse.

The push to rebuild the Luftwaffe's armory proved a costly failure. Only seven Do 335s were delivered in late 1944; only four more were completed in 1945. Only 39 examples of Tank's beautiful high-altitude Ta 152 were ever manufactured.[23] The new types had more than their share of teething troubles, but of greater significance was the cumulative effect of the Allied air offensive on the German war economy. Raw-material shortages, lack of specialized tooling, and labor difficulties all played their part, but the greatest single cause was the chaos that had overtaken the German transportation system. Indeed, the attacks against the marshalling yards of the Deutsche Reichsbahn (German State Railway) and other trans-portation targets brought one of only two unqualified targeting successes for the Allied bomber offensive, the other being the destruction of the Axis petroleum industry.[24] One Luftwaffe general declared,

> The decisive collapse of German air armament production was not due to the efforts of Allied air attacks against the aircraft factories themselves, but was a result of the attacks which destroyed communi-cation routes, to and from the factories and airfields.[25]

Many of the new aircraft ended their days as sub-assemblies which never made it to a final assembly point, or as nearly complete airframes missing vital parts. As a consequence, the output of the advanced piston-engine types was "too insignificant to be considered a factor."[26]

Ironically, the two most advanced aircraft in the production plan were produced in the greatest numbers. In all, 1,433 Me 262s were completed before the end of the war (809 were actually accepted by the Luftwaffe), and 222 Ar 234 jet bombers were manufac-tured. The development, production and deployment of the Me 262 was badly mismanaged, however. The story of Hitler's fixation on the aircraft as a "Blitz bomber" is well known; a new level of absurdity was reached when he placed a senior SS officer in charge of which units were to receive the new aircraft.[27] Yet the real reasons for the failure to deploy sufficient numbers of the Me 262 were more prosaic. There were certainly long-term causes, such as the general muddle in aircraft technical development that charac-terized Udet's early-war tenure as Generalluftzeug-meister. Yet the main problem with the 262 lay in the technical realm—it remained essentially a prototype committed to action before its teething troubles had been cured. Most delays in production resulted not from ill-advised high-level meddling but from raw-material shortages, developmental delays, and the effects of Allied bombing.[28] Even Grabmann, an enthusiastic proponent of the jet, acknowledges that political interference had minimal impact on the type's entry into mass production; factors such as engine reliability and availability were of far greater significance. Although Galland to the end of his life maintained that an earlier combat debut by sufficient numbers of 262s might have had a dramatic impact, other senior Luftwaffe officers were not so adamant. One general noted that earlier deployment of the 262 might have brought about a temporary increase in aerial victories against the USAAF, but would have done little to reverse the overall decline of the Jagdwaffe, which was the result of faulty policy and decision-making dating back several years.[29]

As 1945 began, despite Speer's modernization plans, the RLV squadrons continued to depend upon the two types with which they began the struggle against the USAAF daylight offensive—the Bf 109 and the Fw 190. Over 4,700 new and remanufactured Bf 109s and Fw 190s rolled out of the factories in 1945. Many of these represented the ultimate development of the classic types: the Bf 109K-4 and the Fw 190D-9 and D-12.[30] Contemporary and postwar German assessments maintain that these variants were at least comparable to the latest P-51, P-47, Spitfire, and Tempest models. A host of other factors, however, especially pilot skill, negated their technical strengths. In any case, these products of late-war German industry were a far cry from the precision instruments of 1939–42. Manufacturing standards had declined precipitously. Speer's industrial miracle may have kept the aircraft pouring off the assembly lines, but the dispersed factories, plagued by wartime shortages, ensured that the planes exhibited many defects: nearly opaque armor glass, inferior *ersatz* construction materials, and poor fit and finish.[31] Engine reliability dropped off sharply in the final months of the war. With aviation gasoline scarce, bench and air testing of newly manufactured engines virtually ceased. Poorly trained test and ferry pilots crashed many aircraft before they could ever take their place in the front line. Safety devices, such as the deicers and windscreen defoggers which Allied pilots virtually took for granted, remained unreliable and unsatisfactory. In 1944 the Swiss Air Force took delivery of a number of brand new Bf 109Gs, and was appalled to discover how poorly made they were, compared to an earlier batch received in 1942.[32]

The weapon that most completely captured the *Zeitgeist* was undoubtedly the He 162 *Volksjäger* (People's Fighter).[33] In the fall of 1944, the senior Nazi leadership hit upon the idea of raising the *Volkssturm*, a citizen's militia.[34] The Volkssturm was to be manned by over– and under-aged males and equipped with cheap, mass-produced weapons, including the "People's Rifle," "People's Pistol," and the useless and dangerous concrete "People's Hand Grenade."[35] It would make up for its lack of sophisticated weapons and tactics with National Socialist zeal. It was not long before this initiative acquired an aerial dimension. Saur, as head of the Fighter Staff, sought the rapid development of a small, cheap, high-performance jet fighter which would then be mass-produced in what was termed a "forced action."[36] Saur no doubt hoped that such an action might quickly close the technological gap between the Luftwaffe and the Allied air arms. The Speer ministry pushed the development of the technology, while the *National-sozialistische Fliegerkorps* (National Socialist Flying Corps, NSFK) led by former bomber pilot and Luftflotte commander Genobst. Hans Keller, was responsible for the personnel aspects of the scheme. Keller had made disparaging comments about the evident "lack of guts" of Luftwaffe fighter pilots, and believed that the fanatical boys of the Flying Hitler Youth, an auxiliary of the NSFK, would score a kill on every mission flying the tiny jet.[37] In the original concept, the boys would proceed from glider training directly to a jet-fighter cockpit. Galland correctly diagnosed this proposal as "a sort of levée en masse of the air."[38]

After a hasty competition on September 23, 1944, involving the Junkers, Arado, Heinkel, and Blohm und Voss companies, Göring and Saur selected the

Lt. Hermann Buchner was a successful ground-attack pilot in Fw 190s on the Eastern Front, where he shot down 45 Soviet aircraft and was awarded the Knight's Cross before volunteering for jet service. He was with III./JG 7 from its creation, and shot down a further 12 aircraft, including 11 heavy bombers, in his Me 262. (*Buchner*)

He 162 design as the winner. The aircraft progressed from contract to test flight in 69 days, but had an inauspicious debut. During a test flight before assembled dignitaries at Wien-Schwechat on December 10, 1944, the prototype literally came unglued and disintegrated in flight. Despite this setback, mass production continued. Some 275 of the simple wooden jets were eventually manufactured, mostly in underground assembly halls. Many FHJ boys were detailed to the program, and a new Geschwader, JG 80, was planned to receive them. The glider-to-jet training option proved unrealistic, and a short piston-engine course was added, but by February 1945 the fuel crisis rendered even this rudimentary training impossible. The hapless FHJ were sent into ground

The commanders of JV 44, Oberst Günther Lützow (*left*) and Genlt. Adolf Galland, confer at München-Riem in April. This is one of the last photographs of Lützow before his disappearance on a combat mission. (*Crow*)

combat against the Red Army, and eventually the He 162s went to a conventional fighter unit to be flown by grown-ups. Its design flaws made it a death trap, to be avoided if at all possible, and only a handful ever flew operational missions.

In a similar vein was the Bachem 349 *Natter* (Adder), the ultimate point-defense interceptor. The Natter was a small, vertically launched, rocket-propelled and boosted airplane of largely plywood construction. The craft killed several test pilots and was obviously unready for operational use. In April 1945, ten Natters were nonetheless made ready for action at Kirchheim near Stuttgart, but the arrival of U.S. armored units forced their premature destruction.[39]

Aviation literature is filled with technical descriptions and illustrations of the next generation of Luftwaffe "miracle weapons." Other than the advanced types described in this chapter, however, none was even close to operational testing, much less deployment in any numbers. As fascinating as the Gotha 229 flying wing, or the Messerschmitt P.1101 swept-wing interceptor and the other aircraft of the "Emergency Fighter Competition" of late 1944 undoubtedly are, they were to play no role in our story.[40]

The Me 262s Join the Defenders

The two jet-fighter Geschwader closest to full operational status, JG 7 and KG(J) 54, were up in strength together for the first time on February 9, with results that had to be sorely disappointing to Peltz and the Luftwaffe High Command. The Eighth Air Force flew a maximum-strength mission—1,296 bombers were airborne—against the central German oil targets and railroad viaducts, the latter now considered choke points in Germany's stressed transportation system. The bombers flew in six task forces; three of these encountered German fighters.

Peltz ordered up 67 conventional fighters from six weak Jagdgruppen and an unknown number of Me 262s from III./JG 7 and the Stab and I. Gruppe of KG(J) 54. The Americans noted that the more experienced JG 7 fighters bounced the escorts aggressively, presumably to facilitate attacks on the bombers by the rest of the fighters, but there was no coordinated attack. The battle formation containing the conventional fighters was broken up by P-51s and never reached the bombers in strength, but their pilots' survival skills had improved since the previous month; they lost only 8 pilots KIA, 4 WIA and 13 aircraft, while claiming three P-51s. III./JG 7 claimed four B-17s and one P-51, without loss. KG(J) 54 succeeded in reaching the bombers, and shot down at least one 447th Bomb Group B-17, while claiming four, but the wide turns and tentative tactics of the ex-bomber pilots made them easy prey for the P-51s, which shot down five of the Me 262s and collided with a sixth. The collision killed both a 357th Fighter Group pilot and the KG(J) 54 Kommodore, Obstlt. Volprecht Riedesel Freiherr zu Eisenbach. The other casualties included almost the entire I./KG(J) 54 Stabsschwarm: the Kommandeur was injured, and the adjutant and technical officer were killed.

That night the Luftwaffe commanders sought explanations for the failure of KG(J) 54. The obvious ones, the pilots' inability to cope with the jet fighter's speed or to react like fighter pilots, were unacceptable, and Göring came up with the preposterous theory that the jets had flown too close to the bombers. He issued orders on the 11th that they were to open fire from 1,000 meters rather than 600. The two obvious flaws in his thinking were that the jets had been shot down by fighters, not bombers, and that their gunsights could not compensate for firing their MK 108 cannon from so great a range. The muzzle velocity of the MK 108 was so low that the jet would be required to pull up in a steep angle to lob a few shells at its target. Riedesel's replacement was Major Hansgeorg Bätcher, who had previously commanded II./KG 76, the first operational Ar 234 jet bomber unit. Bätcher was a skilled unit commander, with one of the sharpest minds in the Luftwaffe, but had no experience in fighters.[41]

The RLV fighters were next ordered up on the 14th, to oppose the Eighth Air Force's now-famous raid on Dresden. Peltz scrambled 78 conventional fighters from JG 300, 68 from JG 301, and an unknown number of Me 262s from I and III./JG 7 and KG(J) 54. Although the jet pilots claimed at least three B-17s, no jet attacks were noted by the Americans, who summarized the Luftwaffe reaction as "strikingly weak and almost entirely ineffective." The only successful attack was made by a handful of Fw 190s, probably from JG 301, which caught a single 306th Bomb Group squadron circling to make a second bomb run, shot down one B-17, and severely damaged a second. One Me 262 was apparently lost, but its pilot survived; the conventional units lost 18 pilots KIA, 2 WIA, and 20 aircraft.[42]

Me 262s were now up almost daily, sparring with Allied fighters when they were not ordered to close with the bombers. The Me 262A-1a fighter is credited with a top speed of 845 km/h (525 mph) at 9,000 meters (29,500 ft.), nearly 160 km/h faster than a clean P-51D. The jet fighter was almost invulnerable as long as it kept its speed up; it could be caught if it slowed to attack bombers (a tactic quickly abandoned), if it lost an engine, or when it slowed to land. Allied fighter pilots were alert for any of these events.[43]

The ground infrastructure supporting jet fighters shot to the top of the USSTAF target list. The Fifteenth Air Force had continued its role in the strategic air war, even though it had been ignored by the RLV for months, with a consequent decrease in mentions by this history. On February 16, it struck a major blow against the jets with a raid on the Regensburg Me 262 factory and the jet airfields in the Munich area. III./KG(J) 54 lost 16 Me 262s on the ground. KG(J) 55 was hit even harder, losing at least 23 Me 262s, and never came close to entering operations.[44]

The Allied high command judged that the German transportation system was near collapse. USSTAF ordered Operation Clarion, an all-out attack on road and rail communications, for February 22. Both the Eighth and Fifteenth Air Forces flew full-strength missions. The Eighth ordered visual bombing from 10,000 ft. for those targets with no known Flak defenses. Peltz's response was to keep his conventional fighters well dispersed on the ground, while scrambling 32 Me 262s from the Stab, I. and III. Gruppen of JG 7. Interception was attempted in the Stendal-Salzwedel area, but no more than two B-17s were shot down before every Me 262 Schwarm was involved with Mustangs. Four P-51s were shot down, for the loss of 2 jet pilots KIA, 1 WIA, and six Me 262s.[45]

Adolf Galland had spent the first half of February confined to his home. According to his authorized biography, one night he grew depressed enough to discuss suicide—an honorable escape route for Luftwaffe officers—with his then-current girlfriend. Alarmed, she sneaked out of the house, which was under watch, and telephoned Albert Speer from a public telephone. Speer, who had known nothing of Galland's house arrest, then called Adolf Hitler directly and was put through to him. Hitler, who had always been fond of Galland, was also ignorant of the situation, but knew whom to call next. That same night Galland was startled to receive telephone calls from both SS-Obergruppenführer Ernst Kaltenbrunner, head of the SS Security Service, and his subordinate the Gestapo chief Heinrich Müller, telling him that the investigation had been a mistake, and would he please not kill himself. To cap off the night, a young, embarrassed Luftwaffe officer appeared at Galland's door with orders to confiscate his service pistol and spend the night with him. While this story may seem too outrageous to be believed, the lives of all major Third Reich personalities were full of melodrama in 1945, and no other explanation for Galland's sudden, if partial rehabilitation has come to light.

Within days Göring offered Galland a service posting. Galland asked to be allowed to form a Me 262 fighter unit, choosing its pilots from conventional units that were now flying very little owing to the shortage of aviation fuel. The unit was established on February 24 and given the unusual designation Jagdverband 44 (Fighter Unit 44, JV 44). At Galland's request, he was given the authority of a Jagddivision commander and reported directly to the OKL; he wanted nothing to do with either Gollob or Peltz. He himself drew up the unit's tables of organization, which did not stint on equipment or staff. Reaching its establishment strength of 16 pilots was not a problem—there were many volunteers, and it was joked that a Knight's Cross was a minimum requirement—but it did not become operational until

THE LUFTWAFFE OVER GERMANY

it moved from the JG 7 base at Brandenburg-Briest to München-Riem at the beginning of April. Galland had expected the senior jet unit to offer him its cooperation, but this did not happen. Galland blamed Gollob, but it did not help that Steinhoff, the JV 44 training officer and Galland's good friend, was unpopular with JG 7, which had suffered from lax training standards when he had commanded it.[46]

The Eighth Air Force flew a maximum-strength mission on the 25th against a variety of targets. The entire RLV force was scrambled, to little effect. JG 300 claimed one B-17 and one P-51, for no losses. Of the three JG 301 Gruppen, I. Gruppe was split up by 20th Fighter Group P-51s on takeoff, and lost four pilots killed while downing two Mustangs; II. Gruppe was kept from the bombers by the P-51s, claiming one Mustang for the loss of one pilot; and III. Gruppe followed its leader back to base when he had to abort, and did not make contact with the enemy. Of the jet units, no claims or losses are known for JG 7, while the bad luck of KG(J) 54 continued. Jets from its I. and II. Gruppen were hit by 55th Fighter Group P-51s as they scrambled from Giebelstadt and lost four pilots killed and seven Me 262s; four more jets were destroyed on the ground by strafing. Peltz suggested to Chief of Staff Koller that the Geschwader should withdraw to Austria to oppose the Fifteenth Air Force, while the next two ex-bomber Geschwader in the pipeline, KG(J) 6 and KG(J) 27, were sent east for seasoning. Koller concurred, while pointing out that if the two Geschwader were sent southeast to Luftflotte 4 in Hungary they could attack the Fifteenth Air Force in the flank. The order was recorded in the OKL war diary, but was never carried out.[47]

Major Günther Rall flew to Jüterbog-Damm in late February to take command of JG 300 from Major Hackl, who transferred to JG 11. On his arrival Rall found ". . . fifteen aircraft burning on the field from a P-51 attack. All was chaos. There was no ground control or radar; food and fuel were sought from day to day." He commanded the Geschwader for the rest of the war, and could recall no effective missions being flown by the unit.[48]

In March, the RLV day fighters established a routine. Me 262s from the few fully operational jet fighter units (usually the Stabsschwarm and the I. and III. Gruppen of JG 7) sortied against almost every Eighth Air Force and some Fifteenth Air Force raids, plus a few RAF Bomber Command day raids. The jets could almost always penetrate the escort screen for one rear pass at a bomber box; they became vulnerable if they tried to turn, either for a repeat bomber attack or to battle the escorts. The two conventional Jagdgeschwader were ordered up as fuel permitted, but a few costly missions reduced their strength to such an extent that by month's end the survivors were being used only to screen the jets' airfields. Fuel shortages greatly hampered operations of the tactical Jagdgeschwader on the eastern and western fronts. A call for volunteers to transfer to jets brought such an overwhelming response that the standards were raised; only pilots with a Knight's Cross or a German Cross in Gold could be accepted. Fighter units began to be disbanded, with the best pilots transferring to other units, other men deemed worthy of protection going to the Flak arm, especially the railroad Flak, and the rest going to the paratroops or the nearest infantry unit. The first units to go under were the most junior "fourth Staffeln" of the expanded Jagdgruppe establishment; next came the least effective Gruppe from each four-Gruppe Jagdgeschwader.

The first jet casualties in March came on the first day of the month. The hapless I./KG(J) 54 sortied eight Me 262s for a training mission; they were bounced by 355th Fighter Group P-51s, and lost two aircraft and pilots. On the 2nd JG 7 was allowed to train, while every other RLV unit was ordered up against a full-strength Eighth Air Force raid on the central German synthetic fuel plants. I./KG(J) 54 scrambled 14 Me 262s, which were bounced by a flight of sweeping P-51s from the 354th Fighter Group. Only two of the German pilots pressed on with their mission. They shot down one bomber and one P-51, but both were then shot down and killed by 354th Group Mustangs. JG 300 and JG 301 each sortied for the last time in full four-Gruppe strength—a total of 198 Bf 109s and Fw 190s took off—and their leaders had to look for weak spots in the escort coverage in the absence of any Me 262s to divert the P-51s. By luck or good direction, II.(Sturm)/JG 300 found itself in the rear of the leading 3rd Air Division combat wing and made a close-formation assault attack that downed four 385th Bomb Group B-17s before the P-51s arrived. JG 301 was not as fortunate, even with the brand-new Ta 152s of III./JG 301 flying high cover for the battle formation. The Geschwader was apparently delayed in forming up by the cloud cover, and was split up by P-51s before reaching the bombers. Small groups of Fw 190s were able to reach

1./JG 1 He 162A-2 "white 4" photographed at Kassel-Rothwesten in August 1945, just one of the many pieces of Luftwaffe debris scattered across Germany. (*Rosch*)

the 1st and 2nd Air Divisions and downed at least three B-17s and B-24s. At least four P-51s were shot down in the wide-ranging air combats, but the Bf 109s and Fw 190s suffered grievous losses in return. JG 300, JG 301, and JGr 10 lost 26 pilots KIA, 3 MIA, 10 WIA, and 43 aircraft destroyed. The new IV./JG 301, which had been very slow to join operations, lost eight pilots killed; this was its first and last RLV mission.[49]

The next day the jets were able to put on an impressive show. Major Rudolf Sinner led 29 III./JG 7 Me 262s up from Brandenburg-Briest to counter yet another Eighth Air Force raid on central German oil targets. The jet pilots did not attempt mass attacks, but quickly broke up into flights of three or four aircraft that attacked the combat boxes in echelon formation, almost in trail. Most made rear attacks, but Sinner led his Schwarm in a head-on attack on the 493rd Bomb Group that downed two Fortresses. In response, a bomber gunner hit a jet in the cockpit; it dove to the ground with its dead pilot. Sinner then found the 2nd Air Division stream and attacked the B-24s from the rear. He hit one Liberator which lost control and flew into a second; both crashed to the ground. Sinner's other Schwärme were careful to keep their speed up, flying from one box to the next and not being drawn into fighter combat. As many as eight B-17s and B-24s were shot down on the most successful jet mission to date. There was only the one German loss; P-51 pilots claimed six damaged Me 262s, but apparently all of them reached base.[50]

For the next few days the jets were limited to sorties against reconnaissance aircraft. Major Sinner and his wingman, Obfw. Arnold, were successful on the 7th. Each claimed a P-51; a 7th PRG P-51 was, in fact, shot down. Although J2 jet fuel, which was essentially

kerosene, was still available, high-octane aviation fuel stocks were nearly gone. On the 8th Ultra intercepted a message from Peltz's command stating that "Otto" [piston engine] fighters were to be employed only in situations especially favorable to success, in cooperation with jet units. Otherwise they were to remain camouflaged on their airfields, even when threatened with low-altitude attack by Allied aircraft.[51]

On March 8, the war's most lethal weapon system against heavy bombers—the Me 262 armed with 24 R4M unguided rockets—had its baptism of fire. The small missile, only 55 mm (2.2 in.) in diameter and carrying a 0.5 kg (1.1-pound) impact-fused warhead, had been under test since the previous fall, initially with armor-piercing warheads. Major Georg Christl at JGr 10 saw their promise as air-to-air weapons, had some fabricated with high-explosive warheads, and devised a simple launcher: a wooden rack holding 12 rockets side-by-side. The first launching rails were made from curtain rods. The Me 262 could carry one rack beneath each wing with only a moderate loss in performance, and fire the rockets in various combinations. The firing tests on the 8th by the first converted jet fighter were so successful that the pilots of Stamp's Stabsstaffel and Sinner's III./JG 7 began clamoring for the rockets, and installation of the racks on operational jets began immediately. Jagdgruppe 10 also equipped its own Fw 190D-9s with R4M racks, and used them operationally against both air and ground targets until the unit was disbanded in April.[52]

Major Heinz Bär's jet operational training Gruppe, III./EJG 2, began flying small-scale operational missions against bomber formations, probably at Bär's urging. The Gruppe claimed one B-26 on March 9 and one B-17 on the 12th. On the 14th, ten III./JG 300 Bf 109s scrambled from Jüterbog to protect the Hannover airfield. They were swarmed over by 353rd Fighter Group Mustangs, and lost half of their number. Also on the 14th, two JG 400 Me 163s were allowed up after a reconnaissance aircraft, which they missed. The next day nine rocket fighters were scrambled to protect their airfield. A pilot of the 359th Fighter Group was credited with downing one of them; two more failed to return to base for unknown reasons. This was the last USAAF fighter combat with Me 163s, which according to the RLM daily report were now flying again in small numbers after a long period of inactivity. They had been grounded due to a shortage of rocket fuel, which had been needed to power V-1 launch rockets. Since V-1s were now being launched from aircraft rather than from the ground by these rockets, some fuel was available, and was supplied to the lower-priority Me 163s. On the 14th, III./JG 7 claimed five B-24s and two B-17s; III./EJG 2 claimed one B-17. The Eighth Air Force lost seven B-17s and two B-24s, but reported no encounters with jets; it is conceivable that some bombers that allegedly blew up unexpectedly from anti-aircraft hits were instead hit by R4Ms.[53]

The RLV targets on the 16th were again reconnaissance aircraft. Obfw. Rudolf Glogner of I./JG 400 claimed a photo-reconnaissance Mosquito, for the last but one JG 400 claim of the war. Major Weissenberger, the JG 7 Kommodore, claimed a P-51 (or its F-6 reconnaissance equivalent).[54]

March 18—Berlin

The Eighth Air Force's targets on the 18th were Berlin railroad stations and tank factories. JG 7's jets, aided by hazy cloud and R4M rockets, put on their most impressive show to date. Major Weissenberger led a dozen Me 262s up from Brandenburg-Briest in time to intercept the incoming 1st Air Division, which was leading the stream of 1,300 bombers. Weissenberger attacked an isolated diamond of four 457th Bomb Group B-17s from the rear. One B-17 went down; the others were damaged, but escaped into the contrails and clouds. Weissenberger then led an unusual second pass, right over Berlin, which apparently downed a 401st Bomb Group Fortress. His dozen jets returned to base without damage. A second formation of 12 Me 262s was led to a disorganized section of the 3rd Air Division stream by the 9. Staffel Kapitän, Oblt. Günther Wegmann. His fighters carried R4M rockets which were used to good effect to shoot down four straggling 100th Bomb Group B-17s. Wegmann then led a second pass using 30-mm cannon, but this time he was headed off by a P-51, which hit his cockpit and right engine. The injured Wegmann bailed out safely, but one of his legs later had to be amputated. His wingman was shot down and killed by a B-17 gunner.[55] I./JG 7 scrambled 11 jets from Kaltenkirchen only after the day's formation leader, 1. Staffel Kapitän Oblt. Hans Grünberg, lost a telephone argument with Göring, who insisted that the aircraft take off even though the cloud deck was lower than mandated for the Me 262, which was not cleared for instrument flight. Oblt. Hans-Peter Waldmann, a Knight's Cross holder and the 3. Staffel Kapitän, collided with his wingman in the clouds, killing both

JG 1 officers stand in front of their He 162s at Leck, awaiting the arrival of the British in early May. *From left:* Maj. Werner Zober (I. GrKdr) , Oberst Herbert Ihlefeld (Kdre), Hptm. Heinz Künneke (1. StaKa), Oblt. Emil Demuth (3. StaKa), Maj. Bernd Gallowitsch (4. StaKa), Hptm. Strasen (III./JG 4 Kdr), hidden, Hptm. Wolfgang Ludewig (2. StaKa—in leather coat). (*Heinz Rose via Arno Rose*)

men. Grünberg was unable to assemble the survivors, who made individual attacks that were probably not successful, although two claims were filed by Major Erich Rudorffer, the Gruppenkommandeur, who obviously did not lead this mission and may have been flying alone. The pilots had to be talked back to the ground individually by the local controller. Apparently all made it back safely, although some aircraft may have sustained damage.[56]

The men of the Eighth Air Force knew nothing of the problems faced by I./JG 7, but were highly impressed by the performance of Weissenberger's other pilots, who had pressed through the Berlin Flak zone using contrails and clouds to mask their attacks and evade most of the Mustangs, which had been able to shoot down only a single Me 262. At least six B-17s were shot down, and several others force-landed with severe damage. Had the Americans known that much of the damage was caused by a new weapon, the R4M rocket, they would have been even more concerned.

The next day the Eighth Air Force bombed various targets in Bavaria, including several known jet airfields. Peltz sent up everything he had: jets from JG 7, KG(J) 54, and III./EJG 2; rocket fighters from JG 400; and conventional fighters from JG 300 and JG 301. Although Obstlt. Bär of III./EJG 2 claimed a Mustang, the day's most notable successes were again gained by Sinner's III./JG 7, which attacked in larger formations than before: three waves in line abreast, each of about a dozen jets. The 357th Fighter Group at the rear of the 3rd Air Division stream drove off the first two waves, but the third got past and quickly shot down four B-17s with their R4M rockets. The Mustangs then returned and shot down two of the Me 262s, killing both pilots. The 13 I./JG 7 Me 262s airborne lost one plane and pilot to a 359th Fighter Group Mustang, while claiming one certain B-17 and one probable. KG(J) 54 may have claimed two B-17s, and lost no jets in the air, but B-24 bombs destroyed or damaged 11 of III./KG(J) 54's 16 jets on the ground at Neuburg. These were quickly replaced; this favoured unit had no problems getting aircraft. The two piston-engine Geschwader stayed close to their airfields. The organizational drawdown of the conventional fighter units now hit the two RLV Geschwader; I./JG 300 and IV./JG 301 were ordered to disband. Although JG 300 and JG 301 remained on the IX. Fliegerkorps (Jagd) order of battle for a while longer, they were never again sent up en masse against the heavy bombers. They flew some airfield protection missions, but for the rest of the war were used mainly in support of the ground forces.[57]

Both the Eighth and Fifteenth Air Forces targeted known jet airfields on the 21st. The four jet Gruppen were scrambled, but once again, most of the known successes can be credited to Major Weissenberger and JG 7's Stab and III. Gruppe. Their principal target was the 3rd Air Division stream. The 490th Bomb Group lost four B-17s near Wittenberg—three to R4Ms and a fourth to collision—while the 94th and 100th Groups each lost one bomber to the jets. Weissenberger and his wingman each claimed one B-17; I./JG 7 claimed two B-17s and one P-47, for no losses; III./JG 7 claimed 11 B-17s, while losing two pilots killed and two injured. Bär's III./EJG 2 claimed one B-24 and one P-38, possibly from the Fifteenth Air Force, while I./KG(J) 54 lost one pilot for no claims.[58]

One noteworthy interception on the 21st was made by Lt. Fritz Müller of III./JG 7, who recalled:

I scrambled with my wingman versus the major Leipzig–Dresden incursion. Our radio today was jammed especially heavily by the enemy. I spotted a lone B-17 with four P-51 escorts at 7,500 meters [25,000 ft.] south of Dresden, four kilometers behind the formation. It seemed to me that this machine was on some sort of special mission, and I resolved to attack it. The jamming was so strong that radio communication was impossible. I flew beneath the P-51s,

which were smoking at full throttle, trying to keep up with me. The Boeing was now ahead of me in a left turn. At about 1,000 meters the rear gunner opened up with harassing fire . . . It was all over in seconds. At 300 meters my wingman and I opened fire with our 30-mm and gave it short bursts, allowing a slight lead. We saw a dozen rounds exploding against the fuselage and between the engines. Then we were past him. We banked around, with the Mustangs falling farther behind. The B-17 spun down 2,000 meters, then exploded. The radio jamming stopped when the bomber crashed . . .[59]

Muller's supposition about his "special" target was correct. The 482nd Bomb Group B-17 was testing an experimental radar set, the Micro-H Mk II, on a mission to Oberursel. Allied records do not indicate that the bomber was lost on this date, however.[60]

On the 22nd the Fifteenth Air Force B-17 wing encountered the newly aggressive jets for the first time while bombing a frequent Eighth Air Force target, the Ruhland synthetic fuel plant 120 km (75 miles) south of Berlin. This was a 2,300-km (1,400-mile) round trip for the Italy-based crews, who were told that they had been assigned the target because the Eighth had been unable to destroy it. Three Fifteenth Air Force P-51 groups and an Eighth Air Force group that was sweeping the Berlin area, the 4th, were unable to prevent the initial attack by Weissenberger's 21 Me 262s, which shot down no fewer than six 483rd Bomb Group B-17s on their initial pass through the formation. 31st Fighter Group Mustangs then chased the jets away, downing four. The other jet units made no known claims and lost at least one pilot. Eighth Air Force B-24s bombed the airfields of I./KG(J) 54 and the non-operational II./KG(J) 54, leaving both fields unserviceable for at least a week. The 4th Fighter Group missed the jet action, but went down on the field at Eggersdorf and shot down six Fw 190s of the newly reformed III./JG 54. A repeat raid on the field the next day destroyed six more Focke-Wulfs, and that Gruppe never returned to operations.[61]

All three of the Allied strategic bombing forces attacked the shrinking Reich on the 23rd, stretching the RLV day force even thinner than usual. Major Weissenberger led a small group of Me 262s to Ruhland and Chemnitz, which were being revisited by the Fifteenth Air Force. Major Heinrich Ehrler of the Stabsschwarm claimed two B-24s. The RLV force ignored the Eighth Air Force as it bombed tactical targets in support of Field Marshal Montgomery's massive Rhine crossing, which was scheduled for the next day. Part of RAF Bomber Command attacked similar targets, and was not ignored. I./JG 7 jets shot down two Lancasters, for the loss of one of their own to an RAF Mustang.[62]

On March 24, the Eighth Air Force supported Montgomery's crossing directly, with airfield bombings and supply drops. Three JG 300 Gruppen were ordered west to attack the bridgeheads. Allied fighters tore II.(Sturm)/JG 300 apart, killing 14 Fw 190 pilots. The other two Gruppen used their agile Bf 109s to escape the area with light losses, but the Sturmgruppe was finished, and the Geschwader flew no more major missions as a battle formation.[63]

Peltz reserved his jet force to defend the Daimler-Benz tank factory in Berlin, which was bombed on the 24th by the Fifteenth Air Force on its longest-ever mission, a round trip of some 2,400 km (1,500 miles). The crews were told that this was a vital diversionary raid to draw the attention of the Luftwaffe away from the Rhine operation, but a cynical mind would see this raid as a blatant attempt to gain the "Forgotten Fifteenth" some publicity. Major Weissenberger led the Stab and III. Gruppe of JG 7, and Obstlt. Bär led III./EJG 2 in the interception. The leading 463rd Bomb Group had already lost four B-17s to Flak, which had undoubtedly loosened its formation, and was a logical first target, losing one B-17 to the jets. The 483rd also lost one, but its gunners were credited with downing six Me 262s, three by a single B-17. The 332nd Fighter Group, which took pride in its close escort of the bombers, claimed three of the jets, while losing three P-51s. The 31st Group relieved the 332nd and claimed five jets, for no losses. The intense combat resulted in excessive claims by both sides. JG 7 claimed 12 B-17s, for a loss of four Me 262s and four injured pilots. Bär claimed one B-24 and one P-51 for no losses. That the jets had in reality downed only two B-17s and three P-51s was a source of great pride for the Fifteenth Air Force. The 483rd Bomb Group and the 332nd Fighter Group were awarded Distinguished Unit Citations for this mission.[64]

A Fifteenth Air Force raid on Neuburg airfield on the 24th cost III./KG(J) 54 yet another 14 burned-out and 36 damaged Me 262s on the ground. This most-heavily bombarded Jagdgruppe never to see operations doggedly requested more aircraft and continued training.[65]

The weather over western Europe began to worsen.

The two B-17 divisions dispatched by the Eighth Air Force on the 25th were recalled, leaving only the B-24s of the 2nd Air Division to proceed with the briefed raid on oil targets. Lt. Rudolf Rademacher led 23 Me 262s, mostly from III./JG 7 but including some from I./JG 7 and the KG(J) 54 Stab, in an attack on an isolated 448th Bomb Group squadron that downed four B-24s. III./JG 7 lost four pilots killed on the mission; the pace of operations was undoubtedly beginning to wear them down. One was lost in a takeoff accident, one in the region of the bombers, and two to 56th Group P-47s while attempting to land.[66]

Aerial operations over the Reich were cut back for the next several days owing to weather conditions. On the 26th JG 1 was ordered to give up all of its aircraft to Luftflotte 6 in the east and withdraw for re-equipment with the He 162. The next day Hitler further increased the bureaucratic snarls entangling the Luftwaffe by appointing SS Obergruppenführer Hans Kammler the *Bevollmächtiger der Führer für Strahlflugzeuge* (Führer's Plenipotentiary for Jet Aircraft). Kammler thus took over responsibility for production from Albert Speer; for operations from Göring; and for coordination from Göring's own jet plenipotentiary, Josef Kammhuber. Kammler was responsible to no one but Hitler and acted in full awareness of his authority. The staffs of Speer and Göring now had an additional master, and confusion continued to reign in Berlin.[67]

On the 30th the weather cleared sufficiently to allow the Eighth Air Force to fly a full-scale raid on shipyards in Hamburg, Bremen and Wilhelmshaven that were manufacturing new-design U-boats. The closely spaced targets increased the density of the escorts, and their location on the coast restricted the direction of approach of the RLV jets. I./JG 7 scrambled eight Me 262s from Kaltenkirchen, and III./JG 7 put up 30 from Brandenburg-Briest. Although they claimed four B-17s, three P-51s, and one Mosquito, a single 339th Fighter Group P-51 was apparently the only loss to the jets. One German pilot was killed, and a second lost a leg after he hit his airplane's tail when bailing out. An unknown number of jets were shot down or crash-landed without injury to their pilots. Pilots from six P-51 groups were given credit for destroying Me 262s.[68]

On the 31st, with the weather closing in again, the Eighth Air Force made a raid on central Germany against light opposition, bombing mainly secondary targets, while 469 RAF Bomber Command aircraft made a day raid on the Blohm und Voss U-boat yard in Hamburg. Given a choice, the day RLV always went after the RAF, and so it happened. All serviceable JG 7 aircraft were ordered up. The last formation in the bomber stream, from No. 6 Group (RCAF), had missed rendezvous with its fighter cover and had continued the mission without escort. The hurriedly scrambled jets reached the bombers in at least three groups, but all found the vulnerable Canadians and streaked in on them from the rear. Lt. Grünberg did not try to form up his men, but simply shouted, "*Hinein!*" The turrets of the Canadian bombers could not track the jets. Eleven Lancasters and Halifaxes were lost on the mission; a few were hit by Flak, but most were downed by the jet pilots, who claimed 17. Apparently no JG 7 aircraft were lost to the RCAF bombers; a few JG 7 and KG(J) 54 jets were shot down by the American P-51s swarming over central Germany.[69]

Flying Officer Kenneth Blyth of No. 408 Squadron (RCAF) had taken off late in a spare Halifax and never caught up to his formation. He saw the jets attacking the bombers ahead of him, pressed on, and bombed alone. After turning for England his bomber was suddenly hit from dead astern by a jet's 30-mm shell and caught fire. He quickly ordered the bailout, and his crew of six, called No. 6 Group's "cradle crew" for its average age of 18, got out safely, followed by Blyth, headed for a short stay in POW camp. Long after the war Blyth returned to Bergedorf, the site of his crash, to interview witnesses. One man told him that his uncle had shot him down. A document was produced crediting the victory to Sturmführer Willi Strübing, an instructor in the NSFK. The 53-year-old Strübing had been too old to join the Luftwaffe, but his Nazi supervisors allowed him to fly independent missions from his Buchen base in his Me 262. Blyth's Halifax was his 23rd claim. Strübing's commander nominated him for a Knight's Cross, but the application went nowhere; a copy eventually found its way into his nephew's files.[70]

Also on the 31st, the Fifteenth Air Force bombers hit the main rail station in Linz, while its fighters swept over central Europe on their most successful 1945 mission. Ten P-38s and P-51s were lost for claims of 35 Axis Bf 109s and Fw 190s. One large battle took place just north of Prague. The 17 Mustangs of the 31st Fighter Group's 309th Squadron waded into a large, loose formation of Bf 109s and after a 20-

minute combat returned to Italy to claim 18, without loss. Their victims were from the I. and II. Gruppen of KG(J) 6, which had had to settle for Bf 109s instead of Me 262s. They lost at least 4 KIA, including the Kommandeur of II./KG(J) 6; 6 WIA; and 15 Bf 109s.[71]

Reliable information on Luftwaffe activity is scarce for the last months of the war. The detailed RLM records of victory claims and losses end at the end of January, as previously noted. Personnel records become progressively less reliable, leaving even the names of unit commanders in doubt. Boundaries between the higher commands shifted frequently and are often uncertain today. The RLM daily reports, with their definitive record of sortie, claim and loss totals, peter out in April. RAF Air Intelligence did manage to salvage a document from the Quartermaster General's office with much of the same data; this file is an invaluable aid in sorting out the activities of the RLV in these last chaotic months.[72] But to tell a complete story the historian is forced to resort to secondary sources, which often conflict. The best result to be hoped for is an internally consistent narrative and an accurate "big picture."

Although every German knew by now that the war was lost, the units of the RLV continued to soldier on, with greater or lesser efficiency. The Luftwaffe's internal squabbling actually increased as the Reich crumbled, and a unit's serviceability and operational capabilities came to depend ever more on the political skills of its commander and the scrounging ability of its supply officer. Production facilities fell to the Allies,

3./JG 7 Me 262A-1a "yellow 8," photographed at Stendal on April 15. The airplane carries the Geschwader emblem on the nose and its red and blue fuselage bands. (*Rosch*)

or at least fell into ruins, and the ability of the transportation system to distribute the remaining stocks withered away. As the Allies advanced into the Reich from all sides, the flying units continued to retreat, and their ability to fly often depended on the fuel and ammunition that could be located in the immediate vicinity of their new bases.

A good example of how chaotic things were by April 1 is provided by the status of the rocket-fighter Geschwader, JG 400. Its I. Gruppe had only enough rocket fuel for one Me 163 to sortie every few days. Its II Gruppe, which had never become fully operational, had no fuel at all, although one document states that it now had 80 Me 163s, 60 pilots, and 450 personnel on strength. A Geschwader Stab was certainly not needed, and it was duly disbanded. The JG 400 Kommodore, Major Wolfgang Späte, was recruited by Galland for JV 44, but passed up that honor in favor of JG 7, a unit with a proven record of success. Also on April 1, I./JG 7 was bombed out of its Kaltenkirchen base, and its three Staffeln were dispersed to several airfields in the Brandenburg area. The Kommandeur of I./JG 7, Major Erich Rudorffer, was apparently released from duty on this date, and was never replaced. Details of his tour in the unit are lacking. Rudorffer claimed at least 14 victories while in I./JG 7. Most were not witnessed and never made it farther than his *Flugbuch*. The three Staffeln of the Gruppe operated independently until they were reunited temporarily as a small *Gefechtsverband* on April 25. 1./JG 7 joined the Stab and III./JG 7 at Briest, squeezing out JV 44, which moved south to München-Riem, a base that had previously been scouted and selected by Galland personally.[73]

As JV 44 was setting up shop in Bavaria, Gollob addressed a memo to Göring and Koller complaining that,

JV 44 has not achieved anything so far, although it does have a number of very good pilots. Furthermore, JV 44 has adopted operational methods that detract from those commonly accepted. It is proposed to disband the unit and place the pilots more purposefully with other units.

However, Göring kept his word to Galland, and the unit was allowed to continue on its independent way. It finally claimed its first victory on April 4, during a Fifteenth Air Force raid on Munich. Galland ordered the Rotte of Major Hohagen and Uffz. Schallmoser to

scramble. They encountered a squadron of 14th Fighter Group P-38s due west of Riem. The two sides approached each other head-on. The inexperienced Uffz. Schallmoser could not get his guns to fire. He looked down in the cockpit for the switches, looked up too late, and collided with his target, which crashed. Schallmoser's aircraft was only lightly damaged, and he returned to Riem without incident.[74]

JG 7 was also active on the 4th, operating in full strength against an Eighth Air Force raid on the Kiel shipyards and north German airfields. Ultra picked up a message stating that 30 Me 262s from the Stab, I., and III. Gruppen scrambled from four airfields; nine failed to take off and three returned early owing to technical defects. A dozen of these aircraft had to take off from Parchim directly beneath the Allied fighter screen. So ended the message. These dozen were three III. Gruppe Schwärme under Major Sinner, who evaded the sweeping P-51s and reached the thick overcast safely. When Sinner emerged from the cloud he was shot down by a 339th Fighter Group Mustang; he bailed out but had come partly out of his harness and could not control his descent. He landed in a tree and had to play dead when the Mustangs strafed him. He finally dropped 6 meters (20 ft.) to the ground and rolled into a ditch. Serious facial burns took him out of the war; the newly arrived Major Späte replaced him as III./JG 7 Kommandeur.[75]

Sinner's men evaded the Mustangs in the clouds and succeeded in attacking the very combat box that had targeted Parchim. Three 448th Bomb Group B-24s exploded or broke apart when hit by R4M rockets; a fourth reached England with severe damage. A 93rd Bomb Group B-24 from the same combat wing was also downed. Flights of JG 7 jets

8./JG 301 Fw 190A "blue 22," abandoned at Bad Langensalza in May. The airplane carries the yellow and red identification bands of the Geschwader. (*Rosch*)

cruised across north Germany looking for vulnerable bombers, while squadrons of P-51s attempted to head them off. According to some sources JG 7 pilots claimed a dozen victories in the day; Obstlt. Bär of III./EJG 2 added a P-51. But JG 7 sustained serious losses: four pilots were killed and another injured; at least a dozen of its fighters were destroyed or severely damaged. I./KG(J) 54 was also up, and may have claimed two bombers, but its losses were so severe that it withdrew in a few days to Prague's Rusin airfield.[76]

JV 44 filed its first victory claims for heavy bombers on the 5th. Oberst Steinhoff took five Me 262s up from München-Riem and led a high rear attack on the 379th Bomb Group—6 o'clock high, to the USAAF— that felled one B-17 and damaged two others to the extent that they were scrapped in England. The unit had determined from practice runs on a captured B-17 that an attack from such an angle, followed by a zoom climb, was outside the cone of fire of the B-17 tail gunner and could not be tracked by the top turret, leaving the bomber with no defense. This seems like a minor departure from the standard 6 o'clock level attack, but may have been the "non-standard method" Gollob mentioned in his memo to Göring. One of Steinhoff's men was shot down by P-51s after his engines failed, but survived his bailout.

The records give no clear indication of activities by the other jet units on the 5th or 6th. An Ultra message revealed that Major Christl was keeping the men of his supposedly disbanded JGr 10 busy (and out of the infantry) by having them fabricate and install R4M launchers for all of the Me 262 fighter units, which were eager to get them.[77]

April 7—Sonderkommando Elbe

Sonderkommando Elbe (Special Command Elbe), one of the most bizarre units in the Luftwaffe, flew its only mission on April 7. The unit was the brainchild of Oberst Hajo Herrmann, who resurrected his once-rejected proposal for a bomber-ramming formation in January, after he had joined Gemaj. Peltz's command. With Peltz's approval, Herrmann got Chief of Staff Koller's permission to present his proposal to Göring. He wrote a letter for Göring's signature that solicited volunteers from the advanced training, fighter training and operational fighter units for a special operation "from which there is only the slightest possibility of your return." Somewhat to Herrmann's surprise, since it implicitly condemned Göring's own conduct of the war, the Reichsmarschall signed it.

Göring's letter was read to the fighter units on March 8, and volunteers soon began reporting to Stendal, the Elbe base. On the radio the unit was always referred to as *Schulungslehrgang Elbe* (Training Course Elbe), which confused Allied intelligence as to its purpose.[78]

Although the operation qualified as a *Selbstopfer* (suicide) plan, the pilots did have a real chance of survival. The plan called for the exclusive use of Bf 109 variants with high-altitude engines and metal propellers, to be used as scythes. The tactical unit for the mission was to be the Schwarm, each led by an experienced pilot. It was anticipated that the other pilots would be novices. The fighters were to climb to 11,000 meters (36,000 ft.), out-climbing any escorts encountered, and would receive their orders from the IX. Fliegerkorps (Jagd) transmitter at Treuenbrietzen, which had a 200-km (120-mile) range to this altitude. The fighters would then dive on their targets singly, from above. The bombers' wings and engines were suggested as the aiming points, but Obfw. Willi Maximowitz, an ex-Sturmstaffel "ramming expert" brought in to lecture the pilots, claimed that clipping off the tail section would surely bring down the bomber with less hazard to the German pilots, and that advice was taken by most of them, even though they considered his own experiences in a heavily armored Fw 190 irrelevant to their own situation. Most of the Bf 109s were lightened by removal of their radio transmitters, all guns but a single cowling-mounted MG 131 machine gun, and most of the ammunition. Most pilots also had their Revi gunsights removed, to facilitate bailing out.[79]

Koller scaled down Herrmann's ambitious plan, code-named *Werwolf* (Werewolf), considerably. The requested 1,000 aircraft were reduced to 350, and then to 180. The number of volunteers was restricted to 300. Very few commissioned officers, and no experienced, decorated fighter formation leaders volunteered, so Herrmann was forced to draft some experienced officers from his non-operational KG(J) units. Command was given to Major Otto Köhnke, a bomber pilot who had been awarded the Knight's Cross in KG 54, and had lost a leg in combat. Common characteristics of the true volunteers, according to unit survivor and author Arno Rose, were a lower-middle class, non-religious background; low rank; youth (most were less than 21 years old); loyalty to comrades and the Reich; obedience; and a desire to continue flying rather than be ordered to the infantry. Many sought revenge against the *Terrorflieger* who had

The uniquely marked "white 1" of JV 44 was one of the oldest Me 262s still in service at war's end. It carries the mottled tail camouflage unique to Kommando Nowotny, which was disbanded on December 2, 1944, and the narrow yellow fuselage band and white "S" denoting later service in a school unit. It was photographed at Innsbruck-Hötting, Austria, on May 29, 1945. (*Crow*)

destroyed their homes and killed their families. Their training at Stendal was very scanty, comprising anti-Semitic and nationalist movies, political lectures by college professors, and a single lecture on tactics by Maximowitz. The food and drink at Stendal were very good, however, and were recalled fondly by the survivors.[80]

On the night of April 4–5 the pilots were taken from Stendal to the seven bases chosen for the operation, where they waited for the next major Eighth Air Force raid. This took place on the 7th. Herrmann, in the Treuenbrietzen control room, ordered the Elbe pilots to scramble. It was a clear, very cold day, good considering his pilots' limited flying skills, but bad for their comfort; they were not issued flying suits, and most wore only their light service uniforms. Unfortunately for Herrmann, the Americans had a large number of targets, and the stream split up into no fewer than 60 small formations, creating chaos in his control room as his officers attempted to sort them out. The pilots heard nothing but nationalist songs and exhortations over their one-way radios until and unless they were finally given target instructions. Their fuel tanks had been only partially filled for their one-way flights, and some had to break off their missions early and return to base. Whether successful or not, the day marked the high point of most of the young pilots' military careers, and many survivors have recorded

their impressions. We chose Uffz. Klaus Hahn's account as representative:

I transferred with 30 comrades to Sachau/Gardelegen on the night of April 4–5. I was given my own Bf 109G-6 or G-14 the morning of the 7th. The radio couldn't transmit, only receive the *Jägerwelle*. The tank was half full. My machine was armed with one machine gun with 60 rounds. We took off on the green flare, but I couldn't maintain speed, and fell behind my comrades in the climb. I had no thought of turning back, but kept on. I heard only marches on the radio. My aircraft suddenly gained speed, and I climbed to 10,000 meters [33,000 ft.], entirely alone. I approached four 109s, which proved to be Mustangs. One got on my tail, damaged the aircraft and wounded me in the throat. I decided to bail out despite the -50 degrees C temperature and lack of oxygen. But I saw a Fortress *Pulk* below, and decided to take one with me. My airplane was smoking, and the Mustangs didn't follow. I was able to get up-sun, and dove on the far-right B-17 in the *Pulk*. I don't know what happened next. There was a loud crash. I bailed out automatically, pulled the cord at 1,000 meters [3,300 ft.], apparently lost consciousness with the shock, and hit the ground hard, throwing both thighbones out of their sockets. Witnesses say the bomber didn't crash, but I never found out exactly where I landed. I was wounded severely in one shoulder, arm, and hand. My left arm was amputated in a British POW hospital in June due to an infection. A quick recovery followed, and I was released in August [1945]. I later tried to find the village where I landed, but couldn't—it must be between Steinhuder Meer and Verden, east of the Weser. I'm no longer interested, because the people who helped me are probably all dead now.[81]

Most of the Elbe pilots attacked B-17s of the leading 3rd Air Division, which according to American records lost nine bombers to ramming and three to Me 262s. Four of the ramming victims were from the 452nd Bomb Group, which was awarded the Distinguished Unit Citation for its 40-minute-long combat. The only Luftwaffe fighters seen by the trailing 1st Air Division were two Me 262s, but the 2nd Air Division received some attacks, and according to the Americans lost four B-24s to ramming, two of these in a single attack that is well-documented from both sides. Gefreiter Willi Rösner dove on the 389th

Bomb Group B-24 leading the division and rammed into its nose. Either the B-24 or the Bf 109 then careered into the deputy commander's aircraft. Both B-24s crashed. Rösner bailed out, blacked out, regained consciousness on the ground with a broken collarbone, and returned to Stendal on the evening of the 7th. He was promoted to Unteroffizier and was awarded the Iron Crosses Second and First Class and the German Cross in Gold for this single mission, in violation of all directives.[82]

The OKL war diary contains a bare-bones summary of the mission. Of the 183 fighters prepared for takeoff, 50 returned; 106 pilots had reported in by day's end, claiming 23 successes. There were as yet no reports from 77 pilots. IX. Fliegerkorps (Jagd) was to order the remaining pilots to be released—the operation would not be repeated.[83]

The Elbe mission remained somewhat of a mystery for decades after the war. The survivors were considered naive fools by other Luftwaffe veterans and, often, by their own families. But many of the *Elbe-Männer* eventually concluded that they had a right to take pride in the sacrificial mission for which they had volunteered, and began communicating with one another and cooperating with historians. As a result this is now one of the best-documented Luftwaffe missions of the war. Fritz Marktscheffel was an Elbe volunteer who did not fly on April 7 because he was too junior to be given one of the limited number of airplanes. He has for decades collected documents and pilot's accounts pertaining to the mission, and his figures can be considered the best available. Marktscheffel concludes that about 188 Bf 109s were prepared for the mission at five bases in Germany and one outside Prague. About 143 fighters actually took off; 21 returned early due to technical defects; 15 from Stendal were never given a target and returned to base for lack of fuel; and those from Prague were recalled when the bombers turned north, putting them beyond range. About 90 contacted the enemy; as many as 40 attempted ramming attacks. Marktscheffel can identify the pilots in 18 ramming attacks on B-17s, three on B-24s, and three on unspecified heavy bombers. In addition, one B-17 and one fighter were claimed shot down by the single machine guns of the ram fighters. Casualties to the *Elbe-Männer* were surprisingly light: 18 pilots were killed, six failed to return and remained missing, and 13 were wounded. Sixteen bailed out and landed successfully; two died when their parachutes failed to open; and four were

shot and killed by American fighter pilots while hanging on their chutes. Another pilot was shot at but suffered only a hard landing when his chute was shot through. Known Bf 109 losses total 13 to American escorts, three to German Flak, and 21 in ramming attacks; 14 force-landed for operational reasons after contacting the enemy.[84]

The Elbe plots were told that they would be protected from American fighters by Me 262s, but there is no evidence that the jet pilots knew anything of this. Their primary mission was to attack bombers, not fighters, and this is what they did. Fifty-nine jets from JG 7 and I./KG(J) 54 were scrambled. JG 7 pilots claimed one F-4 (a reconnaissance P-38), two P-51s, one B-17, and one B-24, for no known losses. I./KG(J) 54 reported four victories over B-17s, and lost one Me 262 to a B-17 gunner.[85]

Although the Eighth Air Force lost 17 bombers, the greatest loss on a bombing mission since February 3, and 189 more bombers returned to base with damage, it was certainly not in the Americans' interest to publicize a successful suicide mission in the ETO while the *Kamikazes* were causing great concern in the Pacific, and the casualties due to ramming were downplayed. Allied intelligence professed no knowledge of a special operation. The Eighth Air Force mission summary concluded that,

> While there were a number of instances of fighters ramming bombers, there is no evidence that these were intentional. In all cases the enemy aircraft was either out of control after being hit, or was manned by an inexperienced pilot trying a fly-through attack against a tight formation.

The sacrifices of the *Elbe-Männer* were thus not even acknowledged by the Americans, and certainly did not affect their morale, as Herrmann had hoped. Like Operation Bodenplatte, Werwolf was only a futile, bloody gesture.[86]

The End Game
By the last month of the war the Luftwaffe was a totally spent force. None of its activities could have the least effect on Germany's imminent defeat. It could defend neither the Army, the industrial base, nor the citizenry. Headquarters and combat units were disbanded daily; the survivors moved to stay ahead of the advancing Allied armies, becoming less effective with each move. The jet units were nevertheless up

every day. The performance of the Me 262 was unexcelled, and on most days the claims of the pilots exceeded their losses. The USSTAF was about out of strategic targets, but took a personal interest in the "jet menace," and devoted thousands of tons of bombs to tearing up jet airfields and the remaining shells of jet aircraft production facilities. Parchim, the base for I./JG 1 and its He 162s and a dispersal base for JG 7, was bombed on April 8 and put out of action for a week. JG 7 had four known claims that day, and no known losses. The next day the south German airfields were pasted. Six of JV 44's Me 262s were badly damaged on München-Riem, and casualties to the female anti-aircraft gunners were so high that Galland sent the survivors "away" (destination unknown), having them replaced by men. JV 44 scrambled only one jet to meet this attack, without success. In the north, JG 7 went after RAF Lancasters bombing Hamburg, downing two, while Major Bär and III./EJG 2 were directed to a medium-bomber formation, and downed two 397th Bomb Group B-26s. One jet and pilot are known to have been lost on the 9th.

On April 10, the Eighth Air Force dispatched 1,315 B-17s and B-24s to bomb eight north German airfields suspected of harboring jets. The RLV responded by scrambling 63 Me 262s on what proved to be the high point of Luftwaffe jet activity; their casualties were so great that the effort could never be matched. The 1st and 3rd Air Division streams were both attacked in the Berlin area by Me 262s, which swept in from 6 o'clock high, level or low either individually or in small groups. Ten B-17s were shot down by the jets, which then had to fight through the 905 P-47s and P-51s up over central Germany and find somewhere to land while their own bases were under attack. JG 7 lost 27 Me 262s and at least five pilots, including three Staffelkapitäne. One was Oblt. Franz Schall, a Knight's Cross holder whose jet exploded when he taxied into a new bomb crater when landing on Parchim. Schall had 14 victories as a jet pilot, placing him second in this category to Obstlt. Bär. I./KG(J) 54 lost one KIA, two WIA, and an unknown number of aircraft. The total number of jet pilot casualties is not known; however, the Quartermaster General document states that eight fighters were lost, 24 remained missing, and five were damaged on this day, for claims of 12 Allied aircraft definitely, and one probably destroyed. An unknown number of jets were destroyed on their bases, all of which were now unser-

viceable. JG 7 and KG(J) 54 were ordered to withdraw to the south. The Stab of KG(J) 54 made it to Fürstenfeldbrück near Munich. The aircraft of the other north German units wound up in Prague-Rusin. Pilots without aircraft, including Obfw. Hermann Buchner of III./JG 7, and part of the ground staff, took to the highways, bypassed Prague on their way south, and ended the war in Bavaria or Austria.[87]

According to some sources, even I./JG 400 was able to fly a mission on the 10th, sending up a single Me 163 that downed a straggling B-17 or Lancaster with the Jägerfaust (Hunter's Fist) weapon, which comprised ten vertically mounted 50-mm gun barrels in the wing roots, triggered by a photocell. If true, this was either the ninth or tenth, and last, victory for the Me 163.[88]

Genmaj. Peltz and his IX. Fliegerkorps (Jagd) staff followed the north German jet units to Prague, and after several days of small-scale operations reported on the 15th that 60 Me 262s were on hand at Rusin. The units available were JG 7, with its Stab, I. and III. Gruppen; I./KG(J) 54; and the last bomber-as-fighter unit to become operational, III./KG(J) 6. Most of the remaining KG(J) Gruppen in Oberst Herrmann's Fliegerdivision 9 (Jagd) were ordered to disband, as surplus to requirements.[89]

JV 44 continued its independent war from München-Riem. It intercepted a heavy bomber formation for the last time on the 17th. Uffz. Schallmoser survived yet another aerial collision, this one with a 305th Bomb Group B-17 south of Berlin. Both aircraft went down. Also on the 17th, about 20 JG 7 fighters intercepted the heavy bombers near Prague, and made a number of claims, but apparently only one 91st Bomb Group B-17 went down. These two B-17s were the last 1st Air Division aircraft downed by the Luftwaffe. The German casualty total is unknown, but all of Oblt. Grünberg's Schwarm were shot down by American fighters, with only Grünberg surviving.

JV 44 began paying attention to the medium bombers supporting the advance of the American and French armies into Bavaria. On the 16th the entire unit, 14 Me 262s, attacked a B-26 formation and shot down three. On the 18th, after Galland led his three-plane Kette off the ground without incident, Oberst Steinhoff, leading the second Kette, apparently hit a small bomb crater. He lost control of his airplane, which rolled down an incline at the end of the airfield, overturned, and exploded. Miraculously, Steinhoff lived, emerging from the flames with terrible facial burns which scarred him for life. Galland's other jets reached the bombers and shot down one B-26, while seriously damaging a second. Obstlt. Bär was apparently conducting III./EJG 2 operations from Lechfeld with complete independence. According to his logbook, he shot down one B-26 on the 17th, two P-47s on the 18th, and another B-26 on the 19th.

Prior to the Rhine crossing in March 1945, Schmid's Luftwaffenkommando West, with Flieger-divisionen 14, 15, and 16, conducted tactical fighter operations against the advancing Allied armies, while Stumpff's Luftflotte Reich continued its RLV mission with IX. Fliegerkorps (Jagd). With the Rhine crossing at Remagen and the subsequent Red Army thrust across the Oder, however, the Luftwaffe's field commands began to collapse inward. Luftwaffen-kommando West pulled back into Bavaria, at the same time transferring Fliegerdivisionen 14 and 15 to Luftflotte Reich, which remained in the north.[90] The British Air Ministry historians noted:

> The longstanding division between tactical and strategic fighter forces went by the board, all units now being liable to be put up for all tasks as and when required . . . Still greater confusion was now also being caused in the confined spaces of the Reich by the fact that eastern and western front units found themselves based on the same or on neighbouring airfields.[91]

Stumpff's command was compelled to throw its elite heavy Flak units into the ground battle; whereas in fall 1944 it disposed of over 1,500 heavy batteries, by April it had only 450 remaining.[92] In the last two months of the war, Allied breakthroughs compelled the Luftflotte Reich command to take on a vagabond-like existence across northern Germany. Its battle headquarters relocated four times during that period; first to Stapelburg, then to Quassel, then to Reinsfeld near Lübeck, and finally to Missunde (near Schleswig), where the headquarters staff finally surrendered to units of the British Army.[93] Stumpff himself helped formally to surrender the remnants of the Third Reich in Berlin on May 8, 1945.

Although the Luftwaffe continued operating until VE-Day, May 8, the organized aerial defense of the Reich, which we have designated the RLV, can be said to have ended on April 18. Anticipating that the American and Soviet armies would soon pinch the Reich in two, the Luftwaffe split into northern and

Me 262A-1a "yellow 5" ended the war with JV 44 but carries the red and black checkered fuselage band of KG(J) 54 (checks not visible in this photo). It was captured at München-Riem in May, restored to flying condition, and brought to the U.S.A. Some sources say that this is the Me 262 now on display at the USAF Museum at Wright-Patterson Air Force Base in Ohio. (*Crow*)

southern commands. The northern units were commanded by Genobst. Stumpff's Luftflotte Reich. IX. Fliegerkorps (Jagd), the operational air-defense command that had previously been subordinated to Stumpff, was now in the southern command, as part of Genobst. von Greim's Luftflotte 6. Centralized air defense was no longer possible.[94]

JG 7 flew its last large-scale mission against the Eighth Air Force on April 19. The 3rd Air Division targeted railroad installations in Bohemia. Captain Charles Ailing, piloting the lead bomber of the 93rd Bomb Wing, heard his bombardier describe 12 horses towing Me 262s across an airfield (Prague-Rusin). His tail gunner then watched the jets take off. In seemingly less than a minute, the fighters were called out at 3 o'clock high; they then swept around for a rare head-on attack. Ailing's evasive maneuvers were matched by the rest of the 34th Bomb Group immediately behind him, and his combat box escaped damage. Farther to the rear, however, one 447th and four 490th Bomb Group B-17s blew up, the last heavy bombers to fall to the German jets.[95]

According to the Quartermaster General document, 42 fighters were up on the 19th, claiming seven certain and five probable victories for a loss of four aircraft destroyed, five missing, and three damaged. The sortie total probably includes, in addition to JG 7, I./KG(J) 54, also up against the raid on Bohemia, and III./EJG 2 and JV 44, flying against

B-26s in the south. Bär's B-26 claim has been noted. The JV 44 formation badly damaged two 322nd Bomb Group B-26s before being driven off by 404th Fighter Group P-47s. Other Luftwaffe activity included the formal disbanding of the immobile I./JG 400 at Brandis, just as American tanks appeared on the airfield. Farther north, I./JG 1 flew its first He 162 mission from Leck. The He 162 Gruppe entered service too late to join the strategic air defenses, and was ordered to operate against the RAF's Second Tactical Air Force. This first mission was not a success. Tempests from No. 222 Squadron were intercepted by a single He 162 as they strafed Husum. The jet attempted to turn with them and was shot down. Its pilot used his ejection seat, the first in a service fighter, but his parachute failed to open, and he was killed.[96]

The rundown of the Luftwaffe continued. II./JG 7, which for various reasons had never been declared operational, joined the rest of the Geschwader at Prague-Rusin on April 20, the same day that Kammler radioed Göring that there was only enough jet fuel in the Prague area to transfer away the units already there; he proposed moving them to southern Germany. III./KG(J) 54 was ordered to stand down on the 21st, having never flown a mission. Most of the school commands and operational training units had long since been disbanded, but III./EJG 2 hung on until April 23, on which date Obstlt. Bär, his wingman and instructors quickly made the short flight to München-Riem and reported to Galland. On the 24th Galland's deputy, the highly respected Oberst Günther Lützow, was lost (literally) while battling 365th Fighter Group P-47s after an interception of

Fw 190D-9 "red 1" of the JV 44 *Würger* (Shrike) Staffel, which had the mission of protecting the unit's Me 262s during takeoff and landing. It is parked in front of the unit's Si 204 transport at München-Riem in June. (*Crow*)

17th Bomb Group B-26s—his body has never been found.

Göring was relieved as Luftwaffe Commander-in-Chief on the 24th and placed under arrest. He was succeeded by Ritter von Greim, who was summoned to the Führerbunker in besieged Berlin to receive his field marshal's baton from Hitler. In other Luftwaffe activity worth noting, II./JG 400 was now at Husum and still attempting to become operational on the Me 163. On the 24th its Kommandeur, Major Opitz, crashed on a test flight, surviving with severe burns. On the same day, and on the same airfield, the Kommandeur of II./JG 1, Hptm. Dähne, was killed on his first He 162 flight, which he had postponed as long as he could. Among the vicious features of the *Volksjäger* were twin rudders that could not be used for steep turns because the airflow across them was blanked out by the jet exhaust. Turns had to be made with the ailerons only. Dähne apparently forgot this, and lost control. He ejected; the seat shot upward perfectly, but the canopy did not jettison, and broke Dähne's neck.

On April 25, the U.S. Army met the Soviet Army at Torgau on the Elbe, splitting the dying Reich into northern and southern portions, while two Soviet army groups encircled Berlin and Hitler. The Eighth Air Force flew its last strategic mission on the 25th; RAF Bomber Command flew its last that night; and the Fifteenth Air Force followed suit the following day. Jet operations from Prague tapered off for lack of fuel. In the south, Galland led 12 Me 262s up on the 26th to intercept 17th Bomb Group B-26s that were bombing Lechfeld. Galland claimed two B-26s, for his final victories, but in a moment of inattention was hit and injured by a 50th Fighter Group P-47. He returned to Riem and landed safely, but his leg had to be placed in a cast, and his combat flying was over. Operational control of JV 44 passed to Obstlt. Bär.

The jet units in the Prague area received a timely delivery of J2 fuel on the 26th to allow them to resume operations. Obstlt. Hermann Hogeback, the KG(J) 6 Kommodore, formed a *Gefechtsverband* from the various KG(J) units at Rusin and began attacking Red Army ground targets with R4M rockets. Little is known of JG 7 operations at this time, but the Geschwader is believed to have lost about ten Me 262s during April 28–May 1.[97]

JV 44 remained operational at München-Riem until April 28, but details of its last combats remain anecdotal. Obstlt. Bär claimed a P-47 over Bad Aibling on the 28th, for his last victory. His 16 victories made him the world's top-scoring jet pilot, a record that stood until the final days of the Korean War. Galland was under pressure to move his unit to Prague, which was too close to the Russian lines—and Czech partisans—for his taste, and on the day American forces reached Munich he succeeded in getting permission to move instead to Salzburg.

Hitler's April 30 suicide released the officers of the Wehrmacht from their personal oaths of service, and many of them began to consider how to surrender their units to the Western Allies without falling victim to marauding SS teams who were shooting or hanging suspected deserters. Although Galland attempted to negotiate the surrender of his unit, events overtook him. The war ended relatively smoothly for JV 44, which immobilized its jets at Innsbruck and Salzburg and waited to surrender to the Americans, who arrived on May 4.[98]

Large-scale surrenders began on May 2 on the Italian front, followed on May 4 by the northwestern front. The German high command surrendered unconditionally on the 7th, and Victory in Europe Day (VE-Day) was declared on the 8th. Part of JG 7 was trapped in Prague, from which a few pilots flew a last attack on the Berlin–Cottbus *Autobahn* on the 8th before heading west for forced landings behind the western lines. They were welcomed by the Western Allies, eager to find anything and anyone associated with the German jet program. The fate of the JG 7 personnel remaining in Prague is unclear, but apparently the Soviets respected an informal agreement that they would keep captive only members of Luftwaffe units that had fought primarily on the Eastern Front. Most members of those piston-engine fighter units with long RLV service were released fairly quickly to return home. The bloodiest and most destructive war in European history was over.

Adolf Galland deserves a separate discussion in this narrative. He was by far the dominant personality of the Jagdwaffe, although he had few operational responsibilities while serving as the General der Jagdflieger from early 1942 to January 1945. He saw this job as one of defending the interests of the fighter force within the Luftwaffe High Command. He lasted three years in the position, much longer than one might have expected given his impatience and blunt nature. Galland's relations with Göring and other powerful Luftwaffe chiefs were stormy, yet by earning and cultivating the support of Korten, Milch, Speer,

Saur and even Hitler, he was able to survive in the Byzantine world of the Third Reich. He lost many more battles than he won, but his task was essentially impossible, given the irrational nature of Hitler's war direction and Göring's deep distrust of the Jagdwaffe dating back to its perceived failures in the 1940 Battle of Britain. By early 1943 Galland saw clearly that the air threat posing the greatest danger to the Reich was the American strategic bomber force, which was just then beginning to cross the German border. But it was already too late; the war of production, for which Galland bore no responsibility, was lost by 1942. He tried relentlessly to build up the RLV force, but without command responsibility his role was limited to that of advocate and expediter. The weapons and tactics that he championed achieved some success; but the generation of fighters that was to have won the battle against the *Viermots* was delayed until the course of the war made them irrelevant.

Galland's major failures were sins of omission. Four are listed here; Galland accepted some responsibility for the first three in his post-war interrogation.[99]

1. Fighter pilots received no instrument training at all until very late in the war, after the overall training course had already been cut short by the desperate need for replacements and the fuel shortage. Pre-war Luftwaffe doctrine did not require single-engine fighters to fly in bad weather, or even in heavy cloud. Galland apparently failed to realize that these abilities were absolute prerequisites for a successful home air defense.

2. Outnumbered on all fronts from 1942, the experienced fighter-unit leaders steadily became casualties and dropped from the lists. By mid-1944 a large majority of Jagdwaffe Staffel leaders were former enlisted pilots who had received "battlefield commissions" for their combat skills. Some were given a rudimentary officer's course, but they received no training for their new, crucially important roles as formation leaders until Galland set up a course in late 1943. This lasted only a few months. Galland was quoted as saying that he felt that pilots could learn the art of leading formations as he had, while on the job flying combat missions. He thus blithely ignored their obvious inferiority to him in education, maturity, and flying skills, and most important, glossed over the ever-growing quantitative and

qualitative inferiority of the Jagdwaffe, which allowed few newcomers the time to develop into skilled combat pilots, much less into adequate leaders. Poor combat leadership can be added to the long list of deficiencies that brought the Jagdwaffe low over Germany and the western occupied zone in late 1943 and 1944.

3. The incomparable Me 262, while not a "war winner," could have been a "campaign extender" if it had entered service in the RLV in strength in 1944. The delays owing to Hitler's meddling, engine problems, and misplaced production priorities are well known, but the inexcusable delay between operational testing and true combat status was in large part Galland's fault; his office was responsible for operational testing and training and the development of tactical regulations. His choices to command Kommando Nowotny and JG 7 were weak, and Galland neither came down hard on them nor replaced them. III./JG 7 could theoretically have entered service within one month of the dissolution of Kommando Nowotny instead of three. If this had happened, Göring's decision to give bomber pilots control of the RLV and the new jet-fighter units (the Kampfgeschwader (Jagd) concept), the biggest source of wastage in the Me 262 program, might have been forestalled.

4. New recruits for the Jagdwaffe were lacking in both quality and quantity. Galland recognized the problem, but could not have impacted it without stepping outside organizational lines. Early in the war Galland became aware that the more highly educated pilot trainees, especially those with engineering training, were being selected for the bomber arm; the school staffs did not consider high intelligence important or even desirable for fighter pilots. He made an ineffective effort to educate the selection staffs by sending some of his best pilots to the primary training schools as instructors. Furthermore, Galland believed that the Luftwaffe lost many of the best and brightest young men during their mandatory tour in the Labor Service, where "they were exposed to expert recruiters of the Navy and the Waffen SS." The disorganized Luftwaffe could not match this effort. Galland counted on an innate love of flying to pull German youth toward the Luftwaffe, but this was insufficient. Galland's popularity would have been very important in a Luftwaffe recruiting campaign, had he or anyone else in the RLM seen the need for one.

A two-seat Me 262B-1a trainer of III./EJG 2, photographed at Stuttgart-Echterdingen in June. (*Crow*)

Two fateful decisions by Adolf Hitler, to invade the Soviet Union in June 1941 and to declare war on the U.S.A. that December, doomed Germany to ultimate defeat. But a more effective air defense would certainly have prolonged the war and changed its course in ways impossible to predict. The principal factor in the failure of the RLV was Hitler's and Göring's gross underestimation of the U.S.A.—its production capacity, the capabilities of its aircraft, and its will to force the daylight bombing campaign to a successful conclusion. The most important component of the day air defenses was originally the Jagdwaffe, although the Flak arm was much more important than is generally realized and by late 1944 had certainly displaced the fighters. Early in their post-war interrogation, Adolf Galland and Josef Schmid co-authored an instructive list of the Luftwaffe's biggest mistakes with respect to the Jagdwaffe.[100] All such lists can be accused of special pleading, but this one is objective enough to include some of Galland's and Schmid's own errors:

Mistakes in Organization and Planning

1. At the start of the war the Jagdwaffe was too weak with respect to the other arms of the Luftwaffe for proper expansion.
2. The Jagdwaffe was not a part of the offensive air force, and was thus considered second-rate.
3. The Jagdwaffe had no strong representation in the high command.
4. The Jagdwaffe was never put under unified command (for the prewar build-up, offense, or defense).
5. The Jagdwaffe build-up just before the war was too rapid. Quality suffered.
6. The nine Jagdgeschwader in existence in 1939 were not increased until 1942. 1940 and 1941 were wasted.

7. Only eight new Jagdgeschwader were fully formed. The table of organization strength of all Jagdgeschwader did increase by one-third.
8. All planning by the high command was "reactive."
9. The concept of "control of the air" was never understood by the high command.

Mistakes in Development and Technical Equipment
1. The decisive error was the lack of a Tactical–Technical Section in the OKL [or earlier, in the RLM].
2. Starting in 1940 all planning was short-range as a matter of policy.
3. Technical improvements were not pushed hard enough, as they would have hurt production rates.
4. Obsolete fighter types (like the Bf 109) were kept in production for too long.
5. The inadequate aircraft production rate was not recognized until 1944.
6. Production was not concentrated on fighters until mid-1944.
7. Mistakes with respect to the Me 262 were "especially crass."
8. Mass production of the He 162 was indicative of the "decay in logical thinking." It had a 20-minute endurance!

Mistakes in Pilot Selection and Training
1. The standards for fighter pilots were not tightened to the "elite" level soon enough.
2. The bomber arm was clearly given preference for the best personnel in training.
3. The supply of commissioned pilots for fighters was neglected early; thus there were not enough leaders later.
4. Trainees received too few flying hours. At first there were too few aircraft; then fuel ran low.
5. The emphasis in the flight schools was not shifted soon enough toward the supply of fighter pilots.
6. Gaps in flight training included: hours on operational types, formation flying, gunnery training, combat training, and an almost complete lack of instrument training [fifth on this list!].

Mistakes in Leadership and Staff Training
1. Systematic training of formation leaders was not begun until 1943—far too late.
2. Geschwader Kommodoren were too old at the start of war, but were then replaced by young Turks too quickly.
3. There were no fighter command organizations at the start of the war, and there were never enough good officers to staff those that were set up. There were very few General Staff Officers in the Luftwaffe.
4. Jafü and Jagddivision commanders were relieved too quickly by Göring. They couldn't gain experience.

Mistakes in Strategy and Operational Tactics
1. The Jagdwaffe was overloaded with missions after 1942.
2. On no front was the Jagdwaffe allowed to take the offensive to try to regain air superiority. Tactics were always defensive (for example, escort of army support aviation).
3. Draining of resources from the west for the Eastern Front went on for too long.
4. The build-up of forces for the RLV was a failure. It was too slow and piecemeal, and lacked a formal plan.
5. The high command considered the Jagdgruppen to be organic units, and transferred them without regard to the location of their home Geschwader. This caused confusion and decreased their fighting value.
6. The ground organization and communications networks were neglected when considering unit mobility.
7. Bad weather operations completely overtaxed the fighter units. High losses shook confidence in the high command and caused great uncertainty in the units.
8. The high command never understood the importance of economical employment of strength with respect to the RLV. All incursions had to be met at full strength, rapidly wearing down the defenders.
9. The over-long use of Zerstörer and the 5-cm cannon were mistakes by Hitler and Göring.
10. Three times in 1944 a Jagdwaffe reserve was built up and then destroyed in the west: (a) versus the Invasion; (b) at the end of August; (c) in the Ardennes; (a) was inevitable, but (b) and (c) were inexcusable.
11. Göring permitted no realistic reflection on the loss of air superiority, but squandered time and energy in the most disgusting insults of the fighter force.
12. The high command never understood the

importance of time—for planning, recovery, etc.

13. Giving control of IX. Fliegerkorps to the bomber arm had a disastrous impact when the future hung in the balance. Giving control to Peltz was a dagger thrust into the heart of the Jagdwaffe. Dissolution and ruin were the results.

14. Galland's main rule was ignored. The fighters must maintain the offensive at all times and costs, even when on "defensive" missions (for example, as Sturmgruppe escorts).

15. Absolute integrity of formations in combat is one of the most important requirements for decisive success and low losses. This was frequently disregarded.

16. No fixed scheme should be allowed to take hold of operational tactics and battle techniques. Surprise, cunning and maneuverability must be combined with aggressiveness and dash.

17. Examination of the victory and loss lists, recognizing the enemy's crushing superiority in the air, must leave one with the impression of a hard and courageously fighting German fighter force.

Summing Up

The RLV commanders have had their say—what can the historian, from a vantage point 60 years after the events, conclude about the German day-fighter arm's five and one half year struggle against the Allied bomber offensive? The RLV takes its place alongside the great air-defense efforts in aviation history. Such protracted campaigns are rare; successful ones rarer still. It obviously invites comparison with RAF Fighter Command's victory in the Battle of Britain in 1940. The Luftwaffe General Staff's own historians observed, "In 1940 the English had proven to Germany that an active defense can force the aggressor to lessen his offensive or discontinue it completely."[101] Although the Luftwaffe eventually allocated far greater resources to its air-defense effort than did the RAF in 1940, it failed to commit these resources at a time when the Allied air offensive might still have been checked. As more than one historian has noted, many of the Luftwaffe's key mistakes—notably production and training decisions—that doomed the RLV to defeat were made in 1940, 1941, and 1942.[102] Even so, the RLV was far more successful than the futile Japanese effort to defend the Home Islands against the B-29 onslaught in 1944–5. The air-defense campaign waged by North Vietnam from

Klaus Hahn as a pupil in flight school in 1943. Hahn did not complete his training until early 1945, and had just reported to his first operational posting when he heard the call for volunteers for Sonderkommando Elbe. He volunteered and flew the unit's only mission, which cost him an arm. (*Hahn*)

1965–72, in which an interceptor and ground-based air-defense system exacted a considerable toll from a technically superior adversary over a period of years, may actually be the closest historical parallel.

In evaluating the Luftwaffe's attempts to defend Reich airspace, one finds a mixture of strategic blindness, operational effectiveness, and technological innovation and missteps. Without a doubt, the RLV fell victim to the Luftwaffe senior leadership's chronic failure to develop a coherent air strategy for a long war. While obviously some of this dilemma was caused by even more catastrophic failures at the highest levels of national leadership, the Luftwaffe high command failed to make air defense a priority. It did not absorb the sharp lesson RAF Fighter Command taught it in 1940. The Luftwaffe was caught in a four-front air war, and each theater demanded attention. Jeschonnek is often pilloried, but in a sense he was correct when he observed, on the eve of the Kursk offensive that critical July of 1943, that if the Germans did not win in Russia, they were not going to win at all. Even as clearheaded a participant as Galland believed that the main effort of the air war in 1943 would be in the Mediterranean.[103] Few if any senior Luftwaffe leaders—with the possible exception of Milch—possessed a comprehensive view of the whole war situation.

The Luftwaffe's "Cult of the Offensive" served it well during 1939–41, when it managed to knock the Polish, French and Soviet air forces off balance and pave the way for victory on the battlefield. Yet its reluctance to develop defensive doctrines, technology, production plans and tactics until very late in the war was to cost it dear. Although many of the reasons for the Luftwaffe's defeat could be put down to political meddling or the shortcomings of the supreme Nazi leadership, this specific failing was the Luftwaffe's own. Time and again, the desire to take the offensive undermined defensive efforts. It was the primary reason that Sperrle was allowed to keep Luftflotte 3's fighter forces independent of Lw Bfh Mitte, creating a cumbersome and unnecessarily divided command structure. Even Korten, who is known as a stalwart of the "defensive clique," made rebuilding the bomber arm a priority. The last commander of the Luftkriegsakademie (Air Force War Academy), Generalleutnant Herbert Joachim Rieckhoff, noted just after the war that: "As late as 1944, when the offensive forces of the Luftwaffe had been more or less exhausted, worn down or grounded by lack of fuel, instruction in the art of offensive air tactics continued to dominate the curriculum. It took a tremendous effort to find instructors qualified to teach 'Luftverteidigung' and give the subject the attention it merited."[104] As a result of this thinking, "the Reich's air defense was built on stop-gaps and improvisations" until the final year of the war.[105]

The German military has frequently shown an ability to capitalize on victory, and to subject even successful tactics and procedures to rigorous criticism and evaluation. At key moments, however, this trait deserted the Jagdwaffe. The Luftwaffe leadership's response to victory was to rest on its laurels. The early success above Heligoland Bight led to a near-total

neglect of integrated air defense for many months. Even the transitory victory over the USAAF in fall 1943 did not provide the impetus for continued reforms, and the day-fighter arm found itself outnumbered and outclassed the following spring by American escort fighters, its own Zerstörer units decimated and its cadre of experienced pilots killed off.

Bitter internal struggles within the Luftwaffe's leadership and among its various weapons branches further degraded the home-defense effort. As the bomber arm dwindled, the still powerful representatives of "the embodiment of offensive air warfare" exerted an influence on fighter operations that was at best ill-advised. It is necessary only to mention the names of bomber pilots turned fighter commanders

Fw. Ernst Schröder managed to stay in good spirits while serving as a pilot in a Sturmgruppe, one of the war's most hazardous postings. This snapshot was probably taken in March 1945. (*Schröder*)

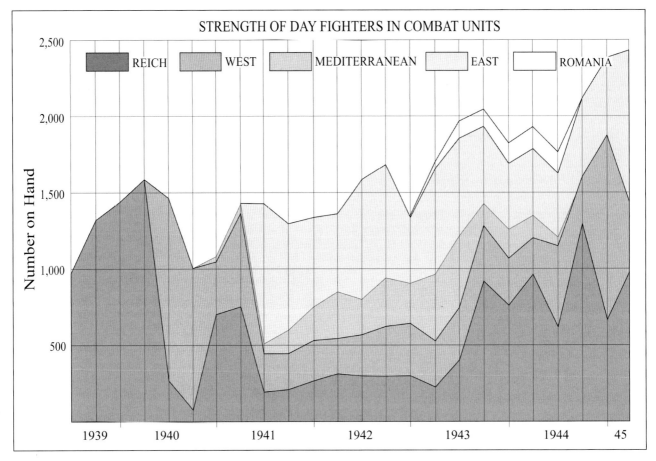

Herrmann and Peltz to strike sparks among surviving Jagdwaffe personnel. The Luftwaffe's own chief historian sadly summed up the convoluted late-war command structure—especially Peltz's IX. Fliegerkorps (Jagd)—as "an eternal puzzle of our time which is so rich in absurdity and crime!"[106] The jaundiced and condescending view of many aviators toward their colleagues in the Flak arm was perhaps even more detrimental to the RLV. This was an attitude totally counterproductive in modern warfare, which depends on effective employment of combined arms.

This work has discussed many notable RLV pilots and given details of their combats. Not mentioned previously was Lt. Emil Hofmann, whose career was more typical of an aspiring RLV pilot. Like most of his contemporaries, Hofmann fulfilled his obligations in the Hitler Youth and *Reichsarbeitsdienst* (German Labor Service) before joining the Luftwaffe. After basic military training, he was selected for the flying branch, and progressed through the various "A" and "B" stages to become a fighter pilot. His *Wehrpass* (service record book) proudly contained the notation for receipt of the pilot's badge . . . and abruptly ends with a terse note of his fatal crash in an Fw 190 while at *Blindflugschule* (Instrument Flying School) 10 on September 9, 1943.[107] Hofmann's abbreviated career was all too typical of German fighter pilots during the later years of the war. Germany began the war with superbly trained pilots but failed to develop an infrastructure capable of turning out the numbers required in modern global war. The story of Luftwaffe pilot training is one of progressive deterioration, in which the training courses were watered down, flying hours curtailed, and the teaching of essential skills reduced or deleted.[108] Aviation enthusiasts will forever debate the relative merits of the P-51D and the Fw 190D; there is no such debate about the quality of pilot trainees from 1943 on. The Allies were unquestionably superior. Lack of trained pilots is one of the primary reasons why the huge increase in German aircraft production in 1944 did not translate into a similar increase in combat power at the front.

Success in modern air combat also depends on an effective balance between quality and quantity. Much

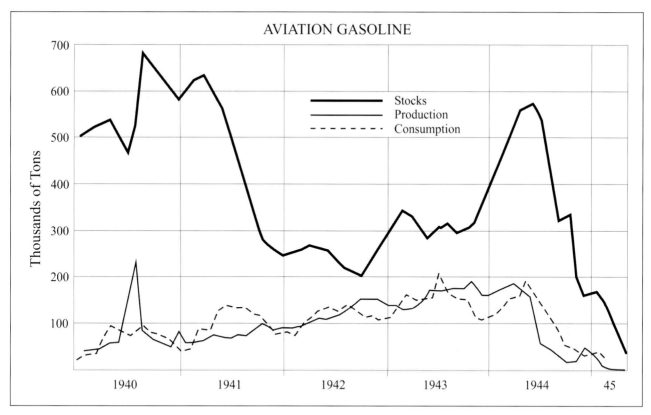

AVIATION GASOLINE

has been written on German aviation technology. In the case of the RLV, the conventional wisdom is correct. The German fighter arm stuck with proven types for too long, while the Allies forged ahead with technically superior air weapons. Coupled with the Allied advantages in numbers and pilot skill, this produced a dilemma the Germans could not resolve. The few vastly improved German types—especially the jet-propelled Me 262—may have scored some spectacular individual successes, but their overall impact was minimal. Indeed, had the Germans not begun to lose air superiority over their home territory, these "miracle weapons" probably would not have been pushed into service use at all.

In the production battle, one can argue that the Luftwaffe leadership did rather better. The tremendous increase in fighter production under very adverse conditions—especially after the Fighter Staff took charge after "Big Week" in February 1944—is remarkable. Yet much of this production surge consisted of obsolescent aircraft. The concurrent effort to bring the advanced types into mass production was largely a failure. The quality of the finished product declined, as dispersed manufacture, use of slave labor, and shortages caused by bombing took their toll. Finally, much of this new production never flew in combat—it either sat with empty fuel tanks, was destroyed on the ground, or was lost in non-combat accidents.

Three graphs produced originally for the postwar United States Strategic Bombing Survey (USSBS) illustrate dramatically the cumulative effects of a number of the factors we have discussed. The diagram on page 290[109] shows the allocation of day fighters among the various combat fronts over the course of the war. The data show the numbers "on hand," and not "operational," which were generally much less, but are consistent. The graph has been redrawn from the original to include the twin-engine Zerstörer. Although the Luftwaffe inventoried them separately from "fighters" (*Jäger*) it is useful to combine them here. The Zerstörer were an appreciable fraction of total Luftwaffe strength during the first year of the war and were returned to service in mid-1943 to bolster the RLV. The graph illustrates the increase in front-line strength made possible by the "Production Miracle." More important, it demonstrates how the demands of the other combat fronts prevented the necessary expansion of the air-defense force. The fighters available for strategic defense were those

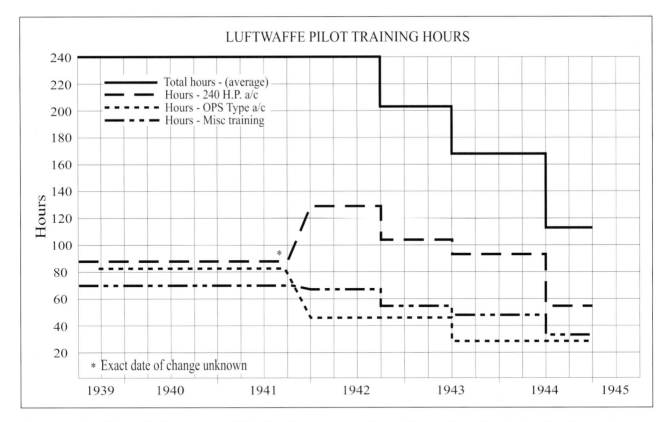

LUFTWAFFE PILOT TRAINING HOURS

Total hours - (average)
Hours - 240 H.P. a/c
Hours - OPS Type a/c
Hours - Misc training

* Exact date of change unknown

shown in the "Reich," those in the "West" prior to D-Day (as needed), and those in "Romania". The Luftwaffe's fighter force was large enough to sustain a successful struggle on any one of the other fronts—but the combination proved more than it could handle. The endgame in Tunisia and the Kursk operation sucked up a large share of the Luftwaffe's fighter force at the precise time that the USAAF daylight bomber offensive might have been turned back. Especially noteworthy are the catastrophic effects of the Normandy invasion and the Ardennes offensive.

Whether obsolescent or state-of-the-art, Germany's fighters were useless without fuel to power them and trained pilots to fly them. The diagram on page 291[110] shows the production, consumption, and inventory of aviation fuel in Germany over the course of the war. The USSTAF can rightfully take credit for this decisive Allied victory. Beginning with the Red Army's occupation of Ploesti at the end of August 1944, the ground armies did capture the remains of numerous Axis oilfields and refineries, but only after they had been reduced to useless rubble by bombing.

The German pilot training program was the first to feel the effects of Spaatz's Oil Campaign, and never recovered. The diagram above[111] shows the nominal number of hours flown by Luftwaffe pilot trainees as the war progressed. With the end in sight, the Luftwaffe leadership decreed that experienced pilots from the disbanded bomber and long-range reconnaissance units would be assigned to jets. The half-trained pilots emerging from the barely functioning training schools were sent to Bf 109 and Fw 190 units. It is hardly surprising that Grabmann observed that by 1945, "It is clearly evident that fighter defense operations with aircraft powered by piston-type engines had become completely uneconomical."[112]

The strategic failure of the Luftwaffe and the RLV should not obscure its notable successes. Although working under the long shadow of "offensive thinking," the leaders of the RLV did a creditable job of cobbling together a defensive command structure that—by day and by night—posed a serious and sustained challenge to the Anglo-American air assault. This command structure did not become truly centralized until very late in the war, but the creation of I. Jagdkorps was one of the more remarkable wartime organizational developments in any air force. When the creation of Luftflotte Reich brought the fighters, Flak, passive defense, and the aircraft-warning service under a single headquarters, a truly integrated, highly developed, day and night air-defense system was in place.

The RLV effort also contained some undeniable accomplishments in terms of tactical and operational innovations. Although the Luftwaffe was inadequately prepared to wage a protracted defensive campaign, its middle level leadership proved imaginative and resourceful in designing effective combat methods. The constant improvements in tactics, culminating in the lethal *Gefechts-verband* and Sturmgruppe attacks, caused great concern at USSTAF headquarters until the end of the war. The use of air-to-air rockets, the development of workable fighter-control procedures (Y-Control and EGON), and the streamlining of the division and Jagdkorps operations centers also deserve mention. If the development process also spawned some failures—extra-large caliber cannon, air-to-air bombing, cable bombs—it was simply the price of innovation, which every air force paid.

The RLV did achieve some transitory victories. It forced RAF Bomber Command to abandon its daylight bombing strategy in 1939, and threw the USAAF effort in fall 1943 into disarray. It compelled the leaders of the USAAF to abandon or modify key elements of their air strategy. On the human plane, the defenders of the Reich made its airspace one of the most dangerous battlefields for American servicemen in the entire Second World War. Eighth Air Force analysts in early 1944 calculated that crews had only one chance in four of surviving their combat tour unscathed. A confidential report to Spaatz maintained that heavy-bomber raids into Germany were "the most hazardous military operations which have been conducted over a sustained period."[113]

Recent scholarship from the German left has argued that from spring 1944 Germany was essentially defenseless; that the Anglo-American bomber fleets could roam at will over Germany and punish a helpless civilian population.[114] The deaths of German civilians are certainly cause for reflection and regret, yet they took place in the context of a titanic aerial struggle. The RLV may have sagged in effectiveness by mid-1944, but, as this account has demonstrated, Flak and fighters defended German airspace to the very last weeks of the war, and exacted a heavy toll from the Allied bombers.

The historians have had their say. The last word in this account will be given to a Sturmgruppe veteran. In an interview with the authors, Ernst Schröder summarized his personal Second World War experience as follows:

Do not forget in any presentation of the 1944–45 Reichsluftverteidigung the circumstances under which we had to fight:

- against an incredible numerical and technical superiority;
- with inadequately trained personnel (my total flying time according to my logbook was 310 hours!);
- against an American foe who sometimes exhibited only a modest fighting spirit (in all of my attacks on American bombers I was only fired at on rare occasions—and then, only at distances greater than 1,000 meters [1,100 yards]!);
- but also against American fighter pilots who had their way with us with tactically skillful maneuvers;
- and at all times with an unprecedented willingness to sacrifice on the part of the German fighter pilots.[115]

This photograph of three Bf 109 pilots' graves was taken late in the war at Döberitz, which had been the Luftwaffe's first fighter base, and symbolizes the fate of a large majority of the pilots who served in the Reich defense force. (*Permann*)

NOTES

Chapter 1: German Air Defense—Early History and Theory (pages 12–30)

1. Hans-Detlef Herhudt von Rohden, "The Battle for Air Supremacy over Germany (German Air Defense), 1939–1945," unpublished typescript, 1946, p. 4.
2. Edward B. Westermann, *Flak: German Anti-Aircraft Defenses, 1914–1945*, University Press of Kansas, Manhattan, KS, 2001, p. 21.
3. James S. Corum, *The Luftwaffe: Creating the Operational Air War*, University Press of Kansas, Manhattan, KS, 1997, p. 41.
4. Keith Rennles, *Independent Force: The War Diary of the Daylight Squadrons of the Independent Air Force, June–November 1918*, Grub Street, London, 2002, pp. 71–2.
5. Georg Paul Neumann, *Die deutschen Luftstreitkräfte im Weltkriege*, Ernst Siegfried Mittler und Sohn, Berlin, 1920, p. 577.
6. Herhudt von Rohden, "Battle for Air Supremacy over Germany," p. 5.
7. "Studie eines Offiziers über die Fliegerwaffe und ihre Verwendung," n.d. (*c.* 1925), p. 10. On the German analysis effort, see James S. Corum, *The Roots of Blitzkrieg: Hans von Seeckt and German Military Reform*, University Press of Kansas, Manhattan, KS, 1992, pp. 153–4.
8. *Richtlinien für die Führung des operativen Luftkrieges* (1926), para 40. A translation of this important directive appears in James S. Corum and Richard R. Muller, *The Luftwaffe's Way of War: German Air Force Doctrine 1911–1945*, Nautical and Aviation, Baltimore, MD, 1998, pp. 91–112.
9. *Führung des operativen Luftkrieges*, para 43.
10. Giulio Douhet, *The Command of the Air*, Coward-McCann, New York, 1942, p. 94.
11. Douhet, *Command of the Air*, p. 55; italics in original.
12. William Mitchell, *Winged Defense: The Development and Possibilities of Modern Air Power, Economic and Military*, Putnam, New York, 1925, p. 199.
13. Hans-Detlef Herhudt von Rohden, "Betrachtungen über den Luftkrieg (I. Teil)," *Militärwissenschaftliche Rundschau*, 2 (1937) Heft 2, p. 204.
14. *Führung des operativen Luftkrieges*, para 127.
15. Karl-Heinz Völker, "Die deutsche Heimatluftverteidigung im Zweiten Weltkrieg (I)," *Wehrwissenschaftliche Rundschau*, 16, 1966, p. 87.
16. Genmaj. a. D. Walther Grabmann, "German Air Defense, 1933–1945," United States Air Force Historical Research Agency (USAFHRA) K. 113. 107–64, p. 25.
17. On the "Risiko-Luftwaffe," see Edward L. Homze, *Arming the Luftwaffe: The Reich Air Ministry and the German Aircraft Industry, 1933–1939*, University of Nebraska Press, Lincoln, NE, 1976, Chap. 3.
18. Hanfried Schliephake, *The Birth of the Luftwaffe*, Henry Regnery Company, Chicago, 1971, p. 38.
19. Beatrice Heuser, *Reading Clausewitz*, Pimlico, London, 2002, pp. 93–5.
20. **Wever, Walther (1887–1936).** The first Chief of the Luftwaffe General Staff and one of Germany's most brilliant air theorists and strategists. Wever began his career in the Army, serving with distinction on the Western Front in World War I and achieving renown as one of Paul von Hindenburg's and Erich Ludendorff's key staff officers. Retained in the 100,000-man Reichswehr, Wever made his mark there as well, rising rapidly to the post of chief of the training branch. In 1933 he was transferred at Göring's request to the still-secret Luftwaffe and became its *de facto* chief of staff. Wever led the team that produced the manual L.Dv. 16 *Conduct of Air Warfare*, crafting the doctrine that would bring the Luftwaffe its most spectacular victories. He championed a Luftwaffe that would be able to function in a wide variety of roles, from direct ground support to air defense to long-range strategic bombardment. All who knew him spoke of his exemplary personal and professional qualities, and he had the rare ability to work effectively with difficult colleagues such as Milch and Göring. For perhaps the only time in the Luftwaffe's short history, the senior leadership, the Technical Office, and the General Staff coexisted free of strife. Wever, like many of the officers transferred from the Army, was determined to master every facet of his new job, and that included learning how to fly at a somewhat advanced age. This professionalism led to his undoing. On June 3, 1936, while flying an unfamiliar aircraft, he crashed to his death on takeoff. His loss was keenly felt; no subsequent General Staff chief was his equal in terms of strategic vision or strength of personality.
21. **Göring, Hermann (1893–1946).** Second in importance only to Adolf Hitler in the foundation and government of the Third Reich. Göring was a successful fighter pilot in World War I, winning the Pour le Mérite and succeeding Manfred von Richthofen in command of the world's first multi-squadron fighter unit, Jagdgeschwader 1. Göring left Germany after the Armistice, but upon his 1922 return quickly fell under the influence of Adolf Hitler. Göring was badly injured in the unsuccessful Munich Beer Hall Putsch of November 1923, resulting in a life-long addiction to morphine and other pain-killing drugs. In 1927 he returned from Italian exile to rejoin Hitler, and soon became the Nazi Party's spokesman to the German upper classes. He was elected to the Reichstag as a delegate from Bavaria, and in 1932 was elected its president. After Hitler became chancellor, Göring was named to

his cabinet as minister without portfolio, becoming the Prussian minister of the interior and the national commissioner of aviation. He used the former position to cement the Nazi hold on power by establishing the Gestapo and the concentration camp system. His second role placed him over all aspects of German aviation, and when the Luftwaffe was established in March 1935, he became its commander-in-chief.

In 1936 Göring became the National Commissioner for the Four-Year Plan for the German Economy. His ruthless energy and intelligence enabled him to carry out all of his official roles with a high degree of success, while at the same time participating in the various prewar inter-service intrigues that ended when Hitler took over direct command of the Wehrmacht.

The invasion of Poland in September 1939 ended Germany's string of bloodless territorial acquisitions, and the subsequent declarations of war by Britain and France took Göring completely by surprise; he had believed Hitler's statement that no major war would begin until 1942. Within four years of its official formation, the Luftwaffe had become one of the world's largest, best organized, and best equipped air forces, but one that was extremely thin in infrastructure and talent. Göring took full credit for its early successes, and Hitler promoted him to a unique rank, Reichsmarschall, and awarded him a unique medal, the Grand Cross of the Iron Cross. But in the summer of 1940 the Luftwaffe failed to win the quick air victory over England that Göring had promised Hitler. Göring blamed his pilots for this failure, rather than taking responsibility for any deficiencies in planning or equipment, and withdrew almost completely from active command of "his" Luftwaffe, leaving this to his deputy Milch and to the Luftwaffe Chief of Staff, Jeschonnek. He remained active in his role as commissioner for the German economy during the invasion of the Soviet Union in mid-1941, approving plans to loot the Ukraine and Belorussia, starve most of the Slavic inhabitants of the region, and exterminate its Jews.

In early 1943 Göring's last broken promise to his Führer, to maintain the Sixth Army at Stalingrad by aerial supply, cost him the last of his credibility, and he spent most of the last two years of the war at his various estates, hunting and admiring his looted art collection. His token appearances at Hitler's staff meetings wearing pancake makeup and gaudy uniforms were greeted with ridicule, and most of his infrequent requests were vetoed or ignored.

In April 1945, after Hitler announced his intention to fight to the last in Berlin, Göring radioed Hitler to inquire if this meant that Göring was to take over the government. An enraged Hitler ordered Göring arrested and stripped him of all his duties, turning the Luftwaffe over to von Greim. Göring spent the remaining few days of the war under SS house arrest, and turned himself over to the American forces on May 8.

Göring, the highest-ranking German prisoner-of-war, inevitably became the foremost defendant in the 1945–6 Nuremberg war crimes trials. Drug-free for the first time in twenty years, his intelligence and arrogance reasserted themselves, and by all accounts his aggressive, forceful defense dominated the proceedings. Found guilty and condemned to death by hanging, he committed suicide the night before his execution by a cyanide capsule that he had hidden among his personal effects for his entire captivity.

22. Wilhelm Deist *et al*, *Das Deutsche Reich und der zweite Weltkrieg*, Band I, *Ursachen und Voraussetzungen der deutschen Kriegspolitik*, DVA, Stuttgart, Germany, 1979, p. 478.

23. Grabmann, "German Air Defense, 1933–1945," p. 22a; Homze, *Arming the Luftwaffe*, n. 71 p. 40.

24. **Milch, Erhard (1892–1972)**. The one individual most responsible for the rapid formation, organization, and growth of the Luftwaffe. Milch joined the German Army in 1910, became an air observer in 1915, and ended World War I in command of a fighter wing. He joined the new Lufthansa airline in 1920 and became its director in 1926. By 1933 Lufthansa was the world's most successful airline. Milch then joined the still-secret Luftwaffe as a colonel at the urging of his friend Göring. He applied his energy to the organization of the new air force, with the full approval of Göring, who was preoccupied with his many other jobs and the ongoing political intrigue within the Third Reich. Milch became Göring's deputy and State Secretary of the RLM. He rose steadily in rank, and was named a field marshal at the conclusion of the 1940 French campaign. After the Battle of Britain in 1940 Göring devoted little time to the Luftwaffe, leaving executive control in Milch's hands. By 1943 he had added Inspector General and Director of Air Armament to his other titles. But his ambition to replace Göring as commander-in-chief became known, and Göring succeeded in taking away many of his responsibilities. In May 1944, Hitler accused Milch of deceiving him with respect to the Me 262 program, and canceled his directive naming Milch as Göring's successor. Milch then withdrew into semi-retirement at his hunting lodge, and in January, 1945 was stripped of his last position and placed in the Führer Reserve. In 1947 Milch was convicted of war crimes at the Nuremberg trials and sentenced to life imprisonment. His sentence was later reduced to fifteen years, and he was released in 1955. He was employed as an adviser by several German industrial firms until shortly before his death in 1972.

25. "Vortrag des Generalmajors Wever bei Eröffnung der Luftkriegsakademie in Berlin-Gatow am 1. November 1935," *Die Luftwaffe: Militärwissenschaftliche Aufsatzsammlung*, Heft 1 (1936), p. 6.

26. Major Hans-Detlef Herhudt von Rohden, *Vom Luftkriege: Gedanken über Führung und Einsatz moderner Luftwaffen*, E. S. Mittler und Sohn, Berlin, 1938, p. 49.

27. On "operational air warfare," see Horst Boog, *Die deutsche Luftwaffenführung 1935–1945*, Deutsche Verlags-Anstalt, Stuttgart, 1982, pp. 151–64; Corum, *Luftwaffe*, pp. 128-144; and Richard Muller, *The German Air War in Russia*, Nautical and Aviation, Baltimore, MD, 1992, pp. 3–15.

28. L.Dv. 16, *Luftkriegführung*, Reichsdruckerei, Berlin, 1935.

29. L.Dv. 16, para. 16.

30. **Galland, Adolf (1912–96)**. The Luftwaffe's General der Jagdflieger (General of the Fighter Arm) for three years and an outstanding fighter pilot and commander. Today Galland is undoubtedly the best-known veteran of the Luftwaffe. A pre-war professional officer, Galland joined the still-secret Luftwaffe in 1934. He gained an excellent reputation in the Spanish Civil War as the leader of a squadron of ground-attack aircraft, and he fought in the Polish campaign in that capacity. He transferred to fighters, and was named Kommodore of Jagdgeschwader 26 (JG 26) in August 1940, one of the first of the younger generation of fighter pilots to be promoted to that level of command. By the end of the Battle of Britain Galland's innovative escort formations had become standard doctrine, and JG 26 had earned a reputation as the best fighter unit in the Luftwaffe. Galland led

JG 26 in France until December 1941, when he was summoned to Berlin to replace Werner Mölders as General der Jagdflieger. after the latter's death. Soon thereafter he was awarded the Oak Leaves with Swords and Diamonds to the Knight's Cross of the Iron Cross, the second member of the Wehrmacht after Mölders to receive this new highest decoration. At age thirty, Galland became the youngest general in the Wehrmacht. His new job was a staff rather than a command position, and Galland spent most of the rest of the war attempting to defend the interests of the fighter force within the Luftwaffe high command. Reichsmarschall Göring tended to blame the failures of his fighter arm on the cowardice of his pilots, rather than deficiencies in numbers, training, and equipment. Galland, although a favorite of Hitler, gradually lost all credibility and influence in his position, and resigned in January 1945. He requested and was granted permission to form a small unit of Me 262 jet fighters, Jagdverband 44, and led it until he was wounded in April 1945. Galland ended the war as a Generalleutnant. His final victory total was 103, all scored against the Western Allies.

Galland served postwar as a technical adviser to the Argentine Air Force, and after his return to Germany became a consultant to the German aviation industry. He remained active until his death in 1996. His classic memoir, *The First and the Last*, established his reputation in the English-speaking world, and remains in print in several languages more than fifty years after its original publication.

31. Adolf Galland, "Defeat of the Luftwaffe: Fundamental Causes," *Air University Quarterly Review* VI (Spring 1953), p. 23.

32. **Schmid, Josef "Beppo" (1901–56).** An officer of the Luftwaffe General Staff, in 1943–4 Schmid held the most important operational command in the RLV, but is best known today for his miscalculations as head of the 5. Abteilung, the Intelligence Section, in 1940. His consistent underestimation of the combat strength of RAF Fighter Command and failure to identify profitable targets were two of the principal reasons the Luftwaffe lost the Battle of Britain. In 1935 Schmid had transferred from the German Army into the Luftwaffe. Unlike many promising staff officers who made this move, Schmid never became a pilot. After a number of staff postings in Berlin, he was given command of the *Hermann Göring* [Luftwaffe armored] Division in Tunisia, where he won the Knight's Cross of the Iron Cross. He was evacuated before the May 1943 Axis surrender in North Africa, and replaced General Josef Kammhuber as commander of XII. Fliegerkorps, which contained all of the fighters defending Germany. Despite his unpromising background, he proved to be a quick learner, and immediately took the decisive measures necessary to restore his command's effectiveness. In the fall of 1943 XII. Fliegerkorps was renamed I. Jagdkorps (I Fighter Corps). Schmid's pleas to the Luftwaffe high command to strengthen and reorganize the Luftwaffe fighter arm led to a strong and lasting relationship with Adolf Galland, a man with whom he otherwise had little in common. In December 1944, he was given command of Luftwaffenkommando West, which comprised the air units supporting the army on the western front. He ended the war in this post, with the rank of Generalleutnant. After the war he was a principal author of the USAF Historical Studies on the German Air Force.

33. Johannes Steinhoff, *Messerschmitts over Sicily*, Nautical and Aviation, Baltimore, MD, 1987, p. 185.

34. Generalstab 8. Abteilung, "Gegenüberstellung der

Kampfführung der eigenen und der anglo-amerk. Luftwaffe," 22 Aug 44, von Rohden 4407-97, National Archives and Records Administration (NARA) microfilm T971/51/334.

35. L.Dv. 16, para 247.

36. L.Dv. 16, para 261.

37. L.Dv. 16, para 246.

38. L.Dv. 16, para. 265.

39. L.Dv. 16, para 267.

40. L.Dv. 16, para 273.

41. Westermann, *Flak*, p. 71.

42. I./Flak-Regiment 12, Betr.: Vortrag Major d. Genst Deichmann, October 29, 1936, Flak 34, NARA T405/61/4834542ff, p. 10.

43. Grabmann, "German Air Defense 1933–1945," Vol. I, p. 93.

44. Höh. Kdr. d. Flakartl. im L. K. II u. Kdr. Im Luftgau 4 Abt. Ia op Nr 3354/36 geh., Betr.: Vortrag Major Raithel, "Vortrag über Technik, Organisation und Einsatz der Jagdflieger," October 22, 1936, NARA T405/6/4834458ff.

45. "Vortrag Major Raithel", p. 8.

46. "Vortrag Major Raithel", p. 9.

47. Grabmann, "German Air Defense, 1933–1945," p. 130.

48. Grabmann, "German Air Defense, 1933–1945," p. 131.

49. "Vortrag Major Raithel", p. 12.

50. Robert Allan Doughty, *The Breaking Point: Sedan and the Fall of France, 1940*, Archon Books, Hamden, CT, 1990, p. 32.

51. Grabmann, "German Air Defense, 1933–1945," p. 63. Italics added.

52. Grabmann, "German Air Defense, 1933–1945," pp. 54–5.

53. Hans Detlef Herhudt von Rohden, "Luftwaffe und Gesamtkriegführung," in Hans Eichelbaum, ed., *Das Buch von der Luftwaffe*, Bong & Co., Berlin, 1938, p. 20.

54. "Vortrag des Generalmajors Wever," p. 8.

55. For an excellent discussion on the effects of Versailles on German air armament, see Homze, *Arming the Luftwaffe*, pp. 39–41.

56. William Green, *The Warplanes of the Third Reich*, Galahad, New York, 1986, p. 26.

57. Schliephake, *Birth of the Luftwaffe*, p. 34.

58. "Vortrag Major Raithel," pp. 2–3.

59. Wolfgang Schenck, personal communication with R. Muller, 1991.

60. R. J. Overy, "The German Prewar Aircraft Production Plans, November 1936–April 1939," *English Historical Review* (October 1975), pp. 778–97; Grabmann, "German Air Defense 1933–1945," pp. 26ff.

61. **Grabmann, Walter (1905–92).** One of the most proficient and influential RLV Jafü and Division-kommandeure. Grabmann learned to fly in the German police force and received a commission in the newly formed Luftwaffe. He soon became the commander of one of JG 26's predecessor units. After a tour in Spain as commander of the Condor Legion's fighter component, he transferred to the new Zerstörer force, and commanded ZG 76 during the French campaign and the Battle of Britain, for which service he was awarded the Knight's Cross. He became Jafü Holland-Ruhrgebiet in August 1942 and in November 1943 was given command of Jagddivision 3, a position he retained until the last chaotic month of the war. His last rank was Generalmajor. After the war he was a principal author of the USAF Historical Studies on the German Air Force.

62. Grabmann, "German Air Defense 1933–1945," pp. 26–7.

63. "Leitfaden für den Unterricht in der Taktik an den Luftkriegsschulen" (1937), quoted in Grabmann, "German Air Defense 1933–1945," pp. 88–9.

64. Hans Arndt, "Die Fliegerwaffe," in Friedrich Seesselberg, ed., *Der Stellungskrieg 1914–1918*, E. S. Mittler & Sohn, Berlin, 1926, pp. 344–6.

65. "Vortrag Major Raithel," p. 27.

66. Major Josef Schmid, "Jagdfliegerverbände" (1937), quoted in Grabmann, "German Air Defense 1933–1945," pp. 90–1.

67. Alan Beyerchen, "From Radio to Radar: Interwar Military Adaptation to Technological Change in Germany, the United Kingdom, and the United States," in Williamson Murray and Allan R. Millett, eds., *Military Innovation in the Interwar Period*, Cambridge University Press, Cambridge, UK, 1996, pp. 272–3.

68. This discussion of the command structure is derived from Karl-Heinz Hummel, "Die Kommandostrukturen in der Reichsluftverteidigung 1939–1945," I. Teil, *Deutsches Soldatenjahrbuch 1986*, Schild-Verlag, Munich, 1986, pp. 350–4; Westermann, *Flak*, pp. 76–8; Grabmann, "German Air Defense 1933–1945," Vol. I, pp. 131ff.; Schliephake, *The Birth of the Luftwaffe*, pp. 44–7; Air Ministry, *The Rise and Fall of the German Air Force*, HMSO, London, 1948, pp. 11, 37. Sources disagree on the precise timing of the many reorganizations.

69. Grabmann, "German Air Defense, 1933–1945," p 132; Schliephake, *Birth of the Luftwaffe*, p. 46

70. Westermann, *Flak*, p. 77.

71. Corum, *Luftwaffe*, p. 243.

72. Herhudt von Rohden, "Battle for Air Supremacy," p. 7.

73. Grabmann, "German Air Defense, 1933–1945," p. 165.

74. Horst Boog, *et al.*, *Germany and the Second World War*, Vol. VI, *The Global War: Widening of the Conflict into a World War and the Shift of the Initiative 1941–1943*, Clarendon Press, Oxford, UK, 2001, p. 479.

75. Hummel, "Kommandostrukturen," I. Teil, p. 353.

Chapter 2: Repelling RAF Bomber Command's Daylight Assault (pages 31–47)

1. Armand van Ishoven, *Messerschmitt Bf 109 at War*, Charles Scribner's Sons, New York, 1977, pp. 42–4.

2. Van Ishoven, *Messerschmitt Bf 109 at War*, p. 44.

3. Grabmann, "German Air Defense, 1933–1945," p. 234.

4. Charles Webster and Noble Frankland, *The Strategic Air Offensive against Germany, 1939–1945*, Vol. I, *Preparation*, HMSO, London, 1961, p. 192.

5. On the state of Bomber Command, see Tami Davis Biddle, *Rhetoric and Reality in Air Warfare*, Princeton University Press, Princeton, NJ, 2002, Chap. 2; Williamson Murray, "Strategic Bombing: The British, American and German Experiences," in Williamson Murray and Allan R. Millett, eds., *Military Innovation in the Interwar Period*, Cambridge University Press, Cambridge, UK, 1996, pp. 118–19; Webster and Frankland, *Strategic Air Offensive against Germany*, Vol. I, pp. 107–26.

6. Alfred Price, *Battle over the Reich*, Charles Scribner's Sons, New York, 1973, p. 12.

7. Details on RAF bomber capabilities may be found in Max Hastings, *Bomber Command*, Dial Press/James Wade, New York, 1979, Append. B; and Denis Richards, *The Hardest Victory: RAF Bomber Command in the Second World War*, W. W. Norton, New York, 1994, Append. III.

8. Philip S. Meilinger, "Trenchard, Slessor and Royal Air Force Doctrine before World War II," in Philip S. Meilinger, ed., *The*

Paths of Heaven: The Evolution of Airpower Theory, Air University Press, Maxwell AFB, AL, 1997, pp. 52–3.

9. Biddle, *Rhetoric and Reality*, pp. 178ff.

10. Hastings, *Bomber Command*, p. 17.

11. Denis Richards, *Royal Air Force 1939–1945*, Vol. I, *The Fight at Odds*, HMSO, London, 1953, p. 40.

12. Richards, *Hardest Victory*, p. 27.

13. Martin Middlebrook and Chris Everitt, *The Bomber Command War Diaries: An Operational Reference Book, 1939–1945*, Penguin, New York, 1990, p. 24.

14. Webster and Frankland, *Strategic Air Offensive against Germany*, Vol. I, p. 193.

15. Christopher Shores, *Fledgling Eagles: The Complete Account of Air Operations during the 'Phoney War' and Norwegian Campaign, 1940*, Grub Street, London, 1991, p. 126.

16. Richards, *The Fight at Odds*, p. 45.

17. Shores, *Fledgling Eagles*, p. 131.

18. Webster and Frankland, *Strategic Air Offensive against Germany*, Vol. I, p. 194.

19. Richards, *Fight at Odds*, p. 45; Webster and Frankland, *Strategic Air Offensive against Germany*, Vol. I, p. 194.

20. Horst Boog, *et al.*, *Germany and the Second World War*, Vol. VI, *The Global War: Widening of the Conflict into a World War and the Shift of the Initiative 1941–1943*, Clarendon Press, Oxford, UK, 2001, p. 494. Webster and Frankland, *Strategic Air Offensive against Germany*, Vol. I, p. 192, makes a similar claim.

21. Hummel, "Kommandostrukturen," I. Teil, pp. 350-3.

22. Grabmann, "German Air Defense 1933–1945," p. 232a.

23. On Luftwaffe–Navy relations, see Sönke Neitzel, "Kriegsmarine and Luftwaffe Co-operation in the War against Britain, 1939–1945," *War in History*, 10 (4), 2003, pp. 448–63.

24. Jochen Prien and Peter Rodeike, *Jagdgeschwader 1 und 11, Teil 1, 1939–1943*, Struve-Druck, Eutin, Germany, n.d., p. 7.

25. Grabmann, "German Air Defense, 1933–1945," pp. 238ff.

26. Prien and Rodeike, *JG 1 und JG 11*, p. 5.

27. TrGr = *Trägergruppe* or "Carrier Group", a unit formed to equip Germany's planned aircraft carrier fleet but which operated from land bases since no carrier was ever completed.

28. The Battle of Heligoland Bight has a considerable literature. This account is derived in the main from Hastings, *Bomber Command*; Prien and Rodeike, *JG 1 und 11*; Eric Mombeek, *Defending the Reich: The History of Jagdgeschwader 1 "Oesau,"* JAC Publications, Norwich, UK, 1992; Donald L. Caldwell, *JG 26: Top Guns of the Luftwaffe*, Orion Books, New York, 1991; Donald L. Caldwell, *The JG 26 War Diary*, Vol. I, *1939–1942*, Grub Street, London, 1996; Webster and Frankland, *Strategic Air Offensive against Germany*, Vol. I; Richards, *The Fight at Odds*; and especially Shores, *Fledgling Eagles*.

29. Ken Merrick, *By Day and by Night: The Bomber War in Europe, 1939–1945*, Ian Allan, London, 1989, p. 13.

30. Webster and Frankland, *Strategic Air Offensive against Germany*, Vol. I, p. 195.

31. Grabmann, "German Air Defense, 1933–1945," p. 240; Prien and Rodeike, *JG 1 und 11*, p. 7.

32. Mombeek, *Defending the Reich*, p. 9.

33. O. K. Dombrowsky, "Der 18. Dezember 1939: Die große Luftschlacht über der Deutschen Bucht," *Jägerblatt*, 63 (4), p. 8.

34. Mombeek, *Defending the Reich*, p. 10.

35. Webster and Frankland, *Strategic Air Offensive against Germany*, Vol. I , p. 199.

36. Richards, *The Fight at Odds*, pp. 46–7.

37. Westermann, *Flak*, p. 89.

38. Williamson Murray, "The German Response to Victory in Poland: A Case Study in Professionalism," in Williamson Murray, *German Military Effectiveness*, Nautical and Aviation Press, Baltimore, MD, 1992, pp. 229–43.

39. Herhudt von Rohden, "Battle for Air Supremacy over Germany," p. 13.

40. Grabmann, "German Air Defense, 1933–1945," p. 233.

41. Grabmann, "German Air Defense, 1933–1945," p. 228.

42. **Jeschonnek, Hans (1899–1943).** The longest-serving Luftwaffe Chief of Staff. Jeschonnek became a pilot at the age of 17 and served with Erhard Milch during World War I. He remained in the inter-war German Army, the Reichswehr, and rose quickly in rank, especially after he and his mentor Milch joined the newly established Luftwaffe. Jeschonnek became Chief of Staff in February 1939, and rose to the rank of Generaloberst, but fell out with both Milch and Göring, who blamed him for the operational failings of the Luftwaffe. Jeschonnek was well-known for his enthusiastic, unquestioning obedience to Hitler, but was unable to hold his own in the cut-throat competition for the Führer's favor. On the morning of August 18, 1943, the day after the USAAF's first raid on Schweinfurt and Regensburg, Jeschonnek received word of the RAF's damaging attack on the German rocket research facility at Peenemünde the previous night. That evening he shot himself, leaving the following note: "I can no longer work together with the Reichsmarschall [Göring]. Long live the Führer."

43. Hauptmann Dierich, *Der Flieger: Dienstunterschrift in der Fliegertruppe*, E. S. Mittler & Sohn, Berlin, 1940, p. 6.

44. L.Dv. 6, *Der Jagdflieger (Vorläufige Richtlinien im Kriege)*, Berlin, 1940.

45. **Sperrle, Hugo (1885–1953).** The long-time commander of Luftflotte 3, which was responsible for the air operations from France and the Low Countries. Sperrle enlisted in the German Army in 1903 and was commissioned the following year. He attended the War Academy in 1914, transferred to the air arm in 1915, and spent the rest of World War I in a variety of staff and command positions. He remained in the armed forces after the war, transferring in 1934 into the still-secret Luftwaffe. In 1936 he was named to head the Condor Legion in Spain, and proved successful in a job that called for great political sensitivity; his blunt professionalism in combination with a willingness to listen to his coalition partners proved popular with Franco and the Spanish generals. On his return to Germany in 1937 Sperrle was double-promoted to General der Flieger and given command of Luftflotte 3, which he led for the next six years. He was promoted to field marshal after the French Campaign. After the end of the Battle of Britain Luftflotte 3 remained in France while the rest of the Luftwaffe moved east for the Russian campaign. Sperrle made Paris his occupation headquarters, and succumbed to the temptations of the good life. By mid-1944 the staff of Luftflotte 3 had apparently grown as bloated and indolent as their commander; their grossly inadequate airfield preparations ruined Berlin's carefully drafted plans for a massive reinforcement of Luftflotte 3 on D-Day. When the Luftwaffe retreated to the German border with the Army in September 1944, Sperrle was relieved of his command and placed in the Führer Reserve. He never returned to active duty.

46. Grabmann, "German Air Defense, 1933–1945," pp. 239–40.

47. Boog, *Global War*, pp. 530–1.

48. Herhudt von Rohden, "Battle for Air Supremacy over Germany," p. 13.

49. Grabmann, "German Air Defense, 1933–1945," p. 309.

50. Karl-Heinz Hummel, "Die Kommandostrukturen in der Reichsluftverteidigung, 1939–1945," II. Teil, *Deutsches Soldatenjahrbuch 1987*, Schild-Verlag, Munich, Germany, 1987, p. 430.

51. Luftflottenkommando Reich, "Report on the Assignments, Activity and Development of the Luftwaffenbefehlshaber Mitte, later Luftflotte Reich, and its changes up to the time of capitulation," Missunde, May 28, 1945, USAFHRA 512. 625L, pp. 1–2.

52. Westermann, *Flak*, p. 118.

53. **Kammhuber, Josef (1896–1986).** A Luftwaffe general best known for establishing Germany's night air defenses. Kammhuber was an infantryman in World War I. He was selected to join the inter-war army, the Reichswehr, attended the school for General Staff officers, and in 1935 transferred to the Luftwaffe. He commanded a bomber wing in the early campaigns of World War II, and was chosen in mid-1940 to set up the German defenses against night bombing. The "Kammhuber Line" that he devised required the close control of each night fighter by a ground operator, and was quite successful until RAF Bomber Command decreased the spacing within its bomber streams and then blinded his radars with the aluminum foil strips code-named "Window." Kammhuber was slow to adapt his defenses to the new realities, and was relieved of his position on September 15, 1943. He was given no important command for the rest of the war. However, when the post-war West German Air Force, the Bundesluftwaffe, was established in 1956, Kammhuber was named as its first *Inspekteur* (commander-in-chief), with the rank of Generalleutnant. He established the organization of the new service and integrated it tightly into the defenses of Western Europe.

54. Boog, *Global War*, p. 538; Herhudt von Rohden, "Battle for Air Supremacy over Germany," p. 15.

55. Grabmann, "German Air Defense, 1933–1945," p. 319.

56. Hummel, "Kommandostrukturen," II. Teil, p. 432.

57. Boog, *Global War*, pp. 544–5, Karl-Heinz Hummel, "Die Kommandostrukturen in der Reichsluftverteidigung, 1939–1945," III. Teil, *Deutsches Soldatenjahrbuch 1988*, Schild-Verlag, Munich, Germany, 1988, p. 239.

58. Grabmann, "German Air Defense, 1933–1945," p. 375.

59. Middlebrook and Everitt, *Bomber Command War Diaries*, p. 191.

60. R. Wallace Clarke, "Bombs from the Stratosphere," *Flypast*, 278 (September 2004), pp. 61–5.

61. H. H. Arnold, *Global Mission*, Harper & Brothers, New York, 1949, pp. 261–3.

62. Webster and Frankland, *Strategic Air Offensive against Germany*, Vol. I, p. 243.

63. Webster and Frankland, *Strategic Air Offensive against Germany*, Vol. I, p. 241.

64. Generalstab 8. Abteilung, "The Douhet Theory and its Application to the Present War," Air Historical Branch translation No. VII/11, USAFHRA 512. 621VII/11, p. 10.

65. Grabmann, "German Air Defense, 1933–1945," p. 379.

66. Boog, *Global War*, p. 549.

Chapter 3: America Enters the War (pages 48–67)

1. Generalstab 8. Abteilung, "A Survey of German Air Operations, 1939–1944," USAFHRA 512. 621 VII/28, pp. 6–7.

2. Völker, "Heimatluftverteidigung (I)," p. 95.
3. Henry Probert, *Bomber Harris: His Life and Times*, Greenhill, London, 2001, p. 139.
4. Middlebrook and Everitt, *Bomber Command War Diaries*, p. 258.
5. John Terraine, *A Time for Courage: The Royal Air Force in the European War*, Macmillan, New York, 1985, p. 492.
6. Hans-Detlef Herhudt von Rohden, "Reich Air Defense 1939–1945: A Strategic-Tactical Survey," unpublished study, August 1946, p. 9.
7. Grabmann, "German Air Defense, 1933–1945" p. 494.
8. Wesley Craven and James Cate, *The Army Air Forces in World War II*, Vol. I, *Plans and Early Operations*, University of Chicago, Chicago, 1948, p. 600.
9. Stephen L. McFarland and Wesley Phillips Newton, *To Command the Sky: The Battle for Air Superiority over Germany, 1942–1944*, Smithsonian Institution Press, Washington DC, 1991, p. 81.
10. DeWitt Copp, *Forged in Fire*, Doubleday, New York, 1982, p. 412.
11. Horst Boog, "German Air Intelligence in the Second World War," *Intelligence and National Security* 5 No. 2 (April 1990), pp. 390–1.
12. Boog, "German Air Intelligence," pp. 390–1.
13. Boog, "German Air Intelligence," pp. 391–2.
14. Richard Suchenwirth, *Command and Leadership in the German Air Force*, Arno Press, New York, 1971, p. 272.
15. Herbert Joachim Rieckhoff, *Trumpf oder Bluff? 12 Jahre deutsche Luftwaffe*, Interavia, Geneva, 1945, p. 274.
16. *Kriegsflugzeuge: Ansprach, Erkennen, Bewaffnung usw.*, Dr. Spohr Verlag, Dresden, Germany, 1942, pp. 122–3.
17. Herhudt von Rohden, "Reich Air Defense, 1939–1945," p. 10.
18. David Irving, *The Rise and Fall of the Luftwaffe: The Life of Field Marshal Erhard Milch*, Little, Brown & Co., Boston, 1973, p. 173.
19. "Answers to Questionnaire V, Training, by Generalmajor [Hubertus] Hitschold, General der Schlachtflieger," USAFHRA 220. 6093-1 vol. 2.
20. Grabmann, "German Air Defense, 1933–1945," p. 500.
21. Galland's interrogation reports and memoirs are filled with such commentary; see Galland, *The First and the Last*, Henry Holt, New York, 1954, pp. 189–90. For a dissenting view, see Rieckhoff, *Trumpf oder Bluff?*, pp. 174ff.
22. Hummel, "Kommandostrukturen, III. Teil, p. 240; Grabmann, "German Air Defense, 1933–1945," pp. 500–3.
23. "Truppengliederung Lw. BeFh. Mitte, Ende 1942," Anlage 4 zu Lfl Reich Nr. 5250/45 vom 29. 5. 45, USAFHRA 512. 619-2 v. 2 1945, Append. 4.
24. Herhudt von Rohden, "The Battle for Air Supremacy over Germany, 1939–1945," p. 25.
25. Grabmann, "German Air Defense, 1933–1945," p. 500.
26. Chef Generalstab 8. Abteilung, Vorstudien zum Luftkrieg Heft 2, 15 Dez 1944, "Luftherrschaft und Luftoffensiv: Eine Analyse der eigenen und feindlichen Luftkriegführung seit 1939," NARA T971/36/914ff.
27. Grabmann, "German Air Defense, 1933–1945," p. 499.
28. Ferenc A. Vajda and Peter Dancy, *German Aircraft Industry and Production*, SAE, Warrendale, PA, 1998, p. 146.
29. Vajda and Dancy, *German Aircraft Industry*, p. 146.
30. Luftwaffe Strength and Serviceability Tables, USAFHRA 512. 621 VII/107.
31. Irving, *Milch*, p. 148.
32. Galland, *The First and the Last*, pp. 136–7.
33. Boog *et al.*, *The Global War*, Vol. VI, pp. 607–8.
34. Grabmann, "German Air Defense, 1933–1945," p. 546.
35. Grabmann, "German Air Defense, 1933–1945," p. 551.
36. Boog *et al.*, *The Global War*, Vol. VI, p. 606.
37. Westermann, *Flak*, p. 170.
38. AI 12/USAFE/M. 116 Intelligence Report No. 116, "Documentary Evidence of Training Difficulties in the GAF," USAFHRA 512. 62152M-116, p. 4.
39. A.D.I.(K) Report No. 163/1943, "GAF Training: Training of a Fighter Pilot," USAFHRA 220. 6093-1, p. 10. In December 1942, IV./KG 77's Ju 88s played the role of the "enemy" bombers for the trainees of Ergänzungsjagdgruppe Süd.
40. Caldwell, *The JG 26 War Diary*, Vol I, 1939-1942, p. 268.
41. Werner Held, *Reichsverteidigung: Die deutsche Tagjagd 1943–1945*, Podzun-Pallas, Friedburg, 1988, p. 43.
42. Adolf Galland, "The Birth, Life & Death of the Jagdwaffe," ADI(K) 373/45, 33.
43. Adolf Galland, interview with D. Caldwell, Remagen, 1991.
44. Josef Priller, *JG 26: Geschichte eines Jagdgeschwaders*, Motorbuch Verlag, Stuttgart, Germany, 1980, p. 171.
45. Johannes Naumann, interview with D. Caldwell, 1995.
46. Priller, *JG 26*, p. 172.
47. Eighth Air Force Mission Folder, 9 Oct 42, USAFHRA.
48. Priller, *JG 26*, p. 169.
49. Al LaChasse, interview with D. Caldwell, 1991.
50. Otto Stammberger, interview with D. Caldwell, 1989.
51. Priller, *JG 26*, p. 170.
52. Copp, *Forged in Fire*, p. 311.
53. "Kampfanweisung für die Jagd- und Zerstörerverbände," BA-MA RL 10/291.
54. Otto Stammberger, personal communication with D. Caldwell, 1989.
55. Eighth Air Force Mission Folder, 20 Dec 42, USAFHRA.
56. Erich Schwarz, personal communication with D. Caldwell, 2000.
57. Galland, "The Birth, Life & Death of the Jagdwaffe."
58. Galland, "The Birth, Life & Death of the Jagdwaffe."
59. Priller, *JG 26*, p. 176.
60. Westermann, *Flak*, p. 180.
61. Grabmann, "German Air Defense, 1933–1945," p. 382.

Chapter 4: The Slow American Build-Up (pages 68–93)

1. Generalstab 8. Abteilung, " Survey of German Air Operations," pp. 5ff.
2. **Peltz, Dietrich (1914–2001)**. One of the most controversial Luftwaffe commanders. Peltz joined the German Army in 1934, transferred to the Luftwaffe in 1935, and was in command of a Staffel of Ju 87 dive bombers during the Polish and French campaigns. He transferred to Ju 88 medium bombers during the Battle of Britain, and won the Knight's Cross of the Iron Cross for his bravery and skill. After leading bomber units on all fronts he was promoted to colonel and named General of the Bomber Arm, a staff position within the Luftwaffe High Command, but returned to combat duty in March 1943, as *Angriffsführer England*. The bombing campaign he led, called the "Baby Blitz" by the British, was ordered by Hitler in revenge for the Allied air attacks on Germany. It was finally called off in early 1944 owing to its ineffectiveness and high German losses, but Peltz was held blameless; he was awarded the Oak Leaves with Swords to the Knight's Cross of the Iron Cross and promoted at age 29 to Generalmajor.

Peltz's career took a startling turn in October 1944, when he was named commander of II. Jagdkorps, which contained all of the fighters on the western front. Peltz had no experience in fighters, and morale among the fighter unit commanders plummeted. German fighter losses over the Ardennes were extremely high, and on January 1, 1945, Operation Bodenplatte, which Peltz had planned, cost the Luftwaffe 214 fighter pilots, including 19 formation leaders, and destroyed the fighter force beyond any hope of rebuilding.

Peltz was next given command of IX. Fliegerkorps (Jagd), which contained all of the Luftwaffe's Me 262 fighters, and in March 1945 was promoted to command the RLV, the position he held at war's end. Postwar his management skills were in great demand, and he had a very successful career in German industry.

3. Hummel, "Kommandostrukturen," III. Teil, pp. 239–40. See also Völker, "Heimatluftverteidigung (I)," pp. 87ff.

4. These fighter divisions would be realigned and renumbered in September 1943 with the creation of I. Jagdkorps.

5. Grabmann, "Luftverteidigung," Band 2, Teil I, p. 393.

6. Grabmann, "German Air Defense, 1933–1945," p. 673.

7. "Truppengliederung LwBefh. Mitte, Ende 1942," USAFHRA 515-619-2 v 2.

8. Westermann, *Flak*, p. 118.

9. Horst Boog, "The German Defenses," in *Reaping the Whirlwind: A Symposium on the Strategic Bomber Offensive 1939–1945*, Royal Air Force Historical Society, 1993, p. 20.

10. Luftflottenkommando Reich, "Report on Development of Luftwaffenbefehlshaber Mitte," pp. 7–9.

11. Grabmann, "German Air Defense, 1933–1945," p. 670.

12. 7. Jagddivision, Anlage 2 zum KTB Nr 1, "Gefechtsberichte—Tagjagd," NARA T971/35/820ff.

13. Befehl für Einsatz der Industriestaffel Me-Regensburg, von Rohden 4406-607, NARA T971/32/372.

14. Industrieschwarm Focke-Wulf Langenhagen/Hann. Flughafen, Betr.: Gefechtsbericht vom 17.4.1943, von Rohden 4406-607, NARA T971/47/874.

15. Jochen Prien and Peter Rodeike, *Jagdgeschwader 1 und 11*, Teil 1, *1939–1943*, Struve-Druck, Eutin, Germany, n.d., p. 208; United States Strategic Bombing Survey (USSBS), Military Analysis Division, Enemy Aircraft Section, German Order of Battle, USAFHRA 137.306-14.

16. USSBS, German Order of Battle.

17. Hans Ring and Werner Girbig, *Jagdgeschwader 27*, Motorbuch Verlag, Stuttgart, 1971, p. 235.

18. USSBS, German Order of Battle.

19. Robert Michulec and Donald Caldwell, *Adolf Galland*, Stratus, Sandomierz, Poland, 2003, p. 69.

20. Caldwell, *JG 26: Top Guns of the Luftwaffe*, p. 154.

21. Priller, *JG 26*, p. 195.

22. Priller, *JG 26*, p. 195.

23. Roger Freeman, *The Mighty Eighth*, Doubleday, Garden City, New York, 1970, p. 20.

24. Prien and Rodeike, *Jagdgeschwader 1 und 11*, p. 221; Eighth Air Force Mission Folder, 27 Jan 1943, USAFHRA.

25. Prien and Rodeike, *Jagdgeschwader 1 und 11*, p. 221.

26. Wesley Craven and James Cate, *The Army Air Forces in World War II*, Vol. II, *Europe: Torch to Pointblank*, University of Chicago Press, Chicago, 1949, p. 323.

27. Eighth Air Force Mission Folder, 27 Jan 1943.

28. Hans-Joachim Jabs, personal communication with D.

Caldwell, 2000.

29. Eighth Air Force Mission Folder, 16 Feb 1943.

30. Erich Schwarz, personal communication with D. Caldwell, 2000.

31. Otto Stammberger, personal communication with D. Caldwell, 1989.

32. Marion Havelaar and William Hess, *The Ragged Irregulars of Bassingbourn: The 91st Bombardment Group in World War II*, Schiffer, Atglen, PA, 1995, p. 25.

33. Dieter Schmidt-Barbo, personal communication with D. Caldwell, 2001.

34. Donald Caldwell, *The JG 26 War Diary*, Vol. 2, *1943–1945*, Grub Street, London, 1998, p. 33.

35. Heinz Knoke, *I Flew for the Führer*, Henry Holt, New York, 1953, p. 97.

36. Eighth Air Force Mission Folder, 18 Mar 1943.

37. **Graf, Hermann (1912–1988)**. The first fighter pilot to claim 200 air victories, and the fifth man to be awarded the Wehrmacht's highest award for valor, the Knight's Cross with Oak Leaves, Swords and Diamonds. Graf was grounded after his 202nd Eastern Front victory and returned to Germany, where this poorly educated son of a baker became a favourite of the Nazi propaganda machine. He was eventually restored to combat status and commanded JG 50, JG 1, and JG 11 in the RLV before he requested and obtained permission to return to the Eastern Front to command his old unit, JG 52. On VE-Day he attempted to surrender to the Americans, but as a prominent member of an *Ostfront* unit he was turned over to the Soviet Army. During his four-year captivity in Russia he apparently signed documents accepting Nazi Germany's guilt for beginning the war. For this transgression he was denounced by the German veterans' associations after his return to West Germany, and remained a controversial figure until his death.

38. Grabmann, "German Air Defense, 1933–1945," pp. 677–8.

39. Knoke, *I Flew for the Führer*, p. 101.

40. Luftflottenkommando 3, Führungsabteilung (I), "Tätigkeitsbericht der Luftflotte 3 für die Monat April 1943," Library of Congress, von Rohden collection 1750 reel 3, p. 7.

41. Heinrich Staniwoga, personal communication with D. Caldwell, 1995.

42. Luftflottenkommando 3, Führungsabteilung (I), "Tätigkeitsbericht der Luftflotte 3 für die Monat Juni 1943," Library of Congress, von Rohden collection 1750 reel 3, p. 8.

43. Prien and Rodeike, *Jagdgeschwader 1 und 11*, p. 267.

44. Francis Marshall, *Sea Eagles: The Messerschmitt Bf 109T*, Air Research Publications, Surrey, UK, 1993, p. 165.

45. "Report of Conference, 22 Feb 43," USAFHRA 512. 621 VII/85, p. 20.

46. Grabmann, "German Air Defense, 1933–1945" p. 679.

47. Irving, *Milch*, p. 399, n. 6.

48. Milch Documents, March 1943–February 1944, "Extracts from Conferences on Problems of Aircraft Production," USAFHRA K-512. 621 VII/140, p. 3.

49. Herhudt von Rohden "Reich Air Defense 1939–1945," p. 39.

50. Westermann, *Flak*, p. 187.

51. **Kreipe, Werner (1904–1967)**. The Luftwaffe Chief of Staff with the shortest term in office, Kreipe enlisted in an artillery regiment after World War I and joined the Nazi Party in time to take part in the 1923 Munich Beer Hall Putsch. He was commissioned in the

Reichswehr, secretly trained as a pilot, and was accepted into the still-camouflaged Luftwaffe in 1934. After the war broke out, he commanded reconnaissance and bomber Gruppen, advanced rapidly, and served as the chief of staff to a Fliegerkorps and a Luftwaffenkommando on the Eastern Front. His most significant appointment was as General der Fliegerausbildung, in charge of all Luftwaffe pilot training during the critical period 1943–4. He became Chief of Staff after Korten's death, but lasted barely two months in office before Hitler banned him from his headquarters. He finished the war as the commander of the Luftkriegsakademie. Postwar, he became a civil servant in the Federal Republic.

52. Air Ministry/USAFE/M. 99, Intelligence Report No. 99, "Review of GAF Training during 1943," USAFHRA 512. 62512M-99, p. 5.

53. Air Ministry, "The Evolution of German Fighter Defenses in 1943: GAF Reactions to Daylight Raids on Germany," 27 Nov 43, USAFHRA 512. 635-1, p. 2; Grabmann, "German Air Defense, 1933–1945" p. 671.

54. Westermann, *Flak*, pp. 205–6.

55. Caldwell, *JG 26: Top Guns of the Luftwaffe*, p. 169.

56. II./JG 1 Kriegstagebuch, BA-MA; Garry Fry and Jeffrey Ethell, *Escort to Berlin: The 4th Fighter Group in World War II*, Arco, New York, 1980, p. 15.

57. Grabmann, "German Air Defense, 1933–1945," p. 681.

58. Caldwell, *The JG 26 War Diary*, Vol. 2, *1943–1945*, p. 47; Prien and Rodeike, *Jagdgeschwader 1 und 11*, p. 291.

59. Priller, *JG 26*, p. 196.

60. Hans-Ekkehard Bob, personal communication with D. Caldwell, 1995.

61. Industrieschwarm Focke-Wulf Langenhagen/Hann. Flughafen, Betr.: Gefechtsbericht vom 17.4.1943, von Rohden 4406-607, NARA T971/47/874.

62. OKL Chef für Ausz. und Disziplin V Film Nr. 3 – Abschuß Übersicht, BA-MA C2027N I. Teil.

63. Eighth Air Force Mission Folder, 17 Apr 1943.

64. Roger Freeman, *Mighty Eighth War Manual*, Jane's, London, 1984, p. 43.

65. Otto Stammberger, personal communication with D. Caldwell, 1989.

66. Luftflottenkommando 3, "Tätigkeitsbericht der Luftflotte 3, April 1943," p. 10.

67. Craven and Cate, *AAF in World War II*, Vol. II, *Torch to Pointblank*, p. 367.

68. Heinrich Staniwoga, personal communication with D. Caldwell, 1995.

69. McFarland and Newton, *To Command the Sky*, p. 100.

70. McFarland and Newton, *To Command the Sky*, p. 106.

71. Steve Pisanos, personal communication with D. Caldwell, 1997.

72. CSDIC(UK) SRAs, USAFHRA 512. 619C.

73. Steve Pisanos, personal communication with D. Caldwell, 1997.

74. Eighth Air Force Mission Folder, 11 Jun 1943.

75. Heinrich Staniwoga, personal communication with D. Caldwell, 1995.

76. Eighth Air Force Mission Folder, 13 Jun 1943.

77. Robert Forsyth and Eddie Creek, *Jagdwaffe: Defending the Reich 1943–44*, Ian Allan, Surrey, 2004, p. 64.

78. Craven and Cate, *The Army Air Forces in World War II*, Vol. II, *Europe: Torch to Pointblank*, p. 672.

79. Adolf Dickfeld, *Footsteps of the Hunter*, J. J. Fedorowicz Publishing, Winnipeg, Manitoba, Canada, 1993, *passim*.

80. Prien and Rodeike, *Jagdgeschwader 1 und 11*, p. 342.

81. Karl-Heinz Hummel, "Die Kommandostrukturen in der Reichsluftverteidigung 1939–1945," IV. Teil, *Deutsches Soldatenjahrbuch 1989*, Schild Verlag, Munich, 1989, p. 294.

82. Hummel, "Kommandostrukturen," IV. Teil, p. 294.

83. Irving, *Milch*, p. 224.

84. United States Air Forces in Europe, Office of Assistant Chief of Staff, "Post Hostilities Investigation: German Air Defenses, Vol. I," USAFHRA 519-601A-01, p. 1.

85. This discussion defaults to the figures contained in Anlage 3 zu Genst. Qu. 6. Abt Nr. 4712/43 gKdos. 17 June 43. Slightly different figures appear in Olaf Groehler, "Stärke, Verteilung und Verluste der deutschen Luftwaffe im zweiten Weltkrieg," *Militärgeschichte 17* (1978), Tabelle 2, pp. 318–9, and "Luftwaffe Strength and Serviceability Tables," USAFHRA K512. 621 VII/107, but the overall trends are consistent.

86. Boog *et al.*, *The Global War*, p. 627.

87. Air Ministry, "GAF Reactions," p. 1.

88. Grabmann, "German Air Defense, 1933–1945," p. 685.

89. Grabmann, "German Air Defense, 1933–1945," p. 694.

90. Irving, *Milch*, p. 222.

Chapter 5: High Tide for the Defenders (pages 94–143)

1. Grabmann, "German Air Defense, 1933–1945," p. 906; Groehler, "Stärke, Verteilung und Verluste der deutschen Luftwaffe," p. 322.

2. Air Historical Branch, "Extracts from Conferences on Problems of Aircraft Production," Translation No. VII/140, USAFHRA 512. 621 VII/140, p. 11.

3. Priller, *JG 26*, p. 139.

4. OKL Chef für Ausz. und Disziplin V Film Nr. 3 – Abschuß Übersicht, BA-MA C2027N I. Teil.

5. Erich Schwarz, personal communication with D. Caldwell, 2000.

6. Ob. d. L. Gen. Q. Gen. 6. Abt., "Flugzeuganfälle und Verluste bei den Verbänden (täglich)," IWM, reel 11.

7. Eighth Air Force Mission Folder, 14 Jul 1943, USAFHRA.

8. Caldwell, *The JG 26 War Diary*, Vol. 2, *1943–1945*, p. 117.

9. Georg-Peter Eder *Abschussmeldung*, author's collection.

10. Ed Burford, personal communication with D. Caldwell, 2000.

11. Craven and Cate, The *Army Air Forces in World War II*, Vol. II, *Europe: Torch to Pointblank*, p. 674.

12. Eighth Air Force Mission Folder, 25 Jul 1943; Martin Middlebrook, *The Battle of Hamburg*, Chas. Scribner's Sons, New York, 1981, p. 145.

13. Caldwell, *The JG 26 War Diary*, Vol. 2, *1943–1945*, p. 121.

14. Eighth Air Force Mission Folder, 26 Jul 1943; Middlebrook, *The Battle of Hamburg*, p. 186.

15. Middlebrook and Everitt, *Bomber Command War Diaries*, p. 414; Middlebrook, *The Battle of Hamburg*, p. 285.

16. Freeman, *Mighty Eighth War Diary*, p. 81; Prien & Rodeike, *Jagdgeschwader 1 und 11*, Teil 1, *1939–1943*, p. 400; Knoke, *I Flew for the Führer*, p. 118.

17. Eberhard Burath, personal communication with D. Caldwell, 1999.

18. Eighth Air Force Mission Folder, 29 Jul 1943.

19. Eighth Air Force Mission Folder, 30 Jul 1943.

20. G. Wegmann, "*Das Oberkommando der Wehrmacht gibt bekannt . . .*," Band 2, Biblio Verlag, Osnabrück, Germany, 1982, p. 529.

21. Craven and Cate, The *Army Air Forces in World War II*, Vol. II, *Europe: Torch to Pointblank*, p. 681.

22. Milch, *Tagebuch*, p. 6648.

23. Horst Boog, in *Das Deutsche Reich und der Zweite Weltkrieg*, Band 7, *Das Deutsche Reich in der Defensive*, Deutsche Verlags-Anstalt, Stuttgart, Germany, 2001, p. 141.

24. Adolf Galland, *Die Ersten und die Letzten*, Franz Schneekluth, Darmstadt, 1953, p. 228.

25. Percy Schramm, ed., *Kriegstagebuch des Oberkommandos der Wehrmacht 1943*, b. 2 (III/6), Bernard und Graefe, Munich, 1982, p. 795.

26. Gebhard Aders, *History of the German Night Fighter Force 1917–1945*, Jane's, London, 1979, p. 94; Hajo Herrmann, *Eagle's Wings*, Motorbooks International, Osceola, WI, 1991, p. 174.

27. Boog, *Das Deutsche Reich in der Defensive*, p. 147.

28. Jochen Prien and Gerhard Stemmer, *Messerschmitt Bf 109 im Einsatz bei der II./JG 3*, Struve-Druck, Eutin, Germany, n.d., p. 249.

29. Gebhard Aders and Werner Held, *Jagdgeschwader 51 "Mölders,"* Motorbuch Verlag, Stuttgart, 1985, p. 142.

30. John Vasco, *The Sting of the Luftwaffe: Schnellkampfgeschwader 210 and Zerstörergeschwader 1 "Wespengeschwader" in World War II*, Schiffer, Atglen, PA, 2001, p. 8.

31. George Punka, *Messerschmitt Me 210/410 in Action*, Squadron/Signal, Carrollton, TX, 1994, p. 28.

32. Klaus Häberlen, *Davongekommen: Als Kampfflieger über den Fronten*, VDM Heinz Nickel, Zweibrücken, Germany, 2001, p. 159; Wolfgang Dierich, *Kampfgeschwader "Edelweiss": The History of a German Bomber Unit 1939–1945*, Ian Allan, London, 1975, p. 86.

33. USSBS, German Order of Battle.

34. Jochen Prien, *et al.*, *Messerschmitt Bf 109 im Einsatz bei der Stab und I./JG 27*, Struve-Druck, Eutin, Germany, n.d., p. 363; Georg Tessin, *Verbände und Truppen der deutschen Wehrmacht und Waffen-SS im Zweiten Weltkrieg*, Band 14, Biblio Verlag, Osnabrück, Germany, 1980, p. 317.

35. Eighth Air Force Mission Folder, 12 Aug 1943; Freeman, *Mighty Eighth War Diary*, p. 88.

36. Martin Middlebrook, *The Schweinfurt–Regensburg Mission*, Chas. Scribner's Sons, New York, 1983, *passim*.

37. Eighth Air Force Mission Folder, 17 Aug 1943.

38. Caldwell, *The JG 26 War Diary*, Vol. 2, *1943–1945*, p. 134.

39. Jörg Kiefner, personal communication with D. Caldwell, 1999.

40. William Binnebose, personal communication with D. Caldwell, 1988.

41. Forsyth and Creek, *Jagdwaffe: Defending the Reich 1943–44*, p. 29.

42. Caldwell, *The JG 26 War Diary*, Vol. 2, *1943–1945*, p. 134.

43. Knoke, *I Flew for the Führer*, p. 122.

44. Middlebrook, *The Schweinfurt–Regensburg Mission*, p. 226.

45. Knoke, *I Flew for the Führer*, p. 124.

46. Heinz Gomann, personal communication with D. Caldwell, 1995.

47. Ed Burford, personal communication with D. Caldwell, 2000.

48. Prien and Rodeike, *Jagdgeschwader 1 und 11*, Teil 1, *1939–1943*, p. 441.

49. Jochen Prien and Gerhard Stemmer, *Messerschmitt Bf 109 in Einsatz bei Stab und I./JG 3*, Struve-Druck, Eutin, Germany, n.d., p. 400.

50. Irving, *Milch*, p. 233.

51. **Korten, Günther (1898–1944)**. Jeschonnek's successor as Luftwaffe Chief of Staff. Korten served as an engineering officer on the western front in World War I, and remained in the 100,000-man Reichswehr after the war. He transferred to the still-secret Luftwaffe in 1934, and served as Milch's Chief of Staff in the Air Ministry 1934–6. After the *Anschluss* with Austria, he helped amalgamate that country's air force into the Luftwaffe, and served as Sperrle's Chief of Staff at Luftflotte 3 during the 1940 campaign in the west. He held a series of increasingly important command positions on the Eastern Front, culminating with the command of Luftflotte 1 in February 1943. As Chief of Staff, he attempted to streamline the Luftwaffe's organization and increase its fighting power, including building up the RLV and creating separate strategic bombing and ground-attack commands. Although a more forceful personality than Jeschonnek, Korten was unable to work effectively with Göring, and confided to Milch that he would resign by August 1944. His career was cut short before that deadline: he was severely wounded by the bomb explosion in the July 20, 1944, plot against Adolf Hitler and died two days later, shortly after being promoted to Generaloberst. For Korten's service record, see "Personal-Nachweis, Gen.d. Fl. Günther Korten," von Rohden 4376/424, NARA T971/6/730.

52. Rieckhoff, *Trumpf oder Bluff?*, p. 274.

53. R. J. Overy, *Göring: The "Iron Man,"* Routledge & Kegan Paul, London, 1984, p. 197.

54. Air Ministry, "Luftwaffe High Command," USAFHRA 512. 6314U v. 2, p. 4.

55. Luftwaffenführungsstab Ia/Flieg Nr 9592/44, "Studie über die Flugzeuglage der Kampfverbände," 5 May 44, NARA T321/10/4746754, p. 4.

56. Generalstab 8. Abteilung, "Development of the German Ground Attack Arm and Principles Governing its Operations up to the End of 1944," 1 Dec 1944, Air Historical Branch Translation No. VII/14, USAFHRA 512. 621 VII/14, p. 8.

57. "Luftwaffe High Command," p. 4.

58. Generalstab 8. Abteilung, OKL, Kriegstagebuch Nr 1, 14 Dec 43–29 Jun 1944, von Rohden 4407-61, NARA T971/49/375ff.

59. Grabmann, "German Air Defense, 1933–1945," p. 716. "The Reichsmarschall states two measures for the Luftwaffe as particularly urgent: 1. Uninterrupted continuation of the work of developing the air defenses; 2. Measures to make offensive forces available for action against the enemy in the west, the south, and the east."

60. Grabmann, "German Air Defense, 1933–1945," p. 918.

61. Quarterly losses for single engine fighters for 1943 were: Jan–Mar 1,310; April–June 2,177, July–Sept 2,804; Oct–Dec 1,995. Twin-engine day-fighter losses were 266, 416, 441, and 240.

62. The best discussion of the effect of attrition on the Luftwaffe remains Williamson Murray, *Luftwaffe*, Nautical & Aviation, Baltimore, 1985, esp. Chaps. V and VI.

63. "Extracts from Conferences on Problems of Aircraft Production," p. 11.

64. Grabmann, "German Air Defense, 1933–1945," p. 696.

65. Recent work by German economic historians has revealed that much of the groundwork for the "production miracle" had been completed prior to the war by the aircraft manufacturers themselves. This view has merit, yet it is also true that Milch and Speer championed the shift from offensive to defensive air armament, and the ruthless reduction of the number of aircraft types in production. See Lutz Budraß, Jonas Scherner, and Jochen Streb, *Demystifying the German "Armaments Miracle" during World War II: New Insights from the Annual Audits of German Aircraft Producers*, Economic Growth Center, Yale University, New Haven, January 2005.

66. Grabmann, "German Air Defense, 1933–1945," pp. 910–14.

67. Air Ministry, *Rise and Fall of the German Air Force: History of the Luftwaffe in World War II*, HMSO, London, 1948, p. 289.

68. USSBS, German Order of Battle.

69. Air Ministry, *Rise and Fall of the German Air Force*, p. 314.

70. Grabmann, "German Air Defense, 1933–1945," p. 956.

71. AI 12/USAFE, "Review of GAF Training during 1943," p. 1.

72. "Stenographische Niederschrift der Besprechung beim Reichsmarschall über Ausbildung am Mittwoch, dem 24. Februar 1943," BA/MA RL3/60, p. 254.

73. AI 12/USAFE, Intelligence Report No, 76, "Schools in the GAF," USAFHRA 512. 62512M-76, p. 5.

74. Murray, *Luftwaffe*, p. 241; Craven and Cate, *Army Air Forces in World War II*, Vol. VI, *Men and Planes*, Office of Air Force History, Washington, DC, 1983, pp. 566ff; Rebecca Hancock Cameron, *Training to Fly: Military Flight Training 1907–1945*, Air Force History and Museums Program, Washington DC, 1999, p. 566.

75. AI 12/USAFE, "Review of GAF Training during 1943," p. 6.

76. Grabmann, "German Air Defense, 1933–1945," p. 962.

77. Grabmann, "German Air Defense, 1933–1945," p. 955.

78. Rieckhoff, *Trumpf oder Bluff?*, p. 194.

79. Adapted from Murray, *Luftwaffe*, p. 172.

80. Hummel, "Kommandostrukturen," IV. Teil, p. 295.

81. Grabmann, "German Air Defense, 1933–1945," pp. 727–8.

82. Hummel, "Kommandostrukturen," IV. Teil, p. 297.

83. GdJ Br. B. Nr. 1467/43, "Bekämpfung feindlicher Kampfverbände," IWM.

84. XII. Fliegerkorps, "Tagjagd Berichte 020843-310843," BA-MA RL 8/88.

85. GdJ Br. B. Nr. 321/43, "Kampfanweisung für die Jagd- und Zerstörerverbände," BA-MA RL 10/191.

86. GdJ Br. B. Nr. 1759/43, "Rammen feindlicher 4-motoriger Kampfflugzeug mit bez. gepanzert. Flugzeuge," IWM; Adolf Galland, interview with D. Caldwell, 1991; Arno Rose, *Radikaler Luftkampf*, Motorbuch Verlag, Stuttgart, 1977, p. 39.

87. Eighth Air Force Mission Folder, 4 Oct 1943; McFarland and Newton, *To Command the Sky*, p. 115; Hans Seyringer, personal communication with A. Price, 2000.

88. Galland, *Die Ersten und die Letzten*, p. 222.

89. Westermann, *Flak*, p. 226.

90. "Stenographische Niederschrift für die Besprechung beim Reichsmarschall am 7. 10. 43, 11,30 Uhr, Atelierhaus Speer, Thema: Heimatverteidigungsprogramm," BA/MA RL 3/60, p. 460.

91. "Heimatverteidigungsprogramm," p. 505.

92. David Irving, *Göring: A Biography*, Morrow, New York, 1989, p. 406.

93. Grabmann, "German Air Defense, 1933–1945," p. 712.

94. Westermann, *Flak*, p. 227.

95. Grabmann, "German Air Defense, 1933–1945," pp. 714–15.

96. Prien and Rodeike, *Jagdgeschwader 1 und 11*, Teil 1, *1939–1943*, pp. 479, 489.

97. Eric Mombeek, *Defenders of the Reich: Jagdgeschwader* Vol. 2, *1943*, Classic Publications, Surrey, UK, 2001, p. 185.

98. Mombeek, *Defenders of the Reich: Jagdgeschwader 1*, Vol. 2, *1943*, p. 185.

99. Galland, *The First and the Last*, p. 248.

100. Eighth Air Force Mission Folder, 8 Oct 1943.

101. Prien and Rodeike, *Jagdgeschwader 1 und 11*, Teil 1, *1939–1943*, p. 501.

102. Christer Bergström, *Graf & Grislawski: A Pair of Aces*, Eagle Editions, Hamilton, MT, 2003, p. 199.

103. I. Jagdkorps Kriegstagebuch, USAFHRA K113. 408-2 v1.

104. Galland, *Die Ersten und die Letzten*, p. 259.

105. This discussion is based primarily on: USSTAF, Air Staff Post Hostilities Intelligence Requirements on German Air Force, 1935–1945, Section IVB, "The German Aircraft Warning and Fighter Control System," USAFHRA 519. 601B-4; Grabmann, "German Air Defense, 1933–1945," and Oberkommando der Luftwaffe Lw-Führungsstab Ausb. Abt Nr 1410/44 geh., "Reichsluftverteidigung" (September 1944), BA./MA RL 2II/366.

106. Luftwaffe Operations Staff, "Tactics and Policy of the German Air Force," Nov 1943(?), USAFHRA 512. 640-1, 29 Mar 1944, p. 1.

107. "Reichsluftverteidigung," Heft 1, para 9.

108. "German Aircraft Warning and Fighter Control System," Vol. I, p. 133.

109. Alfred Price, *Instruments of Darkness: The History of Electronic Warfare*, Charles Scribner's Sons, New York, 1978, p. 69.

110. Grabmann, "German Air Defense, 1933–1945," Vol. III, p. 1067.

111. "German Aircraft Warning and Fighter Control System," Vol. I, p. 167.

112. "German Aircraft Warning and Fighter Control System," Vol. I, p. 145.

113. "Reichsluftverteidigung," Heft 4, para 24.

114. "Vortrag Major Raithel," p. 12.

115. "German Aircraft Warning and Fighter Control System," Vol. I, p. 168.

116. Beirne Lay, Jr., "Smashing the Luftwaffe's Nest," in *The 100 Best True Stories of World War II*, Wise & Co., New York, 1945, p. 691. Lay's account originally appeared in the *Saturday Evening Post*, and remains one of the best eyewitness descriptions of a daylight raid over Germany.

117. Beirne Lay Jr. and Sy Bartlett, *Twelve O'Clock High!*, Harper & Brothers, New York, 1948, pp. 250–1.

118. I. Jagdkorps Kriegstagebuch, USAFHRA K113. 408-2 v3.

119. "German Aircraft Warning and Fighter Control System," Vol. II, Append. IVg.

120. "Reichsluftverteidigung," Heft 2, pp. 23–4; "German Aircraft Warning and Fighter Control System," Vol. II, pp. 127–8, 234–5; Herhudt von Rohden, "The Battle for Air Supremacy over Germany," pp. 84–5.

121. "Tactics and Policy of the German Air Force," p. 1.

122. "German Aircraft Warning and Fighter Control System," p. 146.

123. Ian Hawkins, *Münster: The Way It Was*, Robinson Typographics, Anaheim, CA, 1984, *passim*.

124. Eighth Air Force Mission Folder, 10 Oct 1943.

125. Caldwell, *The JG 26 War Diary*, Vol. 2, *1943–1945*, p. 163.

126. Heinz Gomann, *Und über uns der Himmel: Fliegergeschichten vom JG 26*, Kurt Vowinckel Verlag, Berg-am-See, Germany, 1996, p. 80.

127. Eighth Air Force Mission Folder, 14 Oct 1943.

128. Irving, *Milch*, p. 236.

129. Freeman, *Mighty Eighth War Diary*, p. 129.

130. **Lützow, Günther (1912–45).** An outstanding Luftwaffe fighter pilot and combat commander who was considered an upright "model officer" by his peers and subordinates. "Franzl" Lützow joined the Reichswehr in 1931, received his pilot training at the secret German base in the Soviet Union, and in 1934 joined

the still-unacknowledged Luftwaffe. He led a fighter squadron in the Condor Legion in Spain, was successful in the French campaign, and was promoted to command Jagdgeschwader 3 during the Battle of Britain. He led JG 3 with great success in the early part of the Russian campaign. After his 92nd air victory he became the fourth recipient of the Oak Leaves with Swords to the Knight's Cross of the Iron Cross. He was grounded in October 1941, after his 101st victory, and spent three years as a colonel in fighter-command and staff positions. In January 1945 he led the so-called "Fighter Pilots' Revolt," a frank denunciation of Göring and the Luftwaffe leadership, and narrowly escaped arrest. He was instead named fighter commander for northern Italy, a region that had no German fighters, but was recalled to join Galland's "Jet Unit of the Aces," Jagdverband 44 (JV 44), in March 1945. He began flying missions prior to regaining his fighter pilot's touch or mastering his new aircraft, the Me 262, and failed to return from a mission in late April, probably the victim of a USAAF P-51. Lützow's body has never been found.

131. Grabmann, "German Air Defense, 1933–1945," p. 727.
132. Prien, et al., Messerschmitt Bf 109 im Einsatz bei der Stab und I./JG 27, p. 373.
133. Barry Smith, Storm the Fortresses!, unpublished history of Sturmstaffel 1, 2004.
134. Prien and Stemmer, Messerschmitt Bf 109 in Einsatz bei II./JG 3, p. 237.
135. McFarland and Newton, To Command the Sky, p. 147.
136. Craven and Cate, The Army Air Forces in World War II, Vol. II, Europe: Torch to Pointblank, p. 567.
137. Prien, et al., Messerschmitt Bf 109 im Einsatz bei der Stab und I./JG 27, p. 371.
138. Eighth Air Force Mission Folder, 3 Nov 1943.
139. Ernst Obermaier, Die Ritterkreuzträger der Luftwaffe 1939–1945, Band I, Jagdflieger, Verlag Dieter Hoffmann, Mainz, Germany, 2nd edition, 1989, p. 52; Wolfgang Polster, personal communication with D. Caldwell, 1995.
140. I. Jagdkorps Kriegstagebuch.
141. Jean-Yves Lorant and Richard Goyat, Jagdgeschwader 300 "Wilde Sau," Vol. 1, June 1943–September 1944, Eagle Editions, Hamilton, MT, p. 107.
142. Craven and Cate, The Army Air Forces in World War II, Vol. II, Europe: Torch to Pointblank, p. 707.
143. McFarland and Newton, To Command the Sky, p. 129.
144. Lay, "Smashing the Luftwaffe's Nest," pp. 690–1.
145. 3rd Bombardment Division, Office of A. C of S., A-2, APO 634, "German Fighter Tactics against Flying Fortresses," 11 Nov 1943, USAFHRA 527. 621.
146. USAAF, Informational Intelligence Summary No. 44-3, 20 Jan 1944, USAFHRA 142. 034-1, Jan–Dec 1944, p. 15.
147. USSTAF, "Air Staff Post Hostilities Intelligence Requirements on German Air Force, 1935–1945," Fighter Operations, "Interrogation of Generalleutnant Galland, Obstlt. Bär, Oberst Dahl and Oberst Peterson [sic] on 'Special Weapons for Combatting 4-engine Bombers by Day,'" Append. XXVII, USAFHRA 519. 601B-4, Section IVC, Vol. 2.
148. HQ Eighth Air Force, Annex B, Jan 1944, "Eighth Air Force Narrative of Operations: 182nd Operation, Jan 11, 1944, USAFHRA 520. 01 Jan 1944 Vol. 3, pp. 1–3; USAAF, Informational Intelligence Summary No 44-6, 20 Feb 1944, pp. 3–5.
149. USAAF, Target Germany, Simon and Schuster, New York, 1943, p. 107.
150. USAAF, Informational Intelligence Summary No. 44-4, 30 Jan 1944, "Recent German Tactics Employed against Heavy Bombers," p. 15.
151. Original combat report in file 150 Bomb Squadron, Sept 39–Dec 44, USAFHRA 525. 641.
152. Air Ministry, Rise and Fall of the German Air Force, p. 273.

Chapter 6: The Air War Is Lost (pages 144–189)
1. Grabmann, "German Air Defense, 1933–1945," p. 1182.
2. Air Ministry, Rise and Fall of the German Air Force, p. 239.
3. Boog, Luftwaffenführung, pp. 282 and 582.
4. "Extracts from Conferences on Problems of Aircraft Production," 23 Feb 1944, p. 18.
5. Der Oberbefehlshaber der Luftwaffe, Führungsstab Ia. Ausb. Nr. 570/44 geheim, "Taktische Bermerkungen des Ob. d. L Nr. 2/44," BA/MA RH 11 III/76, pp. 14–15.
6. USSBS, German Order of Battle, p. 39.
7. Boog, Das deutsche Reich in der Defensive, pp. 377–80.
8. Alfred Price, Blitz on Britain, 1939–1945, Ian Allan, London, 1977, pp. 159ff.
9. Generalstab 8. Abteilung, "Survey of German Air Operations," p. 9.
10. Murray, Luftwaffe, Chap. 5.
11. Der Reichsmarschall des Großdeutschen Reiches und Oberbefehlshaber der Luftwaffe, Nr. 8947/43 g. Kdos., 6 Dec 43, Betr.: "Drohende Gefahr West," NARA T321/10/4746474ff.
12. RLV day-fighter units involved in the early planning included I. and III./JG 1, II., III., and IV./JG 3, I. and II./JG 11, II./JG 27, III./JG 26, III./JG 54 , Sturmstaffel 1, I. and II./ZG 26, I. and II./ZG 76.
13. Wesley Craven and James Cate, Army Air Forces in World War II, Vol. III, Europe: Argument to V-E Day, University of Chicago Press, Chicago, 1951, p. 8.
14. Rieckhoff, Trumpf oder Bluff?, p. 176.
15. Schmid, "The GAF vs. the Allies in the West 1943–45: Command Structure," USAFHRA K113. 107-158-160 v5.
16. Schmid, "The GAF vs. the Allies in the West 1943–45: 1 Jan 44–31 Mar 44," USAFHRA K113. 107-158-60 v2.
17. USSTAF, Air Staff Post Hostilities Intelligence Requirements on GAF 1935–45, Sec. IVC, "Fighter Operations," Vol. 2, Append. XXXIII, Adolf Galland, Heinz Bär, and Walther Dahl on "The Evolution of the Defense of the Reich," USAFHRA 519. 601B-4.
18. Jochen Prien and Peter Rodeike, Jagdgeschwader 1 und Jagdgeschwader 11: Einsatz in der Reichsverteidigung von 1939 bis 1945, Teil 2, 1944, Struve-Druck, Eutin, Germany, n.d., p. 651.
19. "Fighter Operations," Append. IV, "Interrogation of Generalleutnant Galland and Generalfeldmarschall Milch on 'History and Development of GAF Fighter Commands.'"
20. "Taktische Bemerkungen Nr. 2/44," p. 11.
21. Luftflotten Kommando Reich, "Report on the assignments, activity, and development of the Luftwaffenbefehlshaber Mitte," p. 12.
22. See Chapter 8 for a full discussion of the final state of RLV command and control methods.
23. Green, Warplanes of the Third Reich, p. 207.
24. McFarland and Newton, To Command the Sky, p. 161.
25. James Doolittle, I Could Never Be So Lucky Again, Bantam Books, New York, 1991, p. 353.
26. Peter Spoden, personal communication with D. Caldwell, 2000.

27. William Hess, *354th Fighter Group*, Osprey, Oxford, UK, 2002, p. 20.

28. Smith, *Storm the Fortresses!* unpublished history of Sturmstaffel 1, 2004.

29. Theo Boiten and Martin Bowman, *Battles with the Luftwaffe*, HarperCollins, London, 2001, p. 86.

30. Caldwell, *The JG 26 War Diary*, Vol. 2, *1943–1945*, p. 198.

31. **Bär, Heinz (1913–1957)**. One of the dominant personalities of the Luftwaffe fighter force, and one of the very few pilots to fly in combat for all of World War II. "Pritzl" Bär scored his first victory on September 25, 1939, as an Unteroffizier, and his 221st and last on April 29, 1945, while serving as an Oberstleutnant in command of JV 44. Bär was the highest-scoring German jet ace, with 16 victories, and the second-highest day scorer against the western Allies. In February 1942 he became the seventh member of the Wehrmacht to be awarded the Oak Leaves with Swords to the Knight's Cross of the Iron Cross, but a disagreement with Göring kept him from any higher decorations, and his outspoken refusal to obey orders that he considered reckless brought him a demotion in 1943. However, his combat record prevented his courtmartial, and in mid-1944 he was given command of, first, JG 1, and later JG 3, two of the most successful units in the RLV. Bär was killed in the crash of a light airplane in 1957.

32. **Steinhoff, Johannes (1913–1994)**. A successful Luftwaffe fighter pilot and combat commander on all fronts. "Macki" Steinhoff joined the German Navy in 1934 as an officer cadet and transferred to the Luftwaffe in 1935. At the beginning of the war he was a pilot in the embryonic night-fighter force, but preferred day fighting, and in mid-1940 was able to transfer to JG 52 as a Staffelkapitän. After a long tour on the Eastern Front he took command of JG 77 in Tunisia just as the Western Allies were wresting air superiority from the Axis. His bitter experiences in Sicily formed the basis of his first book, *Die Strasse von Messina* (The Straits of Messina). In January 1945, after commanding several fighter units, including the jet fighter Geschwader JG 7, he took an active role in the so-called "Fighter Pilots' Revolt" in opposition to Göring, and was sent on leave. He managed to join Galland's "Jet Unit of the Aces," JV 44, and scored six victories in the Me 262, but on April 18, 1945, his heavily loaded fighter crashed on takeoff and burst into flames. He survived with severe burns that kept him in hospital until 1947. Steinhoff was a recipient of the Oak Leaves with Swords to the Knight's Cross of the Iron Cross; his final victory total was 178.

Steinhoff had a very distinguished postwar career. In 1955 he left his job as an advertising salesman and joined the new West German Air Force, the Bundesluftwaffe. He rose swiftly through the ranks, and became Inspekteur (commander-in-chief) in 1966, just in time for the most serious crisis in the force's history. Its new fighter, the Mach 2 Starfighter, was falling from the skies in alarming numbers, provoking a crisis of confidence in the West German government. Steinhoff implemented drastic changes in training and maintenance and succeeded in cutting the Starfighter's accident rate in half in four years. After promotion to full general, Steinhoff capped off his career with a tour as Chairman of the NATO Military Committee, serving from 1971 to 1974.

33. Prien and Rodeike, *Jagdgeschwader 1 und Jagdgeschwader 11*, Band 2, *1944*, p. 672.

34. Doolittle, *I Could Never Be So Lucky Again*, p. 355.

35. McFarland and Newton, *To Command the Sky*, p. 162; Hans Seyringer, personal communication with A. Price, 2000.

36. Schmid, "The GAF vs. the Allies in the West 1943–45: 1 Jan 44–31 Mar 44."

37. Caldwell, *The JG 26 War Diary*, Vol. 2, *1943–1945*, p. 208.

38. Schmid, "The GAF vs. the Allies in the West 1943–45: 1 Jan 44–31 Mar 44."

39. Eighth Air Force Mission Folder, 10 Feb 1944; Air Historical Branch, "ADI(K) Science Memo 2: RLM Gen. Qu. 6 Statistics on RLV Reaction to Anglo-American Bomb Raids," PRO AIR 40.

40. Eighth Air Force Mission Folder, 11 Feb 1944; *ULTRA—Main Series of Signals Conveying Intelligence to Allied Commands*, VL-722X.

41. Fritz Buchholz, personal communication with A. Price, 2000.

42. KTB I. Jagdkorps, USAFHRA K113. 408-2 v3; Schmid, "The GAF vs. the Allies in the West 1943–45: 1 Jan 44–31 Mar 44."

43. David Mets, *Master of Airpower: Gen. Carl A. Spaatz*, Presidio, Novato, CA, 1988, p. 195; Doolittle, *I Could Never Be So Lucky Again*, p. 366.

44. Eighth Air Force Mission Folder, 20 Feb 1944.

45. Air Historical Branch, "COPC Report on Enemy Tactics," PRO AHB 6 files; USSTAF, "German Air Defense 1938–1945," USAFHRA 519. 601A.

46. Heinz Hanke, personal communication with A. Price, 2000.

47. Eighth Air Force Mission Folder, 11 Feb 1944; ADI(K) Science Memo 2.

48. MAAF Intops Summaries Jan–Feb 44, PRO AIR 23/8282; Luftwaffe Daily Loss Summaries, BA-MA RL 2 III/843-872.

49. Fritz Engau, *Frontal durch die Bomberpulks*, Hoppe, Graz, Austria, 1997, p. 91; Fritz Engau, personal communication with D. Caldwell, 2001; D. Shepherd, *Of Men and Wings: the First 100 Missions of the 449th Bombardment Group*, Norfield, Panama City, FL, 1996, p. 58.

50. Index to Missing Air Crew Reports (MACRs), USAFHRA; Oppelmeyer Flugbuch.

51. Schmid, "The GAF vs. the Allies in the West 1943–45: 1 Jan 44–31 Mar 44."

52. MAAF Intops Summaries Jan–Feb 44; Anon., *Defenders of Liberty: 2nd Bombardment Group/Wing 1918–1993*, Turner, Paducah, KY, 1996, p. 1.

53. Eighth Air Force Mission Folder, 24 Feb 1944; ADI(K) Science Memo 2.

54. Fifteenth Air Force, "Fifteenth Air Force in World War II: Vol. II – Appendices," U.S. Library of Congress Reel 1742-6.

55. William Hess, *B-17 Flying Fortress Units of the MTO*, Osprey, Oxford, UK, 2003, p. 52.

56. McFarland and Newton, *To Command the Sky*, p. 196.

57. Alan S. Milward, *The German Economy at War*, The Athlone Press, University of London, 1965, p. 141.

58. "Extracts from Conferences on Problems of Aircraft Production," 23 Feb 1944, p. 20.

59. Milward, *The German Economy at War*, p. 142.

60. Grabmann, "German Air Defense, 1933–1945," p. 1432.

61. Milward, *The German Economy at War*, p. 142.

62. Grabmann, "German Air Defense, 1933–1945," p. 1432.

63. Air Historical Branch, "Fighter Staff Conferences 1944," Translation No. VII/137, USAFHRA K-512. 631 VII/137, 14 Apr 1944, p. 2.

64. "Eröffnungsansprachen im Werk Erla, 14.3.1944," BA/MA RL 3/3, pp. 1081–3.

65. "Fighter Staff Conferences 1944," p. 11. On May 30, Saur chided members who had skipped meetings in order to enjoy a

holiday weekend, sarcastically noting, "Perhaps you Whitsun holidaymakers have heard what has happened." Fourteen major factories had been bombed.

66. R. J. Overy, *War and Economy in the Third Reich*, Clarendon Press, Oxford, 1994, p. 343.

67. R. J. Overy, *Why the Allies Won*, W. W. Norton, New York, 1996, p. 204.

68. Air Ministry, *Rise and Fall of the German Air Force*, p. 309.

69. Overy, *War and Economy in the Third Reich*, p. 358.

70. Milward, *The German Economy at War*, p. 146.

71. Air Ministry, *Rise and Fall of the German Air Force*, p. 309.

72. Overy, *War and Economy in the Third Reich*, p. 363.

73. Grabmann, "German Air Defense, 1933–1945," pp. 1437ff.

74. Der Chef des Luftwaffenführungsstabes Nr. 9207/44 g. Kdos. Ia/Flieg., "Besprechung beim Herrn Reichsmarschall an 9. 7. 44," NARA T971/13/750.

75. Irving, *Milch*, pp. 278–9; Luftwaffenführungsstab Ia, "Studie über die Flugzeuglage der Kampfverbände," NARA T321/10/4746754ff.; Air Historical Branch, "Suggestions from the German Air Force Operations Staff for the Regaining of German Air Supremacy," May 19, 1944, USAFHRA 512. 621VII/48.

76. "Fighter Staff Conferences 1944," 27 Apr 1944, p. 7.

77. Grabmann, "German Air Defense, 1933–1945," p. 1437.

78. Grabmann, "German Air Defense, 1933–1945," p. 1135.

79. Grabmann, "German Air Defense, 1933–1945," p. 1437.

80. "Fighter Staff Conferences," 18 Apr 1944, p. 4.

81. Murray, *Luftwaffe*, p. 292.

82. Herhudt von Rohden, "The Battle for Air Supremacy over Germany," p. 58.

83. Milward, *The German Economy at War*, p. 113.

84. Alan Clark, Barbarossa; *The Russian-German Conflict, 1941–1945*, William Morrow, New York, 1965, p. 321. On the use of concentration camp labor in the aircraft industry, see Lutz Budraß, *Flugzeugindustrie und Luftrüstung in Deutschland 1918–1945*, Droste Verlag, Düsseldorf, Germany, 1998, pp. 777ff.

85. McFarland and Newton, *To Command the Sky*, p. 191.

86. Schmid, "The GAF vs. the Allies in the West 1943–45: 1 Jan 44–31 Mar 44."

87. Charles Johnson, *The History of the Hell Hawks*, Southcoast Typesetting, Anaheim, CA, 1975, p. 31.

88. Jeffrey Ethell and Alfred Price, *Target Berlin – Mission 250: 6 March 1944*, Jane's, London, 1981, *passim*.

89. Map based upon "German Aircraft Warning and Fighter Control System," Vol. II, Append. IIf, p. 345.

90. Caldwell, *The JG 26 War Diary*, Vol. 2, *1943–1945*, p. 226.

91. Fritz Ungar, personal communication with D. Caldwell, 1987.

92. Smith, *Storm the Fortresses!*

93. Günther Wolf, personal communication with D. Caldwell, 2001.

94. Obermeier, *Die Ritterkreuzträger der Luftwaffe 1939–1945*, Band 1, *Jagdflieger*, p. 160.

95. Gerd Wiegand, personal communication with D. Caldwell, 1988.

96. Hans Heitmann Flugbuch.

97. Headquarters 3rd Bombardment Division, May 20, 1944, "German Fighters vs American Heavy Bombers," USAFHRA 527. 641B, Jan–April 1944, p. 3.

98. A report of one especially garrulous POW is: 2 TAF, "Interrogation of Lt Zink, Adjutant and Intelligence Officer of J.G. 3 on 16 Jul 1944," USAFHRA 515. 619-2 v. 1, 1944, pp. 1–4.

99. "German Interception of B-17 Formations," AAF Informational Intelligence Summary No. 44-28, 10 Sep 1944, pp. 7–8.

100. Bert Stiles, *Serenade to the Big Bird*, W. W. Norton, New York, 1952, p. 92.

101. III./ZG 26 KTB Nr. 8, BA-MA RL 10/257.

102. Caldwell, *The JG 26 War Diary*, Vol. 2, *1943–1945*, p. 227.

103. Gerhard Kroll, personal communication with D. Caldwell, 1987.

104. Grabmann, "German Air Defense, 1933–1945," p. 1113.

105. Wegmann, *"Das Oberkommando der Wehrmacht gibt bekannt . . .",* Band 3, p. 51; McFarland and Newton, *To Command the Sky*, p. 220.

106. Eric Mombeek, *Defenders of the Reich: Jagdgeschwader 1*, Vol. 3, *1944–1945*, Classic Publications, Surrey, UK, 2003, p. 227.

107. Werner Held, *Reichsverteidigung—Die deutsche Tagjagd 1943–1945*, Podzun-Pallas Verlag, Friedberg, Germany, 1988, p. 86; Cajus Bekker, *The Luftwaffe War Diaries*, Doubleday, Garden City, NY, 1968, p. 353; Grabmann, "German Air Defense, 1933–1945," p. 1129.

108. Werner Girbig, *Jagdgeschwader 5 "Eismeerjäger,"* Motorbuch Verlag, Stuttgart, Germany, 1976, p. 46.

109. Heinrich von Podewils, personal communication with K. Minor, 2002.

110. KTB I. Jagdkorps, p. 760.

111. Eric Hammel, *Air War Europa*, Pacific Press, Pacifica, CA, 1994, p. 263; Prien, *et al.*, *Messerschmitt Bf 109 im Einsatz bei der Stab und I./JG 27*, p. 387; György Punka, *Hungarian Aces of World War II*, Osprey, Oxford, UK, 2002, p. 45.

112. Eighth Air Force Mission Folder, 18 Mar 1944.

113. MAAF Intops Summaries Mar–Apr 44, PRO AIR 23/8283; Prien, *et al.*, *Messerschmitt Bf 109 im Einsatz bei der Stab und I./JG 27*, p 387.

114. Eighth Air Force Mission Folder, 23 Mar 1944. Obermeier, *Die Ritterkreuzträger der Luftwaffe 1939–1945*, Band 1, *Jagdflieger*, p. 33.

115. Smith, *Storm the Fortresses!*

116. III./ZG 26 KTB Nr. 8, BA-MA RL 10/257.

117. Freeman, *The Mighty Eighth*, p. 129.

118. KTB I. Jagdkorps, p. 858; Schmid, "The GAF vs. the Allies in the West 1943–45: 1 Jan 44–31 Mar 44," p. 398.

119. Aders, *German Night Fighter Force*, p. 115; Tessin, *Verbände und Truppen der deutschen Wehrmacht*, Band 14, p. 367; Boog, *Das Deutsche Reich in der Defensive*, p. 268.

120. Willi Reschke, personal communication with G. Lanio, 2001.

121. Smith, *Storm the Fortresses!*

122. MAAF Intops Summaries Mar–Apr 44; 455th Bombardment Group Mission Report, USAFHRA; "Einsatz der Fliegendenverbände – Luftlage (eig. u. feindl. Luftwaffe)," BA-MA Kart 44, 1692; ADI(K) Science Memo 2.

123. Hammel, Air War Europa, p. 273; Punka, *Hungarian Aces of World War II*, p. 45; Punka, *Messerschmitt Me 210/410 in Action*, p. 20; "Einsatz der Fliegendenverbände – Luftlage (eig. u. feindl. Luftwaffen)," p. 1694.

124. Fritz Engau, personal communication with D. Caldwell, 2001.

125. Eighth Air Force Mission Folder, 8 Apr 1944; William Hess, *Hell in the Heavens: Ill-Fated Eighth Air Force Bomb Group Missions*, Specialty Press, North Branch, MN, 2000, p. 4.

126. Caldwell, *The JG 26 War Diary*, Vol. 2, *1943–1945*, p. 238.

127. Freeman, *Mighty Eighth War Diary*, p. 214; ADI(K) Science Memo 2.

128. Schmid, "The GAF vs. the Allies in the West 1943–45: 1 Apr 44–6 Jun 44," USAFHRA K113. 107-158-160 v3, p. 539.

129. III./ZG 26 KTB Nr. 8, p. 37.

130. Eighth Air Force Mission Folder, 11 Apr 1944; "Einsatz der Fliegendenverbände – Luftlage (eig. u. feindl. Luftwaffen)," p. 1704.

131. Freeman, *Mighty Eighth War Diary*, p. 217; Jochen Prien, *"Pik-As": Geschichte des Jagdgeschwaders 53*, Teil 3, Struve-Druck, Eutin, Germany, 1991, p. 1300.

132. Eighth Air Force Mission Folder, 11 Apr 1944.

133. Mombeek, *Sturmstaffel 1: Reich Defense 1943–44*, p. 75.

134. Paul Andrews and William Adams, *The Mighty Eighth Combat Chronology: Heavy Bomber and Fighter Activities 1942–1945*, Eighth Air Force Memorial Museum Foundation, Warrenton, VA, 1997, p. 114; Hess, *Hell in the Heavens*, p. 56.

135. III./ZG 26 Anlagen u. Gefechtsberichte 24 Aug 43–30 Dez 43, BA-MA RL 10/565, p. 40.

136. Jochen Prien, *IV./JG 3: Chronik einer Jagdgruppe 1943–1945*, Struve-Druck, Eutin, Germany, n.d., p. 96.

137. Schmid, "The GAF vs. the Allies in the West 1943–45: 1 Apr 44–6 Jun 44," p. 552; ADI(K) Science Memo 2.

138. Boiten and Bowman, *Battles with the Luftwaffe*, p. 112; Punka, *Hungarian Aces of World War II*, p. 46.

139. Eighth Air Force Mission Folder, 13 Apr 1944; ADI(K) Science Memo 2.

140. Neil Page, personal archives, 2001.

141. Prien and Rodeike, *Einsatz in der Reichsverteidigung von 1939 bis 1945: Jagdgeschwader 1 und 11*, Teil 2, *1944*, p. 871.

142. **Rall, Günther (1918–).** The third-highest scoring fighter pilot of all time. Rall joined the German Army in 1936 and transferred to the Luftwaffe in 1938. He was assigned to JG 52 in August 1939, and remained in this most successful of all fighter units for the next four years. He scored steadily against the Soviet Air Force, received the Oak Leaves with Swords to the Knight's Cross of the Iron Cross, and on November 28, 1943, became the second Luftwaffe pilot after Nowotny to claim 250 victories. On April 19, 1944, Rall was summoned to Germany to take command of II./JG 11 in the RLV. Like many pilots who transferred from the Eastern Front, Rall quickly became a casualty—on May 12, 1944, after scoring his 275th and last victory, he was shot down by a P-47 and lost a thumb. After his hospital stay he was given a school posting, and then, in February 1945, took command of JG 300, another RLV fighter wing. However, the fuel shortage and the chaos accompanying the war's final days prevented Rall from achieving any success with his new command.

Rall joined the post-war West German Air Force, the Bundesluftwaffe, in 1956, and rose to command it from 1970 to 1974. His final rank was Generalleutnant.

143. Prien and Rodeike, *Einsatz in der Reichsverteidigung von 1939 bis 1945: Jagdgeschwader 1 und 11*, Teil 2, *1944*, p. 878.

144. Ian McLachlan, *Night of the Intruders*, Patrick Stephens, Somerset, UK, 1994, p. 56.

145. Frank Olynyk, *USAAF (Mediterranean Theater) Credits for the Destruction of Enemy Aircraft in Air-to-Air Combat – World War 2*, privately published, 1987, p. 77.

146. Caldwell, *The JG 26 War Diary*, Vol. 2, *1943–1945*, p. 246.

147. Eighth Air Force Mission Folder, 24 Apr 1944.

148. Prien, *IV./JG 3 – Chronik einer Jagdgruppe 1943–1945*, p. 107.

149. Eighth Air Force Mission Folder, 042944; ADI(K) Science Memo 2; "Einsatz der Fliegendenverbände – Luftlage (eig. u.

feindl. Luftwaffen)," p. 1728.

150. Schmid, "The GAF vs. the Allies in the West 1943–45: 1 Apr 44–6 Jun 44," p. 510.

151. Some transcripts record Galland giving a figure of 1,200 pilots lost.

152. Slightly different transcripts of Galland's remarks are extant; this version is drawn from "Fighter Staff Conferences," 25 Apr 1944, pp. 8–9; Grabmann, "German Air Defense, 1933–1945," pp. 1184–7.

153. Murray, *Luftwaffe*, p. 232.

154. Rieckhoff, *Trumpf oder Bluff?*, p. 196.

Chapter 7: The Oil Campaign (pages 190–229)

1. Craven and Cate, *Army Air Forces in World War II*, Vol. III, *Europe: Argument to V-E Day*, p. 172; USSBS, "The Effects of Strategic Bombing on the German War Economy," 31 Oct 1945, pp. 73–82.

2. Mets, *Master of Airpower: Gen. Carl A. Spaatz*, p. 210.

3. John Weal, *Jagdgeschwader 2 "Richthofen,"* Osprey, Oxford, UK, 2000, p. 109.

4. Smith, *Storm the Fortresses!*

5. Schmid, "The GAF vs. the Allies in the West 1943–45: 1 Apr 44–6 Jun 44," USAFHRA K113. 107-158-160 v3, p. 673.

6. Oskar Bösch, personal communication with D. Caldwell, 1999.

7. Berthold Wendler, personal communication with D. Caldwell, 2000.

8. Eighth Air Force Mission Folder, May 11, 1944; Steve Blake, "Mission 351—The Death of Water Oesau," *Fighter Pilots in Aerial Combat*, 9, 1983, p. 14.

9. Eighth Air Force Mission Folder, May 12, 1944.

10. Werner Girbig, ". . . mit Kurs auf Leuna": Die Luftoffensive gegen die Triebstoffindustrie und der deutsche Abwehreinsatz 1944–1945*, Motorbuch Verlag, Stuttgart, Germany, 1980, p. 13; KTB I. Jagdkorps.

11. KTB II./JG 1.

12. Jochen Prien, et al., *Messerschmitt Bf 109 im Einsatz bei der II./Jagdgeschwader 27*, Struve-Druck, Eutin, Germany, n.d., p. 383; Prien, *Jagdgeschwader 53*, Teil 3, p. 1308.

13. Prien, *Jagdgeschwader 1 und 11*, Teil 2, *1944*, p. 927, Prien and Stemmer, *Stab u. I./JG 3*, p. 352; Prien, *IV./JG 3*, p. 125; Hess, *Hell in the Heavens*, p. 63.

14. Günther Rall, personal communication with D. Caldwell, 2004; Hubert Zemke, "The Zemke Fan and the Battle of the Aces," *AAHS Journal*, 41 (2), 1996.

15. Prien and Stemmer, *III./JG 3*, p. 304.

16. Caldwell, *The JG 26 War Diary*, Vol. 2, *1943–1945*, p. 256.

17. Albert Speer, *Inside the Third Reich*, Macmillan, New York, 1970, pp. 346–7.

18. USSBS, "The U.S. Strategic Bombing Survey Over-all Report (European War)," 30 Sep 1945, p. 39; Girbig, ". . . mit Kurs auf Leuna," p. 27; ULTRA—Main Series of Signals Conveying Intelligence to Allied Commands*, KV-6675.

19. "Discussions with Reichsmarschall Göring 5/15-16/44 re Fighters & Personnel," AHB 6 VI/71, PRO AIR 20/7703.

20. John Foreman and S. E. Harvey, *Me 262 Combat Diary*, Air Research Publications, Surrey, UK, 1990, p. 33.

21. Prien, *IV./JG 3*, p. 135.

22. Hans Schreier, JG 52: *Das erfolgreichste Jagdgeschwader des II. Weltkrieges*, Kurt Vowinckel Verlag, Berg-am-See, Germany, 1990, p. 135; Ultra, KV-443X.

23. Ultra, KV-9684.

24. Walther Dahl, *Rammjäger*, Orion Verlag, Heusenstamm, Germany, 1961, p. 40.

25. Freeman, *Mighty Eighth War Diary*, p. 251; Schmid, "The GAF vs. the Allies in the West 1943–45: 1 Apr 44–6 Jun 44," p. 650.

26. Eighth Air Force Mission Folder, May 28, 1944; Ivo De Jong, *Mission 376: Battle over the Reich 28 May 1944*, Hikoki Publications, Crowborough, UK, 2003, p. 206.

27. Prien, *et al.*, *Stab und I./Jagdgeschwader 27*, p. 404.

28. "JG 27 Abschussmeldungen und Anlage," BA-MA RL 10/433.

29. Girbig, ". . . mit Kurs auf Leuna," p. 40; Meldungen über Flugzeugverluste bei den fl. Verbänden, BA-MA RL 2 III/843-872.

30. Norbert Hannig, *Luftwaffe Fighter Ace: From the Eastern Front to the Defense of the Homeland*, Grub Street, London, 2004, p. 122; Eighth Air Force Mission Folder, May 29, 1944; Prien and Stemmer, *Stab und I./JG 3*, p. 502.

31. Craven and Cate, *Army Air Forces in World War II*, Vol. III, *Europe: Argument to V-E Day*, p. 314.

32. III./ZG 26 KTB Nr. 8: 1 Jan 1944–30 Sep 1944, BA-MA RL 10/257, p. 57.

33. Grabmann, "German Air Defense, 1933–1945," pp. 1123ff.

34. Michael Holm, private archive.

35. AI12/USAFE/M. 116, Intelligence Report No. 116, "Documentary Evidence of Training Difficulties in the GAF," USAFHRA 512. 62512M-116, p. 6.

36. Der Reichsmarschall des Großdeutschen Reiches und Oberbefehlshaber der Luftwaffe Nr 2460/44 g. Kdos., 16 Mar 1944, NARA T321/10/4746669.

37. Grabmann, "German Air Defense, 1933–1945," pp. 1345–6.

38. 1st Bomb Division, A.D.I.(K) Report No. 155, 1945, "The Output and Training of G.A.F. Fighter Pilots Sept 39–Dec 44," USAFHRA 525. 641, pp. 7–8.

39. "Output and Training of G.A.F. Fighter Pilots," pp. 1–2.

40. Chef Genst 8. Abteilung, "Gedanken zur 'Beurteilung der Ausbildungslage,'" 17 Sep 1944, von Rohden 4376/323, NARA T971/14/24, p. 4.

41. "Beurteilung der Ausbildungslage," p. 1.

42. "Output and Training of G.A.F. Fighter Pilots," p. 5.

43. "Beurteilung der Ausbildungslage," p. 3.

44. Oberkommando der Luftwaffe, Lw. Führungsstab Nr. 1640/44 geh., (Ia/Ausb), 26 June 1944, "Taktischer Einzelhinweis Nr. 19: Sicherung des Flugbetriebes gegen feindliche Jagdangriffe," BA-MA RL 2 II/127, pp. 3–4.

45. McFarland and Newton, *To Command the Sky*, pp. 229–31.

46. "Taktische Bemerkungen Nr. 2/44," p. 9.

47. "Taktische Bemerkungen Nr. 2/44," p. 4.

48. USSTAF, Air Staff Post Hostilities Investigation: "German Air Defenses, Instructions for the Operation and Command of Battle of the Anti-aircraft Artillery in Air Defense," USAFHRA 519. 601A-14 Vol. 14, Part C, Book 26, p. 4.

49. Oberkommando der Luftwaffe, Lw. Führungsstab Nr. 1411/44 geh. (Ia/Ausb.), "Taktische Bemerkungen des Oberkommandos der Luftwaffe Nr. 4/44," 1 June 1944, BA-MA RH 11 III/76, pp. 11–12.

50. Westermann, *Flak*, p. 270.

51. Oberkommando der Luftwaffe, Lw. Führunggstab Nr 1920/44 geh. (Ia/Ausb.), "Taktische Bemerkungen des Oberkommandos der Luftwaffe Nr. 5/44," 17 July 1944, BA-MA RH 11 III/76, p. 16.

52. Rieckhoff, *Trumpf oder Bluff?*, p. 194.

53. "Output and Training of G.A.F. Fighter Pilots," p. 11.

54. Der Reichsmarschall des Großdeutschen Reiches und Oberbefehlshaber der Luftwaffe Nr. 8947/43 gKdos, (Füst. Ia), Betr: "Drohende Gefahr West," 6 Dec 43, NARA T321/10/4746474.

55. Karl Gundelach, "Drohende Gefahr West: Die deutsche Luftwaffe vor und während der Invasion 1944," *Wehrwissenschaftliche Rundschau* 1959 (Heft 6), p. 306.

56. Der Reichsmarschall des Großdeutschen Reiches und Oberbefehlshaber der Luftwaffe Nr. 9221/44 g. Kdos. Chefsache, Betr. "Drohende Gefahr West," 27 Feb 44, BA/MA RL 2 II/5, p. 5.

57. "The primary task of the [fighters] is the escort of ground-attack aircraft in the face of enemy fighter opposition. Beyond this they may—if sufficient strength is available—operate over a wide area and freely engage enemy aircraft and, in exceptional cases, protect march routes, supply, and other positions from enemy air attack." Panzergruppe West Abt. Ia/Fliegerverbindungsoffizier Nr. 1600/44 geheim, "Merkblatt zur Luftwaffen-Unterstützung (Westverhältnisse)," 22 Mar 44, NARA T321/51/4798880.

58. Oberkommando der Luftwaffe, Führungsstab Ia/Ausb. Nr. 70/44 geh., "Taktische Einzelhinweis Nr. 4, Richtlinien für die Ausbildung von Jagdverbänden im Schlachtfliegereinsatz," 13 Mai 1944, BA/MA RL 2 II/127.

59. "Taktische Bemerkungen Nr. 4/44," p. 13.

60. Martin Mettig, Oberst i. Genst., 1004/44 gKdos., "Erfahrungen aus dem Beginn der Invasion," 18 Oct 44, von Rohden 4407/86, NARA T971/18/296, p. 6.

61. Adolf Galland, "Birth, Life & Death of the Jagdwaffe," ADI(K) 373/45, p. 51.

62. Murray, *Luftwaffe*, p. 265.

63. Price, *Battle over the Reich*, p. 136; Ultra, KV-7138.

64. Caldwell, *JG 26 War Diary*, Vol. 2, *1943–45*; p. 270; Ultra, KV-7815.

65. Oberkommando der Luftwaffe, Lw. Führungsstab Nr. 2300/44 geh. (Ia/Ausb.), 25 Aug 1944, "Taktische Bemerkungen des Oberkommandos der Luftwaffe, Nr. 6/44," BA/MA RH 11 III/76, p. 4.

66. "Erfahrungen aus dem Beginn der Invasion," pp. 3–4.

67. Prien, *IV./JG 3*, p. 367.

68. Willi Reschke, *Jagdgeschwader 301/302 "Wilde Sau,"* Motorbuch Verlag, Stuttgart, Germany, 1998, p. 69.

69. Olynyk, *USAAF (Mediterranean Theater) Credits for the Destruction of Enemy Aircraft*, p. 945; Jiri Rajlich, *et al.*, *Slovakian and Bulgarian Aces of World War II*, Osprey, Oxford, 2004, p. 49; Punka, *Hungarian Aces of World War II*, p. 49.

70. Eighth Air Force Mission Folder, 20 Jun 1944; Girbig, ". . . mit Kurs auf Leuna," p. 56, Allen Blue, *The Fortunes of War*, Aero Publishers, Fallbrook, CA, 1967, p. 32; Hess, *Hell in the Heavens*, p. 75.

71. Mark J. Conversino, *Fighting with the Soviets: The Failure of Operation Frantic, 1944–1945*, University Press of Kansas, Lawrence, KS, 1997, p. 88; Muller, *German Air War in Russia*, pp. 208, 213; Grabmann, "German Air Defense, 1933–1945," p. 1195.

72. Aders and Held, *Jagdgeschwader 51 "Mölders,"* p. 152; Eighth Air Force Mission Folder, 21 Jun 1944.

73. Jochen Prien and Peter Rodeike, *Jagdgeschwader 1 und 11: Ensatz in der Reichsverteidigung von 1939 bis 1945*, Teil 3, *1944–45*, Struve-Druck, Eutin, Germany, n.d., p. 1231.

74. Anon., *The Flight of the Vulgar Vultures: 455th Bomb Group (H) 1943–1945*, privately published, 1991, p. 80; Hans Werner Neulen, *In the Skies of Europe: Air Forces Allied to the Luftwaffe*, Crowood Press, Wiltshire, UK, 1998, p. 138; Jon Guttman, "Tatra

Eagle: Slovakia's Ace of Aces," *Aviation History*, 9 (1), 2001, p. 51.

75. Girbig, ". . . *mit Kurs auf Leuna*," p. 78.

76. MAAF Sigint Summaries Jun 44, PRO AIR 26/382.

77. ADI(K) Science Memo 2; Index to Missing Air Crew Reports.

78. Eighth Air Force Mission Folder, 29 Jun 44; D. L. Bohnstedt and B. J. Bohnstedt, *460th Bomb Group History*, Taylor, Dallas, TX, 1996, p. 3; Dravan Savic and Boris Ciglic, *Croatian Aces of World War 2*, Osprey, Oxford, UK, 2002, p. 66.

79. Jeam-Bernard Frappé, *La Luftwaffe face au débarquement allié: 6 juin au 31 août 1944*, Editions Heimdal, Bayeux, France, 1999, p. 178.

80. USSBS, German Order of Battle.

81. MAAF Intops Summaries; Jon Guttman, "Kidd Hofer: Last of the Screwball Pilots," *American Fighter Aces Bulletin* 18 (1), 2001, p. 22; Einsatz der Fliegendenverbände – Luftlage (eig. u. feindl. Luftwaffen), BA-MA Karte 44/2028.

82. Willi Reschke, personal communication with D. Caldwell, 1997.

83. Robert Goebel, personal communication with D. Caldwell, 1993; Neulen, p. 140.

84. Matthew Cooper, *The German Air Force 1933–1945*, Jane's, London, 1981, p. 346; Ultra XL-1671, XL-4602, XL-4904.

85. Blue, *The Fortunes of War*, p. 36.

86. Girbig, ". . . *mit Kurs auf Leuna*," p. 87.

87. Girbig, *Jagdgeschwader 5 "Eismeerjäger*," p. 236.

88. Dahl, *Rammjäger*, p. 86; Günther Sinnecker, personal communication with D. Caldwell, 2004.

89. Galland, "Birth, Life & Death of the Jagdwaffe," p. 68.

90. Oskar Bösch, personal communication with D. Caldwell, 1999.

91. BA-MA Karte 44/2059.

92. "Taktische Bemerkungen Nr. 6/44," p. 14.

93. Headquarters 3rd Bombardment Division, "Memorandum to Director of Intelligence, Eighth Air Force, AAF Sta. 101," October 17, 1944, USAFHRA 527. 640A, Sept 43–Jan 45, p. 1.

94. 3rd Bombardment Division, "Special Report of Unusual Battle Damage, Mission of 7 October 1944," USAFHRA 527. 640A, p. 2.

95. "Special Report of Unusual Battle Damage," p. 2.

96. David Irving, *Hitler's War*, Viking, New York, 1977, p. 385.

97. An account of this bizarre episode may be found in the memoirs of a U.S. Army intelligence officer. See Frank E. Manuel, *Scenes from the End: The Last Days of World War II in Europe*, Steerforth Press, South Royalton, VT, 2000, pp. 105–111.

98. Rieckhoff, *Trumpf oder Bluff?*, 83.

99. On the bribery issue, see Norman J. W. Goda, "Black Marks: Hitler's Bribery of his Senior Military Officers during World War II," *Journal of Modern History*, 72 (2), 2000, pp. 413–52.

100. Nicolaus von Below, *At Hitler's Side: The Memoirs of Hitler's Luftwaffe Adjutant 1937–1945*, Greenhill, London, 2001, p. 174.

101. Omer Bartov, *Hitler's Army: Soldiers, Nazis and War in the Third Reich*, Oxford University Press, New York and Oxford, 1991.

102. Air Ministry translation, "Maintenance of Morale in the GAF," 22 Dec 1943, USAFHRA 512. 62512TA-13, p. 12.

103. Der Reichsmarschall des Großdeutschen Reiches, 15 Mar 44, Milch 53. 65, NARA T321/154/470; Boog, *Luftwaffenführung*, pp. 290ff.

104. See, for example, a large, poorly organized collection of documents pertaining to the "Nazification of the armed forces," Von Rohden collection, LC 1750/5/no frame #s.

105. "Taktische Bemerkungen Nr. 6/44," p. 3.

106. Air Ministry/USAFE Intelligence Report No. 110, "The GAF in the Grip of the Nazi Party," May 15, 1946, USAFHRA 512.

62512M-110, p. 45.

107. See, for several of many possible examples, the accounts in David P. Williams, *Day Fighters: Hunters of the Reich*, Cerberus, Bristol, UK, 2002.

108. Max Hastings, *Armageddon: The Battle for Germany, 1944–1945*, Knopf, New York, 2004, p. 165.

109. Hannig, *Luftwaffe Fighter Ace*, p. 6.

110. "Output and Training of German Fighter Pilots," p. 7.

111. USSTAF, "Fighter Operations," Vol. II, "Interrogation of Obstlt. Baer at Kaufbeuren, Germany, 6 Sep 1945," Append. IX.

112. Der Oberbefehlshaber der Luftwaffe, Führungsstab Ic, "Frontnachrichtenblatt der Luftwaffe," Nr 50, Mai 1943.

113. USSTAF, "Fighter Operations," Vol. II, "Interrogation of Generalleutnant Galland on 'Decorations and Awards,'" Append. VII.

114. ADI(K) Report No. 473/1944, "Morale and Fighting Spirit of the G.A.F. Since D-Day," USAFHRA 512. 619B20-23, 1944.

115. Headquarters AAF Intelligence Summary No 55-6, 30 Mar 1945, "Morale of the German Air Force," USAFHRA 527. 641A, pp. 22–3.

116. Jean-Yves Lorant and Richard Goyat, *Bataille dans le ciel d'Allemagne: une Escadre de Chasse dans la Débâcle*, Tome 2, *Septembre 1944–Mai 1945*, éditions Larivière, Paris, 2005, p. 102.

117. W. E. Thompson, "Turkey Shoot over Vienna." *Flight Journal*, 8 (3), 2003, p. 64.

118. Eric Mombeek, *Sturmjäger: Zur Geschichte des Jagdgeschwaders 4 und der Sturmstaffel 1*, Band 1, privately published, 1997, p. 152.

119. Prien, *IV./JG 3*, p. 178; Ultra, XL-2951.

120. III./ZG 26 KTB Nr. 8, p 63; Foreman and Harvey, *Me 262 Combat Diary*, p. 34; J. Richard Smith and Eddie Creek, *Me 262*, Vol. 2, Classic Publications, West Sussex, UK, 1998, p. 234.

121. Jack Smith, *Mustangs and Unicorns: A History of the 359th FG*, Pictorial Histories, Missoula, MT, 1997, p. 86; Ultra XL-4137.

122. Prien and Rodeike, *JG 1 und JG 11*, Band 2, p. 1120; Band 3, p. 1251; Ultra XL-4963.

123. Smith, *Storm the Fortresses!*

124. Willi Unger, personal communication with B. Smith, 2000.

125. Freeman, *Mighty Eighth War Diary*, p. 33; ADI(K) Science Memo 2; BA-MA RL 2 III/843-872.

126. ADI(K) Science Memo 2; Gerhard Schöpfel, personal communication with D. Caldwell, 2000.

127. MAAF Intops Summaries; Prien, *et al.*, *II./JG 27*, p. 439.

128. Foreman and Harvey, *Me 262 Combat Diary*, p. 33.

129. Berthold Wendler, personal communication with D. Caldwell, 2000; Smith and Creek, *Me 262*, Vol. 2, p. 363; Ultra XL-5773.

130. Dahl, *Rammjäger*, p. 119; JG 300 Gefechtsbericht, private archive; Gobrecht, *Might in Flight*, p. 508.

131. Eighth Air Force Mission Folder, 16 Aug 44; Jeffrey Ethell and Alfred Price, *The German Jets in Combat*, Jane's, London, 1979, p. 124; Girbig, ". . . *mit Kurs auf Leuna*," p. 121.

132. Hammel, *Air War Europa*, p. 365; Index to MACRs; Reschke, *Jagdgeschwader 301/302 "Wilde Sau*," p. 121.

133. MAAF Intops Summaries; BA-MA Kart 44/2229; BA-MA RL 2 III/843-872.

134. MAAF Intops Summaries; BA-MA Kart 44/2230; BA-MA RL 2 III/843-872.

135. Prien, *Jagdgeschwader 53*, Teil 3, p. 1182.

136. Eighth Air Force Mission Folder, 24 Aug 1944; MAAF Intops Summaries; ADI(K) Science Memo 2.

137. Hans Bott, personal communication with D. Caldwell, 2001.

138. Ethell and Price, *The German Jets in Combat*, p. 127.

139. Fritz Buchholz, "JG 6 am 25. August 1944," *Jägerblatt*, 76/1, 1976, p. 10; L. Lächler and G. Lauser, "Die Geschichte einer Zerstörergruppe." *Jet & Prop*, 5/91, 1991, p. 55; Mombeek, *Sturmjäger*, Band 1, p. 85.

140. Anon., *Defenders of Liberty: 2nd Bombardment Group/Wing 1918–1993*, p. 6; BA-MA RL 2 III/843-872; BA-MA Kart 44/2236; Reschke, *Jagdgeschwader 301/302 "Wilde Sau,"* p. 131.

Chapter 8: The "Big Blow" That Never Fell (pages 230–261)

1. Craven and Cate, *Army Air Forces in World War II*, Vol. III, *Europe: Argument to V-E Day*, p. 658.

2. "Beurteilung der Ausbildungslage," p. 4.

3. Galland, *Die Ersten und die Letzten*, p. 331.

4. Hajo Herrmann, Aktennotiz Betr. Rechnerische Grundlagen f.d. SO-Einsatz, private archive.

5. Robert Jung, *Auf verlorenem Posten: Die Geschichte eines jungen Jagdfliegers*, privately printed, 1994, p. 19.

6. Reschke, *Jagdgeschwader 301/302 "Wilde Sau,"* p. 134.

7. Eighth Air Force Mission Folder, 11 Sep 1944; Girbig, ". . . mit Kurs auf Leuna," p. 132; Lorant and Goyat, *Jagdgeschwader 300 "Wilde Sau,"* Vol. 1, p. 310; Meldungen über Flugzeugverluste bei den fl. Verbänden, BA-MA RL 2 III/843-872.

8. John Sloan, *The Route as Briefed: The History of the 92nd Bombardment Group 1942–1945*, Argus Press, Cleveland, OH, 1946, p. 177.

9. Eric Mombeek, *Sturmjäger: zur Geschichte des Jagdgeschwaders 4 und der Sturmstaffel 1*, Band 2, privately printed, n.d., p. 9; J. Zdiarsky, "The History of the Battle Krusnohori (Ergebirge) 11 Sep 44," private archive.

10. Girbig, ". . . mit Kurs auf Leuna," p. 140; Mombeek, *Sturmjäger*, Band 2, p. 29.

11. Russell Strong, *First over Germany: A History of the 306th Bombardment Group*, privately published, 1990, p. 273.

12. Ellis Woodward, *Flying School: Combat Hell*, American Literary Press, Baltimore, MD, 1998, p. 91; Jung, *Auf verlorenem Posten*, p. 67.

13. Hess, *354th Fighter Group*, p. 90.

14. Dahl, *Rammjäger*, p. 128; Prien, *IV./JG 3*, p. 234.

15. Karl Boehm-Tettelbach, *Als Flieger in der Hexenküche*, v. Hase & Koehler Verlag, Mainz, Germany, 1981, p. 130; Dahl, *Rammjäger*, p. 134; USSTAF, "Evolution of the Defense of the Reich," App. XXXIII.

16. Charles MacDonald, *The Mighty Endeavor: American Armed Forces in the European Theater in World War II*, Oxford University Press, New York, 1969, p. 328.

17. Mombeek, *Sturmjäger*, Band 2, p. 37.

18. *ULTRA—Main Series of Signals Conveying Intelligence to Allied Commands*, HP-486.

19. MacDonald, *Mighty Endeavor*, p. 346.

20. Grabmann, "German Air Defense, 1933–1945," p. 1230.

21. Grabmann, "German Air Defense, 1933–1945," p. 1231.

22. Tony Wood and Bill Gunston, *Hitler's Luftwaffe*, Salamander, London, n.d., p. 112.

23. **Nowotny, Walter (1920–1944)**. One of the most successful of the younger German fighter pilots who entered service after World War II began. Nowotny joined a front-line fighter unit, JG 54, in February 1941, and took part in Operation Barbarossa, the German invasion of the Soviet Union, that June. He remained with JG 54 on the northern sector of the Eastern Front until he was grounded in November 1943, after his 256th air victory, for

which he became the eighth member of the Wehrmacht to receive the Oak Leaves with Swords and Diamonds to the Knight's Cross of the Iron Cross. After a period in a training wing he was chosen by Adolf Galland to command the unit which would introduce the Me 262 jet fighter to combat. The success of this unit was crucially important if the Me 262 was to play the role which Galland envisioned for it in the air defense of Germany. Nowotny scored two victories while flying the jet, but was apparently not an especially skillful unit commander, having received no training for this role. Galland was compelled to visit Nowotny's Achmer base to evaluate his performance, and while there on November 8, 1944, witnessed Nowotny crash to his death on the edge of the airfield after a battle with P-51s.

24. Eighth Air Force Mission Folder, 27 Sep 1944; Hess, *Hell in the Heavens*, p. 85; Anon., *The Kassel Mission Reports: Highest Group Loss in Eighth Air Force History*, privately published, n.d., *passim*.

25. Eighth Air Force Mission Folder, 28 Sep 1944; Ken Blakebrough, *The Fireball Outfit: The 457th Bombardment Group in the Skies over Europe*, Aero Publishers, Fallbrook, CA, 1968, p. 38; Gobrecht, *Might in Flight*, p. 544; Steve Blake, "The P-38's Eighth Air Force Swan Song," *Lightning Strikes* 14 (1), 2001, p. 6; Hess, *Hell in the Heavens*, p. 105.

26. USSTAF, Fighter Operations, "Interrogation of Generalleutnant Galland on 'Plans of the German Fighter Force for the Continuation of World War II,'" App. XII; Alfred Price, *Last Year of the Luftwaffe, May 1944 to May 1945*, Motorbooks International, Osceola, WI, 1991, p. 94.

27. Foreman and Harvey, *Me 262 Combat Diary*, p. 46.

28. Eighth Air Force Mission Folder, 6 Oct 1944; Mombeek, *Sturmjäger*, Band 2, p. 58; Smith, *Storm the Fortresses!*

29. Eighth Air Force Mission Folder, 7 Oct 1944.

30. Ethell and Price, *The German Jets in Combat*, p. 129; Hans Bott, personal communication with D. Caldwell, 2001.

31. Ethell and Price, *The German Jets in Combat*, p. 31; Foreman and Harvey, *Me 262 Combat Diary*, p. 46.

32. Reschke, *Jagdgeschwader 301/302 "Wilde Sau,"* p. 136.

33. Caldwell, *The JG 26 War Diary*, Vol. 2, *1943–1945*, p. 364.

34. Eighth Air Force Mission Folder, 12 Oct 1944.

35. Girbig, ". . . mit Kurs auf Leuna," p. 152; Olynyk, *USAAF (Mediterranean Theater) Credits for the Destruction of Enemy Aircraft in Air-to-Air Combat World War II*, p. 109.

36. Hans Ring and Werner Girbig, *Jagdgeschwader 27*, Motorbuch Verlag, Stuttgart, Germany, 1971, p. 287.

37. Ultra, HP-5147.

38. Smith and Creek, *Me 262*, Vol. 2, p. 408.

39. Generalstab 8. Abteilung, "The Problems of German Air Defense in 1944," Air Historical Branch Translation No. VII/22, November 5, 1944, USAFHRA 512. 621 VII/22, p. 2.

40. "Problems of German Air Defense," p. 1.

41. Grabmann, "German Air Defense, 1933–1945," p. 1348; Gerhard Stamp, *Bomben gegen Bomber*, unpublished manuscript, 1952, pp. 2–4.

42. Generalstab 8. Abteilung, "Survey of the War Situation," November 10, 1944, Air Historical Branch Translation No. VII/27, USAFHRA 512. 621VII/27, p. 7.

43. See the discussion in Chapter 5.

44. Map modified from "German Aircraft Warning and Fighter Control System," Vol. II, App. IIg, p. 347.

45. "German Aircraft Warning and Fighter Control System," p. 206.

46. "German Aircraft Warning and Fighter Control System," p. 52.

47. Luftflotten Kommando Reich, "Report on the assignments, activity, and development of the Luftwaffenbefehlshaber Mitte," p. 14.

48. "German Aircraft Warning and Fighter Control System," p. 206.

49. For technical details of the various radar devices, see "Reichsluftverteidigung," Heft 4, Anlage 1, and Gebhard Aders, *History of the German Night Fighter Force, 1917–1945*, Jane's, London, 1979, p. 206.

50. "Reichsluftverteidigung," Heft 4, p. 18.

51. Josef Schmid, "German Day-Fighting in the Defense of the Reich from Sept. 15, 1943 to the End of the War," USAFHRA 512. 645G , p. 2.

52. "Reichsluftverteidigung," Heft 4, p. 14; italics in original.

53. "Reichsluftverteidigung," Heft 4, p. 17.

54. "Reichsluftverteidigung," Heft 1, p. 18.

55. "Taktische Bemerkungen Nr. 6/44," pp. 7–8.

56. General der Jagdflieger, Gruppe 3, Br. B. Nr. 5838/44 geh., "Richtlinien für die Aufgaben und den Einsatz des Nachrichten-Offiziers in den Jagdgeschwader und Jagdgruppen der Reichsverteidigung," 26 Mar 1944, von Rohden 4376/190, NARA T971/37/742ff, pp. 9–10.

57. Schmid, "German Day-Fighting," p. 5.

58. Diagram modified from "German Aircraft Warning and Fighter Control System," Vol. II, Append. IV, Figure 24.

59. "German Aircraft Warning and Fighter Control System," p. 201.

60. "German Aircraft Warning and Fighter Control System," p. 110, also Figure 24.

61. Herhudt von Rohden, "Battle for Air Supremacy over Germany," p. 84.

62. General der Jagdflieger, "Richtlinien für die Aufgaben und den Einsatz des Nachrichten-Offiziers," pp. 11–12.

63. Schmid, "German Day-Fighting," p. 5; "German Aircraft Warning and Fighter Control System," p. 251.

64. USSTAF, Post-Hostilities Investigation, "German Air Defenses," Vol. 2, USAFHRA 519. 621A-2, p. 57.

65. Merkblatt g. 251, "Instructions for the Operations and Command of Battle of the AAA in Air Defense," 10 Sept 1944, USAFHRA 519. 601A-14 vol 14, pp. 1ff.

66. "Taktische Bemerkungen Nr 5/44," p. 17.

67. Westermann, *Flak*, pp. 263–4.

68. "Reichsluftverteidigung," Heft 2, p. 9.

69. Grabmann, "German Air Defense, 1933–1945," p. 1349.

70. "Survey of the War Situation," p. 8.

71. Harry J. Coleman, personal communications with R. Muller, 1997 and 2005.

72. Craven and Cate, *Army Air Forces in World War II*, Vol. III, *Europe: Argument to V-E Day*, p. 644.

73. Ethell and Price, *The German Jets in Combat*, p. 131.

74. Foreman and Harvey, *Me 262 Combat Diary*, p. 46; Freeman, *56th Fighter Group*, 102.

75. Hess, *Hell in the Heavens*, p. 112.

76. Prien and Stemmer, *Stab u. I./JG 3*, p. 443.

77. Blakebrough, *The Fireball Outfit*, p. 43; Mombeek, *Sturmjäger*, Band 2, p. 72.

78. Prien, *et al.*, *Stab und I./JG 27*, p. 471.

79. Craven and Cate, *Army Air Forces in World War II*, Vol. III, *Europe: Argument to V-E Day*, p. 660; Gerhard Weinberg, ed., *Hitler and his Generals: Military Conferences 1942–1945*, Enigma Books, New York, 2003, p. 513.

80. Galland, "Birth, Life & Death of the Jagdwaffe," ADI(K) 373/45.

81. Foreman and Harvey, *Me 262 Combat Diary*, p. 64; Smith and Creek, *Me 262*, Vol. 2, p. 418.

82. Schmid, "The GAF vs. the Allies in the West 1943–45: Command Structure," USAFHRA K113. 107-158-160 v5, p. 918.

83. Ring and Girbig, *Jagdgeschwader 27*, p. 287; Mombeek, *Sturmjäger*, Band 2, p. 80.

84. Rudolf Sinner, Flugbuch.

85. Galland, *Die Ersten und die Letzten*, p. 331.

86. Werner Girbig, *Start im Morgengrauen*, Motorbuch Verlag, Stuttgart, Germany, 1973, p. 39; Lorant and Goyat, *Bataille dans le ciel d'Allemagne*, Tome 2, p. 75.

87. Smith and Creek, *Me 262*, Vol. 2, p. 428.

88. Eighth Air Force Mission Folder, 26 Nov 1944; ADI(K) 139/45; Frank Olynyk, *USAAF (European Theater) Credits for the Destruction of Enemy Aircraft in Air-to-Air Combat World War II*, privately published, 1987, p. 163.

89. Hess, *Hell in the Heavens*, p. 123; Reschke, *Jagdgeschwader 301/302 "Wilde Sau,"* p. 150.

90. Girbig, *Start im Morgengrauen*, p. 44.

91. Freeman, *Mighty Eighth War Diary*, p. 386; Hermann Buchner, Flugbuch; Foreman and Harvey, *Me 262 Combat Diary*, p. 69; Prien and Rodeike, *JG 1 und JG 11*, Band 3: *1944–1945*, p. 1329.

92. Eighth Air Force Mission Folder, 27 Nov 1944; Girbig, *Start im Morgengrauen*, p. 51.

93. Eighth Air Force Mission Folder, 30 Nov 1944; Dahl, *Rammjäger*, p. 154.

94. Lorant and Goyat, *Bataille dans le ciel d'Allemagne*, Tome 2, p. 103; Dahl, *Rammjäger*, p. 227.

95. "GAF Tactics vs. the 8th AF 2 Dec 1944," USSTAF document in private archive; Prien and Rodeike, *JG 1 und JG 11*, Band 3, p. 1335; Mombeek, *Sturmjäger*, Band 2, p. 89; Reschke, *Jagdgeschwader 301/302 "Wilde Sau,"* p. 160.

96. Eighth Air Force Mission Folder, 5 Dec 1944; Prien and Rodeke, *JG 1 und JG 11*, Band 3, *1944–1945*, p. 1336.

97. Willi Andiel, personal communication with D. Caldwell, 2000.

98. Middlebrook and Everitt, *Bomber Command War Diaries*, p. 628.

99. J. Richard Smith and Eddie Creek, *Me 262*, Vol. 3, Classic Publications, Crowborough, UK, 2000, p. 516.

100. Prien and Stemmer, *Stab u. I./JG 3*, p. 450.

101. Middlebrook and Everitt, *Bomber Command War Diaries*, p. 630; ADI(K) 169/45.

102. John Weal, *Luftwaffe Sturmgruppen*, Osprey, Oxford, UK, 2005, p. 104; Prien, *IV./JG 3*, p. 257.

103. Danny Parker, *To Win the Winter Sky*, Combined Books, Conshohocken, PA, 1994, p. 138.

104. Girbig, "*. . . mit Kurs auf Leuna*," p. 159; Gordon Gollob, personal communication with A. Price, 1976; Punka, *Hungarian Aces of World War II*, p. 59.

105. Steve Blake, "14th Fighter Group Mission 17 December 1944," *Lightning Strikes 13* (1), 2000, p. 7; 461st Bomb Group Mission Report, 17 Dec 44; O. Hommert, "Face to Face at 17,000 Feet," *The 461st Liberaider*, 17 (1), 2000, p. 1.

106. Ernst Schröder, personal communication with D. Caldwell, 2000.

107. Caldwell, *The JG 26 War Diary*, Vol. 2, *1943–1945*, p. 391.

108. Craven and Cate, *Army Air Forces in World War II*, Vol. III, *Europe: Argument to V-E Day*, p. 690; Prien, *IV./JG 3*, p. 267.

109. Boiten and Bowman, *Battles with the Luftwaffe*, p. 184.

110. Girbig, *Start im Morgengrauen*, p. 99.

111. Girbig, *Start im Morgengrauen*, p. 112.

112. Girbig, *Start im Morgengrauen*, p. 132.

113. USSBS, German Order of Battle.

114. Caldwell, *JG 26: Top Guns of the Luftwaffe*, p. 322; Girbig, *Start im Morgengrauen*, p. 139.

Chapter 9: The Final Desperate Expedients (pages 262–293)

1. Caldwell, *The JG 26 War Diary*, Vol. 2, *1943–1945*, p. 403.

2. **Koller, Karl (1898–1951)**. The Luftwaffe's last Chief of Staff. Koller volunteered for service in the Bavarian Army at the start of World War I, and served as a pilot on the Western Front after learning to fly. Koller joined the Bavarian State Police in 1920 and did not reenter the armed forces until 1936, when he joined the Luftwaffe as a major. His entire Luftwaffe career was spent as a staff officer, most notably under Sperrle at Luftflotte 3. He was promoted from head of the Luftwaffe Operations Staff to Chief of Staff when Kreipe was sacked by Hitler in November 1944. Like Kreipe, Koller was totally disgusted with his superior Göring, but he managed to keep his by now meaningless post until war's end. His last rank was General der Flieger; his last official duty was to fly to Berchtesgaden to notify Göring of Hitler's decision to die in Berlin. Göring's carefully worded message to Hitler, inquiring whether this meant that Göring was to take over the government, was apparently suggested by Koller, but resulted in Göring's house arrest and the loss of all his titles.

3. Toliver and Constable, *Fighter General*, p. 274.

4. **Greim, Robert Ritter von (1892–1945)**. The last Commander-in-Chief of the Luftwaffe. An outstanding fighter pilot in World War I, during which he won the Pour le Mérite, Greim had a successful career in civil aviation before re-joining the German armed forces in 1934. He was named the first commander of the first fighter Staffel of the new Luftwaffe. During World War II he commanded Fliegerkorps V in the western campaign and during Operation Barbarossa, ultimately rising to command Luftflotte 6. He was a highly decorated and popular leader. Greim was the last general promoted to field marshal by Hitler. This took place in a bizarre Führerbunker ceremony in besieged Berlin, to which Greim had been summoned at great personal risk to be told that he was to replace Göring as Luftwaffe Commander-in-Chief. An ardent Nazi to the end, Greim committed suicide on May 24, 1945, while in American captivity.

5. Girbig, *Start im Morgengrauen*, p. 257.

6. Baker, *Adolf Galland*, p. 281.

7. Eighth Air Force Mission Folder, 1 Jan 1945; Walter Thom, *The Brotherhood of Courage: The History of the 305th Bombardment Group (H) in World War II*, privately published, 1986, p. 209; Reschke, *Jagdgeschwader 301/302 "Wilde Sau,"* p. 171.

8. *ULTRA—Main Series of Signals Conveying Intelligence to Allied Commands*, BT 1020. BT 1520, BT 1884, BT 1989.

9. Anon., *ULTRA and the History of the USSAFE versus the German Air Force*, University Publications, Frederick, MD, 1980, p. 175.

10. Eighth Air Force Mission Folder, 14 Jan 1945; Caldwell, *The JG 26 War Diary*, Vol. 2, *1939–1945*, p. 419.

11. Reschke, *Jagdgeschwader 301/302 "Wilde Sau,"* p. 183.

12. Girbig, *Start im Morgengrauen*, p. 284; Merle Olmsted, *The 357th over Europe: The 357th Fighter Group in World War II*, Phalanx Publishing, St. Paul, MN, 1994, p. 101.

13. Heinz-Günter Kuring, personal communication with D. Caldwell, 2000. Several B-17 units are known to have experimented in 1945 with fixed rear-firing rocket launchers to counter Me 262 attacks. Details of their use on this mission are unknown.

14. Girbig, *Start im Morgengrauen*, p. 244.

15. Arthur Fiedler, personal communications with D. Caldwell, 2000–3; Reschke, *Jagdgeschwader 301/302 "Wilde Sau,"* p. 189; Robert Forsyth, *Jagdwaffe: Defending the Reich 1944–1945*, Ian Allan, Surrey, UK, 2005, p. 264.

16. Gordon Gollob, "Kritische Anmerkungen u. Ergänzungen z. Buch 'In Letzter Stunde'," *Jägerblatt*, n.d. (via R. Forsyth); Smith & Creek, *Me 262*, Vol. 3, p. 532.

17. Smith and Creek, *Me 262*, Vol. 3, p. 533.

18. Gordon Gollob, minutes of 30 Jan 1945 GdJ. conference (via R. Forsyth).

19. Baker, *Adolf Galland*, p. 281.

20. Eighth Air Force Mission Folder, 3 Feb 1945; Walt Brown, "Back to Berlin," *Eighth Air Force News*, September 2000.

21. Smith and Creek, *Me 262*, Vol. 3, p. 542.

22. Der Chef der Luftwaffenführungsstabes Nr. 3209/44 g. Kdos. Ia/Flieg (T), 10 July 1944, NARA T971/13/750.

23. Figures in Vajda and Dancey, *German Aircraft Industry and Production, 1933–1945*, p. 136, Tables 8-F and 8-G.; also Herhudt von Rohden, "The Battle for Air Supremacy over Germany," p. 89.

24. Alfred C. Mierzejewski, *The Collapse of the German War Economy 1944–1945: Allied Air Power and the German National Railway*, University of North Carolina Press, Chapel Hill, NC, 1988, pp. 182–7.

25. Grabmann, "German Air Defense, 1933–1945," p. 1468.

26. Grabmann, "German Air Defense, 1933–1945," p. 1437.

27. Boog, *Luftwaffenführung*, 326ff; Grabmann, "German Air Defense, 1933–1945," p. 1289.

28. Manfred Boehme, *JG 7: The World's First Jet Fighter Unit 1944/1945*, Schiffer Military History, Atglen, PA, 1992, pp. 180–90.

29. Rieckhoff, *Trumpf oder Bluff?*, p. 196.

30. Herhudt von Rohden, "The Battle for Air Supremacy over Germany," pp. 63, 90.

31. In assessing the decline in German aircraft manufacturing standards, contemporary documents and photographs tell only part of the story. Examining the actual artifacts can also be very revealing. One of the authors spent a year at the National Air and Space Museum as a research fellow in the 1980s and was able to examine the many captured German late war aircraft in the collection. The decline in manufacturing standards was strikingly evident. The Fw 190D currently displayed at the U.S. Air Force Museum has a wooden propeller.

32. Williamson Murray, "Reflections on the Combined Bomber Offensive," *Militärgeschichtliche Mitteilungen*, 51, (Heft 1, 1992), p. 79 n. 22.

33. Grabmann, "German Air Defense, 1933–1945," pp. 1457ff.

34. The best account of this effort is David K. Yelton, *Hitler's Volkssturm: The Nazi Militia and the Defeat of Germany, 1944–1945*, University Press of Kansas, Lawrence, KS, 2002.

35. Yelton, *Hitler's Volkssturm*, p. 110.

36. Ulrich Albrecht, "Military Technology and National Socialist Ideology," in Monika Renneberg and Mark Walker, eds., *Science, Technology and National Socialism*, Cambridge University Press, Cambridge, UK, 1994, p. 109.

37. Albrecht, "Military Technology and National Socialist Ideology," p. 106.

38. Galland, *The First and the Last*, p. 348.
39. Grabmann, "German Air Defense, 1933–1945," pp. 1464–6.
40. Antony L. Kay & J. R. Smith, *German Aircraft of the Second World War*, Naval Institute Press, Annapolis, MD, 2002, pp. 298–304.
41. Eighth Air Force Mission Folder, 9 Feb 1945; RLM Ic-Reich Tagesmeldungen Feb–Mar 45, BA-MA RL II 2/388; Foreman and Harvey, *Me 262 Combat Diary*, p. 95; Manfred Griehl and Steve Blake, "Bomber Pilots in Jet Fighters," *Airfoil*, 4, 1986, p. 27.
42. Eighth Air Force Mission Folder, 14 Feb 1945; RLM Ic-Reich Tagesmeldungen Feb–Mar 45; Strong, *First over Germany*, p. 306.
43. Smith and Creek, *Me 262*, Vol. 2, p. 442.
44. Griehl and Blake, "Bomber Pilots in Jet Fighters," p. 28.
45. RLM Ic-Reich Tagesmeldungen Feb–Mar 45.
46. Adolf Galland, interview with D. Caldwell, 1991; Baker, *Adolf Galland*, p. 283; Robert Forsyth, *JV 44: The Galland Circus*, Classic Publications, West Sussex, UK, 1996, p. 131.
47. RLM Ic-Reich Tagesmeldungen Feb–Mar 45; William Hess, *German Jets vs. the U.S. Army Air Force*, Specialty Press, North Branch, MN, 1996, p. 78; Smith and Creek, *Me 262*, Vol. 3, p. 588.
48. Günther Rall, personal communication with D. Caldwell, 2001.
49. Peter Kassak, *An Ordinary Day in 1945*, Stratus, Sandomierz, Poland, 2005, *passim*; Eighth Air Force Mission Folder, 2 Mar 1945; Girbig, *Start im Morgengrauen*, p. 266; RLM Ic-Reich Tagesmeldungen Feb–Mar 45.
50. Eighth Air Force Mission Folder, 3 Mar 1945; RLM Ic-Reich Tagesmeldungen Feb–Mar 45; Hermann Buchner, Flugbuch; Rudolf Sinner, Flugbuch.
51. Ultra, BT-7304; RLM Ic-Reich Tagesmeldungen Feb–Mar 45; Rudolf Sinner, Flugbuch; Freeman, *Mighty Eighth War Diary*, p. 457.
52. David Brown, personal archives.
53. Hess, *German Jets vs. the USAAF*, p. 88.
54. RLM Ic-Reich Tagesmeldungen Feb–Mar 45.
55. Eighth Air Force Mission Folder, 18 Mar 1945; Smith and Creek, *Me 262*, Vol. 3, p. 616.
56. Gerhard Bracke, *Gegen vielfache Übermacht*, Motorbuch Verlag, Stuttgart, Germany, 1977, p. 194; Erich Rudorffer, Flugbuch.
57. RLM Ic-Reich Tagesmeldungen Feb–Mar 45.
58. RLM Ic-Reich Tagesmeldungen Feb–Mar 45; Hess, *German Jets vs. the USAAF*, p. 95.
59. Price, *Last Year of the Luftwaffe*, p. 137.
60. Freeman, *Mighty Eighth War Diary*, p. 469.
61. Eighth Air Force Mission Folder, 22 Mar 1945; Hess, *German Jets vs. the USAAF*, p. 95; D. G. Stern, *The 483rd Bomb Group (H)*, Turner Publishing, Paducah, KY, 1994, p. 28.
62. RLM Ic-Reich Tagesmeldungen Feb–Mar 45; Middlebrook and Everitt, *Bomber Command War Diaries*, p. 686.
63. W. Bethke and F. Henning, *Jagdgeschwader 300 Wilde Sau*, Teil II, Struve-Druck, Eutin, Germany, 2000, p. 537.
64. Hess, *German Jets vs. the USAAF*, p. 95; Stern, *The 483rd Bomb Group (H)*, p. 28.
65. Foreman and Harvey, *Me 262 Combat Diary*, p. 130.
66. Freeman, *Mighty Eighth War Diary*, p. 474; Hess, *German Jets vs. the USAAF*, p. 95.
67. Smith and Creek, *Me 262*, Vol. 3, p. 632; Prien and Rodeike, *Jagdgeschwader 1 und 11*, Teil 3, p. 1568.
68. Foreman and Harvey, *Me 262 Combat Diary*, p. 134; Hess, *German Jets vs. the USAAF*, p. 95.
69. Foreman and Harvey, *Me 262 Combat Diary*, p. 140; Middlebrook and Everitt, *Bomber Command War Diaries*, p. 690.
70. Kenneth Blyth, *Cradle Crew*, Sunflower University Press, Manhattan, KS, 1997, p. 129; Kenneth Blyth, *Who Shot Down EQ-Queenie*, Fenestra Books, Tucson, AZ, 2004, p. 101.
71. O. Jirovec, "31 Mar 45 combat data – 31st FG vs. KG(J) 6," personal archives.
72. "RLM GenQu 6 statistics on RLV reaction to Anglo-American bomb raids," ADI(K) Science Memo 2 (via S. Coates).
73. Forsyth, *JV 44*, p. 135; J. Richard Smith and Eddie Creek, *Me 262*, Vol. 4, Classic Publications, Crowborough, UK, 2000, p. 682; Rudorffer, Flugbuch.
74. Gollob, "Kritische Anmerkungen . . ."
75. Ultra, KO-432; Held, *Reichsverteidigung—Die deutsche Tagjagd 1943–1945*, p. 167.
76. Andrews and Adams, *Mighty Eighth Combat Chronology*, p. 315; James Hoseason, *The 1,000 Day Battle*, Gillingham Publications, Lowestoft, UK, 1979, p. 231; Griehl and Blake, "Bomber Pilots in Jet Fighters," p. 28; ADI(K) Science Memo 2.
77. Andrews and Adams, p. 316; Hess, *German Jets vs. the USAAF*, p. 126; Smith and Creek, *Me 262*, Vol. 4, p. 684; Ultra, BT-9640.
78. Herrmann, *Eagle's Wings*, p. 253.
79. Arno Rose, *Radikaler Luftkampf*, Motorbuch Verlag, Stuttgart, Germany, 1977, p. 147; Adrian Weir, *The Last Flight of the Luftwaffe: The Fate of Schulungslehrgang Elbe, 7 April 1945*, Arms & Armour Press, London, 1997, p. 50.
80. Arno Rose, personal communication with D. Caldwell, 2002.
81. Klaus Hahn, personal communication with D. Caldwell, 2000.
82. Eighth Air Force Mission Folder, 7 Apr 1945; Rose, *Radikaler Luftkampf*, p. 285.
83. OKL Kriegstagebuch, NARA microfilm series T-321, roll 10.
84. Fritz Marktscheffel, personal communications with D. Caldwell, 1999–2005.
85. Rose, *Radikaler Luftkampf*, p. 268; ADI(K) Science Memo 2.
86. USSTAF, "GAF Tactics vs. 8th AF: 7 Apr 1945" (via G. Permann).
87. Eighth Air Force Mission Folder, 10 Apr 45; Hermann Buchner, *Stormbird*, Hikoki Publications, Aldershot, UK, 2000, p. 140; Foreman and Harvey, *Me 262 Combat Diary*, p. 134; ADI(K) Science Memo 2.
88. Ethell and Price, *The German Jets in Combat*, p. 134; Mano Ziegler, *Rocket Fighter: The Story of the Messerschmitt Me 163*, Arms & Armour Press, London, 1976, p. 148.
88. Schmid, "The GAF vs. the Allies in the West 1943–45: Command Structure," USAFHRA K113. 107-158-160 v. 5; Ultra, KO-1753.
90. "Truppengliederung Luftflotte Reich, Mitte April 1945," Anlage 13, USAFHRA 515. 619-2 vol. 2, 1945.
91. Air Ministry, *Rise and Fall of the German Air Force*, p. 397.
92. "Truppengliederung Luftflotte Reich, Mitte April 1945."
93. "Report on the assignments, activity and development of the Luftwaffenbefehlshaber Mitte," p. 15; Grabmann, "German Air Defense, 1933–1945," p. 1235.
94. Ultra, KO-928; "Flugzeugstärke der deutschen Luftwaffe Ende April/Anfang Mai 1945," USAFHRA K113. 312-2 v. 4.
95. Eighth Air Force Mission Folder, 19 Apr 1945; Charles Ailing, *A Mighty Fortress: Lead Bomber over Europe*, Casemate, Havertown, PA, 2002, p. 127.
96. ADI(K) Science Memo 2; Prien and Rodeike, *Jagdgeschwader 1 und 11*, Teil 3, p. 1586; Chris Thomas and Christopher Shores,

The Typhoon & Tempest Story, Arms & Armour Press, London, 1988, p. 134.

97. Smith and Creek, *Me 262*, Vol. 4, p. 735.

98. Forsyth, *JV 44*, p. 316.

99. Galland, "Birth, Life & Death of the Jagdwaffe," ADI(K) 373/45.

100. USSTAF, Fighter Operations, "Mistakes of the GAF," App. XXXVI.

101. Herhudt von Rohden, "The Battle for Air Supremacy over Germany," p. 77.

102. Murray, *Luftwaffe*, p. 232.

103. Murray, *German Military Effectiveness*, p. 79.

104. Rieckhoff, *Trumpf oder Bluff?*, p. 175.

105. Herhudt von Rohden, "The Battle for Air Supremacy over Germany," pp. 90–1.

106. Herhudt von Rohden, "The Battle for Air Supremacy over Germany," pp. 76.

107. Wehrpass, Lt Emil Hofmann, in authors' possession.

108. United States Strategic Bombing Survey, "The Defeat of the German Air Force" (Military Analysis Division, January 1947), pp. 3–7.

109. USSBS, "The Defeat of the German Air Force," p. 31; USSBS, German Order of Battle.

110. USSBS, "Overall Report (European Air War)," p. 39.

111. USSBS, "The Defeat of the German Air Force," p. 5.

112. Grabmann, "German Air Defense, 1933–1945," p. 1284.

113. Mark K. Wells, *Courage and Air Warfare: The Allied Aircrew Experience in the Second Word War*, Frank Cass, London, 1995, pp. 101–2.

114. Jörg Friedrich, *Der Brand: Deutschland im Bombenkrieg 1940–1945*, Propyläen, Munich, Germany, 2002, pp. 121–2.

115. Ernst Schröder, personal communication with D. Caldwell, 2004.

APPENDICES

TABLE OF EQUIVALENT RANKS
Luftwaffe – United States Army Air Force – Royal Air Force

Luftwaffe Title	Luftwaffe Abbr.	USAAF Title	USAAF Abbr.	RAF Title	RAF Abbr.
COMMISSIONED OFFICERS					
Reichsmarschall	RM.	—	—	—	—
Generalfeldmarschall	GFM.	General (5 star)	Gen.	Marshal of the RAF	
Generaloberst	Genobst.	General (4 star)	Gen.	Air Chief Marshal	ACM.
General der Flieger	Gen. der Flg.	Lieutenant General	LGen.	Air Marshal	AM.
Generalleutnant	Genlt.	Major General	MGen.	Air Vice Marshal	AVM.
Generalmajor	Genmaj.	Brigadier General	BGen.	Air Commodore	Air Cdre.
Oberst	Obst.	Colonel	Col.	Group Captain	Gp. Capt.
Oberstleutnant	Obstlt.	Lieutenant Colonel	LCol.	Wing Commander	Wing Cdr.
Major	Maj.	Major	Maj.	Squadron Leader	Sqd. Ldr.
Hauptmann	Hptm.	Captain	Capt.	Flight Lieutenant	Flt. Lt.
Oberleutnant	Oblt.	First Lieutenant	1st Lt.	Flying Officer	Flg. Off.
Leutnant	Lt.	Second Lieutenant	2nd Lt.	Pilot Officer	Plt. Off.
WARRANT OFFICERS					
Stabsfeldwebel	Stabsfw.	Flight Officer	Flt. Off.	Warrant Officer	Wt. Off.
Oberfähnrich	Ofhr. [sr. ofc. candidate]	—	—	—	—
NON-COMMISSIONED OFFICERS					
Oberfeldwebel	Obfw.	Master Sergeant	MSgt.	Flight Sergeant	Flt. Sgt.
Fähnrich	Fhr. [officer candidate]	—	—	—	—
Fahnenjunker	Fhj. [officer candidate]	—	—	—	—
Feldwebel	Fw.	Technical Sergeant	TSgt.	Sergeant	Sgt.
Unterfeldwebel	Ufw.	Sergeant	Sgt.	—	—
Unteroffizier	Uffz.	Corporal	Cpl.	Corporal	Cpl.
ENLISTED MEN					
Hauptgefreiter	Hptgfr.	—	—	—	
Obergefreiter	Ogfr.	—	—	Leading Aircraftsman	LAC.
Gefreiter	Gefr.	Private 1st Class	PFC.	Aircraftsman 1stCl.	AC.
Flieger	Flg.	Private	Pvt.	Aircraftsman 2ndCl.	AC.

DAY-FIGHTER ORDER OF BATTLE
Luftwaffenbefehlshaber Mitte, March 9, 1943[1]

Command/Unit		Commander[2]	Command Post/Airfield	Type	Strength: Actual (Eff.)
Luftwaffenbefehlshaber Mitte		Weise	Berlin-Dahlem		
XII. Fliegerkorps		Kammhuber	Zeist		
Jagddivision 1		von Döring	Deelen		
	Jafü Holland-Ruhrgebiet	Grabmann	Deelen		
	Stab JG 1	Mix	Schiphol	Fw 190	2 (1)
	II./JG 1	Kijewski	Woensdrecht + Schiphol	Fw 190	35 (29)
	IV./JG 1	Losigkeit	München-Gladbach	Fw 190	30 (20)
Jagddivision 2		Schwabedissen	Stade		
	Jafü Deutsche Bucht	Hentschel	Stade		
	I./JG 1	Beise	Jever	Bf 109	37 (28)
	III./JG 1	Leesmann	Husum	Fw 190	43 (31)
Jagddivision 3		Junck	Metz		
Jagddivision 4		Huth	Döberitz		
	Jafü Mitte	Frommherz	Döberitz		
	III./JG 54	Seiler	Oldenburg	Bf 109	in transit
	Jafü Süddeutschland	von Bülow	Schleissheim		
	elements from 4 training schools	?	various	Bf 109	? (?)
	Industrie-Staffel Messerschmitt	?	Regensburg/Obertraubling	Bf 109	? (?)

Jagddivisionen 1, 2, 3, and 4 were subordinated to XII. Fliegerkorps.

Twin-engine fighters from NJG 1, 3, 4 and 5 were available for use against unescorted daylight bomber formations.

Total day-fighter strength (excluding training and Industrie-Staffeln): 147 (109)

DAY-FIGHTER ORDER OF BATTLE
Luftwaffenbefehlshaber Mitte, December 31, 1943[3]

Command/Unit	Commander	Command Post/Airfield	Type	Strength: Actual (Eff.)
Luftwaffenbefehlshaber Mitte	Weise	Berlin-Dahlem		
I. Jagdkorps	Schmid	Zeist		
Jagddivision 1	Lützow	Döberitz		
III./JG 54	Schnell	Ludwigslust	Fw 190	16 (14)
Ind-St. Erla	Laube	Leipzig-Mockau	Bf 109	8 (7)
Jafü Schlesien	*Witt*	*Kosel*		
Jagddivision 2	Ibel	Stade		
Stab/JG 11	Graf	Jever	Bf 109	6 (2)
I./JG 11	Hermichen	Husum	Fw 190	19 (11)
II./JG 11	Specht	Wunstorf	Bf 109	35 (30)
III./JG 11	Hackl	Oldenburg	Bf 109	34 (21)
11./JG 11	Christmann	Heligoland	Bf 109T	22 (9)
II./JG 3	Sannemann	Rotenburg	Bf 109	10 (0)
Stab/ZG 26	Boehm-Tettelbach	Achmer	Bf 110	2 (1)
I./ZG 26	?	Wunstorf	Bf 110	24 (20)
II./ZG 26	Tratt	Hesepe	Me 410	17 (14)
III./ZG 26	Schulze-Dickow	Achmer	Bf 110	17 (11)
ErprKdo 163	Späte	Bad Zwischenahn	Me 163	0 (0)
(20./JG 1)				
Jafü Dänemark	*Müller-Rienzburg*	*Grove*		
10./JG 11	Sahnwaldt	Aalborg + Lister	Fw 190	11 (8)
Jagddivision 3	Grabmann	Deelen		
Stab/JG 1	Oesau	Deelen	Fw 190	4 (1)
I./JG 1	Schnoor	Dortmund-Brakel	Fw 190	29 (27)
II./JG 1	Hoeckner	Rheine	Fw 190	18 (14)
III./JG 1	Eberle	Volkel	Bf 109	42 (36)
Sturmstaffel 1	von Kornatzki	Dortmund	Fw 190	14 (11)
III./JG 26	Mietusch	München-Gladbach	Bf 109	26 (18)
IV./JG 3	Beyer	Volkel	Bf 109	4 (0)
Jagddivision 7	Huth	Schleissheim		
Stab/JG 3	Wilcke	Neubiberg	Bf 109	4 (2)
III./JG 3	Dahl	Wörishofen	Bf 109	42 (35)
Stab/JG zbV	?	Biblis	Bf 109	0 (0)
II./JG 27	Schroer	Wiesbaden	Bf 109	22 (12)
JG 104 (Einst.)	A. Müller	Fürth	Bf 109	? (?)
Stab/ZG 76	Rossiwall	Ansbach	Bf 110	3 (1)
I./ZG 76	Kaminski	Ansbach	Bf 110	31 (18)
II./ZG 76	Kiel	Neubiberg	Bf 110	43 (28)
III./ZG 76 (-9. St)	Kiel	Öttingen	Bf 110	19 (11)
Jafü Ostmark	*Handrick*	*Wien*		
I./JG 27	Franzisket	Fels-am-Wagram	Bf 109	49 (40)
II./JG 53	Michalski	Wien-Seyring	Bf 109	45 (39)
II./ZG 1	Albrecht	Wels	Bf 110	40 (35)
JG 108 (Einst.)	K. Müller	Bad Vöslau	Bf 109	? (?)

Jagddivisionen 1, 2, & 3 were subordinated to I. Jagdkorps.

Jagddivision 7 reported directly to Luftwaffenbefehlshaber Mitte.

Total day-fighter strength:[4] single-engine: 460 (337)

twin-engine: 196 (139)

DAY-FIGHTER ORDER OF BATTLE
Luftflotte Reich, May 24, 1944[5]

Command/Unit	Commander	Command Post/Airfield	Type	Strength: Actual(Eff.)
Luftflotte Reich	Stumpff	Berlin-Wannsee		
I. Jagdkorps	Schmid	Treuenbrietzen		
Jagddivision 1	Herrmann	Döberitz		
Stab/JG 3	Müller	Salzwedel	Bf 109	6 (4)
I.(Höhen)/JG 3	Mertens	Burg	Bf 109	34 (17)
II./JG 3	Frielinghaus	Sachau	Bf 109	31 (20)
IV.(Sturm)/JG 3	Moritz	Salzwedel	Fw 190	39 (10)
II./JG 5	Weissenberger	Gardelegen	Bf 109	21 (18)
Stab/ZG 26	Boehm-Tettelbach	Königsberg/Neumark	Me 410	5 (0)
I./ZG 26	?	Königsberg/Neumark	Me 410	39 (12)
II./ZG 26	?	Königsberg/Neumark	Me 410	31 (23)
2./JG 400	?	Oranienburg	Me 163	0 (0)
Jafü Ostpreussen	Nordmann	Insterburg		
Jafü Schlesien	Witt	Kosel		
Jagddivision 2	Ibel	Stade		
Stab/JG 11	Specht	Rotenburg	Bf 109, Fw 190	3 (1)
I./JG 11	Koenig	Rotenburg	Fw 190	24 (14)
II.(Höhen)/JG 11	Krupinski	Hustedt	Bf 109	24 (13)
III./JG 11	Hackl	Reinsehlen	Bf 109	27 (19)
1./JG 400	Olejnik	Wittmundhafen	Me 163	8 (2)
Jägerabschnittsführer Dänemark	Bongartz	Grove		
10./JG 11	Grosser	Aalborg	Fw 190, Bf 109	10 (10)
Jagddivision 3	Grabmann	Deelen		
Stab/JG 1	Ihlefeld	Lippspringe	Fw 190	0 (0)
I./JG 1	Ehlers	Lippspringe	Fw 190	28 (11)
II./JG 1	Eder	Störmede	Fw 190	27 (16)
III.(Höhen)/JG 1	Grasser	Paderborn	Bf 109	48 (21)
Jägerabschnittsführer Mittelrhein	Trübenbach	Darmstadt		
JG 102 (Einst.)	Roth	Lachen-Speyersdorf	Bf 109	? (?)
JG 106 (Einst.)	Strümpell	Lachen-Speyersdorf	Bf 109	? (?)
Jagddivision 7	Huth	Schleissheim		
Stab/JG zbV	Dahl	Ansbach	Bf 109	0 (0)
III./JG 3	Langer	Ansbach	Bf 109	38 (20)
II./JG 27	Keller	Herzogenaurach	Bf 109	33 (14)
I.(Höhen)/JG 5	Carganico	Herzogenaurach	Bf 109	18 (12)
III./JG 54	Schroer	Unterschlauersbach	Fw 190	24 (11)
II./JG 53	Meimberg	Öttingen	Bf 109	34 (15)
JG 104 (Einst.)		Fürth	Bf 109	
Jafü Ostmark	Handrick	Wien-Cobenzl		
Stab/JG 27	Rödel	Seyring	Bf 109	8 (4)
I./JG 27	Redlich	Fels-am-Wagram	Bf 109	38 (21)
III./JG 27 (-7. St)	Düllberg	Götzendorf	Bf 109	35 (24)
IV./JG 27	Meyer	Lucko	Bf 109	? (?)
II./JG 51	Rammelt	Zirkle	Bf 109	42 (20)
7./ZG 26	?	Fels-am-Wagram	Bf 110	? (?)
II./ZG 1	Albrecht	Wels	Bf 110	51 (18)
JG 108 (Einst.)	K. Müller	Bad Voslau	Bf 109	? (?)
SG 152 (Einst.)	Kennel	Prossnitz	Fw 190	? (?)
Jägerabschnittsführer Ungarn	Neumann	Budapest		
1/1st Wing (Hung.)	?	Szolnok	Bf 109	? (?)
3/1st Wing (Hung.)	?	Ferihegy	Bf 109	? (?)
2/2nd Wing (Hung.)	?	Klausenburg	Bf 109	? (?)

Total day-fighter strength:[6] single-engine: 592 (315)
twin-engine: 126 (53)
Me 163: 8 (2)

DAY-FIGHTER ORDER OF BATTLE

Luftflotte Reich, June 10, 1944[7]

Command/Unit	Commander	Command Post/Airfield	Type	Strength: Actual (Eff.)
Luftflotte Reich	Stumpff	Berlin-Wannsee		
I. Jagdkorps	Schmid	Treuenbrietzen		
Jagddivision 1	Herrmann	Döberitz		
III./JG 300	Ilk	Jüterbog	Bf 109	46 (21)
Stab/ZG 26	Kogler	Königsberg/Neumark	Me 410	2 (1)
I./ZG 26	?	Königsberg/Neumark	Me 410	33 (9)
II.//ZG 26	?	Königsberg/Neumark	Me 410	39 (30)
Jafü Schlesien	*Witt*	*Kosel*		
Jagddivision 2	Ibel	Stade		
Jägerabschnittsführer Dänemark	*Schalk*	*Grove*		
Jagddivision 3	Grabmann	Deelen		
Jägerabschnittsführer Mittelrhein	*Trübenbach*	*Darmstadt*		
Stab/JG 300	Dahl	Rhein/Main	Fw 190	? (?)
I./JG 300	Stamp	Herzhausen	Bf 109	48 (26)
II./JG 300	Peters	Rhein/Main	Fw 190	46 (14)
JG 102 (Einst.)	Roth	Lachen-Speyerdorf	Bf 109	? (?)
JG 106 (Einst.)	Strümpell	Lachen-Speyerdorf	Bf 109	? (?)
Jagddivision 7	Huth	Schleissheim		
JG 104 (Einst.)	?	Fürth	Bf 109	? (?)
Jafü Ostmark	*Handrick*	*Wien-Cobenzl*		
I./JG 302	Lewens	Götzendorf	Bf 109	39 (23)
II./ZG 1	Albrecht	Wels	Bf 110	31 (15)
Stab/ZG 76	Kowalewski	Seyring	Me 410	3 (2)
I./ZG 76	?	Seyring	Me 410	47 (15)
7./ZG 76	?	Seyring	Me 410	3 (2)
JG 108 (Einst.)	K. Müller	Bad Voslau	Bf 109	? (?)
Jägerabschnittsführer Ungarn	*Neumann*	*Budapest*		
JGr 101 (Hung.)	Heppes	Veszprém	Bf 109	? (?)

Total day-fighter strength:[8] single-engine: 179 (84)
                              twin-engine: 158 (74)

DAY-FIGHTER ORDER OF BATTLE

Luftflotte Reich, September 5, 1944[9]

Command/Unit		Commander	Command Post/Airfield	Type	Strength: Actual (Eff.)
Luftflotte Reich		Stumpff	Berlin-Wannsee		
I. Jagdkorps		Schmid	Treuenbrietzen		
Jagddivision 1		Kleinrath	Döberitz		
	Stab/JG 4	Michalski	Jüterbog	Bf 109	0 (0)
	II.(Sturm)/JG 4	Kornatzki	Welzow	Fw 190	? (?)
	III./JG 4	Eberle	Alteno	Bf 109	68 (58)
	Stabsstaffel/JG 3	Bär	Königsberg	Bf 109	12 (5)
	I./JG 3	Laube	Borkheide	Bf 109	18 (14)
	II./JG 5	Wienhausen	Reinsdorf	Bf 109	24 (9)
	III./JG 300	Ilk	Jüterbog	Bf 109	20 (18)
	Stab/JG 11	Specht	Finsterwalde	Bf 109	8 (5)
	II./JG 27	Keller	Finsterwalde	Bf 109	45 (23)
	III./JG 53	Schnell	Mörtitz	Bf 109	52 (36)
	I./JG 76	Offterdinger	Gahro	Bf 109	62 (50)
	I./JG 302	Fulda	Schafstädt	Fw 190	25 (13)
	Stab/JG 300	Dahl	Erfurt-Bin5dersleben	Bf 109	5 (3)
	I./JG 300	Stamp	Esperstedt	Bf 109	30 (23)
	II.(Sturm)/JG 300	Lindenberger	Erfurt-Bindersleben	Fw 190	48 (35)
	IV.(Sturm)/JG 3	Moritz	Alperstedt	Fw 190	57 (33)
	JGr 10	Chrristl	Parchim +	Bf 109	17 (14)
			Erfurt-Bindersleben		
	I./JG 400	Olejnik	Brandis	Me 163	12 (7)
	Jafü Schlesien	*Witt*	*Kosel*		
	Jafü Ostpreussen	*Nordmann*	*Königsberg/Seewiesen*		
	II./ZG 76	?	Seerappen	Me 410	70 (43)
Jagddivision 2		Ibel	Stade		
	Jägerabschnittsführer Dänemark	*Schalk*	*Grove*		
Jagddivision 3		Grabmann	Deelen		
	4./JGr 10	?	Rheine	Fw 190	? (?)
	Jägerabschnittsführer Mittelrhein	*Trübenbach*	*Darmstadt*		
Jagddivision 7		Huth	Schleissheim		
Jagddivision 8		Handrick	Wien-Cobenzl		

Total day-fighter strength:[10] single-engine: 491 (339)

twin-engine: 70 (43)

Me 163: 12 (7)

DAY-FIGHTER ORDER OF BATTLE

Luftflotte Reich, November 28, 1944[11]

Command/Unit		Commander	Command Post/Airfield	Type	Strength:Actual (Eff.)
Luftflotte Reich		Stumpff	Berlin-Weilburg-am-Lahn		
I. Jagdkorps		Huth	Treuenbrietzen		
Jagddivision 1		Kleinrath	Döberitz		
	Stab/JG 1	Ihlefeld	Greifswald	Fw 190	3 (0)
	I./JG 1	Ehlers	Greifswald	Fw 190	30 (26)
	II./JG 1	Staiger	Tutow	Fw 190	44 (35)
	Stab/JG 300	Dahl	Jüterbog	Fw 190	6 (3)
	I./JG 300	?	Borkheide	Bf 109	46 (28)
	II.(Sturm)/JG 300	?	Löbnitz	Fw 190	44 (26)
	III./JG 300	Nölter	Jüterbog	Bf 109	29 (29)
	IV./JG 300	Puchinger	Reinsdorf	Bf 109	51 (38)
	II./ZG 76	Kaminski	Reinsdorf	Me 410	57 (37)
	Stab/JG 301	Aufhammer	Stendal	Fw 190	4 (?)
	I./JG 301	?	Salzwedel	Fw 190	23 (23)
	II./JG 301	?	Sachau	Fw 190	36 (19)
	III./JG 301	Dietsche	Stendal	Fw 190	51 (40)
	JGr 10	Christl	Redlin + Damm	Bf 109	? (?)
	I./JG 400	Fulda	Brandis	Me 163	37 (9)
	Jafü Schlesien	*Krumm*	*Kosel*		
Jagddivision 2		Ibel	Stade		
	Jägerabschnittsführer Dänemark	*Schalk*	*Grove*		
Jagddivision 3		Grabmann	Wiedenbrück		
	Stab./JG 3	Bär	Störmede	Fw 190	4 (3)
	I./JG 3	Wirges	Werl	Bf 109	66 (32)
	III./JG 3	Langer	Schachten	Bf 109	80 (56)
	IV.(Sturm)/JG 3	Moritz	Stormede	Fw 190	66 (44)
	Stab/JG 27	Rödel	Hopsten	Bf 109	4 (0)
	I./JG 27	v. Eichel-Streiber	Rheine	Bf 109	49 (27)
	II./JG 27	Keller	Hopsten	Bf 109	42 (25)
	III./JG 27	Düllberg	Hesepe	Bf 109	45 (19)
	IV./JG 27	Dudeck	Achmer	Bf 109	55 (34)
	IV./JG 54	Klemm	Vörden	Fw 190	54 (26)
	Jägerabschnittsführer Mittelrhein	*Trübenbach*	*Darmstadt*		
	Stab/JG 4	Michalski	Rhein-Main	Fw 190	1 (1)
	I./JG 4	Steinmann	Darmstadt	Bf 109	44 (28)
	II.(Sturm)/JG 4	Schröder	Mainz-Finthen	Fw 190	72 (54)
	III./JG 4	Eberle	Egelsbach	Bf 109	77 (26)
	IV./JG 4	Wienhausen	Rhein-Main	Bf 109	? (?)
Jagddivision 7		?	Pfaffenhofen-Inn		
Jagddivision 8		Handrick	Wien-Cobenzl		

Total day-fighter strength:[12]
single-engine: 1,026 (642)
twin-engine: 57 (37)
Me 163:   37 (9)

DAY-FIGHTER ORDER OF BATTLE
Luftflotte Reich, February 1, 1945[13]

Command/Unit		Commander	Command Post/Airfield	Type
Luftflotte Reich	Stumpff	Berlin		
IX. Fliegerkorps (Jagd)	Peltz	Treuenbrietzen		
Jagddivision 1		Wittmer	Ribeck	
	Stab/JG 7	Weissenberger	Brandenburg-Briest	Me 262
	I./JG 7	Rudorffer	Kaltenkirchen	Me 262
	III./JG 7	Sinner	Brandenburg-Briest	Me 262
	JGr 10	Christl	Parchim/Rechlin	Fw 190
	II./ZG 76	?	Grossenhain	Me 410
	Stab/JG 300	Hackl	Jüterbog	Fw 190
	I./JG 300	Baier	Borkheide	Bf 109
	II.(Sturm)/JG 300	Radener	Löbnitz	Fw 190
	III./JG 300	Jenne	Jüterbog	Bf 109
	IV./JG 300	Offterdinger	Wittstock	Bf 109
	IV./JG 54	Klemm	Sachau	Fw 190
	Stab/JG 301	Aufhammer	Welzow	Fw 190
	I./JG 301	Posselmann	Finsterwalde	Fw 190
	II./JG 301	Nölter	Welzow	Fw 190
	III./JG 301	Guth	Alteno	Ta 152
	II./JG 3	Baeker	Alperstedt	Bf 109
	Stab/JG 400	Späte	Brandis	Me 163
	I./JG 400	Fulda	Brandis	Me 163
	II./JG 400	Opitz	Brandis	Me 163
Jagddivision 2		Ibel	Stade	
Jagddivision 3		Grabmann	Wiedenbrück	
Jagddivision 7		Janke	Vienna	

Total day-fighter strength (estimated): single-engine: 300–400
Me 262 50–70
Me 163: 40–50

Notes to Orders of Battle

1. Walter Grabmann, "Geschichte der deutschen Luftverteidigung 1933–1945," Band III, 1 Jan 43–27 Jan 1944, USAFHRA K113. 106-164, Vol. 3, pp. 671–5; USSBS, German Order of Battle; "Zuteilung von flg. Verbanden zur Reichsverteidigung," USAFHRA K113. 312-2 v. 4 1943–1945.

2. Our list of combat unit commanders is based on an Internet file by Michael Holm.

3. Grabmann, "Geschichte der Luftverteidigung 1933–1945," Band III, pp. 726–8; USSBS, German Order of Battle; "Zuteilung von flg. Verbanden zur Reichsverteidigung."

4. Excluding training units.

5. Compiled from Grabmann, "Geschichte der Luftverteidigung, 1933–1945," Band IV, pp. 1054–7; Grabmann, "German Air Force Air Defense Operations," USAF Historical Study #164; Boog, *Das deutsche Reich in der Defensive*, pp. 268–9; Price, *Last Year of the Luftwaffe*, pp. 22–5, Wood and Gunston, *Hitler's Luftwaffe*, p. 101.

6. Excluding training units, IV./JG 27, 7./ZG 26, and Hungarian squadrons.

7. Compiled from Grabmann, "German Air Defense, 1933–1945," pp. 1239–41; USSBS, German Order of Battle, pp. 40–1, 68;

"Strength Figures on GAF," USAFHRA 519. 632-1, 1943–1944.

8. Excluding training and Hungarian units.

9. Compiled from Grabmann, "Geschichte der Luftverteidigung 1933–1945," Band IV, pp. 1157–9; USSBS, German Order of Battle, pp. 42–4.

10. Excluding II.(Sturm)/JG 4 and 4./JGr 10.

11. Compiled from Grabmann, "Geschichte der Luftverteidigung 1933–1945," Band IV, pp. 1171–3; USSBS, German Order of Battle, pp. 45–8; Georg Tessin, *Verbände und Truppen der deutschen Wehrmacht und Waffen-SS im Zweiten Weltkrieg 1939–1945*, 14. Band, *Die Landstreitkräfte: Namensverbände/Die Luftstreitkräfte (Fliegende Verbände)/Flakeinsatz im Reich 1943–1945*, Biblio-Verlag, Osnabrück, 1980; Ultra, HP-8296; BA-MA Kart 40/219 via Arno Abendroth.

12. Excluding IV./JG 4 and JGr 10.

13. Compiled from Grabmann, "German Air Defense, 1933–1945," pp. 1279–82; USSBS, German Order of Battle, pp. 45–9; Studiengruppe Geschichte des Luftkrieges Karlsruhe, "Der Einsatz der deutschen Luftwaffe gegen die Alliierten im Westen, 1943–1945," Band VII, USAFHRA K113. 106-160, pp. 376–8.

PUBLISHED SOURCES

Aders, Gebhard, *History of the German Night Fighter Force 1917–1945*, Jane's, London, 1979.

Aders, Gebhard, and Werner Held, *Jagdgeschwader 51 "Mölders,"* Motorbuch Verlag, Stuttgart, 1985.

Ailing, Charles, *A Mighty Fortress: Lead Bomber over Europe*, Casemate, Havertown, PA, 2002.

Air Ministry, *The Rise and Fall of the German Air Force: History of the Luftwaffe in World War II*, HMSO, London, 1948.

Andrews, Paul, and William Adams, *The Mighty Eighth Combat Chronology: Heavy Bomber and Fighter Activities 1942–1945*, Eighth Air Force Memorial Museum Foundation, Warrenton, VA, 1997.

Anonymous, *The Kassel Mission Reports: Highest Group Loss in Eighth Air Force History*, privately published, n.d.

Anonymous, *Kriegsflugzeuge: Ansprach, Erkennen, Bewaffnung usw.*, Dr. Spohr Verlag, Dresden, Germany, 1942.

Anonymous, *Defenders of Liberty: 2nd Bombardment Group/Wing 1918–1993*, Turner Publishing, Paducah, KY, 1996.

Anonymous, *ULTRA and the History of the USSAFE versus the German Air Force*, University Publications, Frederick, MD, 1980.

Anonymous, *ULTRA—Main Series of Signals Conveying Intelligence to Allied Commands*, Clearwater Publishing, New York, *c.* 1988 [104 microfilm rolls].

Anonymous, *The Flight of the Vulgar Vultures: 455th Bomb Group (H) 1943–1945*, privately published, 1991.

Arnold, H. H., *Global Mission*, Harper & Brothers, New York, 1949.

Bartov, Omer, *Hitler's Army: Soldiers, Nazis and War in the Third Reich*, Oxford University Press, Oxford, UK, 1991.

Bekker, Cajus, *The Luftwaffe War Diaries*, Doubleday, Garden City, NY, 1964.

von Below, Nicolaus, *At Hitler's Side: The Memoirs of Hitler's Luftwaffe Adjutant 1937–1945*, Greenhill, London, 2001.

Bergström, Christer, *Graf & Grislawski: A Pair of Aces*, Eagle Editions, Hamilton, MT, 2003.

Bethke, W., and F. Henning, *Jagdgeschwader 300 Wilde Sau*: Teil II, Struve-Druck, Eutin, Germany, 2000.

Biddle, Tami Davis, *Rhetoric and Reality in Air Warfare*, Princeton University Press, Princeton, NJ, 2002.

Blakebrough, Ken, *The Fireball Outfit: The 457th Bombardment Group in the Skies over Europe*, Aero Publishers, Fallbrook, CA, 1968.

Blue, Allen, *The Fortunes of War*, Aero Publishers, Fallbrook, CA, 1967.

Blyth, Kenneth, *Cradle Crew*, Sunflower University Press, Manhattan, KS, 1997.

Blyth, Kenneth, *Who Shot Down EQ-Queenie*, Fenestra Books, Tucson, AZ, 2004.

Boehme, Manfred, *JG 7: The World's First Jet Fighter Unit 1944/1945*, Schiffer Military History, Atglen, PA, 1992.

Bohnstedt, D. L., and B. J. Bohnstedt, *460th Bomb Group History*, Taylor Publishing, Dallas, TX, 1996.

Boiten, Theo, and Martin Bowman, *Battles with the Luftwaffe*, HarperCollins, London, 2001.

Boehm-Tettelbach, Karl, *Als Flieger in der Hexenküche*, v. Hase & Koehler Verlag, Mainz, Germany, 1981.

Boog, Horst, *Die deutsche Luftwaffenführung 1935–1945*, Deutsche Verlags-Anstalt, Stuttgart, 1982.

Boog, Horst, *et al.*, *Germany and the Second World War*, Vol. VI, *The Global War: Widening of the Conflict into a World War and the Shift of the Initiative 1941–1943*, Clarendon Press, Oxford, UK, 2001.

Boog, Horst, *et al.*, *Das Deutsche Reich und der Zweite Weltkrieg*, Band 7, *Das Deutsche Reich in der Defensive*, Deutsche Verlags-Anstalt, Stuttgart, Germany, 2001.

Bracke, Gerhard, *Gegen vielfache Übermacht*, Motorbuch Verlag, Stuttgart, Germany, 1977.

Buchner, Hermann, *Stormbird*, Hikoki Publications, Aldershot, UK, 2000.

Budraß, Lutz, *Flugzeugindustrie und Luftrüstung in Deutschland 1918–1945*, Droste Verlag, Düsseldorf, Germany, 1998.

Budraß, Lutz, Jonas Scherner, and Jochen Streb, "Demystifying the German 'Armaments Miracle' during World War II: New Insights from the Annual Audits of German Aircraft Producers," Economic Growth Center, Yale University, New Haven, CT, January 2005.

Caldwell, Donald, *JG 26: Top Guns of the Luftwaffe*, Orion Books, New York, 1991.

Caldwell, Donald, *The JG 26 War Diary*, Vol. 1, *1939–1942*, Grub Street, London, 1996.

Caldwell, Donald, *The JG 26 War Diary*, Vol. 2, *1943–1945*, Grub Street, London, 1998.

Cameron, Rebecca Hancock, *Training to Fly: Military Flight Training 1907–1945*, Air Force History & Museums Program, Washington DC, 1999.

Clark, Alan, *Barbarossa: The Russian-German Conflict, 1941–1945*, William Morrow, New York, 1965.

Conversino, Mark. J., *Fighting with the Soviets: The Failure of Operation Frantic, 1944–1945*, University Press of Kansas, Lawrence, KS, 1997.

Cooper, Matthew, *The German Air Force 1933–1945*, Jane's, London, 1981.

Copp, DeWitt, *Forged in Fire*, Doubleday, New York, 1982.

Corum, James S., *The Roots of Blitzkrieg: Hans von Seeckt and German Military Reform*, University Press of Kansas, Manhattan, KS, 1992.

Corum, James S., *The Luftwaffe: Creating the Operational Air War*, University Press of Kansas, Manhattan, KS, 1997.

Corum, James S., and Richard R. Muller, *The Luftwaffe's Way of War: German Air Force Doctrine 1911–1945*, Nautical & Aviation, Baltimore, MD, 1998.

Craven, Wesley, and James Cate, *The Army Air Forces in World War II*, Vol. I, *Plans and Early Operations*, University of Chicago Press, Chicago, IL, 1948.

Craven, Wesley, and James Cate, *The Army Air Forces in World War II*, Vol. II, *Europe: Torch to Pointblank*, University of Chicago Press, Chicago, IL, 1949.

Craven, Wesley, and James Cate, *The Army Air Forces in World War II*, Vol. III, *Europe: Argument to V-E Day*, University of Chicago Press, Chicago, IL, 1951.

Craven, Wesley, and James Cate, *The Army Air Forces in World War II*, Vol. VI, *Men and Planes*, Office of Air Force History, Washington, DC, 1983.

Dahl, Walther, *Rammjäger*, Orion Verlag, Heusenstamm, Germany, 1961.

Deist, Wilhelm, *et al.*, *Das Deutsche Reich und der Zweite Weltkrieg*, Band I, *Ursachen und Voraussetzungen der deutschen Kriegspolitik*, DVA, Stuttgart, Germany, 1979.

De Jong, Ivo, *Mission 376: Battle over the Reich 28 May 1944*, Hikoki Publications, Crowborough, UK, 2003.

Dickfeld, Adolf, *Footsteps of the Hunter*, J. J. Fedorowicz Publishing, Winnipeg, Canada, 1993.

Dierich, Hauptmann, *Der Flieger: Dienstunterschrift in der Fliegertruppe*, E. S. Mittler & Sohn, Berlin, 1940.

Dierich, Wolfgang. *Kampfgeschwader "Edelweiss": The History of a German Bomber Unit 1939–1945*, Ian Allan, London, 1975.

Doolittle, James, *I Could Never Be So Lucky Again*, Bantam Books, New York, 1991.

Doughty, Robert Allan, *The Breaking Point: Sedan and the Fall of France, 1940*, Archon Books, Hamden, CT, 1990.

Douhet, Giulio, *The Command of the Air*, Coward-McCann, New York, 1942.

Eichelbaum, Hans, ed., *Das Buch von der Luftwaffe*, Bong & Co., Berlin, 1938.

Engau, Fritz, *Frontal durch die Bomberpulks*, Hoppe Verlag, Graz, Austria, 1997.

Ethell, Jeffrey, and Alfred Price, *The German Jets in Combat*, Jane's, London, 1979.

Ethell, Jeffrey, and Alfred Price, *Target Berlin – Mission 250: 6 March 1944*, Jane's, London, 1981.

Foreman, John, and S. E. Harvey, *Me 262 Combat Diary*, Air Research Publications, Surrey, UK, 1990.

Forsyth, Robert, *JV 44: The Galland Circus*, Classic Publications, West Sussex, UK, 1996,

Forsyth, Robert, and Eddie Creek, *Jagdwaffe: Defending the Reich 1943–1944*, Ian Allan, Surrey, UK, 2004.

Forsyth, Robert, *Jagdwaffe: Defending the Reich 1944–1945*, Ian Allan, Surrey, UK, 2005.

Frappé, Jean-Bernard, *La Luftwaffe face au débarquement allié: 6 juin au 31 août 1944*, Editions Heimdal, Bayeux, France, 1999.

Freeman, Roger, *The Mighty Eighth*, Doubleday, Garden City, NY, 1970.

Freeman, Roger, *Mighty Eighth War Diary*, Jane's, London, 1981.

Freeman, Roger, *Mighty Eighth War Manual*, Jane's, London, 1984.

Friedrich, Jörg, *Der Brand: Deutschland im Bombenkrieg 1940–1945*, Propyläen, Munich, Germany, 2002.

Fry, Garry, and Jeffrey Ethell, *Escort to Berlin: The 4th Fighter Group in World War II*, Arco, New York, 1980.

Galland, Adolf, *Die Ersten und die Letzten*, Franz Schneekluth, Darmstadt, Germany, 1953.

Galland, Adolf, *The First and the Last*, Henry Holt, New York, 1954.

Girbig, Werner, *Start im Morgengrauen*, Motorbuch Verlag, Stuttgart, Germany, 1975.

Girbig, Werner, *Jagdgeschwader 5 "Eismeerjäger,"* Motorbuch Verlag, Stuttgart, Germany, 1976.

Girbig, Werner, *". . . mit Kurs auf Leuna": Die Luftoffensive gegen die Triebstoffindustrie und der deutsche Abwehreinsatz 1944–1945*, Motorbuch Verlag, Stuttgart, Germany, 1980.

Gomann, Heinz, *Und über uns der Himmel: Fliegergeschichten vom JG 26*, Kurt Vowinckel Verlag, Berg-am-See, Germany, 1996.

Green, William, *The Warplanes of the Third Reich*, Doubleday, New York, 1972.

Häberlen, Klaus, *Davongekommen: Als Kampfflieger über den Fronten*, VDM Heinz Nickel, Zweibrücken, Germany, 2001.

Hammel, Eric, *Air War Europa: America's Air War against Germany in Europe and North Africa 1942–1945*, Pacifica Press, Pacifica, CA, 1994.

Hannig, Norbert, *Luftwaffe Fighter Ace: From the Eastern Front to the Defence of the Homeland*, Grub Street, London, 2004.

Hastings, Max, *Bomber Command*, Dial Press/James Wade, New York, 1979.

Hastings, Max, *Armageddon: The Battle for Germany, 1944–1945*, Knopf, New York, 2004.

Havelaar, Marion, and William Hess, *The Ragged Irregulars of Bassingbourn: The 91st Bombardment Group in World War II*, Schiffer Publishing, Atglen, PA, 1995.

Hawkins, Ian, *Münster: The Way It Was*, Robinson Typographics, Anaheim, CA, 1984.

Held, Werner, R*eichsverteidigung—Die deutsche Tagjagd 1943–1945*, Podzun-Pallas Verlag, Friedberg, Germany, 1988.

Herhudt von Rohden, Hans-Detlef, *Vom Luftkriege: Gedanken über Führung und Einsatz moderner Luftwaffen*, E. S. Mittler und Sohn, Berlin, 1938.

Herrmann, Hajo, *Eagle's Wings*, Motorbooks International, Osceola, WI, 1991.

Hess, William, *Zemke's Wolfpack: The 56th Fighter Group in World War II*, Motorbooks International, Osceola, WI, 1992.

Hess, William, *German Jets vs. the U.S. Army Air Force*, Specialty Press, North Branch, MN, 1996.

Hess, William, *Hell in the Heavens: Ill-Fated Eighth Air Force Bomb Group Missions*, Specialty Press, North Branch, MN, 2000.

Hess, William, *354th Fighter Group*, Osprey, Oxford, UK, 2002.

Hess, William, *B-17 Flying Fortress Units of the MTO*, Osprey, Oxford, UK, 2003.

Heuser, Beatrice, *Reading Clausewitz*, Pimlico, London, 2002.

Homze, Edward L., *Arming the Luftwaffe: The Reich Air Ministry and the German Aircraft Industry, 1933–1939*, U. of Nebraska Press, Lincoln, NE, 1976.

Hoseason, James, *The 1,000 Day Battle*, Gillingham Publications, Lowestoft, UK, 1979.

Irving, David, *The Rise and Fall of the Luftwaffe: The Life of Field Marshal Erhard Milch*, Little, Brown & Co., Boston, 1973.

Irving, David, *Hitler's War*, Viking, New York, 1977.

Irving, David, *Göring: A Biography*, Morrow, New York, 1989.

Johnson, Charles, *The History of the Hell Hawks*, Southcoast Typesetting, Anaheim, CA, 1975.

Jung, Robert, *Auf verlorenem Posten: Die Geschichte eines jungen Jagdfliegers*, privately published, 1994.

Kassak, Peter, *An Ordinary Day in 1945*, Stratus, Sandomierz, Poland, 2005.

Kay, Antony L., and J. Richard Smith, *German Aircraft of the Second World War*, Naval Institute Press, Annapolis, MD, 2002.

Knoke, Heinz, *I Flew for the Führer*, Henry Holt, New York, 1953.

Lay, Jr., Beirne, "Smashing the Luftwaffe's Nest," in *The 100 Best True Stories of World War II*, Wise & Co., New York, 1945.

Lay, Jr., Beirne, and Sy Bartlett, *Twelve O'Clock High!*, Harper & Brothers, New York, 1948.

Lorant, Jean-Yves, and Richard Goyat, *Jagdgeschwader 300 "Wilde Sau,"* Vol. 1, *Jun 1943–Sep 1944*, Eagle Editions, Hamilton, MT, 2005.

Lorant, Jean-Yves, and Richard Goyat, *Bataille dans le ciel d'Allemagne: une Escadre de Chasse dans la Débâcle*, Tome 2, *Septembre 1944–Mai 1945*; éditions Larivière, Paris, 2005.

MacDonald, Charles, *The Mighty Endeavor: American Armed Forces in the European Theater in World War II*, Oxford University Press, New York, 1969.

Manuel, Frank E., *Scenes from the End: The Last Days of World War II in Europe*, Steerforth Press, South Royalton, VT, 2000.

Marshall, Francis, *Sea Eagles: The Messerschmitt Bf 109T*, Air Research Publications, Surrey, UK, 1993.

McFarland, Stephen L., and Wesley Phillips Newton, *To Command the Sky: The Battle for Air Superiority over Germany, 1942–1944*, Smithsonian Institution Press, Washington DC, 1991.

McLachlan, Ian, *Night of the Intruders: First-Hand Accounts Chronicling the Slaughter of Homeward Bound USAAF Mission 311*, Patrick Stephens, Sparkford, UK, 1994.

Mehner, Kurt, and Reinhard Teuber, *Die Luftwaffe 1939–1945*, Militär-Verlag Klaus D. Patzwall, Norderstedt, Germany, 1996.

Meilinger, Philip S., ed., *The Paths of Heaven: The Evolution of Airpower Theory*, Air University Press, Maxwell AFB, AL, 1997.

Merrick, Ken, *By Day and by Night: The Bomber War in Europe, 1939–1945*, Ian Allan, London, 1989.

Mets, David R., *Master of Airpower: Gen. Carl A. Spaatz*, Presidio, Novato, CA, 1988.

Michulec, Robert, and Donald Caldwell, *Adolf Galland*, Stratus, Sandomierz, Poland, 2003.

Middlebrook, Martin, *The Battle of Hamburg: Allied Bomber Forces against a German City in 1943*, Allen Lane, London, 1980.

Middlebrook, Martin, *The Schweinfurt–Regensburg Mission*, Allen Lane, London, 1983.

Middlebrook, Martin, and Chris Everitt, *The Bomber Command War Diaries: An Operational Reference Book, 1939–1945*, Penguin, New York, 1990.

Mierzejewski, Alfred C., *The Collapse of the German War Economy 1944–1945: Allied Air Power and the German National Railway*, University of North Carolina Press, Chapel Hill, NC, 1988.

Milward, Alan S., *The German Economy at War*, The Athlone Press (University of London), London, 1965.

Mitchell, William, *Winged Defense: The Development and Possibilities of Modern Air Power*, Economic and Military, Putnam, New York, 1925.

Mombeek, Eric, *Defending the Reich: The History of Jagdgeschwader 1 "Oesau,"* JAC Publications, Norwich, UK, 1992.

Mombeek, Eric, *Sturmjäger: Zur Geschichte des Jagdgeschwaders 4 und der Sturmstaffel 1*; Band 1, privately published, 1997; Band 2, privately published, n.d.

Mombeek, Eric, *Defenders of the Reich: Jagdgeschwader 1*; Vol. 2, *1943*; Vol. 3, *1944–1945*, Classic Publications, Surrey, UK, 2003.

Muller, Richard, *The German Air War in Russia*, Nautical & Aviation, Baltimore, MD, 1992.

Murray, Williamson, *Luftwaffe*, Nautical & Aviation, Baltimore, MD, 1985.

Murray, Williamson, ed., *German Military Effectiveness*, Nautical & Aviation, Baltimore, MD, 1992.

Murray, Williamson, and Allan R. Millett, eds., *Military Innovation in the Interwar Period*, Cambridge University Press, Cambridge, UK, 1996.

Murray, Williamson, and Allan R. Millett, *A War to be Won: Fighting the Second World War*, Belknap/Harvard, Cambridge, MA, 2000.

Neulen, Hans Werner, *In the Skies of Europe: Air Forces Allied to the Luftwaffe*, Crowood Press, Wiltshire, UK, 1998.

Neumann, Georg Paul, *Die deutschen Luftstreitkräfte im Weltkriege*, Ernst Siegfried Mittler und Sohn, Berlin, 1920.

Obermaier, Ernst, *Die Ritterkreuzträger der Luftwaffe 1939–1945*, Band I, *Jagdflieger*, Verlag Dieter Hoffmann, Mainz, Germany, 2nd Edition, 1989.

Olmsted, Merle, *The 357th over Europe: The 357th Fighter Group in World War II*, Phalanx Pulishing, St. Paul, MN, 1994.

Olynyk, Frank, *USAAF (European Theater) Credits for the Destruction of Enemy Aircraft in Air-to-Air Combat in World War 2*, privately published, Aurora, OH, 1987.

Olynyk, Frank, *USAAF (Mediterranean Theater) Credits for the Destruction of Enemy Aircraft in Air-to-Air Combat in World War 2*, privately published, Aurora, OH, 1987.

Overy, R. J., *Göring: The "Iron Man,"* Routledge & Kegan Paul, London, 1984.

Overy, R. J., *War and Economy in the Third Reich*, Clarendon Press, Oxford, UK, 1994.

Overy, R. J., *Why the Allies Won*, W. W. Norton, New York, 1996.

Parker, Danny, *To Win the Winter Sky: Air War over the Ardennes, 1944–1945*, Combined Books, Conshohocken, PA, 1994.

Price, Alfred, *Battle over the Reich*, Charles Scribner's Sons, New York, 1973.

Price, Alfred, *Blitz on Britain, 1939–1945*, Ian Allan, London, 1977.

Price, Alfred, *Instruments of Darkness: The History of Electronic Warfare*, Charles Scribner's Sons, New York, 1978.

Price, Alfred, *Last Year of the Luftwaffe: May 1944 to May 1945*, Motorbooks International, Osceola, WI, 1991.

Prien, Jochen, and Peter Rodeike, *Jagdgeschwader 1 und Jagdgeschwader 11, Einsatz in der Reichsverteidigung von 1939 bis 1945*; Teil 1, *1939–1943*; Teil 2, *1944*; Teil 3, *1944–45*, Struve-Druck, Eutin, Germany, n.d.

Prien, Jochen, and Gerhard Stemmer, *Messerschmitt Bf 109 im Einsatz bei der Stab und I./JG 3: 1938–1945*, Struve-Druck, Eutin, Germany, n.d.

Prien, Jochen, and Gerhard Stemmer, *Messerschmitt Bf 109 im Einsatz bei der II./Jagdgeschwader 3: 1940–1945*, Struve-Druck, Eutin, Germany, 1996.

Prien, Jochen, and Gerhard Stemmer, *Messerschmitt Bf 109 im Einsatz bei der III./Jagdgeschwader 3: 1940–1945*, Struve-Druck, Eutin, Germany, 1996.

Prien, Jochen, *IV./JG 3: Chronik einer Jagdgruppe 1943–1945*, Struve-Druck, Eutin, Germany, n.d.

Prien, Jochen, *et al.*, *Messerschmitt Bf 109 im Einsatz bei der Stab und I./JG 27*, Struve-Druck, Eutin, Germany, n.d.

Prien, Jochen, *et al.*, *Messerschmitt Bf 109 im Einsatz bei der II./Jagdgeschwader 27*, Struve-Druck, Eutin, Germany, n.d.

Prien, Jochen, *"Pik-As": Geschichte des Jagdgeschwaders 53*, Teil 3, Struve-Druck, Eutin, Germany, 1991.

Priller, Josef, *JG 26: Geschichte eines Jagdgeschwaders*, Kurt Vowinckel, Heidelberg, Germany, 1956.

Probert, Henry, *Bomber Harris: His Life and Times*, Greenhill, London, 2001.

Punka, György, *Messerschmitt Me 210/410 in Action*, Squadron/Signal, Carrollton, TX, 1994.

Punka, György, *Hungarian Aces of World War II*, Osprey, Oxford, UK, 2002.

Rajlich, Jiri, *et al.*, *Slovakian and Bulgarian Aces of World War II*, Osprey, Oxford, UK, 2004.

Renneberg, Monika, and Mark Walker, eds., *Science, Technology and National Socialism*, Cambridge University Press, Cambridge, UK, 1994.

Rennles, Keith, *Independent Force: The War Diary of the Daylight Squadrons of the Independent Air Force, June–November 1918*, Grub Street, London, 2002.

Reschke, Willi, *Jagdgeschwader 301/302 "Wilde Sau,"* Motorbuch Verlag, Stuttgart, Germany, 1998.

Richards, Denis, *Royal Air Force 1939–1945*, Vol. I, *The Fight at Odds*, HMSO, London, 1953.

Richards, Denis, *The Hardest Victory: RAF Bomber Command in the Second World War*, Hodder & Stoughton, London, 1994.

Rieckhoff, Herbert Joachim, *Trumpf oder Bluff? 12 Jahre deutsche Luftwaffe*, Interavia, Geneva, Switzerland, 1945.

Ring, Hans, and Werner Girbig, *Jagdgeschwader 27*, Motorbuch Verlag, Stuttgart, Germany, 1971.

Rose, Arno, *Radikaler Luftkampf*, Motorbuch Verlag, Stuttgart, Germany, 1977.

Savic, Dravan, and Boris Ciglic, *Croatian Aces of World War II*, Osprey, Oxford, UK, 2002.

Schliephake, Hanfried, *The Birth of the Luftwaffe*, Henry Regnery Company, Chicago, IL, 1971.

Schramm, Percy, ed., *Kriegstagebuch des Oberkommandos der Wehrmacht 1943*, b. 2 (III/6), Bernard und Graefe, Munich, Germany, 1982.

Schreier, Hans, *JG 52: Das erfolgreichste Jagdgeschwader des II. Weltkrieges*, Kurt Vowinckel Verlag, Berg-am-See, Germany, 1990.

Seesselberg, Friedrich, ed., *Der Stellungskrieg 1914–1918*, E. S. Mittler & Sohn, Berlin, 1926.

Shepherd, D., *Of Men and Wings: the First 100 Missions of the 449th Bombardment Group*, Norfield, Panama City, FL, 1996.

Shores, Christopher, *Fledgling Eagles: The Complete Account of Air Operations during the 'Phoney War' and Norwegian Campaign, 1940*, Grub Street, London, 1991.

Sloan, John, *The Route as Briefed: the History of the 92nd Bombardment Group 1942–1945*, Argus Press, Cleveland, OH, 1946.

Smith, J. Richard, and Eddie Creek, *Me 262*, Vols 2, 3, 4, Classic Publications, Crowborough, UK, 1988, 2000, 2000.

Smith, Jack, *Mustangs and Unicorns: A History of the 359th FG*, Pictorial Histories, Missoula, MT, 1997.

Speer, Albert, *Inside the Third Reich*, Macmillan, New York, 1970.

Steinhoff, Johannes, *Messerschmitts over Sicily*, Nautical & Aviation, Baltimore, MD, 1987.

Stern, D. G., *The 483rd Bomb Group (H)*, Turner Publishing, Paducah, KY, 1994.

Stiles, Bert, *Serenade to the Big Bird*, W. W. Norton, New York, 1952.

Strong, Russell, *First over Germany: A History of the 306th Bombardment Group*, privately published, Charlotte, NC, 1990.

Suchenwirth, Richard, *Command and Leadership in the German Air Force*, Arno Press, New York, 1971.

Swanborough, Gordon, and William Green, *The Focke-Wulf Fw 190*, Arco, New York, 1976.

Terraine, John, *A Time for Courage: The Royal Air Force in the European War*, Macmillan, New York, 1985.

Thom, Walter, *The Brotherhood of Courage: The History of the 305th Bombardment Group (H) in World War II*, privately published, 1986.

Tessin, Georg, *Verbände und Truppen der deutschen Wehrmacht und Waffen-SS im Zweiten Weltkrieg*, Band 14, Biblio Verlag, Osnabrück, Germany, 1980.

Thomas, Chris, and Christopher Shores, *The Typhoon & Tempest Story*, Arms & Armour Press, London, 1988.

USAAF, *Target Germany*, Simon and Schuster, New York, 1943.

Vajda, Ferenc A., and Peter Dany, *German Aircraft Industry and Production*, SAE, Warrendale, PA, 1998.

van Ishoven, Armand, *Messerschmitt Bf 109 at War*, Charles Scribner's Sons, Ian Allen, London, 1977.

Vasco, John, *The Sting of the Luftwaffe: Schnellkampfgeschwader 210 and Zerstörergeschwader 1 "Wespengeschwader" in World War II*, Schiffer Publishing, Altglen, PA, 2001.

Weal, John, *Jagdgeschwader 2 "Richthofen,"* Osprey, Oxford, UK, 2000.

Weal, John, *Luftwaffe Sturmgruppen*, Osprey, Oxford, UK, 2005.

Webster, Charles, and Noble Frankland, *The Strategic Air Offensive against Germany, 1939–1945*, Vol. I, *Preparation*, HMSO, London, 1961.

Wegmann, G., *"Das Oberkommando der Wehrmacht gibt bekannt . . .",* Band 2, Biblio Verlag, Osnabrück, Germany, 1982.

Weinberg, Gerhard, ed., *Hitler and His Generals: Military Conferences 1942–1945*, Enigma Books, New York, 2003.

Weir, Adrian, *The Last Flight of the Luftwaffe: The Fate of Schulungslehrgang Elbe, 7 April 1945*, Arms & Armour Press, London, 1997.

Wells, Mark K., *Courage and Air Warfare: The Allied Aircrew Experience in the Second Word War*, Frank Cass, London, 1995.

Westermann, Edward B., *Flak: German Anti-Aircraft Defenses, 1914–1945*, University Press of Kansas, Manhattan, KS, 2001.

Williams, David P., *Day Fighters: Hunters of the Reich*, Cerberus, Bristol, UK, 2002.

Wood, Tony, and Bill Gunston, *Hitler's Luftwaffe*, Salamander, London, 1977.

Woodward, Ellis, *Flying School: Combat Hell*, American Literary Press, Baltimore, MD, 1998.

Yelton, David K., *Hitler's Volkssturm: The Nazi Militia and the Defeat of Germany, 1944–1945*, University Press of Kansas, Lawrence, KS, 2002.

Ziegler, Mano, *Rocket Fighter: The Story of the Messerschmitt Me 163*, Arms & Armour Press, London, 1976.

GLOSSARIES

Abbreviations

AEAF: Allied Expeditionary Air Force.

CBO: Combined Bomber Offensive—the USAAF and RAF joint strategic bombing campaign.

CO: commanding officer.

e/a: enemy aircraft.

ETO: European Theater of Operations.

IFF: Identification—Friend from Foe.

IP: Initial Point, from which a bomber formation maintained a steady course to its target.

KIA: killed in action.

MIA: missing in action.

MTO: Mediterranean Theater of Operations.

NCO: non-commissioned officer.

POW: prisoner of war.

PFF: Pathfinder Force.

PRU: photo reconnaissance unit.

RAAF: Royal Australian Air Force.

RAF: Royal Air Force.

RCAF: Royal Canadian Air Force.

RNZAF: Royal New Zealand Air Force.

SAAF: South African Air Force.

TAF: (RAF) Tactical Air Force.

USAAF: U.S. Army Air Force.

USSTAF: U.S. Strategic Air Forces—the Eighth and Fifteenth Air Forces; commanded by Gen. Spaatz from England.

Vic: a vee-shaped formation of three aircraft.

WIA: wounded in action.

Aviation Terms

(#–#): (destroyed–damaged beyond economical repair [Cat E]) aircraft losses.

(#–#–#): (destroyed–probable–damaged) aircraft claims (by Allies).

Split-S: a half-roll followed by a dive; results in a reversal of direction and the loss of a great deal of altitude. A common means of breaking off combat.

German Terms

Abschuss: "shootdown"—an air victory.

Abschussmeldung: victory report.

Abschwung: split-S; a half-roll followed by a dive.

Alarmeinheit: "alarm unit"—a small unit drawn from a training school or aircraft factory for air defense.

Alarmstart: scramble; a rapid takeoff for an intercept mission.

Auftragstaktik: mission-oriented tactics; the German concept of allowing battlefield commanders the freedom to select the tactics needed to accomplish the ordered mission.

Benito: Allied code name for *Y-Führung* (q.v.).

Blitzverlegung: rapid transfer of a unit's flying component.

Casino: pilots' mess.

dicken Autos: "fat cars"—Luftwaffe code designation for Allied heavy bombers.

Egon: Erstling long-range control procedure—a method of ground control using the Erstling IFF device; in service from mid-1944.

Einsatzstaffel: operational Staffel (of a training unit).

endgültige Vernichtung (eV): final destruction; the shootdown of a bomber already separated from its formation.

Ergänzungsgruppe (ErgGr): advanced-training group.

Ergänzungsstaffel (ErgSt): advanced-training squadron.

Experte: a fighter pilot proficient in aerial combat; the Allied "ace."

Feindberührung: enemy contact; required in order for a Jagdwaffe pilot to receive credit for a combat mission.

Fliegerdivision (FD): air division—a higher command containing several types of flying units.

Flieger Hitlerjugend (FHJ): Flying Hitler Youth; the air section of the Nazi youth organization.

Fliegerkorps (FK): air corps—a higher command containing several types of flying units; usually contained one or more *Fliegerdivisionen*.

Flugbuch: aircrewman's logbook.

Flugmeldedienst: Aircraft Reporting Service.

Flugwachen: ground observers.

Flugzeugführer: pilot.

freie Jagd: (pl. *freie Jagden*) "free hunt"—a fighter sweep without ground control.

Fühlungshalter: contact keeper; an airborne reporter whose mission was to radio information about enemy bomber formations to ground control.

Führer: leader.

Gefechtsstand: command post.

Gefechtsverband: battle formation; two or more *Jagdgruppen* and/or *Zerstörergruppen* airborne under a single commander.

General der Jagdflieger (GdJ.): General of the Fighter Arm; a staff position in the Luftwaffe General Staff. Werner Mölders and Adolf Galland were the most prominent holders of the position.

Generalluftzeugmeister: Director of the Office of Air Armament; the RLM post responsible for all aspects of aircraft development and production. Prominent holders of the position were Ernst Udet, and, after Udet's suicide, Erhard Milch.

Geschwader: wing (pl. *Geschwader*)—the largest mobile, homogeneous Luftwaffe flying unit.

Geschwadergruppe: wing commodore's group; a fixed but unofficial grouping of two or three Staffeln under the operational command of a *Kommodore*.

Geschwaderkommodore: wing commodore—usually a Major, Obstleutnant, or Oberst in rank.

Gruppe (Gr): group (pl. *Gruppen*)—the basic Luftwaffe combat and administrative unit.

Gruppenkommandeur: group commander—usually a Hauptmann, Major, or Obstleutnant in rank.

Heer: army—refers to the German Army.

Herausschuss (HSS): "shoot-out"—the separation of a bomber from its combat formation.

Höhengruppe: high-altitude group.

Höhenstaffel: high-altitude squadron.

Holzauge: "wooden eye"—a spotter; the last airplane or the top cover unit of a formation.

Indianer: Indians—Luftwaffe code designation for enemy fighters.

Industrieschutzstaffel (or . . . *schwarm*): industry protection squadron or flight—based at aircraft production facilities and dedicated to their defense; commanded by Luftwaffe officers and staffed primarily by test pilots.

Invasionsfront: (Normandy) invasion front.

Jabo: fighter-bomber.

Jagdabschnitt: fighter sector; an independent command smaller than a Jafü.

Jagdbomber (Jabo): fighter-bomber.

Jagddivision (JD): fighter division; an upper-level headquarters that administered the fighter units based within its geographic area and controlled the fighters airborne above it.

Jagdflieger: fighter pilot(s).

Jagdfliegerführer (Jafü): fighter command/control unit or its commander. The Jafü originated as administrative units, but quickly gained operational control responsibilities. Their control functions were surrendered to the larger Jagddivisionen in 1944, and most of the Jafü were disbanded.

Jagdgeschwader (JG): fighter wing, commanding three or four *Gruppen*. The authorized strength of a three-Gruppe Geschwader after the reorganization of October 1, 1943, was 208 aircraft.

Jagdgruppe (JGr): fighter group, containing three or four *Staffeln*. The authorized strength of a Jagdgruppe was originally 40 aircraft; this was upped to 68 after October 1, 1943.

Jagdstaffel: fighter squadron, containing 12 or 16 aircraft (three or four *Schwärme* of four aircraft).

Jagdwaffe: fighter arm or fighter force.

Jäger: originally, a hunter—beginning in World War I, also a fighter pilot.

Jägerführung: fighter ground control.

Jägerstab: Fighter Staff—established in March 1944 under Karl-Otto Saur in Speer's Armaments Ministry to set production goals and maximize fighter production.

Kanalfront: (English) Channel Front.

Kanalgeschwader: the *Geschwader* serving on the English Channel (JG 2 and JG 26).

Kanaljäger: fighter pilot(s) based near the Channel.

Kapitän: "captain"; a command position (usually of a *Staffel*) rather than a rank.

Kette: flight of three aircraft; the basic tactical unit for fighters until Mölders's 1939 reforms, when it was replaced by the *Schwarm*; the Kette remained the basic unit of bomber formations.

Kommandeur: "commander"; a command position (usually of a *Gruppe*) rather than a rank.

Kommodore: "commodore"; a command position (usually of a *Geschwader*) rather than a rank.

Kriegstagebuch (KTB): unit war diary.

Luftflotte (LF): air fleet; a mixed-equipment force corresponding to a numbered American Air Force.

Luftgaukommando (Luftgau, pl. Luftgaue): air force administrative area; a fixed geographic region of the Reich that commanded various aviation resources.

Luftstreitkräfte: the German Air Force of World War I.

Luftverteidigungskommando: air-defense command. The defensive components of a Luftgau; used only until 1940.

Luftverteidigungszone: air-defense zone. A high-level command containing several *Luftverteidigungskommandos*; proposed in 1939 but never fully established.

Luftwaffe: "Air Force"—refers to the German Air Force of the Third Reich (1935–45).

Luftwaffen Befehlshaber Mitte (Lw Bfh Mitte): the German air-defense command in the mid-war period; superseded by Luftflotte Reich.

Möbelwagen: furniture vans, Luftwaffe slang for heavy bombers.

Nachwuchs: "new growth"—the late-war crop of pilot trainees.

Oberbefehlshaber der Luftwaffe (ObdL): Supreme Commander of the Luftwaffe (Reichsmarschall Göring).

Oberkommando des Heeres (OKH): the (German) Army High Command.

Oberkommando der Luftwaffe (OKL): the Luftwaffe High Command; controlled most of the military aspects of German aviation from its establishment in February 1944.

Oberkommando der Wehrmacht (OKW): the (German) Armed Forces High Command.

Ostfront: Eastern Front.

Pulk: "bunch" or "herd"—Luftwaffe slang for one or more combat boxes of heavy bombers.

Reich: "empire"—Hitler's Germany was "the Third Reich."

Reichsjägerwelle: Reich Fighter Frequency, a comprehensive running commentary on each air raid; broadcast on a common radio frequency to all defenders.

Reichsluftfahrtministerium (RLM): German Air Ministry; Göring's headquarters, it controlled all aspects of German aviation.

Reichsluftverteidigung (RLV): "aerial defense of the Reich"—the German air defenses.

Reichsverteidigung: "defense of the Reich"—a general term for the defensive forces in the German homeland, including fighter units, anti-aircraft units, ground-control units, and the civil defense organization.

Reichswehr: the 100,000-man defensive force permitted Germany by the Versailles Treaty.

Richthofen: JG 2's honor title; commemorated Manfred von Richthofen, the famous World War I ace.

Rotte: tactical element of two aircraft.

Rottenflieger: wingman; the second man in a *Rotte.*

Rottenführer: leader of an element of two aircraft.

Schlageter: JG 26's honor title; commemorated Albert Leo Schlageter, a nationalist martyr of the interwar period.

Schlachtflieger: ground-attack aircraft or unit.

Schlachtgeschwader (SG): ground-attack wing.

Schwarm: flight of four aircraft (pl. *Schwärme*); the basic unit of all *Jagdwaffe* tactical formations 1939–45, when it was replaced in some units by the *Kette.*

Schwarmführer: flight leader.

Sitzbereitschaft: "seated readiness"—cockpit readiness; the highest form of alert, with pilots seated in their cockpits for immediate takeoff.

Sonderkommando: special command—used for Sonderkommando Elbe, a ramming unit.

Stab: staff.

Stabsschwarm: staff flight.

Staffel (St): squadron (pl. *Staffeln*).

Staffelführer: squadron leader (temporary or probationary).

Staffelkapitän: squadron leader—usually a Leutnant, Oberleutnant, or Hauptmann.

Sturmbock: "assault billy goat" or "assault battering ram"; the heavily armed and armored Fw 190 variants used by the *Sturmgruppen.*

Sturmgruppe: assault group; a unit whose mission was to attack bomber formations in close formation from the rear to extremely close range.

Sturmjäger: assault pilot, pilots, fighter, or fighters.

Sturmstaffel: assault squadron; Sturmstaffel 1 was an experimental unit used to develop the *Sturmtaktik.*

Sturmtaktik: assault tactics; the tactics adopted by the *Sturmgruppen.*

Wehrmacht: armed forces—refers to the German Armed Forces.

Werkenummer (W. Nr.): aircraft serial number.

Wilde Sau: "Wild Sow"—procedure for using single-engine fighters to engage night bombers over the target; also, the units involved.

Verband: formation.

Verbandsführer: formation leader; the leader of a *Staffel, Gruppe, Geschwader,* or *Gefechtsverband* in the air.

Viermot: "four-engine"—Luftwaffe slang for Allied heavy bomber.

Y-Führung: Y-Control—ground-control procedure requiring two fighters with FuG 16ZY radios, one for transmitting location, and the second for receiving orders.

Zerstörer: "destroyer" (heavy fighter)—Bf 110 or Me 410 twin-engine fighter.

Zerstörergeschwader (ZG): heavy fighter wing.

Zerstörergruppe (ZGr): heavy fighter group.

INDEX